Dictionary of Battles and Sieges

Dictionary of Battles and Sieges

A Guide to 8,500 Battles from Antiquity
through the Twenty-first Century

Volume 1
A–E

Tony Jaques

Foreword by Dennis Showalter

GREENWOOD PRESS
Westport, Connecticut • London

Library of Congress Cataloging-in-Publication Data

Jaques, Tony.
  Dictionary of battles and sieges : a guide to 8,500 battles from antiquity through the twenty-first century /
Tony Jaques ; foreword by Dennis Showalter.
      p. cm.
  Includes bibliographical references and index.
  ISBN 0–313–33536–2 (set : alk. paper)—ISBN 0–313–33537–0 (vol. 1 : alk. paper)—ISBN 0–313–33538–9
(vol. 2 : alk. paper)—ISBN 0–313–33539–7 (vol. 3 : alk. paper)   1. Battles—History—Encyclopedias.   2. Sieges—
History—Encyclopedias.   3. Military history—Encyclopedias.   I. Title.
  D25.J33 2007
  355.403—dc22   2006015366

British Library Cataloguing in Publication Data is available.

Library of Congress Catalog Card Number: 2006015366
ISBN: 0–313–33536–2 (set)   ISBN-13: 978–0–313–33536–5 (set)
       0–313–33537–0 (vol. 1)   978–0–313–33537–2 (vol. 1)
       0–313–33538–9 (vol. 2)   978–0–313–33538–9 (vol. 2)
       0–313–33539–7 (vol. 3)   978–0–313–33539–6 (vol. 3)

First published in 2007

Greenwood Press, 88 Post Road West, Westport, CT 06881
An imprint of Greenwood Publishing Group, Inc.
www.greenwood.com

Printed in the United States of America

The paper used in this book complies with the
Permanent Paper Standard issued by the National
Information Standards Organization (Z39.48–1984).

10 9 8 7 6 5 4 3 2 1

This dictionary is dedicated to the memory of my father, Pat Jaques, 1903–1980.

Contents

Foreword

Why write and publish a book like this? Why, in an age of increasingly-sophisticated electronic search agents, search agents able not merely to compile lists, but categorize and cross-reference their contents, did Tony Jaques and Greenwood Press collaborate on this *Dictionary of Battles and Sieges*?

Utilitarian considerations play a part. It is useful even in the computer age to have a compendium like this one ready to hand. It is convenient to let one's fingers do the walking through actual printed pages; and stimulating to pursue the comparisons across space and time suggested by alphabetical listings of common events. A technologically-oriented critic, however, might be excused for dismissing these arguments as exercises in nostalgia: examples of a vestigial mind-set no less dated than quill pens and typewriters.

Perhaps, then, we might consider this work from an aesthetic perspective, as a tribute to the intelligence and the energy of its author. In that context the *Dictionary* is surely a *tour de force*. Nothing remotely like it exists; nothing remotely like it will be needed in the foreseeable future. Jaques draws references from six continents and four millennia. Their scale extends from epic engagements that lasted weeks and involved millions to frontier skirmishes with a few dozen men to a side. Their location ranges from familiar cockpits and choke points—Flanders in Europe, the Bosporus in Asia Minor, Panipat in northern India—to remote dots on a map, with no discernible significance of any kind. Yet each has its place in a structure whose synergy of complexity and order invites comparison to a mosaic or a tapestry. As an overview of organized violence, the volume is in a class by itself.

Yet the question remains: why? Particularly at a time when military history is turning away from its historic focus on combat, emphasizing instead the structure of armed forces, the relationship of military institutions to their societies, the cultural, intellectual and psychological aspects of war—why reinforce an obsolescent paradigm?

The Dictionary of Battles and Sieges provides convincing evidence that war is an integral part of the human experience. From its emergence as a species, mankind has competed with other species for survival. Individuals and cultures have defended and aggrandized themselves by organized violence. The adjective is as important as the noun. *Homo sapiens* in a pristine state is a poor squib indeed, ill equipped physically by nature either to fight or to run. *Homo faber*, man the tool-maker, is a very different proposition. Archaeological evidence indeed suggests he might more accurately be called "man the weapons-maker." And the human forebrain that enabled the development of weapons enabled as well an understanding that those weapons were most effective when employed cooperatively, even in the random clashes of small hunting parties that probably evolved into the first battles.

That understanding has shaped the nature of war from its beginning—certainly from the beginning of recorded history. Recent debates on the existence of a distinctive "Western way of war," with a unique emphasis on decisive battle, have obscured the universal centrality of fighting to warmaking. Battle can mean different things to different cultures. Its scale and its nature may vary widely. But battle, the direct encounter of competing forces, ultimately structures war's impact and war's consequences, individual and collective. Tony Jaques merits the thanks of the historical community by this massive and eloquent reminder of a fact sufficiently uncomfortable to invite suppression, yet too fundamental to be overlooked.

Dennis Showalter

Preface

It has often been said that there is more to history than kings and battles. But it is equally true that kings and battles are an essential and intriguing part of history, and the study of battles and wars can provide a valuable window to history.

At the very least, battles can be dramatic milestones in the journey of history and can provide insight into the broader understanding of war. Indeed, some battles have proved decisive turning points, not just in the course of a war, but sometimes even dramatic turning points in the history of an entire people, such as the siege and destruction of **Carthage** in 146 BC or the demise of the Aztec Empire at **Tenochtitlan** in 1521.

This book sets out to bring into a single source battles and sieges from all periods of recorded history and across all geographies. The 8,500 battles included are presented in the main alphabetical section, which also contains about 2,500 cross-references, which are mainly alternate names for battles, or the names of battles within a campaign.

Each entry includes the name and date of the battle, the name of the war and the context in which it was fought, the opposing commanders if known, the outcome of the fighting, and any other outstanding detail which can be contained within the necessary constraints of the limited words available. Any mention of a related battle included elsewhere in the book appears in **bold**.

In addition, every battle in the book appears in a Chronological Reference Guide as a finding aid. The only exceptions are Adas 1775 and Dacca 1971, where two battles were fought in the same year but in different wars.

This book was conceived as a dictionary of battles and sieges, not a dictionary of wars and not an encyclopedia of battles. However, some wars which do not have specific recorded battles remain significant in their own right in an historic context. For completeness of the project, a small number of such wars appear in a separate appendix and are also included in the Chronological Reference Guide.

The general principle underlying this book has been comprehensiveness, not selectivity. The objective was to include as many battles as possible, which meant that each entry had to be in very brief dictionary style in order to contain the information within a single publishing project. The entries are not intended to be stand-alone analyses of each battle, but should provide sufficient detail to enable the reader to research the full information elsewhere in the sources, including those referenced in the bibliography.

As a result, the same space is devoted to a brief skirmish as is given to a major strategic encounter. The book makes no attempt to distinguish or categorise different military encounters.

Some writers and historians have attempted to categorise or define what they believe are the most significant or most decisive battles.

One of the earliest and most famous of these works was Sir Edward Creasey's *Fifteen Decisive Battles of the World*, originally published in 1852. Others include the classic *Decisive Battles of the Western World and Their Influence upon History* (J.F.C. Fuller, 1954) and, more recently, *Turning the Tide of War: Fifty Battles That Changed the Course of Modern History from*

1792–1995 (Tim Newark, 2001), *One Hundred Decisive Battles: From Ancient Times to the Present* (Paul K. Davis, 1999), *Fifty Battles That Changed the World: The Conflicts That Most Changed the Course of History* (William Weir, 2001) and *The Seventy Great Battles in History* (Jeremy Black, ed, 2005). But before considering what makes a battle significant, the more fundamental question must be asked, what is a battle?

What is a battle?

At the simplest level, a battle is any clash between organised forces of combatants. While this allows no distinction in scope, scale or significance, considerations such as significance are often applied only in retrospect and may have very little to do with scope or scale. For instance, some battles which were very minor military affairs have gained significance for other reasons, such as the loss of an important political or military leader. Examples would include the siege of **Chalus** (1199), which saw Richard I "the Lionheart" killed by a crossbow bolt in a pointless dispute over some supposed treasure; the otherwise unremarkable siege of **Fredrikshald** (1718), where King Charles XII of Sweden was shot dead (possibly by one of his own soldiers); or the battle of **Klissova** (1826), a struggle over a worthless harbour sandbar near Missolonghi during the Greek War of Independence, noted mainly for the death of the renowned Turkish commander Hussein bey Djertili.

Apart from the loss of an important commander, the level of casualties in a battle does not necessarily impart significance. As Sir Edward Creasey wrote in the introduction to his classic study, "I hardly need remark that it is not the number of killed and wounded in a battle that determines its general historical importance."

There have of course been some important battles with no casualties at all to enemy action, such as **Charleston Harbour** (1863), where the bloodless bombardment of Fort Sumter effectively triggered the American Civil War; or the bloodless escalade and capture of **Gwalior** (1780) by British General Thomas Goddard, which was a major setback to the Maratha army.

Sadly, at the opposite end of the scale, there have been all too many battles, such as on the Western Front during World War I, with losses running into the tens of thousands killed for no tactical or strategic gain whatever.

Some military historians have developed alternative terminology in an attempt to categorise the scale of actions. Such writers have introduced seemingly graduated descriptions such as encounter, skirmish, fight, ambush, raid, action, engagement and combat to expand the vocabulary of actions regarded as less-than-full-scale battles. (An example of a history which uses such distinctions would be the classic 128-volume American Civil War official record, *The War of the Rebellion*, published between 1880 and 1901.) However, the present project eschews such labels, and the simple words "battle" or "siege" are used throughout, regardless of scale, although the text sometimes particularises certain events. It is essential to remember that from the point of view of the man with a rifle or the man with a spear, no battle is less than another, and the individual risk of brutal death or injury is just as great whenever he looks his enemy in the eye. Historians and armchair generals may later debate whether it was a skirmish, an ambush or a battle, but to the companions and family of the fallen, it makes little difference.

In pursuit of comprehensiveness, not selectivity, some actions have been included which might be regarded as marginal to the more narrow definition of a battle.

For example, the "confrontation" between King Charles I and Parliamentary forces at **Turnham Green** (1642) saw only scattered shots fired, but the King was forced to withdraw, saving London. A similar confrontation by Ivan Ivanovich of Moscow at **Ugra** (1480) persuaded the Mongol leader Ahmed Khan to withdraw and is claimed to symbolise the end of Mongol rule.

Standing in contrast to confrontations which involved very large numbers of men, but little or no fighting, are small actions where opposing forces effectively agreed to resolve issues by a clash of champions. Typical of these are the so-called Battle of the **Thirty** (1351), when the English and French garrisons of neighbouring castles in Brittany sent 30 men from either side to fight to the death; the Battle of **North Inch** (1396), when champions from two Scottish clans fought to the death in a judicial battle in the presence of the King himself to resolve a long-running feud; the tournament at **Arcos de Valdevez** (1140), when Portuguese and Galician knights fought to settle an invasion by royal rivals; or the semi-legendary Battle of the **Champions** (547 BC), when 300 men from either side reportedly fought to the death in a failed attempt to resolve a war between Sparta and Argos.

Also included in this project are a number of events which have been described as massacres. But in most cases, they have been included because of their broader historic or military significance.

Such events—with heavy losses inflicted on an ill-armed or even unarmed group—include the **Whitman Massacre** (1847), which triggered the Cayuse War; the **Jamestown** Massacre (1622), which began the Powhatan War; the **Yellow Creek** Massacre (1774), which led to the so-called Cresap's War; the **Amritsar** Massacre (1919), which galvanised Indian opposition to British rule in India and the massacre at **My Lai** (1968), which severely undermined America's war effort in Vietnam.

In other instances, however, the description "massacre" is far more equivocal and politically charged, such as the **Sand Creek Massacre** (1864), when Colonel John Chivington attacked a Cheyenne Indian camp; or the Massacre at **Wounded Knee Creek** (1890), when Colonel James Forsyth attacked a Ghost Dance camp in South Dakota. In both cases, it has been argued by some historians that these were battles, not massacres, because the Indians fought back and inflicted casualties on the American horse-soldiers. Addressing this question in relation to a similar attack at **Sappa Creek** (1875), William Chalfont wrote: "If a massacre is defined as the indiscriminate, wanton and wholesale slaughter of people, then there was a massacre" (1997).

Much less debatable are some other so-called massacres which are self-evidently battles, but in which one side suffered disproportionate or even total loss. Indeed, the description massacre is sometimes applied somewhat indiscriminately to any one-sided military disaster. A good example is the **Fetterman Massacre** (1866). In this battle in Wyoming, two well-armed forces fought a very hard action, but the outnumbered Americans under the impetuous Captain William Fetterman were killed to the last man. Many sources call it a massacre, but this famous defeat is perhaps more accurately described by its Sioux name, the Battle of the Hundred Slain. The same applies with the **Dade Massacre** (1835), in which only three soldiers out of 80 survived an Indian attack.

What battles to include?

Apart from the question of how to define a battle comes the question how to determine which battles should be included. This is equally challenging.

The most self-evident requirement is that the battle must have been recorded in writing, and for inclusion here, it must be cross-referenced in at least two independent sources, with good detail (or at least consensus among authorities) on the date, the event, the participants and the outcome. As a result, battles recorded in oral history alone are generally not included, even recognising that this excludes some extensive historic traditions, such as in parts of pre-European sub-Saharan Africa.

But even accepting that, a number of battles have been included which bear the classification "semi-legendary," such as **Halys** (585 BC), **Fei River** (383), **Bravalla** (735), **Svolde** (1000) or **Calatanazar** (1002).

One major objective of this military history project has been to bring to Western literature the many important battles fought in wars which are little reported in the principal English-language sources, particularly those fought in Central and Eastern Europe, South America, Mesoamerica and Central and East Asia. A typical case would be the Battle of **Cesis**, between Estonian and German forces in the shadow of World War I (19–23 June 1919). While this decisive action is seldom featured in the mainstream western European sources, within Estonia it marked the turning point of their War of Independence and is still celebrated every year as Victory Day.

The challenge of determining what to include is well illustrated by the American Civil War, one of history's most widely studied and documented conflicts. The US Federal Civil War Sites Advisory Commission reported that out of 10,500 armed conflicts in the war, they had chosen 384 as "principal battles," which they then classified according to historic significance. Although Civil War enthusiasts challenge the Federal government selection, the present publication has adhered explicitly to the Commission's determination, and has included just those 384 battles (although some which took place between Indian forces and government troops during the period have been reclassified as being part of various Indian campaigns rather than as specific Civil War battles).

In another example, the Military History Bureau of China's Ministry of National Defence has published a 100-volume *History of the Sino-Japanese War, 1937–1945*, which claimed that the Chinese fought 23 campaigns, 1,117 major battles, 38,531 engagements and, in the course of the war, lost an extraordinarily precise 3,327,916 military casualties and 5,787,352 civilian casualties. In this case, however, the relevant government authority failed to provide its own categorisation of the principal battles, and the selection of battles for inclusion here is once again subjective.

Another complexity regarding what to include is that some quite extensive conflicts had no specific actions at all which can be classified as named battles, but remain of historic interest. As a result, a limited selection of such wars is included in an appendix, and they also appear in the chronological index. This does not include history's large number of low-level wars and insurgencies, such as the Malayan Emergency of 1948–1960, where there were no significant battles. Many such conflicts have occurred, and most in the modern era are well documented elsewhere, especially those since 1945.

Beyond the scope of more traditional land battles, it is also necessary to consider what will be categorised as a naval battle. Is it a ship-to-ship action between just two vessels, such as **Guadaloupe** (1800)? Or does it include only fleet actions, such as **Actium** (31 BC)? Does the carrier-borne aircraft attack on the Italian fleet at **Taranto** (1940) constitute a naval battle? What about the Italian human torpedoes sinking the only two British battleships in the Mediterranean at **Alexandria** harbour (1941)?

The answer in each of these cases is that such actions are included, though of course on a selective basis. Furthermore, the list of naval battles in fact also includes what are effectively prolonged naval campaigns rather than specific actions, such as the Battles of the **Atlantic** in World War I and World War II. In the selection of battles, it must also be remembered that this is not just a dictionary of battles, but also of sieges, and many historic sieges were either wholly or partly naval operations, such as **Thasos** (465–463 BC), **Bari** (1068–1071), **Almeria** (1309) and **Dubrovnik** (1991–1992).

The question of air battles is even more difficult. To be included, the general rule is that there must be reasonably large-scale air forces on either side, which means that no air battles until after World War I are included. Broadly, this has also excluded large-scale air raids as specific battles, unless major forces were deployed from either side, or there were major losses, for example, **Nuremberg** (1944), **Ploesti** (1943), the Battle of **Britain** (1940), **Namsi** (1951); or when there was some other major military or political significance, such as **Guernica** (1937). In reality, however, air warfare is a relatively new technology and has been well covered in other publications.

Before leaving the issue of what constitutes a battle, a modern-day example illustrates the challenge of determining what should be included. In November 2001, during the Afghanistan War, a group of mainly foreign Taliban and al-Qaeda prisoners captured near **Kunduz** overwhelmed guards and seized their prison at **Qala-i-Jangi**. The bloodbath which followed has been variously described as a three-day prison riot, a massacre and a battle. And, while even today the details remain shrouded by often highly politicised reports, it is clear that artillery, tanks and jet aircraft were employed, and that perhaps 400 Taliban were killed along with about 40 Northern alliance troops and an American special forces observer. Was it a battle? Perhaps history will tell, but for now it has been included in this book.

What to call a battle?

Having decided what battles to include, it is by no means self-evident what name to give to each battle. While the great majority of battles are named for their geographic location, even that is subject to considerable variation. Even so famous a battle as **Waterloo** (1815) is known by some French historians as Mont St Jean.

Similarly, the French battle of **Guise** (1914) is known by the Germans as St Quentin; the allied Battle of the **Java Sea** (1942) is the Japanese Battle of Surubaya; the American Battle of **Buenavista** (1847) is the Mexican La Angostura; the German Battle of **Korsun** (1944) is the Russian Battle of the Cherkassy Pocket; the British Battle of **Jutland** (1916) is the German Battle of the Skaggerak; the British Battle of **Omdurman** (1898) is the Sudanese Karala; and one of the most famous battlefields of the American Civil War (1861 and 1862) is called either Manassas or **Bull Run**, depending on which side is describing the event.

Some distinctions arise simply from legitimate differences in the focus of the opposing armies, such as where they were headquartered, or from opposing nations using their own names for the same location, such as German Diedenhofen and French **Thionville** (1639), or the city of Oradea in modern Romania, also known as German Grosswardein and Hungarian **Nagyvarad** (1660).

A good example of the confusion which can arise from different national names is the Battle of **Ebelsberg** (1809), which is located just southeast of Linz. This action is sometimes referred to as Ebersberg, which has led to it being mistakenly located in a number of sources at Ebersberg, which is about 100 miles west near Munich.

A similar challenge arises from the use of modern names for locations. Broadly, the rule has been to use the name which applied at the time (in some cases, with the modern name in parentheses). Thus, for place names in India, for example, Bombay and Madras have been used throughout, not Mumbai and Chennai. And a battle as famous as **Stalingrad** (1942–1943) could hardly appear under its modern name Volgagrad. This distinction is especially difficult with the revised spellings in China. In general, this project uses the modern Pinyin Romanisation of Chinese names throughout—thus, **Zhijiang** (not Chihchiang), and **Tianjin** (not Tientsin), with cross-references where necessary. There are, however, a handful of exceptions, including Chiang Kai-Shek (not Jiang Jieshi) and **Hong Kong** (not Xianggang). The challenge of modern alternatives also applies to many Indian and Arabic place names (as well as personal names), which creates equal difficulties of transliteration into the English alphabet. The estimable *Encyclopedia of Islam* has been used as a reference in the latter cases. Thus, as referred to below, the famous battle in 636 is given here as **Qadisiyya**, with Kadasiya, Kadesiah and Cadesia provided as alternatives. The transliteration of Aztec and other Mesoamerican names is another such challenge (for example, the personal name Motecuhzoma, not Montezuma or Moctezuma).

Sometimes, the choice of name for a battle reflects other events. A classic case is the action at the confluence of the Rosillo and Salado Creeks, southeast of San Antonio, Texas, in 1813. At the time it was known as the Battle of the Salado, but is today usually called the Battle of **Rosillo**, in order to distinguish it from another battle fought at the **Salado** in 1842.

However, some geographic name choices are much more deliberate. A good example of the purely political naming of a battle is the great German victory in East Prussia at **Tannenberg** (1914). According to military historian Basil Liddell Hart, General Erich Ludendorf originally designated his triumph as Frogenau, which is where the battle took place. But his aide, Colonel Max Hoffman, reportedly suggested it should be called Tannenberg to erase the defeat of the Teutonic knights nearby in 1410. Although

Tannenberg was some miles to the southeast, this is the name by which the battle came to be known by both sides—a telling instance of how history is written by the victors.

Apart from geography, battles are also named for many other reasons. Some are named for one of the key participants, such as **Lochrey's Defeat** (1781) in Pennsylvania, named for the unfortunate Colonel Archibald Lochrey; or **Dudley's Defeat** (1813) in Ohio, named for the rashly impetuous Colonel William Dudley; or **Monson's Retreat** (1804), named for the equally rash Colonel William Monson in northwest India. Meanwhile, **Whitman Massacre** (1847) in Washington commemorates the ill-fated missionary Dr Marcus Whitman.

Similarly, both a battle and geography can be named for one of the participants, such as the **Cañón de Ugalde** in West Texas, named for the battle in the Sabinal River Canyon in 1790, between Apache and the Mexican commander General Juan de Ugalde.

An example of how this form of name evolves is provided by the clash on an unnamed island in the dry Arikee River in eastern Colorado in 1848. During this action, an American scouting detachment under Major George Forsyth was attacked by a large war party led by the Cheyenne Chief Roman Nose. One of 23 American casualties was Lieutenant Fredrick Beecher, and Roman Nose was also killed. The army called it the Battle of **Beecher Island**, while the Indians call it the Battle Where Roman Nose Was Killed.

Perhaps the most extreme example of this form is the battle which many historians have come to describe as **Boudicca** (61 AD). The exact location of this decisive Roman victory over Boudicca (or Boadicea) of the Iceni is effectively unknown and remains the subject of extensive academic debate. But it is of such historic importance that the event has widely been assigned simply the name of the British Warrior Queen whose army was crushed.

Another example of an uncertain battle site is the great Roman disaster on the German frontier, known as the Battle of **Teutoborgwald** (9 AD). In the 1980s, the apparent battlefield was finally located some considerable distance away at

Kalkriese, near Osnabruck. However, the traditional name is still generally accepted and retained.

Likewise, historians have traditionally recorded that the Byzantine Emperor Heraclius, in 622, landed on the Plain of Issus in the northeastern Mediterranean to advance into Armenia and defeat the Persian Shahbaraz. Modern scholars believe it is more likely that Heraclius crossed the Sea of Marmara from Constantinople to land in northwestern Turkey, advancing to **Ophlimos** on the Lycus to secure his decisive victory over the Persians.

Another category of battles are those known today by a name assigned after the event, which has become the accepted name for the location, such as **Massacre Canyon** (Nebraska, 1873), **Battle Creek** (Idaho, 1878), **Bloody Ridge** (Guadalcanal, 1942 and Korea, 1951), **Blood River** (Natal, 1838) or **Bloody Nose Ridge** (Peliliu, 1944). The battlefield of **Kepaniwai** (which means "damning of the waters") is named for the action in Hawaii's Iao Valley in 1790 when there were so many dead that they reputedly blocked the stream.

Similarly, the site of the British disaster at Parent's Creek in Detroit in 1763 was subsequently named **Bloody Run**, and the Battle of **Anzac** in the Dardanelles is named for the 1915 landing by the Australian and New Zealand Army Corps (ANZACs) on a previously unnamed stretch of coast just north of Gabe Tepe, identified on allied military maps as Beach Z.

Even the date can provide the name for a battle, such as **Christmas Hill** (also known as Longstop Hill or Djebel Rhar) in Tunisia, where a battle took place on Christmas Eve 1942; or the famous victory at **Puebla** in Mexico in 1862, which is still celebrated as **Cinco de Mayo** (5 May). The great naval battle known as the **Glorious First of June** (1794) was obviously named by the British for the date of their victory. The defeated French call it Ushant (or Ouessant) after the Breton island more than 400 miles to the east.

In addition, there are battles which have gained "popular" names unrelated to date or geography. Typical of these would be **Leipzig**

(1813), which is known by the Germans as the Battle of the Nations, while the French call it the Battle of the Giants. **Austerlitz** (1805) is also known as the Battle of the Three Emperors, while **Alcazarquivir** (1578) is called the Battle of the Three Kings.

Some battles, including many in World War II, Korea and Vietnam, are well known by their code names, such as Operation Market Garden used to describe the attack on **Arnhem** in September 1944, or Operation Buffalo for the battle at **Con Thien** in July 1967. Broadly, this book avoids such operational names, except where there is no adequate or generally accepted geographic name, such as the Operation **Longcloth** incursion in northern Burma in early 1943.

However, in recognition of the different names for particular battles, this book provides the widest possible range of alternates. These are given in the format "Abárzuza, 1874, 2nd Carlist War See Estella," There are over 2,500 such cross-references.

Furthermore, while most battles are described simply by their accepted names, this book has added further distinction where there may be confusion over battlefields of the same name in different countries, such as **Tripoli, Libya** (1551) and **Tripoli, Syria** (1289); **Hyderabad, India** (1709) and **Hyderabad, Pakistan** (1843) or **Barcelona, Spain** (1936) and **Barcelona, Venezuela** (1817). A similar distinction has also been provided where there are battlefields of the same name within one country, such as the Indian battles of **Gheria, Bombay** (1756) and **Gheria, Bengal** (1763); the New Zealand War battles at **Te Ahuahu, Bay of Islands** (1845) and **Te Ahuahu, Taranaki** (1864); the American battles at **Charleston, Massachusetts** (1776), **Charleston, South Carolina** (1781) and **Charlestown, West Virginia** (1864) and, even more confusingly, the battles at **Friedberg, Bavaria** and **Friedberg, Hesse** fought within a few weeks in Germany in 1796.

Finally, where more than one battle has been fought at a particular location, these are commonly referred to elsewhere as, for example, First Bull Run (1861) and Second Bull Run (1862). However, because some locations have

so seen many battles (this book has, for example, 15 entries for Constantinople, 15 for Kabul, 12 for Alexandria and 11 for Adrianople), the designations 1st, 2nd, 3rd etc. are used only for battles fought in the same year. In this way, the two battles of Bull Run are not referred to as first and second, whereas this distinction is used for the two battles at **Babi Wali Kotal** in 1842, the three battles at **Douaumont** in 1916 and the four separate battles at **Cawnpore** in 1857. The same applies to the eleven battles fought on the **Isonzo** between 1915 and 1917.

In the book's chronological index, however, such battles appear only once for each year. The only exception is Dacca, 1971, where two battles were fought in the same year at the same location, but in different wars.

What date to assign?

The seemingly simple question of what date to assign to a battle also gives rise to argument and debate. The most common complication is the overlap of the New and Old Style calendars, which were introduced around the Western world at different times. In general, this book attempts to use the calendar applicable in the country concerned at the time of the battle, though historic records can vary and cause great confusion, especially where opposing combatant countries were using different calendars.

While these calendar variations are usually no more than a few days, much more significant differences can arise from academic debate over the correct interpretation of historic battles, which may rely on ambiguous documents or on varying interpretations of non-Western chronologies, such as certain Muslim or Asian calendar systems.

Where serious academic debate continues, an attempt has been made to assign dates which appear to reflect a consensus among historians, though for battles such as **Kadesh** (1275 BC), **Megiddo** (1468 BC), **Covadonga** (718) and the Siege of **Troy** (1184 BC), the annotation "trad date" has been used to indicate uncertainty. In the case of the vital strategic battle at **Qadisiyya** during the Muslim conquest of Persia, the exact timing is so important and so hotly argued by scholars that this entry has the annotation "disputed date 636 or 637." For a handful of battles in medieval India, where regnal chronologies are the subject of extensive academic debate, the style used is **Pullalur** (disputed date, c 610).

When exact dates are known, historians are most often in agreement about what day a battle started. But when a battle ended can be a subject of considerable debate. A good example is provided by some of the great offensives on the Western Front during World War I. Some historians date such battles as ending when the last advance was halted, but others give a date days or even weeks later, when fighting finally died down.

While determining the exact date for a battle can be challenging, dating a siege can be even more fraught with variables, especially for very prolonged siege campaigns. Some writers, for example, date the start of a siege from when the enemy army first approaches the target town or fort, or when they first meet the defenders in battle outside the walls. Other historians suggest that a siege commences only when the attacking force complete their encirclement, or when they commence the preliminary bombardment, or perhaps when they launch the first major assault. It is similarly debatable when to date a siege reaching its conclusion. Some historians record that a siege ends when a relieving force breaks through the encircling attackers, or at the time of the final assault. Others date as the siege ending when the attacking army finally secures the target town, or when the unsuccessful attackers finally withdraw. It is even more confusing when the attackers storm and seize a city, yet the garrison holds out in the citadel. The difference in dates can be very significant, especially in the case of some historic battles where a defeated or unsuccessful siege force might take weeks or even months before it finally withdraws.

What to call a war?

The final issue to be considered is what name to use for the wars to which battles are assigned. While the names of wars usually seem to be self-evident, this is very often not the case. Some distinctions are simply reflections of national involvement, such as the Swabian War (1499), which the Germans call the Swiss War; the Vietnam War (1963–1972), which the Vietnamese call the American War or the anti-American War; the French-Mexican War (1861–1867), which the Mexicans call the War of the Intervention; or the brutal conflict of 1857–1858, which the British call the Indian Mutiny (or the Sepoy Rebellion), and which some Indian historians call the First Indian War of Independence.

Similarly, the war on the American central plains in 1874–1875, which the Army called the Red River War, is known by the Indians as the War to Save the Buffalo, while the Creek Indian War (1813–1814) is known by the Creek themselves as the Red Stick War. Indeed, some historians do not credit the latter as a separate war at all, but regard it simply as part of the War of 1812.

In some cases, European names have been given to non-European wars. For example, the Japanese refer to the Boshin War (1868–1869) and the Seinan War (1877), which are respectively nominated here as the War of the Meiji Restoration and the Satsuma Rebellion.

Descriptors such as rebellion, mutiny and uprising are widely employed in this book, even though one side's rebellion is often the other side's war of liberation. Similarly, words such as rebel and insurgent have been used in some instances. The broad objective throughout, however, is to conform to common usage, not to express any political or partisan opinion.

Indeed, some wars have been renamed in modern times, specifically in the interests of political sensitivity. Take for instance the series of campaigns fought between the British and the Xhosa people of South Africa between 1779 and 1877, often referred to as the Kaffir Wars. As that term is now regarded as pejorative, they are now sometimes called the Frontier Wars, the Cape Frontier Wars or the Anglo-Xhosa Wars. This book has called them the Cape Frontier Wars, even though Kaffir Wars is undeniably the name by which they were best known at the time. Similarly, the conflicts in New Zealand between

1843 and 1870 were known for 130 years as the Maori Wars. But that nomenclature too is now criticised, and this book has adopted the alternative term New Zealand Wars. By contrast, however, this book has retained throughout the term Indian rather than Native American—as in Sioux Indian Wars and Navajo Indian War.

In other cases, the choice of war name used in this project must sometimes necessarily be little more than arbitrary. For example, the American phase of the War of the Grand Alliance (1688–1697) is referred to as King William's War, and the American phase of the War of the Spanish Succession (1701–1714) has been given its alternate name, Queen Anne's War. However, the War of Netherlands' Independence (1566–1648) is not given its common alternative name, the Eighty Years War, and the name Seven Years War is given only to the great European conflict of 1756–1763, not its alternate use for the Second Seminole War (1835–1842). Nor are either the Russo-Polish War (1654–1667) or the War between Poland and the Teutonic Order (1454–1566) given their common alternative name, the Thirteen Years War. Similarly, the description Wars of the Three Kingdoms is used for the brutal struggle in China in the third century AD, not as the modern alternative for what was once called the English civil wars, now more widely known as the British civil wars.

For some wars, the selection of a "correct" name is made difficult simply by the abundance of choice. The 1973 Arab-Israeli War, for example, is widely also known as the Yom Kippur War, the Ramadan War, the October War and the War of Atonement. And the book *Our Incredible Civil War* (Burke Davis, 1960) records no fewer than 35 different names for the American Civil War, including the War of the Rebellion, the War of Secession, the War between the States, the Confederate War and many others.

For some conflicts, there is simply no generally accepted name. Accordingly, this book categorises such campaigns very broadly, for example, the Greco-Persian Wars (498–450 BC), Goth Invasion of the Roman Empire (402–471), Ottoman Conquest of the Balkans (1363–1396), Maratha Wars of Succession (1762–1775), Co-lombian civil wars (1823–1877) and Persian-Afghan Wars (1711–1755). For very prolonged campaigns, such as the 400 years of intermittent conflict between Byzantium and her Muslim neighbours, the battles have been assigned to three major logical groupings: Early Byzantine-Muslim Wars (645–739), Byzantine-Muslim Wars (778–902) and Later Byzantine-Muslim Wars (961–1038).

These descriptions are necessarily arbitrary and fairly loose, as is the timing of when such campaigns began and finished. A good example of debate over the time frame of a campaign is the Reconquista, or Christian Reconquest of Spain and Portugal. Most historians agree that the campaign concluded with the recapture of Granada in 1492, but there is extensive academic disagreement over when it commenced. Some scholars argue that the Reconquest began with the semi-legendary defeat of the Muslim invaders at **Covadonga** (718), while others argue that the campaign commenced when Alfonso VI of Castile captured **Toledo** (1085). Yet others suggest the Reconquest really began only after Pope Urban's proclamation of Crusade in 1095. For the record, this book defines the first battle of the Reconquest as **Graus** (1063), and for convenience divides the long struggle into Early Christian Reconquest of Spain (1063–1248), Later Christian Reconquest of Spain (1309–1452) and Final Christian Reconquest of Spain (1481–1492). A similar problem arises when wars merge into one another, such as Cresap's War (1774), which soon merged with Lord Dunmore's War (1774), or the eight-year struggle between Japan and China, which commenced in 1937 as the Sino-Japanese War and merged after December 1941 into World War II. Some Chinese historians have overcome this latter problem by referring to the entire campaign as the War of Resistance, though this nomenclature has limited currency outside China.

Names of commanders

The style adopted for naming commanders is usually given name and family name only, but in some cases, a further degree of distinction is needed to avoid misunderstanding, such as dates of birth and death or the use of a middle name.

In this way, dates are used to distinguish the almost exact contemporaries General Sir Charles Napier (1782–1853) and his cousin naval commander Sir Charles Napier (1786–1860), or the cousins Admiral Samuel Hood (1762–1814) and Admiral Samuel Hood (1724–1816). Equally confusing for historians are Sir John Doveton (1768–1847) and Sir John Doveton (1782–1857), who both fought in India, as did General Sir Henry Norman (1818–1899) and Field Marshal Sir Henry Norman (1826–1904).

While American commanders are commonly credited with their middle initial, even more distinction is needed in the case of Henry H. (Hastings) Sibley (1811–1891), who fought the Sioux in Minnesota and Dakota and served as a General in the Union army, while Henry H. (Hopkins) Sibley (1816–1886) was a Confederate General in the same war. A similar American example of the need for further distinction is General James Henry Lane (1833–1907), who led a Confederate brigade in many key battles, while General James Henry "Jim" Lane (1814–1866) was an anti-slavery campaigner who commanded Kansas militia and was later a US Senator.

For ranks and titles, the objective has been to use the rank or title at the time of the particular battle. For example, Stephan Dushan of Serbia is described as Crown Prince when he helped defeat the Byzantines at **Velbuzhde** (1330), while he is referred to as Emperor in his decisive victory over the Byzantine army at **Adrianople** (1355). Similarly, commanders are generally credited with their rank at the time of a particular battle, not their ultimate rank. For example, one of Britain's most famous soldiers is referred to as Colonel Arthur Wellesley in his early battles in Europe and India, as General Sir Arthur Wellesley at the start of the Peninsular Campaign, as Arthur Wellesley Lord Wellington.

I have tried to use the same principle of simplicity in other combinations titles such as Field Marshal Sir Henry Norman after his elevation to the peerage following the great victory at **Talavera de la Reina** (1809) and as the Duke of Wellington in the **Waterloo** Campaign of 1815.

At a broader level, in the interests of brevity, the courtesy rank of General is used throughout, rather than Lieutenant General, Brigadier General and so on. For the same reason, naval flag officers are referred to as Admiral, not Vice Admiral or Rear Admiral, and Field Marshals generally appear simply as Marshal.

The selection of who to name as commander can also be a challenge for such brief battle entries—whether to identify the national military commander or the overall army commander or the field commander. In general, it is the field commander who has been identified.

Accuracy

Military historians and military history enthusiasts are notoriously keen to identify "mistakes" in their field—from arguments about which was in fact the "last cavalry charge in battle" or "the largest tank battle in history," to movie anachronisms such as the 1915-model Webley revolver reportedly carried by Stanley Baker in the movie *Zulu*, set at **Rorke's Drift** in 1879.

It is essential, however, to distinguish between errors of facts and differences of opinion. The preceding discussion of the "correct" name for battles, the "correct" date and even the "correct" location illustrates just a few of the challenging areas which may provide a rich source of claimed "mistakes." Similarly, the reporting of casualties in any particular battle can be highly contentious and politically charged. Apart from the ever-present elements of propaganda and nationalistic exaggeration, even the "facts" can be open to interpretation. A good illustration is provided by the air battle over **Namsi** during the Korean War. The official American record correctly says three B-29 bombers were "shot down." However, two crash-landed after the raid and two more were so badly damaged that they were scrapped. So the Russian record of the same action equally correctly says seven American bombers were "destroyed."

For every battle recorded in this book, extensive effort has been made to cross-reference as many sources as possible for academic and historic consensus and consistency. But even this is difficult. For, as Dr Samuel Johnson said, "Many things which are false are transmitted from book to book and gain credit in the world." Indeed, the research for this project revealed many cases where a clear mistake made in one book was picked up and repeated in others. But, as Napoleon Bonaparte himself said, "What is history but a fable agreed upon." Where there is legitimate disagreement among authorities, there is sometimes little choice but to make a judgment based on the available information. In this respect, a good option is sometimes to fall back on what Lieutenant-Colonel Alfred H. Burne rather nicely calls "Inherent Military Probability" (1952).

Beyond these matters of opinion and legitimate debate, however, there is the reality that in any project of this scope and scale, it is inevitable that there will be errors of fact, despite the extensive cross-referencing of sources, checking of transcription and extensive review by experts in their respective historic periods. Some of the hundreds of individuals, institutions and libraries who kindly provided invaluable assistance are acknowledged below, but all opinions, interpretations and details—right or wrong—remain the sole responsibility of the author. Any legitimate corrections or suggested additional battles will of course be welcome for future editions.

Acknowledgments

Scores of scholars, historians, researchers and enthusiasts around the world (not to mention dozens of mainly anonymous librarians, especially those at the State Library of Victoria) have contributed to this project, particularly in tracking down obscure details such as the full names of lesser known commanders and the exact location and geographic relationship of obscure battlefields. This help was especially appreciated in relation to battles in Central and Eastern Europe, many of which are little known in the mainstream English-language literature.

The following are particularly acknowledged and thanked:

Bob Babcock (22nd Infantry Regiment Society, Marietta, Georgia), John Beauval (Ghent, Belgium), Dr Valdis Berzins (Institute of History of Latvia, Riga), Bernard Browne (National 1798 Centre, Enniscorthy, Ireland), James Burd (Italian-American Military Collector's Association), Scott Chafin (Houston, Texas), Cheat Mountain Club (West Virginia), Jose Correia (Estarreja, Portugal), Professor Rafe de Crespigny (Australian National University, Canberra), Holger Doebold (Spain), Dr Srilal Fernando (Ceylon Society, Melbourne, Australia), Goran Frilund (Nykarleby, Finland), Dr Femme Gaastra (Leiden University, Holland), Chris George (*Journal of the War of 1812*, Baltimore), Wilma Goosen (University Library of Amsterdam, Maastricht), Slawek Grzechnik (California), Mike Guidry (Church Point, Louisiana), Natalya Gutina (Petrozavodsk, Russia), Scott Hartwig (Gettysburg National Military Park), Herki Helves (Viljandi Museum, Estonia), Ara Hakopian (Moscow), Tom Holmburg (Chicago), Esben Høstager (Copenhagen, Denmark), Dr Dexter Hoyos (Sydney University), Chris Hunt (Leicester, England), Ian Jackson (San Francisco), Henrik Stissing Jensen (Danish National Archives, Copenhagen), J. L. Keene (South African National Museum of Military History, Johannesburg), Mikail Khvostov (Russia), Chris Kimball (Orlando, Florida), Jüri Kivimäe (University of Toronto), Bill Latta (USA), Martin Liechty (Zurich), Dr Stewart Lone (Australian Defence Force Academy, Canberra), Philip Mackie (Seven Years War Association, England), Gordon Mackinlay (Sydney, Australia), Adjutant Emilio Condado Madera (Foreign Legion Museum, Aubagne, France), Joan Marsh (South African Military History Society, Kengray), Lidia Martinez (Madrid, Spain), Dr Pat McCarthy (Military History Society of Ireland, Dublin), Earl McGill (Tucson, Arizona), Alexander Mikaberidze (Mississippi State University), Michel Moerenhout (Royal Museum of the Army and Military History, Brussels), Linda Morton-Keithley (Idaho State Historical Society), George Nafziger (West Chester, Ohio), Soeren Noerby (Royal Danish Naval Museum, Copenhagen), Jean-Marie Piquart (Nancy, France), George Razutov (Moscow), Professor Merle Ricklefs (Melbourne University), Bernabe

Saiz (Logrona, Spain), Iwona Sakowicz (University of Gdansk, Poland), Dan Schorr (Maine), Nikolay Semibratov (Russia), Steven H. Smith (California), Julie Somay (Commonwealth War Graves Commission), 8th Tennessee Infantry Reenactment Unit, J. M. Toledo (Leioa, Spain), Geert van Uythoven (Willemstad, Holland), Bernhard Voykowitsch (Vienna), John Wilson (Wellington, New Zealand), Neil Wood (HMS Charybdis Association), Kate Woods (National Army Museum, London), Alexander Zhmodikov (St Petersburg).

Chronological Reference Guide

This semi-chronological reference guide contains every named battle in the main alphabetical section, sorted by the earliest battle recorded in any particular war. The reference guide also has chronological entries for a small number of selected wars which do not have specific recorded battles, but which remain sufficiently significant to be included in a separate appendix (pages 1139 to 1146).

Battles of the Ancient World to 600 AD

Egyptian-Syrian Wars: Megiddo, **1468 BC**

Egyptian-Hittite Wars: Kadesh, **1275 BC**

Trojan War: Troy, **1184 BC**

Philistine-Israel Wars: Eben-ezer, **1050 BC**; Michmash, **1013 BC**; Mount Gilboa, **1010 BC**

Wars of the Western Zhou: Muye, **1045 BC**; Zongzhou, **771 BC**

Early Assyrian Wars: Qarqar, **854 BC**

Nubian Conquest of Egypt, 750–730 BC. See Appendix

1st Messenian War, 736–716 BC. See Appendix

Lelantine War, 725–700 BC. See Appendix

Assyrian Wars: Samaria, **724–722 BC**; Qarqar, Raphia, **720 BC**; Eltekeh, **700 BC**; Khalule, **691 BC**; Khanigalbat, **681 BC**; Azotus, **659–630 BC**; Nineveh, **653 BC**; Babylon (Iraq), **650–648 BC**

Wars of China's Spring and Autumn Era: Xuge, **707 BC**; Han, **645 BC**; Hong, **638 BC**; Chengpu, **632 BC**; Yao, **627 BC**; Bi, **597 BC**; An, **589 BC**; Yanling, **575 BC**; Biyang, **563 BC**; Boju, **506 BC**; Zuili, **496 BC**; Fuqiao, **494 BC**; Lizhe, **478 BC**; Suzhou, **475–473 BC**

Rise of Argos: Hysiae, **669 BC**

2nd Messenian War, 650–630 BC. See Appendix

Babylon's Wars of Conquest: Nineveh, **612 BC**; Harran, **610 BC**; Carchemish, **605 BC**; Jerusalem, **597 BC**; Jerusalem, **587–586 BC**

Egyptian Conquest of Judah: Megiddo, **609 BC**

Egyptian-Nubian War: Napata, **593 BC**

1st Sacred War: Crisa, **590 BC**

Median-Lydian War: Halys, **585 BC**

Median-Persian War, 553–550 BC. See Appendix

Persian-Lydian War: Pteria, **547 BC**; Sardis, Thymbria, **546 BC**

Spartan-Argive Wars: Champions, **547 BC**; Sepeia, **494 BC**

Persian-Babylonian War: Babylon (Iraq), **541–539 BC**

Carthaginian-Greek Wars: Alalia, **535 BC**

Persian Invasion of Egypt: Pelusium, **525 BC**

Persian War of Succession, 521–519 BC. See Appendix

Persia's Scythian Expedition, 516–509 BC. See Appendix

Early Roman-Etruscan Wars: Rome, **505 BC**; Lake Regillus, **496 BC**; Cremera, **477 BC**

Greco-Persian Wars: Ephesus, **498 BC**; Salamis (Cyprus), **497 BC**; Lade, **494 BC**; Marathon, **490 BC**; Artemisium, Salamis (Greece), Thermopylae, **480 BC**; Mycale, Plataea, **479 BC**; Eurymedon, **466 BC**; Papremis, **459 BC**; Prosopitis, **456–454 BC**; Salamis (Cyprus), **450 BC**

Carthaginian Invasion of Sicily: Himera, **480 BC**

Syracusan-Etruscan War: Cumae, **474 BC**

Arcadian War: Tegea, **473 BC**; Dipaea, **417 BC**

Wars of the Delian League: Drabescus, **465–464 BC**; Thasos, **465–463 BC**

3rd Messenian War, 464–455 BC. See Appendix

1st Peloponnesian War: Aegina, **458–457 BC**; Oenophyta, Tanagra, **457 BC**; Coronea, **447 BC**

2nd Sacred War, 449–448 BC. See Appendix

Corinthian-Corcyrean War: Leucimne, **435** BC; Sybota, **433** BC

Great Peloponnesian War: Potidaea, **432–429** BC; Methone, **431** BC; Naupactus, Patras, Spartolus, **429** BC; Plataea, **429–427** BC; Mytilene, **428–427** BC; Corcyra, **427** BC; Olpae, Tanagra, **426** BC; Pylos-Sphacteria, Solygeia, **425** BC; Delium, Megara, **424** BC; Amphipolis, **422** BC; Mantinea, **418** BC; Syracuse, **415** BC; Syracuse, **414–413** BC; Syracuse Harbour, **413** BC; Chios, **412** BC; Miletus, **412** BC; Cynossema, Eretria, Syme, **411** BC; Cyzicus, **410** BC; Arginusae, Notium, **406** BC; Aegospotami, **405** BC; Athens, **404** BC; Munychia, **403** BC

Wars of the Roman Republic: Algidus, **431** BC

Roman-Etruscan Wars: Fidenae, **426** BC; Veii, **405–396** BC

Carthaginian-Syracusan Wars: Himera, Selinus, **409** BC; Acragas, **406** BC

Persian Civil War: Cunaxa, **401** BC

1st Dionysian War: Motya, **397–396** BC; Syracuse, **396** BC

Corinthian War: Haliartus, **395** BC; Corinth, **394–392** BC; Cnidus, Coronea, Nemea, **394** BC; Lechaeum, **390** BC; Cremaste, **388** BC

Gallic Invasion of Italy: Allia, **390** BC

2nd Dionysian War: Elleporus, **389** BC

3rd Dionysian War: Cabala, Cronium, **383** BC

Wars of the Greek City-States: Naxos, **376** BC; Tegyra, **375** BC; Leuctra, **371** BC; Midea, **368** BC; Cynoscephalae, **364** BC; Mantinea, **362** BC; Peparethus, **361** BC

4th Dionysian War: Lilybaeum, **368–367** BC

1st Greek Social War: Chios, **357** BC; Embata, Potidaea, **356** BC

3rd Sacred War: Methone, **355–354** BC; Neon, **354** BC; Thessaly, **353** BC; Pagasae, **352** BC; Olynthus, **348** BC

China's Era of the Warring States: Guiling, **353** BC; Maling, **341** BC; Jimo, **279** BC; Changping, **260** BC; Handan, **259–258** BC; Pingyang, **234** BC

Timoleon's War: Adranum, **344** BC; Crimisus, **340** BC

1st Samnite War: Mount Gaurus, **342** BC

Latin War: Suessa, **339** BC

4th Sacred War: Perinthus, **339** BC; Chaeronea, **338** BC

Archidamian Wars: Mandonium, **338** BC

Conquests of Alexander the Great: Thebes, **335** BC; Granicus, Halicarnassus, Miletus, **334** BC; Issus, **333** BC; Gaza, Tyre, **332** BC; Gaugamela, **331** BC; Jaxartes, **329** BC; Aornos, Sogdian Rock, **327** BC; Hydaspes, **326** BC

Macedonian Conquests: Megalopolis, Pandosia, **331** BC

Lamian War: Lamia, **323–322** BC; Amorgos, Crannon, **322** BC

2nd Samnite War: Caudine Forks, **321** BC; Lautulae, **315** BC; Tarracina, **314** BC; Lake Vadimo, **310** BC; Bovianum, **305** BC

Wars of the Diadochi: Memphis, **321** BC; Paraetacene, **317** BC; Tyre, **315–314** BC; Gaza, **312** BC; Salamis (Cyprus), **306** BC; Rhodes, **305–304** BC; Ipsus, **301** BC; Corupedion, **281** BC

Wars of the Mauryan Empire, 321–232 BC. See Appendix

Agathoclean War: Himera River, **311** BC; Syracuse, **311–307** BC; Carthage (Tunisia), **310–307** BC

3rd Samnite War: Camerinum, Sentinum, **295** BC; Aquilonia, **293** BC

Later Roman-Etruscan War: Arretium, Lake Vadimo, **283** BC

Damascene War, 280–275 BC. See Appendix

Pyrrhic War: Heraclea (Lucania), **280** BC; Asculum (Apulia), **279** BC; Lilybaeum, **277–275** BC; Beneventum, **275** BC; Argos, **272** BC

1st Syrian War, 274–271 BC. See Appendix

Chremonidian War: Corinth, **265** BC; Athens, **264–262** BC

1st Punic War: Messana, **264** BC; Acragas, **262** BC; Lipara, Mylae, **260** BC; Adys, Ecnomus, **256** BC; Hermaeum, Tunis, **255** BC; Panormus (Sicily), **251** BC; Lilybaeum, **250–241** BC; Drepanum, **249** BC; Aegates Islands, **241** BC

2nd Syrian War, 260–255 BC. See Appendix

Macedonian-Egyptian Wars: Cos, **254** BC; Andros, **245** BC

3rd Syrian War: Antioch (Syria), **244** BC

Wars of the Achaean League: Corinth, **243** BC; Pellene, **241** BC

Truceless War: Utica, Bagradas, **240** BC; Saw, Tunis, Leptis, **238** BC

War of Demetrius, 239–229 BC. See Appendix

War of the Brothers: Ancyra, **235** BC

Pergamum-Seleucid Wars: Pergamum, **230** BC; Lake Koloe, Harpasus, **229** BC

1st Illyrian War: Paxos, **229** BC

Cleomenic War: Ladoceia, Mount Lyceum, **227** BC; Hecatombaeum, **226** BC; Sellasia, **222** BC

Gallic Wars in Italy: Faesulae, Telamon, **225** BC; Adda, **223** BC; Clastidium, **222** BC; Cremona, Placentia, **200** BC; Mincio, **197** BC; Lake Como, **196** BC; Mutina, **193** BC

Syrian Civil War: Apollonia, **220** BC

2nd Punic War: Tagus, **220 BC**; Saguntum, **219 BC**; Chevelu, Tarraco, Ticinus, Trebbia, White Rock, **218 BC**; Ebro, Lake Trasimene, **217 BC**; Cannae, Nola, **216 BC**; Ibera, Nola, **215 BC**; Beneventum, Casilinum, Leontini, Nola, **214 BC**; Syracuse, **213–212 BC**; Beneventum, Capua, Herdonea, Saguntum, Silarus, **212 BC**; Baetis, Capua, Ilurci, **211 BC**; Herdonea, Numistro, **210 BC**; Asculum, Apulia, New Carthage, **209 BC**; Baecula, Bantia, Venusia, **208 BC**; Gibraltar, Grumentum, Metaurus, **207 BC**; Ilipa, **206 BC**; Locri, **205 BC**; Agathocles, Crotona, Liguria, **204 BC**; Bagradas, Utica, **203 BC**; Zama, **202 BC**

2nd Illyrian War: Dimale, **219 BC**

2nd Greek Social War, 219–217 BC. See Appendix

4th Syrian War: Raphia, **217 BC**

1st Macedonian War, 215–205 BC. See Appendix

Early Syrian-Parthian War: Arius, **208 BC**

Fall of the Qin Dynasty: Julu, **207 BC**; Xianyang, **207 BC**

Spartan-Achaean Wars: Mantinea, **207 BC**; Scotitas, **199 BC**; Argos, **195 BC**; Gytheum, **194 BC**; Mount Barbosthene, **192 BC**

Chu-Han War: Jingxing, Pengcheng, **205 BC**; Chenggao, **204 BC**; Gaixia, **202 BC**

2nd Macedonian War: Chios, Lade, **201 BC**; Abydos, **200 BC**; Aous, **198 BC**; Cynoscephalae, **197 BC**

Wars of the Former Han: Pingcheng, **200 BC**; Dayuan, **102 BC**; Kangju, **36 BC**

5th Syrian War: Paneas, **198 BC**

Roman-Syrian War: Corycus, Thermopylae, **191 BC**; Eurymedon, Magnesia, Myonnesus, **190 BC**

3rd Macedonian War: Callicinus, **171 BC**; Pydna, **168 BC**

Maccabean War: Beth Horon, Beth Zur, Emmaus, Gophna, **166 BC**; Beth Zachariah, **164 BC**; Adasa, Capharsalma, Elasa, **161 BC**

Lusitanian Wars, 154–138 BC. See Appendix

Celtiberian Wars, 153–133 BC. See Appendix

Seleucid Dynastic War: Ptolemais, **150 BC**

4th Macedonian War: Pydna, **149 BC**

3rd Punic War: Carthage (Tunisia), **148–146 BC**

Roman-Achaean War: Corinth, Scarpheia, **146 BC**

Syrian Dynastic War: Oenaparus, **145 BC**

Syrian-Parthian War, 141–139 BC. See Appendix

1st Servile War: Enna, Tauromenium, **133 BC**

Numantian War: Numantia, **133 BC**

Later Syrian-Parthian War: Zab, **130 BC**; Ecbatana, **129 BC**

Rome's Gallic Wars: Avignon, Isara, **121 BC**; Noreia, **113 BC**; Provence, **109 BC**; Aginnum, **107 BC**; Arausio, **105 BC**; Adige, Aquae Sextiae, **102 BC**; Vercellae, **101 BC**

Chinese Conquest of Vietnam, 111 BC. See Appendix

Jugurthine War: Suthul, **109 BC**; Muthul, **108 BC**; Thala, **107 BC**; Cirta, **106 BC**

2nd Servile War, 104–99 BC. See Appendix

Roman Social War: Acerrae, Teanum, Tolenus, **90 BC**; Asculum (Marche), Fucine Lake, Pompeii, **89 BC**

1st Mithridatic War: Rhodes, **88 BC**; Piraeus, **87–86 BC**; Chaeronea, Orchomenus, **86 BC**; Miletopolis, Tenedos, **85 BC**

Sullan Civil War: Mount Tifata, **83 BC**; Aesis, Colline Gate, Faventia, Sacriportus, **82 BC**

2nd Mithridatic War: Halys, **82 BC**

Sertorian War: Baetis, **80 BC**; Anas, **79 BC**; Ilerda, **78 BC**; Lauron, **76 BC**; Italica, Murviedro, Sucro, Turia, **75 BC**; Calahorra, **74 BC**

Lepidus Revolt, 77 BC. See Appendix

3rd Mithridatic War: Chalcedon, **74 BC**; Cyzicus, Lemnos, **73 BC**; Cabira, **72 BC**; Tigranocerta, **69 BC**; Artaxata, **68 BC**; Zela, **67 BC**; Lycus, **66 BC**

3rd Servile War: Silarus, **71 BC**

Catiline Revolt: Pistoria, **62 BC**

Rome's Later Gallic Wars: Admagetobriga, **61 BC**; Mühlhausen, Arar, Bibracte, **58 BC**; Aduatuca, Aisne, Sambre, **57 BC**; Morbihan Gulf, **56 BC**; Aduatuca, **54 BC**; Agendicum, Alesia, Avaricum, Gergovia, **52 BC**

Roman Invasion of Britain: Deal, **55 BC**; Wheathampstead, **54 BC**

Roman-Parthian Wars: Carrhae, **53 BC**; Gindarus, **38 BC**; Phraaspa, **36 BC**

Wars of the First Triumvirate: Bagradas, **49 BC**; Curicta, **49 BC**; Ilerda, **49 BC**; Massilia, **49 BC**; Utica, **49 BC**; Dyrrhachium, **49–48 BC**; Messana, **48 BC**; Pharsalus, **48 BC**; Vibo, **48 BC**; Alexandria, **48–47 BC**; Nile, **47 BC**; Tauris, **47 BC**; Ruspina, **46 BC**; Thapsus, **46 BC**; Munda, **45 BC**

Roman-Pontian Wars: Nicopolis (Armenia), **48 BC**; Zela, **47 BC**

Wars of the Second Triumvirate: Mutina, **44–43 BC**; Forum Gallorum, **43 BC**; Philippi (Macedonia), **42 BC**; Perusia, **41–40 BC**; Cumae, **38 BC**; Mylae, Naulochus, Tauromenium, **36 BC**; Metulum, Siscia, **34 BC**; Actium, Methone, **31 BC**

Roman-Nubian War: Napata, **23 BC**

Rome's Germanic Wars: Lippe, **11 BC**; Teutoburgwald, **9**; Weser, **16**

Fall of the Xin Dynasty: Kunyang, **23**

Wars of the Later Han: Changlu, **29**; Chengdu, **36**; Lang Bac, **42**; Jiluo Mountain, **90**

Byzantine-Persian Wars: Amida, **502–503**; Apadna, Edessa, **503**; Dara, **530**; Callinicum, **531**; Antioch (Syria), Dara, **540**; Edessa, **544**; Petra, **548–549**; Petra, **551**; Dara, **573**; Melitene, **576**; Solachon, **586**; Hyrcanian Rock, Martyropolis, **588**; Araxes, **589**; Ganzak, **591**; Antioch (Syria), **611**; Jerusalem, **614**; Ophlimos, **622**; Dwin, **624**; Arcesh, Sarus, **625**; Nineveh, **627**

Gothic War in Italy: Horreum Margi, **505**; Rome, **537–538**; Ravenna, **539–540**; Rome, **545–546**; Sinigaglia, **551**; Taginae, **552**; Mount Lactarius, **553**; Casilinum, **554**

Visigothic-Frankish Wars: Vouillé, **507**; Arles, **508–510**

Aksum-Sabaean War: Zabid, **525**

Wei Dynastic Wars: Ye, **528**; Hanling, **532**; Shayuan, **537**; Heqiao, **538**; Mangshan, **543**; Yubi, **546**; Yingchuan, **548–549**; Pingyang, **576–577**; Taiyuan, **577**

Nika Insurrection: Constantinople, **532**

Vandal War in Africa: Ad Decimum, Tricameron, **533**

Sino-Vietnamese Wars: Chu Dien, **547**; Giao-chou, **602**; Tra-khe, **605**

Byzantine-Balkan Wars: Melanthius, **559**; Sirmium, **580–582**; Thessalonica, **586**; Viminacium, **601**; Thessalonica, **615**; Thessalonica, **618**; Constantinople, **626**

"Star" Wars: Tikal, **562**; Dos Pilas, **679**; Calakmul, **695**

Lombard Invasion of Italy: Pavia, **569–572**

Frankish Imperial Wars: Carcassonne, **589**; Wogastisburg, **631**

Anglo-Saxon Territorial Wars: Lindisfarne, **590**; Wodnesbeorg, **592**; Cathraeth, **598**; Daegsaston, **603**; Beandun, **614**; Chester, **615**; Idle, **617**; Cirencester, **628**; Morpeth, **629**; Heathfield, **633**; Heavenfield, **634**; Maserfield, **641**; Bradford, **652**; Winwaed, **655**; Penselwood, **658**; Pontesbury, **661**; Badon, **665**; Biedenheafde, **674**; Trent, **679**; Dunnichen Moss, **685**; Wodnesbeorg, **715**; Camel, **721**; Somerton, **733**; Burford, **752**; Seccandun, **757**; Otford, **775**; Bensington, **779**

Medieval Warfare, 600–1500

Persian-Arab Wars: Dhu-Qar, **610**

Indian Dynastic Wars: Pullalur, **610**; Narmada, **620**; Vatapi, **642**; Kanchi, **655**; Vilande, **731**; Kanchi, **740**; Khandesh, **752**; Pennagadam, **775**

Sino-Korean Wars: Salsu, **612**; Ansi Sung, **644**; Sabi, **660**; Paekchon, **663**; Pyongyang, **668**

Rise of the Tang Dynasty: Huoyi, **617**; Qianshuiyuan, Yanshi, **618**; Luoyang, **620–621**; Hulao, **621**

Campaigns of the Prophet Mohammed: Badr, **624**; Ohud, **625**; Medina, **627**; Khaybar, **628**; Hunain, Mecca, **630**

Muslim Conquest of Syria: Muta, **629**; Ajnadin, Bosra, Marj Rahit, Wadi al-Arabah, Yarmuk, **634**; Damascus, Fihl, Marj as-Suffar, **635**; Yarmuk, **636**; Jerusalem, **638**; Aleppo, **639**

Tang Imperial Wars: Iron Mountain, **630**; Sunqu, **641**; Dafeichuan, **670**; Gilgit, **747**; Talas, **751**

Muslim Civil Wars: Buzakha, Dhu al Quassa, **632**; Akraba, **633**; Camel, **656**; Siffin, **657**; Karbala, **680**; Harra, Mecca, Medina, **683**; Marj Rahit, **684**; Mecca, **692**; Dayr al Jamajm, Maskin, **701**; Akra, **721**; Aqua Portora, **742**; Ain Diar, **744**; Karbala, **749**; Zab, **750**; Medina, **762**; Bakhamra, **763**

Muslim Conquest of Iraq: Hafir (Iraq), Hira, Mazar, Ullais, Walaja, **633**; Ain Tamar, Babylon (Iraq), Bridge, Firadz, Nimaraq, **634**; Buwayb, **635**; Qadisiyya, **636**; Jalula, Madain, **637**

Muslim Conquest of Egypt: Heliopolis, Pelusium, **640**; Babylon (Egypt), **640–641**; Alexandria, **641–642**

Muslim Conquest of Iran: Nehavend, **641**

Egyptian-Nubian War, 641–652. See Appendix

Early Byzantine-Muslim Wars: Alexandria, **645**; Mount Phoenix, **654**; Amorium, **669**; Syllaeum, **677**; Sebastopolis, **692**; Constantinople, **717–718**; Adrianople, **718**; Akroinos, **739**

Muslim Conquest of North Africa: Sufetula, **647**; Biskra, **683**; Mams, **688**; Carthage (Tunisia), **697–698**

Sino-Indian War: Kanauj, **648**

Jinshin War: Yamazaki, **672**

Frankish Civil Wars: Tertry, **687**

Byzantine-Bulgarian Wars: Anchialus, **708**; Marcellae, **759**; Anchialus, **763**; Marcellae, **792**; Verbitza, **811**; Versinikia, **813**

Muslim Conquest of Spain: Ecija, Guadalete, **711**; Merida, Segoyuela, **713**; Covadonga, **718**

Muslim Conquest of Sind: Raor, **712**; Navsari, **738**

Rise of Charles Martel: Ambleve, **716**; Vincy, **717**; Soissons, **719**

Muslim Invasion of France: Toulouse, **721**; Bordeaux, Tours, **732**

Danish War of Succession: Bravalla, **735**

Berber Rebellion: El Asnam, **740**; Badkura, **741**; Wadi Salit, **742**; Tawurgah, **761**

An Lu-shan Rebellion: Luoyang, **755**; Chang'an, **756**; Suiyang, Xiangji, **757**; Xiangzhou, **758**; Luoyang, **762**

Later Tang Imperial Wars: Chang'an, **763**; Fengtian, **783**; Caizhou, **817**

Wars of Charlemagne: Roncesvalles, **778**; Suntel Hill, **782**; Detmold, **783**

Byzantine-Muslim Wars: Hadath, **778–779**; Samalu, **780**; Nicomedia, **782**; Crasus, **805**; Heraclea (Anatolia), **806**; Syracuse, **827–828**; Palermo, **830–831**; Amorium, Dazimon, **838**; Messina, **843**; Ostia, **849**; Castrogiovanni, **859**; Poson, **863**; Bari, **871**; Syracuse, **877–878**; Taormina, **902**

Viking Raids on Britain: Lindisfarne, **793**; Carhampton, **835**; Hingston Down, **837**; Carhampton, **843**; Burnham, **848**; Aclea, Sandwich, Thanet, **851**

Later Indian Dynastic Wars: Bundelkhand, Monghyr, **800**; Tellaru, Vengi, **830**; Vingavelli, **850**; Arisil, **860**; Madura, **862**; Sripurambiyam, **880**; Kanauj, **916**; Vellur, **917**; Takkolam, **949**; Kalighatta, **972**; Koppam, **1054**; Kudalsangamam, **1063**; Talakad, **1116**

Muslim War of Succession: Baghdad, **809–811**

Shi'ite Rebellion, 814–819. See Appendix

Later Wars of Wessex: Ellandun, Gafulford, **825**

Frankish War of Succession: Fontenoy (France), **841**

Scottish Dynastic Wars: Logie, **844**; Duncrub, **965**

Breton Rebellion: Ballon, **845**

Viking Wars in Britain: York, **866–867**; Hoxne, Englefield, **870**; Ashdown, Basing, Merton, Reading, Wilton, **871**; Dollar, **875**; Wareham, **876**; Inverdovat, **877**; Chippenham, Countisbury Hill, Edington, **878**; Farnham, **893**; Buttington, **894**; Dunnottar, **900**; Wimborne, **902**; Holme, **905**; Tettenhall, **910**; Wednesfield, **911**; Corbridge, **914**; Derby, **917**; Corbridge, Tempsford, **918**; Brunanburh, **937**; Castleford, **948**; Stainmore, **954**

Paulician War, 867–872. See Appendix

Christian Recapture of Zamora: Zamora, **873**

Carolingian Imperial Wars: Andernach, **876**

Huang Chao Rebellion: Guangzhou, **879**; Liangtian, **883**; Chenzhou, **883–884**

Viking Raids on Germany: Ebsdorf, **880**; Dyle, La Gueule, **891**

Viking Raids on France: Saucourt, **881**; Paris, **885–886**; Montfaucon, **886**; Sens, **886–887**

Zandj Slave Rebellion: Al-Mukhtara, **883**

German Imperial Wars: Meuse, **900**; Brennaburg, **928**; Lenzen, **929**; Andernach, **939**

Magyar Invasion of Germany: Pressburg, **907**; Augsburg, **910**; Riade, **933**; Lechfeld, **955**

Later Byzantine-Bulgarian Wars: Anchialus, **917**

Christian-Muslim Wars in Spain: San Esteban de Gormaz, **918**; Val-de-Junquera, **920**; Sanguesa, **924**; Simancas, **939**

Franco-Norman Wars: Soissons, **923**; Laon, **941**

Sack of Mecca: Mecca, **930**

Muslim Civil War, 936–944. See Appendix

Sino-Annamese War: Bach Dang, **938**

Masakado Uprising: Kojima, **940**

Sumitomo Uprising: Hakata, **941**

Muslim Civil War, 945–948. See Appendix

Wars of the Five Dynasties: Gaoping, **954**

Later Viking Raids on Britain: Invercullen, **961**; Luncarty, Tara, **980**; Maldon, **991**; Nairn, **1009**; Mortlack, **1010**; Clontarf, **1014**

Later Byzantine-Muslim Wars: Crete, **961**; Aleppo, **962**; Adana, **964**; Tarsus, **965**; Aleppo, Antioch (Syria), **969**; Amida, **973**; Azaz, **1030**; Edessa, **1031**; Rometta, **1038**

Muslim Civil War, 968–978. See Appendix

Byzantine-Russian Wars: Arcadiopolis, **970**; Dorostalon, **971**

Polish-German Wars: Cedynia, **972**; Naklo, Psie Pole, **1109**

Byzantine Military Rebellions: Pancalia, **978**; Aquae Saravenae, **979**; Abydos, **989**

Later Christian-Muslim Wars in Spain: Rueda, **981**; Calatanazar, **1002**

Byzantine Wars of Tsar Samuel: Mount Haemus, **981**; Trajan's Gate, **986**; Spercheios, **996**; Balathista, **1014**

War of Leonese Succession: Portela, **982**

Later German Imperial Wars: Cotrone, **982**; Belkesheim, **983**; Sant'Angelo, **998**

Scandinavian National Wars: Hjorungavag, **985**; Svolde, **1000**; Nesjar, **1016**

Muslim Conquest of Northern India: Lamghan, **989**; Peshawar, **1001**; Bhera, Waihand, **1006**; Waihand, **1008**; Thaneswar, **1011**; Sharwa, **1019**; Somnath, **1026**; Hansi, **1037–1038**

Afghan Wars of Succession: Ghazni, **998**; Fatehabad, **1041**

Eastern Muslim Dynastic Wars: Merv, **999**; Tarq, **1002**; Uk, **1003**; Balkh, **1008**; Hazarasp, **1017**; Samarkand, **1025**; Sarjahan, **1029**; Dabusiyya, **1032**

German War of Succession: Creussen, **1003**

Arduin's Wars, 1004–1014. See Appendix

Revolt of Baldwin of Flanders: Valenciennes, **1006–1007**

Danish Conquest of England: Ashingdon, Penselwood, Sherston, **1016**; Carham, **1018**

Russian Dynastic Wars: Liubech, **1016**; Bug, **1018**; Alta, **1019**; Nemiga, **1067**; Alta, **1068**; Kiev, **1069**; Nezhatina Niva, **1078**; Tripole, **1093**; Chernigov, **1094**

Norman Conquest of Southern Italy: Cannae, **1018**; Montemaggiore, Monte Siricolo, Olivento, **1041**; Monopoli, **1042**; Civitate, **1053**; Messina, **1061**; Cerami, **1063**; Misilmeri, **1068**; Bari, **1068–1071**; Palermo, **1071–1072**; Syracuse, **1085**

German Civil Wars: Vlaardingen, **1018**; Unstrut, **1075**; Merseburg, **1080**; Warmstadt, **1113**; Andernach, **1114**; Welfesholze, **1115**; Weinsberg, **1141**

Chola-Pala War, 1021–1024. See Appendix

Norwegian Wars of Succession: Helgeaa, **1026**; Stangebjerg, **1028**; Stiklestad, **1030**

Anglo-Welsh Wars: Ystradowen, **1032**; Aberdare, **1093**; Coleshill, **1157**

French Barons' War: Bar-le-Duc, **1037**

Spanish Territorial Wars: Tamaron, **1037**; Atapuerca, **1054**

Seljuk Wars of Expansion: Nishapur, **1037**; Dandanaqan, **1040**; Hasankale, **1048**; Isfahan, **1050–1051**; Tarq, **1051**; Manzikert, **1054**; Baghdad, **1055**; Rayy, **1059**; Kufah, **1060**

Scottish War of Succession: Elgin, **1040**; Dunsinane, **1054**; Lumphanan, **1057**; Essie, **1058**

Later Byzantine Military Rebellions: Ostrovo, **1043**; Constantinople, **1047**

German-Magyar War: Raab, **1044**

Rise of William of Normandy: Val-es-Dunes, **1047**; Mortemer, **1054**; Varaville, **1058**

Fall of Ghana: Audaghost, **1054**; Kumbi, **1076**

Earlier Nine Years War: Torinomi, **1057**; Kawasaki, **1058**; Komatsu, Kuriyagawa, **1062**

Early Christian Reconquest of Spain: Graus, **1063**; Coimbra (Portugal), **1064**; Cabra, **1079**; Almenar, **1082**; Ebro, **1084**; Toledo (Spain), **1084–1085**; Zallaka, **1086**; Almodovar del Rio, **1091**; Cuarte, Valencia (Valencia), **1093–1094**; Alcoraz, **1096**; Bairen, **1097**; Mollerusa, **1102**; Uclés, **1108**; Valtierra, **1110**; Saragossa, **1118**; Cutanda, **1120**; Arinsol, **1126**; Cullera, **1129**; Fraga, **1134**; Tortosa, **1148**; Alarcos, **1195**; Las Navas de Tolosa, **1212**; Cordova, **1236**; Seville, **1248**

Norwegian Invasion of England: Fulford, Stamford Bridge, **1066**

Norman Conquest of Britain: Hastings, **1066**; Exeter, **1068**; Durham, **1069**; York, **1069–1070**; Ely, **1071**; Norwich, **1075**; Durham, **1080**

War of the Three Sanchos: Viana, **1067**

War of Castilian Succession: Lantada, **1068**; Golpejerra, Zamora, **1072**

Byzantine-Turkish Wars: Sebastia, **1070**; Manzikert, **1071**; Antioch (Syria), **1085**; Aleppo, **1086**; Co-

tyaeum, **1113**; Philomelion, **1116**; Myriocephalum, **1176**

Franco-Frisian War: Cassel, **1071**

Welsh Dynastic War: Bron yr Erw, **1075**; Mynydd Carn, **1081**; Llandudoch, Llechryd, **1088**

Byzantine Wars of Succession: Nicaea, **1077**; Calavryta, **1079**

Norman Dynastic Wars: Gerberoi, **1080**; Pevensey, Rochester, **1088**; Bamburgh, **1095**; Arundel, Bridgnorth, **1102**; Tinchebrai, **1106**; Brenneville, **1119**; Bourgtherolde, **1126**

1st Byzantine-Norman War: Dyrrhachium, **1081**; Dyrrhachium, **1083**; Corfu, Larissa, **1084**

Later Three Years War: Numa, **1086**; Kanazawa, **1087**

Byzantine-Pecheneg Wars: Mount Leburnion, **1091**; Eski Zagra, **1122**

Anglo-Scottish Territorial Wars: Alnwick, **1093**; Clitheroe, Standard, **1138**

1st Crusade: Civetot, Wieselburg, Xerigordon, **1096**; Albara, Antioch (Syria), Dorylaeum, Heraclea (Anatolia), Nicaea, Tarsus, **1097**; Antioch (Syria), **1097–1098**; Arqa, Edessa, Harenc, Jerusalem, Maarat an-Numan, Orontes, **1098**; Ascalon, Jerusalem, **1099**

Crusader-Muslim Wars: Melitene, **1100**; Heraclea (Anatolia), Mersivan, Ramleh, **1101**; Joppa, Ramleh, Tripoli (Lebanon), **1102**; Acre, Harran, **1104**; Artah, Ramleh, **1105**; Khabar, **1107**; Menbij, **1108**; Tripoli (Lebanon), **1109**; Beirut, Sidon, **1110**; Tyre, **1110–1111**; Tel-Danith, **1115**; Antioch (Syria), **1119**; Ascalon, **1123**; Tyre, **1124**; Azaz, **1125**; Anazarbus, **1130**; Edessa, **1144**; Edessa, **1146**; Inab, **1149**; Ascalon, **1153**; Baniyas, Mallaha, **1157**; Artah, **1164**; Montgisard, **1177**; Baniyas, **1179**

2nd Byzantine-Norman War: Dyrrhachium, **1107**

Jurchen Invasion of Northern China: Songhua, **1114**

Later Eastern Muslim Dynastic Wars: Ghazni, **1117**

Jin-Song Wars: Kaifeng, **1126–1127**; Nanjing, **1129**; Chenjia, Caishi, **1161**; De'an, Xiangyang, **1206–1207**

Portuguese War of Succession: Sao Mamede, **1128**

War of Flemish Succession: Alost, Thielt, **1128**

Moray Rebellion: Stracathro, **1130**

Norman-Papal War: Garigliano, **1139**

Christian Reconquest of Portugal: Ourique, **1139**; Lisbon, Santarem, **1147**; Alcacer do Sol, **1158**; Alcacer do Sol, **1217**

Portuguese-Castilian Wars: Arcos de Valdevez, **1140**

English Period of Anarchy: Lincoln, Oxford, Winchester, **1141**; Wilton, **1143**; Wallingford, **1153**

Wars of the Great Seljuk Sultanate: Samarkand, **1141**; Balkh, **1153**; Shahr Rey, **1194**

2nd Crusade: Dorylaeum, **1147**; Damascus, **1148**; Mopsuestia, **1152**

Ghor-Ghazni Wars: Ghazni, **1148**; Ghazni, **1151**

Frederick's 1st Expedition to Italy: Tortona, **1155**

1st Byzantine-Sicilian War: Apulia, **1155**; Brindisi, **1156**

Hogen War: Shirakawa, **1156**

Danish War of Succession: Grathe Heath, **1157**

Frederick's 2nd Expedition to Italy: Cassano, Milan, **1158**; Crema, **1159–1160**; Milan, **1161–1162**

Heiji War: Rokuhara, **1160**

Swedish Wars of Succession: Upsala, **1160**; Visingo, **1167**; Gestilren, **1210**

Crusader Invasion of Egypt: Alexandria, El Ashmunien, **1167**; Damietta, **1169**

Wars of the Lombard League: Rome, **1167**; Ancona, **1173**; Alessandria, **1174–1175**; Legnano, **1176**

Danish Wars of Expansion: Arkona, **1168**; Stralsund, **1184**; Reval, **1219**; Molln, **1225**; Bornhoved, **1227**

Anglo-Norman Conquest of Ireland: Waterford, **1170**; Dublin, **1171**

Byzantine-Venetian War, 1171–1177. See Appendix

Anglo-Norman Rebellion: Fornham, **1173**; Alnwick, **1174**

Later Muslim Conquest of Northern India: Gujarat (India), **1178**; Taraori, **1191**; Taraori, **1192**; Chandwar, **1194**

Gempei War: Fujigawa, Ishibashiyama, Ujigawa, **1180**; Sunomata, **1181**; Hiuchi, Kurikara, Mizushima, Shinowara, **1183**; Awazu, Hojuji, Ichinotani, Uji, **1184**; Dannoura, Yashima, **1185**; Koromogawa, **1189**

2nd Byzantine-Sicilian War: Strymon, Demetritsa, **1185**

Branas Rebellion: Constantinople, **1187**

3rd Crusade: Cresson, Hattin, Jerusalem, Tyre, **1187**; Acre, **1189–1191**; Arsouf, **1191**; Joppa, **1192**

Byzantine-Serbian War: Morava, **1190**

Imperial Invasion of Sicily: Ascoli, **1190**

Bulgarian Imperial Wars: Berroea, **1190**; Arcadiopolis, **1194**; Adrianople, **1205**; Philippopolis, **1208**; Trnovo, **1218**; Klokotnitsa, **1230**; Adrianople, **1255**

French War of Richard I: Freteval, **1194**; Gisors, **1198**; Chalus, **1199**

Muslim War of Succession, 1196–1200. See Appendix

4th Crusade: Sidon, **1196**; Joppa, **1198**; Zara, **1202**; Constantinople, **1203–1204**

Conquests of Genghis Khan: Kerulen, Khalakhaljit, **1203**; Khangai, **1204**; Irtysh, **1208**; Beijing, **1214–1215**; Jand, Kashgar, **1218**; Otrar, **1219–1220**; Bokhara, Hamadan, Khojend, Samarkand, **1220**; Bamian, Gurganj, Indus, Merv, Nishapur, Parwan, Durrah, **1221**; Herat, **1221–1222**; Kuban, **1222**; Kalka, **1223**; Yellow River, **1227**

Wars of Sosso: Kumbi, **1203**; Kirina, **1235**

Anglo-French Wars: Chateau Gaillard, **1203–1204**; Damme, **1213**; Bouvines, **1214**; Toulouse, **1218**; Saintes, Taillebourg, **1242**; Cape St Mathieu, **1293**

Ghor-Khwarezm War: Andkhui, **1205**

Albigensian Crusade: Beziers, Carcassonne, **1209**; Muret, **1213**; Avignon, **1226**

1st Latin-Byzantine Imperial War: Antioch (Anatolia), Rhyndacus, **1211**

1st English Barons' War: Rochester, **1215**; Dover, **1216–1217**; Lincoln, South Foreland, **1217**; Bytham, **1221**; Bedford, **1224**

Early Russian Dynastic Wars: Lipitsa, **1216**

Wars of the Delhi Sultanate: Taraori, **1216**; Kaithal, **1240**; Deogiri, **1294**; Deogiri, **1307**; Warangal, **1309–1310**; Deogiri, **1318**; Warangal, **1322–1323**; Godaveri, **1326**

5th Crusade: Adiliya, **1218**; Damietta, **1218–1219**; Ashmoun Canal, **1221**

Jokyo Disturbance: Kyoto, **1221**

Latin-Epirote War: Thessalonica, **1224**

Mongol Conquest of Korea, 1231–1241. See Appendix

Mongol Conquest of China: Yuxian, **1232**; Kaifeng, **1232–1233**; Jiangling, **1236**; Diao Yu, **1258**

Rise of Mali, 1235–1332. See Appendix

2nd Latin-Byzantine Imperial War: Constantinople, **1236**

Early Wars of the Teutonic Knights: Siauliai, **1236**; Durbe, **1260**; Rakvere, **1268**; Karuse, **1270**; Aizkraulke, **1279**

Mongol Conquest of Russia: Ryazan, **1237**; Kolomna, Moscow, Sit, Vladimir, **1238**; Kiev, **1240**

Imperial-Papal Wars: Cortenuova, **1237**; Brescia, **1238**; Meloria, **1241**; Parma, **1247–1248**; Fossalta, **1248**

Later Crusader-Muslim Wars: Gaza, **1239**; Jerusalem, La Forbie, **1244**; Ascalon, **1247**; Sarvantikar, **1266**; Antioch (Syria), **1268**; Krak de Chevaliers, **1271**; Marqab, **1285**; Tripoli (Lebanon), **1289**; Acre, **1291**; Rhodes, **1310**; Smyrna, **1344**

Rise of Russia: Neva, **1240**; Lake Peipus, **1242**; Rakvere, **1268**

Mongol Invasion of Europe: Carpathian Passes, Cracow, Liegnitz, Sajo, **1241**

Mongol Invasions of India: Lahore, **1241**; Jalandhar, **1298**; Kili, **1299**; Amroha, **1305**; Ravi, **1306**

Mongol Conquest of Asia Minor: Kose Dagh, **1243**

Austro-Hungarian War: Leitha, **1246**

7th Crusade: Ashmoun Canal, Damietta, **1249**; Fariskur, Mansura (Egypt), **1250**

War of Welsh Succession: Bryn Derwyn, **1255**

Mongol Invasion of the Middle East: Alamut, **1256**; Anbar, Baghdad, **1258**; Ain Jalut, Aleppo, **1260**; Homs, **1281**

Mongol Wars of Kubilai Khan: Thang Long, **1258**; Xiangyang, **1268–1272**; Hakata Bay, **1274**; Hangzhou, **1276**; Ngasaunggyan, **1278**; Yashan, **1279**; Hakata Bay, **1281**; Champa, **1281–1283**; Siming, **1285**; Liao, **1287**; Bach Dang, Noi Bang, **1288**; Singhasari, **1293**

3rd Latin-Byzantine Imperial War: Pelagonia, **1259**; Constantinople, **1261**; Prinitza, **1263**; Makry Plagi, Thessalonica, **1264**

Guelf-Ghibelline Wars: Cassano, **1259**; Montaperti, **1260**; Campaldino, **1289**; Montecatini, **1315**; Altopascio, **1325**

Bohemian Wars: Kressenbrunn, **1260**; Marchfeld, **1278**

Mongol Dynastic Wars: Kuba, **1262**; Terek, **1263**; Karakorum, **1301**

Norwegian Invasion of Scotland: Largs, **1263**

2nd English Barons' War: Lewes, Northampton, Rochester, **1264**; Axholme, Evesham, Kenilworth, Newport, **1265**; Chesterfield, **1266**; Ely, **1267**

Venetian-Genoese Wars: Saseno, **1264**; Trapani, **1266**; Laiazzo, **1294**; Kaffa, **1296**; Curzola, **1298**; Constantinople, **1352**; Sapienza, **1354**

Angevin Conquest of the Two Sicilies: Benevento, **1266**; Tagliacozzo, **1268**

8th Crusade: Carthage (Tunisia), **1270**

Mamluk-Nubian War, 1272–1275. See Appendix

Neapolitan-Byzantine War: Berat, **1281**

War of the Sicilian Vespers: Sicilian Vespers, **1282**; Messina, **1283**; Naples, **1284**

English Conquest of Wales: Aber Edw, Bangor, **1282**; Conwy, **1295**

Genoese-Pisan War: Meloria, **1284**

French-Aragonese War: Gerona, Las Hormigas, **1285**

German Ducal Wars: Worringen, **1288**

Habsburg-Swiss Wars: Winterthur, **1292**; Nafels, **1352**; Sempach, **1386**; Nafels, **1388**

English Invasion of Scotland: Berwick, Dunbar, **1296**

William Wallace Revolt: Stirling, **1297**; Falkirk, **1298**; Roslin, **1303**; Happrew, Stirling, **1304**

Franco-Flemish Wars: Furnes, **1297**; Bruges, Courtrai, **1302**; Mons-en-Pevele, Zieriksee, **1304**; Cassel, **1328**

Habsburg Wars of Succession: Gollheim, **1298**; Gammelsdorf, **1313**; Morgarten, **1315**; Solothurn, **1318**; Mühldorf, **1322**

Hungarian War of Succession, 1301–1308. See Appendix

Byzantine-Ottoman Wars: Baphaeum, **1301**; Brusa, **1317–1326**; Pelacanon, **1328**; Nicomedia, **1331–1337**; Didymoteichon, **1352**; Gallipoli, **1354**; Adrianople, **1362**; Gallipoli, **1366**; Dardanelles, **1399**; Constantinople, **1422**; Constantinople, **1453**

Wars of the Catalan Company: Aprus, **1305**; Cephisus, **1311**

Rise of Robert the Bruce: Dalry, Kirkincliffe, Methven, **1306**; Glentrool, Lochryan, Loudon, Hill, Slioch, **1307**; Brander, Cree, Dee, Inverurie, **1308**; Durham, **1312**; Perth, **1312–1313**; Stirling, **1313–1314**; Bannockburn, Edinburgh, Roxburgh, Rushen, **1314**; Ardscull, **1316**; Dundalk, **1318**; Berwick, **1318–1319**; Myton, **1319**; Byland, **1322**

Wars of the Teutonic Knights: Gdansk, **1308**; Plowce, **1331**; Reval, **1343**

Later Christian Reconquest of Spain: Algeciras, Almeria, **1309**; Genil, Vega, **1319**; Alcalá, Algeciras, Rio Salado, **1340**; Algeciras, **1343–1344**; Higueruela, **1431**; Alporchones, **1452**

Tiepolo's Rebellion: Venice, **1310**

Khalji Invasion of Pandya, 1310–1311. See Appendix

English Invasion of Ireland: Athenry, **1316**; Dysert O'Dea, **1318**

1st Ethiopian-Ifat War, 1320–1332. See Appendix

Rebellion of the Marches: Boroughbridge, **1322**

Serbian Imperial Wars: Velbuzhde, **1330**; Stefaniana, **1344**; Adrianople, **1355**

Genko War: Akasaka, **1331**; Chihaya, Kamakura, Kyoto, **1333**

Anglo-Scottish War of Succession: Annan, Dupplin, **1332**; Berwick, Halidon Hill, **1333**; Dundarg, **1334**; Boroughmuir, Kilblain, **1335**; Lochindorb, **1336**; Crichton, **1337**; Dunbar, **1337–1338**; Perth, **1339**

Ashikaga Rebellion: Kamakura, **1335**; Kyoto, Minatogawa, Tatarahama, **1336**

Hundred Years War: Cadsand, **1337**; Sluys, Tournai, **1340**; Hennebont, **1341–1342**; Brest, Morlaix, Quimperlé, **1342**; Auberoche, **1345**; Aiguillon, Caen, Crecy, St Pol de Léon, **1346**; Calais, **1346–1347**; Roche-Derrien, **1347**; Winchelsea, **1350**; Saintes, Thirty, **1351**; Mauron, **1352**; Poitiers, **1356**; Rennes, **1356–1357**; Rheims, **1359–1360**; Brignais, **1362**; Becherel, **1363**; Auray, Cocherel, **1364**; Navarette, **1367**; Limoges, Pontvallain, **1370**; La Rochelle, **1372**;

Chize, **1373**; Chateauneuf-de-Randon, **1380**; Bruges, Roosebeke, **1382**; Margate, **1387**; Othée, **1408**; Agincourt, Harfleur, **1415**; Harfleur, Valmont, **1416**; Caen, **1417**; Rouen, **1418–1419**; Fresnay, Melun, **1420**; Baugé, **1421**; Meaux, **1421–1422**; Cravant, **1423**; Verneuil, **1424**; Avranches, **1426**; Montargis, **1427**; Orleans, **1428–1429**; Jargeau, Paris, Patay, Rouvray, **1429**; Compiegne, **1430**; Bulgnéville, **1431**; Paris, **1436**; Pontoise, **1441**; Rouen, **1449**; Caen, **1450**; Formigny, **1450**; Bordeaux, Castillon, **1453**

Condottieri Wars: Parabiago, **1339**

Burgundian-Swiss Wars: Laupen, **1339**; Fribourg, **1340**

Florentine-Pisan Wars: Lucca, **1341**

Hungarian-Venetian Wars: Zara, **1346**

Anglo-Scottish Border Wars: Neville's Cross, **1346**; Nesbit, **1355**; Otterburn, **1388**; Homildon Hill, Nesbit, **1402**

Aragonese Civil War: Epila, **1348**

War of the Japanese Emperors: Shijo Nawate, **1348**

Florentine-Milanese Wars: Scarperia, **1351**; Castellazzo, **1391**; Brescia, **1401**

Aragon's Conquest of Sardinia: Alghero, **1353–1354**

Rise of the Ming Dynasty: Nanjing, **1356**; Shaoxing, **1359**; Nanchang, Poyang Lake, **1363**; Suzhou, **1366–1367**

Wars of the Hanseatic League: Visby, **1361**; Copenhagen, Helsingborg, **1362**

Russian-Mongol Wars: Syni Vody, **1362**; Vozha, **1378**; Kalka, Kulikovo, **1380**; Moscow, **1382**

Ottoman Conquest of the Balkans: Maritza, **1363**; Vidin, **1366**; Maritza, Samokov, **1371**; Savra, **1385**; Plotchnik, **1387**; Kossovo, **1389**; Rovine, **1395**; Nicopolis (Bulgaria), **1396**

Egyptian Crusade of Peter of Cyprus: Alexandria, **1365**

Conquests of Tamerlane: Tashkent, **1365**; Balkh, **1370**; Herat, **1383**; Isfahan, **1387**; Syr Darya, **1389**; Kunduzcha, **1391**; Shiraz, **1393**; Terek, **1395**; Delhi, Multan, **1398**; Meerut, Vorskla, **1399**; Aleppo, Baghdad, **1400**; Damascus, **1401**; Angora, Smyrna, **1402**

Vijayanagar-Bahmani Wars: Kauthal, **1367**; Krishna, **1398**; Vijayanagar, **1406**; Pangul, **1418–1420**; Mudgal, **1443**

Castilian War of Succession: Montiel, **1369**

Scottish Clan Wars: Invernahavon, **1370**; North Inch, **1396**; Arbroath, **1446**

Guglers' War: Fraubrunnen, **1375**

War of the Eight Saints, 1375–1378. See Appendix

War of the Swabian League: Ulm, **1376**; Reutlingen, **1377**

War of Chioggia: Antium, **1378**; Pula, **1379**; Chioggia, **1379–1380**

Neapolitan-Papal War: Anagni, **1381**

Portuguese-Castilian Wars: Atoleiros, **1384**; Aljubarrota, **1385**

English Barons' Revolt: Radcot Bridge, **1387**

Padua-Verona War: Castagnaro, **1387**

German Towns War: Doffingen, **1388**; Beraun, **1394**

Wars of Scandinavian Union: Aasle, Falkoping, **1389**

Glendower's Rebellion: Welshpool, **1400**; Pilleth, **1402**

Habsburg-Swiss Wars: Speicher, **1403**; Stoss, **1405**; Bregenz, **1408**

Percy's Rebellion: Shrewsbury, **1403**; Bramham Moor, **1408**

Florentine-Pisan Wars: Pisa, **1406**

Ming Imperial Wars: Kerulen, **1409**; Jing Luzhen, Onon, **1410**; Tumu, **1449**

Later Wars of the Teutonic Knights: Tannenberg, **1410**; Wilkomierz, **1435**

MacDonald Rebellion: Harlaw, **1411**; Lochaber, **1429**; Inverlochy, **1431**; Strathfleet, **1453**; Bloody Bay, **1480**

Ottoman Civil Wars: Chamorlu, **1413**; Yenisehir, **1481**

2nd Ethiopian-Ifat War, 1415. See Appendix

Portuguese Colonial Wars in North Africa: Ceuta, **1415**; Tangier, **1437**; Arsilah, **1471**

Venetian-Turkish Wars: Gallipoli, **1416**; Salonika, **1430**; Mytilene, **1462**; Krujë (Albania), **1466–1467**; Negroponte, **1470**; Scutari, **1474**; Krujë (Albania), **1478**; Scutari, **1478–1479**; Lepanto, **1499**

Hussite Wars: Bor Pansky, Porici, Sudomer, Vitkov Hill, Vysehrad, **1420**; Kutna Hora, Vladar, Zatec, **1421**; Habry, Nebovidy, Nemecky Brod, **1422**; Horice, Kromeriz, Strachuv, Tynec, **1423**; Malesov, Skalice, **1424**; Aussig, **1426**; Tachov, Zwettl, **1427**; Domazlice, **1431**; Lipany, **1434**; Grotniki, **1439**

Swiss-Milanese Wars: Arbedo, **1422**; Giornico, **1478**

Condottieri Wars: Aquila, **1424**

Sino-Vietnamese War: Tot-dong, **1426**; Dong-do, **1426–1427**; Chi Lang Pass, **1427**

Venetian-Milanese Wars: Brescia, **1426**; Casa-al-Secco, Gottolengo, Maclodio, **1427**; Cremona, Soncino, **1431**; Maderno, **1439**; Anghiari, **1440**

Malwa-Bahmani Wars: Kherla, **1428**

Aztec Wars of Conquest: Azcapotzalco, **1428**; Coixtlahuaca, **1458**; Tarascan Frontier, **1478**; Soconusco, **1498–1500**

Thai Invasion of Cambodia: Angkor, **1430–1431**

Scandinavian Revolt, 1433–1439. See Appendix

Aragon's Conquest of Naples: Gaeta, **1435**; Naples, **1442**; Troia, **1462**

Wars of Russian Succession: Skoriatino, **1436**

Anglo-Scottish Border Wars: Piperdean, Roxburgh, **1436**; Sark, **1448**; Roxburgh, **1460**

Transylvanian Peasant Revolt: Bábolna, **1437**

Turkish-Hungarian Wars: Semendria, **1439**; Belgrade, **1440**; Császáhalom, **1441**; Hermannstadt, Vasaq, **1442**; Varna, **1444**; Ialomitsa, **1446**; Kossovo, **1448**; Krusevac, **1454**; Novo Brdo **1455**; Belgrade, **1456**; Jajce, **1464**; Shabatz, **1476**; Villach, **1492**; Belgrade, Shabatz, **1521**; Mohacs, Peterwardein, **1526**

Old Zurich War: St Jakob on the Sihl, **1443**; St Jakob on the Birs, **1444**

Turkish-Hungarian Wars (Long Campaign): Melshtitsa, Nish, Zlatitsa, **1443**; Kunovica, **1444**

Albanian-Turkish Wars: Domosdova, **1444**; Dibra, Krujë (Albania), Svetigrad, **1448**; Krujë (Albania), **1450**; Berat, **1455**; Oranik, **1456**; Albulen, **1457**

Spanish Wars of Succession: Olmedo, **1445**; Aibar, **1452**

Thai-Malacca War: Ulu Muar, **1445**; Batu Pahat, **1456**

Russian-Mongol Wars: Suzdal, **1445**; Aleksin, **1472**; Ugra, **1480**

Albanian-Venetian War: Danj, **1447–1448**

Milanese War of Succession: Caravaggio, **1448**; Borgomanero, **1449**; Milan, **1449–1450**

Portuguese War of Succession: Alfarrobeira, **1449**

Cade's Rebellion: London Bridge, Sevenoaks, **1450**

Hungarian Civil War: Szentkiraly, **1451**

Polish-Bohemian War: Lucenec, **1451**

Douglas Rebellion: Brechin, **1452**; Abercorn, Arkinholm, **1455**

Franco-Burgundian Wars: Gavere, **1453**; Montenaeken, Montlhéry, **1465**; Dinant, **1466**; Brusthem, **1467**; Liège, **1468**; Héricourt, **1474**; Neuss, **1474–1475**

Thirteen Years War: Chojnice, **1454**; Puck, **1462**

Wars of the Roses: St Albans, **1455**; Blore Heath, Ludford Bridge, **1459**; Northampton, Sandwich, Wakefield, **1460**; Dunstable, Ferrybridge, Mortimer's Cross, St Albans, Towton, **1461**; Alnwick, **1462–1463**; Twt Hill, **1463**; Bamburgh, Hedgeley Moor, Hexham, **1464**; Caister Castle, **1469**; Edgecote, **1469**; Lose-Coat Field, Nibley Green, **1470**; Barnet, Ravenspur, Tewkesbury, **1471**; Bosworth Field, **1485**

Muscovite Wars of Expansion: Novgorod, **1456**; Shelon, Shilenga, **1471**

Hungarian National Wars: Baia (Romania), **1467**; Vienna, **1485**

Wars of the Songhai Empire: Timbuktu, **1468**; Anfao, **1493**

Hungarian-Bohemian War, 1469–1478. See Appendix

Vietnamese-Cham War: Vijaya, **1471**

Wars of the Kalmar Union: Brunkeberg, **1471**; Rotebro, **1497**; Hemmingstedt, **1500**; Brännkyrka, **1518**; Bogesund, **1520**; Copenhagen, **1523–1524**

Ottoman-Turkoman War: Terjan, **1472**; Erzincan, **1473**

Genoese-Turkish War: Kaffa, **1475**

Moldavian-Turkish War: Rakhova, **1475**; Valea Alba, **1476**

Portuguese-Castilian Wars: Toro, **1476**

Burgundian-Swiss War: Grandson, Morat, **1476**; Nancy, **1477**

Florentine-Neapolitan War: Poggibonsi, **1479**

Franco-Austrian War: Guinegate, **1479**

Transylvanian-Turkish Wars: Kenyermezo, **1479**

Turkish Imperial Wars: Otranto, Rhodes, **1480**; Cosmin, **1497**; Rhodes, **1522**; Tunis, **1533**; Tripoli (Libya), **1551**; Malta, **1565**

Final Christian Reconquest of Spain: Zahara, **1481**; Alhama, Loja, **1482**; Axarquia, Lucena, **1483**; Malaga, **1487**; Almeria, Baza, **1489**; Granada, **1491–1492**

Polish-Crimean Tatar Wars: Kiev, **1482**; Kleck, **1506**

Anglo-Scottish Royal Wars: Berwick, **1482**; Lochmaben, **1484**; Goodwin Sands, **1511**; Broomhouse, Flodden, **1513**; Hadden Rig, Solway Moss, **1542**; Ancrum Moor, **1545**; Pinkie, **1547**; Leith, **1560**

Simnel's Rebellion: Stoke, **1487**

Russia's Volga Wars: Kazan, **1487**; Kazan, **1552**; Astrakhan, **1554**; Astrakhan, **1569**

Mad War: St Aubin du Cormier, **1488**

Scottish Barons' Rebellion: Sauchieburn, **1488**; Gartalunane, **1489**

Persian-Turkoman Wars: Dartanat, **1488**; Jabani, **1500**; Sharur, **1501**; Hamadan, **1503**

Spanish Conquest of Haiti, 1494–1509. See Appendix

Italian War of Charles VIII: Fornovo, Seminara, **1495**; Aversa, **1496**

Flammock's Rebellion: Blackheath, **1497**

Mughal-Uzbek Wars: Samarkand, **1497–1498**; Sar-i-Pul, **1501**; Akhsikath, **1503**; Herat, Maruchak, **1507**; Kandahar, **1508**; Pul-i-Sanghin, **1511**; Ghujduwan, Kul-i-Malik, **1512**

Swabian War: Bruderholz, Calven, Dornach, Frastenz, Hard, Schwaderloch, Triesen, **1499**

The Early Modern Era, 1500–1750

1st Muscovite-Lithuanian War: Vedrosha, **1500**; Helmed, Mstislavl, Seritsa, **1501**; Lake Smolino, Smolensk, **1502**

Italian War of Louis XII: Novara, **1500**; Taranto, **1501–1502**; Barletta, **1502–1503**; Cerignola, Garigliano, Seminara, **1503**

Early Portuguese Colonial Wars in Asia: Calicut, **1500**; Cochin, **1506**; Chaul, **1508**; Diu, **1509**; Goa, **1510**; Malacca, **1511**

Portuguese Colonial Wars in East Africa: Zanzibar, **1503**; Kilwa, Mombasa, **1505**; Mombasa, **1528**; Mombasa, **1589**

Irish Barons' Wars: Knockdoe, **1504**

Funj-Nubian War, 1504–1505. See Appendix

Mughal Dynastic War: Kabul, **1504**; Kandahar, **1520–1522**

Spanish Colonial Wars in North Africa: Mers el Kebir, **1505**; Oran, **1509**; Bougie, Los Gelves, Tripoli (Libya), **1510**; Algiers, **1511**

Portuguese Colonial Wars in Arabia: Muscat, **1507**; Hormuz, **1507–1508**; Aden, **1513**; Hormuz, **1515**; Bahrain, **1521**

War of the League of Cambrai: Cadore, **1508**; Agnadello, Padua, **1509**

Spanish Conquest of Puerto Rico, 1508–1511. See Appendix

Persian-Uzbek Wars: Merv, **1510**; Damghan, Herat, Torbat-i-Jam, **1528**

Spanish Conquest of Cuba, 1511–1513. See Appendix

Turko-Persian War in Anatolia: Kayseri, **1511**; Chaldiran, **1514**; Turna Dag, **1515**

War of the Holy League: Casalechio, Mirandola, **1511**; Brest, Ravenna, **1512**; Brest, Guinegate, Novara, Vicenza, **1513**; Marignano, **1515**

2nd Muscovite-Lithuanian War: Smolensk, **1512–1514**; Orsha, **1514**

Vijayanagar-Gajapati War: Udayagiri, **1513–1514**; Kondavidu, **1515**

Transylvanian Peasant War: Temesvár, **1514**

Ottoman-Mamluk War: Marj-Dabik, Yaunis Khan, **1516**; Ridanieh, **1517**

Spanish Conquest of Yucatan: Champotón, **1517**; Aké, **1528**; Chichén Itzá, **1531**

Spanish Conquest of Mexico: Cholula, **1519**; Cempoala, Otumba, Tenochtitlan, **1520**; Tenochtitlan, **1521**

Wars of the Deccan Sultanates: Raichur, **1520**; Jamkhed, **1560**; Kondavidu, **1563**; Talikota, **1565**

Comuneros Uprising: Villalar, **1521**

Philippines Expedition: Mactan, **1521**

1st Habsburg-Valois War: Esquiroz, **1521**; Bicocca, Genoa, **1522**; Marseilles, Rebecco, Sesia, **1524**; Pavia, **1524–1525**

German Knights' War: Landstuhl, **1523**

Spanish Conquest of Guatemala: Quetzaltenango, Ututlán, **1524**

German Peasants' War: Böblingen, Frankenhausen, Frauenberg, Ingolstadt, Kempten, Königshofen, Leipheim, Weinsberg, Zabern, **1525**; Schladming, **1526**

Scottish Royalist Wars: Linlithgow Bridge, Melrose, **1526**

Mughal Conquest of Northern India: Panipat, **1526**; Khanua, **1527**; Gogra, **1529**; Chitor, **1534–1535**; Champaner, Mandu, **1535**; Chausa, **1539**; Kanauj, **1540**; Sirhind, **1555**; Delhi, Panipat, **1556**; Chitor, **1567–1568**; Ahmadabad, Sarnal, **1572**; Tukaroi, **1575**; Haldighat, Rajmahal (Bengal), **1576**; Malandarai Pass, **1586**; Nekujyal, **1612**

2nd Habsburg-Valois War: Rome, **1527**; Naples, **1528**; Landriano, **1529**; Florence, **1529–1530**

Turkish-Habsburg Wars: Tokay, **1527**; Buda, Vienna, **1529**; Guns, **1532**; Tunis, **1535**; Valpovo, **1537**; Buda, **1540**; Algiers, Buda, **1541**; Nice, **1543**; Mahdiyya, **1550**; Eger, Temesvár, **1552**; Djerba, **1560**; Hadad, **1562**; Gyula, Szigetvar, **1566**; Lepanto, **1571**; Sissek, Veszprem, **1593**; Komárom, **1594**; Esztergom, **1595**; Keresztes, **1596**; Esztergom, **1605**

Burmese Dynastic Wars: Ava, **1527**; Pegu, **1539**; Pegu, **1551**; Prome, **1552**; Ava, **1555**; Pegu, **1599**; Syriam, **1613**

Adal-Ethiopian War: Shimbra-Kure, **1529**; Wayna Daga, **1543**

Polish-Moldavian War: Gwozdiec, Obertyn, **1531**

Swiss Religious Wars: Kappel, Zug, **1531**

Inca War of Succession: Cuzco, **1532**

Spanish Conquest of Peru: Cajamarca, **1532**

Ottoman Conquest of Persia: Baghdad, **1534**

German Religious Wars: Munster, **1534–1535**

Danish Counts' War: Bornholm, Oksnebjerg, **1535**; Copenhagen, **1535–1536**

3rd Habsburg-Valois War: Marseilles, **1536**

Later Venetian-Turkish War: Corfu, **1537**; Preveza, **1538**; Castelnuovo (Albania), **1538–1539**

Spanish Civil War in Peru: Abancay, **1537**; Salinas (Peru), **1538**; Chupas, **1542**; Anaquito, **1546**; Huarina, **1547**; Xaquixaguana, **1548**; Chuquinga, **1554**

Portuguese Colonial Wars in Asia: Diu, **1538–1539**; Diu, **1546**; Malacca, **1568**; Colombo, **1587–1588**; Mannar, **1591**; Balane, **1594**

Spanish Conquest of Honduras: Cerquin, **1539**

Dacke's Rebellion: Hjortensjon, **1543**

4th Habsburg-Valois War: Ceresole, Serravalle, **1544**

Scottish Clan Wars: Shirts, **1544**

French War of Henry VIII: Boulogne, **1544**; Spithead, **1545**

Maya Revolt, 1546–1547. See Appendix

Mughal Wars of Succession: Kabul, **1546–1549**; Machiwara, **1560**; Khurd-Kabul, **1581**

War of the German Reformation: Mühlberg, **1547**; Sieveshausen, **1553**

Burmese-Siamese Wars: Ayutthaya, **1548**; Ayutthaya, **1568–1569**; Pa Mok, **1585**; Nong Sarai, **1593**

Kett's Rebellion: Dussindale, Norwich, **1549**

Western Rebellion: Exeter, Sampford Courtenay, St Mary's Clyst, **1549**

5th Habsburg-Valois War: Metz, **1552**; Marciano, **1554**; Siena, **1554–1555**; St Quentin, **1557**; Calais, Gravelines, **1558**

Spanish Conquest of Chile: Tucapel, **1553**; Marigüeñu, **1554**; Mataquito, **1557**; Curalaba, **1598**

Wyatt's Rebellion: Temple Bar, Wrotham Heath, **1554**

Sack of Havana: Havana, **1555**

Japan's Era of the Warring States: Miyajima, **1555**; Okehazama, **1560**; Anegawa, Ishiyama Honganji, **1570**; Mikata ga hara, **1572**; Nagashino, **1575**; Kozuki, **1577–1578**; Mimikawa, **1578**; Minamata, **1581**; Takamatsu, Yamazaki, **1582**; Shizugatake, **1583**; Nagakute, Okita Nawate, **1584**; Kagoshima, Sendaigawa, Takashiro, Toshimitsu, **1587**; Odawara, **1590**; Sekigahara, **1600**; Osaka Castle, **1614–1615**

Livonian War: Narva, **1558**; Fellin, Oomuli, **1560**; Polotsk, **1563**; Chashniki, Nevel, **1564**; Reval, **1570–1571**; Reval, Wenden, **1577**; Wenden, **1578**; Polotsk, **1579**; Velikie Luki, **1580**; Narva, **1581**; Pskov, **1581–1582**

Persian-Mughal Wars: Kandahar, **1558**; Kandahar, **1622**; Kandahar, **1637**; Kandahar, **1649**; Kandahar, **1652**; Kandahar, **1653**

1st French War of Religion: Dreux, Rouen, Vassy, Vergt, **1562**; Le Havre, Orleans, **1563**

Huntly Rebellion: Corrichie, **1562**; Craibstane, Tillyangus, **1571**; Glenlivet, **1594**

Nordic Seven Years War: Alvsborg, Gotland, Halmstad, Mared, **1563**; Oland, **1564**; Axtorna, Varberg, **1565**; Oland, **1566**; Varberg, **1569**

O'Neill Rebellion: Coleraine, **1564**; Ballycastle, **1565**; Knockfergus, **1566**; Letterkenny, **1567**

Netherlands War of Independence: Valenciennes, **1566–1567**; Heiligerlee, Jemmingen, Jodoigne, **1568**; Brielle, Goes, Havré, Mons, Naarden, **1572**; Haarlem, **1572–1573**; Middelburg, **1572–1574**; Alkmaar, Zuyder Zee, **1573**; Leyden, **1573–1574**; Mookerheyde, Walcheren, **1574**; Zieriksee, **1575–1576**; Antwerp, **1576**; Gembloux, Rymenant, **1578**; Maastricht, **1579**; Hardenberg Heath, **1580**; Steenwijk, **1580–1581**; Kollum, Noordhorn, Tournai, **1581**; Antwerp, **1584–1585**; Zutphen, **1586**; Bergen-op-Zoom, **1588**; Gertruydenberg, **1588–1589**; Breda, **1590**; Zutphen, **1591**; Steenwijk, **1592**; Gertruydenberg, **1593**; Groningen, **1594**; Turnhout, **1597**; Nieuport, **1600**; Ostend, **1601–1604**; Narrow Seas, **1602**; Sluys, **1603**; Sluys, **1604**; Mulheim, **1605**; Cape St Vincent, **1606**; Gibraltar, **1607**; Breda, **1624–1625**; Grol, **1627**; Hertogenbosch, Wesel, **1629**; Slaak, **1631**; Maastricht, **1632**; Breda, **1636–1637**; Downs, **1639**; Sas van Gent, **1644**; Hulst, **1645**

2nd French War of Religion: St Denis, **1567**

Uprising against Mary Queen of Scots: Carberry Hill, **1567**; Langside, **1568**

Morisco Revolt, 1568–1570. See Appendix

3rd French War of Religion: Jarnac, La Roche-L'Abeille, Moncontour, Orthez, Poitiers, **1569**; Arnay-le-Du, **1570**

Dacre's Rebellion: Gelt, **1570**

Venetian-Turkish War in Cyprus: Nicosia, **1570**; Famagusta, **1570–1571**

Russian-Tatar Wars: Moscow, **1571**; Molodi, **1572**

Tupac Amaru Revolt: Huayna Pucará, **1572**

4th French War of Religion: St Bartholomew's Eve, **1572**; La Rochelle, **1572–1573**

Burmese-Laotian Wars: Vientiane, **1574**

Moldavian Rebellion: Jiliste, Kagul Lagoon, **1574**

Portuguese Colonial Wars in West Africa: Sao Salvador, **1574**; Ambuila, **1665**; Pungu-a-Ndongo, **1671**

5th French War of Religion: Dormans, **1575**

Balkan National Wars: Sinpaul, **1575**; Selimbar, **1599**; Bucov, Khotin, Mirischlau, **1600**; Goraslau, **1601**; Brasov, **1603**; San Petru, **1611**

Gdansk War: Danzig, Lubieszow, **1577**

Portuguese-Moroccan War: Alcazarquivir, **1578**

Geraldine Rebellion: Fort del Or, **1580**; Glen Malure, **1580**

Spanish-Portuguese War: Alcántara, **1580**; Terceira, **1582**; Sao Miguel, **1583**

Russian Conquest of Siberia: Kashlyk, **1582**

Turko-Persian Wars: Vilasa, **1583**; Khoi, **1584**; Tabriz, **1585**; Baghdad, **1587**; Gandzha, **1588**; Tabriz, **1603**; Sufiyan, **1605**; Erivan, **1616–1618**; Baghdad, **1625–1626**; Baghdad, Hamadan, **1630**; Erivan, **1635–1636**; Baghdad, **1638**

Drake's Caribbean Raid: Cartagena (Colombia), Santo Domingo, St Augustine, **1586**

8th French War of Religion: Auneau, Coutras, **1587**

Siamese-Cambodian Wars: Lovek, **1587**; Lovek, **1594**

Anglo-Spanish Wars: Cadiz, Sluys, **1587**; Spanish Armada, **1588**; Burgos, **1589**; Azores, **1591**; Cadiz, **1596**

Habsburg-Polish War: Byczyna, **1588**

Mughal-Uzbek Wars: Herat, **1588–1589**; Balkh, **1646**

9th French War of Religion: Arques, **1589**; Ivry, Paris, **1590**; Rouen, **1591–1592**; Aumâle, Caudebec, **1592**; Fontaine-Française, **1595**; Calais, **1596**; Amiens, **1597**

Moroccan-Songhai War: Tondibi, **1591**

Ningxia Mutiny: Ningxia, **1592**

Japanese Invasion of Korea: Angolpo, Chongju, Hansan, Imjin, Okpo, Pusan, Pyongyang, Sachon, Sangju, Tanghangpo, Tangpo, Tongnae, **1592**; Haengju, Pyokjekwan, Pyongyang, **1593**; Chiksan, Kyo Chong, Myongyang, Namwon, **1597**; Noryang, Sachon, Sunchon, Ulsan, **1598**

Cossack-Polish Wars: Piatka, **1593**; Lubny, **1596**

Later Scottish Clan Wars: Dryfe Sands, **1593**; Glen Fruin, **1603**; Altimarlach, **1680**

O'Donnell's Rebellion: Ford of the Biscuits, **1594**

Wallachian-Turkish War: Calugareni, Giurgiu, Tirgovist, **1595**

Tyrone Rebellion: Clontibret, **1595**; Blackwater, **1598**; Derry, Moyry Pass, **1600**; Kinsale, **1601**

Mughal-Ahmadnagar Wars: Ahmadnagar, Supa, **1596**; Ahmadnagar, **1600**; Asirgarh, **1600–1601**; Roshangaon, **1616**; Bhatavadi, **1624**; Kalinjar, Sironj, **1631**; Daulatabad, **1633**

Persian Reconquest of Khorasan: Rabat-i-Pariyan, **1598**

Swedish War of Succession: Stangebro, **1598**

Spanish Conquest of New Mexico: Acoma Pueblo, **1598–1599**

Cambodian-Spanish War: Phnom Penh, **1599**

1st Polish-Swedish War: Kokenhausen, **1601**; Dorpat, **1603**; Weissenstein, **1604**; Kirkholm, **1605**

Dutch-Portuguese Colonial Wars: Bantam, **1601**; Goa, **1604**; Ambon, **1605**; Malacca, **1606**; Salvador, **1624–1625**; Salvador, **1627**; Recife, **1630**; Recife, **1632**; Porto Calvo, **1635**; Porto Calvo, **1637**; Salvador, **1638**; Itamaraca, **1640**; Malacca, **1640–1641**; Guararapes, Luanda, **1648**; Guararapes, **1649**; Recife, **1650–1654**

Swiss Religious Wars: Geneva, **1602**

Later Portuguese Colonial Wars in Arabia: Bahrain, **1602**; Muscat, **1650**

Russian Time of Troubles: Novgorod Seversk, **1604**; Dobrynitchi, **1605**; Bolkhov, Khodynka, **1608**; Smolensk, **1609–1611**; Klushino, **1610**; Moscow, **1611–1612**; Moscow, **1618**

Zebrzydowski's Rebellion: Janowiec, **1606**; Guzów, **1607**

Dutch-Spanish Colonial Wars: Manila, **1610**; Muysers Bay, **1625**; Matanzas, **1628**

War of Kalmar: Alvsborg, Kringen, Vaxholm, **1612**

Anglo-Portuguese Colonial Wars: Swally Roads, **1612**; Jask, **1620**; Hormuz, **1622**

Anglo-French Wars in North America: Port Royal, **1614**; Quebec, **1629**

Russo-Swedish Wars: Bronnitsa, Gdov, **1614**; Pskov, **1615**; Riga, **1656**

2nd Polish-Swedish War: Riga, **1617**; Riga, **1621**; Mitau, **1621–1622**; Dorpat, **1625**; Mewe, Wallhof, **1626**; Danzig, **1626–1630**; Kasemark, Oliwa, Tczew, **1627**; Gorzno, Sztum, **1629**

Thirty Years War (Bohemian War): Pilsen, **1618**; Sablat, **1619**; White Mountain, **1620**

Early Dutch Wars in the East Indies: Bantam, **1618**; Jakarta, **1619**; Batavia, **1628**; Batavia, **1629**

Later Portuguese Colonial Wars in Asia: Jaffna, **1619**; Radenivela, **1630**; Hooglhy, **1632**; Gannoruwa, **1638**; Trincomalee, **1639**; Colombo, **1655–1656**

Manchu Conquest of China: Niumaozhai, Sarhu, Siyanggiayan, **1619**; Shenyang, **1621**; Ningyuan, **1626**; Dalinghe, Xoaling, **1631**; Kaifeng, **1642**; Beijing, Shanhaiguan, **1644**; Tongguan, Yangzhou, **1645**; Nanjing, **1659**

Swiss-Milanese Wars: Tirano, **1620**

Polish-Turkish Wars: Cecora, Jassy, **1620**; Khotin, **1621**

French Civil War: Ponts-de-Ce, **1620**; Castelnaudary, **1632**

Corsair Wars: Algiers, **1620–1621**; Porto Farina, **1665**; Bougie, **1671**

1st Huguenot Rebellion: Montauban, St Jean d'Angely, **1621**

Early Mughal-Sikh Wars: Rohilla, **1621**; Amritsar, **1634**; Kartarpur, **1635**

Thirty Years War (Palatinate War): Fleurus, Heidelberg, Höchst (Frankfurt), Mannheim, Wiesloch, Wimpfen, **1622**; Stadtlohn, **1623**

Powhatan Indian Wars: Jamestown, **1622**; Pamunkey, **1625**; York River (Virginia), **1644**

Rebellion of Prince Shahjahan: Balochpur, **1623**; Damdama, **1624**

Anatolian Rebellion: Kayseri, **1624**

Polish-Tatar Wars: Martynow, **1624**; Kamieniec, Sasowy Rog, **1633**; Okhmatov, **1644**

2nd Huguenot Rebellion: La Rochelle, **1625**

Turkish-Druse War: Anjar, **1625**

Cossack-Polish Wars: Borovitsa, **1625**; Pereiaslav, **1630**; Kumeiky, **1637**; Zhovnyne, **1638**; Bazavluk, Korsun, Pilawce, Zolte Wody, **1648**; Zborov, **1649**; Beresteczko, Bila Tserkva, **1651**; Batoh, **1652**

Anglo-Spanish Wars: Cadiz, **1625**; Jamaica, Santo Domingo, **1655**; Cadiz, **1656**; Santa, Cruz de Tenerife, **1657**

Thirty Years War (Saxon-Danish War): Dessau, Lutter am Barenberg, **1626**; Stralsund, Wolgast, **1628**

Manchu Conquest of Korea: Pyongyang, **1627**

3rd Huguenot Rebellion: Ile de Ré, **1627**; La Rochelle, **1627–1628**

Thirty Years War (Mantuan War): Casale, **1628–1629**; Casale, Mantua, **1629–1630**; Avigliana, **1630**

Thirty Years War (Swedish War): Magdeburg, **1630–1631**; Breitenfeld, Frankfort on the Oder, Neu-brandenburg, Werben, **1631**; Alte Veste, Lützen, Rain, **1632**; Hessich-Oldendorf, Steinau, **1633**; Landshut, Nördlingen, Regensberg, **1634**

Later Portuguese Wars in East Africa: Mombasa, **1631–1633**; Zanzibar, **1652**; Mahungwe, **1684**; Mombasa, **1696–1698**; Mombasa, **1728–1729**

Russo-Polish "War of Smolensk": Smolensk, **1632–1634**

Thirty Years War (Franco-Habsburg War): Avein, Boulay, Domitz, Goldberg, Kyritz, Mainz, **1635**; Hanau, **1635–1638**; Corbie, St Jean de Losne, Tornavento, Wittstock, **1636**; Monte Baldo, **1637**; Breisach, Brema, Fuentarrabia, Rheinfelden, Sennheim, Vlotho, Wittenweier, **1638**; Brandeis, Chemnitz, Chieri, Thionville, **1639**; Casale, Turin, **1640**; La Marfée, Wolfenbüttel, **1641**; Barcelona (Spain), Breitenfeld, Kempen, Lérida, Olmütz, Schweidnitz, **1642**; Cabo de Gata, Rocroi, Rottweil, Sierck, Thionville, Tuttlingen, **1643**; Freiburg, Gravelines, Juterbog, Kolberg Heath, Lérida, Lolland, **1644**; Jankau, Mergentheim, Nördlingen, Rosas, **1645**; Dunkirk, Isola del Giglio, Lérida, Orbetello, Porto Longone, **1646**; Lérida, **1647**; Lens, Prague, Trancheron, Zusmarshausen, **1648**

Transylvanian-Turkish Wars: Salonta, **1636**

Pequot Indian War: Block Island, **1636**; Mystic, Wethersfield, **1637**

Japanese Christian Rising: Amakusa, **1638**

Shimabara Rebellion: Hara, **1638**

1st Bishops' War: Dee, Megray Hill, **1639**

2nd Bishops' War: Newburn, **1640**

Catalonian Uprising: Barcelona, **1641**; Barcelona, **1652**

British Civil Wars: Brentford, Edgehill, Powick Bridge, Tadcaster, Turnham Green, **1642**; Adwalton Moor, Alton, Braddock Down, Bristol, Chalgrove Field, Gainsborough, Gloucester, Grantham, Highnam, Hopton Heath, Lansdown, Launceston, Newbury, Piercebridge, Reading, Ripple Field, Roundway Down, Rowde Ford, Seacroft Moor, Sourton Down, Stratton, Wakefield, Winceby, **1643**; Arundel, **1643–1644**; Basing House, **1643–1645**; Aberdeen, Alresford, Beacon Hill, Bolton, Cropredy Bridge, Fyvie, Inveraray, Latham, Laugharne, Lostwithiel, Lyme, Marston Moor, Nantwich, Newark, Newbury, Selby, Tippermuir, York, **1644**; Alford, Auldearn, Borough Hill, Bridgwater, Bristol, Colby Moor, Inverlochy, Kilsyth, Langport, Leicester, Naseby, Philiphaugh, Rowton Heath, Taunton, **1645**; Benburb, Inverness, Stow, Torrington, **1646**; Dungan Hill, **1647**; Colchester, Maidstone, Pembroke, Preston, St Fagan's, **1648**; Drogheda, Rathmines, Wexford, **1649**; Carbiesdale, Clonmel, Dunbar, **1650**; Dundee, Inverkeithing, Limerick, Wigan, Worcester, **1651**; Lochgarry, **1654**

Spanish-Portuguese Wars: Montijo, **1644**; Elvas, **1659**; Ameixial, **1663**; Montes Claros, **1665**

Ingle's Rebellion: St Mary's, **1645–1646**

Venetian-Turkish Wars: Khania, **1645**; Candia, **1648–1669**; Dardanelles, **1654**; Dardanelles, **1656**; Dardanelles, **1657**; Castelnuovo (Albania), **1687**; Monemvasia, **1689–1690**; Cattaro, **1690**; Khania, **1692**; Chios, **1694**; Spalmadori, **1695**

Allesi's Insurrection: Palermo, **1647**

Masaniello's Insurrection: Naples, **1647**

Bijapur-Maratha Wars: Gingee, **1648**; Pratabgarh, **1659**; Panhala, **1660**; Panhala, Umrani, **1673**; Nesri, **1674**; Ponda, **1675**; Koppal, Tiruvadi, **1677**; Vellore, **1677–1678**

War of the 1st Fronde: Charenton, **1649**

War of the 2nd Fronde: Champ Blanc, **1650**; Blenau, Etampes, St Antoine, **1652**

1st Dutch War: Dungeness, Elba, Goodwin Sands, Kentish Knock, Plymouth (England), **1652**; Gabbard Bank, Leghorn, Portland (Dorset), Scheveningen, **1653**

Moldavian Civil War: Finta, **1653**

Swiss Peasant War: Gisikon, Herzogenbuchsee, Wohlenschwyl, **1653**

Russo-Polish Wars: Smolensk, Szepiele, **1654**; Lvov, Okhmatov, Ozernoe, **1655**; Kiev, Poltava, Werki, **1658**; Konotop, **1659**; Chudnov, Liubar, Polonka, Slobodyszcze, **1660**; Kushliki, **1661**; Lokhvitsa, **1663**; Podhajce, **1667**

Franco-Spanish War: Arras, **1654**; Valenciennes, **1656**; Cambrai, **1657**; Dunes, Dunkirk, **1658**; Luxembourg, **1684**

1st Northern War: Cracow, Jasna Gora, Nowy Dwor, Opoczno, Sobota, Ujscie, Wojnicz, **1655**; Gnesen, Golab, Sandomierz, Warka, Warsaw, **1656**; Fredericia, **1657**; Funen, Sound, **1658**; Nyborg, **1659**

1st Villmergen War: Rapperswil, Villmergen, **1656**

Transylvanian-Polish War: Trembowla, Warsaw, **1657**

War of the Mughal Princes: Bahadurpur, Dharmat, Samugargh, **1658**; Deorai, Khajwa, Maldah, **1659**

Transylvanian National Revolt: Lippa, **1658**; Gilau, Nagyvarad, **1660**; Nagyszollos, **1662**

Royalist Rising: Winnington Bridge, **1659**

Wallachian-Turkish War: Fratesci, **1659**

1st Dutch-Khoikhoi War, 1659–1660. See Appendix

Dutch Wars in the East Indies: Macassar, **1660**; Macassar, **1667–1668**; Kartosuro, **1705**; Bangil, **1706**

Mughal-Maratha Wars: Chakan, **1660**; Poona, **1663**; Surat, **1664**; Purandar, **1665**; Dindori, Sinhgarh, Surat, **1670**; Salher, **1671–1672**; Bhupalgarh, Bijapur, **1690**; Kanchi, **1692**; Chitaldrug, **1695**; Aiwagudi, Basawapatna, **1696**; Satara, **1699–1700**; Panhala, **1701**; Khelna, **1701–1702**; Raigarh, **1703–1704**; Torna, **1704**; Ratanpur, **1706**

Chinese Conquest of Taiwan: Fort Zeelandia, **1661–1662**; Penghu, **1683**

Later Turkish-Habsburg Wars: Neuhausel, **1663**; St Gotthard, **1664**; Esztergom, Parkany, Vienna, **1683**; Neuhausel, **1685**; Buda, **1686**; Harkany, **1687**; Belgrade, **1688**; Nish, **1689**; Belgrade, Nish, Zernyest, **1690**; Slankamen, **1691**; Lugos, **1695**; Zenta, **1697**

North African War of Louis XIV: Jijelli, **1664**

2nd Dutch War: Dylerschans, **1664**; Bergen (Norway), Lowestoft, **1665**; Four Days Battle, North Foreland, Vlie, **1666**; Martinique, **1667**; Medway, Nevis, **1667**

Lubomirski's Rebellion: Matwy, **1666**

Scottish Covenanter Rebellion: Pentland Hills, **1666**; Bothwell Bridge, Drumclog, **1679**

War of Devolution: Lille, **1667**; Dole, **1668**

Morgan's Raids on Panama: Porto Bello, **1668**; Panama, **1671**

Cossack Rebellion: Simbirsk, **1670**

Revolt of the Three Feudatories, 1671–1681. See Appendix

3rd Dutch War: Aardenburg, Charleroi, Groningen, Nijmegen, Sole Bay, Tolhuis, **1672**; Bonn, Maastricht, Schooneveld, Texel, **1673**; Besançon, Enzheim, Grave, Mühlhausen, Seneffe, Sinsheim, **1674**; Consarbruck, Sasbach, Turckheim, **1675**; Augusta (Sicily), Messina, Palermo, Stromboli, **1676**; Cassel, Kochersberg, **1677**; St Denis (France), **1678**

Turkish Invasion of the Ukraine: Kamieniec, **1672**; Khotin, **1673**; Trembowla, Zloczow, **1675**; Soczawa, Zurawno, **1676**; Chigirin, **1677**; Chigirin, **1678**

2nd Dutch-Khoikhoi War, 1673–1677. See Appendix

King Philip's War: Deerfield, Great Swamp Fight, Swansea, **1675**; Hadley, **1676**; Mount Hope, Seekonk, **1676**

Scania War: Fehrbellin, Rathenow, **1675**; Jasmund, Lund, Oland, **1676**; Koge Bay, Landskrona, **1677**

Bacon's Rebellion: Jamestown, Occaneechee Island, **1676**

Mughal Conquest of the Deccan Sultanates: Indi, **1676**; Bijapur, **1679**; Bijapur, **1685–1686**; Golconda, **1687**

Pueblo Rising: Santa Fé, **1680**

Mughal-Berad Wars: Sagar, **1680**; Wagingera, **1705**

Franco-Barbary Wars: Algiers, **1682–1683**; Algiers, **1688**

Franco-Genoese War: Genoa, **1684**

Monmouth Rebellion: Norton St Philip, Sedgemoor, **1685**

Russo-Chinese Border War: Albazin, **1685–1686**

War of the Grand Alliance: Philippsburg, **1688**; Bantry Bay, Walcourt, **1689**; Beachy Head, Fleurus, Staffarda, **1690**; Mons, **1691**; La Hogue, Leuze, Namur, Steenkirk, **1692**; Baia (Italy), Charleroi, Lagos Bay, Marsaglia, Neerwinden, **1693**; Camaret Bay, **1694**; Barcelona (Spain), Namur, **1695**; Cartagena (Colombia), **1697**

Mughal-Sikh Wars: Bhangani, **1688**; Nadaun, **1691**; Guler, **1696**; Anandpur, **1700**; Anandpur, **1701**; Basoli, Nirmohgarh, **1702**; Anandpur, Chamkaur, Sarsa, **1704**; Muktsar, **1705**; Samana, **1709**; Jalalabad, Lohgarh, Rahon, Sirhind, **1710**; Jammu, **1712**; Gurdas Nangal, **1715**

War of the British Succession in Ireland: Londonderry, Newtown Butler, **1689**; Boyne, Limerick, **1690**; Athlone, Aughrim, Limerick, **1691**

First Jacobite Rebellion: Dunkeld, Killiecrankie, **1689**; Cromdale, **1690**; Glencoe, **1692**

King William's War: Lachine, **1689**; Fort Loyal, Port Royal, Quebec, Salmon Falls, Schenectady, **1690**; La Prairie, **1691**; Wells, York (Maine), **1692**; Oyster, **1694**; Fort William Henry (Maine), **1696**

Chinese-Mongol Wars: Ulan Butong, **1690**; Jaomodo, **1696**; Hoton Nor, **1731**

Russian Invasion of the Crimea: Azov, **1695–1696**

Spanish-Itzá War: Nojpeten, **1698**

2nd "Great" Northern War: Copenhagen, Jungfern-hof, Narva, **1700**; Dunamunde, Riga, **1701**; Erestfer, Hummelshof, Kliszow, Noteborg, **1702**; Nyenskans, Pultusk, Thorn, **1703**; Dorpat, Narva, Punitz, **1704**; Gemauerthof, Kotlin Island, **1705**; Fraustadt, Kalisch, **1706**; Baturin, Grodno, Holowczyn, Lesnaya, **1708**; Poltava, **1709**; Riga, **1709–1710**; Helsingborg, Vyborg, **1710**; Gadebusch, **1712**; Tonning, **1713**; Altona, Hango, Storkyro, **1714**; Stralsund, **1714–1715**; Fredrikshald, **1718**; Osel Island, **1719**; Grengam, **1720**

War of the Spanish Succession: Carpi, Chiari, **1701**; Cadiz, Cremona, Friedlingen, Landau, Luzzara, Santa Marta, Santa Vittoria, Vigo Bay, **1702**; Breisach, Ekeren, Granville, Höchstädt, Munderkingen, Speyer, **1703**; Barcelona, Blenheim, Castelo Branco, Donauwörth, Gibraltar, Malaga, **1704**; Badajoz, Barcelona, Cassano, Marbella, Valencia (Alcántara), **1705**; Alcántara, Alicante, Calcinato, Cartagena (Spain), Ramillies, Turin, **1706**; Almanza, Beachy Head, Denia, Játiva, Lérida, Lizard, Stollhofen, Toulon, **1707**; Cartagena (Colombia), Firth of Forth, Lille, Minorca, Oudenarde, Sardinia, Wynendael, **1708**; Alicante, **1708–1709**; Malplaquet, Mons, Tournai, Val Gudina, **1709**; Almenar, Brihuega, Douai, Rio de Janeiro, Saragossa, Villaviciosa, **1710**; Arleux, Rio de Janeiro, **1711**; Denain, **1712**; Freiburg, Landau, **1713**; Barcelona, **1713–1714**

Queen Anne's War: St Augustine, **1702**; Ayubale, **1703**; Deerfield, Port Royal, **1704**; Charleston (South Carolina), **1706**; Port Royal, **1710**; Quebec, **1711**

Spanish-Algerian Wars: Oran, **1704–1708**; Oran, **1732**; Algiers, **1775**; Oran, **1780–1791**; Algiers, **1783**

Rákóczi Rebellion: Zsibó, **1705**; Trenchin, **1708**

Maratha Civil War: Khed, **1707**

Mughal Wars of Succession: Jajau, **1707**; Hyderabad (India), **1709**; Lahore, **1712**; Agra, **1713**; Hasanpur, **1720**; Gheria (Bengal), **1740**; Daulatabad, **1741**; Rajmahal (Rajasthan), **1747**

Russian Invasion of Moldavia: Stanilesti, **1711**

Persian-Afghan Wars: Kandahar, **1711**; Kandahar, **1714**; Farah, Herat, **1719**; Kerman, **1721**; Gulnabad, Isfahan, Kerman, **1722**; Meshed, **1726**; Herat, Mehmandost, Murchakhar, **1729**; Zarghan, **1730**; Herat, **1731–1732**; Kandahar, **1737–1738**; Kabul, **1738**; Herat, **1750**; Nishapur, **1750–1751**; Torbat-i-Jam, **1751**; Meshed, **1754**; Sabzavar, **1755**

2nd Villmergen War: Bremgarten, Villmergen, **1712**

Tuscarora Indian War: Cotechna, **1712**; Nohoroco, **1713**

Ottoman Invasions of Montenegro: Podgoritza, **1712**; Cevo, **1768**

Jacobite Rebellion (The Fifteen): Preston, Sheriffmuir, **1715**

Yamasee Indian War: Salkehatchie, **1715**

Austro-Turkish War: Peterwardein, Temesvár, **1716**; Belgrade, **1717**

War of the Quadruple Alliance: Cape Passaro, **1718**; Glenshiel, Messina, Vigo, **1719**

Mughal-Hyderabad War: Balapur, Ratanpur, **1720**; Shakarkhelda, **1724**

Spanish-Moroccan Wars: Ceuta, **1720–1721**; Melilla, **1774–1775**

Russian Invasion of the Caspian: Baku, **1723**

Dummer's War: Norridgewock, **1724**; Fryeburg, **1725**

Rise of Dahomey, 1724–1727. See Appendix

Turko-Persian War: Erivan, **1724**; Tabriz, **1724–1725**; Kiemereh, **1726**; Erivan, Hamadan, **1731**

Franco-Barbary Wars: Tripoli (Libya), **1728**

Later Mughal-Maratha Wars: Amjhera, Palkhed, **1728**; Jaitpur, **1729**; Delhi, **1737**; Bhopal, **1737–1738**; Damalcherry Pass, **1740**; Trichinopoly, **1740–1741**; Katwa, **1742**; Trichinopoly, **1743**; Katwa, **1745**; Burdwan, **1747**; Malthan, **1751**; Sindkhed, **1757**; Mangrol, **1761**; Rakshasbhuvan, **1763**

Funj-Ethiopian War, 1730–1755. See Appendix

Maratha Rebellions: Dabhoi, **1731**; Savanur, **1756**

War of the Polish Succession: Danzig, **1733–1734**; Bitonto, Guastalla, Parma, Philippsburg, Secchia, **1734**

Turko-Persian Wars of Nadir Shah: Baghdad, Karkuk, Leilan, **1733**; Baghavand, **1735**; Basra, Mosul, **1743**; Kars, **1745**

Chickasaw-French War: Ackia, Chucalissa, **1736**

Austro-Russian-Turkish War: Azov, Perekop, **1736**; Banyaluka, Nish, Ochakov, Valjevo, **1737**; Bender, Orsova, **1738**; Belgrade, Kroszka, Stavuchany, **1739**

Portuguese-Maratha War: Bassein (India), **1737–1739**; Thana, **1738**

Persian Invasion of India: Jamrud, **1738**; Karnal, **1739**

War of the Austrian Succession: Porto Bello, **1739**; St Augustine, **1740**; Cartagena (Colombia), Mollwitz, Santiago de Cuba, **1741**; Bloody Swamp, Chotusitz, Sahay, **1742**; Braunau, Camposanto, Dettingen, **1743**; Cuneo, Madonna del Olmo, Prague, Toulon, Velletri, **1744**; Amberg, Bassignano, Fontenoy (Belgium), Hennersdorf, Hohenfriedberg, Kesseldorf, Soor, **1745**; Piacenza, Rottofredo, **1746**; Genoa, **1746–1747**; Bergen-op-Zoom, Cape Finisterre, Exilles, Lauffeld, Rocoux, **1747**; Havana, Maastricht, **1748**

Persian-Uzbek Wars: Charjui, Khiva, **1740**

1st Russo-Swedish War: Willmanstrand, **1741**

King George's War: Annapolis Royal, **1744**; Louisbourg, **1745**

Jacobite Rebellion (The Forty-Five): Carlisle, **1745**; Clifton Moor, Inverurie, Prestonpans, **1745**; Stirling, **1745–1746**; Culloden, Falkirk, **1746**

1st Carnatic War: Madras, Negapatam, St Thomé, **1746**; Fort St David, **1746–1748**; Cuddalore, Pondicherry, **1748**

Indian Campaigns of Ahmad Shah: Manupur, **1748**; Lahore, **1752**; Delhi, Gohalwar, **1757**; Lahore, **1759**; Barari Ghat, Kunjpura, Sikandarabad, **1760**; Panipat, Gujranwala, Sialkot, **1761**; Kup, **1762**; Sialkot, **1763**

2nd Carnatic War: Ambur, Devikota, **1749**; Gingee, Tiruvadi, **1750**; Arcot, Arni, Conjeeveram, Volkondah, **1751**; Trichinopoly, **1751–1752**; Bahur, Chingleput, Covelung, Gingee, Kaveripak, Seringham, **1752**; Tiruvadi, Trichinopoly, **1753**

The Century of Revolution, 1750–1850

Pathan War: Farrukhabad, Kasganj, **1750**; Farrukhabad, Qadirganj, **1751**

Later Dutch Wars in the East Indies: Jenar, **1751**; Tjiledug, **1752**

Persian Wars of Succession: Chahar Mahall, **1751**; Asterabad, **1752**; Kermanshah, **1752–1753**; Qomsheh, **1753**; Kamarej, **1754**; Kazzaz, **1756**; Lahijan, Urmiya, **1757**; Shiraz, **1758**; Ashraf, **1759**; Maragheh, **1760**; Qara Chaman, **1762**; Urmiya, **1762–1763**; Shiraz, **1780–1781**

Burmese Civil Wars: Ava, **1752**; Pegu, **1757**

Seven Years War (North America): Fort Necessity, Great Meadows, **1754**; Beauséjour, Belle Isle (Canada), Lake George, Monongahela, **1755**; Oswego, **1756**; Fort William Henry (NY), **1757**; Fort Duquesne, Fort Frontenac, Fort Ticonderoga, Louisbourg, Snowshoes, **1758**; Fort Niagara, Fort Ticonderoga, Montmorency Gorge, Quebec, **1759**; Montreal, **1760**; Quebec, St Francis, **1760**

War against Malabar Pirates: Savandrug, **1755**; Gheria (Bombay), **1756**

Guarani War: Caibaté, **1756**

Seven Years War (India): Calcutta, **1756**; Calcutta, Chandernagore, Plassey, Trichinopoly, **1757**; Cuddalore, Fort St David, Negapatam, Rajahmundry, Tanjore, **1758**; Madras, **1758–1759**; Chinsura, Masulipatam, Patna, Pondicherry, **1759**; Hajipur, Karikal, Masumpur, Sherpur (India), Udgir, Wandewash, **1760**; Pondicherry, **1760–1761**; Suan, **1761**

Seven Years War (Europe): Kolin, Lobositz, Minorca, Pirna, Port Mahon, **1756**; Breslau, Gotha, Gross-Jagersdorf, Hastenbeck, Leuthen, Moys, Prague, Rossbach, Schweidnitz, **1757**; Ile d'Aix, Cancale, Cherbourg, Crefeld, Domstadtl, Hochkirch, Lutterberg, Olmütz, Sandershausen, St Cast, Zorndorf, **1758**; Bergen (Hesse), Kay, Kunersdorf, Lagos Bay,

Maxen, Minden, Neuwarp, Quiberon Bay, **1759**; Carrickfergus, Dresden, Emsdorf, Glatz, Kloster-Kamp, Kolberg, Korbach, Landshut, Liegnitz, Torgau, Warburg, **1760**; Belle Isle (Brittany), Gruneberg, Kolberg, Vellinghausen, **1761**; Almeida, Amoneburg, Burkersdorf, Freiberg, Kassel, Lutterberg, Reichenbach (Poland), Valencia (Alcántara), Vila Velha, Wilhelmstahl, **1762**

Seven Years War (Caribbean): Cap Francais, **1757**; Guadeloupe, Martinique, **1759**; Dominica, **1761**; Havana, Martinique, **1762**

Baluchi Rebellion: Mastung, **1758**

Seven Years War (West Africa): Gorée, Senegal, **1758**

Cherokee Indian Wars: Etchoe, Fort Loudoun, Fort Prince George, **1760**; Etchoe, **1761**

Burmese Invasions of Siam: Ayutthaya, **1760**; Ayutthaya, **1766–1767**

Seven Years War (Philippines): Manila, **1762**

Maratha Wars of Succession: Alegaon, **1762**; Miraj, **1762–1763**; Dhodap, **1768**; Kasegaum, **1774**; Adas, Panchgaum, **1775**

Pontiac's War: Bloody Run, Bushy Run, Devil's Hole, Fort Pitt, Michilimackinac, Point Pelee, **1763**; Detroit, **1763–1764**

Bengal War: Gheria (Bengal), Katwa, Patna, Udaynala, **1763**; Buxar, Patna, **1764**; Kora, **1765**

1st British-Mysore War: Ambur, Chengam, Trinomalee, Vaniyambadi, **1767**; Mulbagal, **1768**

Mamluk Wars: Tanta, **1768**; Cairo, **1772**; Salihiyya, **1773**; Jaffa, **1775**

Polish Rebellion: Orekhovo, **1769**; Lanskroun, Stalowicz, **1771**; Cracow, **1772**

Catherine the Great's 1st Turkish War: Dniester, Khotin, **1769**; Bender, Chesme, Chios, Kagul, Larga, Lemnos, Nauplia, Pruth, Ryabaya Mogila, **1770**; Bucharest, Perekop, **1771**; Hirsov, Silistria, Turtukai, **1773**; Kozludzha, Kurchukai, Turtukai, **1774**

Regulators War: Alamance Creek, **1771**

Maratha-Mysore Wars: Chinkurli, **1771**; Saunshi, **1777**

Mamluk-Ottoman Wars: Damascus, **1771**; Jaffa, **1772–1773**; Rahmaniyya, **1786**

Pugachev Rebellion: Orenburg, Ufa, **1773–1774**; Kazan, Tatishchevo, Tsaritsyn, **1774**

Vietnamese Civil War: Quy Nhon, **1773**; Thang Long, **1789**; Thang Long, **1802**

Cresap's War: Yellow Creek, **1774**

Dunmore's War: Point Pleasant, **1774**

Rohilla War: Miranpur Katra, **1774**

1st British-Maratha War: Thana, **1774**; Adas, **1775**; Wargaom, **1779**; Ahmadabad, Bassein (India), Doogaur, Gwalior, Kalyan, Malang-gad, **1780**; Arnala, **1780–1781**; Bhorghat, Durdah, **1781**; Ratnagiri, **1783**

Turko-Persian Gulf War: Basra, **1775–1776**

War of the American Revolution: Bunker Hill, Chambly, Concord, Crown Point, Fort Ticonderoga, Great Bridge, Hampton, Lexington (Massachusetts), Longueuil, Machias, Montreal, St Johns, **1775**; Boston, Quebec, **1775–1776**; Charleston (Massachusetts), Dorchester Heights, Fort Lee, Fort Sullivan, Fort Washington, Gwynn Island, Harlem Heights, Kip's Bay, Long Island, Moore's Creek Bridge, New Providence, Norfolk, Pell's Point, Throg's Neck, Trenton, Trois Rivières, Valcour Island, White Plains, **1776**; Bennington Raid, Brandywine, Cooch's Bridge, Danbury Raid, Fort Anne, Fort Clinton, Fort Mercer, Fort Mifflin, Fort Stanwix, Fort Ticonderoga, Germantown, Hubbardton, Oriskany, Paoli, Peekskill Raid, Princeton, Saratoga (New York), Somerset Court House, Staten Island, White Marsh, **1777**; Barren Hill, Carrickfergus, Cherry Valley, Dominica, Little Egg Harbour, Monmouth, Newport (Rhode Island), Pondicherry, Rhode Island, Savannah, St Augustine, St Lucia, Ushant, Whitehaven, Wyoming Massacre, **1778**; Baton Rouge, Beaufort, Briar Creek, Charleston (South Carolina), Flamborough Head, Grenada, Kettle Creek, Minisink, Newtown, Paulus Hook, Penebscot, Savannah, St Vincent, Stono Ferry, Stony Point, Vincennes, **1779**; Gibraltar, **1779–1783**; Blackstocks, Camden, Cape Finisterre, Cape St Vincent, Charleston (South Carolina), Charlotte, Fishdam Ford, Fishing Creek, Hanging Rock, King's Mountain, Lanneau's Ferry, Martinique, Mobile, Monck's Corner, Monte Christi, Piqua, Rocky Mount, Ruddle's Station, Rugley's Mill, Springfield (New Jersey), St Louis, St Lucia, Wateree Ferry, Waxhaw, Williamson's Plantation, Young's House, **1780**; Augusta (Georgia), Charleston (South Carolina), Chesapeake Capes, Cowan's Ford, Cowpens, Dogger Bank, Eutaw Springs, Fort Ninety-Six, Fort St Joseph, Guildford Courthouse, Haw River, Hobkirk's Hill, Jamestown Ford, Lochrey's Defeat, Martinique, Pensacola, Porto Praya, Quinby Bridge, Richmond (Virginia), Scilly Isles, St Eustatius, Tappan Zee, Tarrant's Tavern, Ushant, Yorktown, **1781**; Minorca, **1781–1782**; Blue Licks, Dominica, Little Mountain, Negapatam, Providien, Sadras, Saints, St Kitts, Trincomalee, **1782**; Cuddalore, **1783**

Tupac Amaru Revolt, 1780–1782. See Appendix

2nd British-Mysore War: Arcot, Perambakam, **1780**; Negapatam, Pollilore, Porto Novo, Sholinghur, **1781**; Arni, Cuddalore, Kumbakonam, Paniani, Trikalur, **1782**; Bednur, **1783**; Mangalore, **1783–1784**

1st Cape Frontier War: Fish River, **1781**

Anglo-Dutch War: Elmina, **1782**

Hawaiian Wars: Mokuohai, **1782**; Kepaniwai, **1790**

Shays' Rebellion: Petersham, Springfield (Massachusetts), **1787**

Mughal-Maratha War of Ismail Beg: Lalsot, **1787**; Agra, **1787–1788**; Bagh Dera, Chaksana, **1788**; Merta, Patan, **1790**

Catherine the Great's 2nd Turkish War: Kinburn, **1787**; Khotin, Liman, Ochakov, Orsova, Thedonisi Island, **1788**; Belgrade, Focsani, Rimnik, **1789**; Izmail, Tendra, Yenikale Strait, **1790**; Babadag, Cape Kaliakra, Matchin, **1791**

2nd Russo-Swedish War: Hogland, **1788**; Bornholm, Frediksham, Hogfors, Oland, Svenskund, **1789**; Frediksham, Kronstadt Bay, Reval, Svenskund, Vyborg Bay, **1790**

Brabantine Rebellion: Turnhout, **1789**

3rd British-Mysore War: Travancore, **1789**; Calicut, Sathinungulum, Tiagar, **1790**; Koppal, **1790–1791**; Arikera, Bangalore, Gurrumkonda, Nandi Drug, Savandrug, Shimoga, **1791**; Seringapatam, **1792**

Mexican-Apache Wars: Cañón de Ugalde, **1790**

Little Turtle's War: Harmar's Defeat, **1790**; St Clair's Defeat, **1791**; Fallen Timbers, Fort Recovery, **1794**

Polish Rising: Dubienka, Zielenice, **1792**

French Revolutionary Wars (1st Coalition): Baisieux, Jemappes, Lille, Longwy, Mainz, Speyer, Valmy, Verdun, **1792**; Aix-la-Chapelle, Aldenhoven, Avesnes-le-Sec, Condé-sur-l'Escaut, Dunkirk, Froeschwiller, Hondschoote, Kaiserslautern, La Maddalena, Lincelles, Louvain, Lyons, Mainz, Marseilles, Martinique, Menin, Neerwinden, Pirmasens, Le Quesnoy, St Pierre and Miquelon, Tobago, Toulon, Trouillas, Valenciennes, Wattignies, Wissembourg, **1793**; Aldenhoven, Bastia, Beaumont-en-Cambresis, Bellegarde, Bois-le-Duc, Boulou, Boxtel, Calvi, Charleroi, Coullioure, Courtrai, Figueras, First of June, Fleurus, Guadeloupe, Hooglede, Kaiserslautern, Platzberg, Trippstadt, L'Ecluse, Landrécies, Mannheim, Martinique, Mouscron, Nieuport, Ourthe, Pont-à-Chin, Roulers, San Fiorenzo, San Lorenzo (Spain), St Lucia, Tourcoing, Tournai, Villers-en-Cauchies, Willems, **1794**; Luxembourg, Mainz, Rosas, **1794–1795**; Bilbao, Cape Colony, Genoa, Höchst im Odenwald, Hyèyes, Ile de Groix, Loano, Mannheim, Quiberon, Texel, Trincomalee, Ushant, **1795**; Altenkirchen, Amberg, Ambon, Arcola, Aschaffenburg, Augsburg, Bassano, Biberach, Bleichfeld, Borghetto, Caldiero, Calliano, Castelnuovo (Italy), Castiglione, Ceva, Colombo, Cosseria, Dego, Deining, Emmendingen, Friedberg (Bavaria), Friedberg (Hesse), Grenada, Lavis, Lodi, Lonato, Malsch, Millesimo, Mindelheim, Mondovi, Montenotte, Neresheim, Neumarkt, Neuwied, Piacenza, Primolano, Rastatt, Renchen, Roveredo, Saldanha Bay, Schliengen, St Lucia, St Vincent, Uckerath, Wetzlar, Wilnsdorf, Würzburg, **1796**;

Huningue, Kehl, Mantua, **1796–1797**; Altenkirchen, Cape St Vincent, Diersheim, Fishguard, Imola, Kirchberg, La Corona, La Favorita, Malborghetto, Neuwied, Rivoli, Santa Cruz de Tenerif, Tagliamento, Tarvis, Trinidad (West Indies), **1797**; Bern, Civita Castelana, Corfu, Ionian Islands, Minorca, **1798**; Valetta, **1798–1800**; Naples, **1799**

French Revolutionary Wars (Vendée War): Angers, Chatillon-sur-Sevre, Chemille, Cholet, Dol-de-Bretagne, Entrammes, Fontenay, Granville, Laval, Le Mans, Lucon, Montaigu, Nantes, Pallet, Pont de Gravereau, Pornic, Saumur, Savenay, St Fulgent, Thouars, Torfou, **1793**

2nd Cape Frontier War: Trompettersdrift, **1793**

Maratha Territorial Wars: Lakhairi, **1793**; Kharda, **1795**; Agra, Fatehpur, **1799**; Malpura, **1800**; Georgegarh, Indore, Ujjain, **1801**; Hansi, **1801–1802**; Poona, **1802**

Persian Wars of Succession: Kerman, **1794**

War of the 2nd Polish Partition: Brest-Litovsk, Bydgoszcz, Chelmno, Kobylka, Kruptchitsa, Maciejowice, Praga, Raclawice, Szczekociny, Vilna, Warsaw, **1794**

Hawaiian Wars: Nuuanu, **1795**

Persian-Georgian War: Shusha, Tiflis, **1795**

Punjab Campaigns of Shah Zaman: Rohtas, **1795**; Amritsar, Gujrat (Pakistan), **1797**; Amritsar, **1798**

Afghan Wars of Succession: Girishk, **1795**; Kabul, **1800**; Nimla, **1809**; Kabul, **1818**; Kandahar, **1834**

Montenegran-Scutari War: Krusi, Martinici, **1796**

French Revolutionary Wars (Irish Rising): Bantry Bay, **1796**; Camperdown, **1797**; Ballinamuck, Castlebar, Collooney, Donegal Bay, Killala, Rutland, **1798**

Irish Rebellion: Antrim, Arklow, Ballygullen, Ballynahinch, Carlow, Enniscorthy, Gibbet Rath, Kilcullen, Kilcumney Hill, Naas, New Ross, Oulart, Tara, Tubberneering, Vinegar Hill, **1798**

Franco-American Quasi War: Guadeloupe, **1798**; Nevis, **1799**; Guadeloupe, **1800**

French Revolutionary Wars (Middle East): Alexandria, Malta, Nile, Pyramids, Sediman, Shubra Khit, **1798**; Aboukir, Acre, Aswan, Cape Carmel, El Arish, Jaffa, Mount Tabor, Er Ridisiya, Samhud, **1799**; Heliopolis, **1800**; Aboukir, Alexandria, Cairo, Mandora, **1801**

4th British-Mysore War: Malavalli, Seringapatam, Sidassir, **1799**

French Revolutionary Wars (2nd Coalition): Acqui, Airolo, Alessandria, Alkmaar, Bergen-aan-Zee, Cassano, Castricum, Coire, Devil's Bridge, Feldkirch, Groote Keeten, Magnano, Mannheim, Martinsbruch, Modena, Muottothal, Novi Ligure, Ostrach, Ramosch, St Maria, Stockach, Tauffes, Toulouse, Trebbia, Turin,

Verona, Wetzikon, Zurich, Zuyper Sluys, **1799**; Bard, Biberach, Engen, Erbach, Genoa, Höchstädt, Hohenlinden, Ivrea, Marengo, Mincio, Montebello, Montréjeau, Mosskirch, Stockach, Surinam, **1800**; Algeciras Bay, Boulogne, Copenhagen, Elba, **1801**

3rd Cape Frontier War: Roodewal (Cape Province), Sundays, **1802**

Napoleonic Wars (Santo Domingo Rising): Crête-à-Perriot, Gonaives, **1802**; Santo Domingo, **1802–1803**; Port-au-Prince, Vertieres, **1803**

Emmet's Insurrection: Dublin, **1803**

1st British-Kandyan War: Hanwella, Kandy, **1803**

Napoleonic Wars (3rd Coalition): St Lucia, **1803**; Boulogne, Gorée, Pulau Aur, Surinam, **1804**; Amstetten, Austerlitz, Caldiero, Cape Finisterre, Dominica, Durrenstein, Elchingen, Gunzburg, Haslach, Hollarbrunn, Maria Zell, St Kitts, Tagliamento, Trafalgar, Ulm, Wertingen, **1805**

2nd British-Maratha War: Agra, Ahmadnagar, Aligarh, Argaum, Assaye, Delhi, Gawilgarh, Laswari, **1803**; Delhi, Dieg, Farrukhabad, Monson's Retreat, **1804**; Bharatpur, **1805**

Tripolitan War: Tripoli, **1803**; Tripoli, **1804**; Derna, **1805**

Russo-Persian Wars: Echmiadzin, **1804**; Akhalkalaki, **1810**; Aslanduz, **1812**; Lenkoran, **1813**; Shamkhor, Shusha, Yelizavetpol, **1826**; Abbasabad, Echmiadzin, Erivan, **1827**

1st Serbian Rising: Ivanovatz, **1805**; Misar, **1806**; Belgrade, **1807**; Nish, **1809**; Loznitza, Varvarin, **1810**

Rise of Sokoto: Alkalawa, **1806**

Vellore Mutiny: Vellore, **1806**

Napoleonic Wars (4th Coalition): Auerstadt, Blueberg, Buenos Aires, Castelnuovo (Albania), Czarnowo (Mazowieckie), Golymin, Halle, Jena, Lubeck, Magdeburg, Maida, Potsdam, Prenzlau, Pultusk, Saalfield, Santo Domingo, Schleitz, Zehdenick, **1806**; Breslau, **1806–1807**; Alexandria, Bergfriede, Buenos Aires, Constantinople, Copenhagen, Danzig, Eylau, Friedland, Heilsberg, Hof, Konigsberg, Mohrungen, Montevideo, Ostrolenka, Queetz, Rosetta, St Thomas, Stralsund, Waltersdorf, **1807**

Russo-Turkish Wars: Lemnos, **1807**; Silistria, **1809**; Batin, Silistria, **1810**; Loftche, **1810–1811**; Ruschuk, **1811**; Akhaltsikhe, Kars, Varna, **1828**; Adrianople, Kulevcha, Sliven, **1829**

Napoleonic Wars (Russo-Swedish War): Juthas, Kauhajoki, Kokonsaari, Lapuu, Nykarleby, Oravais, Pulkkila, Revolax, Siikajoki, Sveaborg, Vasa, Virta bro, **1808**; Savar, **1809**

Napoleonic Wars (Peninsular Campaign): Alcolea, Baylen, Benavente, Bilbao, Cabezon, Cabrillas, Cadiz,

Cardedeu, Durango, Espinosa, Evora, Gamonal, Gerona, Guenes, Lodosa, Mansilla, Medina del Rio Seco, Mengibar, Molins de Rey, Obidos, Pancorbo, Reynosa, Rolica, Rosas, Sahagun, Saragossa, Somosierra, Tudela, Valencia (Valencia), Valmaseda, Vimeiro, Zornoza, **1808**; Alba de Tormes, Alcaniz, Alcántara, Almonacid, Amarante, Arzobispo, Banos, Belchite, Braga, Cacabellos, Casa de Salinas, Chaves, Ciudad Real, Corunna, Gerona, Grijon, Igualada, Lugo, Maria, Medellin, Meza de Ibor, Miajadas, Monjuich, Monzon, Ocaña, Oitaven, Oporto, Oveida, Santiago, Talavera de la Reina, Tamames, Trepa, Uclés, Valls, **1809**; Hostalrich, **1809–1810**; Alcalá la Real, Almaden, Almazan, Almeida, Astorga, Barba de Puerco, Barquill, Baza, La Bisbal, Bussaco, Ciudad Rodrigo, Coa, El Ronquillo, Fuengirola, Fuente de Cantos, Jaen, La Carolina, Lérida, Manresa, Margalef, Torres Vedras, Vich, Vilafranca del Penèdes, Villagarcia, **1810**; Tortosa, **1810–1811**; Cadiz, **1810–1812**; Albuhera, Albuquerque, Aldea del Ponte, Almeida, Arroyo Molinos, Ayerbe, Badajoz, Barrosa, Benavides, Bornos, Calatayud, Campo Mayor, Carpio de Azaba, Castillejos, Cazal Novo, Coimbra (Portugal), Condeixa, El Bodon, Figueras, Foz d'Aronce, Fuentes d'Onoro, Gebora, Monjuich, Montserrat, Navas de Membrillo, Niebla, Olivenza, Orbigo, Oropesa, Pla, Pombal, Redhina, Sabugal, Sagunto, Tarragona, Usagre, **1811**; Tarifa, Valencia (Valencia), **1811–1812**; Alba de Tormes, Albufera, Alicante, Almaraz, Altafulla, Badajoz, Bilbao, Bornos, Burgos, Castalla, Castrejon, Castrillo, Castro Urdiales, Ciudad Rodrigo, Foix, Garcia Hernandez, Guarda, Guetaria, Huebra, Lequeitio, Llera, Majadahonda, Peñíscola Portugalete, Puente Larga, Roda, Salamanca Forts, Salamanca, Salinas (Spain), Santander, Tordesillas, Venta del Pozo, Villa Muriel, Villagarcia, **1812**; Amposta, Biar, Bidassoa, Buenza, Castalla, Castro Urdiales, Dona Maria, Echalar, Fort Balaguer, Irurzun, Lizasso, Lodosa, Maya, Morales, Nive, Nivelle, Ordal, Osma, Pamplona, Poza, Roncesvalles, La Salud, San Marcial, San Millan, San Sebastian, Sorauren, St Jean de Luz, St Pierre d'Irube, Sumbilla, Tarragona, Tiebas, Tolosa, Vera, Villafranca de Oria, Vitoria, Yanzi, Yecla, **1813**; Aire, Arriverayte, Bayonne, Bordeaux, Croix D'Orade, Garris, Orthez, St Étienne, Tarbes, Toulouse, Vic-de-Bigorre, **1814**

Napoleonic Wars (5th Coalition): Abensberg, Aix, Aspern-Essling, Cayenne, Ebelsberg, Eckmühl, Flushing, Gefrees, Hausen, Landshut, Martinique, Neumarkt-St-Viet, Piave, Raab, Raszyn, Regensberg, Sacile, Santo Domingo, St Michael-Leoben, St Paul, Stralsund, Vienna, Wagram, Walcheren, Znaim, **1809**; Grand Port, Guadeloupe, Ionian Islands, Mauritius, Réunion, **1810**; Anholt, Batavia, Foule Point, Lissa, **1811**

Anglo-Arab Wars: Ras al-Khaimah, **1809**; Ras al-Khaimah, **1819**; Sur, **1820**; Balad Bani Bu Ali, **1821**; Aden, **1839**

West Florida Revolution: Baton Rouge, **1810**

Mexican Wars of Independence: Aculco, Dolores, Guanajuato, Monte de las Cruces, **1810**; Calderón, Zitácuaro, **1811**; Cuautla, Palmar, Zitácuaro, **1812**; Palmar, Valladolid, **1813**; Puruarán, **1814**; San Juan de los Llanos, Sombrero, Soto La Marina, Venadito, **1817**; Los Remedios, **1817–1818**

Argentine War of Independence: Cotagaita, Suipacha, **1810**; Cerro Porteño, Huaqui, Las Piedras, San Nicolás, **1811**; Cerrito, Río Piedras, Tucumán, **1812**; Ayohuma, Salta, San Lorenzo, Vilcapugio, **1813**; Arroyo de la China, Florida (Bolivia), Martín García, Montevideo, **1814**; Puesto del Márquez, Sipe-Sipe, Venta y Media, **1815**; Parí, **1816**; Jujuy, **1821**

Paraguayan War of Independence: Tacauri, **1811**

Tecumseh's Confederacy: Tippecanoe, **1811**

Colombian War of Independence: Palacé, **1811**; Ventaquemada, **1812**; Carillo, Palacé, Santa Fé de Bogotá, **1813**; Bogotá, Calibio, Tacines, **1814**; Balaga, Cartagena, Chire, Palo, **1815**; Cachirí, La Plata, El Tambo, **1816**; Boyacá, Gámeza, Pantano de Vargas, **1819**; Genoy, Tenerife, **1820**; Cartagena, **1820–1821**; Bomboná, **1822**

Turko-Wahhabi War: Hejaz, **1812–1813**

Gutiérrez-Magee Expedition: Nacogdoches, **1812**; La Bahía, **1812–1813**; Alazán Creek, Medina (Texas), Rosillo, **1813**

Napoleonic Wars (Russian Campaign): Berezina, Bolshoi-Stakhov, Borisov, Borodino, Dahlenkirchen, Eckau, Gorodeczno, Inkovo, Jacobovo, Kobryn, Kovno, Krasnoye, Loshnitza, Maloyaroslavetz, Mir, Mogilev, Ostrowno, Polotsk, Romanov, Shevardino, Smolensk, Smoliantsy, Tarontin, Valutino, Vinkovo, Vitebsk, Vyazma, **1812**; Kalisch, **1813**

War of 1812: Bahia, Brownstown, Detroit, Faial, Fort Dearborn, Fort Erie, Madeira, Magagua, Mississinewa, Queenston, Virginia, **1812**; Beaver Dams, Black Rock, Boston Harbour, Buffalo, Chateaugay, Chrysler's Farm, Craney Island, Dudley's Defeat, Florida, Fort George (Quebec), Fort Meigs, Fort Niagara, Fort Schlosser, Fort Stephenson, Frenchtown, Guyana, Lake Erie, Newfoundland, Ogdensburg, Portland (Maine), Sackets Harbour, Stoney Creek, Thames (Ontario), York (Ontario), **1813**; Baltimore, Barataria, Bladensburg, Caulk's Field, Chippewa, Fort Bowyer, Fort Erie, Fort McHenry, Hampden, Lacolle Mill, Lake Borgne, Lake Champlain, Longwood, Lundy's Lane, Michilimackinac, Pensacola, Plattsburg, Prairie du Chien, Rock Island Rapids, St George's Channel, Sandy Creek, Stonington, Valparaiso, Villeré's Plantation, Western Approaches, **1814**; Connecticut, Fort Bowyer, Madeira, New Orleans, Tristan de Cunha, **1815**

Venezuelan War of Independence: Puerto Cabello, **1812**; Araure, Bárbula, Barquisimeto, Los Horcones, Mosquiteros, Niquitao, San Marcos, Taguanes, Vigirima, **1813**; Aragua de Barcelona, Carabobo, La Puerta, La Victoria, San Mateo, Urica, Valencia, **1814**; Angostura, Barcelona, La Hogaza, Mucuritas, San Felix, **1817**; Calabozo, Semen, Sombrero, **1818**; Queseras del Medio, Rincón de los Toros, **1819**; Carabobo, Caracas, **1821**; Maracaibo, **1823**

Creek Indian War: Autossee, Burnt Corn, Fort Mims, Fort Sinquefield, Hillabee, Holy Ground, Littafatchee, Talladega, Tallaseehatchee, **1813**; Calabee Creek, Emuckfaw, Enotachopco, Horseshoe Bend, **1814**

Napoleonic Wars (War of Liberation): Altenberg, Bautzen, Cassel, Colditz, Dennewitz, Dresden, Grossbeeren, Hagelsberg, Hanau, Hoyerswerda, Katzbach, Königswartha, Kulm, Leipzig, Libertwolkwitz, Lindenau, Lowenberg, Luckau, Luneberg, Lützen, Mockern, Pirna, Reichenbach (Germany), Rippach, Sehested, Wachau, Wartenburg, **1813**; Cattaro, Danzig, Hamburg, **1813–1814**

Chilean War of Independence: Cancha Rayada, Roble, Yerbas Buenas, **1813**; Alto de Quilo, Rancagua, **1814**; Chacabuco, Gavilán, Potrerillos, Putaendo, Salala, **1817**; Cancha Rayada, Maipú, Talcahuano, **1818**; Hualqui, Quilmo, **1819**; Valdivia, **1820**; Chiloé, **1826**

Afghan-Sikh Wars: Attock, **1813**; Multan, **1818**; Shupiyan, **1819**; Nowshera, **1823**; Peshawar, **1834**; Jamrud, **1837**

Napoleonic Wars (French Campaign): Arcis-sur-Aube, Bar-sur-Aube, Bergen-op-Zoom, Borghetto, Brienne, Champaubert, Chateau-Thierry, Craonne, Fismes, La Fère-Champenoise, La Rothière, Laon, Maubeuge, Merxem, Montereau, Montmirail, Mortmant, Ourcq, Paris, Rheims, Soissons, St Dizier, Troyes, Vauchamps, **1814**

British-Gurkha War: Kalanga, Mangu, Nalagarh, **1814**; Jaitak, **1814–1815**; Almorah, Jitgargh, Katalgarh, Malaon, Parsa, **1815**; Makwanpur, **1816**

Peruvian War of Independence: Apacheta, Chacaltaya, Huanta, **1814**; Matará, Umachiri, **1815**; Callao, Pisco, **1819**; Cerro de Pasco, **1820**; Callao, **1820–1821**; Torata, **1823**; Ayacucho, Junín, **1824**; Callao, **1824–1826**

Algerine War: Cabo de Gata, **1815**

Napoleonic Wars (The Hundred Days): Ferrara, Huningue, La Souffel, Ligny, Namur, Quatre Bras, Tolentino, Waterloo, Wavre, **1815**

2nd British-Kandyan War: Kandy, **1815**

1st Seminole Indian War: Negro Fort, **1816**; Fowltown, **1817**; Pensacola, **1818**

Corsair Wars: Algiers, **1816**; Algiers, **1824**

3rd British-Maratha War: Kirkee, Mehidpur, Nagpur, Sitibaldi, **1817**; Ashti, Chanda (Maharashtra), Kor-egaon, Malegaon, Rampura, Seoni, Sholapur, Talneer, Kandy, **1818**; Asirgarh, **1819**

Xhosa Civil War: Amalinda, **1818**

Rise of Shaka Zulu: Gqokli, **1818**; Mhlatuze, **1819**

Persian-Afghan Wars: Kafir Qala, **1818**; Herat, **1837–1838**; Herat, **1856**; Herat, **1863**

5th Cape Frontier War: Fish River, Grahamstown, **1819**

Argentine Civil Wars: Barrancas, La Herradura, **1819**; Cepeda, **1820**; Río Seco, **1821**; Navarro, **1828**; Puente de Márquez, San Roque, La Tablada, Vizcacheras, **1829**; Oncativo, **1830**; La Ciudadela, Rio Cuarto, Rodeo de Chacón, **1831**; Cagancha, Chascomús, Pago Largo, Yerua, **1839**; Quebracho Herrado, Sauce Grande, **1840**; Caaguazú, Famaillá, Rodeo del Medio, **1841**; Rincón de Vences, **1847**; Caseros, **1852**; Sierra Chica, **1855**; Pigüé, **1858**; Cepeda, **1859**; Pavón, **1861**; San Ignacio, **1867**; Santa Rosa (Entre Rios), **1870**; Ñaembé, **1871**; San Carlos, **1872**; Santa Rosa (Mendoza), **1874**

Brazilian Occupation of Uruguay: Tacuarembó, Huachi, **1820**; Huachi, Tanizahua, Yaguachi, **1821**; Pichincha, Ríobambo, **1822**; Ibarra, **1823**

Italian Revolt against Austria: Novara, Rieti, **1821**

Turko-Persian War in Azerbaijan: Erzurum, **1821**; Khoi, **1822**

Greek War of Independence: Dragasani, Eressos, Galaxidi, Monemvasia, Navarino, Sekou, Thermopylae, Tripolitza, Valtesti, Vasilika, Vrachori, **1821**; Acropolis, Nauplia, **1821–1822**; Chios, Devernaki, Peta, Stura, **1822**; Missolonghi, **1822–1823**; Anatoliko, Karpenision, **1823**; Bodrum, Kasos, Psara, Samos, **1824**; Krommydi, Lerna, Maniaki, Navarino, Sphakteria, Trikorpha, **1825**; Missolonghi, **1825–1826**; Arachova, Chaidari, Klissova, **1826**; Acropolis, **1826–1827**; Analatos, Distomo, Navarino, **1827**

Brazilian War of Independence: Piraja, **1822**; Salvador, **1822–1823**; Jenipapo, Salvador, **1823**; Montevideo, **1823–1824**

Cape Frontier Wars: Takoon, **1823**

Franco-Spanish War: Trocadera, **1823**

Mexican Civil Wars: Almolonga, **1823**; Gallinero, Posadas, Poza de las Carmelos, Puebla, Tolomé, Vera Cruz, **1832**

Colombian Civil Wars: Catambuco, **1823**; Barbacoas, **1824**; La Ladera, **1828**; Santuario (Antioquia), **1829**; Santuario (Cundinamarca), **1830**; Palmira, **1831**; Buesaco, **1839**; Buesaco, Rionegro, **1851**; Bogotá, **1854**; Manizales, **1860**; Bogotá, Subachoque, **1861**; Los Chancos, Garrapata, **1876**; La Donjuana, Manizales, **1877**

Central American National Wars: Mejicanos, Ochomogo, **1823**; Arrazola, Comayagua, La Trinidad, Milingo, **1827**; Gualcho, San Antonio (El Salvador), **1828**; Guatemala City, **1829**; San José, **1835**; Espiritu Santo, Jicaral, San Pedro Perulapán, Soledad, Tegucicalpa, **1839**; El Potrero, Guatemala City, **1840**; Cartago, **1842**; Danli, Jutiapa, Nacaome, **1844**; Comayagua, Leon, Obrajuela, **1845**; La Arada, **1851**; Atulapa, Omoa, **1853**; Masaguara, **1856**; Coatepeque, San Felipe, San Salvador, Santa Rosa (Honduras), **1863**; Palencia, **1870**; Pasaquina, San Lucas Sacatepéquez, Santa Ana, Tacaña, **1871**; Comayagua, **1872**; Comayagua, **1874**; Apaneca, La Esperanza, Pasaquina, San Marcos (Honduras), **1876**; Chalchuapa, **1885**; Choluteca, Tegucicalpa, **1894**

Karankawa Indian War: Jones Creek, **1824**

1st British-Ashanti War: Bonsaso, **1824**; Dodowa, **1826**

1st British-Burmese War: Kemmendine, Martaban, Rangoon, **1824**; Bassein, Danubyu, Prome, Wattee-Goung, **1825**; Melloone, Pagahm-mew, Sittang, **1826**

Bolivian War of Independence: Tumusla, **1825**

Uruguayan War of Independence: Sarandi, **1825**

British-Maratha Wars: Bharatpur, **1825–1826**

Great Java War, 1825–1830. See Appendix

Argentine-Brazilian War: Los Pozos, Quilmes, **1826**; Bacacay, Ituzaingó, Juncal, Monte Santiago, Quilmes, **1827**

Siamese-Laotian Wars: Nong Bua Lamphu, **1827**

Miguelite Wars: Coimbra (Portugal), Praia Bay, **1828**; Oporto, **1832**; Cape St Vincent, **1833**; Asseiceira, **1834**

Peruvian-Colombian War: Tarqui, **1829**

Spanish Invasion of Mexico: Tampico, **1829**

Chilean Conservative Revolution: Ochagavía, **1829**; Lircay, **1830**

Belgian War of Independence: Antwerp, **1830**; Antwerp, **1832**

French Conquest of Algeria: Algiers, **1830**; Macta, Mascara, **1835**; Constantine, **1836–1837**; Smala, **1843**; Isly, **1844**

Polish Rebellion: Grochow, Ostrolenka, Praga, Siedlce, Warsaw, Wawer, **1831**

1st Turko-Egyptian War: Acre, **1831–1832**; Belen, Homs, Konya, **1832**

Russian Conquest of the Caucasus: Aghdash Awkh, **1831**; Gimrah, **1832**; Akhulgo, Burtinah, **1839**; Darghiyya, **1842**; Darghiyya, **1845**; Girgil, Saltah, **1847**; Zakataly, **1853**; Gunib, **1859**

Blackfoot Indian War: Pierre's Hole, **1832**

Black Hawk Indian War: Bad Axe, Kellogg's Grove, Pecatonica, Rock River, Wisconsin Heights, **1832**

Texan Wars of Independence: Anahuac, Nacogdoches, Velasco, **1832**; Anahuac, Concepcion, Goliad, Gonzales, Grass Fight, Lipantitlán, San Antonio, **1835**; Agua Dulce Creek, Alamo, Coleto Creek, Refugio, San Jacinto, San Patricio, **1836**; Mill Creek, San Gabriels, **1839**; Dawson's Massacre, Laredo, Mier, Salado, San Antonio, **1842**

1st Carlist War: Asarta, Guernica, Los Arcos, Peñacerrada, **1833**; Alegría, Alsasua, Arquijas, Artaza, Gulina, Mayals, Mendaza, Peñas de San Fausto, **1834**; Arquijas, Bilbao, Descarga, Larrainzar, Larremiar, Mendigorría, Orbiso, Ormáiztegui, Villafranca de Oria, **1835**; Arlaban, Bilbao, Fuentarrabia, Hernani, Orduña, San Sebastian, Tirapegui, Zubiri, **1836**; Barbastro, Huesca, Irun, Oriamendi, **1837**; Morella, **1837–1838**; Morella, Peñacerrada, **1838**; Morella, **1840**

6th Cape Frontier War: Ciskei, **1834–1835**

Bolivian-Peruvian War: Yanacocha, **1835**; Socabaya, **1836**; Ingavi, **1841**

2nd Seminole Indian War: Black Point, Dade Massacre, Withlacoochee, **1835**; Dunlawton, Fort Defiance, Fort Drane, San Felasco Hammock, Thonotosassa, Wahoo Swamp, Welika Pond, Withlacoochee, **1836**; Lake Okeechobee, **1837**; Jupiter Inlet, Loxahatchee, **1838**; Caloosahatchee, **1839**; Bridgewater, Fort King, Indian Key, Martin's Point, **1840**; Peliklahaka, **1842**

Ecuadorian Civil Wars: Minarica, **1835**; Bodegas, **1860**

Boer-Matabele War: Vegkop, **1836**; Kapain, Mosega, **1837**

Uruguayan Civil War: Carpinteria, **1836**; Palmar, **1838**

Canadian Rebellion: Toronto, **1837**

French-Canadian Rebellion: St Charles, St Denis, St Eustache, **1837**

Kichai Indian War: Stone Houses, **1837**

Boer-Zulu War: Blood River, Bloukranz, Ethaleni, Retief Massacre, Tugela, Veglaer, **1838**

Pastry War: San Juan de Ulúa, **1838**

Kickapoo Indian Wars: Battle Creek (Texas), Kickapoo Town, Killough Massacre, **1838**; Little Concho, Wichita Agency, **1862**; Dove Creek, **1865**; Naciemiento, **1873**

Chilean War of the Confederation: Yungay, **1839**

Mexican Federalist War: Acajete, Alcantra, Tampico, **1839**; Saltillo, Santa Rita de Morelos, **1840**

2nd Turko-Egyptian War: Nezib, **1839**; Acre, Beirut, **1840**

Cherokee Indian Wars: Neches, San Saba, **1839**; Village Creek, **1841**

1st British-Afghan War: Ali Masjid, Ghazni, Kalat, **1839**; Bamian, Kahan, Parwan Durrah, **1840**; Bemaru,

Charikar, Tezin, **1841**; Jalalabad, Kabul, Kandahar, **1841–1842**; Ali Masjid, **1842**; Babi Wali Kotal, Ghoaine, Haikalzai, Jagdalak, Maidan, Tezin, **1842**

1st Opium War: Chuanbi, Kowloon, **1839**; Dinghai, **1840**; Bogue Forts, Dinghai, Guangzhou, Xiamen, Zhenhai, **1841**; Ningbo, Zhapu, Zhenjiang, **1842**

Comanche Indian Wars: Brushy Creek, **1839**; Colorado, Council House Affair, Plum Creek (Texas), **1840**; Bandera Pass, **1841**; Walker's Creek, **1844**; Antelope Hills, Rush Springs, **1858**; Crooked Creek, **1859**; Prairie Dog Creek, **1860**; Adobe Walls, **1864**; Blanco Canyon, **1871**

Colombian War of Supreme Commanders: Culebrera, Huilquipamba, La Polonia, **1840**; Aratoca, La Chanca, Garcia, Itagüí, Ocaña, Riofrio, Salamina, Tescua, **1841**

Spanish Civil War, 1840–1843. See Appendix

Zulu Wars of Succession: Maqonqo, **1840**; Ndonda-kusuka, **1856**

Natal War: Congella, **1842**

Argentine-Uruguayan War: Arroyo Grande, **1842**; Montevideo, **1843–1851**; Arroyo del Sauce, **1844**; India Muerta, Vuelte de Obligada, **1845**

British Conquest of Sind: Hyderabad (Pakistan), Miani, Shahdadpur, **1843**

British-Gwalior War: Maharajpur (Gwalior), Panniar, **1843**

1st New Zealand War: Wairau, **1843**; Kapotai, Kororareka, Ohaewai, Puketutu, Te Ahuahu (Bay of Islands), **1845**; Ruapekapeka, **1845–1846**; Boulcott's Farm, Horokiri, **1846**; Rutland Stockade, St John's Wood, **1847**

Dominican War of Independence, 1844. See Appendix

Peruvian Civil Wars: Carmen Alto, **1844**; La Palma, **1855**; Arequipa, **1857–1858**

Sonderbund War: Gisikon, **1845**

1st British-Sikh War: Ferozeshah, Mudki, **1845**; Aliwal, Baddowal, Dharmkot, Sobraon, **1846**

French Conquest of Madagascar: Tamatave, **1845**; Tamatave, **1883**; Andriba, Tananarive, Tsarasoatra, **1895**

7th Cape Frontier War: Burnshill, Fort Peddie, Gwanga, **1846**

American-Mexican War: Brazito, Fort Texas, Monterey, Monterrey, Palo Alto, Rancho Dominguez, Resaca de la Palma, San Pascual, Thornton's Ambush, **1846**; Atlixco, Buena Vista, Cerro Gordo, Chapultepec, Churubusco, Contreras, Embudo Pass, Huamantla, Izúcar de Matamoros, La Cañada, Molino del Rey, Mora, Puebla, Pueblo de Taos, Sacramento, San Gabriel (California), Vera Cruz, **1847**; Santa Cruz de Rozales, **1848**

Caste War of Yucatan, 1846–1901. See Appendix

Dutch Conquest of Bali: Singaraja, **1846**; Jagaraga, **1848**; Jagaraga, **1849**; Cakranegara, Mataram, **1894**; Denpasar, **1906**

Cayuse Indian War: Whitman Massacre, **1847**; Deschutes, Willow, Tucannon, **1848**

French Conquest of Indochina: Danang, **1847**; Danang, **1858**; Saigon, **1859**; Chi Hoa, **1860–1861**; Hanoi, **1873**; Hanoi, **1882**; Hue, Nam Dinh, **1883**

Orange Free State War: Boomplaats, **1848**

1st Italian War of Independence: Curtatone, Custozza, Goito, Luino, Morazzone, Santa Lucia, Vicenza, **1848**; Brescia, Catania, Mortara, Novara, Palestrina, Rome, Velletri, Venice, **1849**

Hungarian Revolutionary War: Mór, Schwechat, Pakozd, Vienna, **1848**; Acs, Buda, Hatvan, Isaszeg, Kapolna, Komárom, Nagy Sallo, Pered, Segesvár, Temesvár, Waitzen, **1849**

2nd British-Sikh War: Kineyre, Ramnagar, Sadulapur, Sadusam, **1848**; Multan, **1848–1849**; Chilianwallah, Gujrat (Pakistan), **1849**

1st Schleswig-Holstein War: Bov, Dannevirke, **1848**; Duppel, Eckenforde, Fredericia, **1849**; Friedrichstadt, Idstedt, **1850**

The Rise of Modern Professionalism,
1850–1900

Pit River Indian War: Clear Lake, Russian, **1850**

8th Cape Frontier War: Boomah Pass, Fort White, **1850**; Fish River, Viervoet, Waterkloof, **1851**; Berea Mountain, Iron Mountain, **1852**

Taiping Rebellion: Huazhou, **1850**; Jiangkou, Jintian, Yung'an, **1851**; Changsha, Dadong Mountains, Guilin, Quanzhou, Suo'yi Ford, Wuchang, **1852**; Anqing, Huaiqing, Nanchang, Nanjing, Wuxue, **1853**; Luzhou, **1853–1854**; Wuchang, **1854**; Jiujiang, Wuchang, **1855**; Changshu, Nanjing, Wuchang, Zhenjiang, **1856**; Nanjing, Qingpu, Shanghai, Songjiang, **1860**; Anqing, **1860–1861**; Hangzhou, **1861**; Ningbo, Shanghai, Tzeki, Yuhuatai, **1862**; Nanjing, **1862–1864**; Suzhou, **1863**; Changzhou, Hangzhou, **1863–1864**

1st Chilean Liberal Revolt: Loncomilla, Petorca, **1851**

Apache Indian Wars: Janos Massacre, **1851**; Arizpe, **1852**; Cieneguilla, Rio Caliente, **1854**; Canyon of the Dead Sheep, Gila River, **1857**; Apache Pass, **1862**; Bloody Tanks, **1864**; Chiricahua Pass, **1869**; Camp Grant, **1871**; Skeleton Cave, **1872**; Turret Butte, **1873**; Rattlesnake Springs, Tinaja de las Palmas, Tres Castillos, **1880**; Cibecue Creek, **1881**; Big Dry Wash, **1882**; Aros, **1886**

2nd British-Burmese War: Bassein, Martaban, Pegu, Prome, Rangoon, **1852**; Danubyu, **1853**

Crimean War: Akhaltsikhe, Bashgedikler, Oltenitza, Sinope, **1853**; Alma, Balaklava, Bayazid, Bomarsund, Calafat, Chorokh, Citate, Giurgiu, Inkerman, Kürük-Dar, Odessa, Petropavlosk, Silistria, **1854**; Sevastopol, **1854–1855**; Chernaya, Eupatoria, Ingur, Kars, Kerch, Kinburn, Malakov, Redan, Sveaborg, **1855**

Turko-Montenegran Wars: Ostrog, **1853**; Grahovo, **1858**; Piva, **1861**; Rijeka, **1862**

Eureka Rebellion: Eureka Stockade, **1854**

Sioux Indian Wars: Fort Laramie, **1854**; Ash Hollow, **1855**; Spirit Lake, **1857**; Birch Coulee, Fort Ridgely, New Ulm, Wood Lake, **1862**; Big Mound, Dead Buffalo Lake, Stony Lake, Whitestone Hill, **1863**; Killdeer Mountain, **1864**; Massacre Canyon, **1873**; Crazy Woman Creek, Little Big Horn, Powder, Rosebud, Slim Buttes, War Bonnet Creek, **1876**; Muddy Creek, Wolf Mountain, **1877**; Wounded Knee Creek, **1890**

Mexican Liberal Rising: Acapulco, **1855**

Rogue River War: Hungry Hill, **1855**; Big Meadow, **1856**

3rd Seminole Indian War: Big Cypress Swamp, **1855**; Tillis Farm, **1856**

Yakima Indian Wars: Toppenish, Union Gap, **1855**; Grande Ronde Valley, Satus, **1856**; Four Lakes, Pine Creek, Spokane Plain, **1858**

National (Filibuster) War: Granada (Nicaragua), La Virgen, Rivas, **1855**; Granada (Nicaragua), Masaya, Rivas, San Jacinto (Nicaragua), Santa Rosa de Copán, **1856**; Rivas, San Jorge, **1857**; Trujillo, **1860**

Ute Indian Wars: Poncha Pass, **1855**; Spanish Fork Canyon, **1863**; Red Canyon, White River, **1879**

Anglo-Persian War: Bushire, Reshire, **1856**; Khoosh-Ab, Mohammerah, **1857**

Cheyenne Indian War: Solomon Forks, **1857**

Mormon War: Mountain Meadows, **1857**

Pisacane Rebellion: Sapri, **1857**

Indian Mutiny: Agra, Aligarh, Aong, Arrah, Badli-ki-Serai, Bashiratganj, Bithur, Bulandshahr, Cawnpore, Chanda (Uttar Pradesh), Chatra, Chinhat, Danchua, Delhi, Dhar, Fatehpur, Ghazi-ud-din-Nagar, Goraria, Jagdispur, Jiran, Kasganj, Khajwa, Lucknow, Mainpuri, Manduri, Mangalwar, Meerut, Najafghar, Narnaul, Nimach, Pali, Pandu Nadi, Patiala, Rawal, Shahganj, Sikander Bagh, Sohanpur, Trimmu Ghat, Unnao, **1857**; Alambagh, **1857–1858**; Amorha, Awah, Azamgarh, Badshahganj, Banda, Banki, Bareilly, Barodia, Betwa, Bijapur, Budhayan, Burgidiah, Chanda (Uttar Pradesh), Chanderi, Dalippur, Dundia Khera, Fatehgarh, Garhakota, Gorakhpur, Gwalior, Haraiya, Jagdispur, Jaunpur, Jawra Alipur, Jhansi, Kalpi, Kankar, Kankrauli, Kotah, Kotah-ki-Serai, Kunch, Lucknow, Madanpur, Maniar, Morar,

Muhamdi, Musa Bagh, Musjidiah, Nagal, Nagina, Nawabganj, Rahatgarh, Rajgarh, Ranod, Ruiya, Sagar, Sanganer, Shamsabad, Sirsa, **1858**; Dausa, Rapti, Sikar, **1859**

2nd Opium War: Fatshan Creek, Guangzhou, **1857**; Dagu Forts, **1858**; Dagu Forts, **1859**; Baliqiao, Dagu Forts, **1860**

Diaz Revolt in Uruguay: Cagancha, **1858**

Mexican War of the Reform: Acámbaro, Ahualalco, Atenquique, Guadalajara, Salamanca, **1858**; Colima, La Estancia, Tacubaya, Vera Cruz, **1859**; Calderón, Calpulalpam, Guadalajara, Silao, Toluca, Vera Cruz, **1860**

2nd Chilean Liberal Revolt: Cerro Grande, Loros, **1859**

Venezuelan Federalist Revolt: Santa Inés, **1859**; Cople, **1860**

2nd Italian War of Independence: Magenta, Melegnano, Montebello, Palestro, San Fermo, Solferino, Tre Ponti, Turbigo, Varese, **1859**; Ancona, Calatafimi, Castelfidardo, Milazzo, Palermo, Volturno, **1860**; Gaeta, **1860–1861**; Messina, **1860–1861**

Pyramid Lake Indian War: Pinnacle Mountain, Truckee, **1860**

Spanish-Moroccan War: Castillejos, Guad-el-Ras, Tetuán, **1860**

2nd New Zealand War: Mahoetai, Puketakauere, Waireka, Waitara, **1860**; Te Arei, **1861**; Camerontown, Katikara, Koheroa, Mauku, Poutoko, Pukekohe East, Rangiriri, **1863**; Gate Pa, Kaitake, Mangapiko, Moutoa, Orakau, Rangiaowhia, Sentry Hill, Te Ahuahu (Taranaki), Te Ranga, **1864**; Hungahungatoroa, Nukumaru, Waerenga, **1865**; Otapawa, **1866**; Makaretu, Matawhero, Moturoa, Te Ngutu-o-temanu, **1868**; Mohaka, Ngatapa, Te Porere, **1869**; Waikorowhiti, **1870**

American Civil War (Eastern Theatre): Aquia Creek, Ball's Bluff, Big Bethel, Blackburn's Ford, Bull Run, Camp Allegheny, Carnifex Ferry, Cheat Summit, Cross Lanes, Dranesville, Fort Hatteras, Greenbrier River, Hoke's Run, Philippi (West Virginia), Rich Mountain, Sewell's Point, **1861**; Antietam, Beaver Dam Creek, Bull Run, Cedar Mountain, Chantilly, Cockpit Point, Cross Keys, Drewry's Bluff, Eltham's Landing, Fort Macon, Fredericksburg, Front Royal, Gaines' Mill, Garnett's & Golding's Farm, Goldsboro Bridge, Groveton, Hampton Roads, Hancock, Hanover Court House, Harper's Ferry, Kernstown, Kettle Run, Kinston, Malvern Hill, McDowell, New Bern, Oak Grove, Port Republic, Rappahannock, Roanoke Island, Savage's Station, Seven Days' Battles, Seven Pines, Shepherdstown, South Mills, South Mountain, Thoroughfare Gap, Tranter's Creek, White Hall, White Oak Swamp, Williamsburg, Winchester (Virginia), Yorktown, **1862**; Aldie, Auburn, Boonsboro,

Brandy Station, Bristoe Station, Buckland Mills, Chancellorsville, Droop Mountain, Fort Anderson, Fredericksburg, Gettysburg, Hanover, Kelly's Ford, Manassas Gap, Middleburg (Virginia), Mine Run, Rappahannock Station, Salem Church, Suffolk, Upperville, Washington (North Carolina), Williamsport, Winchester (Virginia), **1863**; Albermarle Sound, Berryville, Cedar Creek, Cedarville, Chester Station, Cloyd's Mountain, Cold Harbour, Cove Mountain, Crater, Cumberland, Darbytown Road, Deep Bottom, Drewry's Bluff, Fair Oaks, Fisher's Hill, Fort Fisher, Fort Stevens, Globe Tavern, Hatcher's Run, Haw's Shop, Jerusalem Plank Road, Kernstown, Lynchburg, Monocacy, Moorefield, Morton's Ford, New Market, New Market Heights, New Market Road, North Anna, Old Church, Opequon, Petersburg, Piedmont, Plymouth (North Carolina), Poplar Springs Church, Port Walthall Junction, Reams Station, Sappony Church, Smithfield, Snicker's Ferry, Spotsylvania Court House, St Mary's Church, Staunton River Bridge, Stephenson's Depot, Summit Point, Swift Creek, Tom's Brook, Totopotomoy Creek, Trevilian Station, Walkerton, Ware Bottom Church, Wilderness, Wilson's Wharf, Yellow Tavern, **1864**; Amelia Springs, Appomattox Court House, Appomattox Station, Dinwiddie Court House, Farmville, Five Forks, Fort Fisher, Fort Stedman, Hatcher's Run, High Bridge, Lewis's Farm.

American Civil War (Lower Seaboard): Fort Sumter, Santa Rosa Island, **1861**; Baton Rouge, Donaldsonville, Fort Jackson and St Philip, Fort Pulaski, Georgia Landing, New Orleans, Secessionville, Simmon's Bluff, St John's Bluff, Tampa, **1862**; Charleston Harbour, Cox's Plantation, Donaldsonville, Fort Bisland, Fort Brooke, Fort McAllister, Fort Wagner, Grimball's Landing, Irish Bend, Lafourche Crossing, Plains Store, Port Hudson, Stirling's Plantation, Vermillion Bayou, **1863**; Olustee, **1864**; Natural Bridge, **1865**

American Civil War (Trans-Mississippi): Bird Creek, Blue Mills Landing, Boonville, Carthage (Missouri), Dry Wood Creek, Fredericktown, Lexington (Missouri), Mount Zion Church, Round Mountain, Shoal Creek, Springfield (Missouri), Wilson's Creek, **1861**; Cane Hill, Clark's Mill, Galveston, Glorieta Pass, Hill's Plantation, Independence, Kirksville, Lone Jack, Newtonia, Old Fort Wayne, Pea Ridge, Prairie Grove, Roan's Tan Yard, Sabine Pass, St Charles (Arkansas), Valverde, **1862**; Baxter Springs, Bayou Fourche, Cabin Creek, Cape Girardeau, Chalk Bluff, Devil's Backbone, Galveston, Hartville, Honey Springs, Lawrence, Pine Bluff, Sabine Pass, Springfield (Missouri), **1863**; Big Blue, Blair's Landing, Elkin's Ferry, Fort Davidson, Fort De Russy, Glasgow, Independence, Jenkins' Ferry, Lexington (Missouri), Little Blue River, Mansfield, Mansura

(Louisiana), Marais des Cygnes, Marks' Mills, Marmiton, Mine Creek, Monett's Ferry, Newtonia, Old River Lake, Pleasant Hill, Poison Spring, Prairie d'Ane, Westport, Yellow Bayou, **1864**; Palmito Ranch, **1865**

American Civil War (Western Theatre): Barbourville, Belmont (Missouri), Camp Wild Cat, Ivy Mountain, Rowlett's Station, **1861**; Chattanooga, Chickasaw Bluffs, Corinth (Mississippi), Fort Donelson, Fort Henry, Hartsville, Hatchie Bridge, Island Number Ten, Iuka, Jackson (Tennessee), Memphis (Tennessee), Middle Creek, Mill Springs, Munfordville, Murfreesboro, Parker's Cross Roads, Perryville, Richmond (Kentucky), Shiloh, **1862**; Stones River, **1862–1863**; Arkansas Post, Bean's Station, Big Black, Blountsville, Blue Springs, Brentwood, Buffington Island, Campbell's Station, Champion Hill, Chattanooga, Chickamauga, Collierville, Corydon, Davis' Cross Roads, Day's Gap, Fort Donelson, Fort Sanders, Franklin, Goodrich's Landing, Grand Gulf, Helena (Arkansas), Hoover's Gap, Jackson (Mississippi), Milliken's Bend, Mossy Creek, Port Gibson, Raymond, Ringgold Gap, Salineville, Snyder's Bluff, Thompson's Station, Vaught's Hill, Vicksburg, Wauhatchie Station, **1863**; Adairsville, Allatoona, Athens (Alabama), Atlanta, Brice's Cross Roads, Buck Head Creek, Bull's Gap, Columbia, Cynthiana, Dallas, Dalton, Dandridge, Decatur, Ezra Church, Fair Garden, Fort McAllister, Fort Pillow, Franklin, Griswoldville, Honey Hill, Johnsonville, Jonesborough, Kennesaw Mountain, Kolb's Farm, Lovejoy's Station, Marietta, Marion, Memphis (Tennessee), Meridian, Mobile Bay, Murfreesboro, Nashville, New Hope Church, Okolona, Paducah, Peachtree Creek, Pickett's Mill, Resaca, Rocky Face Ridge, Saltville, Spring Hill, Tupelo, Utoy Creek, Waynesborough (Georgia), **1864**; Averasborough, Bentonville, Blakely, Kinston, Monroe's Cross Roads, Rivers' Bridge, Selma, Spanish Fort, **1865**

Garibaldi's First March on Rome: Aspromonte, **1862**

Serbo-Turkish Wars: Belgrade, **1862**

Ecuador-Colombia War: Tulcán, **1862**; Cuaspud, **1863**

Mexican-French War: Acultzingo, Orizaba, Puebla, **1862**; Camerone, Piedra-Gorda, Puebla, San Lorenzo, San Luis Potosi, Santa Inés, **1863**; Candelaria, Matehuala, **1864**; Oaxaca, Santa Ana Amatlan, Tacámbaro, **1865**; La Coronilla, La Carbonera, Matamoros, Miahuatlán, Oaxaca, Santa Gertrudis, Santa Isabel (Coahuila), **1866**; Mexico City, Puebla, Querétaro, San Jacinto, San Lorenzo, **1867**

Bear River Indian War: Bear River, **1863**

British-Satsuma War: Kagoshima, **1863**

Pathan Rising: Ambela, **1863**

Dominican War of Restoration, 1863–1864. See Appendix

War of the Meiji Restoration: Kyoto, **1863**; Kyoto, **1864**; Fushimi, Ueno, Wakamatsu, **1868**; Goryokaku, **1869**

American Civil War (High Seas): Cherbourg, **1864**

Navajo Indian War: Canyon de Chelly, **1864**

2nd Schleswig-Holstein War: Alsen, Duppel, Helgoland, **1864**

Shimonoseki War: Shimonoseki, **1864**

Cheyenne-Arapaho Indian War: Ash Creek, Cedar Canyon, Sand Creek, **1864**; Fort Rice, Julesburg, Platte Bridge, Powder, Tongue, **1865**; Plum Creek (Nebraska), **1867**; Beaver Creek, Beecher Island, Washita, **1868**; Summit Springs, **1869**

War of the Triple Alliance: Coimbra (Brazil), **1864**; Paysandú, **1864–1865**; Corrientes, Paso de Cuevas, Mbutuy, Riachuelo, Uruguayana, Yatay, **1865**; Boquerón (Nhembucu), Corrales, Curupaíty, Curuzú, Estero Bellaco, Ilha de Redencão, Tuyutí, Yataití-Corá, **1866**; Estero Rojas, Nhembucu, Potrero Obella, Tatayiba, Tuyutí, **1867**; Angostura (Paraguay), Avaí, Humaitá, Ita Ybate, Tebicauri, Ytororó, **1868**; Acosta-Ñu, Piribebuy, Tupium, **1869**; Cerro Corá, **1870**

British-Bhutanese War: Dewangiri, **1865**

Later Afghan War of Succession: Khujbaz, **1865**; Kabul, Sheikhabad, **1866**; Khujbaz, Kila Alladad, **1867**; Zurmat, **1869**; Herat, **1870**

Russian Conquest of Central Asia: Tashkent, **1865**; Bokhara, **1868**; Khiva, **1873**; Khokand, **1875**; Andizhan, **1876**; Geok Tepe, **1879**; Geok Tepe, **1881**

Peruvian-Spanish War: Callao, Valparaiso, **1866**

Seven Weeks War: Aschaffenburg, Blumenau, Gerchsheim, Gitschin, Hammelburg, Helmstadt, Huhnerwasser, Kissingen, Königgratz, Langensalza, Laufach, Liebenau, Münchengratz, Nachod, Podol, Schweinschadel, Skalitz, Soor, Tauberbischofsheim, Tobitschau, Trautenau, Werbach, Wiesenthal, Würzburg, Zella, **1866**

3rd Italian War of Independence: Bassa, Bezzecca, Custozza, Lissa, Monte Suella, **1866**

Red Cloud's War: Fetterman Massacre, Lodge Trail Ridge, **1866**; Fort Phil Kearney, **1866–1867**; Hayfield Fight, Wagon Box Fight, **1867**

Garibaldi's Second March on Rome: Mentana, Monterotondo, Villa Glori, **1867**

British Expedition to Ethiopia: Arogi, Magdala, **1868**

Canadian River Expedition: Soldier Spring, **1868**

Spanish Revolution: Alcolea, **1868**

1st Cuban War of Independence: Bayamo, **1869**; Virginius Incident, **1873**

Piegan Indian Expedition: Marias, **1870**

Franco-Prussian War: Amiens, Artenay, Bagneux, Bazeilles, Beaugency, Beaumont-en Argonne, Beaune-la-Rolande, Bellevue, Buzancy, Chateaudun, Chatillon-le-Duc, Chatillon-sous-Bagneux, Chatillon-sur-Seine, Chevilly, Colombey, Coulmiers, Dijon, Dreux, Etival, Gravelotte, Gray, Hallue, Le Bourget, Loigny, Malmaison, Mars-la-Tour, Metz, Neu-Breisach, Noiseville, Nouart, Nuits Saint George, Saarbrucken, Schlettstadt, Sedan, Soissons, Spicheren, Strasbourg, Thionville, Toul, Verdun, Villiers, Wissembourg, Wörth, **1870**; Bapaume, Paris, **1870–1871**; Belfort, Dijon, Héricourt, Le Mans, Mont Valerian, Pontarlier, St Quentin, Villersexel, **1871**

Kiowa Indian War: Little Wichita, **1870**; Salt Creek, **1871**

Paris Commune: Paris, **1871**

Egyptian Wars of Expansion: Masindi, **1872**

Modoc Indian War: Lost River (California), **1872**; Lava Beds, Schonchin Flow, **1873**

Red River Indian War: McClellan Creek, **1872**; Adobe Walls, Buffalo Wallow, Lost Valley (Texas), Lyman's Wagon Train, Palo Duro, **1874**; Sappa Creek, **1875**

2nd Carlist War: Oroquieta, **1872**; Alpens, Bocairente, Mañeru, Montejurra, **1873**; Bilbao, **1873–1874**; Caspe, Castellfullit de la Roca, Cuenca, Estella, Gandesa, Oteiza, Somorrostro, **1874**; Lácar, Treviño, **1875**; Estella, Montejurra, **1876**

2nd British-Ashanti War: Abakrampa, Escobea, Essaman, **1873**; Amoafo, Odasu, **1874**

2nd Riel Rebellion: Cypress Hills, **1873**; Batoche, Battleford, Cut Knife Creek, Duck Lake, Eagle Hills, Fish Creek, Frenchman's Butte, Frog Lake, Loon Lake, **1885**

Saga Rebellion: Saga, **1874**

Egyptian-Ethiopian War: Aussa, Gundet, **1875**; Gura, **1876**

Diaz Revolt in Mexico: Icamole, Jazmin, Oaxaca, San Juan Epatlán, Tecoac, **1876**

Serbo-Turkish War: Alexinatz, Djunis, Vucji Do, **1876**

Xinjiang Rebellion: Ürümqi, **1876**; Turpan, **1877**

Nez Percé Indian War: Bear Paw Mountains, Big Hole, Canyon Creek, Clearwater, White Bird Canyon, **1877**

Satsuma Rebellion: Kagoshima, Kumamoto, Shiroyama, **1877**

9th Cape Frontier War: Ibeka, **1877**; Kentani, N'Axama, **1878**

Russo-Turkish War: Aladja Dagh, Ardahan, Gorni-Dubnik, Kars, Kizil-Tepe, Loftche, Mount St Nicholas,

Nicopolis (Bulgaria), Orchanie, Pelischat, Plevna, Shipka Pass, Stara Zagora, Svistov, Tahir, Yahni, Zivin, **1877**; Erzurum, **1877–1878**; Plovdiv, Senova, Tashkessan, **1878**

Austro-Turkish War in Bosnia: Sarajevo, **1878**

Bannock Indian War: Battle Creek (Idaho), Birch Creek, Pendleton, Silver Creek (Oregon), **1878**

2nd British-Afghan War: Ali Masjid, Peiwar Kotal, **1878**; Charasia, Fatehabad, Kabul, Sherpur (Afghanistan), **1879**; Ahmad Khel, Kandahar, Maiwand, Urzu, **1880**

Anglo-Zulu War: Eshowe, **1879**; Gingindlovu, Hlobane, Inyezane, Isandhlwana, Khambula, Myer's Drift, Rorke's Drift, Sihayo's Kraal, Ulundi, **1879**

Baputhi War: Moorosi's Mountain, **1879**

Sheepeater War: Vinegar Hill (Idaho), **1879**

White River Massacre: Meeker Massacre, **1879**

War of the Pacific: Angamos, Iquique, San Francisco (Chile), Tarapacá, **1879**; Arica, Los Angeles (Peru), Tacna, **1880**; Chorrillos, Miraflores, **1881**; Concepción (Peru), Pucará, Tongos, **1882**; Huamachuco, **1883**

1st Anglo-Boer War: Bronkhorstspruit, **1880**; Ingogo, Laing's Nek, Majuba Hill, **1881**

Afghan Civil Wars: Kandahar, **1881**; Ghaznigak, **1888**

Arabi's Egyptian Rebellion: Alexandria, Kassassin, Tel-el-Kebir, Tel-el-Maskhuta, **1882**

Franco-Mandingo Wars: Kéniéra, **1882**; Bamako, **1883**; Sikasso, **1887–1888**; Guélémou, Sikasso, **1898**

War of the Desert: Apeleg, **1883**

Zulu Civil War: Msebe, Ondini, **1883**; Tshaneni, **1884**

Sino-French War: Hanoi, Son Tay, **1883**; Bac Le, Bac Ninh, Chilung, Fuzhou, Tanshui, **1884**; Lang Son, Tuyen-Quang, **1885**

British-Sudan Wars: El Obeid, Tokar, **1883**; El Teb, Sinkat, Tamai, **1884**; Khartoum, **1884–1885**; Abu Klea, Abu Kru, Ginniss, Hashin, Kirkeban, Tofrek, **1885**; Gemaizeh, Handoub, **1888**; Toski, **1889**; Tokar, **1891**; Firket, Hafir, **1896**; Abu Hamed, **1897**; Atbara, Dakhila, Gedaref, Omdurman, **1898**; Um Diwaykarat, **1899**

Russo-Afghan War: Penjdeh, **1885**

Serbo-Bulgarian War: Pirot, Slivnitza, **1885**

3rd British-Burmese War: Bhamo, Minhla, **1885**

Sudanese-Ethiopian War: Kufit, **1885**; Debra Sina, **1887**; Gallabat, **1889**

1st Italo-Ethiopian War: Dogali, **1887**; Halai, **1894**; Amba Alagi, Coatit, **1895**; Makale, **1895–1896**; Adowa, **1896**

Saudi-Rashidi Wars: Riyadh, **1887**; Mulaydah, **1891**; Dilam, Riyadh, **1902**; Bukairiya, Unayzah, **1904**;

Rawdhat al Muhanna, **1906**; Jirab, **1915**; Kinzan, **1915**; Hail, **1921**

Zulu Rebellion: Ceza, Hlophekhulu, Ivuna, **1888**

German Colonial Wars in Africa: Bagamoyo, Pangani, **1889**; Lugalo, **1891**; Hornkranz, **1893**; Iringa, Naukluf, **1894**; Adibo, **1896**

1st Franco-Dahomean War: Atchoupa, Cotonou, **1890**

Chilean Civil War: Caldera Bay, Concón, Huara, Placilla, Pozo Almonte, San Francisco (Chile), **1891**

2nd Franco-Dahomean War: Abomey, Dogba, **1892**

British Conquest of Nigeria: Yemoji, **1892**; Benin, Ugbine, **1897**

Venezuelan Civil Wars: San Pedro, **1892**; Mata Carmelera, **1898**; Tocuyito, **1899**; La Victoria, **1902**; Ciudad Bolívar, **1903**

British Occupation of Sierra Leone: Waima Incident, **1893**

Italo-Sudanese Wars: Agordat, **1893**

Matabele War: Bembesi, Empadine, Shangani, Shangani Incident, **1893**

3rd Franco-Dahomean War: Acheribe, **1893**

War of Melilla: Melilla, **1893–1894**

Sino-Japanese War: Caohekou, Fenghuangcheng, Haiyang, Kangwachai, Phung-tao, Port Arthur, Pyongyang, Songhwan, Yalu, **1894**; Haicheng, **1894–1895**; Kaiping, Niuzhuang, Taipingshan, Weihaiwei, Yingkou, **1895**

Chitral Campaign: Chitral, Malakand, Nisa Col, Panjkora, **1895**

2nd Cuban War of Independence: Coliseo, Dos Ríos, Iguará, Jobito, Mal Tiempo, Manacal, Peralejo, Sao del Indio, **1895**; Artemisa, Cacarajicara, Candelaria, Loma del Gato, Paso Real, Punta Brava, Saratoga, **1896**; Victoria de la Tunas, **1897**

Jameson's Raid: Krugersdorp, **1896**

Philippines War of Independence: Binakayan, Imus, San Isidro, San Juan del Monte, San Mateo, Zapote Bridge, **1896**; Dasmariñas, Imus, Naic, Puray, Silang, Zapote Bridge, **1897**; Baler, **1898–1899**

1st Greco-Turkish War: Domokos, Mati, Nezeros, Pharsalus, Velestino, Vigla, **1897**

Great Frontier Rising: Dargai, Landi Kotal, Malakand, Dargai, Landi Kotal, Shabkadr, **1897**

British Conquest of Northern Nigeria: Ilorin, Bida, **1897**; Burmi, Kano, Rawiya, Sokoto, **1903**

Spanish-American War: Cienfuegos, Coamo, Cuzco Hills, El Caney, Guam, Guánica, Guantánamo Bay, Las Guásimas, Maine, Manila, Manila Bay, Nipe, San Juan Hill, San Juan (Puerto Rico), Santiago Bay, Santiago de Cuba, **1898**

Colombian War of the Thousand Days: Peralonso, **1899**; Palonegro, **1900**

Philippine-American War: Bagbag, Caloocan, Calumpit, Iloilo, Malolos, Manila, Polo, Quinqua, San Isidro, San Mateo, Santa Cruz, Sucat, Tirad Pass, Vigan, Zapote River, **1899**; Balangiga, **1900**; Palanan, **1901**

2nd Anglo-Boer War: Belmont, Chieveley, Colenso, Elandslaagte, Graspan, Magersfontein, Modder, Nicholson's Nek, Rietfontein, Stormberg, Talana Hill, Willow Grange, **1899**; Kimberley, Ladysmith, Mafeking, **1899–1900**; Alleman's Neck, Belfast, Biddulphsberg, Boshof, Bothaville, Diamond Hill, Doornkop, Driefontein, Elands River Post, Elandsfontein, Helvetia, Karee Siding, Lindley, Nooitgedacht, Paardeberg, Poplar Grove, Reddersburg, Roodewal (Orange Free State), Sannah's Post, Spion Kop, Stadt, Tugela Heights, Vaal Kranz, Vryheid, Wagon Hill, Wepener, Zand, Zilikats Nek, **1900**; Bakenlaagt, Belfast, Blood River Poort, Elands River Poort, Fort Itala, Groenkloof, Kleinfontein, Lichtenburg, Moedwil, Tweefontein, Vlakfontein, **1901**; Roodewal (Transvaal), Tweebosch, Yzer Spruit, **1902**

French Colonial Wars in North Africa: Ingosten, **1899**; In Rhar, In Salah, **1900**; Charouine, Timimoun, **1901**; Tit, **1902**; El Moungar, Taghit, **1903**; Casablanca, Taddert, Wadi Kiss, **1907**; Bou Denib, Bou Nouala, Djorf, El Menabba, R'Fakha, Settat, Wadi M'Koun, **1908**; Fez, **1911**; Fez, Sidi Ben Othman, **1912**; El Ksiba, **1913**; El Herri, Khenifra, **1914**; Sidi Sliman, **1915**; Gaouz, **1918**

World War and Revolution, 1900–1939

French Conquest of Chad: Kouno, Niellim, **1899**; Kousséri, **1900**

Ashanti Rising: Ashanti, **1900**

Boxer Rebellion: Beicang, Beijing, Dagu Forts, Langfang, Tianjin, Yangcun, **1900**

Russo-Chinese War: Aigun, Haicheng, Jilin, Liaoyang, Ongon, Qiqihar, Shaho, Xing-an, **1900**

Wars of the Mad Mullah: Ferdiddin, Samala, **1901**; Erego, **1902**; Daratoleh, Gumburu, **1903**; Illig, Jidballi, **1904**; Dul Madoba, **1913**; OK Pass, **1919**; Baran, Galiabur, Taleh, **1920**

Venezuelan Incident: La Guaira, **1902**

American-Moro Wars: Bayan, **1902**; Bacolod, Lake Seit, **1903**; Kudarangan, Pangpang, **1904**; Malala, **1905**; Bud Dajo, **1906**; Bud Bagsak, Mount Talipao, **1913**

Honduran Civil War: Nacaome, **1903**; San Pedro Sula, **1919**; Tegucicalpa, **1924**

British Invasion of Tibet: Guru, Gyantse, Karo Pass, Red Idol Gorge, **1904**

Russo-Japanese War: Chemulpo, Chongju, Dashiqiao, Delisi, Dogger Bank, Hill 203, Liaoyang, Motien Pass, Nanshan, Port Arthur, Shaho, Ulsan, Yalu, Yangzi Pass, Yellow Sea, **1904**; Port Arthur, **1904–1905**; Mukden, Sandepu, Tsushima, **1905**

German Colonial Wars in Africa: Freyer's Farm, Naris, Okaharui, Onganjira, Oviumbo, Owikokorero, Waterberg, **1904**; Hartebeestmund, Mahenge, Namabengo, Vaalgras, **1905**; Van Rooisvlei, **1906**

Bambatha Rebellion: Bobe, Mome, Mpukonyoni, **1906**

Guatemalan-Salvador War: El Jícaro, **1906**

Nicaraguan-Honduran War: Maraita, Namasigue, San Marcos de Colón, **1907**

1st Chinese Revolution: Hankou, Hanyang, Nanjing, Wuchang, **1911**

Italo-Turkish War: Ain Zara, Benghazi, Sidi El Henni, Sidi Mesri, Tripoli (Libya), **1911**; Dardanelles, Derna, Two Palms, Zanzur, **1912**

Mexican Revolution: Casas Grandes, Ciudad Juárez, Cuautla, **1911**; Rellano, **1912**; Chihuahua, Ciudad Juárez, Mexico City, San Andrés, Tierra Blanca, Torréon, **1913**; Ojinaga, **1913–1914**; Paredón, Torréon, Vera Cruz Incident, Zacatecas, **1914**; Naco, **1914–1915**; Agua Prieta, Aguascalientes, Celaya, Trinidad (Mexico), **1915**

1st Balkan War: Chataldja, Jannitsa, Kirk Kilissa, Kumanovo, Lüleburgaz, Monastir, Sarandáporon, **1912**; Adrianople, Jannina, Scutari, **1912–1913**; Bizani, **1913**

Saudi-Ottoman War: Hofuf, **1913**

2nd Balkan (Inter-ally) War: Bregalnica, Kilkis, Kresna, **1913**

2nd Chinese Revolution: Nanchang, Nanjing, **1913**

World War I (Far East): Qingdao, **1914**

World War I (Eastern Front): Augustovo, Galicia, Gnila Lipa, Gorodok, Gumbinnen, Ivangorod, Komárow, Krasnik, Limanowa, Lodz, Masurian Lakes, Orlau-Frankenau, Przemysl, Radom, Rawa Russka, San, Stalluponen, Tannenberg, Warsaw, Zlota Lipa, **1914**; Bolimov, Brest-Litovsk, Carpathians, Dvinsk, Gorlice-Tarnow, Grodno, Kovno, Lemberg, Lutsk, Masurian Lakes, Nowo Georgiewsk, Przasnysz, Triple Offensive, Vilna, Warsaw, **1915**; Strypa, **1915–1916**; Baranovitchi, Brody, Brusilov Offensive, Brzezany, Czernowitz, Lake Naroch, Lutsk, Riga, Stochod, Styr, **1916**; Aa River, Brzezany, Kerensky Offensive, Riga, Stanislau, Tarnopol, **1917**

World War I (African Colonial Theatre): Dar es Salaam, Duala, Kamina, Sandfontein, Tanga, **1914**; Garua, **1914–1915**; Gibeon, Jasini, Rufiji Delta, Windhoek, **1915**; Mora (Cameroon), **1915–1916**; Iringa, Mahiwa, Morogoro, Salaita, Tabora, **1916**; Narungombe, **1917**; Kasama, **1918**

World War I (Balkan Front): Cer, Drina, Kolubara, Sabac, **1914**; Belgrade, Kossovo, Kosturino, Vardar, **1915**; Salonika, **1915–1918**; Arges, Constanta, Flamanda, Florina, Hermannstadt, Mojkovac, Monastir, Rimnic Sarat, Targu Jiu, Tutrakan, **1916**; Doiran, Lake Prespa, Maracesti, **1917**; Dobro Polje, Doiran, Vardar, **1918**

World War I (Caucasus Front): Sarikamish, **1914– 1915**; Karakilise, Malazgirt, **1915**; Bayburt, Bitlis, Erzincan, Erzurum, Koprukoy Trebizond, **1916**; Baku, Sardarapat, **1918**

World War I (Mesopotamia): Qurna, Sahil, **1914**; Ahwaz, Amara, Ctesiphon, Kut-al-Amara, Nasiriya, Shaiba, Umm-at-Tubal, **1915**; Kut-al-Amara, **1915– 1916**; Dujaila, Hanna, Khanikin, Sannaiyat, Sheik Sa'ad, Wadi, **1916**; Baghdad, Istabulat, Kut-al-Amara, Mushahida, Ramadi, **1917**; Khan Baghdadi, Sharqat, **1918**

World War I (War at Sea): Cape Sarych, Coronel, Falkland Islands, Helgoland Bight, Scarborough, Sevastopol, **1914**; Dogger Bank, **1915**; Atlantic, **1915– 1917**; Jutland, **1916**; Dover Straits, Otranto, **1917**; Ostend, Zeebrugge, **1918**

World War I (Western Front): Aisne, Albert, Antwerp, Ardennes, Armentières, Arras, Charleroi, Flanders, Frontiers, Gheluvelt, Givenchy, Guise, Haelen, La Bassée, Langemark, Le Cateau, Liège, Lorraine, Marne, Messines, Mons, Mühlhausen, Namur, Nancy, Néry, Nonne Boschen, Ourcq, Tirlement, Ypres, Yser, **1914**; Champagne, **1914–1915**; Argonne, Artois, Aubers, Bellewaarde, Champagne, Festubert, Frezenberg, Givenchy, Gravenstafel, Hill 60 (Flanders), Loos, Neuve Chappelle, St Julien, Woevre, Ypres, **1915**; Albert, Bazentin, Delville Wood, Douaumont, Flers-Courcelette, Fleury, Guillemont, Le Mort-Homme, Louvement, Morval, Pozières, Somme, Souville, Thiepval, Transloy Ridges, Vaux, Verdun, **1916**; Ancre, **1916–1917**; Aisne, Arras, Broodseinde, Cambrai, Langemark, Menin Road, Messines, Nivelle Offensive, Passchendaele, Pilkem Ridge, Poelcappelle, Polygon Wood, Verdun, Ypres, **1917**; Aisne, Albert, Amiens, Arras, Bapaume, Belleau Wood, Cambrai-St Quentin, Canal du Nord, Cantigny, Chateau-Thierry, Courtrai, Épéhy, Flanders, Hamel, Hindenburg Line, Kemmel, Le Cateau, Lys, Marne, Meuse-Argonne, Noyon-Montdidier, Sambre, Scarpe, Selle, Somme, St Mihiel, St Quentin Canal, **1918**

World War I (Gallipoli): Anzac, Baby 700, Chunuk Bair, Dardanelles, Dardanelles Narrows, Eski Hissarlik, Hill 60 (Gallipoli), Krithia, Kum Kale, Lone Pine, Sari Bair, Scimitar Hill, Suvla Bay, **1915**; Gallipoli, Helles, **1915–1916**

World War I (Italian Front): Isonzo, **1915**; Asiago, Isonzo, **1916**; Caporetto, Isonzo, Monte Grappa, Ortigara, **1917**; Monte Grappa, Piave, Vittorio Veneto, **1918**

World War I (Middle East): Suez Canal, **1915**; Agagia, Beringia, Guiba, Hejaz, Jeddah, Katia, Magdhaba, Rafa, Romani, Taif, Yanbu, **1916**; Medina, **1916–1919**; Aqaba, Beersheba, El Mughar, Gaza, Huj, Jerusalem, Sheria, Siwa, Tel el Ful, Wejh, **1917**; Abu Tellul, Aleppo, Amman, Damascus, Dera, Es Salt, Jericho, Jisr Benat, Maan, Megiddo, Tafileh, Yakub, **1918**

Easter Rising: Dublin, **1916**

United States' Expedition against Villa: Carrizal, **1916**

Villa's Raids: Columbus, Santa Isabel (Sonora), **1916**

Manchu Restoration: Beijing, **1917**

Russian Civil War: Petrograd, **1917**; Orenburg, **1917– 1918**; Belaya Glina, Chelyabinsk, Ekaterinburg, Ekaterinodar, Kazan, Novocherkassk, Perm, Rostov, Samara, Stavropol, Torgovaya, Ufa, **1918**; Alexandrovsk, Chelyabinsk, Don Basin, Ekaterinburg, Kronstadt, Odessa, Omsk, Orel, Peregonovka, Perm, Tobol, Tsaritsyn, Ufa, Velikoknyazheskaya, Voronezh, Zlatoust, **1919**; Chita, Kuban, Melitopol, Novorossisk, Perekop, Rostov, Torgovaya, **1920**

Finnish War of Independence: Aland, Helsinki, Oulo, Porvoo, Rautu, Ruovesi, Sigurds, Tampere, Vilppula, Vyborg, **1918**

D'Annunzio's Insurrection: Fiume, **1919**

Estonian War of Independence: Cesis, Narva, Petrograd, Tallinn, **1919**

Hungarian-Czech War: Nove Zamky, Salgótarján, **1919**

Hungarian-Romanian War: Budapest, Tisza, **1919**

Latvian War of Independence: Riga, **1919**

Polish-Czech War: Teschen, **1919**

Punjab Disturbances: Amritsar, **1919**

Sapoa Revolution: Santa Rosa de Copán, **1919**

3rd British-Afghan War: Bagh, Dakka, Spin Baldak, Thal, **1919**

Russo-Polish War: Minsk, **1919**; Berezina, Kiev, Nieman, Szczara, Vilna, Warsaw, Zamosc, **1920**

Waziristan Campaign: Palosina, **1919**; Ahnai Tangi, Aka Khel, Barari Tangi, **1920**

Lithuanian War of Independence: Vilna, **1919**; Memel, **1923**

Saudi-Hashemite Wars: Turabah, **1919**; Taif, **1924**; Medina, **1925**

Anglo-Irish War: Balbriggan, Bloody Sunday, Cork, Rineen, **1920**

Anhui-Zhihli War: Zhuozhou, **1920**

French Occupation of Syria: Maisalun, **1920**

Iraqi Revolt: Jarbuiyah, Kufah, Rumaithah, Rustumiyah, Samawah, Tel Afar, **1920**

Saudi-Kuwait War: Hamad, Jahrah, **1920**

Hungarian Civil War: Budapest, **1921**

Kronstadt Rebellion: Kronstadt, **1921**

2nd Greco-Turkish War: Eskisehir, Inönü, Sakarya, **1921**; Afyon, Bursa, Smyrna, **1922**

Spanish-Rif War: Anual, **1921**; Tizzi Azza, **1922**; Tizzi Azza, **1923**; Chaouen, **1924**; Alhucemas, **1925**

1st Zhihli-Fengtian War: Changxindian, **1922**

Irish Civil War: Beal na mBlath, Clonmel, Cork, Four Courts, Kilmallock, Limerick, O'Connell Street, Tipperary, Waterford, **1922**; Clashmealcon Caves, **1923**

Corfu Incident: Corfu, **1923**

2nd Zhihli-Fengtian War: Shanhaiguan, **1924**

Druze Rebellion: Damascus, Hama, Kafr, Mazraa, Museifré, Rashaya, Suwayda, **1925**; Damascus, Suwayda, **1926**

Guo Songling's Revolt: Tianjin, Xinmintun, **1925**; Tianjin, **1926**

1st Chinese Revolutionary Civil War: Changsha, Fuzhou, Hesheng, Nanchang, Pingjiang, Tingsiqiao, Tingzu, Wuchang, **1926**; Hangzhou, **1926–1927**; Linying, Luoyang, Nanjing, Shanghai, Zhumadian, **1927**

Chaco War: Sorpresa, **1927**; Vanguardia, **1928**; Boquerón (Gran Chaco), Carlos Antonio López, **1932**; Alihuatá, Campo Vía, Gondra, Nanawa, Pampa Grande, Toledo (Paraguay), **1933**; Ballivian, Cañada el Carmen, Cañada Tarija, Cañada-Strongest, Villazón, Ybibobo, Yrendagüe, **1934**; Boyuibé, Ingavi, **1935**

2nd Chinese Revolutionary Civil War: Guangzhou, Longtan, Xuzhou, **1927**; Baoding, Beijing, Jinan, **1928**; Changsha, **1930**; Guangchang, Xiang, **1934**; Lazikou Pass, Loushan Pass, **1935**

Afghan Reformist War: Kabul, **1929**

Ikhwan Rebellion: Sabalah, Umm Urdhumah, **1929**

Italo-Senussi War: Al Khufrah, **1931**

Manchuria Incident: Mukden, **1931**; Great Wall, **1933**

Shanghai Incident: Shanghai, **1932**

Saudi-Yemeni War: Hudayda, **1934**

2nd Italo-Ethiopian War: Walwal, **1934**; Adowa, Dembeguina, **1935**; Addis Ababa, Amba Aradam, Ganale Doria, Lake Ashangi, Maychew, Ogaden, Shire, Tembien, **1936**

Waziristan Campaign, 1936–1937. See Appendix

Spanish Civil War: Alcazar, Alto de Leon, Badajoz, Barcelona, Boadilla del Monte, Cape Espartel, Chapinería, El Ferrol, Gijon, Ilescas, Larache, Madrid, Majorca, Melilla, Merida, Navalcarnero, Oveida, Somosierra, Talavera de la Reina, Villarreal de Alava, **1936**; Corunna Road, Maria de la Cabeza, **1936–1937**; Belchite, Bilbao, Brunete, Cape Cherchell, Gijon, Guadalajara, Guernica, Jarama, Malaga, Santander, Saragossa, **1937**; Teruel, **1937–1938**; Belchite, Cape Palos, Castellón de la Plana, Ebro, Valencia, Vinaroz, **1938**; Barcelona, **1938–1939**

Russo-Japanese Border Wars: Kanchatzu, **1937**; Changfukeng, **1938**; Khalkan Gol, **1939**

Sino-Japanese War: Beijing, Marco Polo Bridge, Nanjing, Panay Incident, Pingsingguan, Shanghai, Taiyuan, **1937**; Xuzhou, **1937–1938**; Guangzhou, Taierzhuang, Wuhan, **1938**; Changsha, Nanchang, Nanning, **1939**; Anhui Incident, Changsha, Shanggao, **1941**

World War II, 1939–1945

Russo-Finnish War: Helsinki, Mannerheim Line, Petsamo, Suomussalmi, Tolvajärvi, **1939**; Winter War, **1939–1940**; Mannerheim Line, Raate Road, **1940**

World War II (Southern Europe): Albania, **1939**; Greece, **1940**; Malta, **1940–1943**; Balkans, Belgrade, Crete, Greece, Maleme, **1941**; Bari, Catania, Dodecanese Islands, Foggia, Gela, Kos, Leros, Messina, Naples, Ortona, Palermo, Salerno, Sangro, Sicily, Termoli, Troina, Volturno, **1943**; Gustav Line, **1943–1944**; Anzio, Apennines, Bologna, Garigliano, Liri Valley, Monte Cassino, Rapido, Rimini, **1944**; Gothic Line, **1944–1945**; Po Valley, **1945**

World War II (War at Sea): River Plate, Scapa Flow, **1939**; Atlantic, **1939–1945**; Calabria, Cape Passaro, Cape Spada, Cape Spartivento, Glowworm, Taranto, **1940**; Alexandria, *Bismarck*, Cape Bon, Cape Matapan, Sirte, **1941**; Barents Sea, Channel Dash, Convoy Pedestal, Convoy PQ17, Sirte, **1942**; Alten Fjord, North Brittany, North Cape, **1943**

World War II (Western Europe): Bzura, Hel, Kock, Poland, Warsaw, Westerplatte, **1939**; Ardennes, Arras, Belgium, Boulogne, Britain, Calais, Channel Ports, Dunkirk, Dyle Line, Eben Emael, France, Laon, Rotterdam, **1940**; Bruneval, Dieppe, St Nazaire, **1942**; Dams Raid, Ploesti, Schweinfurt, **1943**; Berlin, **1943–1944**; Aachen, Alsace, Antwerp, Arnhem, Avranches, Bastogne, Breskens, Brest, Caen, Cherbourg, Epsom, Falaise, Fort Driant, Goodwood, Marseilles, Metz, Mons, Montélimar, Montrevel, Mortain, Nancy, Normandy, Nuremberg, Paris, Riviera, Scheldt Estuary, Schnee Eifel, St Lo, St Malo, St Vith, Toulon, **1944**; Ardennes, Hürtgen Forest, Siegfried Line, **1944–1945**; Colmar, Granville Raid, Reichswald, Remagen, Rhineland, Ruhr, Wesel, **1945**

World War II (Northern Africa): Dakar, Gallabat, Mers el Kebir, Sidi Barrani, Tug Argan, **1940**; Addis Ababa, Agordat, Amba Alagi, Bardia, Beda Fomm, Debra Tabor, Dessie, El Agheila, Gondar, Keren, Keyes Raid, Massawa, Mechili, Sidi Rezegh, Sollum-Halfaya, Tobruk, Wolchefit Pass, **1941**; Alam Halfa,

Algiers, Bir Hacheim, Casablanca, Cauldron, El Agheila, El Alamein, Gazala, Kidney Ridge, Longstop Hill, Mersa Brega, Mersah Matruh, Oran, Tébourba, Tobruk, Torch, **1942**; Tunisia, **1942–1943**; Bizerte-Tunis, Buerat, El Guettar, Faid Pass, Fondouk Pass, Hunt's Gap, Kasserine, Mareth Line, Médenine, Sidi Nsir, Wadi Akarit, **1943**

World War II (Northern Europe): Altmark Incident, Andalsnes, Narvik, Norway, Oslo, Valdres, **1940**; Karelia, Lofoten, Vaagso, **1941**; Spitzbergen, **1943**; Ihantala, Ilomantsi, Kirkenes, Vuosalmi, Vyborg, **1944**; Lapland, **1944–1945**

World War II (Middle East): Fallujah, Habbaniyah, Iran, Iraq, Lebanon, Palmyra, Syria, **1941**

World War II (China): Hong Kong, Kowloon, **1941**; Changsha, **1941–1942**; Zhejiang-Jiangxi, **1942**; Changde, Western Hubei, **1943**; Central Henan, Changsha, Guilin-Liuzhou, Hengyang, Ichigo, Longling, Songshan, Tengchong, **1944**; Salween, Wanting, **1944–1945**; Laohekou, Manchuria, Zhijiang, **1945**

World War II (Eastern Front): Bialystok, Brody-Dubno, Bryansk, Chernigovka, Kiev, Minsk, Odessa, Perekop, Rostov, Smolensk, Soltsy, Uman, Vyazma, **1941**; Moscow, Sevastopol, **1941–1942**; Leningrad, **1941–1944**; Kerch, Kharkov, Kotelnikovo, Rostov, Rzhev, Voronezh, **1942**; Caucasus, Stalingrad, **1942–1943**; Dnieper, Kharkov, Kiev, Kursk, Melitopol, Novorossisk, Orel, Prokhorokva, Smolensk, Zhitomir, **1943**; Balkans, Belgrade, Belorussia, Bobruysk, Jassy-Kishinev, Kamenets Podolsk, Kerch, Kirovograd, Korsun, Krivoy Rog, Lublin, Lvov, Minsk, Mogilev, Odessa, Perekop, Riga, Sevastopol, Tarnopol, Uman, Vilna, Vitebsk, Warsaw, **1944**; Budapest, **1944–1945**; Berlin, Breslau, Danzig, Königsberg, Lake Balaton, Pillau, Poznan, Prague, Vienna, Vistula-Oder, **1945**

World War II (Pacific): Guam, Jitri, Kota Bharu, Pearl Harbour, Prince of Wales and Repulse, Wake, **1941**; East Indies, Kampar, Malaya, Philippines, **1941–1942**; Aleutians, Bataan, Bismarck Sea, Bloody Ridge, Cape Esperance, Coral Sea, Corregidor, Darwin (Australia), Doolittle Raid, Eastern Solomons, Gemas, Gona, Guadalcanal—Naval, Java Sea, Kokoda Trail, Lombok Strait, Macassar Strait, Madoera Strait, Makin, Matanikau, Midway, Milne Bay, Muar, Palembang, Santa Cruz Islands, Savo Island, Singapore, Slim River, Solomon Islands, Sunda Strait, Tassafaronga, Tenaru, Tulagi, **1942**; Buna, Guadalcanal—Land, Kokumbona, Papua, Sanananda, **1942–1943**; Attu, Cape St George, Empress Augusta Bay, Enogai Inlet, Gilbert Islands, Horaniu, Huon Peninsula, Kolombangara, Komandorski Islands, Kula Gulf, Makin, New Georgia, Piva Forks, Rennell Island, Salamaua, Tarawa, Treasury Islands, Vella Gulf, Vella Lavella—Land, Vella Lavella—Naval, **1943**; Arawe, Bougainville, Cape Gloucester, New Britain, Shaggy Ridge,

Solomon Islands, **1943–1944**; Admiralty Islands, Aitape, Angaur, Biak, Bloody Nose Ridge, Cape Engaño, Eniwetok, Green Islands, Guam, Hollandia, Kwajalein, Leyte, Leyte Gulf, Los Negros, Manus, Mariana Islands, Marshall Islands, Noemfoor, Ormoc Bay, Palau Islands, Palawan Passage, Peliliu, Philippine Sea, Roi-Namur, Saipan, Samar, Sarmi, Sibuyan Sea, Surigao Strait, Tinian, Truk, Wakde, **1944**; Philippines, Wewak, **1944–1945**; Balikpapan, Bataan, Borneo, Brunei Bay, Corregidor, East China Sea, Iwo Jima, Luzon, Manila, Mindanao, Okinawa, Penang, Tarakan, **1945**

World War II (Indian Ocean): Ceylon, Colombo, Madagascar, Trincomalee, **1942**

World War II (Burma-India): Bilin, Burma, Kawkareik, Kuzeik, Lashio, Moulmein, Pegu, Prome, Shwegyin, Sittang, Toungoo, Yenangyaung, **1942**; Arakan, **1942–1943**; Irriwaddy, **1942–1945**; Longcloth, **1943**; Arakan, **1943–1944**; Admin Box, Bhamo, Hukawng, Imphal, Indaw, Kohima, Mogaung, Myitkyina, **1944**; Arakan, **1944–1945**; Mandalay, Meiktila, **1945**

War after 1945

Greek Civil War: Athens, **1944–1945**; Deskarti, Litokhoro, Naoussa, **1946**; Florina, Grevena, Metsovo, **1947**; Konitsa, **1947–1948**; Grammos, Karditsa, Kastoria, Roumeli, **1948**; Naoussa, **1948–1949**; Florina, Grammos, Karpenision, Vitsi, **1949**

Indonesian War of Independence: Surabaya, **1945**; Marga, **1946**; Jogjakarta, **1948**

3rd Chinese Revolutionary Civil War: Handan, Shangdang, Shanhaiguan, **1945**; Changchun, Jiangsu, Mukden, Siping, **1946**; Siping, Songhua, Yan'an, **1947**; Liaoshi, **1947–1948**; Baoji, Changchun, Jinan, Jinzhou, Kaifeng, Liaoshen, Luoyang, Mukden, Nianzhuang, Shuangduiji, Siping, Yichuan, **1948**; Beijing-Tianjin, Huaihai, **1948–1949**; Beijing, Chenguanzhuang, Nanjing, Taiyuan, Tianjin, Xi'an, Yangzi Incident, **1949**

French Indo-China War: Thakhek, **1946**; Cao-Bang, Dong-Khé, Red River Delta, **1950**; Day River, Mao Khé, Nghia Lo, Vinh Yen, **1951**; Hoa Binh, **1951–1952**; Nghia Lo, **1952**; Muong-Khoua, **1953**; Dien Bien Phu, **1953–1954**

Madagascan Insurrection: Moramanga, **1947**

Paraguayan Civil War: Asuncion, **1947**

1st Indo-Pakistan War: Bhatgiran, Shalateng, Uri, **1947**; Poonch, **1947–1948**; Leh, Skardu, Zojila, **1948**

Israeli War of Independence: Asluj, Beersheba, Deganiya, Deir Yassin, Gesher, Haifa, Huleiqat, Jaffa, Jenin, Jerusalem, Kastel, Latrun, Lydda-Ramleh, Manara, Mishmar Hayarden, Nazareth, Safad, Tarshiha, Tiberias, **1948**; Faluja, **1948–1949**

Costa Rican Civil War: Ochomogo, San Isidro del General, **1948**; Santa Rosa de Copán, **1955**

Korean War: Chochiwon, Chongchon, Chosin, Chunchon, Hadong, Han, Inchon, Koto-ri, Kum, Naktong Bulge, Osan, Pusan Perimeter, Pyongyang, Seoul, Taejon, Unsan, Wonju, Yongchon, **1950**; Bloody Ridge, Chipyong, Heartbreak Ridge, Imjin, Kapyong, Namsi, No Name Line, Seoul, Sinuiju, **1951**; Hook, Old Baldy, Triangle Hill, White Horse Hill, **1952**; Hook, Kumsong, Old Baldy, Pork Chop Hill, **1953**

Cuban Revolution: Moncada, **1953**; Alegría del Pío, **1956**; Cienfuegos, El Uvero, La Plata, **1957**; Santa Clara, Sierra Maestra, **1958**

Mau Mau Revolt: Aberdare, Mount Kenya, **1955**

Imam Revolt: Rustaq, **1955**; Jebel Akhdar, **1958**

Arab-Israeli Sinai War: Abu Ageila, Gaza, Mitla Pass, Rafa, Straits of Tiran, **1956**

Suez Crisis: Port Said, **1956**

Algerian War: Algiers, **1956–1957**; Frontier, Souk-Ahras, **1958**; Kabylie, **1959**

Ifni War: Ifni, **1957**

Indonesian Civil Wars: Bukittingi, Manado, **1958**

Western Sahara Wars: El Ayoun, **1958**; Tindouf, **1963**; Amgala, Nouakchott, Smara, **1976**; Oum Droussa, Zouerate, **1977**; Lebouirate, Tan-Tan, **1979**; Zag, **1980**; Guelta Zemmour, **1981**

Laotian Civil War: Vientiane, **1960**; Nam Tha, **1962**; Long Cheng, **1971–1972**; Sala Phou Khoun, **1975**

Bay of Pigs Incident: Bay of Pigs, **1961**

Franco-Tunisian Crisis: Bizerte, **1961**

Congolese Civil War: Elizabethville, **1961**; Elizabethville, **1962–1963**; Stanleyville, **1964**

Brunei Rebellion: Brunei, Limbang, Seria, **1962**

Dutch-Indonesian War: West Irian, **1962**

Sino-Indian War: Bomdila, Namka Chu, Se La, Tseng Jong, **1962**

Venezuelan Porteñazo Uprising: Puerto Cabello, **1962**

Vietnam War: Ap Bac, **1963**; Bien Hoa, Nam Dong, **1964**; Binh Gia, **1964–1965**; Ba Gia, Chu Lai, Dong Xoai, Ia Drang, Phuoc Ha, Pleiku, Plei Me, **1965**; A Shau, Ap Chinh An, Bon Son, Chau Nhai, Dau Tieng, Long Tan, Plain of Reeds, Song Ngan, Toumorong, Tuy Hoa, **1966**; Con Thien, Dak To, Iron Triangle, Khe Sanh, Loc Ninh, Suoi Tre, **1967**; Dong Ha, Hue, Khe Sanh, My Lai, Saigon, Tet Offensive, **1968**; Dong Ap Bia, **1969**; Cambodia, Son Tay, **1970**; Lam Son, **1971**; An Loc, Eastertide Offensive, Kontum, Quang Tri, **1972**; Phuoc Binh, **1974–1975**; Ban Me Thuot, Danang, Hue, Saigon, Xuan Loc, **1975**

Indonesian-Malaysian Confrontation: Mongkus, **1964**; Bau, Plamam Mapu, **1965**

Guinea-Bissau War: Como, **1964**; Guiledge, **1973**

Dominican Civil War: Santo Domingo, **1965**

2nd Indo-Pakistan War: Buttar Dograndi, Chawinda, Chhamb, Haji Pir, Khem Karan, Lahore, Phillora, Sialkot, **1965**

Arab-Israeli Six Day War: Abu Ageila, Bir Gafgafa, Gaza, Golan Heights, Jebel Libni, Jenin, Jerusalem, Mitla Pass, Nablus, Rafa, **1967**

Biafran War: Benin, Calabar, Enugu, **1967**; Onitsha, **1967–1968**; Abagana, Port Harcourt, **1968**; Owerri, **1968–1969**; Umuahia, **1969**

Yemeni Civil Wars: Sanaa, **1967–1968**; Aden, **1986**; Aden, **1994**

Arab-Israeli Border Wars: Karama, **1968**

Bangladesh War of Independence: Dacca, **1971**

3rd Indo-Pakistan War: Chhamb, Dacca, Garibpur, Karachi, Longewala, Shakargarh, **1971**

Dhofar War: Jebel Akhdar, **1971**; Mirbat, **1972**

Arab-Israeli Yom Kippur War: Chinese Farm, Golan Heights, Latakia, Mount Hermon, Suez Canal, **1973**

Turkish Invasion of Cyprus: Kyrenia, **1974**

Cambodian Civil War: Phnom Penh, **1975**

Lebanon Civil War: Tel-el-Zataar, **1976**; Beirut, **1978**; Zahle, **1981**; Beirut, **1982**; Beirut, **1990**

Ogaden War: Gode, Jijiga, Marda, **1977**; Dire Dawa, Harer, **1977–1978**; Jijiga, **1978**

Eritrean War of Independence: Massawa, **1977**; Keren, **1977–1978**; Nakfa, **1977–1986**; Barentu, **1985**; Afabet, **1988**; Massawa, **1990**; Dekemhare, **1990–1991**; Assab, **1991**

Shaba War: Kolwezi, **1978**

Tanzanian-Ugandan War: Kagera, **1978**; Kampala, **1979**

Chad Civil Wars: Ati, **1978**; N'Djamena, **1979**; N'Djamena, **1980**; Abéché, Faya Largeau, Oum Chalouba, **1983**; Iriba, Ouaddai, **1990**

Afghan Civil War: Herat, Kabul, **1978**; Kabul, **1979**; Panjshir Valley, **1982**; Ali Kheyl, Panjshir Valley, **1984**; Khost, Parrot's Beak, **1985**; Zhawar, **1986**; Jalalabad, **1989**; Khost, **1991**; Kabul, **1992**; Kabul, **1996**

Sino-Vietnamese War: Lang Son, **1979**

Vietnamese-Cambodian War: Phnom Penh, **1979**

Iraq-Iran War: Abadan, Ahwaz, Khorramshahr, Susangerd, **1980**; Abadan, Susangerd, **1981**; Basra, Khorramshahr, Mandali, Musian, **1982**; Amara, Haj Omran, Mehran, Panjwin, **1983**; Basra, **1984**; Basra, **1985**; Al Faw, Mehran, **1986**; Basra, Suleimaniya, **1987**; Al Faw, Halabja, Mehran, Salamcheh, **1988**

Falklands War: Goose Green, Mount Longdon, Mount Tumbledown, San Carlos, South Georgia, Stanley, **1982**

American Invasion of Grenada: Grenada, **1983**

Libyan-Chad War: Erdi, **1986**; Zouar, **1986–1987**; Aozou, Fada, Maaten-as-Sarra, Ouadi Doum, **1987**

Angolan War: Cuito Cuanavale, **1987–1988**

Somalian Civil War: Hargeisa, **1988**; Mogadishu, **1990–1991**; Mogadishu, **1993**

American Invasion of Panama: Panama, **1989**

Ethiopian Civil War: Inda Silase, **1989**; Asosa, **1990**; Addis Ababa, **1991**

1st Gulf War: Kuwait, **1990**; As-Salman, Baghdad, Bubiyan, Desert Storm, Khafji, Kuwait, Wadi al-Batin, **1991**

Croatian War: Vukovar, **1991**; Dubrovnik, **1991–1992**; Medak, **1993**; Knin, **1995**

Bosnian War: Bihac, **1992–1995**; Sarajevo, **1992–1996**; Mostar, **1993–1994**; Srebrenica, **1993–1995**; Gorazde, **1994–1995**

Ethiopian-Eritrean War: Badme, **1998**; Badme, Tsorona, **1999**; Barentu, **2000**

Kargil War: Tololing, **1999**

Kossovo War: Kossovo, **1999**

Afghanistan War: Kabul, Kandahar, Kunduz, Mazar-i-Sharif, Qala-i-Jangi, Tora Bora, **2001**

2nd Gulf War: Baghdad, Basra, Najaf, Nasiriya, Tikrit, Umm Qasr, **2003**

A

Aachen ▌ 1793 ▌ French Revolutionary Wars (1st Coalition)
  See **Aix-la-Chapelle**

Aachen ▌ 1944 ▌ World War II (Western Europe)
  American General Courtney Hodges advanced on the **Siegfried Line** and attacked the heavily fortified Aachen sector, defended by General Friedrich Koechling. After severe street fighting, Colonel Gerhard Wilch was forced to surrender Aachen itself, the first German city to fall. Hodges then took his army through the first breach of the West Wall into the **Hürtgen Forest** (2–21 October 1944).

Aardenburg ▌ 1672 ▌ 3rd Dutch War
  Advancing through the neutral Spanish Netherlands, French General Claude de Dreux Comte de la Nancré secured Dutch Flanders and invaded Zeeland, where he was blocked by the small garrison at Aardenburg, southwest of Breskens, under young Elias Beekman. De la Nancré had to retreat after suffering heavy losses in two failed night attacks and Zeeland was saved (26–28 June 1672).

Aa River ▌ 1917 ▌ World War I (Eastern Front)
  After German forces eventually halted the **Brusilov Offensive**, Russian General Radko Dmitriev launched a new offensive in the north along the River Aa, west of Riga. Germans under General Oskar von Hutier were initially forced back, but he soon counter-attacked to

retake the lost ground. Later in the year, he attacked and drove the Russians out of **Riga** (7–29 January 1917).

Aasle ▌ 1389 ▌ Wars of Scandinavian Union
  During a time of rebellion among local nobles, Queen Margaret of Denmark invaded Sweden and at Aasle, near Falkoping, she defeated and captured King Albert of Sweden (Albert of Mecklenburg), bringing an end to the Folkung Dynasty. As a result of the battle, Denmark, Norway and Sweden came under one crown and the Scandinavian Union lasted for 130 years (24 February 1389).

Abadan ▌ 1980 ▌ Iraq-Iran War
  After costly delays attempting a frontal assault on **Khorramshahr**, Iraqi forces tried to encircle and besiege nearby Abadan, on the Shatt al-Arab, one of the largest cities in Iran. The delay enabled Iran to reinforce the island city and, although Iraqis largely surrounded Abadan and seized some suburbs, Iran kept communication open and the invaders settled down to a siege (October 1980).

Abadan ▌ 1981 ▌ Iraq-Iran War
  Following failure at **Susangerd**, Iran's Mullahs overthrew President and Army Chief Beni-Sadr and launched a massive counter-offensive to break the siege of Abadan. While Iran suffered terrible losses, the Iraqis were unwilling to sacrifice their army against "human wave" attacks and retreated across the Karun, leaving

about 35,000 men to hold nearby **Khorram-shahr** (26–29 September 1981).

Abagana I 1968 I Biafran War

Supporting the siege of rebel-held **Onitsha** by Nigerian Federal forces under Colonel Murtala Mohammed, a weakly escorted Federal convoy of almost 100 trucks was ambushed to the northeast at Abagana by Biafran Major Jonathon Uchendu. When the two escorting armoured cars fled, the column was burned and destroyed, cutting supplies to the siege, but Onitsha was already doomed (31 March 1968).

Abakrampa I 1873 I 2nd British-Ashanti War

When Ashanti Chief Amonquatia threatened British territory on the coast of modern Ghana, he was driven off at **Essaman** in October, then led a large-scale attack 15 miles inland at Abakrampa, held by Major Baker Russell. The Ashanti were repulsed with heavy losses and, as General Sir Garnet Wolseley approached with reinforcements, they retreated north through **Amoafo** (5–6 November 1873).

Abancay I 1537 I Spanish Civil War in Peru

In the war between rival Spanish factions in Peru, forces of Diego del Almagro under Rodrigo Orgoñez defeated supporters of the Conquistador Francisco Pizarro at Abancay in southern Peru and captured their commander, Alonzo de Alvarado. The following year, Almagro was defeated by Pizarrist forces at **Salinas** and executed and the Pizarro faction gained control (12 July 1537).

Abárzuza I 1874 I 2nd Carlist War

See **Estella**

Abbasabad I 1827 I Russo-Persian Wars

Russian commander Ivan Paskevich led a new offensive against the Persian invasion of Azerbaijan, where he left a blockade on **Erivan**, then occupied Nakhichevan and took his siege train against Abbasabad. A 40,000-strong relief army under Persian Prince Abbas Mirza was defeated at nearby Dzhevan-Bulak (5 July) and Abbasabad fell two days later (7 July 1827).

Abéché I 1983 I Chad Civil Wars

Well equipped with Libyan heavy arms, rebels loyal to Goukouni Oueddei seized Faya Largeau in northern Chad, then advanced south and took Abéché. Government troops under Idriss Miskine and Idriss Déby launched a bloody counterattack which retook Abéché and checked the rebel offensive. They then pursued rebel General Negue Djogo back to disaster at **Faya Largeau** (8–12 July 1983).

Abensberg I 1809 I Napoleonic Wars (5th Coalition)

Encouraged by French reverses in Spain, Austria sent Archduke Charles Louis to invade Bavaria and trap Napoleon Bonaparte at Regensberg on the Upper Danube. Beaten at **Hausen**, Charles was badly defeated further south at Abensberg by Marshals Louis Davout and Jean Lannes. The divided Austrians were defeated in detail in the next two days at **Eckmühl** and **Landshut** (20 April 1809).

Abercorn I 1455 I Douglas Rebellion

James Earl of Douglas renewed rebellion against James II of Scotland and took an army against Abercorn, near Queensferry on the Firth of Forth. When rebels began to desert, then dispersed without serious fighting, the Earl withdrew and Abercorn Castle surrendered with many of its garrison executed. Earl Douglas fled to England and his brothers were routed at **Arkinholm** (March 1455).

Aberdare, Kenya I 1955 I Mau Mau Revolt (1st)

On the offensive against Mau Mau guerrillas in Kenya, General Sir George Erskine swept Nairobi (Operation Anvil, 24 April 1954), then launched 10,000 troops against a reported 2,000 rebels to the north in the Aberdare Forest. Operation Hammer yielded only 99 killed and 62 captured but was quickly followed by another offensive further east on **Mount Kenya** (6 January–11 April 1955).

Aberdare, Kenya I 1955 I Mau Mau Revolt (2nd)

New commander General Gerald Lathbury followed success at **Aberdare** and **Mount Kenya** by attacking the Mau Mau again in the Aberdare Forest. Despite bombers and artillery, this final, large-scale action achieved little and a British colonel was killed by friendly fire. Anti-insurgent gangs took over much of the fighting and the last British troops left Kenya in November 1956 (July 1955).

Aberdare, Wales I 1093 I Anglo-Welsh Wars

When Welsh King Rhys ap Tewdwr invaded Glamorgan and threatened Cardiff, Norman commander Sir Robert Fitzhamon sent a Norman-Welsh force under Cedrych and Einion (who had escaped at **Llandudoch** in 1088). The King's sons Goronwy and Cynan were both killed in a terrible defeat at Aberdare and Rhys himself was later captured and executed (17–23 April 1093).

Aberdeen I 1639 I 1st Bishops' War
See **Dee**

Aberdeen I 1644 I British Civil Wars

Two weeks after victory at **Tippermuir**, Scottish Royalist forces led by James Graham Marquis of Montrose inflicted a decisive defeat near Aberdeen on non-conformist Covenanters under Robert Balfour Lord Burleigh. The city of Aberdeen suffered a terrible sack before Montrose withdrew through **Fyvie**. Within months, Montrose renewed his offensive at **Inveraray** and **Inverlochy** (13 September 1644).

Aber Edw I 1282 I English Conquest of Wales

Edward I was determined to subdue Llewellyn ap Gruffydd of Wales (who had supported Simon de Montfort in the English Barons' War) and took a large army which was repulsed at **Bangor**. A month later, he defeated Llewellyn at Aber Edw on the Wye in Radnor. Llewellyn was killed in a skirmish at nearby Builth and the Welsh cause was effectively lost (11 December 1282).

Abomey I 1892 I 2nd Franco-Dahomean War

While advancing north into Dahomey (modern Benin) against King Behanzin, French Colonel Alfred Dodds fought off an attack at **Dogba**, then secured the holy city of Kana (6 November) before marching on Abomey. With nearby forts bombarded, the King burned and abandoned his capital. Dodds entered the city to enforce another truce until surrender at **Acheribe** (17 November 1892).

Aboukir I 1799 I French Revolutionary Wars (Middle East)

With British naval support, a large Turkish force led by Said Mustafa Pasha landed from Rhodes at Aboukir at the mouth of the Nile in an attempt to re-establish Allied influence in Egypt. Attacked by a French force only half as large under Generals Jean Lannes and Joachim Murat, the Turkish army was utterly defeated, with thousands drowned attempting to escape (25 July 1799).

Aboukir I 1801 I French Revolutionary Wars (Middle East)

Despite grim losses, a British-Turkish army under General Sir Ralph Abercromby made a successful amphibious landing on the Nile Delta at Aboukir against strong French forces led by General Louis Friant. Two weeks later, Abercromby began advancing towards **Alexandria** and was mortally wounded while defeating the French (8 March 1801).

Aboukir Bay I 1798 I French Revolutionary Wars (Middle East)
See **Nile**

Abraham, Plains of I 1759 I Seven Years War (North America)
See **Quebec**

Abricium I 251 I 1st Gothic War
See **Abrittus**

Abrittus I 251 I 1st Gothic War

Emperor Decius recovered from disaster near **Philippopolis** to attack the Goth leader Kniva in

Thrace a year later and pursue him to the lower Danube, where the Romans were lured onto marshy ground at Abrittus (modern Razgrad, Bulgaria). Decius and his son Herennius Etruscus were killed in a terrible defeat, but the Goths were eventually bought off by a cash tribute and withdrew (June 251).

Abu Ageila I 1956 I Arab-Israeli Sinai War

At the start of Israel's pre-emptive war against Egypt in Sinai, Colonel Yehuda Wallach attacked the strong HQ fortress in the north at Abu Ageila under Brigadier Gaafer el Abd. After heavy fighting for outlying positions, Abu Ageila fell by storm and the Egyptians were forced to withdraw, opening Israel's route south towards the **Straits of Tiran** (29 October–1 November 1956).

Abu Ageila I 1967 I Arab-Israeli Six Day War

On the central axis of Israel's invasion of the Sinai, General Ariel Sharon's tanks advanced on General Sadi Naguib in the sprawling Egyptian fortifications at Abu Ageila. A brilliant encircling attack, supported by paratroops landing to neutralise artillery, saw the Egyptians forced to flee, abandoning their equipment. Sharon then turned southwest towards **Mitla Pass** (5–6 June 1967).

Abu Hamed I 1897 I British-Sudan Wars

During British reconquest of the Sudan, General Sir Herbert Kitchener sent a flying column of British and Sudanese troops under General Sir Archibald Hunter forward from Merowi against the Nile railhead at Abu Hamed. The Mahdist troops were driven out, with 300 killed and commander Muhammad al-Zayn captured, and Kitchener continued on towards the **Atbara** (7 August 1897).

Abu Klea I 1885 I British-Sudan Wars

British troops under General Sir Herbert Stewart advanced up the Nile as part of the failed attempt to relieve **Khartoum** and crossed the desert from Dongola to Metemmeh to reach Jakdul and defeat a much larger Mahdist force at Abu Klea. The adventurer Colonel Frederick Burnaby was among those killed. The British won again two days later, further south at **Abu Kru** (17 January 1885).

Abu Kru I 1885 I British-Sudan Wars

Two days after victory at **Abu Klea** while crossing the desert from Dongola, British troops of the Khartoum Relief Expedition returning to the Nile were attacked by Mahdists further south at Abu Kru. While his British troops successfully held a defensive square, General Sir Herbert Stewart was mortally wounded. **Khartoum** fell a few days later and the failed expedition returned to Cairo (19 January 1885).

Abu Tellul I 1918 I World War I (Middle East)

In a final offensive to recover Jericho, attacking Turkish and German forces seized the strategic village of Abu Tellul in the hills to the north from the Australian Light Horse under General Charles Cox. A rapid counter-attack regained Abu Tellul and the garrison were forced to withdraw with heavy losses and 500 men captured, including over 350 Germans (14 July 1918).

Abydos I 411 BC I Great Peloponnesian War
See **Cynossema**

Abydos I 200 BC I 2nd Macedonian War

Philip V of Macedon captured **Chios** in 201 BC, then ravaged Pergamum and attacked the free city of Abydos, on the Asian side of the Dardenelles. Attalus of Pergamum and his Rhodian allies sent inadequate assistance and the city was forced to surrender after a bitter siege. Abydos regained its freedom in 196 BC under a peace agreement after **Cynoscephalae**.

Abydos I 989 I Byzantine Military Rebellions

Ten years after routing a usurper at **Aquae Saravenae**, Byzantine General Bardas Phocas had proclaimed himself Emperor and marched on Basil II at Constantinople, who sought aid from Prince Vladimir of Kiev. Checked at

Chrysopolis, Bardas Phocas was then decisively defeated at Abydos at the narrowest point of the Hellespont. He died soon afterwards and the rebellion ended (13 April 989).

Acajete | 1839 | Mexican Federalist War

Generals José Urrea and José Antonio Mejía rose against Mexican President Anastasio Busta-mente, who sent General Gabriel Valencia with 1,600 men to meet the Federalists at Acajete, northwest of Jalapa. Urrea fled to Tampico after fierce fighting and heavy losses, while Mejía was captured and shot without trial by newly arrived General Antonio de Santa Anna (3 May 1839).

Acámbaro | 1858 | Mexican War of the Reform

Just weeks after defeat at **Atenquique**, the Liberal offensive resumed in central Mexico, where about 4,000 men led by General Manuel Garcia-Pueblita met a strong Conservative government force under General Leonardo Márquez at Acámbaro. While Márquez withdrew north to Querétaro after a severe yet indecisive action, the Liberals were routed six weeks later at **Ahualalco** (12 August 1858).

Acapulco | 1855 | Mexican Liberal Rising

Liberals under Benito Juarez who supported the reform programme known as the Plan of Ayutla rose against the military dictator General Antonio de Santa Anna and defeated the government at Acapulco in southwest Mexico. Santa Anna then fled the country, ending his 30 years as the dominant personality in Mexican affairs (9 August 1855).

Accra | 1824 | 1st British-Ashanti War
See **Bonsaso**

Accra | 1826 | 1st British-Ashanti War
See **Dodowa**

Acerrae | 90 BC | Roman Social War

At war with Rome over failure to extend citizenship, near **Teanum** the Marsi and Samnites beat Consul Lucius Julius Caesar, who was reinforced and moved south along the Vulturno to relieve Acerrae. When Caesar's Numidian auxiliaries deserted, Samnite commander Papius Mutilus attacked, but was routed with about 6,000 men killed. However, Rome soon lost in the north at **Fucine Lake**.

Achalzie | 1828 | Russo-Turkish Wars
See **Akhaltsikhe**

Achelous | 917 | Later Byzantine-Bulgarian Wars
See **Anchialus**

Acheribe | 1893 | 3rd Franco-Dahomean War

Despite losing his capital at **Abomey**, King Behanzin of Dahomey (modern Benin) continued his resistance and General Alfred Dodds soon returned from France to put an end to the renewed war. Advancing to Acheribe, Dodds forced the King's officers to submit (9 November 1893) and enthroned Behanzin's brother Gouchili. Behanzin himself later surrendered (25 January 1894) and died in exile.

Achi Baba | 1915 | World War I (Gallipoli)
See **Krithia**

Ackia | 1736 | Chickasaw-French War

Advancing up the Mississippi from Louisiana against the hostile Chickasaw, Governor Jean Baptiste le Moyne de Bienville led a mixed French and Chocktaw force to avenge defeat at **Chucalissa** in March 1736. At Ackia, near Tupelo, Mississippi, de Bienville was routed in the worst French defeat at Indian hands and, after a further failure in 1739, returned to New Orleans (26 May 1736).

Aclea | 851 | Viking Raids on Britain

Danish Vikings were beaten at sea off **Sandwich**, but soon attacked London, then moved south of the Thames where they were defeated at Aclea (probably modern Oakley near Gravesend) by Aethelwulf of Wessex and his second son, Aethelbald. However, the invaders then withdrew to a position near the mouth of the Thames and secured their presence later in the year at **Thanet**.

Acoma Pueblo I 1598–1599 I Spanish Conquest of New Mexico

As Governor Don Juan de Oñate campaigned against Pueblo Indians in New Mexico, 30 soldiers were surprised near Acoma Pueblo, with 14 killed, including Commander Juan de Zaldivar. His brother Vicente returned and, in a three-day action, captured the "sky city," east of modern Grants. Up to 800 Indians were massacred, with many more enslaved (December 1598–22 January 1599).

Acosta-Ñu I 1869 I War of the Triple Alliance

Withdrawing from defeat at **Piribebuy**, the rearguard of Paraguay's retreating army under Colonel Florentino Oveida was quickly attacked by Brazilian forces east of Asunción at Acosta-Ñu. The Paraguayan force—comprising mainly teenage boy-soldiers—was routed with terrible losses and Dictator Francisco Solano López himself was killed six months later at **Cerro Corá** (16 August 1869).

Acqui I 1799 I French Revolutionary Wars (2nd Coalition)

After French losses in northern Italy at the hands of Russian General Alexander Suvorov, General Barthélemy Joubert took over command of the French army and managed a sharp victory against an Austrian force at Acqui, south of Genoa. However, facing the combined Austro-Russian army at **Novi Ligure** two days later, the French were heavily defeated and Joubert was killed (13 August 1799).

Acragas I 406 BC I Carthaginian-Syracusan Wars

Carthaginian General Hannibal invaded Sicily to avenge the loss at **Himera** (409 BC). He sacked **Selinus** and Himera, then besieged the Greek city of Acragas, where he died beating a relief force of Spartans under Dexippus and Syracusans led by Daphnaeus. His cousin Himilco finally took the city, and Dionysius of Syracuse ceded half of Sicily. Ten years later, Himilco returned to besiege **Syracuse**.

Acragas I 262 BC I 1st Punic War

When Rome besieged the city of Acragas, on the southwest coast of Sicily, held for Carthage by Hannibal, a Carthaginian relief army under Hanno was narrowly defeated. As the city fell, Hannibal and his supporters escaped, giving Rome control over most of the rich island. The Romans renamed the city, 60 miles southeast of Palermo, Agrigentum (modern Agrigento).

Acre I 1104 I Crusader-Muslim Wars

Following a failed siege of Acre in 1103, Baldwin I of Jerusalem tried again the next year, supported by a large fleet of Genoese galleys in return for commercial privileges and a share of the booty. Cut off by the Genoese blockade, commander Bena Zahr ad-Daulah surrendered Acre after three weeks of assault and the Crusaders secured one of the best harbours in Palestine (6–27 May 1104).

Acre I 1189–1191 I 3rd Crusade

During the two-year siege of Acre, north of modern Haifa, the attacking Crusaders fought at least nine engagements with the defenders and the surrounding army of the Kurdish-Muslim leader Saladin. In June 1191 the Crusaders were reinforced by King Richard I of England, who finally defeated Saladin's relief army and forced the Muslim garrison to surrender (28 August 1189–12 July 1191).

Acre I 1291 I Later Crusader-Muslim Wars

Sultan Khalil led a massive Mamluk army, which besieged, then stormed Acre, the last great Crusader-held city in the Holy Land. While there were scenes of remarkable heroism by knights of the Military Orders as survivors attempted to escape by sea, the dramatic fall of the city effectively ended the Christian Crusader kingdoms of the Middle East (6 April–18 May 1291).

Acre I 1799 I French Revolutionary Wars (Egypt)

Marching from Egypt into Syria, Napoleon Bonaparte besieged Acre, north of modern Haifa, defended by Djezzar, Pasha of Acre, aided at sea by British Captain Sir William Sidney Smith. Despite beating a relief force at **Mount Tabor**, Bonaparte made no headway. With his siege train captured off **Cape Carmel** and his army struck by plague, he withdrew to Egypt (16 March–20 May 1799).

Acre I 1831–1832 I 1st Turko-Egyptian War

Egyptian Viceroy Mohammed Ali invaded Turkish Syria, then sent his son Ibrahim Pasha, who quickly captured Gaza, Jaffa, Jerusalem and Haifa before besieging Pasha Abdallah at Acre. The great fortress fell by storm after a long siege. Following further victories at **Homs** and **Belen**, Ibrahim invaded Anatolia and defeated the Turks at **Konya** (10 November 1831–27 May 1832).

Acre I 1840 I 2nd Turko-Egyptian War

When Egyptian Viceroy Mohammed Ali defeated Turkey at **Nezib** in Syria in June 1839 and accepted the surrender of the Turkish fleet, the European powers intervened to prevent danger to Allied shipping. Having bombarded **Beirut**, a British-Austrian naval force under Admiral Sir Robert Stopford then shelled and seized Acre. Ali gave up the Turkish fleet and evacuated Syria (3 November 1840).

Acroinum I 739 I Early Byzantine-Muslim Wars

See **Akroinos**

Acropolis I 1821–1822 I Greek War of Independence

Early in the war, the Muslims of Athens, besieged in the Acropolis, were relieved after 83 days by Omer Vrioni, advancing through **Thermopylae**. When he withdrew after the fall of **Tripolitza**, 1,150 men, women and children finally surrendered in return for safe passage.

About 400 were butchered in the streets before the survivors were saved by French marines (May 1821–21 June 1822).

Acropolis I 1826–1827 I Greek War of Independence

Ottoman commander Reshid Pasha secured **Missolonghi** and captured Athens (25 August), then besieged the Acropolis, held by Yannis Gouras and later by British Admiral Lord Thomas Cochrane and General Sir George Church. The Acropolis surrendered following defeats at **Chaidari** and **Analatos**, and Turkey regained Greece until October's disaster at **Navarino** (August 1826–5 June 1827).

Acs I 1849 I Hungarian Revolutionary War

Austria was driven out of Hungary by defeat at **Hatvan**, **Isaszeg** and **Waitzen** before Russia intervened to help and, following victory at **Pered**, General Ivan Paskievich and Field Marshal Alfred Windischgratz attacked Hungarian General Artur Gorgey at Acs, outside Komárom, northwest of Budapest. This battle was indecisive but rebellion was later crushed at **Temesvár** (2 July 1849).

Actium I 31 BC I Wars of the Second Triumvirate

In the Roman struggle for power, Octavian's navy under Marcus Agrippa blockaded Mark Antony's massive fleet in the Bay of Actium, on the west coast of Greece near modern Preveza. One of the largest sea battles of the ancient world led to the eventual surrender of Antony's army. He and his wife Cleopatra fled to Egypt, where they committed suicide to avoid capture (2 September 31 BC).

Aculco I 1810 I Mexican Wars of Independence

Turned back from Mexico City at **Monte de las Cruces**, Miguel Hidalgo's peasant army marched on Guadalajara and was intercepted at Aculco by Royalist commander Félix María Calleja marching south from Querétaro. The revolutionaries were defeated and driven out, further dispersing Hidalgo's disheartened force, decisively beaten two months later at **Calderón** (7 November 1810).

Acultzingo ❚ 1862 ❚ Mexican-French War
Determined to establish French-dominated government in Mexico, Napoleon III sent a force under Charles Latrille Comte de Lorencez, whose advance towards the central plateau was blocked in the Cumbres Pass near Acultzingo by Mexican General Ignacio Zaragoza and 4,000 men. With a bold front assault, the French cleared the pass and Zaragoza fell back on **Puebla** (28 April 1862).

Adairsville ❚ 1864 ❚ American Civil War (Western Theatre)
Union commander William T. Sherman marched south through Georgia towards **Atlanta** and drove General Joseph E. Johnston out of **Resaca**, southeast of Chattanooga, then advanced through Calhoun and caught the Confederates at Adairsville. Johnston repulsed an initial Union attack but was forced to continue withdrawing through Cassville to a defensive line near **Dallas** (17 May 1864).

Adana ❚ 964 ❚ Later Byzantine-Muslim Wars
After capturing **Aleppo** in Syria (962), Nicephorus Phocas (now Emperor Nicephorus II) attacked the Muslims in Asia Minor and beat the garrison of the Cilician coastal city of Adana in southern Turkey, held for Sayf ad-Dawla, Emir of Aleppo. Nicephorus seized **Tarsus** and continued his advance across the Seyhan River into northern Syria for victory in 969 at **Antioch** and **Aleppo**.

Adas ❚ 1775 ❚ Maratha Wars of Succession
On campaign against the Peshwa Raghunath Rao, who had murdered his nephew Narayan Rao, the Maratha ministers at Poona recovered from defeat at **Kasegaum** in March 1774 and sent General Hari Pant Phadke against the usurper at Adas, near Napar on the Mahi. Ra-

ghunath was heavily defeated and deposed. A further action at Adas four months later failed to restore him (17 February 1775).

Adas ❚ 1775 ❚ 1st British-Maratha War
Intervening in a Maratha civil war, British forces under Colonel Thomas Keating marched towards **Ahmadabad** to support deposed Peshwa Raghunath Rao. They were intercepted on the Mahi near Napar at Adas by a Maratha government force under Hari Pant Phadke. A hard-fought but indecisive action with heavy losses on both sides saw Phadke eventually driven back (18 May 1775).

Adasa ❚ 161 BC ❚ Maccabean War
Soon after being defeated at **Capharsalma**, north of Jerusalem, by the Hebrew leader Judas Maccabeus, the Seleucid General Nicanor awaited reinforcements before renewing his pursuit of the rebels later that year. Lured once again into the nearby hills, the former elephant-master's troops were ambushed at Adasa. This time Nicanor himself was among those killed in the rout.

Adda ❚ 223 BC ❚ Gallic Wars in Italy
Insubrian Gauls from the north campaigning in central Italy were defeated at **Telamon** and driven back to the Po Valley, where they were pursued and challenged two years later by the successful Roman commander Gaius Flaminius. Consul Flaminius dealt them a heavy defeat at the Adda River but was himself killed in 217 BC in the famous Roman disaster at **Lake Trasimene**.

Adda ❚ 490 ❚ Goth Invasion of Italy
After defeating Odoacer, the German ruler of Italy, on the **Sontius** and at **Verona** and confining him under siege at **Ravenna**, Theodoric of the Ostrogoths was repulsed by a major sortie from Ravenna at **Faenza** and withdrew towards the Alps. In a bold defensive battle at the Adda, Theodoric defeated Odoacer, who was once again driven back to a long siege at Ravenna (11 August 490).

Adda I 1705 I War of the Spanish Succession
 See **Cassano**

Adda I 1799 I French Revolutionary Wars (2nd coalition)
 See **Cassano**

Ad Decimum I 533 I Vandal War in Africa

The celebrated Byzantine General Belisarius was ordered by Emperor Justinian to reconquer North Africa from the Vandals and met Ammatus, brother of King Gelimer, in battle outside Carthage at Ad Decimum. Ammatus was heavily defeated when he launched his force on a premature charge and the Romans retook the city two days later (13 September 533).

Addis Ababa I 1936 I 2nd Italo-Ethiopian War

With Ethiopia's last remaining forces routed in the north at **Maychew** and in the east at **Ogaden**, Italian Marshal Pietro Badoglio rapidly advanced on Addis Ababa. The capital fell following one-sided fighting just three days after Emperor Haile Selassie fled into exile and resistance quickly collapsed. Haile Selassie returned with the Allied counter-offensive in April 1941 (5 May 1936).

Addis Ababa I 1941 I World War II (Northern Africa)

British General Sir Alan Cunningham advanced into Ethiopia from Kenya with armoured forces and defeated the Italian army to seize Addis Ababa, the first enemy-occupied capital to fall to the Allies. Cunningham then continued north through **Dessie** to attack the Italians in their mountain stronghold at **Amba Alagi**. Emperor Haile Selassie returned to Addis Ababa on 5 May (6 April 1941).

Addis Ababa I 1991 I Ethiopian Civil War

Facing defeat in Eritrea, the military government of Colonel Haile Mariam Mengistu came under siege in Addis Ababa by Tigrayan rebels advancing from the north and Oromo forces in the south. When Mengistu fled into exile (21 May), the Ethiopian capital collapsed in bloody disorder with perhaps 600 killed. Rebel tanks then rolled in to end the regime and the war (21–28 May 1991).

Aden I 1513 I Portuguese Colonial Wars in Arabia

The great Portuguese commander Afonso de Albuquerque captured **Goa** and **Malacca**, then took a force to besiege Aden, at the mouth of the Red Sea. He was driven off by Governor Mira Merjão following heavy fighting, but two years later he secured Portugal a foothold in the Persian Gulf by capturing **Hormuz**. Shortly afterwards, Aden itself fell to the Ottomans (March 1513).

Aden I 1839 I Anglo-Arab Wars

When negotiations over naval use of the port of Aden in modern Yemen failed, British ships shelled the city. It was then captured and occupied by British troops from India under Major Thomas Maubourg Bailie. Attempts to retake the city were repulsed in November 1839 and May 1840, after which Aden remained a British protectorate and colony until 1967 (19 July 1839).

Aden I 1986 I Yemeni Civil Wars

Ali Nasir Muhammad al-Husani seized South Yemen by coup in 1984 and later faced violent attack by forces of former President Abdul Fattah Ismail. Severe fighting around Aden saw a claimed 10,000 killed, including Ismail, before Ali Nasir went into exile with many thousands of supporters. A new government moved steadily towards unification with North Yemen (13–24 January 1986).

Aden I 1994 I Yemeni Civil Wars

Despite unification of North and South Yemen in 1990, dissident Vice President Ali Selim al-Baidh created a Democratic Republic of Yemen in the south. President Ali Abdullah Saleh declared war on the secessionists and the heaviest fighting was around Aden, which suffered severe damage from northern shelling. The rebels were forced into exile and unity was restored (5 May–7 July 1994).

Adibo ▌ 1896 ▌ German Colonial Wars in Africa

When Dagomba tribesmen rebelled against German authority in Togoland, Lieutenant Valentin von Massow was sent with about 100 paramilitary police, who came under massive rebel attack at Adibo (now in modern Ghana). The heavily armed German force inflicted massive losses, then burned the nearby capital, Yendi, and the rebellion was soon crushed (30 November 1896).

Adige ▌ 102 BC ▌ Rome's Gallic Wars

Although the Teutones and their Cimbri allies lost in Gaul at **Aquae Sextiae**, King Boiorix of the Cimbri (who had beaten a Roman army in Gaul at **Arausio** in 105 BC) marched across the Brenner Pass into northern Italy and on the Adige defeated Consul Quintus Lutatius Catulus. The following year, the Cimbri were destroyed by a reinforced Roman army in the decisive battle at **Vercellae**.

Adiliya ▌ 1218 ▌ 5th Crusade

Campaigning against Egypt, Crusaders from Palestine and Europe attacked **Damietta**, at the eastern mouth of the Nile, defended by al-Kamil, son of Sultan al-Adil Saif al-Din. Months of indecisive action ended when the Crusaders launched a determined attack and captured the fortress of Adiliya, a few miles to the south, opening the way to enforcing the siege of Damietta (24–25 August 1218).

Admagetobriga ▌ 61 BC ▌ Rome's Later Gallic Wars

A Germanic tribal leader, the Suebian Ariovistus, invaded Gaul at the invitation of the Sequani—supposedly in a dispute over tolls on the Saone—and crushed the Aedui, led by Chief Eporedorix, an ally of Rome. The Germanic victory at Admagetobriga, in modern Alsace, is said to have inspired Julius Caesar to intervene in central Gaul in support of the Aedui and thus launch his great career.

Admin Box ▌ 1944 ▌ World War II (Burma-India)

With British forces advancing in **Arakan**, Japanese General Tadishi Hanaya was reinforced and sent General Tokutaro Sakurai circling north to cut off the strategic Ngakyedauk Pass and besiege Admin Box, near Sinzweya. A tiny garrison under Brigadier Geoffrey Evans held out until General Harold Briggs retook the pass in the claimed first British victory over the Japanese (5–25 February 1944).

Admiralty Islands ▌ 1944 ▌ World War II (Pacific)

As part of the campaign to isolate **Rabaul**, American General Innis Swift invaded the Admiralty Islands, northeast of New Guinea, held by Colonel Yoshio Ezaki. With Australian air support, Swift captured **Los Negros** and then **Manus** with about 300 Americans killed and 1,200 wounded, and about 3,000 Japanese dead. Victory secured the harbour at Seeadler (29 February–25 March 1944).

Adobe Walls ▌ 1864 ▌ Comanche Indian Wars

A well-equipped force led by Colonel Kit Carson marched against Comanche and Kiowa in the Texas panhandle, where they defeated Kiowa under Chief Little Mountain near the trading post at Adobe Walls on the South Canadian River. Carson was then unexpectedly besieged by over 1,000 Comanche. Aided by two mountain howitzers, he broke out and withdrew to New Mexico (24 November 1864).

Adobe Walls ▌ 1874 ▌ Red River Indian War

Fearing the threat of buffalo hunting, 700 Comanche, Kiowa, Cheyenne and Arapaho united under Quanah Parker attacked Adobe Walls trading post, on the South Canadian River in the Texas panhandle. Armed with high-powered buffalo guns, 28 hunters under William Dixon drove off the Indians, killing about 10, with many more wounded. Three whites were killed (27 June 1874).

Adowa ∎ 1896 ∎ 1st Italo-Ethiopian War

Reinforcing the Italian invasion of northern Ethiopia after defeat at **Amba Alagi** and **Makale**, General Oreste Baratieri's Italian-native force was rashly ordered to advance from a strong defensive position, Adowa, to seek victory for national prestige. They were virtually annihilated by Emperor Menelik's hugely superior Ethiopian army, the worst European defeat in Africa (1 March 1896).

Adowa ∎ 1935 ∎ 2nd Italo-Ethiopian War

In supposed response to a border clash at **Walwal**, a year later Mussolini sent an invasion force into Ethiopia under General Emilio de Bono. Next day, General Ruggero Santini captured Adowa, which fell with little resistance but was presented as a major victory to avenge defeat 40 years earlier. De Bono secured much of northern Ethiopia before a local counter-attack at **Dembeguina** (6 October 1935).

Adranum ∎ 344 BC ∎ Timoleon's War

Timoleon of Corinth invaded eastern Sicily to deliver Syracuse from tyranny and attacked Carthaginians under Hicetas of Leontini at Adranum (modern Adano), northwest of Catania. Though badly outnumbered, Timoleon secured a brilliant victory. As a result, Dionysius II of Syracuse yielded eastern Sicily and Timoleon beat the Carthaginians four years later in the west at the **Crimisus**.

Adrianople ∎ 313 ∎ Roman Wars of Succession

See **Tzirallum**

Adrianople ∎ 324 ∎ Roman Wars of Succession

During the resumed Roman War of Succession, Western Emperor Constantine marched with a large army towards the modern Bulgarian border and inflicted a major defeat on Eastern Emperor Valerius Licinius near the Hebrus outside Adrianople (modern Edirne). Licinius fell back under siege in his capital at **Byzantium** (later Constantinople) and was defeated at sea on the Hellespont (3 July 324).

Adrianople ∎ 378 ∎ 5th Gothic War

Ten years after beating Goths at **Noviodunum**, Eastern Emperor Valens entered Thrace to meet Goth Chief Fritigern, who had routed a local Roman army at **Marcianopolis** (377). Without waiting for Western Emperor Gratian and his reinforcements, Valens attacked near Adrianople (modern Edirne). Valens was killed and his army was destroyed in one of Rome's worst military defeats (9 August 378).

Adrianople ∎ 718 ∎ Early Byzantine-Muslim Wars

When the Muslim Generals Maslama and Suleiman besieged **Constantinople**, Khan Tervel of Bulgaria (who had previously fought against the Byzantines at **Anchialus**) entered the war to support Emperor Leo III. The Bulgarians defeated Maslama near Adrianople (modern Edirne, Turkey), after which the Muslims abandoned the siege of Constantinople and withdrew.

Adrianople ∎ 1205 ∎ Bulgarian Imperial Wars

A year after seizing **Constantinople**, the newly established Latin Emperor Baldwin I attempted to suppress a Bulgarian rising in Thrace and besieged Adrianople (modern Edirne). Tsar Kaloyan of Bulgaria arrived with a large relief army and the Crusaders were routed with terrible casualties. Baldwin was captured and died in captivity, and the Bulgarians secured Macedonia (12 April 1205).

Adrianople ∎ 1255 ∎ Bulgarian Imperial Wars

Twenty years after Bulgaria supported Byzantine Nicaea against the Latin Emperors in **Constantinople**, Tsar Michael II Asen of Bulgaria attempted to recover territory lost to the Byzantines in Macedonia and Thrace. In battle at Adrianople (modern Edirne), Michael suffered a heavy defeat at the hands of Theodore II Lascaris of Nicaea, virtually ending the Bulgarian Empire.

Adrianople ▮ 1355 ▮ Serbian Imperial Wars

Despite defeat at **Didymoteichon** in 1352, the great Serbian Emperor Stephan Dushan (Uros IV) seized much of the Balkans, then defeated the Byzantine army in a decisive battle at Adrianople (modern Edirne, Turkey) before capturing the city. However, when Stephan died soon afterwards, his hugely expanded empire began to disintegrate and was destroyed three decades later at **Kossovo**.

Adrianople ▮ 1362 ▮ Byzantine-Ottoman Wars

Ottoman Sultan Murad I expanded his empire in Europe, sending Lala Shahin Pasha into Thrace, where he defeated a weak Byzantine army to seize Adrianople (modern Edirne). Murad then secured Serbia at the **Maritza** and **Kossovo** and Turkish rule was established for the next 500 years. The Ottoman capital moved from **Brusa** to Adrianople until the capture of **Constantinople** (July 1362).

Adrianople ▮ 1829 ▮ Russo-Turkish Wars

Russia crossed the Danube in support of Greek independence and, after victories at **Varna** and **Kulevcha**, General Count Hans von Diebitsch soon passed the Balkan Mountains and advanced on Adrianople (modern Edirne) near the Bulgarian border. Its capture forced Turkey to sue for peace, granting Greece independence and ceding Russia the mouth of the Danube (20 August 1829).

Adrianople (1st) ▮ 1912–1913 ▮ 1st Balkan War

As the main Bulgarian army advanced into Thrace through **Kirk Kilissa**, General Nikola Ivanoff was sent to besiege the powerful fortress of Adrianople (modern Edirne), held by about 60,000 Turks under Shukri Pasha. The siege was suspended during a failed armistice, but when fighting resumed, Ivanoff, with Serb reinforcements, took the city by assault (October 1912–26 March 1913).

Adrianople (2nd) ▮ 1913 ▮ 2nd Balkan (Inter-ally) War

When Bulgaria rashly attacked her former allies—Greece and Serbia—Turkey entered the fray and advanced from the lines at **Chataldja**, outside Constantinople, recently held in the previous war. Advancing into Thrace, General Enver Bey attacked Adrianople, lost just four months earlier. The Bulgarians had to withdraw, and at war's end Turkey retained the valuable prize (22 July 1913).

Ad Salices ▮ 377 ▮ 5th Gothic War

When a local Roman army was defeated south of the Danube at **Marcianopolis**, Emperor Valens sent his Generals Saturninus, Trajan and Profuturus, who drove the Goths into a marshy region near the mouth of the Danube. A bloody but indecisive action at Ad Salices cost the Romans heavily before Goth Chief Fritigern slipped away. A year later the Goths killed Valens himself at **Adrianople**.

Aduatuca ▮ 57 BC ▮ Rome's Later Gallic Wars

Julius Caesar beat the Belgae at the **Aisne** and the **Sambre** and in the same year besieged and captured Aduatuca (modern Tongres), capital of the Aduatuci tribe, in eastern Belgium north of Liège, where he inflicted terrible casualties. Caesar's success effectively completed Roman subjugation of the Belgae, and he soon conquered Brittany with victory at sea in **Morbihan Gulf** (September 57 BC).

Aduatuca ▮ 54 BC ▮ Rome's Later Gallic Wars

The Belgic tribe of the Eburones under Ambiorix rose against Roman rule in northern Gaul, attacking Titurius Sabinus in winter camp at Aduatuca (modern Tongres) in modern Belgium. When the attack failed, the Romans were lured out by a promise of withdrawal under safe conduct southwest to Namur. They were then promptly ambushed, with all 9,000 reportedly massacred.

Aduwa I 1896 I 1st Italo-Ethiopian War
See **Adowa**

Aduwa I 1935 I 2nd Italo-Ethiopian War
See **Adowa**

**Adwalton Moor I 1643 I British
Civil Wars**

A large Royalist army under William Ca-
vendish Earl of Newcastle advanced to relieve
the Parliamentary siege of York and severely defeated a Parliamentary force under Ferdinando
Lord Fairfax and his son Sir Thomas on Adwalton Moor, southeast of Bradford near
Drighlington. The victory secured for the Royalists all of Yorkshire except Hull (30 June 1643).

Adys I 256 BC I 1st Punic War

Soon after beating the Carthaginian fleet off
Cape Ecnomus in southern Sicily, Roman
Consul Atilius Regulus landed a large army in
North Africa, where he won a major victory at
Adys, near Carthage. But Regulus attempted to
impose peace terms so harsh that Carthage
vowed to fight on and he was defeated and
captured by Xanthippus. Carthage was finally
defeated near the **Aegates** in 241 BC.

Aegates Islands I 241 BC I 1st Punic War

In a great naval victory near the Aegates
(modern Egadi) Islands off western Sicily, the
Roman Consul Lutatius Catulus arrived with a
fresh fleet and captured or sank the Carthaginian
fleet of Hanno. Coming soon after the loss of their
nearby fortress at **Lilybaeum**, Carthage agreed to
evacuate Sicily and sued for peace, bringing the
1st Punic War to an end (10 March 241 BC).

**Aegean I 1943 I World War II
(Southern Europe)**
See **Dodecanese Islands**

**Aegelsthrep I 456 I Anglo-Saxon
Conquest of Britain**

Jutes under the semi-legendary warrior brothers Hengist and Horsa were invited to England by
King Vortigern of the Britons to fight the Picts,

but at Aegelsthrep (modern Aylesford, Kent) they
turned on and defeated their former ally. Although Horsa died in the battle, Hengist secured
further victory over Vortigern at **Creccanford** in
457 and eventually occupied Kent and much of
southeast England.

**Aegina I 458–457 BC I 1st Peloponnesian
War**

In 460 BC, the island of Aegina in the Saronic
Gulf joined Corinth and other states to oppose the
increasing power of Athens. In a great naval battle
offshore against Athenian commander Leocrates,
Aegina lost a reported 70 vessels sunk or captured
and her sea power was broken forever. Soon afterwards, Leocrates landed to besiege Aegina,
which fell after blockade by land and sea.

**Aegospotami I 405 BC I Great
Peloponnesian War**

Spartan commander Lysander rebuilt the Peloponnesian fleet with Persian aid after defeat at
Arginusae, then surprised the Athenians at anchor by the Aegospotami stream, on the northern
shore of the Dardenelles. Most of Athenian
Admiral Conon's ships and crews ashore were
destroyed, effectively ending Athenian naval
power. Lysander then sailed to besiege **Athens**
itself (September 405 BC).

Aelia I 133–135 I Bar-Cocheba's Revolt

When Rome constructed a new colony named
Aelia Capitolina on the site of ancient Jersualem,
Jews rebelled against Emperor Hadrian. Led by
Simon Bar-Cocheba (the "second Judas Maccabeus"—claimed by some to be the Messiah), they
seized Aelia and held it for two years until the city
fell by storm to Julius Severus. The Jewish rebellion was then crushed with extreme severity.

Aescesdune I 871 I Viking Wars in Britain
See **Ashdown**

Aesis I 82 BC I Sullan Civil War

As General Lucius Cornelius Sulla advanced
on Rome, his General, Quintus Metellus Pius,
met Loyalist forces to the northeast near Aesis

(modern Iesi) on the Esino, inland from Ancona. The Loyalist army, led by Carrinas, a commander under Gnaeus Carbo, was badly defeated and driven north towards Ariminum (modern Rimini), suffering continued losses in the retreat.

Afabet I 1988 I Eritrean War of Independence

When Liberation forces attacked the northern city of Afabet, on the plain east of **Nakfa**, one of the decisive battles of the 30-year war saw three Ethiopian divisions destroyed, with perhaps 10,000 killed and massive arms and supplies captured. Ethiopian forces abandoned north and west Eritrea and this bloody defeat led directly to a failed military coup in Addis Ababa (17–18 March 1988).

Afyon I 1922 I 2nd Greco-Turkish War

Turkish commander Mustafa Kemal launched his counter-offensive against the Greeks a year after checking their advance into Anatolia at the **Sakarya**. On the Akar at Afyon (Afyonkarahisar), he achieved a decisive victory, and the Greek army suffered heavy losses in the subsequent brutal pursuit to **Smyrna**. A large Turkish detachment then diverted north against **Brusa** (30 August 1922).

Afyonkarahisar I 739 I Early Byzantine-Muslim Wars

See **Akroinos**

Agagia I 1916 I World War I (Middle East)

While facing the Turks east of **Suez**, British forces had to turn west against the pro-Turkish Senussi. After several indecisive actions in late 1915, commander William Peyton sent General Henry Lukin against the rebels at Agagia, on the coast near Barrani. The Senussi were routed, with their leader Jafaar Pasha captured. Other Senussi forces were later defeated at **Siwa** (26 February 1916).

Agathocles I 204 BC I 2nd Punic War

Roman General Publius Scipio the Younger was besieging Carthaginian **Utica**, in modern

Tunisia, when he attacked a nearby encampment, supported by renegade Numidian Prince Masinissias. The Numidian cavalry ambushed and defeated an enemy advance guard near an old fortress known as the Tower of Agathocles. Hanno (son of Hasdrubal Gisco) was among the many Carthaginians killed.

Agendicum I 52 BC I Rome's Later Gallic Wars

Threatened by a fresh rising in central Gaul led by Vercingetorix of the Averni, Julius Caesar's deputy commander Titus Labienus was cut off and outnumbered south of the Seine by Gauls under Camulogenus. Labienus secured a fine defensive victory at Agendicum, near modern Sens, then marched south to join up with Caesar's main army to fight against Vercingetorix at **Avaricum**.

Ager Sanguinis I 1119 I Crusader-Muslim Wars

See **Antioch, Syria**

Aghdash Awkh I 1831 I Russian Conquest of the Caucasus

Facing rebellion in Muslim Dagestan, west of the Caspian, Russian General Grigori Emmanuel advanced to relieve Vnezapnaia, besieged by Imam Ghazi Muhammad. But further south on the Aghdash River at Aghdash Awkh, Emmanuel was ambushed and badly defeated, losing about 400 men. The Imam was killed by a much larger Russian force a year later at **Gimrah** (13 July 1831).

Agheila I 1941 I World War II (Northern Africa)

See **El Agheila**

Aghrim I 1691 I War of the Glorious Revolution

See **Aughrim**

Agincourt I 1415 I Hundred Years War

King Henry V of England was marching from **Harfleur** to Calais when he utterly destroyed a much larger French force under Charles

D'Albret, Marshal of France, at Agincourt. While more than 5,000 knights of the French nobility were slaughtered by the unexpected power of the English longbow, Henry's campaign was seemingly exhausted and he soon returned to England (25 October 1415).

Aginnum I 107 BC I Rome's Gallic Wars
When Germanic tribes invaded Gaul and beat a Roman army in **Provence**, they continued west, and Consul Lucius Cassius Longinus met them on the Garonne. But the Tigurini under Divico ambushed Lucius at Aginnum (modern Agen), northwest of Toulouse, where he was routed and killed. Rome was beaten again at **Arausio**, before destroying the invaders at **Aquae Sextiae** (102 BC) and **Vercellae**.

Agnadello I 1509 I War of the League of Cambrai
In support of the League of Cambrai between Germany, France, Spain and the Papal States, Louis XII of France took a large army to northern Italy, and at Agnadello, near Crema, routed Venetian General Bartolomeo d'Alviano, who had earlier defeated an Imperial army at **Cadore**. After a brutal attack on **Padua**, the anti-Venetian League broke up and Venice recovered lost territory (14 May 1509).

Agordat I 1893 I Italo-Sudanese Wars
Mahdist Emir Ahmed Ali campaigned against the Europeans in eastern Sudan and led about 8,500 men east from Kassala against 2,300 Italians at Agordat, west of Asmara, commanded by Colonel Giuseppe Arimondi. About 3,000 Dervishes, including the Emir, were killed in a complete rout and a year later, Italian forces seized Kassala (21 December 1893).

Agordat I 1941 I World War II (Northern Africa)
After British forces routed Italy's invasion of Egypt at **Sidi Barrani** (December 1940), troops were transferred to the Sudan, where General William Platt invaded Eritrea. Advancing through Kassala and Barentu, Platt attacked Italian General Luigi Frusci at Agordat. Three

days of heavy fighting forced the Italians to withdraw northeast to the mountain stronghold at **Keren** (27–31 January 1941).

Agosta I 1676 I 3rd Dutch War
See **Augusta, Sicily**

Agra I 1707 I Mughal Wars of Succession
See **Jajau**

Agra I 1713 I Mughal Wars of Succession
Amid civil disorder which followed the death of the Mughal Bahadur Shah, the rebel Farokshin (Farrukh Siyar) defeated and killed his uncle, the new Padshah Jahandar Shah, in northern India on the River Jumna at Agra. Farokshin then seized the Mughal throne until he was in turn deposed and brutally put to death six years later by three powerful nobles known as the Sayyid brothers (10 January 1713).

Agra I 1787–1788 I Mughal-Maratha War of Ismail Beg
After deserting the Marathas at **Lalsot** in June 1787, Mughal warlord Ismail Beg and Rohilla Chief Ghulam Kadir besieged Agra, defended by Lakwa Dada Lad. A Maratha relief force was repulsed at **Chaksana**, but a renewed relief attempt at **Bagh Dera**, just outside Agra, routed Ismail Beg, who fled the capture of the city by swimming the Jumna (November 1787–18 June 1788).

Agra I 1799 I Maratha Territorial Wars
When the Maratha Governor of Agra attempted to resist the authority of Daulat Rao Sindhia of Gwalior, General Pierre Perron surprised and seized the city, then besieged the 4,000-strong garrison in the fortress and citadel. A mine destroyed part of the bastion after 58 days, and the garrison surrendered. They were allowed to march out with the honours of war (17 February–16 April 1799).

Agra I 1803 I 2nd British-Maratha War
Within weeks of beating the Marathas at **Aligarh** and **Delhi**, General Sir Gerard Lake

marched south to the fortress city of Agra, on the Jumna River, where he defeated a large force under Daulat Rao Sindhia. He then besieged and occupied the fort, capturing a massive treasure. Lake's subsequent victory further west at **Laswari** effectively ended the so-called Hindustan Campaign (4–18 October 1803).

Agra I 1857 I Indian Mutiny

Colonel Edward Greathed marched south from **Delhi** to relieve Agra (besieged following defeat at **Shahganj**) and routed the rebels at **Bulandshahr** and **Aligarh**, before meeting a large force of mutineers outside Agra, on the Jumna River. Greathed inflicted severe casualties in a substantial and decisive action before entering the city next day to raise the siege (7 July–10 October 1857).

Agrigentum I 406 BC I Carthaginian-Syracusan Wars
See **Acragas**

Agrigentum I 262 BC I 1st Punic War
See **Acragas**

Agua Dulce Creek I 1836 I Texan Wars of Independence

After Colonel Francis W. Johnson was defeated on the Texas Gulf Coast at **San Patricio** by General José Urrea's invading Mexican army, a foraging party under Dr James Grant was attacked by cavalry 23 miles to the southwest at Agua Dulce. Six escaped and six were captured, but Grant and 14 others were killed. Urrea then continued through **Refugio** towards **Coleto Creek** (2 March 1836).

Agua Prieta I 1915 I Mexican Revolution

When the United States recognised President Venustiano Carranza, Francisco (Pancho) Villa attacked the Mexican border town of Agua Prieta, held by Federal General Plutarco Elías Calles since victory at **Naco**. Watched by American forces at Douglas, Arizona, Villa's cavalry were destroyed against cannon and barbed wire. He later raided into the USA at **Columbus** (1–3 November 1915).

Aguascalientes I 1915 I Mexican Revolution

Mexican rebel Francisco (Pancho) Villa was defeated by government forces at **Celaya** and **Trinidad**, and withdrew to Aguascalientes. He soon counter-attacked General Álvaro Obregón and encircled his position in the nearby semi-desert. With brilliant tactics, Obregón broke out and finally destroyed Villa's force. The rebel fought back four months later at **Agua Prieta** (6–10 July 1915).

Ahmadabad I 1572 I Mughal Conquest of Northern India

On a campaign of conquest into Gujarat, in northwest India, Mughal Emperor Akbar took just 3,000 horsemen against Sultan Muzaffar II in Ahmadabad, where he defeated a reported 20,000 Gujarati clansmen. Following a further victory at **Sarnal** (24 December), Akbar annexed the rich province, which remained part of the Mughal Empire for the next 200 years (2 September 1572).

Ahmadabad I 1780 I 1st British-Maratha War

One month after British defeat at **Wargaom** at the hands of the Maratha Confederacy, General Thomas Goddard attacked the strong fortress of Ahmadabad, on the Sabarmati in Gujarat. Defended by Maratha and Scinde troops, the city fell to a brave assault by Colonel James Hartley, with 106 British and 300 Maratha dead. Goddard went on to capture other key Maratha fortresses (15 February 1780).

Ahmad Khel I 1880 I 2nd British-Afghan War

As General Sir Donald Stewart marched from Kandahar in southern Afghanistan to support General Sir Frederick Roberts in Kabul, his force was attacked at Ahmad Khel, west of Ghazni, by Afghan Ghilzais. A one-sided engagement saw the British form a defensive square and inflict heavy casualties before continuing towards Ghazni and attacking the Afghans at **Urzu** (19 April 1880).

Ahmadnagar I 1596 I Mughal-Ahmadnagar Wars

Emperor Akbar campaigned to extend Mughal control into Deccan India and sent forces under his son Murad to besiege the great fortress of Ahmadnagar, east of Bombay. In one of India's great heroic exploits, the warrior-Queen Chand Bibi of Bijapur, Regent for the infant Sultan, personally led the defence which saved the city. However, it fell to superior forces four years later.

Ahmadnagar I 1600 I Mughal-Ahmadnagar Wars

After years of warfare to extend Mughal control into Deccan India, Emperor Akbar besieged the great fortress of Ahmadnagar, east of Bombay, previously defended by Chand Bibi, Queen Dowager of Bijapur. But she was later killed by the mob and, just as Mughal troops breached the massive walls, the war came to an end, and the Muslim Sultans made peace (21 April–28 August 1600).

Ahmadnagar I 1803 I 2nd British-Maratha War

General Arthur Wellesley restored the deposed Peshwa Baji Rao II of **Poona**, then marched east into the Deccan against the large French-trained army of Daulat Rao Sindhia of Gwalior and Raja Raghuji Bhonsle of Berar. He defeated the Maratha army near the junction of the Jua and Kelna Rivers, then captured Ahmadnagar, and went on to famous victory in September at **Assaye** (8 August 1803).

Ahmedabad I 1572 I Mughal Conquest of Northern India
See **Ahmadabad**

Ahmedabad I 1780 I 1st British-Maratha War
See **Ahmadabad**

Ahmednugger I 1596 I Mughal-Ahmadnagar Wars
See **Ahmadnagar**

Ahmednugger I 1803 I 2nd British-Maratha War
See **Ahmadnagar**

Ahnai Tangi I 1920 I Waziristan Campaign

After heavy losses at **Palosina**, Mahsud tribesmen in Waziristan withdrew north to a defensive line at the steep Ahnai Tangi Gorge. Fighting in extreme winter conditions, an Indian army striking force under General Andrew Sheen launched night attacks on the heights. In the face of further losses, the rebels abandoned their positions and fell back further north to **Barari Tangi** (7–15 January 1920).

Ahualalco I 1858 I Mexican War of the Reform

After an indecisive action at **Acámbaro**, northwest of Mexico City, Conservative Government forces under Generals Miguel Miramón and Tomás Mejía occupied San Lui Potosi (12 September), then marched against Liberal commander Santiago Vidaurri northwest at Ahualalco. Vidaurri was routed, losing 400 killed, 3,000 prisoners, 33 guns and 120 wagons of supplies (29 September 1858).

Ahvenanmaa I 1714 I 2nd "Great" Northern War
See **Hango**

Ahwaz I 1915 I World War I (Mesopotamia)

While British forces under General Sir John Nixon advanced up the Euphrates from **Basra** towards **Amara**, a column under General George Gorringe marched northeast along the Korun to protect the key city of Ahwaz and secure the area's oilfields for Britain. A heavy Turkish assault was repulsed, and Gorringe later campaigned on the opposite British flank at **Nasiriya** (24–27 April 1915).

Ahwaz I 1980 I Iraq-Iran War

At the start of the war, invading Iraqi forces from Basra and Amara converged on Ahwaz, capital of Khuzestan and a major Iranian military base. Heavy fighting saw the Iraqi tanks repulsed and many were lost when Iran flooded key defensive areas. A smaller invading force was also halted further north outside Dezful, and Iran soon struck back at **Susangerd** (September–October 1980).

Ahzab I 627 I Campaigns of the Prophet Mohammed
See **Medina**

Aibar I 1452 I Spanish Wars of Succession
When Blanche of Navarre married Prince Juan of Aragon and Castile, he assumed her patrimony, but she died leaving him the title, while the Governorship of Navarre went to their only son, Prince Charles of Viana. In a bitter family dispute, Juan defeated his son in battle at Aibar near Pamplona and made him prisoner. Charles was later recognised as heir, but predeceased his father.

Aiglaesthrep I 456 I Anglo-Saxon Conquest of Britain
See **Aegelsthrep**

Aiguillon I 1346 I Hundred Years War
John of Valois, Duke of Normandy, marched into English-held Gascony and besieged the small garrison at Aiguillon on the Garonne, held by Ralph Stafford, who took the castle in December 1345. Holding out against costly assaults, Stafford was finally relieved when Edward III of England led a fresh invasion, culminating in the great English victory a week later at **Crecy** (2 April–20 August 1346).

Aigun I 1900 I Russo-Chinese War
In the aftermath of the Boxer Rebellion, Russians on the Amur under General Deian Subotich advanced through Sakhalin on the Chinese at Aigun (in modern Heihe in Heilongjiang). In very heavy house-to-house fighting, Aigun was stormed by General Pavel Rennenkampf. The Russians then marched south through Mergen (Nenjiang) to the Chinese Eastern Railway at **Qiqihar** (2–5 August 1900).

Ain Diar I 744 I Muslim Civil Wars
Following the death of the Umayyad Caliph Yazid III, his former ally Governor Marwan of Armenia marched into Syria and utterly defeated the Caliph's army in a narrow valley at Ain Diar, near the modern Turkish border. Yazid's designated successor fled Damascus and Marwan seized the throne as Marwan II, the last of the Umayyad Caliphs.

Ain Jalut I 1260 I Mongol Invasion of the Middle East
After Mongols captured **Baghdad** (1258), Kitbuqa invaded Syria, then advanced into Palestine, where his Mongol army was met by the Mamluk Baibars, supported by Mamluk Sultan Kutuz from Egypt. A decisive battle near Nazareth at Ain Jalut—the Pools of Goliath—saw Kitbuqa routed and executed. The Mamluks regained Syria and Mongol expansion was halted (3 September 1260).

Ain Tamar I 634 I Muslim Conquest of Iraq
Muslim General Khalid ibn al-Walid advanced up the Euphrates from **Hira** to take Anbar, then marched west against the powerful fortress of Ain Tamar, defended by Persian Governor Mahran and Christian Arabs under Oqba (who was defeated and captured nearby). The fort capitulated after a brutal siege. Khalid then executed Oqba and other Arab leaders and advanced on **Firadz** (August 633).

Ain Zara I 1911 I Italo-Turkish War
With Tripoli secured in the east at **Sidi Mesri** and **Sidi El Henni**, Italian General Guglielmo Pecori-Giraldi soon led 12,000 men south against the Turko-Arab position at Ain Zara. An artillery barrage and very heavy fighting saw the town taken and large quantities of guns and supplies captured, but the Italian flanking movement was too slow and the Turks escaped (4 December 1911).

Aire I 1814 I Napoleonic Wars (Peninsular Campaign)
Defeated at **Orthez**, Marshal Nicolas Soult withdrew to the Upper Adour to make a stand on

the mid-river island of Aire. Attacked days later by General Sir Rowland Hill, supported by Generals Edward Barnes and John Byng, the French Generals Bertrand Clausel, Jean Isidore Harispe and Eugène Villatte were defeated south of the river, and Soult withdrew southeast (2 March 1814).

Airolo I 1799 I French Revolutionary Wars (2nd Coalition)

While crossing the Alps from Italy to support General Alexander Korsakov in Switzerland, Russian General Alexander Suvorov met stubborn French resistance from General Claude Lecourbe at Airolo, guarding St Gotthard Pass. Suvorov broke through at heavy cost, and won again next day at the **Devil's Bridge**, but Korsakov lost at **Zurich** and Suvorov turned to the Rhine (23 September 1799).

Aisne I 57 BC I Rome's Later Gallic Wars

With the Germans expelled from Gaul at **Mühlhausen** in 58 BC, Belgic tribes in northeast Gaul formed an alliance against Rome. When Julius Caesar started south, King Galba of the Suessiones led a large force trying to block him at the River Aisne. A hard-fought action secured Caesar decisive victory, and he then advanced across the river against the Nervii and destroyed them at the **Sambre**.

Aisne I 1914 I World War I (Western Front)

After the Battle of the **Marne** blunted the German advance into France, French Generals Louis d'Esperey and Michel Maunoury and British General Sir John French counter-attacked across the Aisne against Erich von Falkenhayn's army. The Allied offensive stabilised the front, and began the outflanking "Race to the Sea" through **Albert** and **Arras** to the coast (13–28 September 1914).

Aisne I 1917 I World War I (Western Front)

French commander Alfred Micheler spearheaded the **Nivelle Offensive** with a massive attack along a 50-mile front on the Aisne against

Generals Max von Boehn and Fritz von Bulow. The first days cost over 100,000 French casualties and, despite limited British success further north around **Arras**, the attack ended with shocking losses on both sides for no gain (16 April–9 May 1917).

Aisne I 1918 I World War I (Western Front)

After bloody offensives on the **Somme** and **Lys**, German commander Erich von Ludendorff attacked again across the Chemin des Dames and the Aisne. Generals Bruno von Mudra and Max von Boehn routed Anglo-French forces under General Denis Duchene, but were halted on the Marne at **Chateau-Thierry**. Ludendorff's next offensive was at **Noyon-Montdidier** (27 May–6 June 1918).

Aitape I 1944 I World War II (Pacific)

Supporting the landing in northern New Guinea at **Hollandia**, American General Jens Doe landed 120 miles further east at Aitape against light resistance (22–24 April). When General Hotazo Adachi later counter-attacked at the nearby Driniumor River against General Charles Hall, the Japanese were driven off with very heavy losses and withdrew east to **Wewak** (28 June–5 August 1944).

Aiwagudi I 1696 I Mughal-Maratha Wars

During the epic Mughal siege of Maratha King Rajaram at **Gingee**, northwest of Pondicherry, the ambitious Maratha General Santaji Ghorpade fell out with his King and was dismissed as Senapati. Santaji defeated his successor Dhanaji Jadhav in battle at Aiwagudi, near **Kanchi**, but the great warrior was eventually forced to flee. He was hunted down and killed two years later (June 1696).

Aix I 1809 I Napoleonic Wars (5th Coalition)

British Captain Sir Thomas Cochrane led a courageous night attack against French Admiral Zacharie Allemand in the Aix Roads off Brest, taking explosive-filled fire ships which shattered the anchorage boom. But deliberate delay by

Lord James Gambier's Channel Fleet next day meant just four French ships were destroyed, resulting in a bitter dispute and court-martial (11–12 April 1809).

Aix, Ile de ▌ 1758 ▌ Seven Years War (Europe)
See **Ile d'Aix**

Aix-en-Provence ▌ 102 BC ▌ Rome's Gallic Wars
See **Aquae Sextiae**

Aix-la-Chapelle ▌ 1793 ▌ French Revolutionary Wars (1st Coalition)
Four months after France captured Aix-la-Chapelle (modern Aachen), French under the Venezuelan-born General Francisco de Miranda were defeated and driven out by Austrians led by Friedrich Josias, Prince of Saxe-Coburg. Defeated again two weeks later at **Neerwinden**, Miranda was dismissed for suspected treason and returned to Venezuelan revolutionary politics (3 March 1793).

Aiyina ▌ 458–457 BC ▌ 1st Peloponnesian War
See **Aegina**

Aizkraulke ▌ 1279 ▌ Early Wars of the Teutonic Knights
Having beaten the Livonian Order at **Karuse** (1270), Duke Traidenis of Lithuania attacked Livonian knights withdrawing after a raid into Lithuania. Near Aizkraulke, on the Daugava southeast of modern Riga, the knights suffered a costly defeat, including Livonian Master Ernst von Rassburg killed. Traidenis died soon afterwards, but resistance to the German Crusaders continued (5 March 1279).

Aiznadin ▌ 634 ▌ Muslim Conquest of Syria
See **Ajnadin**

Aizu ▌ 1868 ▌ War of the Meiji Restoration
See **Wakamatsu**

Ajnadin ▌ 634 ▌ Muslim Conquest of Syria
With the Muslim invasion of Byzantine Syria and Palestine stalling after victory at **Wadi al-Arabah**, Muslim General Khalid ibn al-Walid marched across the desert from Mesopotamia. After victory at **Marj Rahit** he joined Amr ibn al-As and at Ajnadin, between Jerusalem and Gaza, they decisively defeated the Byzantines under Theodorus. They won again at the **Yarmuk** (30 July 634).

Akaba ▌ 1917 ▌ World War I (Middle East)
See **Aqaba**

Aka Khel ▌ 1920 ▌ Waziristan Campaign
Defeated at **Barari Tangi**, Mahsud in Waziristan sought aid from Afghanistan, and Shah Doula arrived with reinforcements and two six-pounders. General Andrew Sheen's Strike Force routed the tribesmen at Aka Khel, destroying the guns, and the Mahsud and their allies dispersed. Tribal villages in the Makin Valley were destroyed and the main fighting was over by the end of May (1 February 1920).

Akasaka ▌ 1331 ▌ Genko War
Attempting to restore Imperial power, Japanese Emperor Go-Daigo left Kyoto and raised support from Samurai warriors under Kusunoki Masashige, who was besieged at Akasaka, in Kawachi, west of Nara, by the forces of Japanese Regent Hojo Takatoki. Most of the Imperialist garrison escaped after a bloody defence, and Kusunoki led an heroic defence two years later at **Chihaya**.

Akbarpur ▌ 1857 ▌ Indian Mutiny
See **Danchua**

Aké ▌ 1528 ▌ Spanish Conquest of Yucatan
After incursions into Yucatan by Juan de Grijalva (1518) and Hernán Cortés (1519), Francisco de Monteja led an expedition which took Cozumel Island in the northeast. Monteja then advanced inland against strong resistance and battle at Aké (near Tizimin) cost many Spaniards and over 1,000 Northern Maya killed. Despite his costly victory, Monteja could not make headway and withdrew to Mexico.

Akhalkalaki I 1810 I Russo-Persian Wars

In the Russian campaign to annexe Persian Georgia, Russian forces were driven off from the siege of **Erivan** in 1804. The war dragged on inconclusively until Russian General Marquis Filippo Paulucci defeated a major Persian force at Akhalkalaki, southwest of Tbilisi. However, fighting continued for another two years until the decisive Persian defeat at **Aslanduz** (1 September 1810).

Akhaltsikhe I 1828 I Russo-Turkish Wars

Russians under General Count Ivan Paskevich, in support of Greek independence, attacked Turkey in the Caucasus, where they captured **Kars**, then besieged the fortress of Akhaltsikhe, close to the modern Turkish border. Akhaltsikhe fell by assault after three weeks with heavy losses on both sides and Russian forces marched into Turkey against **Adrianople** (8–27 August 1828).

Akhaltsikhe I 1853 I Crimean War

Advancing north from Ardahan, a Turkish force of 30,000 was met near the Russian border by Prince Ivan Malkhazovich Andronikov and only 7,000 men. Outside Akhaltsikhe, the outnumbered Russians launched an immediate attack, and the Turks were defeated and dispersed. A Russian counter-offensive a few days later saw another victory further south at **Bashgedikler** (14 November 1853).

Akhsikath I 1503 I Mughal-Uzbek Wars

Driven back from Samarkand at **Sar-i-Pul** in 1501, the young Mughal Babur joined his uncles Sultan Mahmud of Tashkent and Sultan Ahmad Mirza of northern Mughalstan against the Uzbek conqueror Muhammad Shaybani Khan. But Babur and the Khans were defeated in a decisive action on the Syr Darya at Akhsikath, east of Tashkent and Ferghana Province was lost (June 1503).

Akhulgo I 1839 I Russian Conquest of the Caucasus

Russian Baron Pavel Grabbe was sent to destroy the Muslim Imam Shamil of Dagestan and advanced through **Burtinah** against the rebel stronghold at Akhulgo, on the Andi Koysu. Following two costly assaults, Grabbe was joined by General Evgeny Golovin, and Akhulgo was stormed at heavy Russian cost. Shamil escaped and eventually regained much of Dagestan (24 June–2 September 1839).

Akra I 721 I Muslim Civil Wars

Continuing internal conflict involving the Umayyad Caliphate saw a major force raised against the Caliph Yazid II by Yazid ibn al-Muhallab, the ambitious and powerful Governor of Iraq. However, in battle at Akra, on the left bank of the Euphrates near Wasit, the rebel was defeated and killed by the Umayyad Prince, Maslama ibn Abd al-Malik (August 720).

Akraba I 633 I Muslim Civil Wars

In Muslim wars of succession following the death of Mohammed (June 632), the false prophet Musaylima was massively defeated by General Khalid ibn al-Walid at Akraba in the eastern Najd Province of modern Saudi Arabia. Musaylima was killed, and the bloody victory—in the so-called Garden of Death—effectively established the authority of the caliphate in Medina (January 633).

Akroinos I 739 I Early Byzantine-Muslim Wars

The great soldier-Emperor Leo III had driven back a massive Muslim siege of **Constantinople** in 718, and later counter-attacked into Asia Minor, where he inflicted a terrible defeat on part of an Arab army under Suleiman at Akroinos (modern Afyonkarahisar) in west central Turkey. The victory gave Leo time to consolidate his power and rebuild the walls of Constantinople.

Akshehr I 1116 I Byzantine-Turkish Wars
See **Philomelion**

Akspoel I 1128 I War of Flemish Succession
See **Thielt**

Alabama vs *Kearsage* I 1864 I **American Civil War (High Seas)**
See **Cherbourg**

**Alacab   1212   Early Christian
Reconquest of Spain**
    See **Las Navas de Tolosa**

Aladja Dagh   1877   Russo-Turkish Wars
    Advancing against Turkey in the Caucasus,
Russian Grand Duke Michael and General Mikhail Loris-Melikov attacked Ahmed Mukhtar
Pasha holding a strongly established position on
the Aladja Dagh, near **Kars**. Defending overex-
tended lines, the Turks lost 6,000 casualties before
10,000 survivors surrendered. The defeat led directly to the fall of Kars (14–15 October 1877).

Alalia   535 BC   Cathaginian-Greek Wars
    Carthage was determined to block Greek ex-
pansion into the western Mediterranean and secured an unlikely ally in Etruria to jointly attack
the Phocian Greek colony of Alalia (Aleria), on
the east coast of Corsica. Defeated by the Car-
thaginian-Etruscan fleet, the Greeks were forced
to abandon the colony to Etruria. The action has
been called the first major naval engagement
since ancient Egypt.

**Alamana, Bridge of   1821   Greek War
of Independence**
    See **Thermopylae**

**Alamance Creek   1771   American
Colonial Wars**
    When Irish-Scottish settlers in northern Car-
olina, calling themselves Regulators, resisted
British rule, they provoked a military response
and were put down at Alamance Creek, in the
north of the state, by cavalry and militia sent by
Governor William Tryon under General Hugh
Waddell. Casualties were minor, though some of
the captured rebels were subsequently hanged
(16 May 1771).

**Al Amarah   1915   World War I
(Mesopotamia)**
    See **Amara**

Al Amarah   1983   Iraq-Iran War
    See **Amara**

Alambagh   1857–1858   Indian Mutiny
    British General Sir Henry Havelock advanced
through **Mangalwar** to relieve **Lucknow**, and
overwhelmed rebels at Alambagh, two miles
south of the city. General Sir James Outram
then held the town against attack by mutineers
under Ahmadullah Shah, Maulvi of Faizabad,
throughout the siege, evacuation and eventual
recapture of Lucknow (23 September 1857–
March 1858).

**Alamein   1942   World War II
(Northern Africa)**
    See **El Alamein**

**Alam Halfa   1942   World War II
(Northern Africa)**
    Checked west of Cairo at **El Alamein**, Field
Marshal Erwin Rommel circled south to attack
Alam Halfa Ridge. A brilliant defensive action,
planned by Sir Claude Auchinleck and adopted
by General Bernard Montgomery, saw heavy
losses on both sides. Rommel was forced to
withdraw and soon began to retreat after the
Allied offensive at **El Alamein** (30 August–5
September 1942).

**Alamo   1836   Texan Wars of
Independence**
    Determined to retake Texas after the loss of
San Antonio (December 1835), Mexican General Antonio de Santa Anna besieged about 200
irregulars led by Colonel William Travis and
James Bowie at nearby Alamo mission. When
the Alamo fell by assault, every surviving male
defender was murdered. This defeat and the
ensuing **Goliad Massacre** became watchwords
for the Texan cause (6 March 1836).

**Alamut   1256   Mongol Invasion of
the Middle East**
    The Mongol conqueror Hulegu advanced into
Persia, where he attacked the Assassins, an Ismaili Muslim religious-political sect which had
been active for 200 years. Hulegu defeated the
Assassins and destroyed their main mountain
fortress at Alamut, near Kasvin in central Iran,

ending their power in Persia. This sect in Syria was finally suppressed 15 years later by the Mamluk Sultan Baibars.

Aland ▌ 1714 ▌ 2nd "Great" Northern War
See **Hango**

Aland ▌ 1918 ▌ Finnish War of Independence
Landing to secure Aland, between Finland and Sweden, White forces from Turku under Colonel V. J. Forssell unexpectedly found the island defended by about 1,000 Russians. The town of Godby was taken by assault, but in a confusion over orders, the Whites surrendered their arms and were taken off by Swedish ships. Days later, they rejoined the fight at **Ruovesi** (14–20 February 1918).

Alarcos ▌ 1195 ▌ Early Christian Reconquest of Spain
During the reconquest of southern Spain, King Alfonso VIII of Castile led a major campaign against the Almohad Caliph Yakub Almansour. Attacking without waiting for his allies—the Kings of Leon and Navarre—Alfonso's Christian army suffered a disastrous defeat at Alarcos, near Cuidad Real. Castile itself then came under direct Muslim attack (18 July 1195).

Alazán Creek ▌ 1813 ▌ Gutiérrez-Magee Expedition
To recover Spanish Texas from Republican Bernardo Gutiérrez and American "Filibusters" led by Major Henry Perry, Colonel Ignacio Elizondo and General Joaquin de Arredondo besieged San Antonio, which had fallen after Royalist defeat at **Rosillo**. Marching out to nearby Alazán Creek, Perry surprised and routed Elizondo, but the Republicans were later destroyed at the **Medina** (20 June 1813).

Alba de Tormes ▌ 1809 ▌ Napoleonic Wars (Peninsular Campaign)
Spanish General Lorenzo Duke del Parque was withdrawing from capturing Salamanca after victory at **Tamames** (18 October), when he was pursued by the large French force under Generals Francois Kellermann and Jean-Gabriel Marchand. Surprised at Alba de Tormes, on the Tormes River south of Salamanca, the Spaniards were heavily defeated and scattered in retreat (28 November 1809).

Alba de Tormes ▌ 1812 ▌ Napoleonic Wars (Peninsular Campaign)
During the Allied retreat towards Portugal after the failed siege of **Burgos**, Anglo-Portuguese troops under Arthur Wellesley Lord Wellington held the river crossing on the Tormes at Alba. French Marshals Nicolas Soult and Jean-Baptiste Jourdan broke off the action after two days' fighting to cross higher up the river, and Wellington was forced to pull back (10–11 November 1812).

Albania ▌ 1939 ▌ World War II (Southern Europe)
In the months before World War II started, Benito Mussolini decided to finally invade Albania, which was already a virtual Italian dependency. After a naval bombardment, the Albanian army was quickly overcome and King Zog went into exile in Britain. Mussolini annexed Albania, which in October 1940 provided a bridgehead for the failed Italian invasion of **Greece** (7 April 1939).

Albara ▌ 1097 ▌ 1st Crusade
During the long Crusader siege of **Antioch, Syria**, a large-scale foraging party was sent south under the command of Bohemund of Taranto and Robert of Flanders. At the village of Albara, they were attacked by Duqaq of Damascus. Despite heavy losses, the Crusaders drove Duqaq's relief army back towards Hama. Another attempt to relieve Antioch was repulsed at **Harenc** (31 December 1097).

Al Basra ▌ 656 ▌ Muslim Civil Wars
See **Camel, Iraq**

Al Basra ▌ 1743 ▌ Turko-Persian Wars of Nadir Shah
See **Basra**

Al Basra ▮ 1775–1776 ▮ Turko-Persian Gulf War
    See **Basra**

Al Basra ▮ 1982 ▮ Iraq-Iran War
    See **Basra**

Albazin ▮ 1685–1686 ▮ Russo-Chinese Border War
    With China in disorder, Russians penetrated the Amur Valley and established a fortress at Albazin (modern Albazino), where they were later attacked by a large Manchu force. Initially driven out, the Russians regained the fortress and held out against siege until the Chinese withdrew. The Russians eventually destroyed and abandoned the fort and made peace (July 1685–December 1686).

Albe ▮ 1268 ▮ Angevin Conquest of the Two Sicilies
    See **Tagliacozzo**

Albeck ▮ 1805 ▮ Napoleonic Wars (3rd Coalition)
    See **Haslach**

Albermarle Sound ▮ 1864 ▮ American Civil War (Eastern Theatre)
    Continuing the Confederate offensive in North Carolina after the capture of **Plymouth**, the ram vessel *Albermarle* under Captain James W. Cooke attacked seven Union gunboats commanded by Captain Melancton Smith in Albermarle Sound, at the mouth of the Roanoke. Cooke inflicted heavy damage before withdrawing, and *Albermarle* was sunk later that year by a spar torpedo (5 May 1864).

Albert ▮ 1914 ▮ World War I (Western Front)
    During battle at the **Aisne**, French General Noel de Castelnau advanced northwest against the German flank and captured Noyon (21 September). There was then a massive German counter-attack under Prince Ruprecht around Albert, southeast of Amiens. French commander Joseph Joffre was driven back and attempted another flanking attack at **Arras** (25–30 September 1914).

Albert ▮ 1916 ▮ World War I (Western Front)
    General Sir Henry Rawlinson followed six days' bombardment by launching a massive offensive northeast from Albert against German commander Fritz von Below. The historic "First Day on the **Somme**" cost an unprecedented 58,000 British casualties—one-third killed—but Below was forced back and was replaced before the next phase of the offensive through **Bazentin** (1–13 July 1916).

Albert ▮ 1918 ▮ World War I (Western Front)
    In the second phase of the offensive east from **Amiens**, British Generals Julian Byng and Sir Henry Rawlinson advanced around Albert, strongly held by Germans under General Georg von de Marwitz. Very heavy fighting was supported by attacks to the north on the **Scarpe** and further south at **Bapaume**, and the German forward defence eventually had to withdraw (21–29 August 1918).

Albuera ▮ 1811 ▮ Napoleonic Wars (Peninsular Campaign)
    See **Albuhera**

Albufera ▮ 1812 ▮ Napoleonic Wars (Peninsular Campaign)
    As part of his siege campaign against the Spanish eastern seaport of **Valencia**, French Marshal Louis Suchet defeated Spanish forces under General Joachim Blake nearby, on the coast close to the Albufera Lagoon. Valencia itself surrendered five days later. Suchet was created Duke of Albufera in recognition of his success (4 January 1812).

Albuhera ▮ 1811 ▮ Napoleonic Wars (Peninsular Campaign)
    A bloody encounter near the Spanish border saw French Marshal Nicolas Soult's attempt to relieve the Allied siege of **Badajoz** driven off at nearby Albuhera by British, Spanish and

Portuguese troops under General Sir William Beresford. British infantry repulsed the relief army, holding firm despite very heavy casualties, but the Allied siege eventually failed (16 May 1811).

Albulen I 1457 I Albanian-Turkish Wars

A third Turkish advance against **Krujë** in central Albania saw 80,000 men under Isa Bey Evrenos surprised at nearby Albulen by Albanian George Kastriote Skanderbeg. The Turks lost thousands of prisoners (including Skanderbeg's renegade nephew Hamza Kastriote) in a disastrous defeat and Ottoman Sultan Mehmed II agreed to a three-year truce (2 September 1457).

Albuquerque I 1811 I Napoleonic Wars (Peninsular Campaign)

Setting out from **Badajoz**, French Marshal Édouard Mortier crossed the Portuguese border and, while besieging the bravely defended fortress of **Campo Mayor**, approached nearby Albuquerque, garrisoned by about 800 regular troops under General Don José Cagigal. In a notoriously shameful capitulation, Cagigal surrendered the fortress and 17 guns without a fight (15 March 1811).

Alcacer do Sol I 1158 I Christian Reconquest of Portugal

King Alfonso I of Portugal took advantage of internal instability among the Muslims of Portugal and Spain by making considerable advances against the Moors and taking **Lisbon**. Aided by Crusader forces from England, he then marched southeast against the key fortress of Alcacer do Sol on the Sado Estuary. The fortress was seized and held by Christian forces for 40 years (24 June 1158).

Alcacer do Sol I 1217 I Christian Reconquest of Portugal

Campaigning against the Moors in southern Iberia, King Alfonso II of Portugal attempted to recover Alcacer do Sol on the Sado River estuary, south of Lisbon, previously captured by his grandfather Alfonso I. With support from a

Crusader fleet under the Counts of Holland and of Weid, the stronghold was besieged for two months before it was finally captured (18 October 1217).

Alcalá I 1340 I Later Christian Reconquest of Spain

Soon after the Christian victory at **Rio Salado**, Alfonso XI of Castile advanced against other frontier positions with a large-scale siege of Alacalá de Benzaide (modern Alcalá la Real), northwest of Granada. Alcalá surrendered after Christians captured the nearby castle of Locubin and drove off a Muslim relief force under King Yusuf I of Granada. Alfonso then turned his attention to **Algeciras**.

Alcalá la Real I 1810 I Napoleonic Wars (Peninsular Campaign)

French General Francois Sébastiani captured **Jaen** and Cordova, then pursued the survivors of General Carlos Areizaga's army, who had meanwhile been reinforced by cavalry units under General Manuel Freire. Sébastiani routed the Spanish forces at Alcalá la Real, northwest of Granada, inflicting over 500 casualties, and Granada surrendered to him next day (28 February 1810).

Alcañiz I 1809 I Napoleonic Wars (Peninsular Campaign)

Attempting to secure Aragon, newly appointed French commander General Louis Suchet launched an ill-advised offensive from Saragossa against a Spanish army under General Joachim Blake. Attacking a strong defensive position at Alcañiz on the Guadalope River, west of Teruel, Suchet was driven back and his offensive broken up, but Blake did not pursue (23 May 1809).

Alcántara I 1580 I Spanish-Portuguese War

King Philip II of Spain took advantage of a disputed succession in Portugal to send an invasion force under Fernando Alvarez Duke of Alva. The rival claimant, Dom Antonio, at the head of a largely peasant army, was heavily defeated near the border at Alcántara, and Spain ruled Portugal for the next 60 years. Spain also seized the Portuguese Azores with victory off **Terceira** (25 August 1580).

Alcántara I 1706 I War of the Spanish Succession

In a fresh offensive from the west, Anglo-Portuguese forces under Henri de Massue Earl of Ruvigny and Antonio de Sousa Marquis de Minas captured the Spanish border city of Alcántara held by French troops of Marshal James Duke of Berwick. The Allies then advanced to occupy Madrid, but their victory was decisively reversed a year later at **Almanza** (14–18 April 1706).

Alcántara I 1809 I Napoleonic Wars (Peninsular Campaign)

Two days after Marshal Nicolas Soult was driven out of Portugal following defeat at **Oporto**, Marshal Claude Victor smashed into the Lusitania Legion and Portuguese militia holding the bridge at Alcántara, on the Tagus just inside Spain. Led by Colonel William Mayne, the Allies fought bravely but were forced back by French artillery and Victor seized the bridge (14 May 1809).

Alcantra I 1839 I Mexican Federalist War

General Antonio Canales Rosillon assumed command of the Federalist rebellion after the loss of **Tampico** in June, and, with Texan and Indian aid, attacked Centralist commander José Ignacio Pávon at Alcantra, on the Alamo River, southwest of Mier. Pávon was decisively defeated and was later replaced by General Mariano Arista, who turned the tables at **Santa Rita Morelos** (3–4 October 1839).

Alcazar I 1936 I Spanish Civil War

In the opening days of the war, the military academy at Alcazar in Toledo declared for the insurgent cause. While government forces quickly secured the city, the fortress held out under Colonel José Moscardó. The siege was relieved after two months by Nationalist General José Varela, who took Toledo by assault and massacred many of the defenders (20 July–27 September 1936).

Alcazarquivir I 1578 I Portuguese-Moroccan War

Dreaming of a Christian empire in Africa, King Sebastian of Portugal invaded Morocco to support a Moorish pretender to the throne of Fez. Sebastian was routed south of Tangier at Alcazarquivir, and the expedition failed. This was known as the "Battle of Three Kings" as it involved Sebastian, the Royal pretender and the King of Fez, all of whom were killed (4 August 1578).

Alcolea I 1808 I Napoleonic Wars (Peninsular Campaign)

At the start of Napoleon's campaign in Spain, a few Spanish regulars and a large force of peasant levies under Colonel Pedro de Echavarri attempted to make a stand at the Alcolea Bridge over the Guadalquivir in front of Cordova. The Spanish force was defeated and destroyed by General Pierre Dupont de L'Etang's French regulars, who next day stormed and sacked Cordova (6 June 1808).

Alcolea I 1868 I Spanish Revolution

In revolt against the despotism of Queen Isabela of Spain, rebels under General Francisco Serrano routed the Royal army under Manuel Pavía, Marques de Novaliches, at Alcolea near Cordova. Isabela fled to France and a provisional government, with Serrano as President of the Ministry, ruled until the Duke of Aosta came to the throne in 1871 as King Amadeo (28 September 1868).

Alcoraz I 1096 I Early Christian Reconquest of Spain

When Sancho Ramirez of Aragon was killed at a failed siege of the strategic Muslim city of Huesca, in northeast Spain (1094), his son Pedro I renewed the offensive and, at nearby Alcoraz, met a large Muslim relief army led by al-Mustain. Despite support from Castilian nobles, al-Mustain was utterly defeated. Besieged Huesca surrendered to Pedro nine days later (18 November 1096).

**Aldea del Ponte I 1811 I Napoleonic Wars
(Peninsular Campaign)**

Marshal Auguste Marmont advancing from **Salamanca** to relieve the Anglo-Portuguese blockade of **Ciudad Rodrigo** was repulsed at **El Bodon** and withdrew southwest to Aldea del Ponte, where he attacked General Sir Edward Pakenham. Arthur Wellesley Lord Wellington arrived with reinforcements and the town changed hands twice before Marmont retired south (27 September 1811).

**Aldenhoven I 1793 I French
Revolutionary Wars (1st Coalition)**

Within months of his victories at **Valmy** and **Jemappes**, French General Charles-Francois Dumouriez was defeated at Aldenhoven by Austrian Prince Friedrich Josias of Saxe-Coburg advancing across the Roer towards Maastrich. Dumouriez negotiated an armistice after further defeats at **Aix-la-Chapelle**, **Neerwinden** and **Louvain**, then defected to the Austrians (1 March 1793).

**Aldenhoven I 1794 I French
Revolutionary Wars (1st Coalition)**

Austrian Count Charles von Clerfayt fell back from Aix-la-Chapelle and took a strong position on the River Ruhr near Aldenhoven, covering Cologne with an army of more than 75,000 men. French forces under General Jean-Baptiste Jourdan attacked along a very wide front and Clerfayt withdrew, crossing the Rhine south of Cologne four days later (2 October 1794).

**Aldie I 1863 I American Civil War
(Eastern Theatre)**

As Robert E. Lee's invasion advanced north towards Gettysburg, part of General James "Jeb" Stuart's Confederate cavalry screen to the east under Colonel Thomas Munford came under attack at Aldie, south of Leesburg, Virginia, by Union cavalry led by General Judson Kilpatrick. After an indecisive action, Munford fell back west towards Stuart, under attack at **Middleburg** (17 June 1863).

**Alegaon I 1762 I Maratha Wars of
Succession**

Following the death of Maratha Peshwa Balaji Rao, his teenage son Madhav Rao fell out with his ambitious uncle Raghunath Rao, who established an alliance with Nizam Ali of Hyderabad. Madhav Rao was heavily defeated at Alegaon in central Maharashtra and submitted to his uncle, while Nizam Ali was rewarded with land he had lost after defeat at nearby **Udgir** (12 November 1762).

Alegría I 1834 I 1st Carlist War

Carlists Tomás Zumalacárregui and Francisco de Iturralde eluded pursuit after victory at **Artaza** and **Peñas de San Fausto** in August, then surprised Liberal Brigadier Manuel O'Doyle at Alegría, northern Spain, between Vitoria and Salvatierra. O'Doyle fled to nearby Arrieta, where a relief column from Vitoria under General Joaquín de Osma was beaten next day (27–28 October 1834).

Alegría del Pío I 1956 I Cuban Revolution

Amnestied from prison after a failed attack on the **Moncada** in 1953, Fidel Castro led a small force from Mexico, which landed at Niquero in eastern Cuba. He was attacked by Batista troops under Colonel Ramón Cruz Vidal at nearby Alegría del Pío, where the rebels suffered very heavy losses in action and the subsequent round-up. The survivors regrouped to strike back at **La Plata** (5 December 1956).

Aleksin I 1472 I Russian-Mongol Wars

With Moscow distracted by war against Novgorod, Mongol leader Ahmed Khan advanced to the Oka, where he attacked and burned Aleksin, east of Kaluga. But garrison commander Semen Beklemishev then fought a bold defensive action. Without promised Lithuanian aid and facing massive Russian reinforcements, Ahmed withdrew. In 1480, he advanced again as far as the **Ugra** (30 July 1472).

Aleksinac I 1876 I Serbo-Turkish War
See **Alexinatz**

Aleppo I 639 I Muslim Conquest of Syria

Muslim conqueror General Khalid ibn al-Walid, captured **Damascus** (635) and **Jerusalem** (638), and later marched north to seize Aleppo, near the modern border between Syria and Turkey. However, Aleppo's citadel held out against a bloody five-month siege. The citadel finally fell by storm and the capture of Aleppo effectively ended Byzantine resistance to the Muslim invaders in Syria.

Aleppo I 962 I Later Byzantine-Muslim Wars

On a major offensive against Muslim military power, Byzantine General Nicephorus Phocas drove the Arabs out of **Crete**, then invaded Syria to besiege Aleppo, capital of the Hamdanid Sayf ad-Dawla. Aleppo was taken by storm, with the population killed or enslaved, and the city was razed. Nicephorus (later Emperor) then attacked **Adana** and **Tarsus** in Cilicia (December 962).

Aleppo I 969 I Later Byzantine-Muslim Wars

After driving the Arabs out of Asia Minor at **Adana** and **Tarsus** (965), Emperor Nicephorus II Phocas invaded Syria to capture **Antioch**, then marched to retake Aleppo from the Chamberlain Karguyah, who had overthrown the Hamdanid Sayf ad-Dawla. Although Nicephorus was assassinated, Aleppo fell to his General, Michael Burtzes, and became a Byzantine protectorate (December 969).

Aleppo I 1030 I Later Byzantine-Muslim Wars

See **Azaz**

Aleppo I 1086 I Byzantine-Turkish Wars

As parts of the Byzantine Empire fell after disaster at **Manzikert** in 1071, Sultan Malik Shah seized Anatolia, but lost it to his rival, Sulaiman ibn Kutalmish, who became the first Seljuk ruler of Rum. Sulaiman seized the last Byzantine outpost at **Antioch**, **Syria**, but outside Aleppo he was defeated and killed by the Sultan's brother Prince Tutush, securing Turkish control of Anatolia and Syria.

Aleppo I 1119 I Crusader-Muslim Wars

See **Antioch, Syria**

Aleppo I 1260 I Mongol Invasion of the Middle East

Hulegu, Mongol Il-Khan of Iran, sacked **Baghdad** in 1258, then invaded Syria and invested the fortress city of Aleppo, defended by Turanshah, uncle of Sultan an-Nasir Yusuf. The city fell after six days' assault (20 January), and the citadel a month later. The capture of Aleppo and its massive treasure induced the Sultan to flee Damascus, which then fell to the Mongols (January–February 1260).

Aleppo I 1400 I Conquests of Tamerlane

When Mongols under Tamerlane invaded Syria, they inflicted a devastating defeat on the Mamluks, who unwisely marched out from the city of Aleppo to meet the Mongols in the open. Having routed his enemy in the field, Tamerlane then sacked Aleppo and marched south against **Damascus** to complete his conquest of Syria (30 October 1400).

Aleppo I 1516 I Ottoman-Mamluk War

See **Yaunis Khan**

Aleppo I 1839 I 2nd Turko-Egyptian War

See **Nezib**

Aleppo I 1918 I World War I (Middle East)

Weeks after seizing **Damascus**, British commander Sir Edmund Allenby continued a more cautious advance further north, supported by troops of the Northern Arab Army, and attacked Aleppo. The Turks withdrew but fought a bitter defence near the city under Mustapha Kemal. However, Turkey signed an armistice just a few days later to end the war in the Middle East (24–25 October 1918).

Aleria I 535 BC I Carthaginian-Greek Wars

See **Alalia**

Alesia ∎ 52 BC ∎ Rome's Later Gallic Wars

Despite a costly loss at **Gergovia** in central Gaul, Julius Caesar surrounded hilltop Alesia (modern Alise Ste. Reine), northwest of Dijon, with a double wall. In the largest campaign of the war, he fought off a huge counter-siege by Vercingetorix, Chief of the Arverni. Starving Alesia surrendered after heavy casualties and Gaul was effectively conquered. Vercingetorix was taken to Rome and executed.

Alessandria ∎ 1174–1175 ∎ Wars of the Lombard League

Emperor Frederick Barbarossa was campaigning in northern Italy for the Lombard League when he attacked Alessandria, at the junction of the Tanaro and Bormida Rivers. Frederick withdrew after a brutal six-month siege when the defenders sortied and burned his siege machines. Following fruitless truce negotiations, he was defeated a year later at **Legnano** (November 1174–April 1175).

Alessandria ∎ 1391 ∎ Florentine-Milanese Wars

See **Castellazzo**

Alessandria ∎ 1799 ∎ French Revolutionary Wars (2nd Coalition)

Attempting to join the French army marching from southern Italy, General Jean Victor Moreau was blocked at the northern town of Alessandria by a much larger Austrian-Russian force led by Count Heinrich von Bellegarde. Moreau defeated von Bellegarde, but his delay contributed to a French defeat at the **Trebbia**. Alessandria surrendered to the Austrians on 22 July (20 June 1799).

Aleutians ∎ 1942 ∎ World War II (Pacific)

As a diversion from **Midway**, Japanese Admiral Boshiro Hosogaya took a large fleet towards the Aleutians. While Admiral Robert Theobald manoeuvred to protect Alaska, the Japanese landed on the outer Aleutian islands of Attu and Kiska. Naval battle near the **Komandorski Islands** a year later blocked reinforcements for **Attu**, which was retaken after a bloody action (5–7 June 1942).

Alexandria ∎ 48–47 BC ∎ Wars of the First Triumvirate

Julius Caesar pursued Pompey to Egypt after victory at **Pharsalus** (48 BC) and found his rival had been assassinated. Caesar was then besieged in part of Alexandria by General Ponthinus for Ptolemy XII, Egyptian co-ruler with his sister Cleopatra VII (Caesar's lover). The Roman garrison repulsed repeated attacks for five months before they were finally relieved after victory at the mouth of the **Nile**.

Alexandria ∎ 296 ∎ Roman Military Civil Wars

In a local rising in Egypt provoked by new tax laws and reform of the coinage, Roman General Achilleus established himself in Alexandria as Emperor in Egypt. His rebellion was put down by Emperor Diocletian after an eight-month siege of the Egyptian capital. Achilleus was subsequently executed, reputedly by being fed to lions.

Alexandria ∎ 641–642 ∎ Muslim Conquest of Egypt

Following the surrender of **Babylon** on the Nile in April 641, Muslim General Amr ibn al-As marched north against Byzantine Alexandria, which was captured at the cost of very heavy Greek casualties after a 14-month siege. The surrender of the Egyptian capital by Byzantine Patriarch Cyrus virtually completed the Muslim conquest of Egypt (July 641–September 642).

Alexandria ∎ 645 ∎ Early Byzantine-Muslim Wars

Just three years after the fall of Alexandria to Muslim Arabs under Amr ibn al-As, Emperor Constans sent a fresh army under Manuel, who recovered the Egyptian city, with the assistance of the remaining Greek residents. Following a short siege, Amr once again captured Alexandria and expelled the Greeks, ending almost 1,000 years of Greco-Roman occupation.

Alexandria ∎ 1167 ∎ Crusader Invasion of Egypt

Having captured Cairo, Crusader King Amalric of Jerusalem, aided by deposed Egyptian Vizier

Shawar, recovered after **El Ashmunien** (18 March) and besieged Kurdish General Shirkuh and his nephew Saladin in Alexandria. Though Shirkuh escaped with much of his army, Saladin was starved into surrendering the city. In 1169, the struggle for Egypt resumed at **Damietta** (April–4 August 1167).

Alexandria I 1365 I Egyptian Crusade of Peter of Cyprus

Seventy years after the end of the principal Christian Crusades, King Peter of Cyprus launched his own campaign against Muslim Egypt. He captured and sacked Alexandria with a terrible slaughter of the population of all races and the capture of massive booty. However, his campaign stalled and was ended by his assassination in Nicosia a few years later (9–11 October 1365).

Alexandria I 1798 I French Revolutionary Wars (Middle East)

Napoleon Bonaparte began his Egyptian campaign by landing his army near Alexandria, where he defeated its Mamluk defenders in a short but bloody action in which Generals Jacques Menou and Jean-Baptiste Kléber were severely wounded. Bonaparte then seized Alexandria and advanced towards Cairo where, three weeks later, he won the decisive Battle of the **Pyramids** (2 July 1798).

Alexandria (1st) I 1801 I French Revolutionary Wars (Middle East)

A British-Turkish army led by Sir Ralph Abercromby, which landed in Egypt through battle at **Aboukir** (8 March), found their way to Alexandria blocked by General Jacques Menou. The French were defeated with heavy losses, though General Abercromby was fatally wounded. The victory led to the eventual surrender of Alexandria and the French were driven out of Egypt (21 March 1801).

Alexandria (2nd) I 1801 I French Revolutionary Wars (Middle East)

Following victory outside Alexandria, newly appointed British commander Sir John Hely-Hutchinson marched to seize **Cairo**, leaving General Sir George Eyre to blockade Alexandria. Hutchinson later returned to the attack and, after Coote captured the western fortress of Marabout against stiff opposition, General Jacques Menou surrendered the city (April–30 August 1801).

Alexandria I 1807 I Napoleonic Wars (4th Coalition)

In order to undermine Turkey, which had switched to the French cause, Britain unwisely sent an expedition under General Alexander Mckenzie Fraser to North Africa to seize Turkish Egypt. Although Alexandria was attacked and captured, the small British force was insufficient for its task and, after defeat at **Rosetta**, they were forced to surrender and withdraw (21 March 1807).

Alexandria I 1882 I Arabi's Egyptian Rebellion

War Minister Arabi Pasha attempted to assert Egyptian sovereignty and began building forts at Alexandria to control the approaches to the Suez Canal. British Admiral Sir Beauchamp Seymour then bombarded the fortresses and occupied the city. A month later an expeditionary force under General Sir Garnet Wolseley landed at the canal and crushed the rebels at **Tel-el-Kebir** (11–12 July 1882).

Alexandria I 1941 I World War II (War at Sea)

One of Italy's most famous naval exploits saw three two-man human torpedoes enter Alexandria Harbour and place charges under units of the British fleet. The only British battleships in the Mediterranean–*Queen Elizabeth* and *Valiant*—were sunk and a tanker and destroyer damaged, briefly changing the balance of power. Both battleships were eventually repaired (18–19 December 1941).

Alexandrovsk I 1919 I Russian Civil War

Supporting White counter-revolutionaries in the Russian civil war, British ships based at

Persian ports fought a Bolshevik navy attempting to seize the Caspian, where battle off Alexandrovsk (modern Alexandro-Nevskaya) in the western Caspian saw a British victory. The following year, the ships were handed to the Whites, who lost them to a renewed Bolshevik offensive (21 May 1919).

Alexinatz ∎ 1876 ∎ Serbo-Turkish War

When Serbia declared war on Turkey to support Christian Bosnia-Herzogovina, a large Turkish force under Abdul Kerim advanced from Nis to Alexinatz (modern Aleksinac), southeast of Belgrade. Serbia's army, under Russian General Mikhail Chernyayev (aided by Russian volunteers), was badly defeated and a brief armistice ensued before fighting resumed at **Djunis** (1 September 1876).

Al Fallujah ∎ 1941 ∎ World War II (Middle East)

See **Fallujah**

Alfarrobeira ∎ 1449 ∎ Portuguese War of Succession

The Regent of Portugal, Dom Pedro Duke of Coimbra, seized government from his 17-year-old nephew Alfonso V, and the young King took a large army against his uncle, whose heavily outnumbered force was entrenched along the Alfarrobeira River, near Santarem. The Duke of Coimbra and most of his supporters were killed and the war of succession came to an end (21 May 1449).

Al Faw ∎ 1986 ∎ Iraq-Iran War

While a diversionary attack went in north of Basra, Iran launched a surprise amphibious assault across the Shatt al-Arab and seized the strategic Al Faw (Fao) Peninsula to threaten the Iraqi naval base at Umm Qasr. Despite the use of chemical weapons, desperate Iraqi counterattacks failed. Iran dug in to hold the bridgehead against all assault until near the end of the war (9–14 February 1986).

Al Faw ∎ 1988 ∎ Iraq-Iran War

With Iran exhausted by war and threatened by superpower intervention in the Persian Gulf,

Iraqi forces with numerous tanks, guns and chemical weapons launched a major amphibious offensive to regain the Al Faw Peninsula. The vastly outnumbered Iranians were overwhelmed, and a further Iraqi victory east of Basra at **Salamcheh** soon effectively ended the war in the south (17–18 April 1988).

Alford ∎ 1645 ∎ British Civil Wars

Scottish Covenanters under General Sir William Baillie attempted to intercept an advance on Aberdeen by Royalist commander James Graham Marquis of Montrose, but were lured into battle across the River Don. Taken in ambush at Alford, 25 miles west of Aberdeen, Baillie's Parliamentary force was heavily defeated. Baillie was beaten again a month later at **Kilsyth** (2 July 1645).

Algeciras ∎ 1309 ∎ Later Christian Reconquest of Spain

At the same time as Aragon was besieging **Almeria**, a Castilian expedition attacked Algeciras, just west of Gibraltar, held by Marinid Muslims from North Africa. In an unexpected defeat, the Castilian noble Juan Manuel led his Christian knights off the field of battle. Castile withdrew from the siege and, shortly afterwards, the Aragonese gave up their assault on Almeria (November 1309).

Algeciras ∎ 1340 ∎ Later Christian Reconquest of Spain

In a renewed offensive in Granada, the Moors inflicted a severe defeat on King Alfonso XI of Castile at Algeciras, across the Bay of Algeciras, west of Gibraltar. Castilian Admiral Alfonso Jofre Tenorio was defeated and killed at sea and the Muslims then captured the city. It was held by the Moors until a Christian counter-offensive three years later.

Algeciras ∎ 1343–1344 ∎ Later Christian Reconquest of Spain

After a fresh Muslim invasion of southern Spain, King Alfonso XI of Castile launched a major counter-offensive and, following his victory at **Rio Salado** in 1340, the King besieged

Algeciras, west of Gibraltar. The Moroccan fleet was defeated off Algeciras by Genoese Admiral Egidio Boccanegra and Alfonso destroyed much of the city before forcing a costly Muslim surrender (26 March 1344).

Algeciras Bay I 1801 I French Revolutionary Wars (2nd Coalition)

British ships under Admiral Sir James Saumarez attacked the French naval squadron in the Mediterranean at Algeciras Bay, off southeast Spain, and defeated Admiral Charles Durand de Linois. Six days later, Saumarez renewed the attack in a confused night action. Linois, reinforced by Spanish Admiral Don Juan Moreno, was again defeated with heavy loss of life (6 & 12–13 July 1801).

Alghero I 1353–1354 I Aragon's Conquest of Sardinia

King Pedro IV of Aragon resolved to capture Sardinia from Genoa and sent a naval force which utterly defeated the Genoese fleet off Alghero in the northwest of the island. The following year, Pedro led another large force, which besieged and captured Alghero itself. Mariano de Arborea, who had claimed the title of King of Sardinia, surrendered and Sardinia became a long-time Aragonese possession.

Algidus I 431 BC I Wars of the Roman Republic

The Republic's early years saw the Italian Aequi and Volsci tribes join forces against Rome, and the Aequi set up a fortified position southeast of Rome at Mount Algidus, controlling the key road near Tusculum. There they were attacked and dislodged by Aulus Postumius Tubertus after stubborn defence. The tribes were eventually subdued and admitted to citizenship (trad date 18 June 431 BC).

Algiers I 1511 I Spanish Colonial Wars in North Africa

A year after taking **Bougie** and **Tripoli**, Spanish forces sailed for Algiers and captured the offshore island of Peñon, effectively blockading the harbour. Pasha Salim al-Tumi sought

aid from the Turkish Corsair Arudj, who repulsed Spanish attacks on Algiers in 1516 and 1519. In 1529, his brother Khayr al-din retook Peñon and Algiers became a key base for Muslim raids on Christian shipping.

Algiers I 1541 I Turkish-Habsburg Wars

Emperor Charles V defeated Muslim Corsairs in **Tunis** in 1535 and later took a large force against Algiers, defended by Hassan Agha. However, a great storm wrecked over 150 ships, and the Emperor's attempted siege was heavily driven off by a bloody counter-attack by Algerian Turks and Arab tribesmen. Facing total failure, the starving survivors returned to Europe (24–26 October 1541).

Algiers I 1620–1621 I Corsair Wars

An intended action against Muslim pirates saw British Admiral Sir Robert Mansell sail to Algiers, supported by Sir Richard Hawkins and Sir Thomas Button. Forty British captives were freed after negotiations (November 1620), but a renewed attack the following year failed miserably when inadequate fireships were driven off. Mansell withdrew and was recalled to England (24 May 1621).

Algiers I 1665 I Corsair Wars
See **Porto Farina**

Algiers I 1682–1683 I Franco-Barbary Wars

Determined to punish the Barbary pirates of Algiers, Louis XIV of France sent Marquis Abraham Duquesne to besiege Algiers. The North African city was bombarded from 30 August to 8 September 1682, killing about 500, and again in June and August 1683, before Dey Husayn Pasha forced Duquesne to withdraw. Husayn made peace in 1684, giving up captured ships and prisoners.

Algiers I 1688 I Franco-Barbary Wars

When Algeria broke the peace, Louis XIV of France sent Admiral Jean d'Estrées, who bombarded Algiers for five days and caused massive damage. But with renewed war in Europe, d'Es-trées was recalled (August 1688), and Corsair Admiral Husayn Pasha retaliated by attacking French shipping. In May 1689, Louis made a new peace, with further concessions (22–27 June 1688).

Algiers ∎ 1775 ∎ Spanish-Algerian Wars

With **Oran** secured, Charles III of Spain de-termined to capture Algiers and sent 500 ships and 20,000 men under Irish-born Count Alex-ander O'Reilly (who had led Spanish forces in crushing French rebellion in Louisiana). Despite heavy naval bombardment, the disastrous land-ing was driven off with over 500 killed and 2,000 wounded. A month later the expedition had to withdraw (8 July 1775).

Algiers ∎ 1783 ∎ Spanish-Algerian Wars

Spain's North African enclave at **Oran** came under siege by Algerian troops and Spain re-acted by sending a force of 10 frigates and over 60 smaller ships against Algiers. A nine-day bombardment caused heavy damage but nothing else. A second Spanish bombardment in 1784 was driven off before much damage could be caused. Oran fell to the Algerians in 1791 (1–9 August 1783).

Algiers ∎ 1816 ∎ Corsair Wars

Responding to North African piracy, 18 Brit-ish ships under Admiral Edward Pellew Baron Exmouth, supported by Dutch Admiral Theo-dore van Capellen, bombarded Algiers and de-stroyed the local fleet. Surrender by Omar Pasha, Dey of Algiers, released more than 3,000 Chris-tian prisoners, largely Spanish and Italian, and Pellew was created Viscount Exmouth (27 August 1816).

Algiers ∎ 1824 ∎ Corsair Wars

British Captains Sir Robert Spencer (*Naiad* 46) and James Burton (*Cameleon* 12) led a re-newed offensive against Barbary pirates, at-tacking the port of Algiers, where they destroyed the pirate corvette *Tripoli*. With the subsequent loss of an Algerine brig off Boma (23 May), and Admiral Sir Harry Neale threatening to bombard

the city, the Dey of Algiers sued for peace (31 January 1824).

Algiers ∎ 1830 ∎ French Conquest of Algeria

After three years blockading the pirate port of Algiers, France launched a major invasion, led by Marshal Louis de Bourmont, who captured the port in a decisive action three weeks later. Hussein, Dey of Algiers, was deposed, and Al-geria was gradually conquered at **Mascara**, **Constantine**, **Smala** and elsewhere. It remained French for the next 130 years (29 June–5 July 1830).

Algiers ∎ 1942 ∎ World War II (Northern Africa)

As part of **Torch** in French northwest Africa, 32,000 Anglo-American troops of the Eastern Task Force landed at Algiers under US General Charles Ryder and Britain's General Kenneth Anderson. Vichy General Alphonse Juin sur-rendered after sporadic resistance, and the Allies went east through Bougie and Bone before en-tering **Tunisia** and stalling at **Tébourba** (8–9 November 1942).

Algiers ∎ 1956–1957 ∎ Algerian War

Facing increasing terrorism in Algiers, Para-troop General Jacques Massu assumed civil control of the city and began a fierce urban campaign against the FLN under Ramdane Abane and later Saadi Yacef. Both sides saw escalating brutality, and the Battle of Algiers ended only with the capture of Yacef. The mil-itary focus of war then moved to the countryside (September 1956–October 1957).

Alhama ∎ 1482 ∎ Final Christian Reconquest of Spain

In retaliation for Muslim capture of **Zahara** late in 1481, Rodrigo Ponce de Leon Marquis of Cadiz soon seized the fortress of Alhama, southwest of Granada, and massacred many residents. Mulei Abdul Hassan, King of Gran-ada, immediately besieged the fortress, but was eventually driven off by the approach of a large

Spanish army under King Ferdinand V of Castile (28 February–14 May 1482).

Alhandega ▮ 939 ▮ Christian-Muslim Wars in Spain

See **Simancas, Vallalolid**

Alhucemas ▮ 1925 ▮ Spanish-Rif War

In a final offensive against Rif rebel Abd el Krim in Morocco, a Spanish amphibious force under General José Sanjurjo landed at Alhucemas, west of Melilla. About 12,000 men required almost a month of heavy fighting to capture the Rif capital Ajdir, just seven miles from the coast. Squeezed by French attacks in the south, Abd el Krim surrendered to end the war (8 September–3 October 1925).

Alicante ▮ 1706 ▮ War of the Spanish Succession

British Admiral Sir John Leake took the Spanish port of **Cartagena** (13 June), then sailed north to besiege Spanish-Irish General Daniel O'Mahony at Alicante. Troops under General Richard Gorges and later Sir John Jennings eventually took the city by storm (29 July) after a naval bombardment by Sir George Byng. A month later, O'Mahony surrendered the citadel (26 June–24 August 1706).

Alicante ▮ 1708–1709 ▮ War of the Spanish Succession

When Claude Francois Bidal, Chevalier d'Asfeld, laid siege to Alicante, General John Richards refused to surrender and the French exploded a massive mine which killed Richards and about 50 others (3 March). However, the English and Huguenot garrison held out for six weeks until Admiral Sir George Byng arrived and evacuated the survivors (1 December 1708–18 April 1709).

Alicante ▮ 1812 ▮ Napoleonic Wars (Peninsular Campaign)

With insufficient troops available, French General Louis Montbrun attempted to storm the well-fortified port city of Alicante, on the southeast Mediterranean coast of Spain, de-fended by Spanish troops under General Nicolas Mahy. Montbrun was repulsed at the cost of many needless French casualties and returned northwest to Toledo (16 January 1812).

Alicudi ▮ 1676 ▮ 3rd Dutch War

See **Stromboli**

Aligarh ▮ 1803 ▮ 2nd British-Maratha War

General Sir Gerard Lake invaded Hindustan with British regulars and native troops and attacked the powerful fortress of Aligarh, southeast of **Delhi**, defended by a Maratha army under French Colonel Pedron. Aligarh was captured after heavy fighting and, with Pedron and other officers having surrendered, Lake continued his advance towards **Delhi** (4 September 1803).

Aligarh ▮ 1857 ▮ Indian Mutiny

Marching south from the capture of **Delhi**, within weeks Colonel Edward Greathed secured Molaghur after victory at **Bulandshahr**, then approached Aligarh, which was largely evacuated at his advance. Pursuing the rebels in an extended running action, Greathed killed over 200, then pressed on to relieve the besieged British garrison 40 miles to the south at **Agra** (5 October 1857).

Alihuatá ▮ 1933 ▮ Chaco War

As part of a major new offensive against Bolivian forces in the Chaco Real, Paraguayan commander Colonel José Félix Estigarribia attacked Bolivia's General Hans Kundt in the vicinity of Alihuatá and Zenteno. Estigarribia occupied Alihuatá after prolonged fighting and, three days later, the retreating Bolivians surrendered further south at **Campo Vía** (23 October–8 December 1933).

Ali Kheyl ▮ 1984 ▮ Afghan Civil War

Following the successful government offensive against Mujahaden rebels north of Kabul in the **Panjshir Valley**, about 12,000 Afghan and Soviet troops relieved Soviet forces under guerrilla attack at Ali Kheyl, southeast of Kabul, in Paktia Province. Supported by an air assault flown in directly from the Soviet Union, the offensive succeeded and the rebels were driven back (August 1984).

Ali Masjid ▌ 1839 ▌ 1st British-Afghan War

Concerned at Russian influence in Afghanistan, the British Army of the Indus marched from Kandahar to **Ghazni** to reinstate Amir Shah Shuja, while Colonel Sir Claude Wade led a second force from the east through the Khyber Pass, supported by Shuja's son Timur. As Wade advanced towards **Kabul**, he lost almost 200 casualties in a sharp action taking the fortress of Ali Masjid (26 July 1839).

Ali Masjid ▌ 1842 ▌ 1st British-Afghan War

After retreating British troops and civilians from **Kabul** were massacred at **Jagdalak**, Afghani commander Akbar Khan immediately sent troops against the British-held fortress of Ali Masjid in the Khyber Pass. When a relief force under Colonel Charles Wild was badly defeated and driven back at the entrance to the Pass, the British garrison withdrew and fell back on Jamrud (January 1842).

Ali Masjid ▌ 1878 ▌ 2nd British-Afghan War

Britain responded to Russian influence over Amir Sher Ali Khan of Afghanistan by sending General Sir Samuel Browne into the Khyber Pass towards Kabul. At the eastern entrance to the Pass, Browne shelled and captured the hill fortress of Ali Masjid held by Faiz Muhammad, while further to the south, General Sir Frederick Roberts advanced through **Peiwar Kotal** (21 November 1878).

Aliwal ▌ 1846 ▌ 1st British-Sikh War

A large Sikh army which crossed the Sutlej into British East Punjab was defeated at **Mudki** and **Ferozeshah** before part of the invading force under Ranjur Singh was met at Aliwal, near the Sutlej, by an Anglo-Indian army under General Sir Harry Smith. A brilliantly led action threw the Sikhs back across the river and they were defeated again two weeks later at **Sobraon** (28 January 1846).

Aljubarrota ▌ 1385 ▌ Portuguese-Castilian Wars

João of Aviz claimed the throne of Portugal after victory at **Atoleiros** (April 1384), then faced another invasion by rival claimant Juan I of Castile. With English support, João and his General, Nuno Alvares Pereira, won an overwhelming victory north of Lisbon at Aljubarotta to secure not only Portugal's independence but also England's longest standing diplomatic alliance (14 August 1385).

Alkalawa ▌ 1806 ▌ Rise of Sokoto

Leading a jihad to establish Islam east of the River Niger, Uthman ibn Fudi of the Fulani attacked the Kingdom of Gobir. After a bloody campaign, the Emir of Gobir was defeated at Alkalawa and his kingdom collapsed. Shaykh Uthman then overthrew the other major rulers of Hausaland to create the new Empire of Sokoto, which reached its zenith under his son Muhammudu Bello (September 1806).

Al Khufrah ▌ 1931 ▌ Italo-Senussi War

Determined to crush renewed Bedouin resistance to Italian occupation of Libya, General Rodolfo Graziano began a forced relocation policy, then marched on the last Senussi stronghold at Al Khufrah in southeast Cyrenaica. Sultan Omar al-Mukhtar was defeated and captured, and a reported 20,000 Bedouin were forced to witness his execution, effectively ending the war (12 September 1931).

Alkmaar ▌ 1573 ▌ Netherlands War of Independence

Campaigning to re-establish Spanish supremacy in the Netherlands, Don Fadrique Alvarez of Toledo (son of the Duke of Alva) captured **Haarlem**, then suffered heavy losses assaulting Alkmaar, defended by Jakob Cabeljau. He had to lift his siege when the Dutch opened dykes to flood the area to the east, and Spanish ships were defeated days later on the **Zuyder Zee** (21 August–8 October 1573).

Alkmaar I 1799 I French Revolutionary Wars (2nd Coalition)

British and Russians under Frederick Augustus Duke of York and General Ivan Hermann, trying to take the initiative in the low country, were beaten at **Bergen-aan-Zee** in North Holland. Two weeks later at Egmont-op-Zee, just west of Alkmaar, they defeated French General Guillaume Brune and seized Alkmaar. However, the Allies soon lost at **Castricum** and had to withdraw (2 October 1799).

Allatoona I 1864 I American Civil War (Western Theatre)

Confederate General John B. Hood marched north from the fall of **Atlanta**, Georgia, and detached General Samuel G. French to attack Colonel John E. Tourtellotte at Allatoona, where Union General John M. Corse had arrived with the famous instruction to "Hold the Fort." After about 700 casualties on either side, French withdrew west to support the advance on **Decatur** (5 October 1864).

Alleman's Nek I 1900 I 2nd Anglo-Boer War

As General Sir Redvers Buller invaded the Transvaal, Christiaan Botha tried to block him in the Drakenbergs, west of Volkrust. Attacking at Alleman's Nek, General Henry Hildyard secured the strategic pass with the bayonet, outflanking the powerful position at nearby Laing's Nek, which fell without fighting. The Boers withdrew and the next day Buller occupied Volkrust (11 June 1900).

Allen's Farm I 1862 I American Civil War (Eastern Theatre)
See **Savage's Station**

Allen's Hill I 1863 I 2nd New Zealand War
See **Poutoko**

Allerheim I 1645 I Thirty Years War (Franco-Habsburg War)
See **Nördlingen**

Allia I 390 BC I Gallic Invasion of Italy

While attempting to hold a line northeast of Rome on the Allia River, a tributary on the left bank of the Tiber, Quintus Sulpicius was heavily defeated near Fidenae, between the Tiber and the Anio (modern Aniene), in a wild charge by Gauls under Brennus. The invaders went on to sack and burn Rome (except the Capitol) before withdrawing after payment of a large tribute (18 July 390 BC).

Allis I 633 I Muslim Conquest of Iraq
See **Ullais**

Alltacoileachan I 1594 I Huntly Rebellion
See **Glenlivet**

Ally Ghur I 1803 I 2nd British-Maratha War
See **Aligarh**

Ally Ghur I 1857 I Indian Mutiny
See **Aligarh**

Alma I 1854 I Crimean War

Defending the heights south of the Alma against the Allied advance on **Sevastopol**, Russian Prince Alexander Menshikov was defeated by a large Anglo-French army under General Fitzroy Somerset Lord Raglan and Marshal Armand Saint-Arnaud. Both sides suffered heavy losses, with severe British casualties in an heroic uphill bayonet-charge which carried the day (20 September 1854).

Al Madain I 637 I Muslim Conquest of Iraq
See **Madain**

Almaden I 1810 I Napoleonic Wars (Peninsular Campaign)

Two months after Spain's disastrous defeat at **Ocaña**, King Joseph Napoleon marched south from Madrid to invade Andalusia. Across the Guadiana, in the Sierra Morena Mountains at Almaden, Marshal Claude Victor intercepted and smashed an outnumbered Spanish force under General Tomás de Zerain, before continuing south to meet the main Spanish army at **La Carolina** (15 January 1810).

Almanara I 1082 I Early Christian Reconquest of Spain
See **Almenar**

Almanara I 1710 I War of the Spanish Succession
See **Almenar**

Almanza I 1707 I War of the Spanish Succession
English, Portuguese and Dutch troops under Henri de Massue Earl of Ruvigny, who invaded Spain to support Archduke Charles of Austria as King, were routed at Almanza near Valencia by the Franco-Spanish army of Marshal James Duke of Berwick. The battle reversed the Anglo-Portuguese victory at **Alcántara** a year earlier and substantially extended French control of Spain (25 April 1707).

Almaraz I 1812 I Napoleonic Wars (Peninsular Campaign)
Arthur Wellesley Lord Wellington secured the border fortresses of **Ciudad Rodrigo** and **Badajoz**, then despatched Anglo-Portuguese troops under General Sir Rowland Hill to seize the forts guarding the pontoon bridge on the Tagus at Almaraz. Hill overwhelmed the French garrisons, who fled east in panic.The victor was later created Baron Hill of Almaraz (19 May 1812).

Almazan I 1810 I Napoleonic Wars (Peninsular Campaign)
A large-scale guerrilla action in old Castile saw Spanish insurgent leader Father Geronimo Merino—known as El Cura—attack two battalions of French marine reinforcements on the march at Alamazan, near Soria. The outnumbered marines fought back bravely, but lost 200 men before the guerrillas were eventually driven off (10 July 1810).

Almeida I 1762 I Seven Years War (Europe)
In support of France, Spanish troops under Don Pedro Abarca Count of Aranda invaded Portugal and besieged the key border fortress of Almeida. Before England could send aid to her

ally, the town capitulated after nine days. When British reinforcements did arrive, General John Burgoyne soon dispersed the Spanish invasion at **Valencia d'Alcantara** and **Vila Velha** (August 1762).

Almeida I 1810 I Napoleonic Wars (Peninsular Campaign)
Following the fall of the Portuguese border fortress of **Ciudad Rodrigo**, and battle at the **Coa**, French Marshal André Masséna besieged the nearby fortress of Almeida, garrisoned by Portuguese troops under Governor Colonel William Cox. The garrison surrendered after an enemy shell destroyed the main powder magazine and Masséna advanced to **Bussaco** (26 August 1810).

Almeida I 1811 I Napoleonic Wars (Peninsular Campaign)
During his siege of the key Portuguese fortress of Almeida, on the Portuguese-Spanish border, Arthur Wellesley Lord Wellington marched eight miles south to defeat a relief effort by Marshal André Masséna at **Fuentes d'Onoro**. Meanwhile, the garrison under General Antoine Brennier blew up the fortifications and escaped to rejoin the French lines (4 April–10 May 1811).

Almenar I 1082 I Early Christian Reconquest of Spain
In the confused alliances of the war in Spain, al-Hayib, Muslim ruler of Lerida, supported by King Sancho Ramirez of Aragon and Count Ramon II of Barcelona, besieged the fortress of Almenar, held by al-Hayib's brother, al-Mutamin, ruler of Saragossa. Spanish warrior Rodrigo Diaz de Bivar—El Cid—in service with al-Mutamin, defeated the invaders and captured Count Ramon.

Almenar I 1710 I War of the Spanish Succession
Persisting in the attempt to install Archduke Charles of Austria as King of Spain, an Anglo-Austrian force under General James Stanhope and Guido von Starhemberg heavily defeated the much larger Franco-Spanish army of Philip V under Ventura de Amezaga at Almenar, just

north of Lérida. The Allies also suffered badly and did not pursue as the Spaniards fled to Lérida (27 July 1710).

Almeria ▌ 1309 ▌ Later Christian Reconquest of Spain

In a fresh offensive against newly crowned King Nasr of Granada, a huge siege by land and sea was launched by Aragon against Almeria, in southeast Spain. Although the Christians were able to collapse part of the wall and drive off a Granadan relief force, the final assault failed. Aragon sued for peace and played little further part in the war against Muslim Granada (August–December 1309).

Almeria ▌ 1489 ▌ Final Christian Reconquest of Spain

The strategic fortress port of Almeria in southeastern Spain was a vital Mediterranean outlet for Muslim Granada, held by Al-Zaghal (sometimes Mohammad XIII). While Al-Zaghal fought a war of disputed succession against his nephew Boabdil, the city was captured by Ferdinand V of Castile, leading directly to the siege and capture of the Muslim capital at **Granada** (22 December 1489).

Almodovar del Rio ▌ 1091 ▌ Early Christian Reconquest of Spain

King Alfonso VI of Castile and Leon suffered a terrible and decisive defeat at **Zallaka** in 1086, but eventually made a belated attempt to resist the advance into Spain of the victorious Almoravids from North Africa. General Alvar Fanez was sent to relieve the siege of Seville and was routed at Almodovar del Rio, west of Cordova. The new Muslim invaders then reaffirmed their control of southern Spain.

Almolonga ▌ 1823 ▌ Mexican Civil Wars

After General Agustin de Iturbide overthrew the Spanish Viceroy and was proclaimed Emperor of Mexico, he faced Republicans under General Antonio de Santa Anna. At Almolonga, east of Chilpancingo, Imperial commander Gabriel de Armijo was defeated by Generals Vicente Guerrero (severely wounded) and

Nicolás Bravo. Iturbide soon abdicated and was later shot (23 January 1823).

Almonacid ▌ 1809 ▌ Napoleonic Wars (Peninsular Campaign)

As General Sir Arthur Wellesley began his withdrawal to Portugal after victory at **Talavera de la Reina**, King Joseph Bonaparte of Spain and a French force under General Francois Sébastiani met Spanish General Francisco Venegas at Almonacid, near Toledo. Venegas was heavily defeated and driven back into La Mancha, effectively ending the Talavera campaign (11 August 1809).

Almorah ▌ 1815 ▌ British-Gurkha War

Three weeks after a costly loss at **Katalgarh**, Britain sent reinforcements under Colonel Jasper Nicolls into the Kumaun to join Colonel William Gardner's advance on the fortified city of Almorah, held by Gurkha forces since 1790. Decisive action at nearby Sitoli led to the fall of Almorah, and Gurkha commander Brahma Shah withdrew east of the Kali into modern Nepal (25 April 1815).

Al-Mukhtara ▌ 883 ▌ Zandj Slave Rebellion

Black slaves in southern Iraq rose in revolt led by Ali ibn Muhammad (869), and won great success before a protracted offensive by Regent al-Muwaffaq and his son (later Caliph al-Mu'tadid). The decisive action was their siege and storming of the rebel capital at al-Mukhtara, southeast of Basra. Ali ibn Muhammad was killed and many survivors were executed as the rising was crushed (11 August 883).

Aln ▌ 1093 ▌ Anglo-Scottish Territorial Wars

See **Alnwick**

Alnwick ▌ 1093 ▌ Anglo-Scottish Territorial Wars

Malcolm III of Scotland renewed his quarrel with William II Rufus of England and led his forces across the border. He was surprised and defeated with heavy losses on the Alne near

Alnwick Castle, north of Newcastle, by Robert de Mowbray Earl of Northumberland. Malcolm and his son Edward were killed in the fighting and the invasion collapsed (13 November 1093).

Alnwick ▮ 1174 ▮ Anglo-Norman Rebellion

Supporting rebellious English Barons and Henry II's son "Young King Henry," King William I of Scotland—the Lion—invaded Northumberland, besieging Alnwick Castle, north of Newcastle-upon-Tyne. He was defeated by a Royalist relief army and held captive at Falaise, in Normandy, until he acknowledged Henry's authority over Scotland, and the rebellion ended (13 July 1174).

Alnwick ▮ 1462–1463 ▮ Wars of the Roses

When Alnwick Castle, north of Newcastle-upon-Tyne, declared for Margaret of Anjou, Robert Lord Hungerford and a mainly French garrison were besieged by William Neville Earl of Kent and Anthony Woodville Earl Rivers. But when George Douglas Earl of Angus and Pierre de Brézé intervened from Scotland, the Yorkists withdrew and the garrison escaped (December 1462–6 January 1463).

Alost ▮ 1128 ▮ War of Flemish Succession

In a war of succession over Flanders, William Clito (son of Duke Robert of Normandy and grandson of William the Conqueror) defeated Theodoric of Alsace (Dietrich von Elsass) at **Thielt** to secure the county. Only weeks later, while besieging Alost, northwest of modern Brussels, Clito was fatally wounded in skirmishing and Theodoric became Count of Flanders as Thierry I (27 July 1128).

Alpens ▮ 1873 ▮ 2nd Carlist War

Campaigning in Catalonia, a government column under General José Cabrinety was ambushed at Alpens, 15 miles east of Berga, by Carlists under General Francisco Savalls. Heavy fighting saw Cabrinety killed and virtually his entire column of 800 killed or captured. Savalls was created Count of Alpens, and the following

year he destroyed another opposing force at **Castellfullit** (9 July 1873).

Alporchones ▮ 1452 ▮ Later Christian Reconquest of Spain

King Muhammad IX of Muslim Granada was unwisely raiding into Christian Murcia, in southeast Spain, when Castilian General Alfonso Fajardo responded by taking a large army east from his base at Lorca. Muhammad's army was routed at the nearby village of Alporchones with heavy losses in killed and prisoners. The survivors fled into the Sierra de Almenara (16 March 1452).

Al-Rahmaniyya ▮ 1786 ▮ Mamluk-Ottoman Wars

See **Rahmaniyya**

Alresford ▮ 1644 ▮ British Civil Wars

Despite heavy losses, Parliamentary forces under Sir William Waller and Sir William Balfour defeated the Royalists of Ralph Lord Hopton and Patrick Ruthven Earl of Forth and Brentford at Cheriton near Alresford in central Hampshire. Although Hopton managed to carry off his guns, the Parliamentarians regained most of Hampshire and Wiltshire (29 March 1644).

Alsace ▮ 1944 ▮ World War II (Western Europe)

As Germany's **Ardennes** offensive stalled, further south General Hans von Obsterfelder advanced into Alsace, north of Strasbourg. Fighting in intense cold and mud, American General Alexander Patch halted the initial offensive and also a second attack towards the Hagenau Forest. South of Strasbourg, the Allies then crushed the **Colmar** Pocket (31 December 1944–25 January 1945).

Al-Salihiyya ▮ 1773 ▮ Mamluk Wars

See **Salihiyya**

Alsasua ▮ 1834 ▮ 1st Carlist War

Spanish Liberal commander Vicente Jenaro de Quesada, marching from Vitoria in Navarre to Pamplona with a large convoy, was attacked outside Alsasua by Carlist leader Tomás Zuma-lacárregui. Although saved from disaster by the arrival of Gaspar Jáuregui, Quesada suffered perhaps 200 casualties and 100 prisoners. He was later replaced by José Rodil (2 May 1834).

Alsen I 1864 I 2nd Schleswig-Holstein War

After the fall of the Danish coastal fortress of **Duppel** in April 1864, the defeated garrison withdrew to the nearby island of Alsen. When an armistice expired, Prussian General Herwarth von Bittenfeld stormed the island at night and General Peter Steinmann surrendered the battery and 2,400 prisoners. The action ended the war and Prussia gained the province of Schleswig (29–30 June 1864).

Alta I 1019 I Russian Dynastic Wars

Prince Yaroslav of Novgorod recovered from defeat at the **Bug** in 1018 and determined to recapture Kiev from his stepbrother Sviatopolk. Abandoned by his Polish allies, Sviatopolk turned for aid to the Pecheneg Turks, but at the Alta, southeast of Kiev, his army was defeated and he was killed in the pursuit. Yaroslav regained the throne and became one of the greatest Princes of Kiev (24 July 1019).

Alta I 1068 I Russian Dynastic Wars

Pecheneg horsemen who invaded Russian territory were met at the Alta River, southeast of Kiev, by Kievan Princes Iziaslav, Sviatoslav and Vsevolod (sons of Yaroslav). The Russians were routed. Kiev's citizens then overthrew Iziaslav and elected Vseslav of Polotsk (captured at **Nemiga**). Iziaslav fled to Poland but soon recaptured **Kiev**. The Pecheneg won again 25 years later at **Tripole**.

Altafulla I 1812 I Napoleonic Wars (Peninsular Campaign)

Six months after French capture of the major Spanish port of **Tarragona**, the city was blockaded by Spain. When Spanish troops under General Baron Jaime Eroles attempted to drive off a relief column under General Maurice Mathieu at nearby Altafulla, the much larger French force smashed all resistance and Tarragona was relieved (24 January 1812).

Altaku I 700 BC I Assyrian Wars
See **Eltekeh**

Alt Breisach I 1703 I War of the Spanish Succession
See **Breisach**

Altdorf I 1799 I French Revolutionary Wars (2nd Coalition)
See **Muottothal**

Altenberg I 1813 I Napoleonic Wars (War of Liberation)

Prussian General Johann Thielmann raided French communications along the Saale, where he took Weissenfels and Merseberg before facing General Charles Lefebvre-Desnouettes at Altenberg, near Pirna. Supported by Austrian Count Emmanuel Mensdorf and General Matvei Platov's Cossacks, Thielmann defeated the French, taking over 1,000 prisoners (28 September 1813).

Alten Fjord I 1943 I World War II (War at Sea)

Following previous failed attempts on the battleship *Tirpitz* in northern Norway's Alten Fjord, six British midget submarines attacked, and Lieutenants Basil Place and Donald Cameron exploded charges under the ship. *Tirpitz* was disabled for six months and moved south to Tromsö Fjord, where she was bombed and sunk (12 November 1944) with over 1,200 men lost (22 September 1943).

Altenkirchen (1st) I 1796 I French Revolutionary Wars (1st Coalition)

In a fresh invasion of Germany, French General Jean-Baptiste Jourdan crossed the Rhine, and General Jean-Baptiste Kléber defeated Prince Eugene of Württemberg at Altenkirchen, north of Coblenz, capturing 3,000 prisoners and 12 guns. The Austrians began withdrawing east, but won a victory on the same battlefield in the counter-offensive just three months later (4 June 1796).

Altenkirchen (2nd) I 1796 I French Revolutionary Wars (1st Coalition)

Continuing his victorious counter-offensive against the French invasion of Germany, Archduke Charles Louis of Austria moved northwest from victory at **Aschaffenburg** to defeat General Jean-Baptiste Jourdan just days later near the Rhine at Altenkirchen. The brilliant General Francois-Severin Marceau was fatally wounded and Jourdan withdrew across the Rhine next day (19 September 1796).

Altenkirchen I 1797 I French Revolutionary Wars (1st Coalition)

In a renewed French offensive, General Louis Lazare Hoche crossed the Rhine near Coblenz and sent his left wing under Generals Jean-Étienne Championnet and Nicolas Soult north against Altenkirchen. Austrian Field Marshal Franz Werneck was driven back on the town and, after learning of General Paul Kray's defeat east of **Neuwied**, he withdrew to Herborn (18 April 1797).

Alte Veste I 1632 I Thirty Years War (Swedish War)

Having secured southern Bavaria after victory at **Rain** in April, Gustavus Adolphus of Sweden occupied Nuremberg, across the Regnitz, from Imperial commander Albrecht von Wallenstein camped at Furth. Crossing the river, the Swedes were repulsed near the old castle of Alte Veste and both Wallenstein and Gustavus withdrew from the area two weeks later (24 August–8 September 1632).

Altimarlach I 1680 I Later Scottish Clan Wars

Disputing the Earldom of Caithness, the legal claimant Sir John Campbell of Glenorchy was upheld against the heir George Sinclair of Keiss, who then took land by force. In the reputed last clan battle in Scotland, Campbell defeated Sinclair at Altimarlach, just west of Wick, inflicting heavy casualties. The courts later found for Sinclair and Campbell was instead created Earl Breadalbane.

Altmark Incident I 1940 I World War II (Northern Europe)

With the battleship *Graf Spee* sunk off the **River Plate**, her auxiliary transport *Altmark*, with prisoners from ships sunk, escaped to Jossing Fjord in neutral Norway. Captain Philip Vian in the British destroyer *Cossack* boarded *Altmark* and recovered about 300 men. The bloodless incident boosted Allied morale and helped precipitate the German invasion of **Norway** (16 February 1940).

Altobiscar I 1813 I Napoleonic Wars (Peninsular Campaign)
See **Roncesvalles**

Alto de la Alianza I 1880 I War of the Pacific
See **Tacna**

Alto de Leon I 1936 I Spanish Civil War

After a failed Nationalist rising in **Madrid**, Colonel Ricardo Serrador fought a brutal action for the strategic Alto de Leon Pass to the northwest in the Guadaramma Mountains. The war's first full battle saw Republican Colonel Enrique Castillo shot and General José Riquelme driven back to Madrid. The Nationalists held the pass and also the eastern pass at **Somosierra** (21–22 July 1936).

Alto de Quilo I 1814 I Chilean War of Independence

Spanish General Gavina Gainza took over the Royalist army after defeat at **Roble** (October 1813), and met Patriot commander Bernardo O'Higgins on the Heights of Quilo, outside Concepción, where he was heavily repulsed. An attack next day on Colonel Benjamin Mackenna at Membrillar, near Chillan, was also repulsed when O'Higgins arrived and Gainza had to withdraw (19 March 1814).

Alton I 1643 I British Civil Wars

Sir Ralph Hopton's Royalists advanced into Hampshire and Sussex to take Alton, then marched on Arundel, leaving a garrison under Ludovic Lindsay Earl of Crawford. Marching south from Farnham, Sir William Waller attacked Alton, where Crawford was driven off and Colonel Richard Bolle was heavily defeated, losing over 1,000 prisoners. Waller then turned east to **Arundel** (13 December 1643).

Altona ▮ 1714 ▮ 2nd "Great" Northern War

While campaigning in northern Germany, the Swedish army of General Magnus Stenbock defeated Danish and Saxon troops, but was overwhelmed at Altona, near Hamburg, by the Russian army of Tsar Peter I. Although the Tsar then withdrew to winter quarters, his victory led to Russia securing the whole of Pomerania the following year.

Alto Palacé ▮ 1813 ▮ Colombian War of Independence
See **Palacé**

Altopascio ▮ 1325 ▮ Guelf-Ghibelline Wars

Ten years after the great pro-Imperial Ghibelline victory at **Montecatini**, Castruccio Castracani of Lucca invaded Florentine territory and defeated the pro-Papal Guelf army under Raymond of Cardona at Altopascio, east of Lucca. The victory gave the Ghibellines most of Tuscany, but Castracani's death in 1328 signalled an end to Luccan power (23 September 1325).

Al-uqab ▮ 1212 ▮ Early Christian Reconquest of Spain
See **Las Navas de Tolosa**

Alvsborg ▮ 1563 ▮ Nordic Seven Years War

Frederick II of Denmark resolved to reestablish the Kalmar Union and invaded Erik XIV's Sweden with a largely German mercenary army under Gunther von Schwartzburg, which besieged the port of Alvsborg. Erik Kagge surrendered after 14 days, losing Sweden's access to the North Sea (though Alvsborg was ransomed after the war). Erik later attacked **Halmstad** (4 September 1563).

Alvsborg ▮ 1612 ▮ War of Kalmar

Determined to regain Sweden, Christian IV of Denmark seized Kalmar, then attacked the strategic fortress at Alvsborg, guarding Goteborg. With the fortress walls smashed by artillery and the Swedish fleet nearby scuttled, garrison commander Olof Strale surrendered. After a Danish check at **Vaxholm** the war ended and Alvsborg was again redeemed for a crippling ransom (5–24 May 1612).

Amakusa ▮ 1638 ▮ Japanese Christian Rising

A doomed resistance against the Shogun Iemitsu saw up to 35,000 Japanese Christians, mainly peasants from the Shimbara area on Kyushu Island, besieged in the castle at Amakusa. Following the fall of Amakusa, the Shogun's men massacred the entire garrison and Christianity in Japan was largely suppressed (28 February 1638).

Amalinda ▮ 1818 ▮ Xhosa Civil War

Climaxing the great rivalry between the Xhosa Chief Ngqika and his uncle Ndlambe, their armies met on Amalinda Plain, near Debe Nek, East London, where Ndlambe's army under Nxele secured a bloody and decisive victory over Ngqika's generals Nteyi and Makoyi. British forces later attacked Ndlambe's camp, provoking a massive assault on **Grahamstown** (June 1818).

Amara ▮ 1915 ▮ World War I (Mesopotamia)

New British commander Sir John Nixon was encouraged by success over the Turks at **Shaiba**, and despatched General Charles Townshend up the Euphrates from Basra against Amara. Supported on the river by "Townshend's Regatta," he took the city virtually by coup and Turks arriving from **Ahwaz** were surprised and captured. Townshend then continued upriver to **Kut-al-Amara** (3–4 June 1915).

Amara ▮ 1983 ▮ Iraq-Iran War

Determined to launch a "final" offensive north of Basra after losses near **Musian**, Iranians advanced on a 25-mile front across the plain towards Amara (Al Amarah) with good air and artillery support. But Iraq's defence was stiffened due to their air force performance, and the Iranians were repulsed with severe losses. Another attempt in April at nearby Musian also failed (6–10 February 1983).

Amarante **I** 1809 **I** Napoleonic Wars (Peninsular Campaign)

Following French capture of **Oporto**, Portuguese Brigadier Francisco Silveira held off French General Louis Loison's repeated attempts to cross the vital bridge at Amarante on the Tamega River, northeast of Oporto. Loison eventually stormed the bridge, but Silveira's three-week delaying action helped provide time for British reinforcements to reach Portugal (12 April–2 May 1809).

Amatola Mountain **I** 1846 **I** 7th Cape Frontier War

See **Burnshill**

Amba Alagi **I** 1895 **I** 1st Italo-Ethiopian War

With Ethiopian rebels defeated by the Italians at **Halai** and **Coatit**, Emperor Menelik gathered an army, and his commander Ras Makonnen surprised an advance column under Major Pietro Toselli at Amba Alagi. Toselli was overwhelmed and killed and, following another unit loss at **Makale**, the main Italian army was utterly destroyed further north in March 1896 at **Adowa** (7 December 1895).

Amba Alagi **I** 1941 **I** World War II (Northern Africa)

Italian forces came under massive pressure in Ethiopia, and Amadeo Umberta Duke of Aosta determined on a last stand in mountains at Amba Alagi against British General Sir Alan Cunningham advancing north through **Addis Ababa** and General Sir William Platt driving south from **Keren**. Aosta surrendered after hard fighting, but remaining Italians held out at **Gondar** (4–19 May 1941).

Amba Aradam **I** 1936 **I** 2nd Italo-Ethiopian War

A month after defeating Ras Seyoum in the **Tembien**, Marshal Pietro Badoglio sent 70,000 men south from Makale to encircle Ras Mulugeta at Amba Aradam. Badoglio bombed and shelled the mountain stronghold until the Ethiopians had to withdraw, with perhaps 6,000 killed. Ras Mulugeta was killed in the pursuit as the survivors fled south towards **Maychew** (10–17 February 1936).

Ambato **I** 1821 **I** Ecuadorian War of Independence

See **Huachi**

Ambela **I** 1863 **I** Pathan Rising

On campaign against Pathan tribesmen in western Pakistan, General Sir Neville Chamberlain's 6,000-strong force was blocked north of Peshawar at Ambela Pass. Nearby Crag Picquet changed hands several times before the Pathans were defeated when reinforcements arrived under General Sir John Garvock. Their stronghold at Malka was later destroyed (22 October–17 December 1863).

Amberg **I** 1745 **I** War of the Austrian Succession

In a surprise mid-winter action, Austria invaded Bavaria and defeated her army at Amberg, east of Nuremberg. Elector Maximilian III Joseph had to abandon Munich, effectively knocking Bavaria out of the war, and he then renounced any claim to the Austrian crown. This left France and Prussia alone against the Quadruple Alliance of Austria, Saxony, England and Holland (7 January 1745).

Amberg **I** 1796 **I** French Revolutionary Wars (1st Coalition)

As French General Jean-Baptise Jourdan advanced across the Rhine into Germany, Archduke Charles Louis of Austria counter-attacked from the Danube, joined by General Alexander Wartensleben from the Raab. After French defeats at **Deining** and **Neumarkt**, Jourdan was heavily defeated at

Amberg, east of Nuremberg, and was forced to retire towards the Rhine (24 August 1796).

Amblef I 716 I Rise of Charles Martel
See **Ambleve**

Ambleve I 716 I Rise of Charles Martel
Charles Martel consolidated his position as leader of the reunified Frankish kingdom after the death of his father Pepin, confirming his control of Austrasia by defeating rebel Neustrian nobles at Ambleve, near Liège. This was followed the next year by another major Frankish victory at **Vincy**, and Martel's position was finally secured in 719 by victory at **Soissons**.

Ambon I 1605 I Dutch-Portuguese Colonial Wars
Dutch Admiral Steven van de Haghen sailed to the East Indies, where he defeated a Portuguese fleet off **Goa**, then seized the clove-growing island of Ambon, in the Moluccas, east of modern Indonesia (held by Portuguese since 1521). The island was central to the Dutch spice trade and, after being taken by the British during the Napoleonic War, was restored to Holland in 1814 (23 February 1605).

Ambon I 1796 I French Revolutionary Wars (1st Coalition)
Advancing against Dutch possessions in the East Indies, British Admiral Peter Rainer took the island colony of Ambon without loss. Its vast booty made him a wealthy man, and he then took neighbouring Banda (7–9 March). Ambon was restored to Holland in 1802, then reoccupied in 1810, before being finally restored to Dutch government in 1814 (16–18 February 1796).

Amboor I 1749 I 2nd Carnatic War
See **Ambur**

Amboor I 1767 I 1st British-Mysore War
See **Ambur**

Ambracian Gulf I 435 BC I Corinthian-Corcyrean War
See **Leucimne**

Ambu Alagi I 1895 I 1st Italo-Ethiopian War
See **Amba Alagi**

Ambu Alagi I 1941 I World War II (Northern Africa)
See **Amba Alagi**

Ambuila I 1665 I Portuguese Colonial Wars in West Africa
With political instability threatening the slave trade in Angola, Portuguese under Luis Lopes de Sequeira marched from Luanda against the Kongo army led by Portuguese mercenary Pedro Dias de Cabral. At Ambuila (Mbwila in northern Angola), King Antonio I was defeated and killed, ending the once-mighty African kingdom of Kongo. Angola remained Portuguese until 1975 (29 October 1665).

Ambur I 1749 I 2nd Carnatic War
Using local conflict to gain advantage in southeastern India, French under Colonel Louis d'Auteil and the Marquis Charles de Bussy supported Chanda Sahib as Nawab of Arcot and Muzaffar Jang as Nizam of Hyderabad. At Ambur, southwest of Vellore, the French and their allies defeated and killed Anwar-ud-din, Nawab of Arcot, who held his throne with British support (3 August 1749).

Ambur I 1767 I 1st British-Mysore War
Early in the war, Haidar Ali of Mysore recovered from defeat at **Trinomalee** to besiege Ambur on the Palar River in the Carnatic region of southeastern India, southwest of Vellore. Captain Matthias Calvert of the Madras Army was forced to withdraw to the city's upper fort, but held out until relieved by the main army under Colonel Joseph Smith (10 November–10 December 1767).

Amegial I 1663 I Spanish-Portuguese Wars
See **Ameixial**

Ameixial I 1663 I Spanish-Portuguese Wars
Moving to reconquer Portugal, Philip IV of Spain invaded his lost kingdom and at Ameixial,

near Estremos, General Don John of Austria was defeated by an Anglo-Portuguese force under Sancho de Villa Flor and Marshal Frederick Herman Schomberg. A second invasion two years later was defeated at **Montes Claros**, and Spain eventually recognised Portuguese independence (8 June 1663).

Amelia Springs ∎ 1865 ∎ American Civil War (Eastern Theatre)

Confederate commander Robert E. Lee was retreating west from **Petersburg**, Virginia, when his rearguard under Generals Thomas L. Prosser and Fitzhugh Lee met a Union force led by General George Crook at Amelia Springs, near Amelia Court House. An inconclusive fight continued south through Jetersville as the main Confederate army advanced towards **Sayler's Creek** (5 April 1865).

Amethyst ∎ 1949 ∎ 3rd Chinese Revolutionary Civil War

See **Yangzi Incident**

Amgala ∎ 1976 ∎ Western Sahara Wars

As Spain prepared to leave Western Sahara, divided between Morocco and Mauritania, Algeria sent troops to assist refugees evacuating through the border town of Amgala, where they clashed with Moroccan regulars. The Algerians were routed and withdrew to avoid a major war, but Algeria continued to support local guerrillas, who briefly retook Amgala a few weeks later (29 January 1976).

Amida ∎ 359 ∎ Later Roman-Persian Wars

The Sassanid Shapur II ended the truce signed after **Nisibis** (350) and marched towards the Euphrates, then diverted to attack Amida (modern Diyabakir) on the Tigris. After a 73-day siege, the Roman garrison agreed to surrender, but was massacred. However, heavy Persian losses made Shapur withdraw. A new Roman offensive a few years later ended in disaster after **Ctesiphon** (6 October 359).

Amida ∎ 502-503 ∎ Byzantine-Persian Wars

Renewing Persia's campaign in Roman Mesopotamia, Sassanid ruler Kawad refused payment to withdraw. Supported by Arabs and Ephthalites, the Persian ruler advanced to the Tigris and besieged Amida (modern Diyabakir), before taking it by assault. Amida's fall was followed by three days of slaughter. Kawad later defeated the Romans again at nearby **Apadna** (October 502–11 January 503).

Amida ∎ 973 ∎ Later Byzantine-Muslim Wars

After a successful expedition against Mesopotamia, Byzantine Emperor John Tzimisces left General Mleh to rule the area. But in a campaign the following spring against the city of Amida (modern Diyabakir), Mleh was utterly defeated by the Arab Amir of Mosul. Previous Byzantine gains were lost and the wounded Mleh died in captivity (4 July 973).

Amiens ∎ 1597 ∎ 9th French War of Religion

Spanish troops of Phillip II invaded northern France from the Netherlands to seize **Calais**, then took Amiens (11 March). In the final major battle of the protracted French Wars of Religion, Henry IV of France took his army against Amiens and defeated the Spanish invaders. The war ended the following May with religious freedom granted to Protestants (25 September 1597).

Amiens ∎ 1870 ∎ Franco-Prussian War

Prussian troops under General Edwin von Manteuffel drove towards Paris after the fall of **Metz**, advancing through Rheims and Compiègne against the small Army of the North. French General Jean-Joseph Farre suffered heavy casualties just east of Amiens at Villers-Bretonneaux and was forced to withdraw north through Arras. Amiens was captured next day (27 November 1870).

Amiens ∎ 1918 ∎ World War I (Western Front)

Following success on the **Marne**, Allied commander Ferdinand Foch launched a new offensive east from Amiens against Generals Georg von de Marwitz and Oscar von Hutier. Attacked by Sir Henry Rawlinson, the German army suffered a decisive defeat, called its "Black Day." The Allied offensive finally stalled, but was renewed further north at **Arras** and **Albert** (8–15 August 1918).

Amjhera | 1728 | Later Mughal-Maratha Wars

On campaign in central India against Giridhar Bahadur, the Mughal Subadar of Malwa, the Maratha Peshwa Baji Rao I and his brother Chimnaji Appa invaded Malwa, and Chimnaji met the Mughal army at Amjhera, west of Dhar. Giridhar Bahadur and his cousin Daya Bahadur were defeated and killed, and Chimnaji went on to a failed siege of Ujjain (29 November 1728).

Amman | 1918 | World War I (Middle East)

In support of the great British offensive north from Jerusalem through **Megiddo**, New Zealand General Edward Chaytor took Colonial and Imperial forces east across the Jordan to capture Amman and reinforce the Arab offensive along the Hejaz Railway. Two previous expeditions towards Amman had been halted at **Es Salt**, but this time Chaytor took the city by storm (25 September 1918).

Amoafo | 1874 | 2nd British-Ashanti War

When Ashanti Chief Amonquatia threatened British territory in modern Ghana, he was defeated at **Essaman** and **Abakrampa** in late 1873, and was then pursued inland by African auxiliaries under General Sir Garnet Wolseley. Amonquatia was defeated and killed in a large-scale action at Amoafo, 15 miles south of the Ashanti capital at Kumasi, and Wolseley advanced through **Odasu** (31 January 1874).

Amoneburg | 1762 | Seven Years War (Europe)

The Prussian-British army of Duke Ferdinand of Brunswick defeated the French in Hesse at **Wilhelmstahl** (24 June), then continued cam-paigning against the French east of the Rhine. At Amoneburg, just east of Marburg in Hesse, Ferdinand suffered an unexpected and costly check. However, by the end of the year, the French had been driven back across the Rhine (21 September 1762).

Amorgos | 322 BC | Lamian War

Following the death of Alexander the Great, Athens and other Greek cities rose against the Macedonian Regent Antipater. With the Greek cities crushed at **Crannon**, the naval phase of the revolt ended later the same year when Macedonian Admiral Clitus utterly destroyed the Athenian fleet at Amorgos in the Aegean. As a result, Athens ceased to be a maritime power in the Mediterranean.

Amorha | 1858 | Indian Mutiny

After rebel defeat at **Gorakhpur**, Colonel Francis Rowcroft marched west to Amorha, near Faizabad, where he was blocked by a huge force under Mehndi Husain, Nizam of Sultanpur, at Belwar. An attack on Rowcroft's camp was repulsed with about 400 rebel casualties. Reinforced, he defeated the rebels twice more (17 and 25 March), then withdrew. He later won at **Haraiya** (5 March 1858).

Amorium | 669 | Early Byzantine-Muslim Wars

In a fresh advance against Byzantium following the death of Emperor Constans, Caliph Mu'awiyah sent a large army towards Constantinople under his son Yazid, who occupied Amorium, southwest of Ankara. But Byzantine General Andreas led a bold counter-offensive and the Arabs were defeated and driven out. A renewed Arab offensive a few years later was defeated at sea at **Syllaeum**.

Amorium | 838 | Byzantine-Muslim Wars

Abbasid Caliph al-Mutasim invaded Byzantine Anatolia, where he beat Emperor Theophilus at **Dazimon**, then seized Ancyra and attacked Amorium (modern Hissar) near the Sakarya. After a bitter siege, with heavy losses on both sides, the Muslims seized and sacked the city, massacring large numbers of Christians. Byzantine commander Aetius was captured and later executed (1–13 August 838).

Amorium I 978 I Byzantine Military Rebellions
See **Pancalia**

Amoy I 1841 I 1st Opium War
See **Xiamen**

Ampfing I 1322 I Habsburg Wars of Succession
See **Mühldorf**

Amphipolis I 422 BC I Great Peloponnesian War
In a courageous Spartan counter-offensive against Athens, the Spartan hero Brasidas invaded Macedonia and captured Amphipolis (modern Amfipolis) at the mouth of the Struma River. Athenian General Cleon was defeated in a decisive battle outside the city and, with both Cleon and Brasidas killed in the fighting, Cleon's rival Nicias made a temporary peace with the Spartans.

Amposta I 1813 I Napoleonic Wars (Peninsular Campaign)
As Lord Frederick Bentinck's abortive Anglo-Sicilian expedition to Catalonia fell back before French Marshal Louis Suchet, General Samuel Whittingham and Lorenzo Duke del Parque came under attack crossing the Ebro at Amposta. General Louis-Benoit Robert, Governor of nearby Tortosa, attacked the Allies in an unexpected sortie, causing over 400 Spanish casualties (18 August 1813).

Amritsar I 1634 I Early Mughal-Sikh Wars
Campaigning against Sikh Guru Hargobind near Amritsar, where he was reputedly arranging his daughter's wedding, Mughal commander Mukhlis Khan engaged in heavy fighting with the Guru's troops under Bhai Bhanno. While both sides suffered very heavy losses, Mukhlis Khan and his lieutenant Shamas Khan were

killed, and the Mughals were forced to withdraw.

Amritsar I 1797 I Punjab Campaigns of Shah Zaman
Shah Zaman of Kabul led a renewed invasion of the Punjab after capturing **Rohtas** in 1795 to secure Lahore, then advanced on the Sikh Ranjit Singh near Amritsar. A terrible battle outside the city—claimed to have cost 20,000 Afghans and 15,000 Sikhs—saw Shah Zaman driven back to Lahore. When he returned to Kabul, his local Governor in India was defeated at **Gujrat** (12 January 1797).

Amritsar I 1798 I Punjab Campaigns of Shah Zaman
Despite Afghan defeat at **Amritsar** and **Gujrat**, the following year Shah Zaman of Kabul led a fresh invasion of the Punjab, then sent 10,000 men against Amritsar, where they were defeated outside the city by the Sikh leader Ranjit Singh. Besieged at Lahore, Zaman Shah returned home, where he was overthrown and blinded. Ranjit Singh was later crowned Maharaja (24 November 1798).

Amritsar I 1919 I Punjab Disturbances
More a massacre than a battle, Gurkha troops under General Reginald Dyer opened fire on an unauthorised assembly of rebellious demonstrators, many armed with Kirpans (daggers), in the city of Amritsar, east of Lahore. With 379 people killed and more than 1,200 wounded, the incident was significant in rousing Indian opinion against British rule (13 April 1919).

Amroha I 1305 I Mongol Invasions of India
Recovering from Mongol defeat in 1299 outside Delhi at **Kili**, 50,000 Mongols invaded northern India, led by Ali Beg (a descendant of Genghis Khan) and Tartaq. At Amroha, on the Ganges Plain east of Delhi near Moradabad, they were heavily defeated by the army of Sultan Ala-ad-din under Malik Kafur. Both the defeated Mongol generals were captured and later executed (20 December 1305).

Amstetten I 1805 I Napoleonic Wars (3rd Coalition)

As Prince Mikhail Kutuzov withdrew towards Vienna after the Austrian disaster at **Ulm**, his Russian rearguard under Prince Pyotr Bagration was mauled at Amstetten, southeast of Linz in Lower Austria, by French Marshals Joachim Murat and Nicolas Oudinot. Ten days later, Napoleon Bonaparte entered Vienna, then advanced to his great victory a month later at **Austerlitz** (5 November 1805).

Amur Incident I 1937 I Russo-Japanese Border Wars
See **Kanchatzu**

An I 589 BC I Wars of China's Spring and Autumn Era

With Jin (Chin) defeated at **Bi** (597), Prince Qing (Ch'ing) of Qi (Ch'i) began to expand his power and invaded neighbouring Lu, where he seized the city of Long and repulsed a relief force sent by Wei. Jin then sent a large army under Xi Ke and Shi Xie, who joined with the forces of Wei and Lu to secure a crushing victory at An in Qi. Prince Qing sued for peace and Jin enjoyed renewed authority.

Anagni I 1381 I Neapolitan-Papal War

When the childless Queen Joanna of Naples attempted to name the King of France's brother as her heir, Pope Urban VI in Rome instead supported her cousin Charles of Durazzo. Charles defeated Joanna's fourth husband, Otto of Brunswick, at Anagni, near Naples, then seized the Neapolitan throne as Charles III. Joanna herself was captured and murdered.

Anahuac I 1832 I Texan Wars of Independence

Having arbitrarily arrested about 20 prominent Texans at Anahuac, on Galveston Bay, Mexican Colonel Juan Bradburn faced patriots under John Austin and Francis W. Johnson in a tense armed confrontation. Colonel José de las Piedras from Nacogdoches relieved Bradburn and released the prisoners without bloodshed, but there was a costly action at nearby **Velasco** (May–June 1832).

Anahuac I 1835 I Texan Wars of Independence

When Mexican officials attempted to enforce customs duties at the Texan port of Anahuac, on Galvestan Bay, William B. Travis and about 25 adherents of his hawkish "war party" forced the surrender of the local garrison under Captain Antonio Tenorio. Travis had to apologise for his rash action, but it helped trigger the subsequent Mexican surrender at **San Antonio** (30 June 1835).

Anaiza I 1904 I Saudi-Rashidi Wars
See **Unayzah**

Analatos I 1827 I Greek War of Independence

In a final effort to relieve the **Acropolis**, Greek forces under Yannis Makriyannis landed at night and attempted to advance at Analatos. However, Kitsos Tzavellas ignored orders for a simultaneous attack from Piraeus and the Greeks were routed on open ground by Turkish cavalry, with 700 killed and 240 captured (most later murdered), ending any hope of success (7 May 1827).

Analipsis I 1897 I 1st Greco-Turkish War
See **Nezeros**

Anandpur I 1700 I Mughal-Sikh Wars

In a fresh offensive against the Sikhs of the northern Punjab, Emperor Aurangzeb sent 10,000 men under Painda Khan and Dina Beg, who joined forces with the hill Chiefs led by Raja Ajmer Chand of Bilaspur. In the course of a long action near Anandpur, northeast of Ludhiana, Painda Khan was killed—reputedly in single combat by Guru Gobind Singh—and the Imperial army fled to Ropar.

Anandpur I 1701 I Mughal-Sikh Wars

The hill Rajas of the northern Punjab regrouped after defeat at **Anandpur** the previous year and resumed their campaign against Sikh Guru Gobind Singh, joining forces with Gujar tribesmen to besiege Anandpur, northeast of Ludhiana. Gujar leader Jagatullah was killed on the first day and the Rajas were driven off after a brilliant defence led by the Guru's son Ajit Singh.

Anandpur (1st) | 1704 | Mughal-Sikh Wars

In renewed war against Sikh Guru Gobind Singh after a costly repulse at **Chamkaur** earlier in the year, Mughal Emperor Aurangzeb sent a fresh force into the northern Punjab under General Saiyad Khan, later replaced by Ramjan Khan. Ramjan was mortally wounded in further very heavy fighting around the Sikh stronghold at Anandpur, northeast of Ludhiana, and his force again withdrew.

Anandpur (2nd) | 1704 | Mughal-Sikh Wars

Imperial troops were repulsed in northern Punjab at **Basoli** and **Anandpur**, and Emperor Aurangzeb sent Generals Wazir Khan and Zaberdast Khan to besiege Sikh Guru Gobind Singh in his stronghold at Anandpur, northeast of Ludhiana. Facing starvation, the Guru capitulated in return for safe passage, but the Sikhs were treacherously attacked at the **Sarsa** (20 May–20 December 1704).

Anaquito | 1546 | Spanish Civil War in Peru

With reforms to control the power of the original Conquistadors, Blasco Nuñez Vela, Spanish Viceroy of Peru, provoked a rebellion led by Gonzalo Pizarro, half-brother of the former Conquistador Francisco Pizarro. At Anaquito, near Quito in modern Ecuador, Nuñez Vela was defeated and killed. Pizarro became Governor of Peru but was overthrown at **Xaquixaguana** in 1548 (8 January 1546).

Anas | 79 bc | Sertorian War

Roman General Quintus Sertorius began his rebellion against Rome by seizing much of Further Spain at the **Baetis**, and the following year his lieutenant Lucius Hirtuleius attacked Lucius Domitius Ahenobarbus in Nearer Spain. At the Anas (modern Guadiana) River, Domitius was defeated and killed. Sertorius soon con-

trolled most of Nearer Spain and Hirtuleius won again a year later at **Ilerda**.

Anatoliko | 1823 | Greek War of Independence

Despite losses at **Karpenision** (August 1822), Mustai Pasha joined Omer Vrioni besieging Anatoliko (modern Aitolikón), five miles northwest of Missolonghi. Although virtually unfortified, Anatoliko was bravely defended by about 600 Greeks, with six old cannon under the English seaman William Martin. Mustai eventually abandoned the siege and withdrew (October–11 December 1823).

Anazarbus | 1130 | Crusader-Muslim Wars

Bohemund II of Antioch marched north to regain territory in Cilicia and was ambushed as he advanced towards the Ceyhan River in Armenian Cilicia. Attacked near Anazarbus (modern Anavarza) by the Roupenian Armenian Prince Leo, with support from Danishmendid Turks, Bohemund's small army was overwhelmed. Bohemund was killed and his embalmed head was sent to the Caliph.

Anbar | 634 | Muslim Conquest of Iraq
See **Ain Tamar**

Anbar | 1258 | Mongol Invasion of the Middle East

Two years after destroying the dangerous Assassin sect in central Iran at **Alamut**, Hulegu, Mongol Il-Khan of Iran and grandson of Genghis Khan, sent his army towards **Baghdad**. Marching out to meet the invasion, the Caliph's General Aibeg encountered Mongol General Baichu at Anbar, on the Euphrates. The Muslims were routed and the advance on Baghdad continued (11–12 January 1258).

Anchialus | 708 | Byzantine-Bulgarian Wars

Campaigning against Byzantium, the Bulgar Khan Tervel inflicted a heavy defeat on troops of the Byzantine army in eastern Thrace at Anchialus (modern Pomoriye), on the Black Sea, northeast of Burgas. However, a decade later, he entered into an alliance with the Byzantine Empire to defend Constantinople against a Muslim siege and defeated the Muslims at **Adrianople**.

Anchialus ❙ 763 ❙ Byzantine-Bulgarian Wars

After the expiry of a truce agreed in 759 following defeat at **Marcellae**, the Bulgars under Khan Telets resumed attacks on the Byzantine Empire and Emperor Constantine V marched to the Black Sea to meet the new threat. Northeast of Burgas at Anchialus (modern Pomoriye, Bulgaria), Telets was heavily defeated. He was later overthrown and killed by his own followers (30 June 763).

Anchialus ❙ 917 ❙ Later Byzantine-Bulgarian Wars

The Bulgar Tsar Symeon launched a successful series of attacks on the declining Byzantine Empire, inflicting a heavy loss on the Byzantines in Thrace, then defeated General Leo Phocas at Anchialus (modern Pomoriye), northeast of Burgas. The rulers in Constantinople paid Symeon off with tribute while they turned their attention to the Muslim threat from the east (20 August 917).

Ancona ❙ 1173 ❙ Wars of the Lombard League

In support of Emperor Frederick Barbarossa campaigning in northern Italy, Christian of Buch, Archbishop of Mainz, attacked the east coast city of Ancona, southernmost ally of the Lombard League. When a terrible six-month siege almost starved the population into surrender, a relief army approached from Lombardy and Bishop Christian was forced to withdraw (April–September 1173).

Ancona ❙ 1860 ❙ 2nd Italian War of Independence

A combined naval and land operation saw Piedmontese ships and troops under Admiral Carlo di Persano and General Enrico Cialdini attack Papal forces defending the Adriatic city and harbour of Ancona. Recovering from defeat

to the south at **Castelfidardo**, the Papal garrison under French General Léon Louis Lamoricière held out for a week before surrendering (29 September 1860).

Ancre ❙ 1916–1917 ❙ World War I (Western Front)

Though winter halted most action on the **Somme**, General Hubert Gough in the north launched a large-scale assault along the Ancre. Attacking in heavy mud, he broke through at Beaumont Hamel and took extensive ground. German reinforcements halted his advance but later abandoned their salient and withdrew to the Hindenburg Line (13 November 1916–24 February 1917).

Ancrum Moor ❙ 1545 ❙ Anglo-Scottish Royal Wars

In support of his war against France, Henry VIII attempted to impose his overlordship on the French ally, Scotland, and sent English Borderers and foreign mercenaries under Sir Ralph Evers to attack Edinburgh. However, the English army was defeated at Ancrum Moor, near Jedburgh, by Archibald Douglas Earl of Angus after the Borderers deserted during the battle (17 February 1545).

Ancyra ❙ 235 BC ❙ War of the Brothers

Seleucid King Seleucus II "Callinicus" (Victorious) had secured his throne after his mother Laodice poisoned his father Antiochus II. But he later faced rebellion by his younger brother Antiochus Heirax, aided by their mother and Galatian allies. Seleucus was defeated in battle at Ancyra (Ankara in modern Turkey) and was forced to yield part of his realm in Asia Minor to his brother.

Ancyra ❙ 1402 ❙ Conquests of Tamerlane
See **Angora**

Andalsnes ❙ 1940 ❙ World War II (Northern Europe)

To assist Norway, Anglo-French forces under General Adrian de Carton Wiart landed north of Trondheim at Namsos and south at Andalsnes, where General Bernard Paget progressed along the Gudbrandsdal towards Lillehammer. Badly beaten by Germans advancing from Oslo, the Allies evacuated central Norway, while fighting continued further north at **Narvik** (8 April–3 May 1940).

Anderida I 491 I Anglo-Saxon Conquest of Britain

Following an inconclusive engagement at **Mearcredesburn** in 485, the Saxon warrior Aella and his son Cissa received reinforcements across the English Channel and besieged the former Roman walled fortress of Anderida, near modern Pevensey. Having captured Anderida, Aella reputedly slaughtered the entire British garrison and was established as undisputed King of the South Saxons.

Andernach I 876 I Carolingian Imperial Wars

In the breakup of the Carolingian Empire after the death of Charlemagne in 814, his grandson Charles the Bald attempted to reunify Germany to his French territory. But on the Rhine at Andernach, he was utterly defeated and his West Frankish army was destroyed by his nephew, who then took the throne as Louis II (8 October 876).

Andernach I 939 I German Imperial Wars

The German Emperor Otto I consolidated his leadership of what became the Holy Roman Empire, using French support to fight off rebellious nobles. In his defeat of the rebels at Andernach, near modern Coblenz, his half-brother Tankmar was killed, along with Duke Eberhard of Franconia and Duke Gilbert of Lorraine. Lorraine was subdued and Otto's younger brother Henry had to submit.

Andernach I 1114 I German Civil Wars

Despite a rebellion of nobles being ruthlessly putting down at **Warmstadt**, German Emperor Henry V faced renewed rebellion the following year led by Lothar Duke of Saxony and Adalbert Archbishop of Mainz. Henry was heavily defeated

at Andernach, near Coblenz in Westphalia, and a further defeat at **Welfesholze** four months later led him to abandon Saxony (1 October 1114).

Anderson's Plantation I 1836 I 2nd Seminole Indian War
See **Dunlawton**

Andizhan I 1876 I Russian Conquest of Central Asia

Russian forces captured the Khanate of **Khokand** in 1875, and the self-proclaimed Khan Pulat-bey withdrew to Andizhan, where he was attacked by new Russian commander Mikhail Skobelev. Following heavy shelling the stronghold fell and, after further fighting at nearby Assake, Pulat-bey was captured and executed. In August 1879, Russia attacked the Turkomans at **Geok Tepe** (8 January 1876).

Andkhui I 1205 I Ghor-Khwarezm War

Muhammad of Ghor in Afghanistan invaded the Khwarezmian Empire in modern Turkmenistan and Uzbekistan, where he suffered a heavy defeat at the hands of Shah Ala ud-Din Mohammed of Khwarezm on the Qaisar River at Andkhui. Victory enabled Ala ud-Din to expand his empire south of the Oxus to absorb the Afghan provinces of Ghor and Ghazni. He later also conquered eastern Persia.

Andriba I 1895 I French Conquest of Madagascar

General Jacques Duchesne advanced into Madagascar through **Tsarasoatra** in June, and later met the Hova army of General Rainianjalahy in a strong position at Andriba, blocking the route onto the central plateau. The French stormed the ridge under heavy artillery fire and the Hova fled, abandoning their guns and supplies. Duchesne then led an advance party racing for **Tananarive** (22 August 1895).

Andros I 245 BC I Macedonian-Egyptian Wars

While his troops were successfully invading Seleucid-held Syria and Asia Minor, Ptolemy III of Egypt suffered a sharp setback at sea in the Aegean, where Antigonus II Gonatus of Macedon recovered Corinth, despite Egyptian ships supporting Alexander of Corinth. Antigonus then attacked and defeated the Ptolemaic fleet near Andros, most northerly of the Cyclades, and retook nearby Delos.

Anegawa I 1570 I Japan's Era of the Warring States

Oda Nobunaga established a puppet Shogun in Kyoto, then marched east against his brother-in-law Asai Nagamasa of Omi, who had allied himself with Asakura Yoshikaga of Echizen. With Tokugawa Ieyasu and Toyotomi Hideyoshi, Nobunaga attacked and routed the rebels at the Anegawa, near Odani outside Yokohama Castle. Four months later he was checked at **Ishiyama Honganji** (30 July 1570).

Anfao I 1493 I Wars of the Songhai Empire

In his bid to seize the Songhai Empire of West Africa, rebel General Muhammad Askia defeated and deposed the legitimate ruler Sonni Baru at Anfao, outside the capital of Gao, on the upper Niger, near the southern edge of the Sahara Desert. The victory ended the Sonni Dynasty and enabled Askia to impose "true Islam" on the great sub-Saharan Empire (12 April 1493).

Angamos I 1879 I War of the Pacific

After successfully raiding along the Chilean Coast, including the action in May off **Iquique**, the Peruvian gunship *Huascar* (Rear Admiral Miguel Grau) was hunted down by Chilean ships at Angamos Point, among southern Chile's offshore islands. A hard-fought action saw Grau killed and *Huascar* was forced to surrender, later entering service with the Chilean Navy (8 October 1879).

Angaur I 1944 I World War II (Pacific)

When American forces invaded the **Palaus**, 500 miles east of the Philippines, there was brutal fighting on **Peliliu**, but eight miles south on Angaur, General Paul Mueller managed to clear most of the island in three days, although

last pockets of resistance held out for weeks. Mueller lost 265 killed, while the 1,400-strong Japanese garrison was virtually wiped out (17 September–21 October 1944).

Angers I 1793 I French Revolutionary Wars (Vendée War)

The weakened and demoralised Royalist rebel army of Henri de la Rochejaquelein retreated back to the Loire, where they attempted to recapture the city of Angers. Lacking sufficient men and siege equipment, the Vendéeans were driven off, with more than 2,000 men lost. They then withdrew across the Loire in the face of an approaching relief army and were crushed at **Le Mans** (3–6 December 1793).

Anghiari I 1440 I Venetian-Milanese Wars

Facing a counter-offensive by Venice after **Maderno** in 1839, Milanese commander Niccolo Piccinino led a diversionary attack into Tuscany against the Venetian ally, Florence. Southeast of Florence at Anghiari, near Arezzo, Piccinino was defeated by a Florentine-Papal army under Micheletto Attendolo and Giampaolo Orsini. He was forced to withdraw and peace soon followed (29 June 1440).

Angkor I 1430–1431 I Thai Invasion of Cambodia

On an aggressive campaign of expansion, King Boromoraja II of Ayutthaya (north of modern Bangkok) led an invasion of the Khmer Kingdom (broadly modern Cambodia), where he besieged the capital at Angkor. The city was captured after seven months and, when the Thai were eventually driven out, Angkor was so badly damaged that the Khmer capital was moved to Phnom Penh.

Angolpo I 1592 I Japanese Invasion of Korea

Two days after a victory off southern Korea at **Hansan** Island, Korean Admiral Yi Sun-shin attacked 42 Japanese ships under Kuki Yoshitaka and Kato Yoshiaki off Angolpo, just west of Pusan. A brilliant action saw this second fleet also destroyed. Two months later, Yi was checked attacking **Pusan** itself, but his victories helped force Japan's army to abandon plans to invade China (16 August 1592).

Angora I 1402 I Conquests of Tamerlane

In his last great victory after capturing **Baghdad**, Tamerlane invaded Anatolia and defeated a large Ottoman Turkish army at Angora (modern Ankara). Sultan Bayazid was taken prisoner and died a few months later in captivity. Tamerlane returned to Samarkand after capturing **Smyrna** and receiving tribute from the Mamluk Sultan of Egypt and Syria and the Byzantine Emperor (20 July 1402).

Angostura, Paraguay I 1868 I War of the Triple Alliance

Paraguayan President Francisco Solano López withdrew north after the fall of **Humaitá** in July and ordered Colonel William Thompson, a British officer in his service, to fortify and hold Angostura, on the Paraguay, just south of Asunción. Thompson defended courageously, but after the defeat further east at **Ita Ybate**, he surrendered and Asunción fell a few days later (28–30 December 1868).

Angostura, Venezuela I 1817 I Venezuelan War of Independence

Campaigning on the Orinoco in eastern Venezuela, Revolutionary General Manuel Piar assaulted then besieged the key city of Angostura (later Ciudad Bolívar). A Royalist relief force was heavily defeated at **San Felix** (11 April) and, after Piar was joined by Patriot leader Simón Bolívar, the starving Spanish garrison evacuated and fled west towards **Calabozo** (January–17 July 1817).

Angostura Pass I 1847 I American-Mexican War

See **Buenavista, Mexico**

Anholt I 1811 I Napoleonic Wars (5th Coalition)

Two years after British Captain Aiskew Hollis occupied the strategic island of Anholt, in the Kattegat between Denmark and Sweden (18 May 1809), Governor James Maurice and Captain Robert Torrens faced a courageous Danish landing supported by 12 gunboats. More than 500 Danes surrendered after sharp fighting, with five boats captured and one sunk (27 March 1811).

Anhui Incident I 1941 I Sino-Japanese War

Relations between Nationalist and Communist Chinese were already strained when Chiang Kai-shek ordered Red commander Ye Ting to withdraw north of the Yangzi. Ye Ting was reluctantly complying when Nationalist Gu Zhutong attacked his camp at Maolin, in Anhui, west of Hangzhou. Ye Ting was captured and many of his men died, damaging the anti-Japanese alliance (1–7 January 1941).

Anjar I 1625 I Turkish-Druse War

With Ottoman support, Druse Chieftain Fakhr-al-Din returned from exile to Lebanon and united Druse and Maronite forces to defeat local tribes and Hafiz Ahmed Pasha, Beylerbey of Damascus, in a decisive action at Anjar, in the Bekaa Valley south of Zahlah. He seized much of Syria, Lebanon and Palestine but was finally defeated by Damascus and sent to Constantinople for execution.

Anjou I 1421 I Hundred Years War
See **Baugé**

Ankara I 235 BC I War of the Brothers
See **Ancyra**

Ankara I 1402 I Conquests of Tamerlane
See **Angora**

Anking I 1853 I Taiping Rebellion
See **Anqing**

Anking I 1860–1861 I Taiping Rebellion
See **Anqing**

Ankol I 1592 I Japanese Invasion of Korea
See **Angolpo**

An Loc | 1972 | Vietnam War

During the **Eastertide Offensive**, North Vietnamese and Viet Cong forces in the south crossed from Cambodia and overran Loc Ninh before driving on An Loc, just 65 miles north of Saigon. They seized part of An Loc, but after heavy attack by American bombers and desperate defence by South Vietnamese reinforcements, the invaders were finally forced to withdraw (13 April–11 July 1972).

Annagudi | 1782 | 2nd British-Mysore War

See **Kumbakonam**

Annam | 1285 | Mongol Wars of Kubilai Khan

See **Siming**

Annan | 1332 | Anglo-Scottish War of Succession

Four months after seizing Scotland's throne with victory at **Dupplin**, English-backed Edward Baliol faced united opposition under Sir Archibald Douglas (Regent for young David II), Robert the Steward (later Robert II) and John Randolph Earl of Moray. Surprised at Annan, Dumfriesshire, Baliol had to flee half-dressed. He regrouped six months later to besiege **Berwick** (16 December 1332).

Annapolis Royal | 1710 | Queen Anne's War

See **Port Royal, Nova Scotia**

Annapolis Royal | 1744 | King George's War

Captain Joseph Dupont Duvivier led a French attempt to retake Acadia (modern Nova Scotia)—lost in the War of the Spanish Succession—where he took Canso, then besieged the port of Annapolis Royal, held by a small British garrison under Major Paul Mascarene. Denied promised support from Louisbourg, Duvivier had to withdraw. The next year **Louisbourg** itself fell (May–June 1744).

Anqing | 1853 | Taiping Rebellion

Taiping commander Shi Dakai advanced down the Yangzi through **Wuxue** and quickly took Jiujiang, then attacked Anqing, bravely defended by Governor Jiang Wenqing when Imperial Commissioner Lu Jianying fled. The city fell by storm after Jiang was killed in a doomed sortie and the rebels captured massive supplies before continuing northeast to **Nanjing** (24 February 1853).

Anqing | 1860–1861 | Taiping Rebellion

On a massive offensive in Anhui Province, the great Imperial commander Zeng Guofan attempted to recover Anqing, where he eventually faced Li Xiucheng, driven back from **Shanghai**. After a complex campaign, with heavy losses on both sides, the Taiping garrison was inexplicably permitted to withdraw and the civilian population was massacred (June 1860–4 September 1861).

Anshan | 1900 | Russo-Chinese War

See **Shaho**

Ansi-song | 645 | Sino-Korean Wars

A renewed Chinese advance on the North Korean kingdom of Koguryo after disaster at **Salsu** saw Tang Emperor Taizong attack the stronghold of Ansi-song, in modern Liaodong, China. A Korean counter-offensive was heavily repulsed, but Ansi held out and, after terrible Tang losses, Taizong had to withdraw. Koguryo fell 23 years later with the loss of **Pyongyang** (18 July–13 October 645).

Anson's Bay | 1841 | 1st Opium War

See **Bogue Forts**

Antelope Hills | 1858 | Comanche Indian Wars

Crossing the Red River into Indian Territory, 100 Texas Rangers led by John "Rip" Ford and 100 Indian allies attacked 300 Comanche under Iron Jacket near Antelope Hills, on the Canadian River, in the west of modern Oklahoma. Iron Jacket was shot down, and in the battle which followed, 76 Comanche were killed, with 18 women and children and 300 horses captured (12 May 1858).

Antietam ▮ 1862 ▮ American Civil War (Eastern Theatre)

Confederate commander Robert E. Lee crossed the Potomac into Maryland and was driven off **South Mountain**. Two days later, he met General George B. McClellan's Union army on Antietam Creek near Sharpsburg, where both sides suffered about 12,000 casualties. Lee withdrew into Virginia after one of the war's bloodiest actions, and McClellan claimed strategic victory (16–18 September 1862).

Antioch, Anatolia ▮ 1211 ▮ 1st Latin-Byzantine Imperial War

With the Byzantine Theodore Lascaris established in Nicaea, the Latin Crusader rulers in Constantinople sent troops to assist former Emperor Alexius III and the Seljuq Sultan Kaykhusraw in southwest Anatolia. The Sultan was killed in a decisive battle near Antioch (modern Yalvac), and Alexius died in captivity. However, Theodore was soon defeated on the **Rhyndacus** and made peace.

Antioch, Syria ▮ 244 BC ▮ 3rd Syrian War

Ptolemy III Euergetes of Egypt invaded Syria in 245 BC to avenge the murder in a dynastic intrigue of his sister Berenice (widow of the Seleucid King Antiochus II) and, on the Orontes at Antioch (Antakya in modern southern Turkey), he routed Seleucid King Seleucus II "Callinicus." Victory gave Ptolemy control of the Levant and he then marched as far as Babylon, which he briefly occupied.

Antioch, Syria ▮ 218 ▮ Roman Military Civil Wars

See **Immae**

Antioch, Syria ▮ 271 ▮ Roman-Palmyrean War

See **Immae**

Antioch, Syria ▮ 540 ▮ Byzantine-Persian Wars

In breach of the "Endless" Peace signed with Justinian in 533, Chosroes I campaigned up the Euphrates, where he captured Sura and Beroea, and besieged Antioch. When the city refused to surrender, it was taken by storm, then sacked and burned. Antioch's population and much of its movable wealth was relocated to build a new city near Ctesiphon. Chosroes returned home via **Dara** (June 540).

Antioch, Syria ▮ 611 ▮ Byzantine-Persian Wars

Having already conquered much of Syria and Mesopotamia, the Sassanid King Chosroes II used a period of Byzantine political turmoil to renew his efforts to expand the Persian Empire westward, capturing the key Byzantine city of Antioch, in Syria. While Emperor Heraclius failed to retake Antioch in 622, it was evacuated by the Persians in 628, following the overthrow of Chosroes (May 611).

Antioch, Syria ▮ 969 ▮ Later Byzantine-Muslim Wars

Emperor Nicephorus II Phocas drove the Arabs out of central Asia Minor by 965 at **Adana** and **Tarsus**, then invaded Syria, where the fortress city of Antioch fell to General Michael Burtzes after more than three centuries of Arab rule. **Aleppo** was then also captured by the Byzantines, forcing Caliph al-Muti to sue for peace, although Nicephorus was assassinated before Aleppo fell (28 October 969).

Antioch, Syria ▮ 1085 ▮ Byzantine-Turkish Wars

In the years following Christian disaster at **Manzikert** in 1071, Turkish Sultan Malik Shah seized Byzantine Anatolia, which was lost to his rival, Sulaiman ibn Kutalmish, who became Seljuk ruler of Rum. During a large-scale offensive, Sulaiman attacked and seized Antioch, the last Byzantine fortress in the east. A year later he was killed at **Aleppo** by Malik Shah's brother Tutush (June 1085).

Antioch, Syria ▮ 1097 ▮ 1st Crusade

During the long siege of Antioch, the Emir Yaghi-Siyan waited until many of the Crusaders departed on a foraging expedition and sortied against the remaining siege army under Raymond of Toulouse. The Turks inflicted heavy casualties in a brilliant night foray, before being driven back into the city. The Christian forage party was attacked two days later at **Albara** (29 December 1097).

Antioch, Syria I 1097–1098 I 1st Crusade

When Crusader forces reached Syria they besieged the fortified city of Antioch, defended by Turkish Emir Yaghi-Siyan. Led by Bohemund of Taranto, they repulsed costly sorties but lacked heavy siege equipment until reinforcements arrived by sea. The city fell by treachery just as a massive relief army appeared. Yaghi-Siyan was killed in the final bloody assault (21 October 1097–3 June 1098).

Antioch, Syria I 1119 I Crusader-Muslim Wars

Artuqid Turkish ruler Ilghazi of Mardin took a huge army against the Crusader Principality of Antioch, and Roger of Antioch marched out to meet the invaders at nearby Balat. On the so-called Field of Blood, Roger was defeated and killed. However, rather than taking the opportunity to seize Antioch itself, Ilghazi returned to Aleppo with his prisoners and reputedly tortured them to death (28 June 1119).

Antioch, Syria I 1268 I Later Crusader-Muslim Wars

As the Crusader states came to an end, the Mamluk Sultan Baibars exerted inexorable pressure against the remaining Christian outposts. Raising a massive army, he captured the fortress of Antioch by storm, then massacred the garrison and demolished its defences. This disaster left only **Acre** and **Tripoli** as Crusader cities and led directly to the Eighth Crusade (18 May 1268).

Antioch-in-Pisidia I 1211 I 1st Latin-Byzantine Imperial War
See **Antioch, Anatolia**

Antium I 1378 I War of Chioggia

In the renewed trade war between Genoa and Venice, a Genoese squadron found itself engaged by a much larger Venetian force south of Rome off Antium (modern Anzio). Venetian Admiral Vittoria Pisani sank six Genoese galleys and captured their commander Luigi Fieschi in a major victory. Genoa never again rivalled Venice (30 May 1378).

Antoine I 1652 I War of the 2nd Fronde
See **St Antoine**

Antrain I 1793 I French Revolutionary Wars (Vendée War)
See **Dol-de-Bretagne**

Antrim I 1798 I Irish Rebellion

At the start of the rebellion in Kildare, about 6,000 rebels under wealthy cotton manufacturer Henry Joy McCracken assembled at Donegore Hill and marched on Antrim, held by Clotworthy Skeffington Earl of Massareene. A premature charge by dragoons allowed rebels into the town, but they were then smashed by reinforcements from Belfast and driven off with heavy losses (7 June 1798).

Antwerp I 1576 I Netherlands War of Independence

During the bloody campaign to re-establish Spanish supremacy in the Netherlands, troops under Sancho d'Avila defeated Walloon defenders and captured Antwerp, in modern Belgium. Perhaps 8,000 civilians were massacred over three days in the notorious sack which followed, subsequently known as "The Spanish Terror" (4 November 1576).

Antwerp I 1584–1585 I Netherlands War of Independence

In the outstanding siege of the Spanish Netherlands offensive, Viceroy Alexander Farnese, later Duke of Parma, attacked Antwerp, and engineer Sebastian Baroccio constructed a fortified bridge to block the Scheldt and cut off the Dutch fleet. The bridge was rebuilt when partially destroyed by an explosive-filled fireship (5 April 1585) and Antwerp finally surrendered (June 1584–17 August 1585).

Antwerp I 1830 I Belgian War of Independence

Following a Belgian Declaration of Independence from Dutch rule in early October 1830, Dutch troops under General David Hendryk Chassé invaded Belgium and bombarded Antwerp. The city resisted, but Chassé seized the Citadel of Antwerp and held it for two years before it was eventually taken by storm (27 October 1830).

Antwerp I 1832 I Belgian War of Independence

After international recognition of Belgian independence from Dutch rule in 1830, a Dutch invasion of Belgium was repulsed by the French troops under Marshal Maurice-Étienne Gérard. However, Dutch General David Chassé held out in the Citadel of Antwerp for over two years, surrendering only after two-month assault by Gérard with British naval support (23 December 1832).

Antwerp I 1914 I World War I (Western Front)

King Albert and 150,000 Belgians fell back before the German onslaught through **Liège** and **Brussels**, withdrawing to the port of Antwerp. Under attack by General Hans von Beseler with massive siege guns, Belgian General Victor Deguise eventually had to surrender, but Albert and most of his army escaped to support the Allies at **Ypres** and the **Yser** (28 September–10 October 1914).

Antwerp I 1944 I World War II (Western Europe)

As Allied forces broke out from **Normandy**, British commander Sir Bernard Montgomery seized Amiens (31 August), then raced for Antwerp. While the Belgian river port was surprised and taken undamaged, Montgomery's neglect of opposing forces downstream let a German army escape through **Breskens** and delayed capture of the vital **Scheldt Estuary** (3 September 1944).

Anual I 1921 I Spanish-Rif War

One of Spain's most famous military disasters occurred when General Manuel Fernández Silvestre in Morocco allowed his army of 20,000 to be surrounded at Anual, southwest of Melilla, by Rif rebel Abd el Krim. A disgraceful panic saw up to 12,000 Spanish troops killed, with thousands more captured, and Silvestre later committed suicide. Spain fought back in 1923 at **Tizzi Azza** (21 July 1921).

Anzac I 1915 I World War I (Gallipoli)

Opening the Gallipoli campaign, British forces landed at **Helles**, while further north, General William Birdwood's Australian and New Zealand Army Corps landed near Gaba Tepe, on a beach which became Anzac Cove. Later reinforced by British troops, the Anzacs suffered heavy losses in offensives such as **Lone Pine** and **Chunuk Bair**, and were evacuated 18–20 December (25 April 1915).

Anzio I 1944 I World War II (Southern Europe)

The Anglo-American landing on the Italian coast at Anzio, south of Rome, was intended to outflank the German **Gustav Line**, but undue caution by General John P. Lucas permitted costly counter-attacks by General Eberhard von Mackensen. The beachhead became besieged and suffered unnecessarily heavy casualties before the final breakout towards **Rome** (22 January–24 May 1944).

Aong I 1857 I Indian Mutiny

General Sir Henry Havelock's British and Sikh troops advanced northeast from Allahabad to recapture Cawnpore and won at **Fatehpur**, then met a larger rebel force entrenched at the village of Aong. The Sepoys suffered a decisive defeat, abandoning substantial stores, and were beaten again the same day at **Pandu Nadi**. Havelock defeated Nana Sahib next day at **Cawnpore** (15 July 1857).

Aornos I 327 BC I Conquests of Alexander the Great

Having recently secured the **Sogdian Rock**, Alexander the Great's advance into India was blocked by the powerful fortress of Aornos (Pir-Sar) on a natural ridge near the Buner River, west of the upper Indus, in modern Pakistan. Seizing a nearby hill to threaten the use of heavy siege weapons against the stronghold, Alexander forced the defenders to retreat, when many were captured and killed.

Aous I 198 BC I 2nd Macedonian War
Rome declared war on King Philip V of Macedon and sent legions under Titus Quintius Flaminius to support her allies in northwestern Greece. Near Antigoneia, on the Aous River (Vijose in modern Albania), Flaminius attacked Philip in a strongly defended position and drove him from the field. Flaminius then advanced into Thessaly for an even greater victory a year later at **Cynoscephalae**.

Aozou I 1987 I Libyan-Chad War
On the offensive to recover northern Chad, forces loyal to President Hissen Habré advanced into the mineral-rich Aozou Strip, occupied by Libya since 1973. Aozou town was taken with over 600 Libyans killed, then lost in the face of massive Libyan air-strikes. Libya abandoned Aozou after defeat at **Maaten-as-Sarra**. In 1994 the disputed border area was awarded to Chad (8–27 August 1987).

Apache Pass I 1862 I Apache Indian Wars
In the one pitched battle of the war, Chiricahua Apache led by Mangas Coloradas defended Apache Pass, east of Tucson, Arizona, against a large force of Californian volunteers raised by General James Carleton. Mangas was wounded and decisively defeated by howitzer fire and was later captured. His son-in-law, Cochise, continued the war and in 1869 fought at **Chiricahua Pass** (15 July 1862).

Apacheta I 1814 I Peruvian War of Independence
Leading a rising in Cuzco, the Indian Chief Mateo Pumacahua and Vicente Angulo marched towards Arequipa and were intercepted to the northeast at Apacheta by Spanish Royalists. Brigadier Francisco Picoaga y Arbiza and Intendente José Moscoso were defeated and cap-

tured. Pumacahua held Arequipa until after the defeat at **Chacaltaya**, and was later crushed at **Umachiri** (9 November 1814).

Apadna I 503 I Byzantine-Persian Wars
Emperor Anastasius determined to recover Mesopotamia from Shah Kawad of Sassanid Persia and sent an army to besiege **Amida** (modern Diyabakir in eastern Turkey). The Byzantine army was driven off and, at the nearby fortress of Apadna, General Patricius and the Emperor's nephew Hypatius were utterly defeated by a large Persian army. Kawad then moved against **Edessa** (August 503).

Apaneca I 1876 I Central American National Wars
Two years after securing a friendly government in Honduras at **Comayagua**, President Justo Ruffino Barrios of Guatemala turned and invaded former ally El Salvador. Outside Apaneca, near Ahuachapán, he routed Salvadoran General Francisco Menéndez. Further east, another Guatemalan column won at **Pasequina**, and Barrios appointed his friend Rafael Zaldivar as President (15 April 1876).

Ap Bac I 1963 I Vietnam War
South Vietnamese Colonel Biu Dinh Dam was determined to bring the Viet Cong to battle and, with US advisor Colonel John Paul Vann, he attacked near Ap Bac, in the Mekong Delta southwest of Saigon. Despite huge numerical superiority, the incompetent Colonel Dam was routed, with over 60 killed. The Viet Cong then slipped away, allowing the Allies to naively claim victory (1–2 January 1963).

Ap Bia I 1969 I Vietnam War
See **Dong Ap Bia**

Ap Cha Do I 1966 I Vietnam War
See **Dau Tieng**

Ap Chinh An I 1966 I Vietnam War
With North Vietnamese regulars threatening a key highway north of Hue, American and South Vietnamese marines landed north and south of

their opponents (Operation Jay). Counter-attacking near the village of Ap Chinh An, the Communists inflicted costly losses, but they were finally defeated with the aid of naval guns and aerial attack and withdrew, with about 80 killed (25 June–2 July 1966).

Apeleg I 1883 I War of the Desert

Renewing the campaign in the deserts of Patagonia, Argentine General Conrado Villegas took a large force against rebellious Mapuche or Araucanos Indians. Decisive action near the Chilean border at Apeleg saw Colonel Nicolás Palacios defeat over 1,000 Indians, who were then crushed and dispersed. Chubut Province was secured and handed over for white settlement (22 February 1883).

Apennines I 1944 I World War II (Southern Europe)

While British forces in northeast Italy attacked at **Rimini**, American General Mark Clark's Fifth Army attacked General Joachim Lemelsen at the **Gothic Line** in the Apennines. The Il Giogio and Funta Passes were taken, but the Americans lost heavily taking Monte Battaglia (27 September–1 October), and the offensive stalled south of **Bologna** (10 September–13 October 1944).

Aphek I 1050 BC I Philistine-Israel Wars
See **Eben-ezer**

Apollonia I 220 BC I Syrian Civil War

Governor Molon of Media rose against Syrian Emperor Antiochus III, launching a powerful offensive in Mesopotamia, seizing Seleucia itself. Personally leading a large army across the Tigris, Antiochus brought Molon to battle at Apollonia and crushed him. Molon and his followers were killed and the victory secured Syrian authority, allowing Antiochus to turn against the Parthians.

Apple River Fort I 1832 I Black Hawk Indian War
See **Kellogg's Grove**

Appomattox Court House I 1865 I American Civil War (Eastern Theatre)

Withdrawing west from **Petersburg**, Virginia, Confederate commander Robert E. Lee was surrounded at Appomattox Court House by General Ulysses S. Grant. After a failed breakout attempt by Generals John B. Gordon and Fitzhugh Lee, and with his supply train destroyed the previous day at **Appomattox Station**, Lee surrendered his army and the war was virtually over (8–9 April 1865).

Appomattox Station I 1865 I American Civil War (Eastern Theatre)

As defeated Confederates withdrew west from **Petersburg**, Virginia, Union commander Philip Sheridan sent General George A. Custer to seize a Confederate supply train and 25 guns at Appomattox Station. Confederate troops under General Lindsay Walker were driven off and Lee surrendered the following day, three miles northeast at **Appomattox Court House** (8 April 1865).

Aprus I 1305 I Wars of the Catalan Company

Byzantine Emperor Michael IX used Catalan troops to assist against the Turks in Asia Minor, then found himself at war with his former mercenaries. At Aprus, in the ancient province of Caenice near the Black Sea, the Imperial army was heavily defeated. The Catalans went on to ravage much of Thrace before they invaded Crusader-held Greece and won at **Cephisus** in 1311 to seize control of Athens.

Aptaat-Kalessi I 251 I 1st Gothic War
See **Abrittus**

Apulia I 1155 I 1st Byzantine-Sicilian War

When Byzantine Emperor Manuel I invaded southern Italy with Papal support against William I—the Bad—of Sicily, his cousin Michael Palaeologus defeated William in the southern Adriatic Sea off Apulia. While the naval victory permitted the Byzantines to gain a foothold on the Italian mainland, they were heavily defeated on land the following year at **Brindisi** and had to withdraw.

Aqaba I 1917 I World War I (Middle East)

Having secured the Red Sea port of **Wejh**, Arab leader Prince Feisal (supported by British Major T. E. Lawrence) marched north to attack the small port of Aqaba. In a much-exaggerated action, the Arabs attacked from the landward side and routed the small Turkish garrison, providing a base for improved Arab support to the British in Egypt and Palestine (6 July 1917).

Aqraba I 633 I Muslim Civil Wars
See **Akraba**

Aquae Saravenae I 979 I Byzantine Military Rebellions

In support of Emperor Basil II against the usurper Bardas Sclerus, the Byzantine warrior Bardas Phocas was defeated at **Pancalia**. The next year, heavily reinforced by Armenians from Tayk, he met and decisively defeated the usurper at Aquae Saravenae, near the Halys, outside modern Yozgat, Turkey. Phocas himself later usurped the throne and was beaten in 989 at **Abydos** (24 March 979).

Aquae Sextiae I 102 BC I Rome's Gallic Wars

Three years after Roman disaster in Gaul at **Arausio**, the Senate sent Consul Gaius Marius against Germanic invaders, and near Aquae Sextiae (modern Aix-en-Provence), his Legions confronted the allied Teutones and Cimbri. Reversing previous victory, the Teutones were totally destroyed and King Teutobodus was captured. Marius soon returned to Italy to destroy the Cimbri at **Vercellae**.

Aqua Portora I 742 I Muslim Civil Wars

During civil war between rival Muslim forces in Spain, Baldj ibn Bishr (invited from Syria to combat Berber revolt) executed Governor Abd-al-Malik ibn Qatan of al-Andalus, then defeated his sons Ummaya and Katan, at Aqua Portora, just north of Cordova. Though Baldj was killed, the victory secured government for the so-called Syrian faction under Thalaba ibn Salama (6 August 742).

Aquia Creek I 1861 I American Civil War (Eastern Theatre)

In support of the Union blockade of Chesapeake Bay following action at **Sewell's Point**, Union commander James H. Ward led three gunboats against the Confederate battery at Aquia Creek, on the Potomac near Stafford, held by Colonel Daniel Ruggles. While the Union bombardment produced little result, it was followed ten days later by a land attack at **Big Bethel** (31 May–1 June 1861).

Aquidaban I 1870 I War of the Triple Alliance
See **Cerro Corá**

Aquila I 1424 I Condottieri Wars

The Condottiere Muzio Attendolo Sforza campaigned on behalf of Naples against Aragon, attacking his rival Braccio da Montone at Aquila, in Abruzzi. After Sforza was drowned crossing the Pescara River (4 January), his son Francesco besieged Aquila, where Montone was defeated and killed. Twenty years later, Francesco Sforza seized **Milan** and established a dynasty (2 June 1424).

Aquileia I 166 I German Invasion of Italy

Germanic tribes crossing the Alps into northeast Italy besieged the city of Aquileia, at the head of the Adriatic. Marching south into Italy they were repulsed by Roman Emperor Marcus Aurelius, who drove them back to Aquileia, where he defeated the invaders and raised the siege. However, Rome's weak military position meant the survivors were allowed to settle within the empire.

Aquileia I 240 I Roman Military Civil Wars

Following the murder of Roman Emperor Severus Alexander in 235, the Thracian Gaius Julius Maximinus was proclaimed Emperor by his soldiers. With support from the Rhine armies he marched on Rome, but at Aquileia, at the head of the Adriatic, the claimant's army was defeated by the Senate with heavy losses. His troops then mutinied and murdered Maximinus and his son.

Aquileia ∎ 340 ∎ Roman Wars of Succession

Amid rivalry for Imperial control following the death of Constantine the Great, Constantine II was slain in battle at Aquileia, northwest of Trieste, at the head of the Adriatic, by his brother and co-Emperor Constans, who became Emperor in the West as Constans I. Following the death of Constans in 350, the third brother, Constantius II, became the sole Emperor.

Aquileia ∎ 388 ∎ Later Roman Military Civil Wars

Theodosius, Emperor in the East, marched against Magnus Clemens Maximus, who had advanced from Britain to usurp control in Italy, routing his forces in the Balkans at **Siscia** and Poetovio. He then drove Maximus into a siege at Aquileia, near the Adriatic, where his supporters murdered him in order to surrender. Theodosius restored Valentinian II as Emperor in the West (28 July 388).

Aquileia ∎ 394 ∎ Later Roman Military Civil Wars

See **Frigidus**

Aquileia ∎ 452 ∎ Hun Invasion of the Roman Empire

The year following his defeat at **Chalons** by a joint Roman-Goth army, Attila the Hun invaded Italy. Attacking Aquileia, northwest of modern Trieste, he overcame the garrison before sacking and burning the city. The residents escaped to islands off the coast where they eventually founded the city of Venice. Attila then secured much of upper Italy, but died the following year.

Aquilonia ∎ 293 BC ∎ 3rd Samnite War

Despite a costly defeat at **Sentinum** in 295 BC and their allies suing for peace, the Samnites of

the central Apennines fought on against Rome until they met Consuls Lucius Papirius and Spurius Carvilius Maximus at Aquilonia, an uncertain site near Bovianum. The Romans secured a decisive victory, storming nearby Cominium, and the Samnites eventually acknowledged the authority of Rome.

Arabah, Wadi al- ∎ 634 ∎ Muslim Conquest of Syria

See **Wadi al-Arabah**

Arachova ∎ 1826 ∎ Greek War of Independence

Georgios Karaiskakis failed at **Chaidari** to relieve the besieged **Acropolis** and withdrew to the mountains to attack Ottoman supply lines. At a pass near Arachova, west of Levadia, he cut off 2,000 Turks under Mustapaha Bey, and bloody hand-to-hand fighting in a snowstorm saw only 300 Turks escape alive. Karaiskakis soon attacked again to the southwest at **Distomo** (5 December 1826).

Aragua de Barcelona ∎ 1814 ∎ Venezuelan War of Independence

Revolutionary leader Simón Bolívar followed his defeat at **La Puerta** in June by retreating to Aragua on the northern Venezuelan coast, where he and José Bermudez led a final stand against Spanish General Tomás Morales. With most of his remaining force destroyed in battle, Bolívar fled into exile with a massive treasure in silver, and the revolution temporarily collapsed (18 August 1814).

Arakan ∎ 1942–1943 ∎ World War II (Burma-India)

The first British counter-attack in Burma saw General Wilfred Lloyd advance into the Arakan, where he forced the Japanese to withdraw from the outpost line Maungdaw-Buthidaung. New commander Takashi Koga then stopped the advance at Donbaik-Rathedaung, and hooked behind the outnumbered British to cripple them and drive them back into India (23 October 1942–12 May 1943).

Arakan | 1943–1944 | World War II (Burma-India)

Despite previous British losses in the Arakan, General Alexander Christison advanced down the Mayu Peninsula against General Tadishi Hanaya. Very heavy fighting saw General Harold Briggs seize Maungdaw (9 January) before Hanaya was reinforced and counter-attacked at **Admin Box**. Hanaya was finally driven off and British forces went north to **Imphal** (December 1943–April 1944).

Arakan | 1944–1945 | World War II (Burma-India)

On a final offensive in southwestern Burma, General Alexander Christison launched a fresh advance down the Arakan coast towards strategic Akyab Island. Supported by amphibious landings on the mainland and on nearby Ramree and Chedube Islands, Christison slowly forced General Shozo Sakurai to withdraw. Rangoon itself then fell without resistance (12 December 1944–April 1945).

Araquil | 1813 | Napoleonic Wars (Peninsular Campaign)

See **Irurzun**

Arar | 58 BC | Rome's Later Gallic Wars

Defending Gaul against a massive Helvetian migration from the area approximating modern Switzerland, Julius Caesar surprised the invaders in a night attack as they attempted to cross the Arar (modern Saone) River. Despite heavy casualties, the Helvetians recovered for a major confrontation at **Bibracte** a month later, where they were decisively defeated (June 58 BC).

Aras | 1775 | 1st British-Maratha War

See **Adas (2nd)**

Aratoca | 1841 | Colombian War of Supreme Commanders

With rebel forces under Colonel Manuel Gonzáles repulsed outside Bogotá at **Culebrera**, General Tomás Cipriano de Mosquera for the government marched north and, supported by Colonel Joaquín Barriga, met the rebels at Ara-

toca, south of Floridablanca. A major action saw González decisively defeated and Mosquera soon won again at **Tescua** (9 January 1841).

Araure | 1813 | Venezuelan War of Independence

Patriot leader Simón Bolívar recovered from defeat near **Barquisimeto** in western Venezuela to check a Royalist army at **Vigirima**, then he met Juan Domingo Monteverde's forces under Colonels José Ceballos and José Yáñez southeast of Cartagena at Araure. Bolívar secured a brilliant and decisive victory, but had to flee after a defeat six months later at **La Puerta** (5 December 1813).

Arausio | 105 BC | Rome's Gallic Wars

After reaching Gaul from central Europe, the Cimbri and Teutone tribes won in **Provence** and at **Aginnum** (107 BC), before King Boiorix destroyed Consul Mallius Maximus on the Rhone north of Avignon at Arausio (modern Orange). Followed by massive non-combatant deaths, it was one of Rome's worst defeats. Within three years, Rome was avenged in Gaul at **Aquae Sextiae** and in Italy at **Vercellae**.

Arawe | 1943–1944 | World War II (Pacific)

As part of the campaign to isolate Rabaul, Americans under General Julian Cunningham landed around the Arawe Peninsula on the southwest coast of **New Britain** in New Guinea as a diversion from the subsequent main assault at **Cape Gloucester**. After struggling for the local airfield against Major Shinjiro Komori, further troops arrived to help secure the area (15 December 1943–16 January 1944).

Araxes | 589 | Byzantine-Persian Wars

Persian General Bahram Chobin beat the Turks on behalf of the Sassanid King Hormizd IV at **Hyrcanian Rock**, and a year later turned against the Romans in Lazica. At the Araxes (modern Aras) River, on the northern border of modern Iran, he suffered a decisive defeat at the hands of Byzantine General Romanus. In 590

Bahram overthrew Hormizd, but was then defeated at **Ganzak**.

Arbadil ∎ 1618 ∎ Turko-Persian Wars
  See **Erivan**

Arbedo ∎ 1422 ∎ Swiss-Milanese Wars
  Duke Filippo Maria Visconti of Milan intervened in Swiss politics and attempted to seize the city of Bellinzona near Lake Maggiore. At nearby Arbedo, Swiss halberdiers and pikemen were defeated by Milanese cavalry under the soldier of fortune Francesco Bussone (known as the Count Carmagnola), and Bellinzona was given up by treaty (30 June 1422).

Arbela ∎ 331 BC ∎ Conquests of Alexander the Great
  See **Gaugamela**

Arbroath ∎ 1446 ∎ Scottish Clan Wars
  In a clan dispute over the post of Ballie of Arbroath, Alexander Lindsay, Master of Crawford, led an army against Alexander Ogilvie of Inverquharity. When the two forces met outside Arbroath, northeast of Dundee, Lindsay's father, David Earl of Crawford, was killed attempting to prevent fighting. The Ogilvies were routed in the ensuing battle, triggering a prolonged feud (13 June 1446).

Arcadiopolis ∎ 970 ∎ Byzantine-Russian Wars
  A Russian army under Prince Sviatoslav of Kiev was marching towards Constantinople when they were met and heavily defeated west of the capital near Arcadiopolis (modern Lüleburgaz) by Byzantine General Bardas Sclerus. The invaders were driven out of Thrace and, after a further defeat on the Danube at **Dorostalon** in 971, Sviatoslav was killed while returning home to Kiev.

Arcadiopolis ∎ 1194 ∎ Bulgarian Imperial Wars
  With Byzantine Emperor Isaac II defeated in 1190 at **Berroea**, Tsar Ivan Asen of Bulgaria expanded south into the Balkans and was met by Isaac at Arcadiopolis (modern Lüleburgaz). The Bulgarians secured a decisive victory and, when Isaac tried to raise yet another army, he was overthrown and blinded by his brother, Alexius III, who eventually persuaded the Bulgarians to make peace.

Arcesh ∎ 625 ∎ Byzantine-Persian Wars
  Following success in Armenia at **Dwin**, Byzantine Emperor Heraclius faced three separate Persian armies in the Armenian Highlands where he defeated two then attacked the main Persian camp at Arcesh, north of Lake Van. Persian General Shahbaraz escaped with his life, though most of his army was destroyed. King Chrosroes II was finally overthrown after Heraclius won at **Nineveh** (February 625).

Arcis-sur-Aube ∎ 1814 ∎ Napoleonic Wars (French Campaign)
  In the last substantial battle he was personally involved in before abdication, Napoleon Bonaparte marched south from **Rheims** to challenge a much larger Austrian force under Prince Karl Philipp Schwarzenberg advancing towards **Paris**. Although the battle near Troyes at Arcis-sur-Aube was tactically a victory for Bonaparte, he was forced to withdraw (20–21 March 1814).

Arcola ∎ 1796 ∎ French Revolutionary Wars (1st Coalition)
  Facing another Austrian attempt to relieve the French siege of **Mantua**, Napoleon Bonaparte was checked at **Caldiero** but a few days later met Baron Josef Alvinzi in a marshy area near the Alpone and Adige Rivers, southeast of Verona. While Bonaparte suffered heavy losses in a bloody three-day battle around the village of Arcola, he forced the Austrians to retreat (15–17 November 1796).

Arcos de Valdevez ∎ 1140 ∎ Portuguese-Castilian Wars
  A year after defeating the Muslims at **Ourique**, Afonso Henriques of Portugal pursued his late mother's claim to Galicia and provoked an invasion by Alfonso VII of Castile. It was agreed to settle the matter by tournament, and at Arcos

de Valdevez, north of Braga, the Portuguese knights prevailed. The Castilian King conceded Galician land and recognised his cousin as King Afonso I of Portugal.

Arcot I 1751 I 2nd Carnatic War

To distract the French siege of **Trichinopoly**, Englishman Robert Clive and a small force seized Arcot in eastern Madras, capital of the French-appointed Nawab Chanda Sahib. Besieged by a massive Indian force led by the Nawab's son, Raza Sahib, the British-Indian garrison inflicted heavy casualties and Arcot held out until they were finally relieved (11 September–25 November 1751).

Arcot I 1780 I 2nd British-Mysore War

Soon after the Nawab of Arcot attacked Mysore in southeast India, Haidar Ali of Mysore struck back against the Nawab and his British allies. Having secured a victory at **Perambakam** (10 September), he besieged Arcot in eastern Madras and took the city by storm. He then went on to besiege Wandewash and Vellore, but was defeated at **Porto Novo** (31 October 1780).

Ardahan I 1877 I Russo-Turkish Wars

Russian commander Mikhail Loris-Melikov advanced into the Caucasus shortly after war was declared and attacked the fortress of Ardahan on the River Kura, defended by the incompetetent Hasan Sabri Pasha. Hasan fled after the Russians seized the Guylaberti Heights to the southeast and Ardahan fell with the loss of over 1,000 prisoners (16–17 May 1877).

Ardennes I 1914 I World War I (Western Front)

Just as German forces launched a counter-attack in **Lorraine**, further northwest French Generals Pierre Ruffey and Fernand de Langle de Cary attacked in the Ardennes against Duke Albrecht and Prince Wilhelm. Despite local success at Virton, confused fighting in thick fog saw the French badly defeated and they retreated south to stabilise the line at **Verdun** (21–23 August 1914).

Ardennes I 1940 I World War II (Western Europe)

While the Allies marched north to face the German advance through **Belgium**, seven Panzer divisions under General Gerd von Rundstedt invaded France through the supposedly impassable Ardennes Forest. French Generals André Corap and Charles Huntziger were crushed, and the Germans seized the Meuse along a 50-mile front north from Sedan, then raced for the coast (12–15 May 1940).

Ardennes I 1944–1945 I World War II (Western Europe)

Marshal Walther Model led the last great German offensive in the west, striking through the Ardennes towards Antwerp and creating the so-called Bulge. Undermanned American forces were badly surprised, but after losses including **Schnee Eifel** and **St Vith**, they held the line at **Bastogne**. The Allies then regained the initiative and halted the offensive (16 December 1944–25 January 1945).

Ardscull I 1316 I Rise of Robert the Bruce

Extending the Scottish War to Ireland, Edward Bruce, brother of Robert the Bruce, invaded against a large but poorly co-ordinated Anglo-Irish force under the Justiciar Edward Butler, John Fitzthomas of Ofally and Arnold le Poer of Kilkenny. At Ardscull, near Athy in Kildare, Edward drove his enemy from the field. In 1318 he was crowned King of Ireland at **Dundalk** (26 January 1316).

Arequipa I 1857–1858 I Peruvian Civil Wars

Former Dictator Manuel Ignacio de Vivanco returned from exile after defeat at **Carmen Alto** in 1844 and tried to raise a fresh Conservative revolt against President Ramón Castilla. Driven back to his power base at Arequipa, Vivanco withstood an eight-month siege. After a bloody assault, Castilla eventually took the town by storm, and Vivanco returned to exile (August 1857–5 March 1858).

Argaum ▌ 1803 ▌ 2nd British-Maratha War

Two months after his decisive victory over the Marathas at **Assaye** in Deccan India, General Arthur Wellesley inflicted a further defeat on Daulat Rao Sindhia of Gwalior and Raja Raghuji Bhonsle of Berar at the village of Argaum, north of Akola. He then pursued the defeated Marathas into the mountains, and weeks later attacked their fortress at **Gawilgarh** (28 November 1803).

Argentan ▌ 1944 ▌ World War II (Western Europe)
  See **Falaise**

Argentoratum ▌ 357 ▌ Alemannic Invasion of Roman Gaul

Appointed to lead Roman forces in Gaul, the Caesar Julian, cousin of Emperor Constantius, advanced into the Rhine Valley against the invading German Alemanni under King Chnodomar. Although heavily outnumbered, Julian inflicted heavy losses near Argentoratum (modern Strasbourg) and chased the invaders beyond the Rhine, capturing their King.

Argentoratum ▌ 378 ▌ Alemannic Invasion of Roman Gaul

Resisting renewed tribal invasion across the Rhine, the young Western Roman Emperor, Flavius Gratianus, son of Valentinian, sent his army against the German Alemanni at Argentoratum (modern Strasbourg). A decisive action saw his Generals Nannienus and Mellobaudes the Frank virtually destroy the invaders. The Alemanni ruler Priarius was killed in the fighting.

Arges ▌ 1916 ▌ World War I (Balkan Front)

Romanian commander Alexandru Averescu was driven back on all fronts and concentrated his forces on the Arges, west of Bucharest, against Erich von Falkenhayn advancing from the north and west and August von Mackensen from the south. Despite heroic defence, the Romanians were forced to withdraw northeast through **Rimnic Sarat** and Bucharest fell two days later (1–4 December 1916).

Argesul ▌ 1916 ▌ World War I (Balkan Front)
  See **Arges**

Arginusae ▌ 406 BC ▌ Great Peloponnesian War

A decisive naval engagement off the coast of Asia Minor near the island of Arginusae saw Peloponnesian triremes led by Spartan Admiral Callicratidas engage the Athenian fleet which was trying to raise the blockade of Conon in Mytilene on Lesbos. Callicratidas was killed and the Peloponnesian fleet was destroyed, but was quickly rebuilt to win a year later at **Aegospotami** (August 406 BC).

Argoan ▌ 1803 ▌ 2nd British-Maratha War
  See **Argaum**

Argonne ▌ 1915 ▌ World War I (Western Front)

Soon after the French offensive in **Artois** died down, Crown Prince Wilhelm launched his own offensive further south in the Argonne against General Maurice Sarrail. General Bruno von Modra's Corps took some territory but was eventually repulsed and the attack eased after their failure to break the French line. In September the French struck back in **Champagne** (26 June–4 July 1915).

Argonne ▌ 1918 ▌ World War I (Western Front)
  See **Meuse-Argonne**

Argos ▌ 272 BC ▌ Pyrrhic War

Repulsed in Italy at **Beneventum** in 275 BC, King Pyrrhus of Epirus invaded the Peloponnese against Antigonus II of Macedonia. Repulsed at Sparta by King Areus, who ambushed and killed his son Ptolemaeus, Pyrrhus marched on Antigonus at Argos. Pyrrhus was killed in heavy street fighting and his army surrendered. Areus soon fell out with Antigonus, who killed him seven years later at **Corinth**.

Argos ▌ 195 BC ▌ Spartan-Achaean Wars

The Tyrant Nabis led a fresh Spartan offensive against the Achaean League, whose leader

Philopoemen sought aid from Roman General Titus Quinctius Flamininus, victor two years before at **Cynoscephalae**. Near Argos, the combined Roman-Pergamene-Rhodian force inflicted a heavy defeat on the Spartan Tyrant's son-in-law Pythagorus of Argos. The Allies soon won again at **Gytheum**.

Argus vs *Pelican* ❙ 1813 ❙ War of 1812
See **St George's Channel**

Arica ❙ 1880 ❙ War of the Pacific
After Chilean forces invaded Peru and secured a decisive victory at **Tacna** in May, Bolivia effectively withdrew from the war, and the Peruvians fell back on the port of Arica. The fortress at Morro was taken by infantry assault following heavy bombardment by land and sea, and Arica fell. When peace talks failed, Chile resumed the offensive early the next year and advanced on **Lima** (16–17 June 1880).

Arichit ❙ 860 ❙ Later Indian Dynastic Wars
See **Arisil**

Arikera ❙ 1791 ❙ 3rd British-Mysore War
When Tipu Sultan of Mysore renewed war against the British, Indian Governor-General Earl Cornwallis took personal command and, two months after capturing **Bangalore**, advanced towards **Seringapatam** and attacked Tipu's army at night a few miles away at Arikera. Although Cornwallis inflicted heavy losses, the rainy season forced him back to Bangalore (13–14 May 1791).

Arinsol ❙ 1126 ❙ Early Christian Reconquest of Spain
King Alfonso I of Aragon established his reputation against Muslim Spain to become known as El Batallador—the fighter. When he had liberated Moorish Saragossa, Alfonso campaigned through Valencia and eastern Andalusia and, at Arinsol south of Lucena, inflicted a major defeat on a Muslim army under Abu Bakr, son of the local Emir Ali (10 March 1126).

Arisil ❙ 860 ❙ Later Indian Dynastic Wars
Amid one of the great dynastic rivalries in medieval India, Crown Prince Nripatunga of the Pallavas took an army against Srimara of Pandya. On the banks of the Arisil (Arichit), a tributary of the Kaveri, Nripatunga secured a bloody and decisive victory. Pallava's ally Sena II of Ceylon later launched an attack on the Pandyan capital **Madura**, where Srimara was defeated and killed.

Arius ❙ 208 BC ❙ Early Syrian-Parthian War
Re-establishing the powerful Seleucid Empire, King Antiochus III the Great invaded Parthia to confront King Arsaces III. At the Arius (Harirud) River, west of Herat in modern Afghanistan, Antiochus won a crushing victory over a Parthian-Bactrian army. However, he was unable to secure the whole country and made peace with Arsaces, recognising him as King of Parthia.

Arizpe ❙ 1852 ❙ Apache Indian Wars
To avenge the Mexican attack at **Janos** (5 March 1851), 200 Chiricahua Apache advanced on Arizpe in northwest Mexico and killed a patrol of eight. The garrison of 100 Mexican cavalry then rode out to meet the Indians and were routed with 26 dead and 46 wounded. During this action the Apache leader (whose family were massacred at Janos) won the nom de guerre Geronimo (January 1852).

Arkansas Post ❙ 1863 ❙ American Civil War (Western Theatre)
With Union forces beaten on the Mississippi at **Chickasaw Bluffs** in December 1862, General John A. McClernand led a land and naval assault upstream in Arkansas against Confederate Arkansas Post, held by General Thomas J. Churchill. McClernand lost over 1,000 men taking the fort, but it had no strategic value to the assault on **Vicksburg**, and he was ordered to withdraw (11 January 1863).

Arkinholm ❙ 1455 ❙ Douglas Rebellion
As James II of Scotland moved to crush a rebellion by James Earl of Douglas, the Earl's

brothers were defeated at Arkinholm, near Langholm, by Royalists under their kinsman Archibald Earl of Angus. Archibald Earl of Moray was killed, Hugh Earl of Ormonde was captured and executed, and the third brother, John Lord Balvenie, fled to join Earl Douglas in England (May 1455).

Arklow | 1798 | Irish Rebellion

Four days after the disastrous rebel defeat at **New Ross**, up to 20,000 poorly armed peasants led by Father John Murphy of Boulvogue seized Wexford and marched against Arklow on Ireland's southeast coast. However, they were repulsed with heavy losses by about 1,600 militia under General Francis Needham. Dublin was saved and the rising in the north was effectively over (9 June 1798).

Arkona | 1168 | Danish Wars of Expansion

Waldemar I secured the Danish throne in 1157 at **Grathe Heath**, then fought an indecisive campaign against the Wends (of modern northeast Germany). Eventually, Bishop Absalon took a large force against their stronghold on Rügen Island, where he seized the key port of Arkona, after which Garz town surrendered. Denmark subsequently held Rügen under treaty with Duke Henry the Lion of Saxony.

Arlaban | 1836 | 1st Carlist War

On a fresh advance in Navarre, Liberal General Baldomero Espartero, supported by the British Legion of General Sir George de Lacy Evans, marched northeast from Vitoria against the Carlists near Arlaban. Heavy fighting secured the village of Mendijur for the Allies, but Carlist General Bruno de Villareal counterattacked and forced Espartero to withdraw to Vitoria (17–18 January 1836).

Arles | 411 | Later Roman Wars of Succession

Having claimed recognition as joint Roman Emperor, usurper Flavius Claudius Constantinus unsuccessfully invaded Italy from Gaul and was driven back to Arles, where he was besieged by the Imperial General Constantius. With his son Constans killed at **Vienne** and a Frank relief army under Edobic repulsed, Constantinus surrendered and was put to death (September 411).

Arles | 425 | Goth Invasion of the Roman Empire

Theodoric the Visigoth, King of Toulouse, broke his peace with Rome and invaded Gaul to besiege Arles, in modern Provence—known as the "Little Gallic Rome." However, after he was defeated and driven off by the Roman General Flavius Aetius and his Hunnic allies, Theodoric made peace again and turned instead against the Vandals in Spain. He was finally defeated in 437 near **Narbonne**.

Arles | 435 | Goth Invasion of the Roman Empire

Once more breaking the peace with Rome after his defeat ten years earlier at **Arles**, Theodoric the Visigoth made a fresh advance on Arles, in Provence. For a second time, he was repulsed by the Roman General Flavius Aetius and his largely Hun army. Two years later, Theodoric was again defeated in an even more decisive battle to end the Visigoth siege of **Narbonne**.

Arles | 471 | Goth Invasion of the Roman Empire

Alarmed at Visigoth expansion from Aquitaine after victory over the Bretons at **Deols** in 469, Western Emperor Anthemius sent a fresh army across the Alps against Euric the Visigoth, who was besieging Arles. The Imperial army was crushed in battle nearby and Euric then captured Arles and secured much of southern Gaul. Defeat in Gaul for Anthemius led directly to his overthrow in **Rome**.

Arles | 508–510 | Visigothic-Frankish Wars

A year after Visigoth leader Alaric died at **Vouillé**, Clovis, King of the Salian Franks, advanced through Gaul to besiege Arles, west of Marseilles. An Ostrogoth relief force under Tuluin was driven off (24 June 508), and Clovis continued his siege. The Franks were eventually defeated by Ibbas, General of the new Ostrogoth ruler, Theodoric, who secured control of Provence (June 508–510).

Arleux I 1711 I War of the Spanish Succession

John Churchill Duke of Marlborough attempted to penetrate the French Ne Plus Ultra lines—protective fortifications and flooded swamps south of Paris—where he first captured the Sensee Valley causeway at Arleux. The town was then lost and regained as Marlborough manoeuvred to deceive Marshal Claude Villars and to capture the important fortress further west at Bouchain (21 June 1711).

Armada, Spanish I 1588 I Anglo-Spanish Wars

See **Spanish Armada**

Armageddon I 609 BC I Egyptian Conquest of Judah

See **Megiddo**

Armentières I 1914 I World War I (Western Front)

While British forces attacked the Germans in Flanders at **La Bassée**, just to the north General William Pulteney drove east from Armentières against the Sixth Army of Prince Ruprecht. The British were eventually driven back, but the line stabilised in front of Armentières. Further north, fighting around **Messines** spread into the actions around **Ypres** (13 October–2 November 1914).

Arnala I 1780–1781 I 1st British-Maratha War

General Thomas Goddard was besieging **Bassein**, off Bombay, when he sent forces north against the small Maratha island fortress of Arnala. Even after the fall of Bassein, Madhav Rao Belose held out and repulsed a very costly assault. But he had run out of ammunition and was forced to surrender. The other nearby land forts quickly followed suit (November 1780–18 January 1781).

Arnay-le-Duc I 1570 I 3rd French War of Religion

Six months after the Protestant disaster at **Moncontour**, Huguenot Admiral Gaspard de Coligny led a fresh offensive into south and central France, repulsing a Catholic attack by Marshal Artus de Cosse at Arnay-le-Duc, southwest of Dijon. However, as Coligny advanced towards Paris, Queen Mother Catherine de Medici negotiated a new treaty, and war was again suspended (25 June 1570).

Arnee I 1751 I 2nd Carnatic War

See **Arni**

Arnhem I 1944 I World War II (Western Europe)

Attempting to outflank the **Siegfried Line**, Sir Bernard Montgomery sent British, Polish and American airborne troops to seize key bridges in Holland on the canals near Eindhoven, on the Waal at Nijmegen and the Rhine at Arnhem. Meeting unexpected resistance at Arnhem, British paratroopers briefly held the bridge, then withdrew with over 7,000 killed or captured (17–24 September 1944).

Arni I 1751 I 2nd Carnatic War

Following the relief of **Arcot** in southeast India, British East India Company troops under Robert Clive, with Maratha cavalry in support, pursued the French-Indian force led by Raza Sahib 20 miles further south to Arni. The Indians and their French allies attempted to make a stand but were driven out with over 200 casualites and withdrew towards **Pondicherry** (3 December 1751).

Arni I 1782 I 2nd British-Mysore War

A year after inflicting heavy defeats on Haidar Ali of Mysore at **Porto Novo**, **Pollilore** and **Sholinghur**, British troops under Sir Eyre Coote clashed with him again in an inconclusive engagement at Arni in central Madras. Haidar died six months later, though his less able son, Tipu Sultan, fought on until January 1784 at **Bednur** and **Mangalore** (7 June 1782).

Arogee ∎ 1868 ∎ British Expedition to Ethiopia

See **Arogi**

Arogi ∎ 1868 ∎ British Expedition to Ethiopia

Leading a punitive expedition against Emperor Theodore (Tewodros) of Ethiopia, General Sir Robert Napier and an Anglo-Indian army marched inland from the Red Sea and were attacked by the Ethiopian army near the Beshlio at Arogi. Napier inflicted a decisive defeat, with 700 killed and about 1,200 wounded, then stormed the nearby mountain fortress of **Magdala** (10 April 1868).

Aros ∎ 1886 ∎ Apache Indian Wars

Captain Emmet Crawford crossed into Mexico in pursuit of Geronimo and captured the Apache camp on the Aros River, near Nacori, where he was attacked by Mexican Federal troops, allegedly mistaking his scouts for hostiles. Crawford was fatally wounded and the Federals lost four killed. Mexico later claimed the attack was a response to American border infringements (11 January 1886).

Arqa ∎ 1098 ∎ 1st Crusade

Advancing from **Antioch** towards **Jerusalem**, Raymond of Toulouse besieged Arqa, north of Tripoli. But even when reinforced by the main army under Godfrey of Bouillon, the Crusaders were unable to capture the town. They abandoned the siege after three months, marching directly against Tripoli, where the Emir sued for peace and opened their route south (14 February–13 May 1098).

Arques ∎ 1589 ∎ 9th French War of Religion

Soon after the assassination of Henry III of France, the Huguenot Henry of Navarre claimed the throne and at Arques, near Dieppe, was challenged by Duke Charles of Mayenne, leader of the Holy League. Ambushing the much larger Catholic army on marshy ground near the Bethune River, Henry achieved a great victory and secured his claim to the throne (21 September 1589).

Arquijas ∎ 1834 ∎ 1st Carlist War

The Spanish Liberal army of General Luis Fernández de Córdova pursued Carlist commander Tomás Zumalacárregui through Navarre and secured a hard-fought victory at **Mendaza**, northeast of Logroño. Three days later, when Córdova attempted to force the pass at Arquijas, five miles to the northwest, he suffered a costly repulse and fell back towards Los Arcos (15 December 1834).

Arquijas ∎ 1835 ∎ 1st Carlist War

In a renewed attack on Carlist commander Tomás Zumalacárregui, northeast of Logroño in Navarre near **Mendaza**, Spanish Liberal forces under General Manuel Lorenzo made a second attempt to force the pass at Arquijas. With only half as many men, Zumalacárregui dealt the Liberals a very costly defeat. He soon took the offensive at **Villafranca de Oria** and **Bilbao** (5 February 1835).

Arrah ∎ 1857 ∎ Indian Mutiny

Besieged by Kunwar Singh, Raja of Jagdispur, a small British force defended a fortified compound at Arrah (modern Ara), west of Patna, belonging to railway engineer Vicars Boyle. When a relief attempt by General George Lloyd was repulsed, Major Vincent Eyre defeated the mutineers at nearby Gujraganj to relieve the town and drove them towards **Jagdispur** (25 July–3 August 1857).

Arras ∎ 1654 ∎ Franco-Spanish War

While campaigning in northern France at the head of a Spanish army with French support, renegade nobleman Louis II de Bourbon Prince of Condé attempted to besiege Arras, 100 miles north of Paris, but was attacked at night by a French relief army under Marshal Henri de Turenne. The Spanish troops suffered heavy casualties and Condé was driven off (24–25 August 1654).

Arras ∎ 1914 ∎ World War I (Western Front)

Days after action at **Albert**, French commander Joseph Joffre sent General Louis de

Maud'huy on a fresh attempt to outflank the Germans between Arras and Lens. A German counter-attack under Prince Ruprecht retook Lens, and the French withdrew on Arras. The "Race to the Sea" soon ended at the Channel port of Nieuwport and the battle for **Flanders** began (1–4 October 1914).

Arras ∎ 1917 ∎ World War I (Western Front)

British Generals Edmund Allenby and Henry Horne began the **Nivelle Offensive** by attacking east from Arras against German commander Ludwig von Falkenhausen. While Vimy Ridge was taken, the action cost 150,000 British and 100,000 German casualties before stalling with the capture of Bullecourt (17 May). Further south, the French were defeated on the **Aisne** (9–14 & 23–25 April 1917).

Arras ∎ 1918 ∎ World War I (Western Front)

In the second phase of the offensive from **Amiens**, British commander Sir Douglas Haig opened a new attack in the north from Arras along the **Scarpe**. With heavy fighting further south around **Albert** and **Bapaume**, the offensive secured extensive ground and about 34,000 prisoners in just two weeks, opening the way for the advance on **Cambrai** (26 August–2 September 1918).

Arras ∎ 1940 ∎ World War II (Western Europe)

Counter-attacking against the German Panzer sweep across **France**, British tanks and infantry under General Harold Franklyn struck back at General Erwin Rommel at Arras. Briefly surprised, Rommel used 88-mm anti-aircraft guns to repulse the British armour, but the action is claimed to have helped delay the advance of German tanks towards **Dunkirk** (21–23 May 1940).

Arrazola ∎ 1827 ∎ Central American National Wars

After election as first President of the Central American Confederation, Manuel José Arce began to exercise dictatorial powers and faced an advancing Liberal army from El Salvador under Mariano Prado. President Arce secured a bloody victory at Arrazola, outside Guatemala City, but his subsequent counter-offensive into El Salvador in May was heavily repulsed at **Milingo** (23 March 1827).

Arretium ∎ 283 BC ∎ Later Roman-Etruscan War

With Senonian Gauls besieging the Etruscan fortress of Arretium (near modern Arezzzo) in central Italy, Rome sent a relief army under Consul Lucius Caecilius Metellus. The Roman force was utterly destroyed, with over 13,000 men killed, including Metellus. The defeat encouraged the Etruscans to abandon their former ally and they joined the Senones against Rome at **Lake Vadimo**.

Arriverayte ∎ 1814 ∎ Napoleonic Wars (Peninsular Campaign)

As the Allies closed in on **Bayonne** in southwestern France, General Jean Isidore Harispe withdrew north from the Bidouse at **Garris**, and left General Jean-Baptiste Paris to defend the River Saison at Arriverayte, southeast of Sauveterre. However, General Sir Rowland Hill advanced in time to prevent Paris destroying the bridges, and the French were forced to retreat next day (17 February 1814).

Arroyo de la China ∎ 1814 ∎ Argentine War of Independence

Spanish naval commander Jacinto de Romarate was defeated off Buenos Aires near **Martín García**, then immediately pursued north up the Uruguay River by Argentine Patriot ships under Tomás Notter (the American Thomas Nother). Notter was defeated and killed in action at Arroyo de la China, near Concepción del Uruguay, but his officers effected a courageous withdrawal (28 March 1814).

Arroyo del Sauce ∎ 1844 ∎ Argentine-Uruguayan War

Marching into Uruguay against President Fructuoso Rivera, Argentine General Justo José

Urquiza crossed the Yi, and Colonel Manuel Antonio Urdinarrain attacked Rivera's vanguard under General Anacleto Medina at Arroyo del Sauce. Urquiza's cavalry arrived to secure the victory, and Rivera withdrew towards Tacuarembo. Months later he lost again at **India Muerta** (24 January 1844).

Arroyo Grande I 1842 I Argentine-Uruguayan War

Argentine Dictator Juan Manuel de Rosas intervened in Uruguay and sent former Uruguayan President Manuel Cerefino Oribe against Fructuoso Rivera, who had forced him out of office. At Arroyo Grande, northwest of Montevideo, supported by Argentine Generals Angel Pacheco and Justo José Urquiza, Oribe defeated Rivera, who withdrew to siege in **Montevideo** (5–6 December 1842).

Arroyo Molinos I 1811 I Napoleonic Wars (Peninsular Campaign)

While most fighting was taking place in the south and east of Spain, General Sir Rowland Hill surprised a French division under General Jean-Baptiste Girard at Arroyo Molinos, near the Spanish frontier northwest of Merida in Estremadura. In a one-sided diversionary engagement, Girard's massively outnumbered force lost over 1,000 casualties (28 October 1811).

Arsanias I 62 I Later Roman-Parthian Wars

The Roman General Caesennius Paetus was sent to repulse a Parthian invasion of Armenia but allowed himself to be surrounded and forced to surrender on the Arsanias (modern Murat) River in eastern Turkey. Victory over the Roman army enabled Parthian leader Vologesus I to make his brother Tiridates King of Armenia, while recognising Roman Emperor Nero as overlord.

Arsilah I 1471 I Portuguese Colonial Wars in North Africa

Determined to avenge a disastrous Portuguese repulse at **Tangier** in 1437, and again in 1464, King Alfonso V took a large-scale expedition against the Muslim fortress of Arsilah, on the Atlantic coast of Morocco. Arsilah fell, followed by a deliberate massacre, which induced the Muslims to abandon nearby Tangier. Alfonso then seized Tangier and his courtiers hailed him "Africanus."

Arsissa I 625 I Byzantine-Persian Wars
See **Arcesh**

Arsouf I 1191 I 3rd Crusade

Crusaders led by King Richard I of England advancing along the Palestine coast towards Jerusalem were met at Arsouf, north of Jaffa, by a huge Syrian-Egyptian force under Saladin. Despite initial losses, a Crusader charge scattered their enemy, causing massive casualties. Saladin evacuated **Jaffa** and Richard set to restore it, losing a chance to advance and seize Ascalon (7 September 1191).

Artah I 1105 I Crusader-Muslim Wars

In a renewed Crusader offensive in northern Syria, Tancred, Regent of Antioch, attempted to recover the fortress of Artah, between Antioch and Aleppo. At the nearby village of Tizin, he destroyed a large Turkish army under Ridwan of Aleppo, inflicting massive casualties. Ridwan quickly sued for peace and Tancred consolidated his authority in the Orontes Valley (20 April 1105).

Artah I 1164 I Crusader-Muslim Wars

After Nur ed-Din, Emir of Aleppo, was driven off from besieging Harenc, east of Antioch, he was pursued north by Bohemund III of Antioch, Raymond of Tripoli and Constantine Coloman, Byzantine Governor of Cicilia. Aided by the army of Mosul, he ambushed and destroyed the pursuing army at Artah. All three Christian leaders were captured and later ransomed (10 August 1164).

Artaxata I 68 BC I 3rd Mithridatic War

With Pontus secured at **Cabira** in 72 BC, Roman commander Lucius Licinius Lucullus invaded Armenia, pursuing Mithridates VI of Pontus, who fled to his son-in-law Tigranes.

Following victory at **Tigranocerta**, Lucullus marched northeast and defeated Tigranes again at Artaxata (modern Artashat), ancient capital of Armenia. Lucullus was replaced by Gnaeus Pompey, who won in 66 BC at **Lycus**.

Artaxata I 58 I Later Roman-Parthian Wars

Vologeses of Parthia overthrew the Roman-supported ruler of Armenia in favour of his brother Tiridates, and veteran General Gnaeus Domitius Corbulo was sent to re-establish Roman authority. Advancing into Armenia, Corbulo defeated Tiridates and captured and burned Artaxata (modern Artashat), the ancient capital of Armenia, south of Yerevan near Lake Sevan.

Artaza I 1834 I 1st Carlist War

Soon after Don Carlos V arrived in Spain, Liberal General José Ramon Rodil led perhaps 8,000 men into the rugged Améscoa Valley, where he was attacked at Artaza by just 2,000 Carlists under General Tomás Zumalacárregui. Rodil suffered heavy losses in a one-sided action before the Carlists withdrew, but he continued his campaign in pursuit of the pretender (31 August 1834).

Artemisa I 1896 I 2nd Cuban War of Independence

Driven off from **Candelaria** by troops sent by acting Spanish commander Sabás Marín, insurgent leader Antonio Maceo determined to ambush the Spanish column at Artemisa, 35 miles southwest of Havana. Despite initial success, the Cubans suffered costly losses when reinforcements arrived, but Maceo stubbornly refused to withdraw until fighting ended at nightfall (30 January 1896).

Artemisium I 480 BC I Greco-Persian Wars

In support of the famous defence at **Thermopylae** against Persian invaders, the Greek fleet anchored at Artemisium was attacked by Persian ships. The two fleets clashed indecisively for three days off Euboea until Thermopylae fell. However, severe storms caused heavy Persian losses, as they had no safe harbour. The

Greeks withdrew to later support the great victory off **Salamis** (August 480 BC).

Artenay I 1870 I Franco-Prussian War

During the Prussian advance towards Paris, Baron Ludwig von der Tann led his Bavarian Corps of 28,000 men and 160 guns against the French Army of the Loire under General Joseph Edouard de la Motterouge. Smashing through the French defences north of Orleans at Artenay, the Germans captured **Orleans** next day, along with its crucial supplies and rolling stock (10 October 1870).

Arthuret I 573 I Anglo-Saxon Conquest of Britain

When King Peredur of York united with Dunaut of the Pennines against their Royal kinsman Gwendolou of Carlisle, Gwendolou was defeated and killed at Arderydd (modern Arthuret or Longtown) on the Esk, north of Carlisle. In the ensuing struggle for power, the semi-legendary Urien of Rheged became Lord of Carlisle and eventually the most powerful northern Prince.

Artois (1st) I 1915 I World War I (Western Front)

The so-called Second Battle of Artois saw French General Henri Pétain attack between Lens and Arras towards Vimy Ridge, supported by the British in the north at **Aubers**. After initial French success, German reinforcements created a battle of attrition, with heavy fighting around Souchez. The failed offensive cost 100,000 French and 75,000 German casualties (9 May–18 June 1915).

Artois (2nd) I 1915 I World War I (Western Front)

While French forces attacked in **Champagne**, further north in Artois, General Auguste Dubail advanced towards Vimy Ridge, aided by the British attacking at nearby **Loos**. The so-called Third Battle of Artois saw a powerful German counter-attack under Crown Prince Rupprecht and the French were eventually driven back with about 120,000 casualties (25 September–15 October 1915).

Arundel I 1102 I Norman Dynastic Wars

In the face of renewed rebellion by the powerful Robert of Beleme, Earl of Salisbury, Henry I took a large force against the Norman Earl's castle at Arundel in Sussex. In a siege noted for the use of major works known as counter-castles, Salisbury was unable to send aid to his captains and, after three months, he allowed the garrison to surrender in return for safe conduct back to Normandy.

Arundel I 1643–1644 I British Civil Wars

Sir Ralph Hopton's Royalists believed that Sussex was preparing to rise for the King and marched south to seize Alton and Arundel. But Parliamentary General Sir William Waller retook **Alton** and marched east to besiege the great castle, which was badly damaged by heavy bombardment. When Arundel finally fell, half the 1,000 prisoners changed sides (20 December 1643–6 January 1644).

Arvenanmaa I 1714 I 2nd "Great" Northern War
See **Hango**

Arzila I 1471 I Portuguese Colonial Wars in North Africa
See **Arsilah**

Arzobispo I 1809 I Napoleonic Wars (Peninsular Campaign)

Withdrawing into Portugal after **Talavera de la Reina**, British General Sir Arthur Wellesley and Spanish forces under General Gregorio Cuesta crossed the Tagus at Arzobispo, pursued by Marshal Nicolas Soult. The French Marshal defeated Cuesta's rearguard under General Louis Bassecourt and seized the bridge, but King Joseph Bonaparte refused permission to invade Portugal (4 August 1809).

Arzu I 1880 I 2nd British-Afghan War
See **Urzu**

Asal Uttar I 1965 I 2nd Indo-Pakistan War
See **Khem Karan**

Asan I 1894 I Sino-Japanese War
See **Phung-tao**

Asarta I 1833 I 1st Carlist War

Early in war against Spanish Regent Maria Cristina, Carlist commander Tomás Zumalacárregui tried to hold a position between Asarta and Nazar against General Manuel Lorenzo and Colonel Marcelino Oráa. In his first major victory, Zumalacárregui's half-trained Carlists inflicted heavy Cristino casualties before withdrawing. He soon fought again at **Alsasua** (29 December 1833).

Ascalon I 1099 I 1st Crusade

When Crusaders seized **Jerusalem**, the Fatimid Caliphate of Egypt felt threatened and sent a large army north under the Vizier al-Afdal Shahinshah. On the plain of al-Majdal, outside the coastal city of Ascalon, the outnumbered Crusader army, led by Godfrey of Bouillon, utterly defeated the Fatimid Egyptians and seized massive treasure, but was unable to capture Ascalon (12 August 1099).

Ascalon I 1123 I Crusader-Muslim Wars

In return for promised commercial advantage, Venice despatched a large squadron of galleys to assist the Crusaders in Palestine. Her ships intercepted a large Egyptian fleet off the Muslim fortress of Ascalon, in southern Palestine, and sank or captured virtually every vessel. The Venetians then sailed on to support the siege of **Tyre** (May 1123).

Ascalon I 1153 I Crusader-Muslim Wars

Egyptian forces were defeated by Crusaders near Ascalon in 1099, but they held the strategic coastal fortress until besieged by a large Crusader army under King Baldwin III of Jerusalem. Despite heavy losses—especially among his Knights Templar—Baldwin seized the city, the last Fatimid Egyptian possession in Syria, and gave it to his brother Amalric (25 January–19 August 1153).

Ascalon I 1247 I Later Crusader-Muslim Wars

Following Crusader defeat at **La Forbie** near Gaza in 1244 by Khwarezmian Turks supported by Ayyubid Mamluks, the Egyptians turned on the Turks and drove them out of Jerusalem before launching a massive siege of the Crusader fortress at Ascalon. A bloody assault saw Ascalon taken by storm with heavy Crusader losses, and the city's defences were dismantled (August–October 1247).

Aschaffenburg I 1796 I French Revolutionary Wars (1st Coalition)

With French General Jean-Baptiste Jourdan defeated at **Amberg** and **Würzburg**, Archduke Charles Louis of Austria pursued the French west to Aschaffenburg, in modern Bavaria, where the Austrians achieved their third victory in just three weeks. Archduke Charles then drove northwest towards the Rhine for further victory within days at **Altenkirchen** (13 September 1796).

Aschaffenburg I 1866 I Seven Weeks War

Attacking Austria's German allies, Prussian General August von Goeben marched through **Laufach** towards Aschaffenburg, southeast of Frankfurt, held by Count Erwin von Neipperg with Federal troops and some Hessians. While Alexander of Hesse remained with his army at Seiligenstadt, Aschaffenburg fell with over 2,000 prisoners taken. Frankfurt fell two days later (14 July 1866).

Aschersleben I 1644 I Thirty Years War (Franco-Habsburg War)

See **Juterbog**

Ascoli I 1190 I Imperial Invasion of Sicily

Tancred, the illegitimate grandson of Roger II, seized Sicily's throne and was challenged by Henry VI of Germany, who sent an Imperial army under Marshal Henry of Kalden to support Count Roger of Andria. At Ascoli Satriano, south of Foggia in Apulia, Tancred defeated and later killed Andria, but could not sustain his success. On Tancred's death in 1194, Henry overran Sicily.

Asculum, Apulia I 279 BC I Pyrrhic War

Campaigning in southern Italy against a large Roman army, King Pyrrhus of Epirus won a costly victory at **Heraclea**, then another hard-fought battle on the Aufidus, south of Foggia, at Asculum (modern Ascoli Satriano). However, because his casualties were much harder to replace than the Roman losses, the costly tactical wins spelled strategic defeat, hence the expression "Pyrrhic Victory."

Asculum, Apulia I 209 BC I 2nd Punic War

With Hannibal besieging Canusium (modern Canosa), his Roman rival Marcus Marcellus approached, and Hannibal withdrew up the Aufidus, where Marcellus attacked the Carthaginian camp at Asculum (modern Ascoli Satriano). Initially repulsed, Marcellus renewed his attack next day, and Hannibal suffered terrible losses and withdrew. A year later Marcellus died in ambush at **Venusia**.

Asculum, Marche I 89 BC I Roman Social War

When the Marsi and Samnites of central Italy revolted against Roman rule over citizenship, a Roman force was routed at **Fucine Lake**, and the Italian allies under Judacilius seized Asculum (modern Ascoli Piceno), northwest of Pescara, and massacred its inhabitants. However, Gnaeus Pompeius Strabo routed the rebels in battle, and a further victory in the south at **Pompeii** soon ended the revolt.

Asemus I 443 I Hun Invasion of the Roman Empire

While Attila the Hun campaigned near **Constantinople**, the local garrison at Asemus (modern Osma) surprised a group of Huns escorting booty back to the Hungarian Plain. Roman defeat at **Chersonesus** soon led Emperor Theodosius to sue for peace, but the people of Asemus refused Attila's demands to return the liberated captives, even though Emperor Theodosius II supported the demand.

Ashanti I 1900 I Ashanti Rising

In a final show of independence after defeat at **Odasu** in 1874, Ashanti tribesmen in modern

Ghana supporting King Prempeh rebelled against British efforts to suppress the Royal cult of the Golden Stool. The revolt was put down by General Sir William James Willcocks, who eventually seized the Ashanti capital at Kumasi, and the northern provinces were formally annexed (15 July 1900).

A Shau I 1966 I Vietnam War

Crossing the demilitarized zone, three North Vietnamese battalions attacked the small special forces base in the A Shau Valley, near the Laotian border southwest of Hue. Following heroic defence, the South Vietnamese irregulars, with American support, were boldly evacuated by air. Communist forces built up in the valley until an Allied offensive two years later at **Dong Ha** (9–10 March 1966).

A Shau I 1968 I Vietnam War
See **Dong Ha**

Ash Creek I 1864 I Cheyenne-Arapaho Indian War

Following an army victory at **Cedar Canyon**, Lieutenant George Eayre marched southeast from Denver towards Fort Larned, Kansas. To the north at Ash Creek, he met a large Cheyenne group hunting buffalo. Chief Lean Bear attempted a parley but was killed and, when Eayre opened fire with mountain howitzers, 28 Indians and four soldiers died, triggering war on the Arkansas (May 1864).

Ashdod I 659–630 BC I Assyrian Wars
See **Azotus**

Ashdown I 871 I Viking Wars in Britain

Defeated by Viking invaders at **Reading**, King Aethelred of Wessex and his brother Alfred regrouped northwest of Reading at Ashdown, on the Ridgeway near Lowbury Hill. Danish leader Bagsecq was defeated and killed in a decisive engagement and King Halfdan and his Viking survivors fled to Reading. However, within weeks the Saxons lost at **Basing** and **Merton** (8 January 871).

Ash Hollow I 1855 I Sioux Indian Wars

In retribution for the destruction of Lieutenant John Grattan's platoon near **Fort Laramie**, reputedly in a dispute over a stolen cow, a large cavalry column from Fort Leavenworth under General William S. Harney cornered and defeated Brulé Sioux warriors under Little Thunder at Ash Hollow, Nebraska. More than 130 Indians were killed, virtually the entire fighting force (3 September 1855).

Ashingdon I 1016 I Danish Conquest of England

King Edmund Ironside attempted to resist the Danish conquest of England and met Knut, son of Sweyn Forkbeard, at **Penselwood** and **Sherston**. Later in the year at Ashingdon (Assunden), north of Southend in Essex, Edmund was heavily defeated following the desertion of his brother-in-law Edric. When Edmund died soon after making peace, Knut became King of England (18 October 1016).

Ashkelon I 1099 I 1st Crusade
See **Ascalon**

Ashkelon I 1153 I Crusader-Muslim Wars
See **Ascalon**

Ashkelon I 1247 I Later Crusader-Muslim Wars
See **Ascalon**

Ashmoun Canal I 1221 I 5th Crusade

Having captured **Damietta** at the eastern mouth of the Nile in late 1219, Franks of the Fifth Crusade, under Papal Legate Cardinal Pelagius, attempting to march on Ayubbid Cairo, were heavily defeated at the Ashmoun Canal. Cut off from Damietta as the Nile flooded, they sued for peace. After being forced into surrender, the Crusade was abandoned, having achieved nothing (July–August 1221).

Ashmoun Canal I 1249 I 7th Crusade

In a reprise of the Fifth Crusade, King Louis IX of France took **Damietta** on the eastern Nile Delta and quickly advanced towards Cairo.

A large Ayyubid Muslim army under the Emir Fakr-ed-din repulsed the Crusaders in a brilliant defensive victory on the Ashmoun Canal. The Arabs held out for two months against continuous attack until the Crusader defeat at nearby **Mansura** (20 November 1249).

Ashmunien ∎ 1167 ∎ Crusader Invasion of Egypt
See **El Ashmunien**

Ashraf ∎ 1759 ∎ Persian Wars of Succession
Mohammad Hasan Khan of Qajar recovered from defeat at **Shiraz** in 1758 and advanced south of the Caspian towards Ashraf (modern Bihshahr) to attack Shaykh Ali Khan's Zand army before Regent Karim Khan Zand could bring reinforcements from Tehran. Mohammad Hasan was routed, then killed in the pursuit towards Asterabad, which quickly surrendered to Karim (14 February 1759).

Ashrafieh ∎ 1978 ∎ Lebanon Civil War
See **Beirut**

Ashtee ∎ 1818 ∎ 3rd British-Maratha War
See **Ashti**

Ashti ∎ 1818 ∎ 3rd British-Maratha War
With Peshwa Baji Rao II routed near Poona at **Koregaon** (6 January), British General Michael Smith advanced towards Bombay and met the Maratha army to the east at Ashti. The Peshwa fled before the battle, which saw his cavalry defeated and his commander Bapu Gokla killed. Later that year, the Peshwa suffered one further defeat at **Seoni** before he started negotiating peace (25 February 1818).

Asiago ∎ 1916 ∎ World War I (Italian Front)
Austrian General Conrad von Hotzendorf launched an offensive from the Trentino Bulge, attacking towards Padua to overrun General Roberto Brusati. Asiago and Arserio fell (31 May), but Italian commander Luigi Cadorna brought reinforcements from the **Isonzo** and

drove the Austrians almost back to their starting point with about 80,000 casualties on each side (15 May–25 June 1916).

Asirgarh ∎ 1600–1601 ∎ Mughal-Ahmadnagar Wars
On his last great campaign, Mughal Emperor Akbar captured Burhanpur in Khandesh, then besieged the nearby fortress of Asirgarh, said to be the most powerful of its age. Akbar treacherously seized commander Bahadur Shah after eight months with a false promise of safe negotiations, but the garrison held out until starvation and bribery produced surrender (9 April 1600–6 January 1601).

Asirgarh ∎ 1819 ∎ 3rd British-Maratha War
After the apparent end of the hostilities, deposed Raja Appa Sahib of Berar and Maharaja Mulhar Rao Holkar of Indore renewed the fighting. Asirgarh, north of Burhanpur, the last stronghold of the Maratha Confederacy, was besieged by British forces under Generals Sir John Malcolm and Sir John Doveton (1768–1847) and fell after three weeks, finally concluding the war (18 March–6 April 1819).

Askalon ∎ 1099 ∎ 1st Crusade
See **Ascalon**

Askalon ∎ 1153 ∎ Crusader-Muslim Wars
See **Ascalon**

Askalon ∎ 1247 ∎ Later Crusader-Muslim Wars
See **Ascalon**

Askultisk ∎ 1828 ∎ Russo-Turkish Wars
See **Akhaltsikhe**

Aslanduz ∎ 1812 ∎ Russo-Persian Wars
Following annexation of Persian Georgia, Russia invaded to support its claim and met mixed success at **Echmiadzin** (1804) and **Akhalkalaki** (1810). After years of confused warfare, Russian General Pyotr Kotliarevski crossed the Aras and decisively defeated a much larger army under Crown Prince Abbas Mirza at

Aslanduz. He then captured the key fortress at **Lenkoran** (19–20 October 1812).

Asluj I 1948 I Israeli War of Independence

Israeli commander Ygal Allon seized **Beersheba**, then feinted towards the coast at Rafa while launching his main armoured attack inland towards Asluj. Heavy fighting saw Asluj and nearby El Auja fall on the same day. There was further action around Rafa and south towards the Gulf of Aqaba, but the Egyptians were effectively defeated, and the war soon came to an end (22–27 December 1948).

Asmara I 1990–1991 I Eritrean War of Independence
See **Dekemhare**

Asosa I 1990 I Ethiopian Civil War

Oromo rebels took the offensive in the west, joining with Eritrean forces in a major attack on Asosa, near the Sudanese border. The Ethiopian army was driven out but retaliated with aerial bombing, and the rebels withdrew. However the attack helped establish the Oromo as a viable military force. In May 1991, they would help topple the government in **Addis Ababa** (5–10 January 1990).

Aspendus I 190 BC I Roman-Syrian War
See **Eurymedon**

Aspern-Essling I 1809 I Napoleonic Wars (5th Coalition)

Driving back the Austrian invasion of Bavaria, Napoleon Bonaparte crossed the Danube near **Vienna**, and attacked Aspern and Essling on the Plain of Marchfeld. The French were repulsed after extreme casualties on both sides by a huge Austrian army under Archduke Charles and withdrew to the mid-river island of Lobau. The battle is regarded as Bonaparte's first major defeat (21–22 May 1809).

Aspromonte I 1862 I Garibaldi's First March on Rome

When French-supported Rome held out against the unification of Italy, revolutionary leader Giuseppe Garibaldi crossed from Sicily to lead his Red-Shirts against the Papacy. Concerned about the possibility of French intervention, newly proclaimed King Victor Emmanuel II defeated the rebels in the extreme south of Italy at Aspromonte, capturing Garibaldi and many others (29 August 1862).

Assab I 1991 I Eritrean War of Independence

As rebels advanced on the Eritrean capital **Asmara**, a new rebel offensive began south along the Red Sea coast, towards the port of Assab. After a fierce tank battle at Bera'isole (2 April) and severe fighting at Beylul (4 April), Ethiopian forces attempted a counter-offensive north of Assab but were driven back with costly losses. The port then fell by storm and the war came to an end (25 May 1991).

Assake I 1876 I Russian Conquest of Central Asia
See **Andizhan**

As-Salman I 1991 I 1st Gulf War

On the eve of the Allied offensive into Iraq, French General Bernard Janvier on the western flank, with American support, crossed the border and raced for the strategic As-Salman airfield. Advancing rapidly with helicopters against tanks, the French overwhelmed the defence and seized the airfield, choking air support for the Republican Guard at **Wadi al-Batin** (23–26 February 1991).

Assaye I 1803 I 2nd British-Maratha War

In the decisive battle of the British campaign in Deccan India, General Sir Arthur Wellesley advanced from victory at **Ahmadnagar** to Assaye on the Kelna, where he utterly routed the Maratha army of Daulat Rao Sindhia of Gwalior and Raja Raghuji Bhonsle of Berar. Many years later, as Duke of Wellington, Wellesley nominated Assaye as his bloodiest battle (24 September 1803).

Asseiceira I 1834 I Miguelite Wars

Dom Miguel, brother of the King, seized the throne of Portugal against the interests of his

niece Maria da Gloria. However, he was eventually defeated at Asseiceira, near Santarem in
Portugal, by General Antonio de Souza Duke
of Terceira. Threatened by a large Portuguese-
Spanish army at Evora, Dom Miguel capitulated
two weeks later, relinquishing his claim to the
throne (12 May 1834).

Assens ❙ 1535 ❙ Danish Counts' War
  See **Oksnebjerg**

**Assiette ❙ 1747 ❙ War of the Austrian
Succession**
  See **Exilles**

**Assinarus ❙ 413 BC ❙ Great
Peloponnesian War**
  See **Syracuse Harbour**

**Assunden ❙ 1016 ❙ Danish Conquest of
England**
  See **Ashingdon**

As Suwayda ❙ 1925 ❙ Druze Rebellion
  See **Suwayda**

**Asta ❙ 402 ❙ Goth Invasion of the
Roman Empire**
  Marching through the Alps from Gaul to raise
the Goth siege of Milan, the Roman-Vandal General Flavius Stilicho clashed with the Goth leader
Alaric at Asta (modern Asti) on the Tanarus,
southeast of Turin. While the outcome was inconclusive, Alaric was forced to withdraw and, within
months, the battle was followed by major defeats
for the Goth leader at **Pollentia** and **Verona**.

**Asta's Creek ❙ 1844 ❙ Comanche Indian
Wars**
  See **Walker's Creek**

**Asterabad ❙ 1752 ❙ Persian Wars of
Succession**
  Amid struggle for control of Persia after the
assassination of Nadir Shah, Regent Karim
Khan Zand defeated Ali Mardan Khan in 1751 at
Chahar Mahall, then blockaded the Qajar
Mohammad Hasan Khan, at Asterabad (modern

Gorgan), southeast of the Caspian. Aided
by Turkoman allies, Mohammad Hasan Khan
heavily defeated the Zands in a powerful sortie,
and they withdrew to Tehran.

**Astorga ❙ 1810 ❙ Napoleonic Wars
(Peninsular Campaign)**
  French General Androche Junot was repulsed
from Astorga, on the Tuerto River in northwestern Spain (11 February), then returned with
a force of 26,000 infantry and 8,000 cavalry, as
well as substantial artillery. Spanish commander
José Maria Santocildes held out for a month, but
the city finally fell by storm. It was retaken by
Santocildes in August 1812 (21 March–21 April
1810).

Astrakhan ❙ 1554 ❙ Russia's Volga Wars
  Expanding Russia's empire southwards, Tsar
Ivan IV—the Terrible—conquered **Kazan** in
1552, then sent a large force against the Tatar
fortress of Astrakhan, at the mouth of the Volga.
The city fell to prolonged siege, after which
Khan Yamgurchi was deposed and replaced by
the Russian vassal Khan Darwish Ali. Darwish
was soon overthrown by Yamgurchi, and Russia
returned to seize control.

Astrakhan ❙ 1569 ❙ Russia's Volga Wars
  In support of his scheme to cut a canal between
the Volga and Don Rivers to allow Turkish naval
access from the Black Sea to the Caspian, Ottoman Sultan Selim II attacked Astrakhan. The
Russian garrison held out until a relief force sent
by Tsar Ivan IV—the Terrible—drove off the
Turkish siege army under Grand Vizier Sokollu
Mehmet Pasha. Selim then withdrew.

Asuncion ❙ 1947 ❙ Paraguayan Civil War
  Six years after seizing power, Paraguayan
Dictator Higinio Moringo faced armed rebellion
by former President Rafael Franco and the
Febrersista Party, who marched on Asuncion.
The capital held out in fierce fighting until
Loyalist reinforcements arrived and the rebels
were routed with over 1,600 killed. Moringo
was himself overthrown in a coup the following
year (20 August 1947).

Aswan I 1799 I French Revolutionary Wars (Middle East)

Having routed General Murad Bey near the **Pyramids** (July 1798), Napoleon Bonaparte sent General Louis Desaix to defeat the Mamluk leader on the Upper Nile at **Sediman**. Desaix then marched south and at Aswan, reinforced by cavalry under General Louis-Nicolas Davout, destroyed the last remnants of the Mamluk army and drove Murad Bey beyond the First Cataract (1 February 1799).

Atapuerca I 1054 I Spanish Territorial Wars

Garcia III of Navarre was determined to extend his territory and marched against his younger brother, Ferdinand I, King of Leon and Castile. Garcia was killed in a decisive battle at Atapuerca, near Burgos in northern Castile, and his Navarrese army and its Muslim auxiliaries were routed. Ferdinand seized part of Navarre and gave the rest to Garcia's son, Sancho III (15 September 1054).

Atbara I 350 I Axum-Meroite War

King Ezana of Aksum, on the upper reaches of the Nile, progressively defeated his neighbours, then marched north against the declining Nubian kingdom of Meroe, about 100 miles downstream of modern Khartoum. In a decisive battle near Atabara, Ezana defeated the army of Meroe and overthrew the kingdom. His adoption of Coptic Christianity established a lasting Christian tradition in Ethiopia.

Atbara I 1898 I British-Sudan Wars

Advancing up the Nile to recapture the Sudan, General Sir Herbert Kitchener's Anglo-Egyptian force turned up the Atbara and met a much larger Mahdist army under Emir Mahmoud. Attacking against a thorn-bush stockade near Nakheila, Kitchener inflicted a major defeat—with over 2,000 Dervishes killed—and continued his march towards **Omdurman** (8 April 1898).

Atchoupa I 1890 I 1st Franco-Dahomean War

Reinforced after costly actions in Dahomey at **Cotonou**, Colonel Sébastien Terrillon advanced northwest to Atchoupa, where he was attacked by King Behanzin himself with 9,000 troops (including 2,000 Amazons). French rifles inflicted terrible losses, but Terrillon had to withdraw when his native auxiliaries broke. A truce was soon agreed ceding Cotonou and Porto Novo to France (20 April 1890).

Atella I 1496 I Italian War of Charles VIII

See **Aversa**

Atenquique I 1858 I Mexican War of the Reform

Liberal Generals Leandro Valle and Santos Degollado recovered from early set-backs and attempted to retake Guadalajara, which had been lost at **Salamanca** (10 March). In a ravine at Atenquique, to the south near Ciudad Guzmán, they were driven off by a larger Conservative force under General Miguel Miramón, who won decisively three months later at **Ahualalco** (2 July 1858).

Athenry I 1316 I English Invasion of Ireland

Consolidating the English presence in Ireland, Anglo-Irish troops under William de Burgh and Richard de Bermingham destroyed the undisciplined peasant army of Feidlim O'Connor, King of Connaught, at Athenry in County Galway. A reputed 11,000 men were slaughtered, including 29 Chiefs of the clan, and the O'Connors never again exercised power in Ireland (10 August 1316).

Athens, Alabama I 1864 I American Civil War (Western Theatre)

Confederate cavalry Colonel Moses W. Hannon led a fresh offensive in northern Alabama, where he crossed the Tennessee River to attack Athens, northwest of Huntsville, held by Captain Emil Adam for General Grenville M. Dodge. The early morning attack was driven off after a brief, sharp action, and the Confederates were forced to withdraw (26 January 1864).

Athens, Greece I 404 BC I Great Peloponnesian War

With the Athenian fleet destroyed at **Aegospotami**, Athens itself was besieged by Spartan commander Lysander. Facing starvation after six months, the Athenian Council deposed and executed the hawkish leader Cleophon and surrendered the city. Its defensive long walls were destroyed and the fall of Athens ended the war. Lysander set up an oligarchy but was soon overthrown after **Munychia**.

Athens, Greece I 264–262 BC **I Chremonidian War**

In a revolt against Antigonus II of Macedonia, Athenians led by Chremonides and his brother Glaucon formed an alliance with Sparta and Egypt. However, Antigonus routed the Spartans at **Corinth** (265 BC), then laid siege to Athens. Following an heroic two-year resistance, Athens was starved into surrender. Glaucon and Chremonides fled to Egypt and Athens became a Macedonian province.

Athens, Greece I 87–86 BC **I 1st Mithridatic War**
    See **Piraeus**

Athens, Greece I 1821–1822 I Greek War of Independence
    See **Acropolis**

Athens, Greece I 1827 I Greek War of Independence
    See **Acropolis**

Athens, Greece I 1944–1945 I Greek Civil War

As German forces evacuated Greece, Communists seized most of the north, then attacked Athens, defended by British General Sir Reginald Scobie. Within days, General Manolis Mandakas (later Aris Veloukhiotis) took police stations, the Town Hall, and the road to Piraeus. When British reinforcements arrived, the insurgents accepted a ceasefire (5 December 1944–15 January 1945).

Atherton Moor I 1643 I British Civil Wars
    See **Adwalton Moor**

Athlone I 1691 I War of the Glorious Revolution

Despite a decisive Protestant victory at the **Boyne** in July 1690, Catholic Athlone in County Roscommon held out for James II under Governor Colonel Richard Grace. However, Grace was killed during the siege and the city fell by assault to William III's General Godert de Ginkel. After completing the conquest of Ireland, Ginkel was created Earl of Athlone and Baron **Aughrim** (19–30 June 1691).

Ati I 1978 I Chad Civil Wars

Northern rebels united under Ahmat Acyl, who led an offensive into the south. President Félix Malloum called for aid from France, which sent troops and fighter-bombers. Northeast of the capital at Ati, on the road to Abéché, French and Chadian government forces launched a severe attack, which halted the rebel advance. A year later, Malloum was overthrown in **N'Djamena** (May 1978).

Atlanta I 1864 I American Civil War (Western Theatre)

Two days after a failed sortie north of Atlanta, Georgia, at **Peachtree Creek**, Confederate commander John B. Hood sent General William J. Hardee on a second sortie to the east. Although Union General James A. McPherson was killed, commander William T. Sherman secured a bloody victory. Atlanta was under virtual siege until the decisive action at **Jonesborough** (22 July 1864).

Atlantic I 1915–1917 I World War I (War at Sea)

In the first great underwater campaign, Germany blockaded Britain and attacked shipping in the Atlantic. Unrestricted submarine warfare was declared on 1 February 1917, but by late that year American intervention and effective implementation of the convoy system largely ended the offensive. The Germans had sunk over 8 million tons of shipping at a cost of more than 50 U-boats lost.

Atlantic I 1939–1945 I World War II (War at Sea)

Attempting to repeat the nearly successful blockade of Britain in World War I, German U-boats, supported by surface raiders and aircraft, waged a bitter campaign against merchant shipping. Allied convoys, anti-submarine measures and closing the air gap virtually won the battle in mid-1943. By war's end, U-boats sank 14 million tons of shipping, mainly in the Atlantic, for 780 U-boats lost.

Atlixco I 1847 I American-Mexican War

American General Joseph Lane relieved the siege of **Puebla**, then pursued General Joaquin Rea 18 miles southwest to Atlixco, where Rea's large Mexican force attempted to make a stand. The hillside town surrendered following a heavy artillery bombardment and the guerrillas dispersed with over 200 killed. They were defeated again next month at **Izúcar de Matamoros** (19 October 1847).

Atoleiros I 1384 I Portuguese-Castilian Wars

During a disputed succession in Portugal, João of Aviz and his General Nuno Alvares Pereira seized key cities, provoking an invasion by Juan I of Castile, who claimed the throne through his wife Beatrice. North of Sousel at Atoleiros, the Castilians were defeated and withdrew. When João later formally claimed the throne, Juan invaded again and was routed in 1385 at **Aljubarrota** (6 April 1384).

Atra I 199 I Wars of Emperor Severus

A year after the great Roman victory at **Ctesiphon**, Emperor Septimius Severus attacked the Parthian city of Atra (Al Hathr), famous for its wealthy sun temple, in the desert west of the Tigris. The Roman siege train was destroyed during the three-week siege and Severus withdrew after two major assaults were repulsed with heavy losses. This was a major blow to Roman prestige.

Attleboro I 1966 I Vietnam War

See **Dau Tieng**

Attock I 1813 I Afghan-Sikh Wars

Afghan Vizier Fateh Khan captured Kashmir, then advanced towards Attock, which had been occupied by the great Sikh leader Ranjit Singh. At Haidru, on the Mansur Plain northeast of the fort, General Dewan Mokham Chand routed the Afghans with a decisive cavalry charge and Fateh Khan returned to Kabul. It was the first significant Punjabi victory over the Afghans (13 July 1813).

Attu I 1943 I World War II (Pacific)

When battle at the **Komandorski Islands** blocked Japanese reinforcements to the **Aleutians**, American General Albert Brown landed 11,000 men to retake Attu, held by 2,400 men under Colonel Yasuyo Yamazaki. Only 29 Japanese survived fierce fighting and a suicide charge and the Americans lost 600 killed and 1,200 wounded. The Japanese then evacuated Kiska (11–30 May 1943).

Atulapa I 1853 I Central American National Wars

A stubborn border dispute between President José Trinidad Cabañas of Honduras and President Rafael Carrera of Guatemala saw Honduran forces cross into eastern Guatemala. Near Esquipulas at Atulapa, they were defeated and driven back across the border by General Vicente Cerna. Guatemalan forces then launched an unexpected assault in the west at **Omoa** (July 1853).

Auberoche I 1345 I Hundred Years War

After English forces seized the powerful castle of Auberoche, east of Perigueux, it was held against French siege by Alexander de Caumont from English-ruled Gascony. Marching with a relief force from Bordeaux, Henry Duke of Lancaster routed the besiegers. Louis of Poitiers was fatally wounded and many other French nobles were captured for ransom (21 October 1345).

**Aubers ▌ 1915 ▌ World War I
(Western Front)**

In support of the British in the north around **Ypres**, and the French in the south in **Artois**, General Sir Douglas Haig again advanced against Aubers Ridge, south of Lille. Prince Rupprecht's Sixth Army had been heavily reinforced after **Neuve Chappelle** and Haig lost over 11,000 men in two failed assaults. Four days later he attacked further south at **Festubert** (9–10 May 1915).

**Auburn ▌ 1863 ▌ American Civil War
(Eastern Theatre)**

Confederate commander Robert E. Lee manoeuvred in Virginia after **Gettysburg**, trying to outflank the Union army of General George G. Meade, and sent General James "Jeb" Stuart against his rearguard under General Gouvernor K. Warren. After an inconclusive action near Auburn, Meade kept withdrawing north and repulsed the Confederates at **Bristoe Station** (14 October 1863).

Audaghost ▌ 1054 ▌ Fall of Ghana

When the great West African Empire of Ghana seized the Berber trading city of Audaghost (in modern Mauretania) in 1050, the Almoravid leader Abu Bakr ibn Umar marched south from Morocco, determined to spread Islam. Crossing the Sahara, he captured Audaghost after heavy fighting, then continued a long campaign into Ghana, culminating in the capture of **Kumbi** in 1076.

**Auerstadt ▌ 1806 ▌ Napoleonic Wars
(4th Coalition)**

As Napoleon Bonaparte's army converged on Prussia, Marshal Louis Davout met Karl Wilhelm Ferdinand Duke of Brunswick at Auerstadt, near Weimar. Despite terrible casualties, Davout's outnumbered French Corps won a decisive victory and Brunswick was killed. Bonaparte's victory the same day 15 miles away at **Jena** virtually knocked Prussia out of the war (14 October 1806).

**Aughrim ▌ 1691 ▌ War of the Glorious
Revolution**

A year after the decisive Irish loss at the **Boyne**, the Irish-French army of Patrick Sarsfield Lord Lucan and Charles Marquis de Saint-Ruth renewed the struggle against William III in County Galway, western Ireland. At Aughrim, west of Ballinasloe, the Allies were routed by General Godert de Ginkel's Protestant army. Saint-Ruth was killed and Lucan fled to **Limerick** (12 July 1691).

**Augsburg ▌ 910 ▌ Magyar Invasion of
Germany**

Having secured victory at **Pressburg** in 907, Magyar invaders continued to ravage Germany, culminating in a decisive battle against a large Christian army under the nominal leadership of German King Ludwig III—The Child. The Hungarian cavalry won a crushing victory at Augsburg, on the Lech, west of Munich, and the 17-year-old King was forced into a peace treaty, paying tribute for ten years.

**Augsburg ▌ 955 ▌ Magyar Invasion of
Germany**
    See **Lechfeld**

**Augsburg ▌ 1796 ▌ French Revolutionary
Wars (1st Coalition)**

Advancing against the forces of Archduke Charles Louis of Austria, French General Jean Victor Moreau sent General Laurent Gouvion Saint-Cyr against Austrian forces at Augsburg. When the Bavarian city closed its gates, Austrian General Maximilian Latour was defeated and driven back across the Lech. He was heavily defeated two days later at **Friedberg** (22 August 1796).

**Augusta, Georgia ▌ 1781 ▌ War of the
American Revolution**

American commander Nathanael Greene pursued the British into South Carolina after battle at **Guildford Courthouse**, and sent General Andrew Pickens and Colonel Henry Lee west to besiege Augusta, Georgia, boldly defended by

Colonel Thomas Brown at Fort Cornwallis. Brown had to surrender after continuous bombardment, and Lee marched to **Fort Ninety-Six** (16 April–5 June 1781).

Augusta, Sicily ∎ 1676 ∎ 3rd Dutch War
Three months after indecisive naval action off **Stromboli**, French Admiral Abraham Duquesne, sent to support Sicilian rebellion against Spain, engaged the Dutch-Spanish fleet of Michiel de Ruyter and Don Franscisco de la Cerda in the Gulf of Augusta off Syracuse. Duquesne broke off the action but, due to Spanish irresolution, de Ruyter could not secure victory and later died of wounds (22 April 1676).

Augustovo ∎ 1914 ∎ World War I (Eastern Front)
Despite massive losses at the **Masurian Lakes**, General Paul von Hindenberg checked the advancing Russians at Augustovo, and General Pavel Rennenkampf withdrew behind the Nieman to regroup. Rennenkampf then launched a massive counter-attack and the Germans fell back through Augustovo, abandoning East Prussia with about 60,000 casualties (26 September–9 October 1914).

Auldearn ∎ 1645 ∎ British Civil Wars
After a raid on Dundee, Scottish Royalist James Graham Marquis of Montrose marched towards the east coast, pursued by Covenanters under Colonel Sir John Hurry. Instead of waiting for the main army under General Sir William Baillie, Hurry accepted battle near Nairn at Auldearn and was heavily defeated, leaving the Highlanders to meet Baillie two months later at **Alford** (9 May 1645).

Aumâle ∎ 1592 ∎ 9th French War of Religion
Alessandro Farnese Duke of Parma was advancing through Amiens to relieve the siege of **Rouen**, when he met the Royalist forces of Henry of Navarre to the northeast at Aumâle. The King was wounded in a sharp action, but Henry was saved by his reserves under Louis

Gonzaga Duke of Nevers. The over-cautious Parma allowed the Spanish advance to be delayed (3 February 1592).

Auneau ∎ 1587 ∎ 8th French War of Religion
Just weeks after the Catholic defeat at **Coutras**, northeast of Bordeaux, the leader of the Catholic cause, Duke Henry of Guise, defeated German Protestants marching to assist the French Huguenots at Aneau, east of Chartres. King Henry III fled after the battle, and the ambitious Guise seized Paris. He was soon assassinated (24 November 1587).

Aurangabad ∎ 1724 ∎ Mughal-Hyderabad War
See **Shakarkhelda**

Auray ∎ 1364 ∎ Hundred Years War
Supporting John IV de Montfort's claim for the Duchy of Brittany, an Anglo-Gascon army under de Montfort, and Sir John Chandos besieged Auray, east of Lorient. Bertrand de Guesclin and rival claimant, Charles of Blois, attempted to relieve the port, but Blois was killed and Guesclin was captured. De Montfort became Duke, ending the disputed Breton Succession (29 September 1364).

Aussa ∎ 1875 ∎ Egyptian-Ethiopian War
An Egyptian force of about 350 under the Swiss officer Johann Munzinger Pasha, on campaign in eastern Ethiopia against Yohannes IV, marched inland from Tajoura in modern Djibouti towards Aussa near Lake Assal. Betrayed by the local Governor Walad Lehata, the Egyptians were attacked by Danakil tribesmen and over 200 were killed, including Munzinger (14 November 1875).

Aussig ∎ 1426 ∎ Hussite Wars
Facing a threatened invasion of Moravia by Hussite heretics, a fresh crusade of Catholic Germans marched into northwest Bohemia (in the modern Czech Republic) against former priest, Prokob the Bald, who commanded following the

death of the great leader Jan Zizka. Prokob achieved a decisive victory on the Elbe at Aussig (modern Usti nad Labem) and won again next year at **Tachov**.

Austerlitz I 1805 I Napoleonic Wars (3rd Coalition)

One of Napoleon Bonaparte's greatest victories saw him destroy a Russian-Austrian attempt to cut off his advance from Vienna. On the Pratzen Plateau near Brno at Austerlitz (modern Slavkov), Bonaparte's outnumbered army stormed the heights and inflicted massive casualties on the Allies. Francis II of Austria sued for peace and Tsar Alexander I of Russia withdrew (2 December 1805).

Autossee I 1813 I Creek Indian War

General John Floyd built on victory at **Talladega** and **Hillabee** by leading 950 Georgia militia and 400 Indian allies against the Creek at Autossee, on the Tallapoosa in Alabama. Floyd fell on the town, with 250 Creek Indians killed and 400 houses destroyed in a virtual massacre. Further decisive actions soon followed at **Holy Ground** and **Horseshoe Bend** (29 November 1813).

Autun I 58 BC I Rome's Later Gallic Wars

See **Bibracte**

Autun I 532 I Burgundian-Frankish War

Despite defeat at **Vézeronce** in 524, Godomar of Burgundy recovered his kingdom, then faced a third Frankish invasion, led by Childebert and Clotaire (who had killed the sons of their late brother Clodomir and divided the kingdom with their brother Theodoric). The Franks won a decisive victory near besieged Autun, northwest of Chalons, then annexed the Kingdom of Burgundy.

Ava I 1527 I Burmese Dynastic Wars

Campaigning south along the Irriwaddy, the Shan State of Mohnyin in northern Burma attacked the independent kingdom of Ava, where King Shwenankyawshin was defeated and killed

in a final massive assault. The Shan then seized and sacked Ava, causing terrible destruction, and installed Prince Thohanbwa as King. They held Ava until it fell in 1555 to Bayinnaung of Burma.

Ava I 1555 I Burmese Dynastic Wars

King Bayinnaung of Burma defeated Mon rebels at **Pegu** and **Prome** (1552), then determined to crush the Shan Chiefs, who had advanced down the Irriwaddy and sacked the ancient capital of Ava. With a powerful force, he seized Ava and forced the Shan to submit, dismissing King Sithkyawhtin and securing Burmese overlordship until 1599. Bayinnaung then invaded Siam and won at **Ayutthaya**.

Ava I 1752 I Burmese Civil Wars

Climaxing a prolonged campaign to conquer northern Burma, the Mon King Binnya Dala, with French aid, seized Pegu (1751), then led a final massive offensive against the capital, Ava. The city was captured, with the last Toungoo King taken and later executed, marking the end of the 250-year Toungoo Dynasty. Binnya Dala himself was overthrown in 1757 after the fall of **Pegu** (April 1752).

Avaí I 1868 I War of the Triple Alliance

Falling back from the courageous defence of the **Ytororó**, Paraguayan General Bernadino Caballero turned on the advancing Brazilians under General Manuel Osório. Despite costly Brazilian losses in battle at Avaí, on the Paraguay, south of Asunción near Villeta, Caballero was defeated. His survivors withdrew towards the defensive position near Angostura at **Ita Ybate** (11 December 1868).

Avarayr I 451 I Christian Rising in Armenia

When Persian Shah Yazdgard II tried to impose Zoroastrianism on Christian Armenia, he sparked revolt led by hereditary leader Vardan Mamikonean. But without Roman support, the revolt was doomed. On the Plain of Avarayr, in northeastern Iran near modern Maku, the

Armenians were crushed with terrible losses, including Vardan killed. He was later honoured as a saint (2 June 451).

Avaricum I 52 BC I Rome's Later Gallic Wars

Julius Caesar was determined to put down rebellion against Rome and advanced into central Gaul to besiege the key rebel city of Avaricum (modern Bourges). Driving back relief efforts by Arverni chieftain Vercingetorix, Caesar stormed the city and massacred its inhabitants. Caesar then marched south against Vercingetorix at **Gergovia**, where he suffered a costly repulse (March 52 BC).

Avein I 1635 I Thirty Years War (Franco-Habsburg War)

Marching through Liège to join with the Dutch against Spain in the Netherlands, Armand du Plessis Cardinal Richelieu sent the French army under Marshal Urbain de Maillé-Brézé. The Spanish, led by Prince Thomas of Savoy, suffered a heavy defeat at Avein, north of the Mehaigne near Wasseiges, and the French went on to temporarily threaten Brussels (20 May 1635).

Averasborough I 1865 I American Civil War (Western Theatre)

As Union commander William T. Sherman marched east across North Carolina, his left flank was checked at Averasborough, northeast of Fayatteville, by Confederate General William Hardee. Heavily reinforced by General Henry Slocum, the Union army renewed the advance, driving back a Confederate counter-attack, then marching east to a decisive action at **Bentonville** (16 March 1865).

Aversa I 1496 I Italian War of Charles VIII

After invading Italy in support of his claim for the throne of Naples, Charles VIII of France ravaged much of the country before leaving control with his kinsman, Gilbert Duke of Montpensier, Viceroy at Naples. Montpensier was utterly defeated at Aversa, just north of Naples, by a Spanish-Italian alliance under Gonsalvo de Cordoba and France was temporarily driven out (23 July 1496).

Avesnes-le-Sec I 1793 I French Revolutionary Wars (1st Coalition)

In a brilliant unsupported cavalry action in northern France, Austrian squadrons under Prince Johann Liechtenstein and Count Heinrich von Bellegarde attacked a French force of infantry and artillery at Avesnes-le-Sec, just northeast of Cambrai. The French under General Nicolas Declaye were routed with costly casualties and most of their guns were captured (12 September 1793).

Avigliana I 1630 I Thirty Years War (Mantuan War)

When Savoy intervened in the Mantuan succession, Cardinal Richelieu sent Duke Henry of Montmorency against Savoy and its Imperial allies. West of Turin at Avigliana, the French army routed the Spanish, inflicting 700 casualties and taking 600 prisoners including commander Don Carlo Doria. However, Montmorency could not stop the Imperials taking **Mantua** a week later (10 July 1630).

Avignon I 121 BC I Rome's Gallic Wars

At the start of the Roman campaign in Transalpine Gaul, Consul Domitius Ahenobarbus took a large army, including elephants, against the powerful Allobroges people. The two forces met during the spring on the Rhone, apparently near modern Avignon, where the Gauls suffered a terrible defeat. Later the same year, Rome sent a fresh force to join Ahenobarbus against the Arverni people at the **Isara**.

Avignon I 500 I Burgundian-Frankish War

Frankish King Clovis intervened in Burgundian affairs and defeated King Gundobad at **Dijon** on the River Ouche before pursuing him to a long siege at Avignon on the River Rhone. However, Gundobad resisted so effectively that Clovis eventually recognised his authority and withdrew from Burgundy. A fresh offensive by the next generation of Franks won in 524 at **Vézeronce**.

Avignon ∎ 1226 ∎ Albigensian Crusade

The resumed Crusade against the Albigensian heretics of southern France saw King Louis VIII of France—the Lion—send a large army into the Languedoc to besiege the city of Avignon on the River Rhone. Despite Louis losing a reported 20,000 men to disease and enemy action, the city surrendered after three months and the sect was suppressed. Louis died soon afterwards.

Avranches ∎ 1426 ∎ Hundred Years War

As England completed its conquest of northern France, John Duke of Bedford, Regent in France for Henry VI, defeated Arthur de Richemont, Constable of France, near the village of St James, south of Avranches on the Bay of St Michel. The defeat forced Richemont's brother, Jean V Duke of Brittany, to submit to England (6 March 1426).

Avranches ∎ 1944 ∎ World War II (Western Europe)

In the breakout from **Normandy**, with German armour diverted by the British at **Caen**, American General Omar Bradley attacked southwest from **St Lo** towards Avranches. Despite costly losses to their own bombing, the Americans took 20,000 prisoners in six days and seized Avranches, opening the way to **St Malo** and **Brest**. The Germans struck back at **Mortain** (25–31 July 1944).

Awah ∎ 1858 ∎ Indian Mutiny

Kusal Singh, rebel Thakur of Awah, defeating Jodhpur's army at **Pali** but failed in a siege of **Nimach** (November 1857) and fell back on Awah, east of Mandasur, where he was later attacked by 1,100 men under Colonel John Holmes. Just as an assault was about to be launched after a five-day bombardment, the rebels fled, abandoning guns and extensive military stores (19–24 January 1858).

Awan Erigo ∎ 1902 ∎ Wars of the Mad Mullah

See **Erego**

Awazu ∎ 1184 ∎ Gempei War

Determined to punish his rebellious cousin Minamoto Yoshinaka in Kyoto, Yoritomo in Kamakura sent his brothers Yoshitsune and Noriyori who routed Yoshinaka at the **Uji**, then pursued him to the Awazu, near Otsu, east of Kyoto. Yoshinaka committed seppuku after a brutal final stand and the Minamoto brothers then marched west against the Taira clan at **Ichinotani** (February 1184).

Axarquia ∎ 1483 ∎ Final Christian Reconquest of Spain

A Spanish force under Rodrigo Ponce de Leon Marquis of Cadiz marching towards Malaga was ambushed to the north in the pass at Axarquia by Moorish commander Abdul Hassan, former King of Granada. The destruction of the flower of Spanish chivalry encouraged the new King Abu Abdallah (Boabdil) on a disastrous invasion of Christian territory, leading to defeat at **Lucena** (20 March 1483).

Axholme ∎ 1265 ∎ 2nd English Barons' War

Prince Edward, son of Henry III, defeated and killed Simon de Montfort Earl of Leicester at **Evesham**, then pursued the rebel Barons to siege on the Isle of Axholme in the Fens of Lincolnshire. Some rebels eventually surrendered when Edward promised to spare their lives, but de Montfort's son Simon the Younger fled into exile and others escaped to **Ely** (28 December 1265).

Axone ∎ 57 BC ∎ Rome's Later Gallic Wars

See **Aisne**

Axtorna I 1565 I Nordic Seven Years War

Withdrawing from **Varberg** in Danish Halland, 8,000 Danes and Germans led by Daniel Rantzau were attacked near Axtorna by 12,000 Swedish reinforcements under Jakob Henriksson Hästesko. Despite initial Swedish success in the war's largest action, their cavalry were badly handled and a bold Danish counter-attack saw the Swedes flee, abandoning all their guns (20 October 1565).

Ayacucho I 1824 I Peruvian War of Independence

Five months after victory at **Junín**, Patriot leader General José de Sucre led Peruvians and Colombians against Spanish Viceroy José de la Serna and General José Canterac in Peru's Ayacucho Valley, near Huamanga. De la Serna was routed and surrendered, along with his entire army, securing Peruvian independence and virtually ending Spanish rule in South America (9 December 1824).

Ayerbe I 1811 I Napoleonic Wars (Peninsular Campaign)

When a French-Italian column of fewer than 1,000 men under Colonel Luigi Ceccopieri was marching to relieve the town of Ayerbe, near Huesca in northeastern Spain, it was attacked and overwhelmed by a large force of Spanish guerrillas. The unfortunate Ceccopieri was killed and his entire force was killed or captured (11 October 1811).

Aylesford I 456 I Anglo-Saxon Conquest of Britain

See **Aegelsthrep**

Ayohuma I 1813 I Argentine War of Independence

Royalist General Joaquín de la Pezuela regained the initiative in Spanish Upper Peru (modern Bolivia) to defeat Patriot General Manuel Belgrano at **Vilcapugio**, then pursued him south towards Potosi. To the northeast at Ayohuma, Belgrano suffered another terrible defeat and was replaced in command of Argen-

tina's Army of the North by General José de San Martin (14 November 1813).

Ayubale I 1703 I Queen Anne's War

In order to punish the Spanish for inciting Indian attacks against English settlers, a force of whites and Indians under James Moore, the former Governor of South Carolina, attacked Spanish troops at the Ayubale Mission, near Tallahassee, Alabama. The capture of the mission and devastation of nearby country constituted a major setback for Spanish Florida (14 December 1703).

Ayutthaya I 1548 I Burmese-Siamese Wars

King Tabinshwehti united the kingdoms of Burma at **Pegu** in 1539, then invaded Siam, aided by Portuguese mercenaries. After withdrawing from a failed offensive against Arakan, he returned east with a massive force and besieged the capital Ayutthaya, north of modern Bangkok. Despite heavy Siamese losses, Tabinshwehti was forced into an ignominious withdrawal. He was assassinated in 1550.

Ayutthaya I 1568–1569 I Burmese-Siamese Wars

After crushing rebellion in Burma at **Ava** (1555), King Bayinnaung invaded Siam, seizing the capital Ayutthaya and taking the royal family hostage (1564). Facing rebellion, he later returned in force to besiege Ayutthaya, which fell after heavy fighting. Thousands were deported to slavery and Siam became a virtual vassal state until victory in 1593 at **Nong Sarai** (November 1568–30 August 1569).

Ayutthaya I 1760 I Burmese Invasions of Siam

On a campaign to conquer Siam, King Alaungpaya of Burma led a massive force which besieged the capital Ayutthaya, 50 miles north of modern Bangkok, held by Prince Uthumphon for King Borommaracha. Unable to breach the city's defences in the wet season, Alaungpaya was mortally hit and died on the march home.

His son Hsinbyushin took the city seven years later (April 1760).

Ayutthaya ▌ 1766–1767 ▌ Burmese Invasions of Siam

When King Hsinbyushin of Burma besieged Siam's capital of Ayutthaya, north of Bangkok, Prince Uthumphon defended the city, and Burmese commander Maha Nawrahta was killed. But Ayutthaya fell and was destroyed. King Suriyamurin died and Uthumphon was exiled, ending a 400-year dynasty. Siamese General Phya Taksin soon retook the city (February 1766–7 April 1767).

Azagal ▌ 1086 ▌ Early Christian Reconquest of Spain
See **Zallaka**

Azamgarh ▌ 1858 ▌ Indian Mutiny

British and Sikh troops under General Sir Edward Lugard, advancing from Lucknow to relieve the garrison at Azamgarh, north of Benares, dispersed a rebel force near **Jaunpur**, then routed Kunwar Singh's Danapur mutineers outside Azamgarh. Kunwar Singh's badly mauled force managed to slip away to the east but was soon defeated again at **Maniar** and **Jagdispur** (15 April 1858).

Azaz ▌ 1030 ▌ Later Byzantine-Muslim Wars

Resolved to achieve military success in Syria, Emperor Romanus III Argyrus led a large expedition to secure Antioch, then marched east against Aleppo. In a disastrous defeat just north of Aleppo at Azaz, the Byzantine army was routed by Mirdasid Arabs and fled with perhaps 10,000 killed. The Emperor escaped to Constantinople and Byzantine prestige was soon restored by capture of **Edessa**.

Azaz ▌ 1125 ▌ Crusader-Muslim Wars

When Aqsonqor Il-Bursuqi, Governor of Mosul, unified Muslim rulers and launched a major offensive in northern Syria, King Baldwin II of Jerusalem took the combined forces of Antioch, Tripoli and Edessa to relieve the siege of Zerdana. Baldwin then destroyed the Muslim army in a decisive battle at Azaz, north of Aleppo. Bursuqi sued for peace and withdrew to Mosul (May 1125).

Azcapotzalco ▌ 1428 ▌ Aztec Wars of Conquest

During a disputed Tepanec succession, Maxtla killed his brother and usurped the throne then laid siege to Tenochtitlan. An alliance of opponents under Nezahualcoyotl drove Maxtla back to siege at Azcapotzalco, which fell after 114 days, and the tyrant was executed. Tenochtitlan, Texcoco and Tacuba then created the Triple Alliance, which became the foundation of the powerful Aztec Empire.

Azimghur ▌ 1858 ▌ Indian Mutiny
See **Azamgarh**

Azores ▌ 1591 ▌ Anglo-Spanish Wars

Sent to the Azores to intercept the Spanish treasure fleet, British commander Lord Thomas Howard was surprised by warships under Admiral Don Alonso de Bassan. When Howard was forced to withdraw, Sir Richard Grenville in *Revenge* was cut off and tried to fight. In a classic action, he resisted until fatally wounded. *Revenge* surrendered, but was lost in a storm (31 August 1591).

Azotus ▌ 659–630 BC ▌ Assyrian Wars

King Psammetichus (Psamthek) of Egypt freed Egypt of Assyrian rule, then used Greek mercenaries to attack Azotus, 22 miles north of Gaza in Palestine, to protect his northern border. The strategic city (Greek Ashdod) was taken from the Assyrians after a 29-year siege, one of the longest ever recorded. Egypt was later driven out of Palestine at **Carchemish** (trad date c 659–630 BC).

Azov ▌ 1695–1696 ▌ Russian Invasion of the Crimea

Having failed with a siege in 1695, Tsar Peter I of Russia launched a large-scale land and naval siege of the Crimean fortress of Azov, controlling the southern mouth of the Don River and access to the Black Sea. Despite stubborn Turkish resistance and heavy Russian casualties, General

Boris Sheremetev captured the fort and the Tsar set about improving its defences (28 July 1696).

Azov I 1736 I Austro-Russian-Turkish War

In Russia's renewed campaign against the Crimean Tatars, **Perekop** fell (May 1736), then Irish-born General Count Peter Lacy and Admiral Pyotr Bredal attacked the strategic city of Azov, defended by the Seraskier Tiagya. It fell after a brutal seven-week siege, but the victory led to war with Turkey, at the end of which Russia retained Azov but agreed to demolish its fortifications (1 July 1736).

B

Babadag ▌ 1791 ▌ Catherine the Great's 2nd Turkish War

Russian General Mikhail Kutuzov led a spring offensive at the mouth of the Danube, where he advanced south from **Izmail** and crossed the delta with 12,000 men to attack the Turks at Babadag, in modern Romania. The Turks were driven out of their camp with costly losses and Kutuzov then marched northwest to join the main Russian army in its victory at **Matchin** (3 June 1791).

Bab el Wed ▌ 1948 ▌ Israeli War of Independence

See **Latrun**

Babi Wali Kotal (1st) ▌ 1842 ▌ 1st British-Afghan War

While Akbar Khan, son of deposed Amir Dost Muhammad, besieged **Kabul**, other Afghans besieged **Kandahar**, defended by British General William Nott, who sent Colonel (later Sir) George Wymer on a sortie to Babi Wali Kotal, three miles to the northwest. Wymer heavily defeated the Shahzada Saftar Jang, and Nott himself led a larger sortie two months later (25 March 1842).

Babi Wali Kotal (2nd) ▌ 1842 ▌ 1st British-Afghan War

After being reinforced in **Kandahar** by Brigadier Sir Richard England, who overcame defeat at **Haikalzai**, British General William Nott attacked the besieging Afghans just to the northwest at Babi Wali Kotal. With just 1,500 men against a claimed 8,000, Nott repulsed the Afghans with heavy losses and drove them across the Argand-ab River. But he later evacuated Kandahar (29 May 1842).

Babi Wali Kotal ▌ 1880 ▌ 2nd British-Afghan War

See **Kandahar**

Bábolna ▌ 1437 ▌ Transylvanian Peasant Revolt

Romanian serfs in Transylvania, led by the poor nobleman Antal Budai Nagy, rebelled against Sigismund of Hungary and the avaricious Bishop Gyorgy Lépes, decisively defeating the forces of the Hungarian Governor near Bábolna (modern Bana, east of Gyor). Victory won the peasant army restored rights, though the church and nobility eventually forced them to accept less (6 June 1437).

Baby 700 ▌ 1915 ▌ World War I (Gallipoli)

Determined to break out from **Anzac**, Australian and New Zealand forces under General Alexander Godley attacked up Monash Valley towards a hill known as Baby 700. Despite massive naval bombardment of the Turkish positions, the Allies were driven off with terrible losses. Many Anzacs were then transferred down the coast to support an attack at **Krithia** (2–3 May 1915).

Babylon, Egypt I 640–641 I Muslim Conquest of Egypt

Muslim General Amr ibn al-As defeated the Byzantine army at **Heliopolis**, then besieged the heavily fortified citadel of Babylon, near modern Cairo. Despite treacherous negotiations between the Arabs and Cyrus, Patriarch of **Alexandria**, the citadel held out until the death of Emperor Heraclius ended hope of relief and fell after seven months (October 640–9 April 641).

Babylon, Iraq I 650–648 BC I Assyrian Wars

With Crown Prince Shamash-shum-ukin of Babylon leading a revolt against his brother, King Ashurbanipal of Assyria, the Assyrian King sent a large force to besiege the city. Starved into surrender, Shamash-shum-ukin killed himself and Assyria regained control. Within a few years the Chaldean Nabopolassar seized Babylon, and in 612 BC he overthrew Assyria itself at **Nineveh**.

Babylon, Iraq I 541–539 BC I Persian-Babylonian War

As King Cyrus "The Great" of Persia marched his army east against the decaying kingdom of Babylonia, King Nabonidus withdrew his troops behind the massive walls of Babylon. Cyrus reputedly diverted the Euphrates after a two-year siege, and his troops stormed the city along the riverbed. The fall of Babylon made the Persian Empire the largest then known (541–539 BC).

Babylon, Iraq I 634 I Muslim Conquest of Iraq

When Muslim General Khalid ibn al-Walid returned to Syria after **Firadz**, leaving Muthanna in command in Mesopotamia, a fresh Persian army under Hormuz was sent to recover lost territory on the Euphrates. Near Babylon, the outnumbered Muslims nearly panicked against Persian war-elephants, but eventually won. Later that year they met new Persian commander Rustam at **Nimaraq** (July 634).

Bacacay I 1827 I Argentine-Brazilian War

Just days after a Brazilian naval defeat in the Rio de la Plata at **Juncal**, a Brazilian column of 1,200 men led by Colonel Bentos Manuel Ribiero was attacked at Bacacay, near Neuvo de Julio, by Argentine Colonels Juan Galo Lavalle and José Maria Videla. Lavalle secured a decisive victory and was promoted to General. Argentina soon won again in the north at **Ituzaingó** (13 February 1827).

Bach Dang I 938 I Sino-Annamese War

When the northern Vietnamese province of Giao Chau rebelled, Liu Gong of the Southern Han sent a massive expedition under his son Hong Cao, who was met on the Bach Dang, near Haiphong, by General Ngo Quyen (founder of the Ngo Dynasty). With his ships impaled on stakes in the riverbed, Hong Cao was routed and killed, the defeat ending over 1,000 years of Chinese rule.

Bach Dang I 1288 I Mongol Wars of Kubilai Khan

To avenge defeat at **Siming** in 1285, Kubilai Khan sent his son Toghon and grandson Esen Temur with perhaps 300,000 men to finally subdue the Vietnamese. After initially falling back, General Tran Hung Dao attacked and destroyed General Omar's Mongol fleet at the mouth of the Bach Dang, north of Haiphong. The invaders withdrew, routed at **Noi Bang** as they fled in defeat (3 April 1288).

Bac Le I 1884 I Sino-French War

General Charles Millot campaigned northeast from **Hanoi** to secure **Bac Ninh**, then unwisely sent Captain Alphonse Dugenne with 800 men on towards Lang Son. Advancing through terrible rain and mud, the French crossed a river near the hamlet of Bac Le and were attacked by a large Chinese force. They lost 22 killed and 60 wounded in a humiliating defeat and had to retreat (23 June 1884).

Bac Ninh I 1884 I Sino-French War

Following French victory west of Hanoi at **Son Tay**, new commander General Charles

Millot attacked northeast towards the Chinese Guangxi Army at Bac Ninh. Millot secured high ground nearby after heavy fighting, and the Chinese withdrew northeast towards **Lang Son**, abandoning 10 modern cannon. Three months later the French were bloodily checked at **Bac Le** (16–19 March 1884).

Bacolod | 1903 | American-Moro Wars

A year after Muslim Moros in the southern Philippines were defeated at **Bayan**, Captain John Pershing led a fresh campaign and attacked Bacolod fortress, overlooking Lake Lanao in central Mindanao. About 70 Moros died in a three-day bombardment, but the Sultan of Bacolod escaped before the fortress fell. Fighting on Mindanao soon resumed at **Kudarangan** (5–8 April 1903).

Badajoz | 1705 | War of the Spanish Succession

An Anglo-Dutch army advancing into southwestern Spain under Henri de Massue Earl of Ruvigny and Baron Nicolas Fagel besieged Badajoz, but withdrew when Marshal Count René de Tessé sent cavalry reinforcements. In a second siege, Galway lost an arm and Fagel was recalled to Holland after he withdrew, allowing the French to pull back with all their guns (June and October 1705).

Badajoz (1st) | 1811 | Napoleonic Wars (Peninsular Campaign)

In the first modern siege of the strategic Spanish border fortress of Badajoz, the garrison under General Rafael Menacho held out against French Marshal Nicolas Soult until Menacho was killed on a sortie. Even though he knew relief was on the way, his successor General José Imaz surrendered a week later, along with a large quantity of stores (26 January–10 March 1811).

Badajoz (2nd) | 1811 | Napoleonic Wars (Peninsular Campaign)

Following French capture of the frontier fortress of Badajoz, a costly Anglo-Portuguese siege under Arthur Wellesley Lord Wellington and General Sir William Beresford was repulsed by General Armand Phillipon. Although a French relief attempt by Marshal Nicolas Soult was driven off at **Albuhera** (16 May), the poorly equipped Allied siege was abandoned (20 April–10 June 1811).

Badajoz | 1812 | Napoleonic Wars (Peninsular Campaign)

Despite previous failure, Arthur Wellesley Lord Wellington determined to capture the Spanish fortress of Badajoz. Breaching the walls with improved siege equipment, his Anglo-Portuguese army launched a bloody night-time assault. French General Armand Phillipon surrendered next morning, after which Badajoz was subjected to a notorious sack by the victors (16 March–7 April 1812).

Badajoz | 1936 | Spanish Civil War

Nationalist Colonel Juan Yagüe and forces from the Army of Africa secured **Merida**, and just days later marched north against Badajoz. Despite costly losses, the outnumbered Nationalists captured the city, after which hundreds of Republicans were brutally executed. The fall of the last remaining Republican city on the border effectively cut off reinforcement through Portugal (14 August 1936).

Badara | 1759 | Seven Years War (India)

See **Chinsura**

Bad Axe | 1832 | Black Hawk Indian War

Soon after being driven back at **Wisconsin Heights**, the Sauk Chief Black Hawk was attacked on the Mississippi at the mouth of the Bad Axe, near modern Victory, Wisconsin, by 1,300 regulars and volunteers under General Henry Atkinson. Black Hawk was decisively defeated, with about 300 killed, including women and children, and he was later captured, bringing an end to the war (3 August 1832).

Baddowal | 1846 | 1st British-Sikh War

When a large Sikh army crossed the Sutlej into British East Punjab, they lost at **Mudki** and

Ferozeshah. As Anglo-Indian troops under General Sir Harry Smith marched through **Dharmkot** to relieve Ludhiana, their rear was attacked at nearby Baddowal by Ranjur Singh. Smith lost his baggage and stores in a sharp action, but a week later he routed the Sikhs at **Aliwal** (21 January 1846).

Badenoch I 1429 I MacDonald Rebellion
See **Lochaber**

Badli-ki-Serai I 1857 I Indian Mutiny
At the outbreak of the mutiny rebels seized **Delhi**, and a small British force under General Sir Henry Barnard was quickly despatched to restore control. About five miles away at the village of Badli-ki-Serai, the greatly outnumbered British drove out a large force of mutineers, enabling Barnard to take position next day on the strategic ridge commanding the northwestern approach to Delhi (8 June 1857).

Badme I 1998 I Ethiopian-Eritrean War
Economic differences between Eritrea and Ethiopia triggered war in 1998, and Eritrean troops seized the small town of Badme, in disputed territory on the Ethiopian border southwest of Asmara. Fighting soon died down to border skirmishing, but Ethiopia later launched a massive attack at Badme, beginning one of the largest wars in Africa, involving over half a million men (6 May 1998).

Badme I 1999 I Ethiopian-Eritrean War
In a dramatic escalation of their border war, Ethiopia launched a massive offensive to retake disputed territory around Badme southwest of Asmara, seized by Eritrea in May 1988. While an initial assault was repulsed with heavy losses on both sides, a second Ethiopian attack with tanks and aircraft broke through after human-wave assaults. The Eritreans then withdrew (6–10 & 25–26 February 1999).

Badoeng Strait I 1942 I World War II (Pacific)
See **Lombok Strait**

Badon I 497 I Anglo-Saxon Conquest of Britain
See **Mons Badonicus**

Badon I 665 I Anglo-Saxon Territorial Wars
After defeating Wessex at **Pontesbury**, the Welsh Prince Morgan Mwynfawr ap Arthrwys of Glevissig (modern Glamorgan) joined with Dunnonia (modern Devon and Cornwall) and crossed the Severn to meet the Saxons at Badon, probably Caer Vadon near Bath. While Morgan was killed, the outcome of the battle is not recorded, though the expansion of Wessex appears to have been checked.

Badr I 624 I Campaigns of the Prophet Mohammed
Just two years after fleeing from Mecca (the Hegira), the Prophet Mohammed attacked a wealthy caravan from Syria at Badr, near Medina in modern Saudi Arabia, where his Meccan refugees utterly defeated the escorting army of Abu Sufyan. The battle is regarded as the first great military exploit in founding Islam. The victors became known as Badriyun (13 January 624).

Badshahganj I 1858 I Indian Mutiny
Campaigning against Mehndi Husain, self-proclaimed Nizam of Sultanpur, General Thomas Franks won at **Chanda (Uttar Pradesh)** and **Hamirpur**, then advanced northwest on Sultanpur itself. Two miles from the city at Badshahganj, Mehndi Husain took a strong position, supported by artillery under Mirza Gaffar Beg. However, he was routed and fled, opening the road to **Lucknow** (23 February 1858).

Badshahpur I 1737 I Later Mughal-Maratha Wars
See **Delhi**

Badung Strait I 1942 I World War II (Pacific)
See **Lombok Strait**

Baecula I 208 BC I 2nd Punic War

Sent by Rome to restore order in Spain, Publius Scipio the Younger captured **New Carthage**, then won a brilliant tactical victory over the Carthaginian army of Hasdrubal Barca at Baecula (probably modern Bailen, Andalusia). However, casualties were not heavy and Hasdrubal slipped away with his army through Gaul and across the Alps in a failed attempt to reinforce his brother Hannibal in Italy.

Baecula I 206 BC I 2nd Punic War

See **Ilipa**

Baetis I 211 BC I 2nd Punic War

Publius Scipio campaigning against the Carthaginian Hasdrubal in Andalusia had no choice but to split his force against three separate Carthaginian armies. Publius was defeated and killed in battle on the Upper Baetis (Guadalquivir). Shortly afterwards, his brother Gnaeus Scipio was killed in the same region at **Ilurci**, after which Rome withdrew north of the Ebro, effectively ceding southern Spain.

Baetis I 80 BC I Sertorian War

In support of his former commander Gaius Marius against Lucius Cornelius Sulla in civil war in Rome, veteran General Quintus Sertorius raised a rebellion in Spain and attacked Sulla's appointee Lucius Fufidius in Further Spain. Fufidius was heavily defeated in battle at the Baetis (modern Guadalquivir) River and, the following year, Nearer Spain was secured with victory at the **Anas**.

Bagamoyo I 1889 I German Colonial Wars in Africa

When Arab slave traders in German East Africa (now Tanzania) rebelled under Abushiri ibn Salim and attacked Bagamoyo (September 1888), Commissioner Hermann von Wissmann and a force of 600 Sudanese troops attacked and stormed the rebel stronghold at nearby Jahazi. The rebels were then driven out of Sadani and were defeated at their northern stronghold at **Pangani** (8 May 1889).

Bagbag I 1899 I Philippine-American War

Two days after the setback at **Quinqua**, American commander Arthur MacArthur advanced north from **Malolos**, and Colonel Irving Hale's Brigade on his right wing met Philippine General Antonio Luna defending the Bagbag River, where he had cut an important bridge. While both sides suffered heavy losses in fierce fighting, Luna eventually fell back on **Calumpit** (25 April 1899).

Bagbrades I 203 BC I 2nd Punic War

See **Bagradas**

Bagh I 1919 I 3rd British-Afghan War

Weeks after the incident at **Amritsar** in the Punjab, Amir Amanullah of Afghanistan sent Saleh Mohammad across the "Durand Line" to occupy the Indian village of Bagh, which controlled water supply for Landi Kotal. British troops under General George Crocker advancing from Landi Kotal were driven off by a strong Afghan defence, but succeeded in a second assault (9–11 May 1919).

Baghavand I 1735 I Turko-Persian Wars of Nadir Shah

Regent Nadir Kuli fought to recover Persian territory from Turkey and won a great victory at **Leilan** in 1733, then made peace with Baghdad. However, Sultan Mahmud I assembled a fresh army at Kars, in modern Armenia, and on the nearby Plain of Baghavand near Erivan, Nadir defeated and killed Turkish commander Abdula Koprulu. Threatened by Russia, Turkey quickly made peace (19 June 1735).

Baghdad I 809–811 I Muslim War of Succession

Following the death of the Abbasid Caliph Harun al-Rashid, civil war broke out between his sons—al-Amin, the new Caliph, and al-Ma'mun, subordinate ruler of Khorasan. The rebel Khorasan army, under Tahir ibn Husain, besieged Baghdad for two years, and, when it fell, al-Ma'mun replaced his brother as Caliph. The deposed al-Amin was later killed attempting to escape.

Baghdad I 1055 I Seljuk Wars of Expansion

When his offensive into Byzantine Armenia failed at **Manzikert** (1054), the Seljuk Toghril Beg turned west against the key city of Baghdad, which had seen civil unrest by Sunni demonstrators. After minor fighting against Abbasid forces outside the city, Toghril was invited in and ended the Buwayid Dynasty. A brief attempt to establish Shi'ite rule was later crushed at **Kufah** (December 1055).

Baghdad I 1258 I Mongol Invasion of the Middle East

Within days of the Caliph's army being destroyed at **Anbar**, Hulegu, the Mongol Il-Khan of Iran (grandson of Genghis Khan) struck at the heart of Islam by seizing and sacking Baghdad. The deliberate devastation and impoverishment of the city after a month-long siege is regarded as one of history's most destructive assaults on Islamic learning and culture (18 January–15 February 1258).

Baghdad I 1401 I Conquests of Tamerlane

The Turko-Mongol Tamerlane captured Baghdad in 1393 as part of his massive campaign of conquest in the west. But shortly after his conquest of Syria following victory at **Aleppo** in October 1400, Baghdad rose in revolt. In a terrible retribution, Tamerlane returned to Baghdad and reconquered it in a violent assault. He then massacred the population as punishment and destroyed the city (July 1401).

Baghdad I 1534 I Ottoman Conquest of Persia

While Ottoman Sultan Suleiman I of Turkey campaigned in central Europe, Shah Tahmasp of Persia seized Tabriz and Baghdad. Returning to put down the rebellion, Suleiman and his commander Ibrahim Pasha, defeated the Safavid Persians. Although the war continued sporadically for 20 years, the fall of Baghdad marked the start of almost continuous Turkish rule until 1917 (December 1534).

Baghdad I 1587 I Turko-Persian Wars

Following up the costly Turkish capture of **Tabriz** (23 September 1585), the new Turkish commander Ferhad Pasha led a fresh invasion and advanced towards Baghdad, where he surprised and defeated a 15,000-strong Persian army in a bloody three-day battle. This decisive victory and the prior fall of Tabriz gave Turkey effective control of western Persia.

Baghdad I 1625–1626 I Turko-Persian Wars

Ottoman Grand Vizier Hafiz Ahmed Pasha attempted to recapture Baghdad twenty years after Persians under Shah Abbas had routed the Turkish army at **Sufiyan** to take the city and also Tabriz. But Hafiz was hampered by internal dispute and lack of artillery and, when a large Persian relief army approached after six months, he withdrew with heavy losses (November 1625–4 July 1626).

Baghdad I 1630 I Turko-Persian Wars

Five years after Turkish forces were repulsed outside Baghdad, Grand Vizier Khuzrev Pasha led a fresh invasion into western Persia where he captured **Hamadan**, then made another attempt to recapture Baghdad. However, a shortage of supplies and Persian raids forced him to again abandon the siege. The city did not fall until eight years later (6 October–14 November 1630).

Baghdad I 1638 I Turko-Persian Wars

Following years of inconclusive fighting, the great Sultan Murad IV resolved to recover lost Turkish territory occupied by the Persians. With a mighty and well-equipped expedition, the Sultan marched east against Baghdad. The city fell to a brutal assault after a siege and devastating artillery bombardment and the war was virtually over (15 November–24 December 1638).

Baghdad I 1733 I Turko-Persian Wars of Nadir Shah

When Tahmasp II of Persia was routed by the Turks in 1731 at **Hamadan**, General Nadir Kuli deposed the Shah and declared himself Regent for the infant Abbas III. Nadir then invaded Ottoman territory and defeated Ahmad Pasha, Governor of Baghdad, at nearby Adana. His siege was driven off after defeat at **Karkuk** and Baghdad did not fall until after victory at **Leilan** (January–July 1733).

Baghdad I 1917 I World War I (Mesopotamia)

Anglo-Indian General Sir Frederick Maude recaptured the Tigris city of **Kut-al-Amara**, then advanced upriver against Baghdad with 42,000 infantry, 4,000 cavalry and 174 guns. After attempting to hold entrenchments across the Diyala, outnumbered Turkish commander Khalil Pasha withdrew north from Baghdad through **Mushahida** and **Istabulat** (5–11 March 1917).

Baghdad I 1941 I World War II (Middle East)

See **Iraq**

Baghdad I 1991 I 1st Gulf War

On the first day of **Desert Storm** against Iraq, American aircraft began a prolonged air campaign against Baghdad. Hoping to force President Saddam Hussein to the negotiating table, the bombing continued throughout the war, with over 100,000 sorties against Baghdad and other cities. The reputed heaviest raid on Baghdad was on the last night of the war (17 January–28 February 1991).

Baghdad I 2003 I 2nd Gulf War

War began with the "shock and awe" bombardment of Baghdad, which continued as Allied ground forces converged on the Iraqi capital. By 3 April, Americans seized the airport, then raided into the city two days later. Toppling of Saddam Hussein's statue in the city centre symbolised the fall of Baghdad, and the subsequent capture of **Tikrit** effectively ended the war (20 March–9 April 2003).

Bagh Dera I 1788 I Mughal-Maratha War of Ismail Beg

The Maratha army of Rana Khan Bai and Benoit de Boigne advancing to relieve the Mu-

ghal siege of **Agra**, in northern India, faced the renegade Ismail Beg Hamadani, who was alone after his Pathan allies had withdrawn a month earlier following battle at **Chaksana**. Ismail was routed in a decisive action at Bagh Dera, a suburb of Agra, then fled by swimming the Jumna (18 June 1788).

Ba Gia I 1965 I Vietnam War

Following actions at **Binh Gia** and **Pleiku**, Viet Cong forces attacked in the north against Ba Gia, near Quang Ngai, where government troops panicked and fled. After heavy fighting, the Viet Cong were eventually driven off by American air attack, but further failure at **Dong Xoai** helped convince the United States that only major military intervention would save South Vietnam (29 May–14 July 1965).

Bagneux I 1870 I Franco-Prussian War

Two weeks after being repulsed at **Chevilly**, French General Joseph Vinoy led a renewed reconnaissance in force south from besieged **Paris**. His force of 25,000 men and 80 guns surprised the Prussians at Bagneux, but after the loss of about 400 men on either side, Vinoy was forced to withdraw. The next major sortie from Paris was a week later towards **Malmaison** (13 October 1870).

Bagradas I 240 BC I Truceless War

When Carthaginian General Hanno was defeated outside **Utica** by former mercenaries now in revolt, his rival Hamilcar Barca was soon appointed to lead another relief force from Carthage towards the besieged city. A large-scale action at the Bagradas saw rebel leader Spendius heavily defeated, forcing him to raise the siege, and Hamilcar pursued the rebels into the interior.

Bagradas I 203 BC I 2nd Punic War

Having defeated the Numidians outside **Utica** in modern Tunisia, the Roman General Publius Scipio the Younger pursued Carthaginian Hasdrubal Gisco and King Syphax of Numidia southwest along the Bagradas (modern Medjerda) River. In a classic cavalry action at an area known as Great Plains, Hasdrubal and his

Numidian allies were defeated and Scipio marched to attack Carthage itself.

Bagradas I 49 BC I Wars of the First Triumvirate

While Julius Caesar fought the armies of his rival Pompey in Spain at **Ilerda**, Gaius Curio defeated Publius Atius Varus outside **Utica** in modern Tunisia, then ill-advisedly marched inland against a relief force under Pompeian ally Juba of Numidia. At the Bagradas (modern Medjerda), Curio was killed and his army crushed. His forces then abandoned the siege of Utica (24 July 49 BC).

Bahadurpur I 1658 I War of the Mughal Princes

In bitter conflict between the sons of the ailing Mughal Emperor Shahjahan, Dara Shikoh the eldest sent his son Sulaiman Shikoh against the second brother Shuja. Aided by the Rajput General Jai Singh, the Imperial army met and routed Shuja near Benares at Bahadurpur. However, Imperial forces were much less successful two months later at **Dharmat** (24 February 1658).

Bahia I 1624–1625 I Dutch-Portuguese Colonial Wars
See **Salvador**

Bahia I 1812 I War of 1812

The American frigate *Constitution* (Captain William Bainbridge) met the British frigate *Java* (Captain Henry Lambert) and the prize *William* in action off Bahia in Brazil. Lambert was fatally wounded in a classic and bloody ship-to-ship duel, which cost about 150 British casualties. The utterly wrecked British ship had no choice but to surrender (29 December 1812).

Bahia I 1822–1823 I Brazilian War of Independence
See **Salvador**

Bahía de Cochinos I 1961 I Bay of Pigs Incident
See **Bay of Pigs**

Bahia de Nipe I 1898 I Spanish-American War
See **Nipe**

Bahrain I 1521 I Portuguese Colonial Wars in Arabia

When Portuguese forces took **Hormuz** in the Persian Gulf (1515), commander Diogo Lopes de Sequeira determined to enforce tribute from Mocrin, King of Lasah (modern El-Hassa), and sent Antonio Correa west against Bahrain. Supported by troops from Hormuz under Raez Zarafa, Correa won a bloody victory after Mocrin fell wounded and Portugal held the strategic island for 80 years.

Bahrain I 1602 I Later Portuguese Colonial Wars in Arabia

Having secured the strategic Persian Gulf island of Bahrain, the Portuguese ruled with difficulty over years of unrest until there was a full-scale rising by the trader Rukn-el-Din, whose brother had been executed by the Portuguese Governor. Defeated by Persian troops sent by Shah Abbas, the Portuguese were expelled. Twenty years later Shah Abbas sought British aid to also capture **Hormuz**.

Bahur I 1752 I 2nd Carnatic War

Following defeat at **Trichinopoly** in April, French forces advancing on Fort St David, on the coast south of Madras, were intercepted at the nearby village of Bahur by Major Stringer Lawrence and a British-Sepoy force. The French fled after a fierce hand-to-hand struggle, with commander Jacques Kerjean captured. France soon lost again at **Covelung** and **Chingleput** (6 September 1752).

Baia, Italy I 1693 I War of the Grand Alliance

French Admiral Victor Marie Comte d'Estrées and a squadron of 20 ships moved the focus of the naval campaign from the Atlantic to the Mediterranean, where they surprised the Spanish fleet refitting at Baia, near Pozzuoli in southern Italy. Although they inflicted heavy damage, the French ships were driven off and failed to completely disable the Spanish fleet (June 1693).

Baia, Romania I 1467 I Hungarian National Wars

Shortly after becoming Hopsodar of Moldavia, Stephen the Great was attacked by a greatly superior Hungarian army and fell back into modern northeast Romania. Stephen's largely peasant army won a decisive victory in a brilliant night-time assault on the Hungarian camp at Baia, near Falticeni. Ten years later he was strong enough to defeat the Turks at **Rakhova** (14 December 1467).

Bailen I 208 BC I 2nd Punic War
See **Baecula**

Bainsizza I 1917 I World War I (Italian Front)
See **Isonzo (2nd)**

Bairen I 1097 I Early Christian Reconquest of Spain

Spanish General Rodrigo Diaz de Bivar—El Cid—seized **Valencia** as his personal fief in 1094 and, after defeating a Muslim counter-attack at nearby **Cuarte**, faced another major offensive 40 miles to the south, on the coast at Bairen. The Almoravid army of King Yusuf ibn Tashfin was again defeated, but El Cid died two years later and Valencia was re-occupied by the Muslims.

Baisieux I 1792 I French Revolutionary Wars (1st Coalition)

In the first weeks of the war, Irish-born French General Theobald Comte de Dillon, leading over 2,000 men southeast from Lille towards Tournai, was met by Austrian troops near the Pas de Baisieux. Dillon ordered a retreat which degenerated into a panicked rout and he was killed by his own troops, reportedly while attempting to rally them. Austrians later invaded to besiege **Lille** (29 April 1792).

Bajhura I 1575 I Mughal Conquest of Northern India
See **Tukaroi**

Bajo Palacé I 1811 I Colombian War of Independence
See **Palacé**

Bakdura I 741 I Berber Rebellion

After disastrous defeat at the hands of the Berber Khalid ibn Hamid al-Zanatai at **El Asnam** in 740, the Umayyad Caliph sent a 30,000-strong Arab army under Kulthum ibn Iyad al-Kushayri and his nephew Baldj ibn Bishr. At Bakdura on the Wadi Sebou in northern Morocco, Kulthum was defeated and killed, along with about 10,000 of his army, and Baldj's cavalry fled to Ceuta.

Bakenlaagte I 1901 I 2nd Anglo-Boer War

In response to the experienced Colonel George Benson implementing a scorched-earth policy in the Transvaal highveld, south of Middelburg, his convoy was attacked by Louis Botha's commando at Bakenlaagte, just west of Bethal. The British lost 66 killed (including Benson) and 165 wounded in a courageous rearguard action, but the main column managed to withdraw (30 October 1901).

Baker Massacre I 1870 I Piegan Indian Expedition
See **Marias**

Baker's Cabin Massacre I 1774 I Cresap's War
See **Yellow Creek**

Baker's Zareba I 1884 I British-Sudan Wars
See **El Teb (1st)**

Bakhamra I 763 I Muslim Civil Wars

The Abbasid Caliph's General, Isa ibn Musa, killed Shi'ite rebel Muhammad ibn Abd'Allah at **Medina, Saudi Arabia**, then turned east against his brother Ibrahim, who had raised a larger revolt at Basra. In battle south of Kufa at Bakhamra, Ibrahim repulsed the Abbasid vanguard before he was thoroughly defeated. Ibrahim was seriously wounded and, when he died a month later, the rebellion ended (21 January 763).

Baksar I 1539 I Mughal Conquest of Northern India
See **Chausa**

Baksar I 1764 I Bengal War
See **Buxar**

Baku I 1723 I Russian Invasion of the Caspian
Tsar Peter I wanted to secure the western Caspian and, after seizing Derbent without resistance in 1722, sent a flotilla from Astrakhan under General Mikhail Matyushkin against Baku. The city had to surrender following a four-day bombardment by land and sea, but the financial burden of the settlement eventually became too great and in 1735 Baku was returned by treaty to Persia (26 June 1735).

Baku I 1918 I World War I (Caucasus Front)
With Armenian independence declared after **Sardarapat**, local nationalists seized the Caspian city of Baku and British General Lionel Dunsterville marched northeast from Baghdad to support them against the Turkish "Army of Islam." Dunsterville withdrew after bloody fighting, though armistice in November forced Turkey to give up Baku and most of the Caucasus (4 August–14 September 1918).

Balad Bani Bu Ali I 1821 I Anglo-Arab Wars
To avenge Britain's defeat in a rash attack against the Banu Bu Ali at **Sur** in November, a fresh expedition under General Lionel Smith was sent against the Arabs in northeast Oman. Battle at Balad Bani Bu Ali, southwest of Sur, saw costly losses on both sides before the Arabs were heavily defeated. Smith razed their fortress and more prominent prisoners were sent in captivity to India (2 March 1821).

Balaga I 1815 I Colombian War of Independence
A month after defeat at **Chire**, Spanish Colonel Sebastián Calzada advanced with 1,800 infantry and a cavalry corps on the Rio Chitagá, east of Bucaramanga, held by Patriot forces of Governor Custodio García Rovira under General Rafael Urdaneta. Heavy fighting at nearby Balaga saw Urdaneta decisively defeated and Calzada soon met García Rovira in battle at **Cachirí** (25 November 1815).

Balaguer I 1813 I Napoleonic Wars (Peninsular Campaign)
See **Fort Balaguer**

Balaklava I 1854 I Crimean War
Russian Prince Alexander Menshikov attempted to break the Anglo-French siege of **Sevastopol** at nearby Balaklava, where his cavalry was repulsed by the Heavy Brigade (General Sir James Scarlett) and the infantry stand of the 93rd Highlanders (Sir Colin Campbell). However, British cavalry (Lord Cardigan) were destroyed in the pointless Charge of the Light Brigade (25 October 1854).

Balane I 1594 I Portuguese Colonial Wars in Asia
Attempting to influence the succession in Kandy, in central Ceylon (modern Sri Lanka), Portuguese Pedro Lopes de Sousa enthroned Sinhalese Princess Kusumasana Devi (the Catholic convert Dona Catherina). However, the legitimate ruler Konappu Bandara repulsed the Portuguese and de Sousa was defeated and killed near Balane. Konappu then married Devi and ruled as Vimala Dharma.

Balangiga I 1900 I Philippine-American War
As guerrilla war dragged on, Philippine General Vicente Lukban surprised the American garrison at Balangiga, on Samar, where Captain Thomas W. Connell and 48 men were hacked to death. Only 23 survived, most wounded. Captain Edwin V. Bookmiller then arrived to avenge the "Balangiga massacre" and General Jacob H. Smith inflicted bloody retaliation (28 September 1900).

Balapur I 1720 I Mughal-Hyderabad War
Following his victory at **Ratanpur** (19 June), the ambitious Nizam-ul-Mulk faced another Imperial army under Alam Ali Khan, nephew of

king-maker Husain Ali Khan. Near Balapur, southwest of Akola, the Imperials fled after Alam Ali Khan was killed. The Mughal Governor of Hyderabad submitted to Nizam-ul-Mulk, who founded the independent state of Hyderabad (10 August 1720).

Balarath I 591 I Byzantine-Persian Wars
See **Ganzak**

Balat I 1119 I Crusader-Muslim Wars
See **Antioch, Syria**

Balathista I 1014 I Byzantine Wars of Tsar Samuel
Bulgarian Tsar Samuel again invaded Byzantine territory after a repulse at **Spercheios** in 996, and Emperor Basil II launched a decisive counter-offensive, crushing Bulgaria's army at Balathista in the Struma Valley. A claimed 15,000 Bulgarian prisoners were blinded and sent home to Tsar Samuel, who reputedly died of shock. Bulgaria was soon absorbed into the Byzantine Empire (29 July 1014).

Balaton I 1945 I World War II (Eastern Front)
See **Lake Balaton**

Balbergkamp I 1940 I World War II (Northern Europe)
See **Andalsnes**

Balbriggan I 1920 I Anglo-Irish War
When two Royal Irish Constabulary officers were murdered by Republicans, their "Black and Tan" colleagues from Gormanston Barracks attacked Balbriggan, 20 miles north of Dublin, where it had happened. The notorious "Sack of Balbriggan" saw the small town virtually destroyed and, three months later, similar punishment was meted out to the Sinn Fein city of **Cork** (20 September 1920).

Baler I 1898–1899 I Philippines War of Independence
Despite Spain ceding the Philippines to America, a tiny Spanish garrison at Baler, in

eastern Luzon, held out under Captain Enrique de las Morenas and, later, Lieutenant Saturnio Martin Cerezo. When a relief party under American naval Lieutenant James C. Gillmore was captured by Filipino troops, Cerezo finally surrendered with the full honours of war (1 July 1898–2 June 1899).

Balikpapan I 1942 I World War II (Pacific)
See **Macassar Strait**

Balikpapan I 1945 I World War II (Pacific)
In the last Allied landing of the war, Australian General Edward Milford took 32,000 men against Balikpapan in eastern **Borneo**, where there was severe fighting to secure the port and the "Milford highway" inland. Australia's largest operation cost 221 Australians and about 1,800 Japanese dead and Admiral Shoichi Kamada held out until the end of the war (1 July–15 August 1945).

Baliqiao I 1860 I 2nd Opium War
With the **Dagu Forts** secured, British General Sir James Hope Grant and French General Charles Cousin-Montauban were blocked southeast of Beijing near Tongzhou by Prince Senggelinqin. A brilliant action at the Baliqiao (Palikao) Bridge saw the Chinese routed. Beijing surrendered, conceding foreign trade to end the war, and the French commander became Comte de Palikao (21 September 1860).

Balkans I 1941 I World War II (Southern Europe)
Marshal Wilhelm List was sent to secure Germany's Balkan flank before invading Russia, and launched a brilliant campaign against Yugoslavia and Greece. The Yugoslav capital **Belgrade** fell within a week. German Panzers then swept though **Greece**, forcing British and Commonwealth forces to withdraw to **Crete**, where they were defeated by an airborne assault (April–May 1941).

Balkans ∎ 1944 ∎ World War II (Eastern Front)

With Soviet forces sweeping across the Dnieper at **Jassy-Kishinev**, Romania changed sides and Bucharest was occupied (31 August). Bulgaria did the same with the fall of Sofia (8 September) and Marshal Fedor Tolbukhin invaded Yugoslavia. Aided by partisan forces, Tolbukhin took **Belgrade** after heavy fighting (20 October). The Germans soon evacuated Yugoslavia, Albania and Greece.

Balkh ∎ 1008 ∎ Eastern Muslim Dynastic Wars

Ilek Nasr bin Ali of the Karakhan Dynasty invaded northern Afghanistan to capture Balkh and Herat and, in response, Mahmud of Ghazni took a force of Afghans to the Oxus. Ilek Khan's General, Subashi-Tagin, and Qadir Khan of Khotan were routed in a decisive defeat at the Sharkiyan Bridge, on the Plain of Katar near Balkh, and Ilek Nasr did not cross the Oxus again during Mahmud's reign (4 January 1008).

Balkh ∎ 1153 ∎ Wars of the Great Seljuk Sultanate

Forced out of their traditional land in Turkestan by the Kara Khitai, the Ghuzz (Oghuz Turks) took land south of the Oxus near Balkh, where they later rebelled against the Seljuk Sultan Sanjar of Khorasan in a dispute over tribute. Sanjar took a reported 100,000 men against the rebels, but near Balkh he was defeated and captured. The Sultan escaped after two years and died soon afterwards.

Balkh ∎ 1370 ∎ Conquests of Tamerlane

In the early struggle for Mongol domination, Tamerlane turned against his brother-in-law and former ally Husayn at Balkh in northern Afghanistan. The city fell by storm after a terrible assault and its citadel and palace were destroyed. Tamerlane offered Husayn safe surrender but allowed his rival to be murdered. Tamerlane was then enthroned as Khan of the local Mongol tribes.

Balkh ∎ 1646 ∎ Mughal-Uzbek Wars

When the Uzbek leader Imam Kuli was deposed by Nazr Muhammad, Mughal Emperor Shahjahan marched on Balkh and beat Nazr Muhammad, who was defeated again to the west at Shirbarghan and fled to Persia. The following year, Nazr Muhammad's son Abdul Aziz was beaten trying to retake the city from Mughal Prince Aurangzeb, but the Emperor made peace and withdrew.

Ballinamuck ∎ 1798 ∎ French Revolutionary Wars (Irish Rising)

General Joseph Humbert—now with fewer than 850 French and about 1,000 Irish—continued his advance through Sligo and was trapped at Ballinamuck, near Longford, between General Charles Earl Cornwallis (Lord Lieutenant of Ireland) and General Gerard Lake. Humbert surrendered at nearby Cloone after a brief resistance, ending French intervention on British soil (8 September 1798).

Ballivian ∎ 1934 ∎ Chaco War

Commander General José Félix Estigarribia continued Paraguay's offensive through the Chaco Boreal against Bolivia, with a decisive victory at **Cañada el Carmen**, then advanced on the nearby strategic fortress at Ballivian. The fortress fell early next day after a brief assault, and retreating Bolivians fled across the nearby Pilcomayo into Argentine territory (17 November 1934).

Ballon ∎ 845 ∎ Breton Rebellion

With Norse Vikings raiding up the rivers of western Europe, Bretons under Nomenoe took the opportunity to rise against Frankish Emperor Charles the Bald. Nomenoe's rebels crushed an Imperial army on the plain of Ballon, near the Vilaine River in Brittany, and the hard-pressed Charles was forced to recognise Brittany as an independent kingdom (22 November 845).

Ball's Bluff ∎ 1861 ∎ American Civil War (Eastern Theatre)

Union General Charles F. Stone and Senator Colonel Edward D. Baker led an unwise offensive in northern Virginia following defeat at **Bull Run**, attempting to cross the Upper Potomac and march on Leesburg. But at Ball's Bluff they were ambushed and routed by General Nathan G. Evans, with 50 killed (including Baker), 160 wounded and about 700 captured (21 October 1861).

Ballycastle I 1565 I O'Neill Rebellion

Campaigning against Anglo-Scots colonisation of Ulster, Shane O'Neill Lord of Tyrone routed the outnumbered MacDonnells at Ballycastle, Antrim, capturing James MacDonnell and his brother Sorley Boy. The victory made O'Neill master of the north, and while James died a few months later, Sorley Boy remained a prisoner for two years until O'Neill's defeat at **Letterkenny** (2 May 1565).

Ballygullen I 1798 I Irish Rebellion

Ending the Irish Rising, Wexford rebels gathered at Whiteheaps, near Gorey, came under attack by Loyalist Generals Francis Needham and Sir Thomas Duff. The rebels were driven out of nearby Ballygullen with about 300 killed and the United armies soon officially surrendered. Rebel leaders Anthony Perry and Father Mogue Kearns were later captured and hanged (5 July 1798).

Ballymore I 1798 I Irish Rebellion
See **Tubberneering**

Ballynahinch I 1798 I Irish Rebellion

As the Irish Rising continued, rebels under a draper named Henry Munro occupied Ballynahinch, south of Belfast, in County Down. Loyalist General Sir George Nugent marched from Belfast through Saintfield with 1,600 men and eight guns and drove the rebels out. The town was pillaged and fired, and Munro was later court-martialled and hanged (13 June 1798).

Balochpur I 1623 I Rebellion of Prince Shahjahan

At a time of war against Persia in Afghanistan, Mughal Prince Shahjahan rebelled against his father Emperor Jahangir and raised an army of dissident nobles. However, at Balochpur, south of Delhi, the rebel army was heavily defeated by Imperial General Mahabat Khan. After further defeat at **Damdama**, Shahjahan later made peace with his father and succeeded to the throne (March 1623).

Baltimore I 1814 I War of 1812

British General Robert Ross burned Washington after **Bladensburg**, then sailed east to capture Baltimore from General Samuel Smith. General John Stricker blocked his advance and, after Ross was mortally wounded, Colonel Arthur Brooke was beaten at North Point. A naval bombardment next day of Baltimore's defence at **Fort McHenry** failed and the entire force withdrew (12 September 1814).

Bamako I 1883 I Franco-Mandingo Wars

Continuing the French offensive against Mandingo leader Samory Touré after a narrow victory in 1882 at **Kéniéra**, French Colonel Gustave Borgnis-Desbordes attacked Samorian forces at Bamako, in modern Mali. With just 242 men against about 5,000, Borgnis-Desbordes won a remarkable victory to secure French presence on the Niger. Samory agreed to withdraw east of the river (2–5 April 1883).

Bamburgh I 1095 I Norman Dynastic Wars

Facing rebellion by Robert de Mowbray Earl of Northumberland, William II Rufus captured Newcastle and Tynemouth, then besieged the coastal fortress of Bamburgh. Mowbray was captured after a false offer of negotiation and his wife Mothilde de Laigle surrendered the castle after a threat to blind her husband in front of her. The Earl was dispossessed and imprisoned for 30 years.

Bamburgh I 1464 I Wars of the Roses

With the Lancastrians recently defeated at **Hedgeley Moor** and **Hexham**, Richard Neville Earl of Warwick and his brother John Lord Montagu (now Earl of Northumberland) besieged the last Yorkist stronghold at Bamburgh, held by Sir Ralph Grey and Sir Humphrey Neville. The castle surrendered after heavy bombardment and Grey was executed, ending the war in the north (25 June–10 July 1464).

Bamian | 1221 | Conquests of Genghis Khan

The Mongol Genghis Khan marched into Afghanistan to meet a counter-offensive by Prince Jalal-ud-din of Khwarezm and was blocked at the once-important Bhuddist centre of Bamian, northwest of Kabul. When the Khan's grandson Moetuken was killed after taking Bamian by storm, the city and its population were destroyed. Genghis Khan pursued Jalal-ud-din to battle months later at the **Indus**.

Bamian | 1840 | 1st British-Afghan War

Campaigning against deposed Amir Dost Muhammad and the Wali of Khulum, Brigadier William Dennie and about 1,000 men defeated a reported 10,000-strong Afghan army near Bamian, about 80 miles northwest of Kabul. Dost Muhammad and his son Afzal Khan escaped the defeat, but a further loss at **Parwan** soon persuaded the former Amir to surrender in Kabul (18 September 1840).

Banbury | 1469 | Wars of the Roses
See **Edgecote**

Banda, India | 1858 | Indian Mutiny

Advancing northeast from the capture of **Sagar** in February, a force of only about 1,000 under General Sir George Whitlock met the rebel Nawab of Banda and 7,000 men outside Banda, 50 miles south of Cawnpore. Nawab Ali Bahadur was routed, losing 17 guns and over 400 killed, and fled with his army to **Kalpi**, abandoning Banda and its palace for Whitlock's army to plunder (19 April 1858).

Banda, Indonesia | 1796 | French Revolutionary Wars (1st Coalition)
See **Ambon**

Bandera Pass | 1841 | Comanche Indian Wars

Ambushed by Comanche northwest of San Antonio at Bandera Pass, a badly outnumbered Texas Ranger patrol under Captain Jack Coffee Hayes drove off the Indians with heavy losses, perhaps the first success with the newly introduced five-shot Patterson Colt revolvers. This semi-legendary action was later immortalised as an engraving on the new six-shot Walker revolvers (June 1841).

Bandoeng Strait | 1942 | World War II (Pacific)
See **Lombok Strait**

Bangalore | 1791 | 3rd British-Mysore War

When Tipu Sultan of Mysore renewed war against Britain, Governor-General Charles Earl Cornwallis took command and besieged Bangalore on the Deccan Plateau. After capturing the town and killing Bahadur Khan, Earl Cornwallis attacked and stormed Tipu's nearby camp, inflicting heavy casualties. He then advanced towards **Seringapatam** and **Arikera** (5–21 March 1791).

Bang Bo | 1885 | Sino-French War
See **Lang Son**

Bangil | 1706 | Dutch Wars in the East Indies

Intervening in a Javanese war, Dutch forces won at **Kartosuro** in 1705 to install the pliant Pakubuwana and pursued his dethroned nephew Amangkurat II into eastern Java, where he had fled to the warrior Surapati. When Surapati was killed in battle at Bangil, south of Surubaya, Amangkurat was eventually pardoned. But he was later treacherously arrested and exiled (16 October 1706).

Bangor | 1282 | English Conquest of Wales

Attempting to subdue Llewellyn ap Gruffydd of Wales, who had supported Simon de Montfort against him, Edward I attacked the Welsh Prince in Anglesea. Royal forces built a bridge of boats across the Straits of Menai near Bangor, but commander Lord Luke de Tany was killed in a disastrous attack when the bridge broke. Edward withdrew, then attacked next month at **Aber Edw** (6 November 1282).

Baniyas I 198 BC I 5th Syrian War
See **Paneas**

Baniyas I 1157 I Crusader-Muslim Wars
Having captured Damascus, Sultan Nur-ed-Din of Aleppo marched southwest to besiege the Crusader fortress at Baniyas, in the upper Jordan Valley. A Christian army was heavily defeated in a major battle nearby and Baniyas Township fell three days later. The Muslims then withdrew before a Crusader army under Baldwin III of Jerusalem and the citadel held out for seven years (18 May 1157).

Baniyas I 1179 I Crusader-Muslim Wars
Sultan Saladin was campaigning west from Damascus when he was challenged in the Jordan Valley by Baldwin IV of Jerusalem and Raymond of Tripoli. Near the Templar fortress of Baniyas, Saladin put the Crusaders to flight with heavy losses. King Baldwin and Count Raymond escaped, but Templar Grandmaster Odo de Saint-Armand was captured. He died soon after in prison (10 June 1179).

Banki I 1858 I Indian Mutiny
Concluding his campaign north of the Gaghara, British commander Sir Colin Campbell drove the rebels out of **Musjidiah**, then attacked northeast of Nanpara at Banki (near modern Nepalganj) on the Nepal border. After a brief action, with further losses at nearby Sidonia Ghat, Nana Sahib fled across the river into Nepal. Rebel leader Mehndi Husain surrendered a week later (31 December 1858).

Ban Me Thuot I 1975 I Vietnam War
After preliminary success in the south at **Phuoc Binh** in January, North Vietnam began its final offensive to conquer the south, with General Van Tien Dung's men and tanks storming into the central highlands to converge on Ban Me Thuot. The Darlac provincial capital fell in two days of heavy fighting and the main Communist force swung south through **Xuan Loc** towards **Saigon** (10–11 March 1975).

Bannikatti I 1565 I Wars of the Deccan Sultanates
See **Talikota**

Bannockburn I 1314 I Rise of Robert the Bruce
Edward II marching north to relieve the Scots siege of **Stirling** was defeated two miles away by Robert the Bruce, whose spearmen destroyed the English cavalry in marshy ground as they attempted to cross the stream at Bannock (Bannockburn). It was England's worst defeat against Scotland and war dragged on with further Scots victories in 1319 at **Myton** and in 1322 at **Byland** (24 June 1314).

Banos I 1809 I Napoleonic Wars (Peninsular Campaign)
Marching west from **Talavera de la Reina** towards Portugal, a small Anglo-Portuguese force led by General Sir Robert Wilson crashed into French Marshal Michel Ney returning to Salamanca after supporting Marshal Nicolas Soult pursuing the British out of Spain. Attempting to hold the mountain pass at Banos, north of the Tagus, Wilson's Lusitania Legion was utterly routed (12 October 1809).

Bantam I 1601 I Dutch-Portuguese Colonial Wars
Portuguese Admiral Andre Furtado de Mendonça launched an effort to secure western Java and blockaded the new Dutch factory at Bantam, where his 28-strong fleet was attacked by just five Dutch ships from Sumatra under Admiral Wolphert Harmensz. A prolonged action saw the Portuguese driven off with two ships lost and Harmensz sailed on to the Moluccas (27–30 December 1601).

Bantam ▪ 1618 ▪ Early Dutch Wars in the East Indies

Determined to capture the spice trade, Dutch forces attacked the British trading outpost at Bantam, in northwest Java. However, a British fleet under Sir Thomas Dale arrived to save Bantam, and Dutch Governor Jan Pieterszoon Coen was defeated in a three-day naval action and withdrew to the Moluccas. In May 1619 Coen returned to attack nearby **Jakarta** (27–30 December 1618).

Banten Bay ▪ 1942 ▪ World War II (Pacific)
See **Sunda Strait**

Bantia ▪ 208 BC ▪ 2nd Punic War

With the war in Italy stalling, Consuls Titus Crispinus and Marcus Marcellus were marching south to support the siege of Locri, when Hannibal sent a Carthaginian force which ambushed the Romans near their camp at Bantia, southeast of Venusia. In sharp fighting, Marcellus was killed, depriving Rome of one of its most effective Generals, and Crispinus was mortally wounded.

Bantry Bay ▪ 1689 ▪ War of the Grand Alliance

In support of deposed James II of England, Louis XIV of France sent a large fleet to Ireland with supplies and reinforcements. While Marquis Francois de Chateaurenault was unloading in Bantry Bay, County Cork, he was attacked by Admiral Arthur Herbert Earl of Torrington. The English squadron was badly mauled and the French returned safely to Brest (1 May 1689).

Bantry Bay ▪ 1796 ▪ French Revolutionary Wars (Irish Rising)

Attempting to land French troops in Ireland, Commodore Morard de Galles sailed from Brest with 43 ships and about 15,000 troops under General Lazare Hoche, supported by Irish rebel Wolfe Tone. In heavy weather, the fleet took refuge in Bantry Bay, southwestern Ireland, then abandoned the invasion. Eleven ships were lost to further storms and British naval action (24–27 December 1796).

Banyaluka ▪ 1737 ▪ Austro-Russian-Turkish War

While Austrian commander Count Friedrich von Seckendorff marched down the Morava against **Nish**, Prince Joseph Hildberghausen took a second force and overran Bosnia. But when the Prince attempted to besiege Banyaluka he was heavily defeated by Bosnian Vizier Ali Pasha Hekimoghlu. Seckendorff came to his aid and was soon defeated at **Valjevo** (4 August 1737).

Banyas ▪ 1157 ▪ Crusader-Muslim Wars
See **Baniyas**

Banyas ▪ 1179 ▪ Crusader-Muslim Wars
See **Baniyas**

Banyuls ▪ 1794 ▪ French Revolutionary Wars (1st Coalition)
See **Figueras**

Baoding ▪ 1928 ▪ 2nd Chinese Revolutionary Civil War

As Chiang Kai-shek conquered northern China, Manchurian warlord Zhang Zuolin in Beijing arrayed his armies to defend the capital. To the southwest, Nationalist General Feng Yuxiang besieged Baoding. He was driven off by a massive counter-attack by Zhang's army and reinforcements from Li Zongren restored the front. **Beijing** soon fell (17–25 May 1928).

Baoji ▪ 1948 ▪ 3rd Chinese Revolutionary Civil War

Two months after victory at **Yichuan**, Communist General Peng Dehuai's over-ambitious advance towards Sichuan was blocked in southern Shaanxi near Baoji (Paoki) by Muslim cavalry under General Ma Pufang, while pursuing Nationalist divisions from Yan'an attacked his rear. Peng lost almost half his force, but had his revenge against Ma a year later near **Xi'an** (27–28 April 1948).

Bapaume I 1870–1871 I Franco-Prussian War

General Louis Léon Faidherbe led a midwinter French offensive on the Somme to secure a tactical victory on the **Hallue** in December and later advanced to relieve besieged Péronne. At nearby Bapaume, he outnumbered and defeated General August von Goeben (3 January). But facing German reinforcements he abandoned Péronne, which fell five days later (26 December 1870–9 January 1871).

Bapaume I 1918 I World War I (Western Front)

In the main attack of the Allied offensive east from Amiens, British Generals Julian Byng and Sir Henry Rawlinson crossed the Ancre to outflank Albert and attacked Bapaume, southeast of Arras. After the fall of Bapaume (29 August), German forces tried to make a stand and were driven off in very heavy fighting, then fell back to the Hindenburg Line (22 August–2 September 1918).

Baphaeum I 1301 I Byzantine-Ottoman Wars

Expanding rapidly west along the Black Sea's southern shore, the Ottoman ruler Osman's horsemen attacked outlying possessions of Emperor Andronicus II, whose son Micheal was commander in Asia. At Baphaeum (near Nicomedia) an Imperial army under General Muzalon was crushed and fled before the Turks, who advanced to the Asian shore of the Bosphorus (27 July 1301).

Baran I 1920 I Wars of the Mad Mullah

Determined to crush Muhammad Abdullah Hassan of Somaliland, a large British force attacked his northern forts. Although Medishe was abandoned after heavy bombing, Dervishes held firm at Baran. Colonel John Wilkinson took the key fort at bayonet point, and Jidali to the west also fell. Access to the coast was then cut off at **Galiabur**, and the Mullah withdrew south to **Taleh** (23–24 January 1920).

Baranovitchi I 1916 I World War I (Eastern Front)

Russian General Aleksei Evert opened the second phase of the **Brusilov Offensive** by attacking the salient north of Pinsk around Baranovitchi. Despite unprecedented artillery bombardment, the Austro-German Divisions held firm and, after the failed action had cost 80,000 Russian casualties, General Aleksei Brusilov moved the offensive south towards **Brody** and **Kovel** (2–9 July 1916).

Barari Ghat I 1760 I Indian Campaigns of Ahmad Shah

As Afghans moved into the decaying Mughal Empire, Afghan General Ahmed Shah Durrani—on his fifth invasion—was checked at **Lahore**, then met Maratha Chief Dattaji Sindhia at Barari Ghat on the Jumna River north of Delhi. The Maratha army was destroyed in a surprise attack and Dattaji was killed. The victory led directly to the great Afghan triumph a year later at **Panipat** (9 January 1760).

Barari Tangi I 1920 I Waziristan Campaign

Following failed peace talks after defeat at **Ahnai Tangi**, Mahsud in Waziristan reinforced a position on the Tank Zam River at Barari Tangi, including the strong bluff "Gibraltar." General Andrew Sheen launched two night assaults under General Frederic Lucas, who drove the tribesmen off. They turned for aid to Afghanistan, but were soon beaten again at **Aka Khel** (23–25 January 1920).

Barataria I 1814 I War of 1812

Concerned by British overtures to the pirates and smugglers of Barataria, on Grand Terre off the Mississippi Delta, Louisiana Governor William Claiborne sent a combined force under Commodore Daniel Patterson and Colonel George Ross. The pirate stronghold fell after a brief bombardment and their Chief Jean Lafitte later supported the Americans at **New Orleans** (16 September 1814).

Barbacoas ▮ 1824 ▮ Colombian Civil Wars

Despite defeat in 1823 at **Ibarra** and **Catambuco**, Colonel Augustín Agualongo renewed the Royalist rebellion in Pasto against Governor Juan José Flores. West of Pasto at Barbacoas, the rebels were routed by Patriot Colonel Tomas Cipriano de Mosquera (who was badly wounded). Agualongo was captured and executed and the Royalist rising was finally crushed (1 June 1824).

Barba de Puerco ▮ 1810 ▮ Napoleonic Wars (Peninsular Campaign)

With British forces under General Robert "Black Bob" Craufurd defending the Agueda, northwest of Ciudad Rodrigo, General Claude-Francois Ferey took 600 men across the bridge at San Felice de los Gallegos to surprise the British at Barba de Puerco. Colonel Sydney Beckwith repulsed Ferey after costly losses, but within months **Ciudad Rodrigo** fell to the French (19–20 March 1810).

Barbastro ▮ 1837 ▮ 1st Carlist War

A week after defeat at **Huesca**, new Spanish commander General Marcelino Oráa and French Foreign Legion Colonel Joseph Conrad attacked Spanish pretender Carlos V northwest of Monzón at Barbastro. Despite massive superiority, Oráa was repulsed with very heavy losses, including Conrad killed. The "old" Legion was effectively destroyed as a fighting force (2 June 1837).

Barbosthene Mtns ▮ 192 BC ▮ Spartan-Achaean Wars

See **Mount Barbosthene**

Barbourville ▮ 1861 ▮ American Civil War (Western Theatre)

Advancing into southeastern Kentucky from Cumberland Ford, Confederate General Felix K. Zollicoffer sent Colonel Joel A. Battle against Union forces training near Barbourville. After the recruits withdrew, a rearguard of 300 militia under Captain Isaac J. Blacks attempted to block Battle. However, the militia were dispersed and he destroyed the Union camp (19 September 1861).

Bárbula ▮ 1813 ▮ Venezuelan War of Independence

Loosely blockaded in Puerto Cabella after defeat in July at **Taguanes**, Spanish General Juan Domingo Monteverde received 1,300 reinforcements under Colonel José Miguel Salomón and counter-attacked Simón Bolívar's Republicans. At Bárbula, north of Valencia, Monteverde was defeated and wounded. Salomón's regulars lost three days later at Las Trincheras (30 September 1813).

Barbury ▮ 556 ▮ Anglo-Saxon Conquest of Britain

See **Beranbyrg**

Barcelona, Spain ▮ 1641 ▮ Catalonian Uprising

Pedro Santa Coloma, Spanish Viceroy in Catalonia, arrested one of the Catalonian deputies and was murdered in the riots and uprising which followed (sometimes known as the Reapers War for the agricultural workers who took part). A Royalist army under the Marques de los Velez sent to suppress the rebels was defeated outside the walls of Barcelona.

Barcelona, Spain ▮ 1642 ▮ Thirty Years War (Franco-Habsburg War)

Cruising off Catalonia, French Admiral Jean-Armande de Maillé-Brézé and Chevalier de Cangé met a slightly smaller Spanish fleet near Barcelona under Admiral Sancho de Urdanivia. A confused and indecisive action ensued, in which the Spanish lost two vessels and Cangé went down with his ship. The Spanish withdrew to Minorca and Brézé eventually returned to Toulon (30 June 1642).

Barcelona, Spain ▮ 1652 ▮ Catalonian Uprising

Following years of peasant rebellion in Catalonia, King Philip IV took advantage of the devastation caused when the area was struck by famine and plague, to recapture Barcelona. After a terrible siege, the city was starved into surrender. Against the advice of his counsellors, the Spanish King then wisely granted a general amnesty and the area returned to allegiance to the Crown.

Barcelona, Spain ▎ 1695 ▎ War of the Grand Alliance

Louis Duke de Vendôme took French command in Spain from Marshal Anne-Jules de Noailles and laid siege to Barcelona, supported at sea by Admiral Jean d'Estrées. The city was well provisioned and strongly garrisoned, but after a large Spanish relief force under Viceroy Francisco de Velasco was surprised and heavily defeated, Barcelona quickly capitulated (4 June–10 August 1695).

Barcelona, Spain ▎ 1704 ▎ War of the Spanish Succession

When an Anglo-Dutch fleet under Admiral Sir George Rooke arrived off Barcelona, a small marine force led by Prince George of Hesse landed and demanded the city's surrender. However, Governor Francisco de Velasco refused to yield. The inadequate force re-embarked after a half-hearted bombardment and the Allies withdrew, returning to try again a year later (17–30 May 1704).

Barcelona, Spain (1st) ▎ 1705 ▎ War of the Spanish Succession

Despite previous Allied failure, Admiral Sir Clowdesley Shovell and Charles Mordaunt Lord Peterborough besieged Barcelona, where Prince George of Hesse was killed capturing the nearby fortress of Montjuich (2 September). Governor Francisco de Velasco surrendered Barcelona after some bombardment and Archduke Charles was proclaimed King (11 August–28 September 1705).

Barcelona, Spain (2nd) ▎ 1705–1706 ▎ War of the Spanish Succession

Following the fall of Barcelona in September 1705 to Charles Mordaunt Lord Peterborough,

the city suffered a renewed siege by Philip V of Spain and Marshal Count René de Tessé. With Admiral Louis de Bourbon Comte de Toulouse repulsed by Admiral Sir John Leake, and a threatened English invasion from Portugal, Philip abandoned the siege (November 1705–30 April 1706).

Barcelona, Spain ▎ 1713–1714 ▎ War of the Spanish Succession

As hostilities came to an end, the Catalans continued fighting and a large Franco-Spanish Royalist army, led by General Antonio de Villaroel, was sent against Barcelona. Following a 13-month siege, with terrible losses and no quarter on either side, Marshal James Duke of Berwick took command and stormed the city, forcing a surrender to end the war in Spain (August 1713–11 September 1714).

Barcelona, Spain ▎ 1808 ▎ Napoleonic Wars (Peninsular Campaign)
See **Cardedeu**

Barcelona, Spain ▎ 1936 ▎ Spanish Civil War

When Nationalist forces attempted to secure the key cities of Spain, cavalry General Fernández Burriel met strong opposition trying to seize Barcelona. He was then reinforced by General Manuel Goded from **Majorca**, but very heavy urban fighting against militia and anarchists saw the rebels overrun, with Goded captured and executed. The rising also failed in **Madrid** (18–19 July 1936).

Barcelona, Spain ▎ 1938–1939 ▎ Spanish Civil War

Having blunted the Republican offensive on the **Ebro** in November, about 350,000 Nationalist troops counter-attacked across the river into Catalonia. General Juan Yagüe seized Tortosa after heavy fighting (13 January), then advanced on Barcelona, where Prime Minister Juan Negrín fled. The city fell two days later, and within two months the war was over (23 December 1938–26 January 1939).

Barcelona, Venezuela I 1817 I Venezuelan War of Independence

Patriot leader Simón Bolívar returned to Venezuela and fortified the city of Barcelona, which successfully held off a siege by the forces of Spanish commander Pablo Morillo under General Pascual del Real and later General Juan Aldama. Bolívar later departed to besiege **Angostura**, and General Raimundo Freites was left to eventually surrender the city (January–5 August 1817).

Bard I 1800 I French Revolutionary Wars (2nd Coalition)

As Napoleon Bonaparte crossed the Alps into northern Italy, he was held up leaving the St Bernard Pass by the stubbornly defended fortress of Bard. While the village fell on 22 May and some troops were able to pass, the Austrian garrison continued to delay the advance of Bonaparte's main army and heavy equipment, until the fortress was forced to surrender (21 May–1 June 1800).

Bardia I 1941 I World War II (Northern Africa)

General Richard O'Connor crushed Italy's invasion of Egypt at **Sidi Barrani**, then pursued Marshal Rudolfo Graziano into Libya and attacked General Annibale Bergonzoli at Bardia. Following land and naval bombardment, Bardia was stormed by General Iven Mackay's Australians, who took almost 40,000 prisoners, and O'Connor raced west towards **Tobruk** (3–5 January 1941).

Bareilly I 1858 I Indian Mutiny

With **Lucknow** secured in March, General Sir Colin Campbell marched into Rohilkhand, where the rebels had appointed Khan Bahadur Khan as viceroy. In an early morning attack on Bareilly, Campbell defeated Khan outside the city. The rebel leader fled during the night, ending his rule in Rohilkhand, and Bareilly was captured next day after a brief bombardment (5–6 May 1858).

Barents Sea I 1942 I World War II (War at Sea)

When Admiral Oskar Kummetz led the heavy cruiser *Hipper*, pocket battleship *Lützow* and six destroyers against convoy JW51B in the Barents Sea near Bear Island, he met fierce resistance from the destroyer escort (Captain Robert Sherbrooke) and Admiral Robert Burnett's cruisers. The timid Kummetz withdrew with heavy damage and one destroyer lost (31 December 1942).

Barentu I 1985 I Eritrean War of Independence

On a fresh offensive in southwest Eritrea, rebel forces used captured Ethiopian tanks and artillery to help storm the strategic stronghold of Barentu. Responding with huge reinforcements, the Ethiopians suffered perhaps 2,000 killed in repeated failed assaults, before air-strikes forced the Eritreans to withdraw. However, Ethiopia then failed yet again to take **Nakfa** (6 July–25 August 1985).

Barentu I 2000 I Ethiopian-Eritrean War

In order to break a stalemate in their bloody border war, Ethiopia launched a massive offensive, reportedly with over 100,000 men, southwest of Asmara. Pushing deep into Eritrea, they stormed the strategic town of Barentu and bombed the capital. Within days, Eritrea pledged to withdraw from disputed border territory and, after further scattered action, war came to an end (17–18 May 2000).

Barfleur I 1692 I War of the Grand Alliance

See **La Hogue**

Bari I 871 I Byzantine-Muslim Wars

Although Muslim forces had long been active in southern Italy, an attack on Rome provoked a joint intervention by Western Emperor Louis II and Byzantine Emperor Basil I. Driven back under siege to the Adriatic port of Bari, the Arabs reputedly resisted for three years until a fresh expedition by Louis, supported by the

Byzantine navy, finally took the city by storm (2 February 871).

Bari ∎ 1068–1071 ∎ Norman Conquest of Southern Italy

With the Byzantine Empire distracted by a Turkish invasion, the fortified Adriatic port of Bari was subjected to a three-year siege and naval blockade by Norman leader Robert Guiscard. The Emperor Romanus IV Diogenes had already left the campaign and, when the city was finally forced to submit, its surrender marked the end of Byzantine presence in Italy (5 August 1068–April 1071).

Bari ∎ 1943 ∎ World War II (Southern Europe)

A German air-raid on the port of Bari, being used to support the Allied invasion of Italy, triggered a bizarre incident involving the military use of poison gas. Among 16 Allied ships destroyed was the ammunition carrier *John Harvey*, which blew up with its cargo of 2,000 mustard gas bombs. Hundreds were killed or injured by the gas, including many Italian civilians (2 December 1943).

Bar-le-Duc ∎ 1037 ∎ French Barons' War

After failing in an attempt to gain the throne of Burgundy, the military adventurer Odo (Eudes) II, Count of Blois and Champagne, marched against the principality of Lorraine. Near the city of Bar-le-Duc, on the river Ornain in northeastern France, Odo's army was destroyed by Gozelo (Gothelon) Duke of Upper Lorraine. Odo himself was killed on the battlefield (15 November 1037).

Barletta ∎ 1502–1503 ∎ Italian War of Louis XII

When France and Spain resumed war over Naples, Spanish General Gonsalvo de Cordoba was driven back to Barletta by Louis d'Armagnac Duke of Nemours. The outnumbered Cordoba defeated the French and their Swiss mercenaries in repeated engagements, though Barletta remained under loose blockade for eight months until reinforcements arrived, leading to Spanish victory at **Cerignola**.

Barnet ∎ 1471 ∎ Wars of the Roses

Returning to England after escaping his ambitious younger brother George Duke of Clarence and Richard Neville Earl of Warwick, Edward IV landed at **Ravenspur**. When Clarence came over to his side, the brothers attacked Warwick just north of London at Barnet, where Warwick was defeated and killed. After victory at **Tewkesbury**, Edward had Clarence murdered to secure the throne (14 April 1471).

Barodia ∎ 1858 ∎ Indian Mutiny

General Sir Hugh Rose and about 3,000 men advancing into central India to relieve the small British garrison at **Sagar** defeated the army of the Rajah of Banpur at **Rahatgarh**. However, most of the rebels escaped to a new defensive position at Barodia, northwest of Sagar. The rebels were driven out in a sharp action, but again most escaped, and Rose advanced to Sagar (30 January 1858).

Barquilla ∎ 1810 ∎ Napoleonic Wars (Peninsular Campaign)

Two days after **Ciudad Rodrigo** fell, French General Roch Godart sent a raid west to where General Robert "Black Bob" Craufurd attempted an ambush on the heights of Barquilla, north of Villar de Puerco. The badly outnumbered French under Captain Pierre Gouache repulsed the attack, inflicting costly losses, though Craufurd's reputation was restored two weeks later at the **Coa** (11 July 1810).

Barquisimeto ∎ 1813 ∎ Venezuelan War of Independence

After victory at **Mosquiteros** in October, Republican General Vicente Campo Elías sent Colonel Rafael Urdaneta towards Barquisimeto, where he was blocked by Royalists under Colonel José Ceballos. Revolutionary leader Simón Bolívar himself joined Urdaneta for the attack, but they were heavily defeated—losing 400 killed and 400 captured—and retired on San Carlos (10 November 1813).

Barra I 1308 I Rise of Robert the Bruce
See **Inverurie**

Barranca de Atenquique I 1858 I Mexican War of the Reform
See **Atenquique**

Barrancas I 1819 I Argentine Civil Wars
In a fresh government offensive against Estanislao López of Sante Fe, beaten in February at **La Herradura**, General Juan José Viamonte sent Colonel Rafael Hortiguera, who was met at Barrancas, west of the Parana near Galvez, by the Sante Fe vanguard under Irish-born Pedro Campbell. Hortiguera was badly defeated and the troops of Buenos Aires withdrew from Santa Fe (10 May 1819).

Barraza I 1817 I Chilean War of Independence
See **Salala**

Barren Hill I 1778 I War of the American Revolution
Preparing to evacuate Philadelphia, British General Sir Henry Clinton marched against an American force under the Marquis Marie de Lafayette about 12 miles away at Barren Point. Despite an attempted flanking movement by Generals James Grant and Charles Grey, Lafayette slipped away with little fighting. A month later Clinton defeated the Americans at **Monmouth** (20 May 1778).

Barrier Field I 1600 I Japan's Era of the Warring States
See **Sekigahara**

Barriers I 1814 I Napoleonic Wars (French Campaign)
See **Paris**

Barrosa I 1811 I Napoleonic Wars (Peninsular Campaign)
British General Thomas Graham marched west from Gibraltar to relieve the French siege of Barrosa and attacked Marshal Claude Victor's blockade, while the besieged garrison led a powerful sortie. Graham's outnumbered Anglo-Portuguese force won a brilliant victory, but Spanish General Manuel la Pena failed to provide support and the blockade continued (5 March 1811).

Barros Negros I 1851 I 1st Chilean Liberal Revolt
See **Loncomilla**

Bar-sur-Aube I 1814 I Napoleonic Wars (French Campaign)
After victory at **Montereau**, Napoleon Bonaparte marched north against General Gebhard von Blucher, leaving Marshal Nicolas Oudinot to face Prince Karl Philipp Schwarzenberg and the Allies southeast of Paris near **Troyes**. Advancing through Bar-sur-Aube, Prince Ludwig Wittgenstein outnumbered and defeated Oudinot, who fell back through Troyes towards Paris (27 February 1814).

Bartow I 1861 I American Civil War (Eastern Theatre)
See **Greenbrier River**

Basain I 635 I Muslim Conquest of Syria
See **Fihl**

Basawapatna I 1696 I Mughal-Maratha Wars
During the epic siege of the Maratha fortress of **Gingee**, west of Pondicherry, the Mughal army was in turn besieged by Santaji Ghorpade. Emperor Aurangzeb sent a fresh force under Himmat Khan and, near Basawapatna, Himmat Khan and his son were defeated and killed. However, the ambitious Santaji soon fell out with King Rajaram and was dismissed from service (20 January 1696).

Bashgedikler I 1853 I Crimean War
Advancing into eastern Turkey from Alexandropol following Russian victory at **Akhaltsikhe** (14 November), Prince Vassily Osipovich Bebutov and about 10,000 veteran troops reached Bashgedikler, near the Armenian border, where they met a Turkish force of about 30,000. The

Turks were utterly routed and fled to **Kars**, leaving behind 26 of their guns (1 December 1853).

Bashiratganj (1st) I 1857 I Indian Mutiny

After relieving **Cawnpore**, General Sir Henry Havelock crossed the Ganges towards besieged **Lucknow**, and after a costly victory at **Unnao**, met a strong rebel force later the same day holding the fortified town of Bashiratganj. While the rebels fled following further heavy fighting, Havelock was forced to withdraw west to Cawnpore with heavy losses in casualties and to cholera (29 July 1857).

Bashiratganj (2nd) I 1857 I Indian Mutiny

Crossing the Ganges from Cawnpore northeast towards besieged **Lucknow**, General Sir Henry Havelock made a renewed advance on the fortified town of Bashiratganj, where he again drove the rebels out. However, with no cavalry to pursue and Cawnpore itself threatened by fresh mutineer forces, he overruled his impetuous son Major Henry Havelock and fell back on Mangalwar (5 August 1857).

Bashiratganj (3rd) I 1857 I Indian Mutiny

General Sir Henry Havelock led a renewed attempt to decisively defeat rebel forces besieging **Lucknow**, once more crossing the Ganges towards Bashiratganj, just east of the city. Advancing through waist-deep swamp, his outnumbered force drove the rebels out anew, but casualties and cholera again forced his withdrawal to Cawnpore to meet a fresh rebel threat from **Bithur** (12 August 1857).

Bashkent I 1473 I Ottoman-Turkoman War

See **Erzincan**

Basing I 871 I Viking Wars in Britain

Only two weeks after Aethelred of Wessex led the great Saxon victory northwest of Reading at **Ashdown**, the defeated Vikings under King Halfdan resumed the offensive south of Reading at Basing. The army of the West Saxons was heavily defeated and lost again within a year at **Merton** and **Wilton** (22 January 871).

Basing House I 1643–1645 I British Civil Wars

Blocking the road west from London, massive Basing House was held by Royalist John Paulet Marquis of Winchester against brutal attacks by Sir William Waller and Colonel Richard Norton. Oliver Cromwell then led a third siege and Basing was taken by ferocious assault, looted and burned to the ground (7–12 November 1643, June–November 1644 & 8–14 October 1645).

Basoli I 1702 I Mughal-Sikh Wars

With a Mughal Imperial army repulsed in bloody battle on the Sutlej at **Nirmohgarh**, Sikh Guru Gobind Singh withdrew to Basoli, west of Chamba, where he was supported by the Raja Dharampul of Basoli. An alliance of rival hill Rajas under Ajmer Chand of Kahlur launched a heavy attack on the Sikhs, but they were driven off and Ajmer Chand made a tactical peace with the Guru.

Basque Roads I 1809 I Napoleonic Wars (5th Coalition)

See **Aix**

Basra I 656 I Muslim Civil Wars

See **Camel, Iraq**

Basra I 1743 I Turko-Persian Wars of Nadir Shah

Nadir Shah of Persia campaigned in northern Mesopotamia, where he laid siege to **Mosul**, then sent Qoja Khan Shaikhanlu against Basra, near the mouth of the Tigris, defended by Deputy Governor Rustam Aqa. Lacking sufficient artillery, the Persians' assaults were repulsed and, when Nadir Shah faced a rising at home and made peace, the siege was withdrawn (28 August–8 December 1743).

Basra I 1775–1776 I Turko-Persian Gulf War

Jealous of the Turkish port of Basra, Persian Regent Kharim Khan sent a siege force under his brother Sadiq Khan. An Omani fleet broke the blockade, but a relief force from Baghdad was repulsed and Governor Sulaiman Aqa was finally starved into surrender. When Kharim Khan died, Sadiq withdrew in order to claim the throne and the Persian Gulf Port was lost (8 April 1775–16 April 1776).

Basra I 1914 I World War I (Mesopotamia)

See **Sahil**

Basra I 1915 I World War I (Mesopotamia)

See **Shaiba**

Basra I 1982 I Iraq-Iran War

Iran refused peace feelers after defeating Iraq at **Khorramshahr** in May and determined to invade Iraq itself, launching the massive Operation Ramadan offensive towards Basra. In the claimed largest land battle since World War II, three separate "human wave" assaults were driven off by Iraqi artillery and poison gas. The Iranians lost perhaps 30,000 casualties for no real gain (13 July–3 August 1982).

Basra I 1984 I Iraq-Iran War

In a massive campaign to cut the Basra-Baghdad Road and secure the oil complex at Majnoon, Iran launched overlapping offensives north of Basra, which developed into a giant battle of attrition in the Hawizeh Marshes. Iranian forces seized considerable territory but suffered terrible casualties, many to chemical attack, and Iraq's defence finally exhausted the offensive (15 February–19 March 1984).

Basra I 1985 I Iraq-Iran War

After its costly "human wave" offensives of 1984, Iran launched a smaller attack north of Basra. Well protected against chemical attack, the Iranians advanced out of the Hawizeh Marshes behind heavy artillery fire and reached the strategic Basra-Baghdad Road. Stubborn Iraqi defence, aided by powerful air support, eventually drove them back with further costly losses (11–18 March 1985).

Basra I 1987 I Iraq-Iran War

Having failed south of Basra around Khorramshahr in December 1986, Iran launched another massive offensive north of the city, which inflicted heavy Iraqi losses and almost reached Basra itself before being driven off with shocking Iranian casualties. A second, smaller attack was also a costly failure and proved to be Iran's last "human wave" assault (8 January–26 February & 6–9 April 1987).

Basra I 2003 I 2nd Gulf War

With the fall of **Umm Qasr**, more British troops advanced on Iraq's southern city of Basra. While fierce fighting outside Basra saw heavy Iraqi losses in tanks and prisoners, a direct assault was delayed to allow a supposed popular rising. But amid reports of the rising crushed and a humanitarian crisis, the British stormed the city in their largest single attack of the war (21 March–7 April 2003).

Bassano I 1796 I French Revolutionary Wars (1st Coalition)

Facing a renewed Austrian attempt to relieve the French siege of **Mantua**, Napoleon Bonaparte won at **Calliano**, then immediately turned against General Dagobert Wurmser advancing down the Brenta Valley. After an initial loss at **Primolano**, Wurmser was routed next day at Bassano de Grappa. He then fought his way into Mantua, where he surrendered five months later (8 September 1796).

Bassano I 1866 I 3rd Italian War of Independence

Archduke Albert of Austria defeated the Italians at **Custozza** (24 June) but withdrew north to defend Vienna from the advancing Prussians. Pursued across the Po at Borgoforte by Enrico Cialdini Duke of Gaeta, the Austrians were attacked near Bassano del Grappa, northwest of Venice. Suffering heavy losses they continued withdrawing and peace with Italy soon followed (21 July 1866).

Bassein, Burma ∎ 1825 ∎ 1st British-Burmese War

When Burma conquered Arakan and attacked British India, General Sir Archibald Campbell defeated Maha Bundoola at **Rangoon**, then sent Major Robert Sale west against the river port of Bassein. Supported by naval commander Captain Frederick Marryat, Sale stormed the stockade and seized the town, then marched north to join the advance against **Danubyu** (26 February 1825).

Bassein, Burma ∎ 1852 ∎ 2nd British-Burmese War

After Britain resumed war with Burma for commercial gain, General Henry Thomas Godwin captured **Martaban** and **Rangoon**, and within days advanced west against the river port of Bassein. With naval forces under Commodore George Robert Lambert in support, he captured fortresses on both sides of the river following strong resistance, then advanced north against **Pegu** (19 April 1852).

Bassein, India ∎ 1737–1739 ∎ Portuguese-Maratha War

Maratha forces besieging the Portuguese island fortress of Bassein (modern Vasai) near Bombay gradually captured the outlying positions and repulsed a counter-attack at Thana. Reinforced by Chimnaji Appa, the final attack went in after destruction by massive mines. The four-day battle cost over 5,000 Maratha lives before the Portuguese finally surrendered (March 1737–5 May 1739).

Bassein, India ∎ 1780 ∎ 1st British-Maratha War

British General Thomas Goddard attempted to secure the approaches to Bombay Harbour, besieging the former Portuguese coastal fortress of Bassein (modern Vasai) seized by the Marathas in 1739. Visaji Pant Lele's 4,000-strong garrison held out against terrible bombardment but surrendered when a massive Maratha relief force

was defeated at **Doogaur** (November–12 December 1780).

Bassianae ∎ 468 ∎ Hun-Ostrogoth Wars

Recovering from the terrible Hun defeat at the **Nedao** in 454, Attila's son Dengizich crossed the Danube with a large Hun-Goth force and attempted to capture Bassianae, between Belgrade and Sremska Mitrovica. According to Gothic tradition, he suffered a heavy defeat at the hands of the Ostrogoth Walamer and was killed a year later on the lower Danube by the Roman-German General Anagastes.

Bassignano ∎ 1745 ∎ War of the Austrian Succession

Spanish General Count Juan de Gages and French Marshal Jean-Baptiste Desmarets Marquis de Maillebois joined forces in northern Italy to meet an Austro-Sardinian army led by Prince Johann Christian von Lobkowitz at Bassignano, south of Piacenza. Lobkowitz was decisively defeated and was replaced before Austria turned the tables on Maillebois (June 1746) at **Piacenza** (27 September 1745).

Bastia ∎ 1794 ∎ French Revolutionary Wars (1st Coalition)

With the British navy forced out of **Toulon** in late 1793, Admiral Sir Samuel Hood (1724–1816) invaded Corsica, where he captured **San Fiorenzo**, then sent seamen and marines under Captain Horatio Nelson against the northeastern port of Bastia. Bastia surrendered after a seven-week siege, along with a French frigate in the port, and Hood moved west to attack **Calvi** (4 April–21 May 1794).

Bastogne ∎ 1944 ∎ World War II (Western Europe)

As German Panzer forces advanced into the **Ardennes**, General Heinrich von Lüttwitz besieged the strategic Belgian road and rail centre at Bastogne, defended by American General Anthony McAuliffe. Refusing to surrender with the famous reply "Nuts," McAuliffe held out in bitter cold until relieved by American tanks, and the Germans eventually withdrew (20–26 December 1944).

Bataan ▌ 1942 ▌ World War II (Pacific)
When General Masaharu Homma invaded the **Philippines** and seized Manila, Filipino and American forces withdrew west to the Bataan Peninsula and held off initial assaults. After a renewed attack, General Edward King surrendered 77,000 men, of whom up to 10,000 died on the "Death March" to prison camp. After the war, Homma was executed for war crimes (7 January–9 April 1942).

Bataan ▌ 1945 ▌ World War II (Pacific)
With Americans facing fierce resistance on **Luzon**, General Charles Hall landed in the southwest (29 January) to isolate the Bataan Peninsula, aided by Filipino guerrillas under Captain Ramon Magsaysay. A small Japanese force under Colonel Sanenobu Nagayoshi resisted strongly as Hall secured Bataan, while also moving against nearby **Corregidor** (15–21 February 1945).

Batavia ▌ 1628 ▌ Early Dutch Wars in the East Indies
Sultan Agung of Mataram was determined to regain central Java and sent a large army against the new Dutch city of Batavia (modern Jakarta), defended by Governor Jan Pieterszoon Coen. At the end of a long siege, the Javanese were driven off with terrible losses. General Suriangalaga was forced to return to Mataram, where he was executed for his costly failure (28 August–27 November 1628).

Batavia ▌ 1629 ▌ Early Dutch Wars in the East Indies
In a renewed offensive in central Java, Sultan Agung of Mataram sent a reported 120,000 men against the Dutch city of Batavia (modern Jakarta). While Governor Jan Pieterszoon Coen died during the siege, Antonie van Diemen drove off repeated assaults with very heavy losses. The shattered Javanese withdrew, devastated by starvation and disease (21 August–20 October 1629).

Batavia ▌ 1811 ▌ Napoleonic Wars (5th Coalition)
A British force under General Sir Samuel Auchmuty landed on the Dutch island of Java, where they captured the city of Batavia (modern Jakarta) after storming the nearby position at Fort Cornelius, held by Dutch General Jan Willem Janssens. Java and the neighbouring islands were surrendered to Britain but were returned to Holland at the end of the war (4–28 August 1811).

Batin ▌ 1810 ▌ Russo-Turkish Wars
Returning to the Danube, Russian General Nikolai Kamenskoi captured **Silistria** and besieged Ruschuk and Giurgiu, then attacked a large Turkish relief force under Mukhtar Pasha, entrenched at the mouth of the Yantra, east of Svistov at Batin. The Turks were heavily defeated, with their cannon and 5,000 men captured, and **Ruschuk** and Giurgiu fell three weeks later (7 September 1810).

Batoche ▌ 1885 ▌ 2nd Riel Rebellion
General Frederick Middleton led Canadian forces against rebellion in Saskatchewan, advancing north through **Fish Creek** to besiege the Méti at Batoche, southwest of Prince Albert. When the government forces were reinforced, Batoche was seized with costly losses on both sides. Gabriel Dumont fled to the United States, but Louis Riel surrendered and was hanged (9–12 May 1885).

Batoh ▌ 1652 ▌ Cossack-Polish Wars
Renewing war in the Ukraine after **Bila Tserkva** (1651), Polish Hetman Martin Kalinowsky tried to prevent Cossack leader Bogdan Chmielnicki and his Tatar allies joining Moldavia. However, at Batoh, west of Uman, Kalinowksy was routed and killed along with most of his staff. The Tatars changed sides and the Cossacks made peace, placing the Ukraine under Tsar Alexis II (23 May 1652).

Baton Rouge ▌ 1779 ▌ War of the American Revolution

When Spain entered the war against Britain in June 1779, Don Bernardo de Galvez, Spanish Governor of Louisiana, secured Manchac (7 September), then attacked and defeated the British garrison at Baton Rouge. He later secured Natchez (30 September) and, the following year, **Mobile** in British West Florida. Louisiana remained Spanish until sold to France in 1800 (21 September 1799).

Baton Rouge ▌ 1810 ▌ West Florida Revolution

Although the United States purchased Louisiana from France in 1803, Spain refused to give up the fortress at Baton Rouge. Residents and frontiersmen from nearby American territory defeated the garrison in a sharp engagement and proclaimed the independent State of West Florida. The disputed area was annexed into the United States a few weeks later (23 September 1810).

Baton Rouge ▌ 1862 ▌ American Civil War (Lower Seaboard)

Confederate forces under General John C. Breckinridge advanced on Baton Rouge in an attempt to recover Louisiana, supported by the ram vessel *Arkansas*. The Union troops initially fell back with General Thomas Williams killed, then regrouped under Colonel Thomas W. Cahill. After scuttling their disabled ship, the Confederates withdrew with almost 500 casualties (5 August 1862).

Battleaxe ▌ 1941 ▌ World War II (Northern Africa)

See **Sollum-Halfaya**

Battle Creek, Idaho ▌ 1878 ▌ Bannock Indian War

When the Bannock Chief Buffalo Horn led his starving people west off the Fort Hall Reservation in southeast Idaho, he was attacked at Battle Creek, south of Boise, by a small force of volunteers from Silver City under Captain Joel Harper. The ill-trained volunteers were driven off, but Buffalo Horn was killed. His people were soon defeated at **Silver Creek, Oregon** (8 June 1878).

Battle Creek, Texas ▌ 1838 ▌ Kickapoo Indian Wars

In an outbreak of warfare in eastern Texas, a band of about 300 mainly Kickapoo warriors and followers under Chief Benito attacked a survey party of 23 at Richland Creek (renamed Battle Creek) near modern Dawson, northeast of Waco. Seventeen Texans were killed and five injured, and a month later the Kickapoo joined Mexican forces in the **Killough Massacre** (8 September 1838).

Battleford ▌ 1885 ▌ 2nd Riel Rebellion

Encouraged by the success of Métis (Canadian half-breeds) at **Duck Lake**, Cree Chief Poundmaker (Pitikwahanapiwiyin) took 200 warriors against Battleford on the North Saskatchewan River. With the residents besieged in a fortified stockade, the Cree looted the town before withdrawing when a substantial force approached under Colonel William Otter (30 March–24 April 1885).

Battle Ground ▌ 1811 ▌ Tecumseh's Confederacy

See **Tippecanoe**

Battle Mountain ▌ 1878 ▌ Bannock Indian War

See **Birch Creek**

Batu Pahat ▌ 1456 ▌ Thai-Malacca War

A Thai offensive overland against Melaka (modern Malacca) was routed at **Ulu Muar** (1445) and, eleven years later, Siamese General Awi Dichu led a fresh offensive by sea. An epic naval battle off Batu Pahat saw the forces of Melaka under Bendahara (Chief Minister) Tun Perak secure a decisive victory. Tun Perak served under four Sultans and helped establish Melaka as a maritime power.

Baturin ∎ 1708 ∎ 2nd "Great" Northern War

Charles XII of Sweden invaded Russia for victory at **Holowczyn** in July then turned to the Ukraine, where Cossack leader Ivan Mazeppa declared for the Swedish King. Russian Prince Alexander Menshikov immediately stormed the Cossack capital of Baturin, with its vital stores, destroying the city and its population. Six months later Mazeppa was defeated at **Poltava** (3 November 1708).

Bau ∎ 1965 ∎ Indonesian-Malaysian Confrontation

Indonesian forces attempting to establish a guerrilla base inside Borneo at Bau, southwest of Kuching, were attacked by Gurkhas under Captain Charles Maunsell. Very heavy fighting saw at least 24 Indonesians killed before they withdrew across the border. Three Gurkhas were also killed and Lance Corporal Rambahadur Limbu won the only Victoria Cross of the war (21 November 1965).

Bauds ∎ 961 ∎ Later Viking Raids on Britain

See **Invercullen**

Baugé ∎ 1421 ∎ Hundred Years War

When Henry V of England was recognised by Charles VI of France as his heir, the disinherited son—the Dauphin Charles VII—gathered troops (including Scottish mercenaries) and at Baugé, in Anjou, attacked an English force led by Henry's brother Thomas Duke of Clarence. The Duke was defeated and killed and the victory rallied support for the Dauphin (22 March 1421).

Bautzen ∎ 1813 ∎ Napoleonic Wars (War of Liberation)

Following **Lützen** and the capture of Dresden, Napoleon Bonaparte pursued the Allies to the Spree and attacked them at Bautzen. While lacking cavalry for a decisive victory, Bonaparte defeated General Gebhard von Blucher's Prussians and Prince Ludwig Wittgenstein's Russians, driving them into Bohemia. However, the costly French victory yielded neither guns nor prisoners (20–21 May 1813).

Bavay ∎ 57 BC ∎ Rome's Later Gallic Wars

See **Sambre**

Baxar ∎ 1539 ∎ Mughal Conquest of Northern India

See **Chausa**

Baxar ∎ 1764 ∎ Bengal War

See **Buxar**

Baxter Springs ∎ 1863 ∎ American Civil War (Trans-Mississippi)

On a fresh raid into Kansas after his outrage in August at **Lawrence**, Confederate guerrilla Colonel William C. Quantrill was driven off from the stockade at Baxter Springs, east of Hopefield, then intercepted a headquarters column nearby under Union commander James G. Blunt. While Blunt and a handful escaped, 80 of his escort were killed, some reportedly in cold blood (6 October 1863).

Bayamo ∎ 1869 ∎ 1st Cuban War of Independence

Opening the Ten Years War, Cuban revolutionaries seized Bayamo, and Donato Mármol was later attacked further north at Saladillo by a large Spanish force under Blas Villate Conde de Valmaseda and Colonel Valeriano Weyler. The rebels lost a reported 2,000 casualties, then burned and evacuated Bayamo. However, war did not end until 1878 with false promises of reform (7 January 1869).

Bayan ∎ 1902 ∎ American-Moro Wars

When Muslim Moros attacked American planters on Mindanao, in the southern Philippines, Colonel Frank Baldwin took 500 men to Bayan on the southern shore of Lake Lanao and captured Fort Bindayan. Next day, the Sultan of Bayan was defeated and killed at Fort Pandapatan. Over 300 Moros died and, a year later, another force defeated them again at nearby **Bacolod** (2–3 May 1902).

Bayazid ∎ 1854 ∎ Crimean War

In a fresh invasion of Armenia, Russian forces under Prince Vassily Osipovich Bebutov attacked a Turkish division at Bayazid (modern Dogubayazit), southwest of Mount Ararat. The Turks were defeated, with heavy losses in men and equipment, and fell back on the great fortress at **Kars**. An unwise Turkish counter-offensive from Kars a week later was defeated at **Kürük-Dar** (29 July 1854).

Bayburt ∎ 1916 ∎ World War I (Caucasus Front)

Russian commander Nikolai Yudenich resumed his advance across the Caucasus from **Erzurum** in February, determined to attack through Bayburt, and split the Turkish forces in front of Erzincan. After very heavy fighting on his left flank around Dumanli Dag, Yudenich drove Turkish General Abdul Kerim back to defeat at **Erzincan**, then turned south towards **Bitlis** (2–8 July 1916).

Baylen ∎ 1808 ∎ Napoleonic Wars (Peninsular Campaign)

Repulsed south of the Guadalquivir at **Mengibar**, French General Dominique Vedel fell back on Baylen to join commander General Pierre Dupont de L'Etang against the offensive by Spanish General Francisco Castanos. Outnumbered and disorganised, Dupont could not break through, and four days later he surrendered 20,000 men, a third of Napoleon Bonaparte's force in Spain (16–19 July 1808).

Bay of Bengal ∎ 1758 ∎ Seven Years War (India)

See **Cuddalore**

Bay of Biscay ∎ 1781 ∎ War of the American Revolution

See **Ushant**

Bay of Pigs ∎ 1961 ∎ Bay of Pigs Incident

Concerned over Communist influence in Cuba, US President John Kennedy supported about 1,500 Cuban exiles to land at Bahía de Cochinos (Bay of Pigs). Facing massive opposition, and denied adequate Amercan aid, the ill-advised expedition lost 114 killed and the others captured. While Cuba's army suffered several hundred killed, America bore a humiliating political defeat (17–20 April 1961).

Bayonne ∎ 1814 ∎ Napoleonic Wars (Peninsular Campaign)

Two months after Allied forces defeated Marshal Nicolas Soult on the **Nive**, near Bayonne, British General Sir John Hope crossed the Adour to encircle the French fortress. Governor Pierre Thouvenot stubbornly held out and a sortie on 14 April (after Napoleon Bonaparte had abdicated) cost 800 casualties on each side before the city finally surrendered (27 February–26 April 1814).

Bayou Fourche ∎ 1863 ∎ American Civil War (Trans-Mississippi)

Advancing into eastern Arkansas towards Little Rock, Union Generals John W. Davidson and Frederick Steele were blocked five miles away at the Bayou Fourche by Confederate forces under General John S. Marmaduke. Davidson captured Little Rock that night after heavy fighting, and Marmaduke withdrew southeast down the Arkansas River towards **Pine Bluff** (10 September 1863).

Baza ∎ 1489 ∎ Final Christian Reconquest of Spain

Ferdinand of Castile and Aragon led the final drive into Muslim Granada, where he laid siege to the key fortress of Baza, west of Granada, held by Sidi Yahya for Abdallah el Zagal, uncle and bitter rival of King Abu Abdallah. Baza surrendered on honourable terms after six months, removing Zagal's forces from the war and permitting Ferdinand to advance on **Granada** (June–December 1491).

Baza ∎ 1810 ∎ Napoleonic Wars (Peninsular Campaign)

In a fresh offensive against General Francois Sébastiani in Granada, Spanish forces under General Joachim Blake advanced as far as Baza in eastern Granada Province before being surprised by French Dragoons and Polish Lancers led by General Édouard Milhaud. Blake was routed with over 1,000 casualties and rapidly withdrew northeast into Murcia (4 November 1810).

Bazavluk I 1648 I Cossack-Polish Wars

At the start of a Cossack rebellion in the Ukraine against John II Casimir of Poland, Bogdan Chmielnicki led a small force against Bazavluk, on the Dnieper, northwest of Nikopol, where the Polish garrison was overwhelmed. Following this success, Chmielnicki was elected Hetman, and he was joined by Crimean Tatars for victories later that year at **Zolte Wody** and **Pilawce** (21 January 1648).

Bazeilles I 1870 I Franco-Prussian War

Marshal Marie MacMahon withdrawing along the Meuse from **Beaumont-en-Argonne** was attacked at Bazeilles by Baron Ludwig von der Tann's Bavarians. Next day, the village was abandoned in flames and the French fell back on Balan. MacMahon was severely wounded and General Auguste Ducrot took command for the decisive battle later the same day at **Sedan** (31 August–1 September 1870).

Bazentin I 1916 I World War I (Western Front)

Recovering from unprecedented losses east of **Albert** at the start of the battle of the **Somme**, General Sir Henry Rawlinson launched a rare night attack towards Bazentin-le-Petit. Advancing after minimal bombardment, the British surprised the Germans and captured Bazentin and 2,000 prisoners. Further east, other forces advanced through **Delville Wood** (14–17 July 1916).

Beachy Head I 1653 I 1st Dutch War
See **Portland, Dorset**

Beachy Head I 1690 I War of the Grand Alliance

When French Admiral Anne Comte de Tourville entered the English Channel with a powerful fleet, outnumbered English-Dutch ships

under Arthur Herbert Earl of Torrington were ordered out to battle. Off Beachy Head, in Sussex, Torrington had 12 ships destroyed for no French losses before de Tourville broke off the pursuit. The English Admiral never again served at sea (30 June 1690).

Beachy Head I 1707 I War of the Spanish Succession

Cruising close to the English coast, French Admiral Claude Chevalier de Forbin attacked a Portugal convoy west of Beachy Head, escorted by three warships led by Captain Baron Wyld. During a fierce action two British captains died and their ships were captured, along with 22 merchantmen. Wyld's ship was heavily damaged, but later that year he met Forbin again off the **Lizard** (1 May 1707).

Beacon Hill I 1643 I British Civil Wars
See **Launceston**

Beacon Hill I 1644 I British Civil Wars

Following victory at **Cropredy Bridge** (29 June), Charles I pursued Robert Devereux Earl of Essex to siege at **Lostwithiel** in Cornwall. Partway through the siege Royalist forces under Prince Maurice and Patrick Ruthven Earl of Forth launched a brilliant attack from the east and captured the strategic Beacon Hill. This action led directly to the fall of Lostwithiel (21 August 1644).

Beal na mBlath I 1922 I Irish Civil War

Soon after the strategic capture of **Cork**, General Emmet Dalton and Free State commander Michael Collins were ambushed by Republicans to the west at Beal na mBlath, between Macroom and Bandon. Confused fighting saw Collins killed—possibly by "friendly fire." While the Republican cause in the field had been lost, bitter guerrilla war continued until May 1923 (22 August 1922).

Beandun I 614 I Anglo-Saxon Territorial Wars

Facing an advance across the Cotswolds by a strong British-Welsh force, Cynegils of Wessex and his son Cwichelm met the invaders at a site identified as Beandun (possibly modern Bampton just west of Oxford, or Bindon near Axmouth on the Devon-Dorset border). The Britons were defeated with more than 2,000 killed and were forced to withdraw.

Bean's Station ▌ 1863 ▌ American Civil War (Western Theatre)

Confederate General James Longstreet withdrawing northeast from Knoxville, Tennessee, after defeat at **Fort Sanders** reached Rogersville, then turned against pursuing Union forces under General James M. Shackelford. Heavy fighting on the Holston at Bean's Station forced Shackelford to retire, and Longstreet went into winter quarters further east at Russellville (14 December 1863).

Bear Paw Mountains ▌ 1877 ▌ Nez Percé Indian War

Leading the Nez Percé people across Montana from **Canyon Creek** towards Canada, Chief Joseph was intercepted short of the border in the Bear Paw Mountains by a large force under General Nelson Miles. After very heavy fighting, Joseph was forced to surrender at the end of his epic march of almost 2,000 miles. He died on a reservation in 1904 (30 September–4 October 1877).

Bear River ▌ 1863 ▌ Bear River Indian War

Resisting Mormon expansion in northern Utah, Shoshoni under Bear Hunter made a stand on the Bear River against 300 California volunteers led by Colonel Patrick E. Connor. In deep snow near Preston, Idaho, the soldiers lost almost 70 casualties. But Bear Hunter and more than 200 Shoshoni were killed, with about 160 women and children captured, virtually ending the war (29 January 1863).

Beattie's Prairie ▌ 1862 ▌ American Civil War (Trans-Mississippi)

See **Old Fort Wayne**

Beaufort ▌ 1779 ▌ War of the American Revolution

Facing American commander Benjamin Lincoln on the Savannah, British General Augustine Prevost sent 200 men under Colonel Thomas Gardiner to land in the American rear at Beaufort, on Port Royal Island, South Carolina. Met by militia under Colonel William Moultrie, Gardiner was repulsed with heavy losses. Three months later, Prevost attacked **Charleston** itself (3 February 1779).

Beaugé ▌ 1421 ▌ Hundred Years War

See **Baugé**

Beaugency ▌ 1870 ▌ Franco-Prussian War

Grand Duke Friedrich Franz II of Mecklenburg retook **Orleans** just days after victory near **Loigny**, then marched southwest against General Antoine Eugène Chanzy near Beaugency. The outnumbered Germans took Beaugency despite a costly initial repulse, and the French withdrew towards **Le Mans** when Prince Friedrich Karl approached with reinforcements (7–10 December 1870).

Beaumont-en-Argonne ▌ 1870 ▌ Franco-Prussian War

Manoeuvring near the Meuse, southeast of **Sedan**, French Marshal Marie MacMahon moved north through **Bazeilles**, leaving General Pierre-Louis de Failly to cover his movement. At Beaumont-en-Argonne, de Failly was surprised and heavily defeated by German troops under the Crown Prince Albert of Saxony, losing more than 7,000 men before falling back through Mouzon (30 August 1870).

Beaumont-en-Cambresis ▌ 1794 ▌ French Revolutionary Wars (1st Coalition)

During the French attempt to drive off the Anglo-Austrian siege of **Landrécies**, a French infantry column under General Renee-Bernard Chapuis was defeated to the west near Troisville and Beaumont-en-Cambresis by British and Austrian cavalry under Major General Karl Ott. Following a similar loss at **Villers-en-Cauchies**, the defeat helped ensure the fall of Landrécies (26 April 1794).

Beaumont Hamel ▌ 1916–1917 ▌ World War I (Western Front)
See **Ancre**

Beaune-la-Rolande ▌ 1870 ▌ Franco-Prussian War
Following French recapture of Orleans after victory at **Coulmiers**, General Joseph-Constant Crouzat was immediately sent northeast against Beaune-la-Rolande, held by outnumbered Hanoverians under General Constantin von Voigts-Rhetz. When Prince Friedrich Karl arrived with reinforcements, Crouzat had to withdraw with heavy losses. **Orleans** itself fell a week later (28 November 1870).

Beauport ▌ 1759 ▌ Seven Years War (North America)
See **Montmorency Gorge**

Beauséjour ▌ 1755 ▌ Seven Years War (North America)
Threatened by increased French presence on the St Lawrence, an expedition of British regulars and colonials under Colonels Robert Monckton and John Winslow was sent from Boston to besiege Beauséjour, at the head of the Bay of Fundy. Captain Louis Dupont de Duchambon de Vergor surrendered after four days and Britain secured Acadia, part of modern Nova Scotia (13–16 June 1755).

Beaver Creek ▌ 1868 ▌ Cheyenne-Arapaho Indian War
Three weeks after relieving **Beecher Island**, a squadron of Buffalo Soldiers under Captain Louis Carpenter, escorting Major Eugene Carr, were ambushed on Beaver Creek, just inside the border of northwest Kansas. The black troopers held off the attackers for eight hours of courageous action before relief arrived. Carpenter and Carr later disputed who was due the credit (17 October 1868).

Beaver Dam Creek ▌ 1862 ▌ American Civil War (Eastern Theatre)
In the second of the **Seven Days' Battles** east of Richmond, Virginia, General Robert E. Lee followed the inconclusive action at **Oak Grove** by a bold assault on the Union flank north of the Chickahominy at Beaver Dam Creek. The Confederates were repulsed in a costly defeat with over 1,300 men lost, but Union General Fitz-John Porter had to withdraw to **Gaines' Mill** (26 June 1862).

Beaver Dams ▌ 1813 ▌ War of 1812
With his forces driven back to the Niagara after defeat at **Stoney Creek** (6 June), American General John Boyd sent Colonel Charles Boerstler southeast from **Fort George, Quebec**, towards the British outpost at Beaver Dams, held by Lieutenant James Fitzgibbon. Ambushed by Indians under Captain Dominique Ducharme, Boerstler and 450 men surrendered to Fitzgibbon (24 June 1813).

Bécherel ▌ 1363 ▌ Hundred Years War
Having driven the English out of Normandy, the Breton champion Bertrand du Guesclin, in support of Charles of Blois, marched to the siege of Bécherel, northwest of Rennes, and defeated John IV de Montfort, who was contesting the Duchy of Brittany. Despite being driven off, de Montfort was later recognised as Duke, his title confirmed after the death of Blois in battle a year later at **Auray**.

Beda Fomm ▌ 1941 ▌ World War II (Northern Africa)
Driving southwest from **Tobruk**, General Richard O'Connor crossed Cyrenaica through **Mechili** to trap the retreating Italians south of Benghazi at Beda Fomm. Marshal Rudolfo Graziani tried to break through, but had to surrender 25,000 men, about 100 tanks and over 1,000 trucks. The British were then diverted to **Greece**, and the Germans struck back at **El Agheila** (5–7 February 1941).

Bedcanford I 571 I Anglo-Saxon Conquest of Britain

After Ceawalin of the West Saxons and his brother Cutha defeated Aethelbert of Kent at **Wibbandun** in 568, another brother, Cuthwulf, took a force north of the Thames and defeated the Britons at Bedcanford (modern Bedford). The Saxons then captured Limbury, Aylesbury, Bensington and Eynsham. Cuthwulf died later the same year.

Bedford I 571 I Anglo-Saxon Conquest of Britain

See **Bedcanford**

Bedford I 1224 I 1st English Barons' War

Following the decisive Baronial defeat in 1217 at **Lincoln**, further rebellion flared at **Bytham** and later at Bedford, where the King's Justiciar Hubert de Burgh besieged Bedford Castle, held by William de Breaute for his brother, the rebel leader Falke. William was hanged when the castle fell after two months, while Falke de Breaute was later dispossessed and banished (20 June–14 August 1224).

Bednur I 1783 I 2nd British-Mysore War

When Tipu Sultan of Mysore continued his father's war against Britain, General Richard Mathews recaptured the South Indian towns of Bednur and Mangalore, but was besieged at Bendur (modern Nagar) by a massive Mysorean army. Mathews was forced to surrender after ten days' fighting and died in prison, while Tipu went on to besiege **Mangalore** (17–30 April 1783).

Bedr I 624 I Campaigns of the Prophet Mohammed

See **Badr**

Bedriacum (1st) I 69 I Vitellian Civil War

After overthrowing Galba, new Roman Emperor Otho faced Vitellius invading from the Rhineland and attempted to block him at the Po, south of Cremona near Bedriacum. The Vitellian Marshals Aulus Caecina Alienus and Fabius Valens secured a decisive victory and Otho killed himself, ending just eight weeks' reign. Vitellius himself was soon defeated at the same location (14 April 69).

Bedriacum (2nd) I 69 I Vitellian Civil War

Vitellius overthrew Otho at **Bedriacum** in April, then faced rebellion from his own troops, with Marcus Antonius Primus invading from the Danube. The Vitellians were defeated at Bedriacum, near Cremona, and Primus reached Rome, where Vitellius was discovered in hiding and killed. The instability of the "Year of the Four Emperors" ended with the accession of Vespasian (24 October 69).

Beecher Island I 1868 I Cheyenne-Arapaho Indian War

Advancing from Kansas into eastern Colorado, a scouting party under Major George Forsyth was attacked by a large war party under the Cheyenne Roman Nose on the dry Arikaree River. Besieged on a mid-stream island, Forsyth held out until relieved for nine days, with 23 casualties including Lieutenant Frederick Beecher killed. Roman Nose was also killed (17–25 September 1868).

Beersheba I 1917 I World War I (Middle East)

Rebuilding losses suffered at **Gaza**, new British commander Sir Edmund Allenby ordered a diversionary bombardment of Gaza, then attacked the other end of the line at Beersheba, now under General Erich von Falkenhayn. Mounted infantry circled north and came from the rear to take the town and 2,000 Turkish prisoners, while further west, Allenby advanced through **Sheria** (31 October 1917).

Beersheba I 1948 I Israeli War of Independence

Egyptian forces driven out of **Huleiquat** fought a stubborn defence further east around Suweidan and **Faluja**, while Israeli commander Ygal Allon swung south against Beersheba, capital of the Negev. The 500-strong garrison was overwhelmed after five hours of intense action, cutting off supplies to Egyptians in the north and opening the way south towards **Asluj** (20–21 October 1948).

Bees I 1914 I World War I (African Colonial Theatre)
See **Tanga**

Beicang I 1900 I Boxer Rebellion
With the legations in **Beijing** besieged by anti-foreign Boxers, a fresh 20,000-strong international relief force set out from **Tianjin** and was blocked next day by 25,000 Chinese under General Song Qing on the Bei He at Beicang (Pei-ts'ang). Fighting in flooded fields, the Allies lost almost 300, mainly Japanese, before Song fell back upriver to **Yangcun** (5 August 1900).

Beijing I 1214–1215 I Conquests of Genghis Khan
After Genghis Khan besieged Beijing (then called Zhongdu), he accepted a massive tribute and withdrew. However, when Jin Emperor Xuan Zong moved his capital south, Genghis and the Khitan defector Shimo Mingan renewed the siege. When a relief army was defeated near Hejian, the starving city surrendered and was sacked, securing northern China for the Mongols (April 1214–May 1215).

Beijing I 1644 I Manchu Conquest of China
As the Ming Dynasty stumbled towards its end, rebel leader Li Zicheng seized much of Henan, Hubei and Shanxi Provinces before marching on Beijing itself. When Li captured the capital, the last Ming Emperor Chongzhen committed suicide. A month later, after defeat at **Shanhaiguan** by Ming and Manchu forces, Li burned part of Beijing and abandoned the city to the Manchu (25 April 1644).

Beijing I 1900 I Boxer Rebellion
In a campaign against foreigners, Boxers in Beijing murdered German Minister Klemens von Ketteler, then besieged the legations, where British Minister Sir Claude MacDonald led a defence force of troops and volunteers. They

held out against heavy attack for two months until a relief force arrived from **Tianjin**. China was forced to make peace and pay reparations (20 June–14 August 1900).

Beijing I 1917 I Manchu Restoration
Chinese warlord Zhang Xun took advantage of confusion after Russia's revolution to seize Beijing, and restored 11-year-old Manchu Emperor Puyi (Xuan Tong), overthrown in 1912. General Duan Qirui (with American, Japanese and British aid) took Beijing by assault and the Emperor abdicated again. The Republic then formally declared war on Germany and Austria (1–12 July 1917).

Beijing I 1920 I Anhui-Zhili War
See **Zhuozhou**

Beijing I 1922 I 1st Zhili-Fengtian War
See **Changxindian**

Beijing I 1928 I 2nd Chinese Revolutionary Civil War
Recovering from Nationalist losses at **Baoding**, Chiang Kai-shek and Feng Yuxiang advanced on Beijing, held by warlord Zhang Zuolin and General Sun Zhuanfang. After nearby cities fell, Zhang fled and was killed when Japanese forces mined his train to Mukden. Beijing was occupied, effectively ending the war with northern and southern China united under Chiang (9 April–3 June 1928).

Beijing I 1937 I Sino-Japanese War
Days after the incident at **Marco Polo Bridge**, Japanese forces under General Kanichiro Tashiro launched a large offensive on the axis Beijing-Tianjin (Tientsin). Very heavy fighting saw Tianjin and Dagu fall (30 July) and General Zhang Zizhong soon abandoned Beijing. The Japanese then advanced southwest into Shanxi towards **Taiyuan** (10 July–4 August 1937).

Beijing I 1949 I 3rd Chinese Revolutionary Civil War
During the great offensive by Generals Lin Biao and Nie Rongzhen, up to 200,000

Nationalists under General Fu Zuoyi were besieged in Beijing (then called Peiping). Following the loss of Zhangjiakou to the north and the violent fall of **Tientsin** to the southeast, Fu surrendered to save the city from destruction, giving the Communists virtually all of China north of the Yangzi (22 January 1949).

Beijing-Tianjin ▎ 1948–1949 ▎ 3rd Chinese Revolutionary Civil War

General Lin Biao secured Manchuria with the **Liaoshen** offensive, then crossed the Great Wall to join General Nie Rongzhen in a Communist offensive in northern China. Following capture of besieged Zhanjiakou (Kalgan), **Tianjin** was taken by storm and Beijing surrendered, leaving **Taiyuan** the only Nationalist stronghold in the north (5 December 1948–31 January 1949).

Beirut ▎ 1110 ▎ Crusader-Muslim Wars

Following Crusader capture of the Lebanese port of **Tripoli** in July 1109, King Baldwin I of Jerusalem besieged the port of Beirut in modern Lebanon, supported by ships from Pisa and Genoa. Although the Italian naval blockade prevented aid arriving, Beirut held out for four months before it fell by assault. The Governor was executed and the city was sacked (February–13 May 1110).

Beirut ▎ 1840 ▎ 2nd Turko-Egyptian War

When Egyptian Viceroy Mohammed Ali defeated Turkey at **Nezib** in Syria and accepted the surrender of the Turkish fleet (24 June 1839), the European powers intervened to prevent danger to Allied shipping. A British-Austrian naval force under Admiral Sir Robert Stopford bombarded Beirut and, after a further attack on **Acre**, Ali gave up the Turkish fleet and evacuated Syria (10 October 1840).

Beirut ▎ 1941 ▎ World War II (Middle East)

See **Lebanon**

Beirut ▎ 1978 ▎ Lebanon Civil War

Amid confused alliances in Lebanon, Syria turned on Christian militias they had helped at **Tel-el-Zataar** and attacked Christian positions in East Beirut. Fighting began in July, before Syria launched a massive offensive with devastating artillery fire. Perhaps 1,200 militia were killed, as well as up to 200 Syrians, before Syria withdrew when Israel threatened to intervene (27 September–7 October 1978).

Beirut ▎ 1982 ▎ Lebanon Civil War

On 6 June about 60,000 Israeli troops with tanks invaded Lebanon in a strike against the Palestine Liberation Organisation. After brief action with Syrian forces a cease-fire was agreed and the Israelis besieged Beirut. Severe action caused heavy guerrilla and civilian losses before the PLO went into exile. Israel withdrew from southern Lebanon in June 1985 (13 June–13 August 1982).

Beirut ▎ 1990 ▎ Lebanon Civil War

Christian militia General Michael Aoun declared war on Syrian forces in Lebanon and their Lebanese allies (14 March 1989). The ensuing struggle tore Beirut apart. Aoun later turned on rival militias, before a massive Syrian offensive beat him in a day of terrible fighting to end the 15-year war. In May 1991 Syria and Lebanon signed a treaty confirming Lebanese independence (13 October 1990).

Beisan ▎ 635 ▎ Muslim Conquest of Syria

See **Fihl**

Belasitza ▎ 1014 ▎ Byzantine Wars of Tsar Samuel

See **Balathista**

Belaya Glina ▎ 1918 ▎ Russian Civil War

On the offensive in the Kuban, White commander Anton Denikin captured **Torgovaya** (25 June), then advanced on Belaya Glina, held by Bolshevik General Dmitrii Zhloba. Splitting his army into converging columns, Denikin secured a brilliant victory, taking 5,000 prisoners (most drafted into the White Army). Red commander Ivan Sorokin then fell back on **Ekaterinodar** (6 July 1918).

Belaya Tserkov | 1651 | Cossack-Polish Wars

See **Bila Tserkva**

Belchite | 1809 | Napoleonic Wars (Peninsular Campaign)

Three days after his advance on Saragossa was repulsed at **Maria**, Spanish General Joachim Blake made a stand south of the Ebro at Belchite, supported by Asturian General Carlos Areizaga. Attacked by General Louis Suchet, Blake's force was again defeated and fled, effectively conceding Aragon and the Ebro Valley to French control (18 June 1809).

Belchite | 1937 | Spanish Civil War

As part of the Republican offensive into Aragon towards **Saragossa**, the fortified town of Belchite to the southeast became a key position behind the battlefront. Nationalist Generals Eduardo Buruaga and Fernando Barrón were driven off attempting to relieve the besieged garrison and the ruined town eventually fell by storm. It was retaken six months later (24 August–6 September 1937).

Belchite | 1938 | Spanish Civil War

General Fidel Dávila started a Nationalist offensive on the Ebro by sending a large force with aircraft and tanks against the strategic town of Belchite, lost six months earlier. General José Solchaga retook Belchite after heavy fighting and the International Brigade withdrew towards the coast as the Nationalists advanced through Lerida and **Vinaroz** towards **Castellón de la Plana** (10 March 1938).

Belen | 1832 | 1st Turko-Egyptian War

When Egyptian forces under Ibrahim Pasha seized **Acre** in Turkish Syria and defeated the Pasha of Aleppo at **Homs** (8–9 July), Ottoman Sultan Mahmud II sent a fresh force under Aga Hussein Pasha. At Belen, south of Alexandretta on the Pass into Anatolia, the Ottoman army was routed. The Sultan then sent a further force against Ibrahim in Anatolia at **Konya** in December (29 July 1832).

Belfast | 1900 | 2nd Anglo-Boer War

In a fresh offensive east from Pretoria, General Sir Redvers Buller advanced against Louis Botha defending the railway between Belfast and Machadodorp. After early action at Dalmanutha, General Neville Lyttleton attacked the salient at Bergendal, outside Belfast. Lyttleton breached the line in a bloody action and President Paul Kruger fled east to Delagoa Bay (22–28 August 1900).

Belfast | 1901 | 2nd Anglo-Boer War

After attacks in eastern Transvaal in December at **Vryheid** and **Helvetia**, Boer commanders Louis Botha and Ben Viljoen led an ambitious attack on the Delagoa Railway defended by General Horace Smith-Dorrien. Heavy fighting at Belfast and neighbouring stations cost 100 British killed and 70 prisoners, but the Boers were repulsed and later invaded Natal (7 January 1901).

Belfort | 58 BC | Rome's Later Gallic Wars

See **Mühlhausen**

Belfort (1st) | 1871 | Franco-Prussian War

Campaigning in eastern France, German General Karl August von Werder besieged Belfort, heroically defended by Colonel Pierre-Philippe Denfert-Rochereau. A French relief force under General Charles-Denis Bourbaki, which had won at **Villersexel**, was routed at nearby **Héricourt**. But Belfort held out until the war's end and capitulated with honour (3 November 1870–17 February 1871).

Belfort (2nd) | 1871 | Franco-Prussian War

See **Héricourt**

Belgium | 1940 | World War II (Western Europe)

Faced by an overwhelming German invasion of Belgium, and loss of the key fortress at **Eben Emael**, Belgian forces fell back to the **Dyle Line**. Despite British and French aid, they were driven back towards the coast and Brussels fell (17 May). King Leopold surrendered his army (about 225,000 troops) and capitulated, though a few thousand troops escaped through **Dunkirk** (10–28 May 1940).

Belgrade I 1440 I Turkish-Hungarian Wars

Ottoman Sultan Murad II led a fresh invasion of Serbia and seized most of the country, though Belgrade held out under Zovan Thallóczi, Hungarian Military Governor of Croatia. Although Murad laid siege by land and water, the fortress was well equipped with artillery, which caused heavy Turkish losses. The Sultan withdrew his army and flotilla after six months, returning 16 years later.

Belgrade I 1456 I Turkish-Hungarian Wars

Having captured **Constantinople** in 1453, Sultan Mehmed II took 150,000 men against Belgrade, defended by Janos Hunyadi. A week after Hunyadi defeated a Turkish flotilla on the Danube (14 July), reinforcements raised by Giovanni de Capistrano helped defeat the Turks. Mehmed lifted his siege and Hungary was temporarily saved, though Hunyadi died a few days later (2–22 July 1456).

Belgrade I 1521 I Turkish-Hungarian Wars

Determined to invade Hungary against Louis II, Sultan Suleiman I and Grand Vizier Mehmed Piri Pasha had first to seize the Balkan fortresses, and laid siege to Belgrade. When reinforcements arrived from the fall of **Sabac**, mining breached the walls and Belgrade fell by storm. However, the invasion of Hungary was delayed five years until the advance through **Mohacs** (July–29 August 1521).

Belgrade I 1688 I Later Turkish-Habsburg Wars

Campaigning in Hungary after victory at **Vienna** (1683), Charles V of Lorraine won again at **Harkany** (1687) before Maximilian

Emanuel, Elector of Bavaria, took command and marched against the Turkish stronghold of Belgrade, abandoned by General Yegen Osman. The citadel fell after a 21-day bombardment and most of Serbia and Transylvania fell to the Habsburg army (20 August 1688).

Belgrade I 1690 I Later Turkish-Habsburg Wars

Despite Turkish defeats over five years at **Vienna**, **Harkany** and **Belgrade**, Grand Vizier Fazil Mustafa Pasha led a renewed Turkish offensive in Europe and, after recapturing **Nish** (1689), marched against the key city of Belgrade. At the end of a six-day siege, a Turkish shell destroyed the main Austrian powder magazine and the Serbian capital returned to Turkish hands (8–14 October 1690).

Belgrade I 1717 I Austro-Turkish War

A year after beating Turkey on the Danube at **Peterwardein**, Austrian Prince Eugène of Savoy marched into the Balkans and besieged Belgrade. When a huge relief army approached under Grand Vizier Khalil Pasha, it was defeated with massive losses (16 August). Belgrade's Turkish garrison of 30,000 quickly surrendered and Sultan Ahmed III soon sued for peace (July–21 August 1717).

Belgrade I 1739 I Austro-Russian-Turkish War

In a Turkish offensive on the Danube, Grand Vizier Al-Haji Mohammed routed Austrian Marshal Count Georg Oliver von Wallis at **Kroszka** (22 July), then besieged Belgrade, defended by General Jakob von Succow. Wallis manoeuvred outside the city, but after months of negotiation, Austria made peace, yielding Belgrade, Serbia and Wallachia to the Turks (26 July–18 September 1739).

Belgrade I 1789 I Catherine the Great's 2nd Turkish War

Austrian Baron Gideon Ernst von Laudon supported Russia against Turkey by invading Bosnia to besiege Belgrade, which had been seized by Turks. The city fell after three weeks, but Emperor Leopold, faced by threats in the west, eventually made a separate peace with Turkey and returned Belgrade in exchange for a small part of Bosnia (15 September–8 October 1789).

Belgrade ▮ 1807 ▮ 1st Serbian Rising

When Belgrade fell to Serbian patriot George Kara in 1805, the citadel held out under the Turkish Governor Pasha Suleiman. The Pasha was abandoned by his own forces following the defeat at nearby **Misar** (August 1806) and finally surrendered the city on condition of free passage. He was however shamefully attacked and killed nearby, along with all his followers (7 March 1807).

Belgrade ▮ 1862 ▮ Serbo-Turkish Wars

Prince Michael III of Serbia attempted a rebellion against his Turkish overlords and led a revolt in the capital Belgrade. The Turkish garrison withdrew into the citadel but re-established control after bombarding the city for four hours. Michael was murdered a few years later, apparently at Turkish instigation, to be succeeded by his 14-year-old cousin Milan (15–16 June 1862).

Belgrade ▮ 1914 ▮ World War I (Balkan Front)
See **Kolubara**

Belgrade ▮ 1915 ▮ World War I (Balkan Front)

With an Austrian advance into Serbia repulsed at **Kolubara** in December 1914, forces under General August von Mackensen led a fresh invasion and Austrian General Herman Kovess von Kovesshaza fought his way into Belgrade. The capital fell after bloody fighting and, despite an Anglo-French intervention at **Salonika**, the Serbians fell back south towards **Kossovo** (7–9 October 1915).

Belgrade ▮ 1941 ▮ World War II (Southern Europe)

At the start of Germany's lightning campaign into the **Balkans**, Generals Maximilian von Weich and Ewald von Kleist stormed into Yugoslavia. Massive aerial bombing of Belgrade caused terrible casualties, and the capital fell within a week (12 April). With its airforce crushed and 300,000 troops captured, Yugoslavia capitulated and the Axis focussed on **Greece** (6–17 April 1941).

Belgrade ▮ 1944 ▮ World War II (Eastern Front)

When Romania and Bulgaria defected to the Allies after **Jassy-Kishinev**, Soviet Marshal Fedor Tolbukhin invaded Yugoslavia, defended by General Maximilian von Weichs. Aided by Yugoslav partisans under Tito, the Russians liberated much of the country, then attacked Belgrade. The capital fell after heavy fighting and the Germans evacuated the **Balkans** (14–20 October 1944).

Belkesheim ▮ 983 ▮ Later German Imperial Wars

German Emperor Otto II was campaigning in Italy when heathen Bohemians and Slavs in his eastern territories rebelled against German authority and destroyed a number of churches. At Belkesheim, near the Elbe, Saxon Princes under the Margrave Dietrich defeated and drove back the heathen tribes. However, Christianity was virtually extinguished east of the Elbe.

Belle Alliance ▮ 1815 ▮ Napoleonic Wars (The Hundred Days)
See **Waterloo**

Belleau Wood ▮ 1918 ▮ World War I (Western Front)

Two days after the German offensive across the **Aisne** halted on the Marne at **Chateau-Thierry**, American General Omar Bundy launched a major counter-attack further west at Belleau Wood, which was seized by his Marine Brigade. The Americans fought off repeated

German attacks, before the area was secured at a cost of over 1,800 killed and another 7,000 wounded (6–26 June 1918).

Bellegarde ▌ 1794 ▌ French Revolutionary Wars (1st Coalition)

A Spanish army under Don Antonio Ricardos invaded southeastern France, where he captured the powerful frontier fortress of Bellegarde (22 June 1793), before a counter-offensive the following year by General Jacques Dugommier. The Marquis Dominique de Perignon recaptured Bellegarde after a five-month siege, and Dugommier advanced into Spain (May–17 September 1794).

Belle Grove ▌ 1864 ▌ American Civil War (Eastern Theatre)

See **Cedar Creek**

Belle Isle, Brittany ▌ 1761 ▌ Seven Years War (Europe)

In a large-scale assault on the fortress at Belle Isle, off the coast of Brittany, Britain sent a naval squadron under Commodore Augustus Keppel, supported by 10,000 troops under Major General Studholme Hodgson. After an initial repulse (7 April), a fresh assault settled into an heroic siege before the citadel finally surrendered, securing the strategic island for the Allies (22 April–7 June 1761).

Belle Isle, Canada ▌ 1755 ▌ Seven Years War (North America)

Admiral Sir Edward Boscawen attempted to interdict massive French reinforcements for Canada, capturing three transports near Belle Isle, off Newfoundland. However, the remaining ships—with Governor Pierre Rigaud Marquis de Vaudreuil and General Louis de Montcalm—arrived safely. Admiral Emmanuel de Cahideuc Comte Dubois de la Motte returned unscathed to Brest (10 June 1755).

Bellevue ▌ 1870 ▌ Franco-Prussian War

Determined to secure food for his besieged army at **Metz**, French Marshal Achille Bazaine sent a large-scale sortie north towards Bellevue,

where the Moselle harvest was stored. Both sides lost over 1,000 casualties in heavy fighting near Maizières and the French were driven back to Metz empty-handed. Metz capitulated three weeks later (7 October 1870).

Bellewaarde (1st) ▌ 1915 ▌ World War I (Western Front)

In the final assault of the Second Battle of **Ypres**, Germans under Duke Albrecht, checked east of the city at **Frezenberg** (13 May), attacked further south around Bellewaarde. Advancing behind the largest gas attack to date, the Germans made progress in the north around Mouse Trap Farm, but the Allied line at Bellewaarde held firm and the great German offensive came to an end (24–25 May 1915).

Bellewaarde (2nd) ▌ 1915 ▌ World War I (Western Front)

Coinciding with a British attack at **Givenchy** to support the French in **Artois**, further north British General Edmund Allenby led a smaller supporting attack north from Hooge against Bellewaarde Ridge, east of Ypres. Despite initial success, Allenby's assault stalled and the Second Battle of Artois soon came to an end (16 June 1915).

Belmont, Missouri ▌ 1861 ▌ American Civil War (Western Theatre)

Union General Ulysses S. Grant advancing down the Mississippi towards Columbus, Kentucky, attacked the Confederate garrison under General Gideon T. Pillow across the river at Belmont, Missouri. The Confederates were driven out, but in the face of a counter-attack by General Leonidas Polk, Grant withdrew from Columbus for little tactical advantage (7 November 1861).

Belmont, South Africa ▌ 1899 ▌ 2nd Anglo-Boer War

Attempting to relieve besieged **Kimberley**, British General Lord Paul Methuen attacked a strong Boer position to the southwest at Belmont under Jacobus Prinsloo. The Boers were driven off with a disciplined frontal assault, which cost about 300 British casualties and about 100 Boers. The Boers then fell back through **Graspan**, and across the **Modder** to **Magersfontien** (23 November 1899).

Belorussia I 1944 I World War II (Eastern Front)

On a massive summer offensive against German Army Group Centre, four Soviet armies advanced into Belorussia. Decisive victories including **Vitebsk**, **Mogilev**, **Bobruysk**, **Minsk** and **Vilna** opened the way to East Prussia and the Baltic, while the fall of **Lublin** threatened **Warsaw**. The Germans suffered shocking losses and Marshal Ernst Busch was dismissed (22 June–24 July 1944).

Bemaru I 1841 I 1st British-Afghan War

More than two years after Amir Dost Muhammad of Afghanistan was deposed following defeat at **Ghazni**, his son Akbar Khan besieged the British in Kabul. Colonel John Shelton drove the Afghans from the nearby village of Bemaru, but on a second sortie ten days later, Shelton was routed with heavy losses, helping trigger the disastrous evacuation of **Kabul** (13 & 23 November 1841).

Bembesi I 1893 I Matabele War

Advancing into Matabeleland (in modern Zimbabwe) through victory at the **Shangani**, British Major Patrick Forbes was attacked days later at Bembesi, 30 miles northeast of Bulawayo, by an even larger force under Mjaan. The Matabele were again routed by cannon and Maxim guns and King Lobengula fled. His capital quickly fell and he died of fever while escaping north (1 November 1893).

Bemis Heights (1st) I 1777 I War of the American Revolution

See **Saratoga, New York (1st)**

Bemis Heights (2nd) I 1777 I War of the American Revolution

See **Saratoga, New York (2nd)**

Benavente I 1808 I Napoleonic Wars (Peninsular Campaign)

French cavalry under General Charles Lefebvre-Desnouettes pursuing Sir John Moore's British army towards Corunna in northwest Spain caught up with the Allied rearguard on the Esla at Benavente. General Henry Paget's cavalry turned to savage the French advance units, capturing Lefebvre-Desnouettes and permitting Moore to reach **Corunna** (26 December 1808).

Benavides I 1811 I Napoleonic Wars (Peninsular Campaign)

General Jean-Andre Valletaux advanced north from Benavente into Galicia, where he unwisely attacked Spanish commander José Maria Santocildes at Benavides, nine miles northeast of Astorga. The French were taken in the flank by fresh Spanish forces under General Frederico Castanon. In the resulting defeat Vellataux was killed, along with about 300 of his men (23 June 1811).

Benburb I 1646 I British Civil Wars

Renewing the rebellion of his uncle Hugh O'Neill (crushed at **Kinsale** in 1601), Owen Roe O'Neill faced an offensive by a Scottish Puritan army under Sir Robert Monroe, which landed to support the Protestant colonists of Ulster. O'Neill routed Monroe on the Blackwater at Benburb and Dublin later fell. The rising was eventually crushed as part of the British Civil Wars (5 June 1646).

Bender I 1738 I Austro-Russian-Turkish War

Russian Marshal Count Burkhard Christoph von Münnich advanced into Turkish Moldavia and was heavily repulsed attempting to cross the Dniester at Bender (modern Bendery). Thwarted by poor supplies and lack of support he withdrew, with his army decimated by casualties, disease and starvation. The Count returned the following year for a decisive victory at **Stavuchany**.

Bender I 1770 I Catherine the Great's 1st Turkish War

While the invading Russian army under General Pyotr Rumyantsev established a strong defensive position on the **Pruth**, General Pyotr Panin was sent east to the Dniester against the fortress of Bender (modern Bendery). The Turkish stronghold fell by storm after a three-month siege, followed by a bloody massacre of the garrison (28 July–16 September 1770).

Benevento I 1266 I Angevin Conquest of the Two Sicilies

Encouraged by successive Popes, Charles I of Anjou led a French army into the Kingdom of the Two Sicilies, held by Manfred, illegitimate son of Emperor Frederick II. On the Plain of Grandella, near Benevento northeast of Naples, Manfred's largely German and Saracen army was crushed and Manfred was killed. Charles then seized the twin throne for Anjou (26 February 1266).

Beneventum I 275 BC I Pyrrhic War

King Pyrrhus of Epirus returned to Italy from Sicily after failure at **Lilybaeum** and met Roman General Manius Curius Dentatus at Beneventum, where Pyrrhus was defeated and withdrew south to Tarentum (modern Taranto). Threatened by a reinforced Roman attack, he abandoned Italy, confirming Rome as the principal power, and returned to Greece, where he was killed in 272 BC at **Argos**.

Beneventum I 214 BC I 2nd Punic War

Marching north to join his brother Hannibal northeast of Naples near **Nola**, Carthaginian General Hanno was intercepted further east near Beneventum (modern Benevento) by a slightly larger force under Tiberius Gracchus. Hanno's army of 18,000, comprising mainly native Italian troops with some Numidian cavalry, suffered a terrible defeat and he was driven back to Bruttium (Calabria).

Beneventum I 212 BC I 2nd Punic War

Two years after a previous defeat at **Beneventum**, the Carthaginian General Hanno was attempting to escort supplies to Capua, when he was attacked in camp northeast of Naples near Beneventum (modern Benevento) by Roman Consul Quintus Fulvius Flaccus. Hanno was heavily defeated and Flaccus and Consul Appius Claudius then moved west to besiege **Capua**.

Benghazi I 1911 I Italo-Turkish War

With **Tripoli** secured, Italy sent Admiral Augusto Aubry east against Benghazi, which refused to surrender to General Ottavio Briccola. General Giovanni Ameglio landed after an early morning bombardment and lost over 100 men to hot resistance before a second bombardment forced the surrender. Heavy fighting took place in March 1912 outside Benghazi at **Two Palms** (19 October 1911).

Beni Boo Ali I 1821 I Anglo-Arab Wars
  See **Balad Bani Bu Ali**

Benin I 1897 I British Conquest of Nigeria

Avenging the massacre at **Ugbine** (4 January), a 1,200-strong British Punitive Expedition under Admiral Harry Rawson converged on King Oba at Benin City in modern Nigeria, whose army was destroyed by Maxim guns and artillery. King Oba's capital was razed and he was exiled. His son-in-law Ologbosheri was eventually captured and executed for the attack at Ugbine (18 February 1897).

Benin I 1967 I Biafran War

When Colonel Chukwuemeka Ojukwu declared independent Biafra in southeast Nigeria, his ally Colonel Victor Banjo launched a rash offensive across the Niger into Midwest State and seized the capital Benin. Further west at Ore, the Biafrans were checked by Federal Colonel Murtala Mohammed and driven back to **Onitsha**. Banjo was later executed for abandoning Benin (August–October 1967).

Bennington Raid I 1777 I War of the American Revolution

Over-confident after victory at **Hubbardton**, British General John Burgoyne sent Colonels Friedrich Baum and Heinrich Breymann against Bennington, on the Vermont-New York border. The Brunswickers were routed after Baum was defeated and killed by General John Stark, and Breymann was defeated by Colonel Seth

Warner. Burgoyne soon lost again at **Saratoga** (16 August 1777).

Bensington I 779 I Anglo-Saxon Territorial Wars

King Offa of Mercia determined to rebuild the power of Mercia, which had lost land north of the Thames after defeat at **Burford** in 752. Attacking the West Saxons in Oxfordshire at Bensington (modern Benson) near Wallingford, Offa inflicted a heavy defeat on King Cynewulf of Wessex. Mercia expanded to dominate southern England until the decisive battle in 825 at **Ellandun**.

Ben Suc I 1967 I Vietnam War
See **Iron Triangle**

Bentonville I 1865 I American Civil War (Western Theatre)

As Union commander William T. Sherman marched east across North Carolina, he was checked at **Averasborough**, then advanced three days later against the main Confederate army of General Joseph E. Johnston further east at Bentonville, near Goldsborough. Johnston suffered a costly defeat in the decisive action of the campaign and, a month later, he surrendered his army (19–21 March 1865).

Beorora I 1858 I Indian Mutiny
See **Rajgarh**

Beranbyrg I 556 I Anglo-Saxon Conquest of Britain

Consolidating his control in the area of modern Wiltshire following victory at **Searobyrg** in 522, King Cynric of the West Saxons attacked the Britons at Beranbyrg (Barbury Castle), just south of Swindon. Supported by his son Ceawlin, Cynric defeated the Britons and, a few years later, Ceawlin succeeded to the Saxon crown of Wessex.

Berat I 1281 I Neapolitan-Byzantine War

Charles of Anjou, King of Naples, entered an alliance with Venice to capture Constantinople, but before their full expedition could be assembled, a smaller Neapolitan force under Solimon Rossi attacked the Adriatic coast and besieged Berat, south of Tirana. A relief army sent by Emperor Michael VIII crushed Rossi's force, though a rising in Sicily aborted the great enterprise.

Berat I 1455 I Albanian-Turkish Wars

George Kastriote Skanderbeg attempted to resume the initiative in central Albania and besieged Berat, south of Tirana, supported by about 1,000 men supplied by Alfonso V of Naples. However, he was surprised by a Turkish army under Isa Bey Evrenos and the Neapolitan troops were killed almost to a man. Skanderbeg had his revenge two years later at **Albulen** (26 July 1455).

Beraun I 1394 I German Towns War

When battle at **Doffingen** in 1388 settled war between the Princes and the cities, the weak German King Wenceslas faced continued opposition from dissident nobles, including his cousin Jobst, Margrave of Moravia and Brandenburg. Jobst defeated the Imperial army in battle at Beraun, southwest of Prague, and held Wenceslas prisoner until he agreed to make Jobst Regent of Bohemia.

Berea Mountain I 1852 I 8th Cape Frontier War

Determined to chastise Basutho Chief Moshoeshoe after defeat at **Viervoet** in 1851, Governor Sir George Cathcart led 2,500 British troops north into the Orange River Sovereignty. Outnumbered and surrounded at Berea Mountain, Cathcart narrowly escaped defeat by withdrawing west to the Caledon. Britain later yielded the territory to the Boers as the Orange Free State (20 December 1852).

Beresteczko I 1651 I Cossack-Polish Wars

On a fresh Ukraine offensive against Cossack leader Bogdan Chmielnicki, Polish General Stefan Czarniecki attacked a much larger rebel force at Beresteczko, on the Styr, northeast of Lvov. As at **Zborov**, Chmielnicki's Crimean Tatar allies deserted him and he was decisively beaten. Another action at **Bila Tserkva** soon forced the Cossacks to accept a disadvantageous peace (28–30 June 1651).

Berezina I 1812 I Napoleonic Wars (Russian Campaign)

Retreating from Moscow, Napoleon Bonaparte's army was attacked by Prince Mikhail Kutuzov and Admiral Paul Tchitchakov at the Berezina near Borisov. Despite the courage of Marshal Michel Ney, and a desperate rearguard action by Marshal Claude Victor, the French passage across the icy river was a disaster, with perhaps 25,000 killed or drowned (26–28 November 1812).

Berezina I 1920 I Russo-Polish War

With **Kiev** secured (7 May), Polish commander Josef Pilsudksi was preparing a fresh advance when Russian General Mikhail Tukhachevski struck in a brilliant offensive across the Berezina, supported in the south by 18,000 Cossack cavalry under Semyon Budenny. The Polish army was nearly destroyed west of Kiev around Zhitomir before retreating towards **Warsaw** (14 May–4 June 1920).

Bergamo I 464 I Goth Invasion of the Roman Empire

The Alan King Beorgor led a fresh invasion of northern Italy and marched his force onto the Plain of Lombardy. At Bergamo, northeast of Milan, Beorgor was met by troops under the Suevic-Roman kingmaker Ricimer. The King of the Alans was defeated and killed in fierce fighting and his invasion was repulsed (6 February 464).

Bergen, Hainault I 1572 I Netherlands War of Independence

See **Mons**

Bergen, Hesse I 1759 I Seven Years War (Europe)

On the offensive in Hesse after victory during 1758 at **Sandershausen** and **Lutterberg**, French Duke Victor-Francois of Broglie occupied Bergen, northeast of Frankfurt, and came under attack by Prussians, Brunswickers and British led by Duke Ferdinand of Brunswick. However, the Allies were repulsed with heavy losses and the French advanced through Westphalia to **Minden** (13 April 1759).

Bergen, Norway I 1665 I 2nd Dutch War

Following success in June off **Lowestoft**, Edward Montagu Earl of Sandwich sent Admiral Sir Thomas Teddeman to pursue a Dutch convoy under Commodore Pieter de Bitter into neutral Bergen, Norway. Shore batteries opened fire, and after two hours Teddeman was driven off. A month later after refit, Teddeman and Sandwich captured nine Dutch East Indiamen in just two days (13 August 1665).

Bergen-aan-Zee (1st) I 1799 I French Revolutionary Wars (2nd Coalition)

After the British expedition to northern Holland repulsed the French at **Groote Keeten** and **Zuyper Sluys**, Frederick Augustus Duke of York arrived with the main force and joined General Ivan Hermann's Russians against General Guillaume Brune outside Bergen, near Alkmaar. The Allies were repulsed, with the Russian division suffering very heavy losses in men and guns (19 September 1799).

Bergen-aan-Zee (2nd) I 1799 I French Revolutionary Wars (2nd Coalition)

See **Castricum**

Bergendal I 1900 I 2nd Anglo-Boer War

See **Belfast**

Bergen-op-Zoom I 1588 I Netherlands War of Independence

Alexander Farnese Duke of Parma followed destruction of the **Spanish Armada** in July by besieging Bergen-op-Zoom, the last major town in Brabant still held for the United Provinces, defended by commander Peregrine Bertie Lord Willoughby. Parma was forced to abandon the siege after a brilliant counter-assault by Francis Vere, who won a knighthood (14 September–12 November 1588).

Bergen-op-Zoom I 1622 I Thirty Years War (Palatinate War)
See **Fleurus**

Bergen-op-Zoom I 1703 I War of the Spanish Succession
See **Ekeren**

Bergen-op-Zoom I 1747 I War of the Austrian Succession
Two weeks after crushing the Anglo-Austrian army at **Lauffeld**, French Marshal Maurice de Saxe sent General Ulrich de Lowendahl against the powerful Dutch fortress of Bergen-op-Zoom, held by 86-year-old Isaac Kock Baron Cronstrom. Bergen fell by storm after a bitter and very costly siege, and was subjected to a terrible pillage and destruction (15 July–18 September 1747).

Bergen-op-Zoom I 1814 I Napoleonic Wars (French Campaign)
While the European Allies were crumbling before a French offensive east of Paris, British General Sir Thomas Graham commanding in Holland launched an unwise night-time attack on the fortress of Bergen-op-Zoom (in French hands since 1795). Having forced their way in, the British started plundering, and at dawn most of them were killed or captured (8 March 1814).

Bergfriede I 1807 I Napoleonic Wars (4th Coalition)
At the start of Russia's mid-winter offensive against Napoleon Bonaparte in eastern Prussia, part of General Levin Bennigsen's army was attacked by Marshal Nicolas Soult at the Bergfriede crossing of the Alle, north of Ionkovo. Having withstood a large-scale assault, the Russians slipped away during the night north to Königsberg, ready for **Eylau** five days later (3 February 1807).

Beringia I 1916 I World War I (Middle East)
Encouraged by Turkey, Sultan Ali Dinar of Darfur, in western Sudan, raised rebellion and threatened Khartoum. Pursued by British and Egyptians under Colonel Philip Kelly, the Sultan's entrenched army was defeated at Beringia, north of El Fasher, which fell next day. Darfur was annexed to Anglo-Egyptian Sudan and Ali Dinar was pursued and killed in November at **Guiba** (22 May 1916).

Berlin I 1943–1944 I World War II (Western Europe)
The British attacked Berlin as early as August 1940, but their first sustained air offensive on the German capital saw 16 major raids from November 1943 to March 1944, with more than 1,000 British bombers lost. American forces joined in and lost 200 bombers in just three raids in March–April 1944. While attacks continued into 1945, the Battle of Berlin proved the costliest air campaign of the war.

Berlin I 1945 I World War II (Eastern Front)
Soviet Marshals Georgi Zhukov and Ivan Konev drove deep into eastern Germany, advancing on Berlin itself against intense resistance. Russian losses are estimated at up to 100,000 dead, along with perhaps 150,000 German soldiers killed and maybe as many civilians. After Hitler shot himself, General Karl Weidling finally surrendered the shattered city (16 April–2 May 1945).

Bern I 1339 I Burgundian-Swiss Wars
See **Laupen**

Bern I 1798 I French Revolutionary Wars (1st Coalition)
Facing threatened insurrection in Switzerland, Napoleon Bonaparte sent General Guillaume Brune with troops from Italy and the Rhine. Supported by General Alexis Schauenbourg, Brune defeated Swiss General Karl von Erlach at Bern, which was captured next day along with massive booty. Brune then proceeded to establish a single Swiss Republic (5 March 1798).

Berroea I 250 I 1st Gothic War
See **Philippopolis**

Berroea I 1190 I Bulgarian Imperial Wars

Byzantine Emperor Isaac II defeated rebel Serbs at the **Morava**, and later that year marched against Tsar Ivan Asen of Bulgaria and besieged Trnovo. Facing a large Kipchaq Turkish army, Isaac withdrew and was ambushed and routed in the Balkan Mountains near Berroea (modern Stara Zagora). Isaac had to concede Bulgaria and Wallachia and in 1194 he was defeated again at **Arcadiopolis**.

Berryville I 1864 I American Civil War (Eastern Theatre)

Marching east from Winchester in the Shenandoah Valley, Confederate General Richard H. Anderson was met near Berryville, Virginia, by part of Union commander Philip Sheridan's army under General George Crook. Confederate commander Jubal A. Early arrived to reinforce Anderson, but after inconclusive fighting they withdrew west behind the **Opequon** (3–4 September 1864).

Berwick I 1296 I English Invasion of Scotland

When Scotland allied herself with France and invaded Cumberland, Edward I advanced over the border and stormed the Scots-held city of Berwick-on-Tweed, followed by a terrible sack and massacre. Edward then sent his army further north to meet the Scots at **Dunbar**. Berwick remained in English hands for twenty years (28–30 March 1296).

Berwick I 1318–1319 I Rise of Robert the Bruce

In the aftermath of **Bannockburn**, Robert the Bruce blockaded the remaining English stronghold at Berwick, which fell to Sir James Douglas in 1318. Facing a renewed invasion a year later by Edward II, the Scottish King's son-in-law Walter Stewart defended Berwick against a massive siege, until the English had to withdraw after defeat at **Myton** (28 March 1318 & 24 July–September 1319).

Berwick I 1333 I Anglo-Scottish War of Succession

Advancing into Scotland, Edward III joined his ally Edward Baliol besieging Berwick, held for young David II by Sir Alexander Seton, while the castle was defended by Patrick Dunbar Earl of March. Regent Sir Archibald Douglas approached to relieve the siege but was defeated and killed at nearby **Halidon Hill** (18 July), and both city and castle fell into English hands (June–July 1333).

Berwick I 1482 I Anglo-Scottish Royal Wars

Edward IV ordered a fresh invasion of Scotland, despatching his brother Richard of Gloucester and Alexander Duke of Albany, brother of James III of Scotland. The invaders captured the key fortress of Berwick and went on to seize Edinburgh but eventually withdrew, though Berwick remained permanently English. Duke Alexander was defeated two years later at **Lochmaben** (24 August 1482).

Besançon I 1674 I 3rd Dutch War

On a renewed offensive against the Spanish Netherlands, Louis XIV of France and Marshal Sebastien Vauban returned to Franche-Comte, which they had conquered in 1668 and then conceded by treaty. Besançon, near the Swiss border, which previously capitulated without fighting, held out against siege for nine days. The entire province was captured in under six weeks (April–May 1674).

Bethel Church I 1861 I American Civil War (Eastern Theatre)

See **Big Bethel**

Beth Horon I 166 BC I Maccabean War

Hebrew rebel Judas Maccabeus defeated the Seleucid army of Apollonius in the mountains at **Gophna**, then faced a larger force later that year under General Seron, who avoided the dangerous hills by marching down the Mediterranean coast before turning towards Jerusalem. Coming under attack while crossing the low pass at Beth

Horon, Seron's army was routed and driven back towards the sea.

Beth Horon ▌ 66 ▌ Jewish Rising against Rome

When Zealots massacred the garrison in Jerusalem, Governor Cestius Gallus of Syria took a legion to Judea but was driven off trying to take the Temple in Jerusalem. Attacked in the northern suburb of Bezetha, Gallus retreated through Gabaon to Beth Horon, losing up to 6,000 men and his siege train. He withdrew to Syria, but fresh Roman troops soon arrived to storm **Jotapata** and later **Jerusalem**.

Beth Zachariah ▌ 164 BC ▌ Maccabean War

In a final attempt to suppress the Hebrew rebellion of Judas Maccabeus, Seleucid King Antiochus V Eupator and General Lysias took a huge army, supported by war-elephants, and besieged Beth Zur, south of Jerusalem. Maccabeus rashly accepted a set-piece battle at nearby Beth Zachariah and was badly defeated. Seleucid forces occupied Jerusalem, but civil war forced them to return home.

Beth Zur ▌ 166 BC ▌ Maccabean War

Soon after Seleucid defeats at **Beth Horon** and **Emmaus** at the hands of the Hebrew Judas Maccabeus, Seleucid Viceroy Lysias personally led a large army circling south of Judea to take the rebels in the rear. But he faced a greatly reinforced Maccabean army at Beth Zur, near modern Hebron, and after suffering severe losses was driven back towards the coast. Judas went on to capture Jerusalem.

Betio ▌ 1943 ▌ World War II (Pacific)
See **Tarawa**

Betwa ▌ 1858 ▌ Indian Mutiny

While besieging the great rebel stronghold at Jhansi, General Sir Hugh Rose turned west to meet a massive relief army of perhaps 20,000 under Tantia Topi. A brilliant action at the Betwa saw Rose and Brigadier Charles Stuart rout the much larger rebel force, which fled across the Betwa to Kalpi. Two days later, the British launched their final assault on **Jhansi** (1 April 1858).

Beverly Ford ▌ 1863 ▌ American Civil War (Eastern Theatre)
See **Brandy Station**

Beveziers ▌ 1690 ▌ War of the Grand Alliance
See **Beachy Head**

Bexar ▌ 1835 ▌ Texan Wars of Independence
See **San Antonio**

Beylan ▌ 1832 ▌ 1st Turko-Egyptian War
See **Belen**

Beymaroo ▌ 1841 ▌ 1st British-Afghan War
See **Bemaru**

Bezetha ▌ 66 ▌ Jewish Rising against Rome
See **Beth Horon**

Beziers ▌ 1209 ▌ Albigensian Crusade

When Pope Innocent III proclaimed a Crusade against Albigensian heretics in southern France, the warrior Arnaud Amalric attacked the city of Beziers, defended by Raymond Roger Viscount of Beziers and Carcassonne. A major counter-attack by the garrison was routed, and the city fell, followed by large-scale massacre of the population. The Viscount then fled to **Carcassonne** (22 July 1209).

Bezzecca ▌ 1866 ▌ 3rd Italian War of Independence

Despite being wounded near Lake Garda at **Monte Suella** (3 July), Giuseppe Garibaldi sent his forces on a resumed offensive in the Tyrol against Austrian General Franz Kuhn. At Bezzecca, northeast of Storo, the Garibaldini under General Giuseppe Avezzano fought a fierce action before both sides withdrew with about 500 casualties. The war ended a few days later (21 July 1866).

Bhamo I 1885 I 3rd British-Burmese War

British General Sir Harry Prendergast defeated the Burmese at **Minhla** on the Irriwaddy (17 November) and captured Mandalay. King Thebaw then surrendered, ending Burmese independence. However, some troops and tribal groups continued the struggle. Prendergast eventually beat them near the Chinese border at Bhamo, though guerrilla war continued for some years (28 December 1885).

Bhamo I 1944 I World War II (Burma-India)

With **Myitkyina** secured in August, Chinese divisions under General Daniel Sultan advanced north and besieged about 1,200 Japanese at Bhamo. General Masaki Honda sent a large-scale relief column, but it was driven off (9 December), and the garrison later broke out. The capture of Bhamo, along with **Wanting** to the east, reopened the land route to China (14 November–15 December 1944).

Bhangani I 1688 I Mughal-Sikh Wars

When Sikh Guru Gobind Singh was invited into the Nahan in northern Punjab, he found himself in conflict with the hill Rajas, including Raja Fateh Khan of Srinagar and Raja Bhim Chand of Kahlur. Despite the desertion of his Pathans, the greatly outnumbered Guru achieved a decisive victory in battle near Bhangani, seven miles east of Paonta on the Jumna (18 September 1688).

Bharatpur I 1805 I 2nd British-Maratha War

Having captured **Dieg** (December 1804), British General Sir Gerard Lake besieged the Maratha fortress of Bharatpur, west of Agra, defended by a garrison and field army under Jaswant Rao Holkar of Indore and Jat infantry. Lake had insufficient guns, and after four assaults cost him over 3,000 men, he withdrew, ending the war. The stronghold was finally taken 20 years later (7 January–10 April 1805).

Bharatpur I 1825–1826 I British-Maratha Wars

Twenty years after General Sir Gerard Lake was repulsed at the Jat fortress of Bharatpur, west of Agra, the siege was renewed by a much better equipped force under Stapleton Cotton Lord Combermere. The town fell by storm after heavy bombardment and destruction of part of the bastion by mines. The usurper Durgan Sal surrendered, ending the war (11 December 1825–18 January 1826).

Bhatavadi I 1624 I Mughal-Ahmadnagar Wars

Emperor Jahangir resolved to prevent external involvement in a Mughal civil war and sent Prince Parwiz to join Adil Shah of Bijapur against Ahmadnagar. In a famous battle at Bhatavadi, 10 miles east of Ahmadnagar, Malik Ambar and General Shahji utterly routed the Imperial army, avenging the defeat in 1616 at **Roshangaon**. Ambar soon died, and Ahmadnagar was eclipsed (November 1624).

Bhatgiran I 1947 I 1st Indo-Pakistan War

Advancing north from Srinagar after victory at **Shalateng** (7 November), Indian regular forces repulsed the Pakistan-backed tribal invaders of southwest Kashmir and retook the key city of Uri. At nearby Bhatgiran, a large-scale Indian patrol was ambushed, and heavy fighting cost the Sikhs 63 killed and 60 wounded. India's advance stalled and the war dragged on for another year (12 December 1947).

Bhera I 1006 I Muslim Conquest of Northern India

As he crossed the Indus for the first time, the Muslim ruler Mahmud of Ghazni attacked Bhera on the Jhelum, northwest of Lahore. Raja Biji Rai withdrew into Bhera under siege after a four-day battle outside the fortress. But he was later cornered attempting to flee and killed himself to avoid capture. Bhera was annexed and Mahmud captured massive treasure, including 280 elephants.

Bhogniwala I 1858 I Indian Mutiny
See **Nagal**

Bhopal I 1737–1738 I Later Mughal-Maratha Wars

Nizam-ul-Mulk of Hyderabad invaded Malwa at the head of a large Imperial army, but allowed himself to be besieged at Bhopal by a massive army of about 80,000 Marathas under Baji Rao I. When a Mughal relief force under Safdar Jang was driven off by Mulhar Rao Holkar, the Nizam sued for peace and granted Baji Rao the whole of Malwa (14 December 1737–7 January 1738).

Bhorghat I 1781 I 1st British-Maratha War

Having captured **Bassein**, north of Bombay, General Thomas Goddard attempted to march southeast against the Marathas at Poona with about 6,000 European and Indian troops. After being harried and cut off at Bhorghat Pass by superior Maratha forces under Hari Pant Phadke, Goddard's advance was halted and he was forced to retreat with over 500 casualties (18 January–23 April 1781).

Bhupalgarh I 1679 I Mughal-Maratha Wars

Aided by Sambhuji, rebel son of Maratha King Shivaji, Mughal Viceroy Dilir Khan attacked Bhupalgarh (modern Banur), near Khanapur, south of Poona, defended by Phirangoji Narsala. After terrible fighting, the Mughals captured the fortress and its stores and enslaved the garrison. Dilir Khan then defeated Maratha reinforcements nearby and razed the fort to the ground (2 April 1679).

Bhurtpore I 1805 I 2nd British-Maratha War
See **Bharatpur**

Bhutan I 1865 I British-Bhutanese War
See **Dewangiri**

Bi I 597 BC I Wars of China's Spring and Autumn Era

When King Zhuang of Chu attacked the small state of Zheng, just south of the Yellow River, Jin (Chin) sent a relief army under Xun Linfu. The Jin arrived too late to save Zheng, but Jin General Xiangu impulsively crossed the river and the main army had to follow. Caught unprepared by the Chu on the battlefield at Bi, the Jin were routed and the survivors fled in disorder back across the river.

Biak I 1944 I World War II (Pacific)

A week after securing **Wakde**, off northern New Guinea, American General Horace Fuller leapfrogged west to seize Biak Island and its key airfield from Colonel Kuzume Naoyuki. In some of the hardest fighting of the war, the Americans lost 430 killed and 2,000 wounded for 7,000 Japanese killed. Fierce resistance dragged on for months and Fuller was dismissed (27 May–29 July 1944).

Biala Cerkiew I 1651 I Cossack-Polish Wars
See **Bila Tserkva**

Bialy Kamien I 1604 I 1st Polish-Swedish War
See **Weissenstein**

Bialystok I 1941 I World War II (Eastern Front)

Opening the German invasion of Russia, Army Group Centre under Marshal Fedor von Bock sent forces north through Grodno and from the south to surround the Russians at Bialystok and Volkovysk. Two entire Soviet armies were encircled and destroyed in the Bialystok Pocket, while an overlapping encirclement further east trapped more Russians at **Minsk** (22 June–3 July 1941).

Biar I 1813 I Napoleonic Wars (Peninsular Campaign)

During a new offensive in Valencia, Marshal Louis Suchet routed a Spanish force at **Yecla**, then next day attacked the rearguard of the withdrawing Allies in the pass at Biar, east of

Villena. British, Italian and German forces under General Frederick Adam held Suchet for five hours in a courageous defensive action, before falling back to the Allied position at **Castalla** (12 April 1813).

Bias Bay | 1938 | Sino-Japanese War
See **Guangzhou**

Biberach | 1796 | French Revolutionary Wars (1st Coalition)
Having defeated General Jean-Baptiste Jourdan's invasion of northern Germany, Archduke Charles Louis of Austria turned his counter-offensive south against General Jean Victor Moreau. On the Lahn at Biberach, south of Ulm, Moreau checked General Maximilian Latour but continued falling back before the Austrians and was defeated two weeks later at **Emmendingen** (2 October 1796).

Biberach | 1800 | French Revolutionary Wars (2nd Coalition)
Pursuing the Austrians after their twin defeats at **Engen** and **Stockach**, French General Jean Moreau continued his offensive across the Rhine by sending General Laurent Gouvion Saint-Cyr pursuing the Austrians withdrawing east towards the River Riss. St-Cyr marched down-river after cutting up the Austrians at Oberndorf and defeated a counter-offensive at **Biberach** (9 May 1800).

Bibracte | 58 BC | Rome's Later Gallic Wars
Julius Caesar defended Gaul against a massive Helvetian migration across the Jura, defeating the invaders at the **Arar**, then a month later renewed the attack near Bibracte, on Mount Beuvray near Autun. Caesar inflicted a crushing defeat—slaughtering perhaps 130,000 including warriors and their families—and forced the Helvetii back to their home in modern Switzerland (July 58 BC).

Bicocca | 1522 | 1st Habsburg-Valois War
Following defeat at **Marignano** in 1515, French Marshal Odet de Lautrec renewed the offensive in northern Italy after Milan was lost to Francesco Sforza. Lautrec's Swiss mercenaries insisted on attacking Spanish General Prospero Colonna at Bicocca, just outside Milan, and were repulsed with humiliating losses. Their defeat led to a complete French withdrawal from Lombardy (27 April 1522).

Bida | 1897 | British Conquest of Northern Nigeria
In order to impose a British protectorate on northern Nigeria, Sir Charles Goldie of the Royal Niger Company took 500 African troops and 30 British officers against Emir Abubakr of Nupe. Some towns quickly fell, but outside Bida he faced a determined Nupe army. The ill-armed warriors were routed by Maxim guns and artillery, and Goldie then turned against **Ilorin** (27 January 1897).

Bidassoa | 1813 | Napoleonic Wars (Peninsular Campaign)
Arthur Wellesley Lord Wellington captured the vital northern Spanish port of **San Sebastian** in September, then began advancing against the French defences along the Bidassoa. A massive assault across the Bidassoa estuary saw Wellington defeat General Antoine-Louis Maucune to outflank the French lines, and Marshal Nicolas Soult began to fall back towards the **Nivelle** (7 October 1813).

Biddulphsberg | 1900 | 2nd Anglo-Boer War
On campaign northeast of Bloemfontein, General Sir Leslie Rundle occupied Senekal after a sharp skirmish (25 May), then led 4,000 men against Andries de Villiers at Biddulphsberg on the Senekal-Bethlehem road. Fighting in the midst of a bush fire, the British were driven off with about 180 casualties, while the Boers lost just two men killed, one of them de Villiers himself (29 May 1900).

Biderra | 1759 | Seven Years War (India)
See **Chinsura**

Biedenheafde ▮ 674 ▮ Anglo-Saxon Territorial Wars

In a dispute over the Kingdom of Lindsey, Wulfhere of Mercia invaded Northumbria against Ecgfrith, son of Oswy (who killed Wulfhere's father Penda in 655 at **Winwaed**). Wulfhere was repulsed at Biedenheafde by the smaller Northumbrian army and was forced to yield Lindsey. However, his brother Aethelred defeated Ecgfrith on the **Trent** five years later and recovered the disputed kingdom.

Bien Hoa ▮ 1964 ▮ Vietnam War

When B-57 bombers arrived at Bien Hoa airbase, north of Saigon, the Viet Cong launched their first major attack on an American facility. The predawn assault saw six bombers destroyed and 20 aircraft damaged, with five Americans and two Vietnamese killed and nearly 100 injured. A further attack on the airbase at **Pleiku** led directly to US retaliation against North Vietnam (1 November 1964).

Big Bethel ▮ 1861 ▮ American Civil War (Eastern Theatre)

Supported by blockade in Chesapeake Bay, Union Generals Ebenezer Pierce and Benjamin F. Butler converged on Confederate Colonels John B. Magruder and Daniel H. Hill at Big Bethel, Virginia, northwest of Newport News. In the claimed first land battle of the war, the larger Union force was driven off with 80 casualties, including Major Theodore Winthrop killed (10 June 1861).

Big Black River ▮ 1863 ▮ American Civil War (Western Theatre)

In a failed offensive east from besieged Vicksburg, on the Mississippi, Confederate General John C. Pemberton fell back from **Champion Hill**, and his rearguard under General John S. Bowen attempted to defend the Big Black River, Mississippi. Overwhelmed by General John A. McClernand, who captured 1,800 men and 18 guns, the Confederates retreated to **Vicksburg** (17 May 1863).

Big Blue River ▮ 1864 ▮ American Civil War (Trans-Mississippi)

Confederate General Sterling Price crossed Missouri to reach **Independence**, then found himself between two Union armies southeast of Kansas City. While he attacked **Westport**, Generals Joseph O. Shelby and John S. Marmaduke failed in an attempt to hold the Big Blue River against Generals James G. Blunt and Alfred Pleasanton, and retreated south (22–23 October 1864).

Big Cypress Swamp ▮ 1855 ▮ 3rd Seminole Indian War

When a survey patrol under Lieutenant George L. Hartsuff entered the Big Cypress Swamp, in southwest Florida, there was a confused dispute with the Seminole leader Billy Bowlegs, and the troops were attacked. Four soldiers were killed and three wounded, including Hartsuff, before the survivors returned north to Fort Myers, triggering renewed war with the Seminole (19 December 1855).

Big Dry Wash ▮ 1882 ▮ Apache Indian Wars

Refusing to surrender after defeat at **Cibecue** (August 1881), 60 Apache under Natiotish ambushed Captain Adna Chaffee in the Big Dry Wash, on the East Clear Creek near the Verde River in Arizona. Reinforced by Major Andrew Evans, the troops outflanked and defeated the Indians, killing Natiotish and about 25 others. The shattered survivors fled back to the reservation (17 July 1882).

Big Hole River ▮ 1877 ▮ Nez Percé Indian War

Nez Percé Chief Joseph leading the epic retreat from the **Clearwater River** was attacked at the Big Hole River, near Wisdom, Montana, by General John Gibbon advancing from the east. Joseph boldly besieged Gibbon but, with almost 90 killed and General Oliver Howard's force approaching, the Indians continued east through Yellowstone Park towards **Canyon Creek** (9–11 August 1877).

Big Meadow ▪ 1856 ▪ Rogue River War

In an attempt to intervene between warring settlers and Indians on the Rogue River in southern Oregon, 350 troops under Captain Andrew Jackson Smith were ambushed by Takelma Chief Old John at Big Meadow. When Smith was reinforced next day by Captain Christopher Augur, the Indians were routed and sent to reservations. Old John was imprisoned on Alcatraz (27–29 May 1856).

Big Mound ▪ 1863 ▪ Sioux Indian Wars

Marching into central North Dakota after defeating the Santee Sioux at **Wood Lake**, General Henry Hastings Sibley repulsed an attack on his camp by a joint force of Santee and Teton under Inkpaduta, then counter-attacked at Big Mound in modern Kidder County. Driven out by artillery fire, the Indians withdrew and were beaten again two days later at **Dead Buffalo Lake** (24 July 1863).

Big Sandy ▪ 1814 ▪ War of 1812
See **Sandy Creek**

Bihac ▪ 1992–1995 ▪ Bosnian War

When Serbs attacked the largely Muslim Bihac Pocket in northwest Bosnia, a long siege saw massive shelling and costly fighting. In a perceived failure of international policy, much of the UN "safe haven" was over-run by Serbs and renegade Muslim Fikret Abdic. Bihac town held out under General Artif Dudakovic until relieved by Croatia's offensive towards **Knin** (21 April 1992–6 August 1995).

Bihar ▪ 1761 ▪ Seven Years War (India)
See **Suan**

Bijapur ▪ 1679 ▪ Mughal Conquest of the Deccan Sultanates

Having captured the Maratha fortress of **Bhupalgarh** in April, Mughal Viceroy Dilir Khan attacked Muslim Bijapur, held by his former ally Regent Sidi Mas'ud, who had joined forces with the Marathas. After a failed bombardment, and with Shivaji attacking the Mughal forces in the rear, Dilir Khan was forced to retire, ravaging the region as he withdrew (18 August–15 November 1679).

Bijapur ▪ 1685–1686 ▪ Mughal Conquest of the Deccan Sultanates

Imperial forces advancing against the Muslim sultanates of central India again besieged the powerful fortress of Bijapur, which had resisted them five years earlier. Sultan Sikander Adil Shah, who had hired Maratha auxiliaries, was finally forced to surrender after Emperor Aurangzeb himself arrived to take command, ending the independent kingdom of Bijapur (27 March 1685–12 September 1686).

Bijapur ▪ 1858 ▪ Indian Mutiny

At war with rebel forces in Gwalior after victory at **Kankrauli** (14 August), Major George Robertson pursued Ajit Singh (uncle of Man Singh, Rajah of Narwar) to Bijapur, on the Parbati, 25 miles west of Guna. Roberston surprised the rebel camp after forced marches, and the force of about 600 mutineers was destroyed, with more than 400 reported killed or wounded (4 September 1858).

Bila Hora ▪ 1620 ▪ Thirty Years War (Bohemian War)
See **White Mountain**

Bila Tserkva ▪ 1651 ▪ Cossack-Polish Wars

Just months after disaster at **Beresteczko**, Cossack leader Bogdan Chmielnicki gathered about 50,000 men for a fresh offensive in the Ukraine. After a bloody yet indecisive action against Poles led by Mikolaj Potocki just south of Kiev at Bila Tservka, both sides withdrew exhausted. Chmielnicki accepted an unfavorable truce until renewing the war in May 1652 at **Batoh** (24–25 September 1651).

Bilbao ▪ 1795 ▪ French Revolutionary Wars (1st Coalition)

French General Bon Adrien de Moncey renewed the offensive in Spain, marching into the Province of Biscay against forces under General Joachim Crespo. A week of hard fighting, culminating in victory at Irurzun, drove Crespo beyond the Ebro, and Bilbao fell on 17 July. A few days later, on 22 July, peace was concluded with Spain and the campaign ended (12–18 July 1795).

Bilbao | 1808 | Napoleonic Wars (Peninsular Campaign)

Facing rebellion by Basques, Marshal Jean-Baptiste Bessières sent General Christophe-Antoine Merlin to Bilbao, where he drove off the rebels, with over 1,000 killed, while English ships in the harbour only just eluded capture. The sacked city was recovered by Spanish General Joachim Blake early in October, then promptly retaken by Marshal Francois Lefebvre (16 August 1808).

Bilbao | 1812 | Napoleonic Wars (Peninsular Campaign)

Admiral Sir Home Popham campaigned in northern Spain to relieve pressure on the Allied campaign around **Salamanca**, attacking **Portugalete** and **Lequeitio**, while Spanish General Gabriel Mendizabal captured Bilbao from General Claude-Pierre Rouget. A French counter-attack by Generals Rouget and Louis Caffarelli two weeks later recaptured the town (13 & 27–29 August 1812).

Bilbao | 1835 | 1st Carlist War

Over-confident after the capture of **Villafranca de Oria** in Navarre, Spanish pretender Don Carlos V sent Tomás Zumalacárregui against Bilbao, where he was badly wounded and died ten days later. The siege was continued by Juan Benito Eraso until he was driven off by approaching Liberals under General Jéronimo Valdés. The Carlists were soon routed at **Mendigorría** (13 June–1 July 1835).

Bilbao | 1836 | 1st Carlist War

Leading a fresh Carlist siege of Bilbao in Navarre, Fernando Modet Count of Casa Eguía eventually came under attack at nearby Luchana by the new Liberal Commander-in-Chief General Baldomero Espartero. When the Carlists were routed and raised their siege, Espartero

entered Bilbao next day. He was later created Count of Luchana (9 November–23 December 1836).

Bilbao | 1873–1874 | 2nd Carlist War

On campaign in Navarre, pretender Don Carlos VII and General Joaquín Elío besieged Bilbao, held by General Ignacio del Castillo. Despite defeat at nearby **Somorrostro**, Republican commander Marshal Francisco Serrano, supported by Generals Manuel de la Concha and Arsenio Martínez Campos, broke the siege and de la Concha marched on **Estella** (27 December 1873–2 May 1874).

Bilbao | 1937 | Spanish Civil War

Having crushed a Basque offensive at **Villarreal de Alava** in late 1936, Nationalist forces under Generals Emilio Mola (killed in an air crash), and later Fidel Dávila, launched a massive attack on the Basque capital at Bilbao, held by General Francisco Llano de la Encomienda. With the defensive "Ring of Iron" broken, the city fell and Dávila turned west against **Santander** (1 April–19 June 1937).

Bilgram | 1540 | Mughal Conquest of Northern India

See **Kanauj**

Bilin | 1942 | World War II (Burma-India)

As the Japanese swept into Burma, General Shozo Sakurai advanced from **Kuzeik** towards Yinon, on the Bilin, while General Hiroshi Takeuchi drove north from Moulmein. British General John Smythe sent in his last reserves to try and hold the river but, after delaying the invaders for four days, the badly outnumbered British fell back towards the **Sittang** (17–21 February 1942).

Binakayan | 1896 | Philippines War of Independence

Spanish Governor Ramon Blanco recovered from defeat at **Imus** (5 September), and personally led a large force against the outer defences of Cavite, held by Emilio Aguinaldo.

Despite a bold bayonet assault, Colonel José Marino was repulsed from the strong trenches at Binakayan and, after General Diego de los Rios was driven off at Noveleta, Blanco had to retire (9–11 November 1896).

Binh Gia I 1964–1965 I Vietnam War

After success at **Bien Hoa** in November, Viet Cong Colonel Ta Minh Kham turned to Binh Gia, 40 miles southeast of Saigon, where an undermanned assault was driven off. A larger attack took the village, and government reinforcements suffered very heavy losses before the Viet Cong withdrew. Actual losses on both sides remain hotly disputed (2–9 & 28–31 December 1964–3 January 1965).

Birch Coulee I 1862 I Sioux Indian Wars

Having relieved **Fort Ridgely**, Minnesota (22 August), Colonel Henry Hastings Sibley sent Major John Renshaw Brown to bury bodies at the nearby Sioux agency overrun by Santee Chief Little Crow. Camped at Birch Coulee, Brown was attacked by Big Eagle and Mankato. By the time Sibley arrived and drove the Indians off, the soldiers had suffered 24 dead and 76 wounded (2–3 September 1862).

Birch Creek I 1878 I Bannock Indian War

Soon after Buffalo Horn was killed at **Battle Creek, Idaho**, his Bannock people marched into Oregon and joined the Paiute under Chief Egan and medicine man Oytes. After action at **Silver Creek**, they were heavily defeated by General Oliver Howard and Captain Reuben Bernard north of the Blue Mountains at Birch Creek (Battle Mountain) and soon lost again near **Pendleton** (8 July 1878).

Bird Creek I 1861 I American Civil War (Trans-Mississippi)

Confederate Colonel Douglas H. Cooper pursued Chief Opothleyahola and his pro-Union Creeks and Seminoles after action at **Round Mountain** (19 November), and attacked again at Chusto-Talasah, on the Horsehoe bend of Bird Creek, eastern Oklahoma. Cooper finally drove Opothleyahola across the river, followed by a decisive action a few weeks later at **Shoal Creek** (9 December 1861).

Bir Gafgafa I 1967 I Arab-Israeli Six Day War

With **Rafa** secured, General Israel Tal turned inland through **Jebel Libni** and advanced west on major Egyptian concentrations around Bir Gafgafa. Tal's small force intercepted and destroyed Arab tanks withdrawing from the Sinai, then faced fresh Egyptian armour arriving from Ismaili to counter-attack. The modern Russian tanks were also destroyed and Tal raced for the Suez Canal (7 June 1967).

Bir Hacheim I 1942 I World War II (Northern Africa)

As Axis commander Erwin Rommel launched a massive attack on the British line at **Gazala**, a powerful encircling movement swung inland around the desert flank at Bir Hacheim. A Free French brigade under General Marie-Pierre Koenig fought a bold defence before they were forced to withdraw and the Germans swept into the British rear to establish the **Cauldron** (28 May–11 June 1942).

Bir Lahfan I 1967 I Arab-Israeli Six Day War

See **Jebel Libni**

Birpur I 1760 I Seven Years War (India)

See **Hajipur**

Birten I 939 I German Imperial Wars

See **Andernach**

Biskra I 683 I Muslim Conquest of North Africa

In the Arab conquest of North Africa, the Umayyad General Uqbah ibn Nafi conquered as far west as the Atlantic coast of Morocco. On his return, part of his army was ambushed south of Biskra at Tahuda, in northeastern Algeria, by the Berber "King" Kusayla, supported by Byzantine troops. Uqbah was defeated and killed and the Berbers expelled the Arabs from Ifrikiya (roughly modern Tunisia).

Bismarck I 1941 I World War II
(War at Sea)

The German battleship *Bismarck* and heavy cruiser *Prince Eugen* sank the British battle-cruiser *Hood* and damaged the battleship *Prince of Wales* in the Denmark Strait. Subsequently damaged by a torpedo and heading for Brest, *Bismarck* was dramatically pursued by a large force under Admiral Sir John Tovey and sunk with heavy loss of life, including Admiral Günther Lütjens (23–27 May 1941).

Bismarck Sea I 1942 I World War II
(Pacific)

Sailing from Rabaul to reinforce the garrison at **Lae** in **Papua**, 7,000 Japanese soldiers were intercepted in the Bismarck Sea by Australian and American aircraft under US Air Force General George Kenney and by American PT boats. The three-day action saw four destroyers and all eight transports sunk, with 3,000 troops drowned. Only 1,000 reached Lae (2–4 March 1942).

Bithur I 1857 I Indian Mutiny

General Sir Henry Havelock secured victory east of the Ganges at **Bashiratganj** and four days later had to march northwest from Cawn-pore against a fresh rebel force of over 4,000 under Tantia Topi at Bithur. The rebels were driven from the field following very heavy fighting, and Havelock returned to Cawnpore to find he had been superseded by General Sir James Outram (16 August 1857).

Bitlis I 1916 I World War I
(Caucasus Front)

While Russian General Nikolai Yudenich seized **Erzincan**, Ahmet Izzet Pasha's Sec-ond Army advanced against the Russian left flank, where his corps commander Mustafa Kemal seized Bitlis and Mus. Yudenich counter-attacked and, after prolonged combat west of Lake Van, he retook Bitlis and the Turks aban-doned Mus before winter ended the fighting (2 & 23 August 1916).

Bitonto I 1734 I War of the Polish
Succession

In support of France against Austria, Don Carlos, son of Philip V of Spain, invaded Austrian-held southern Italy. Having seized Naples he advanced towards Bari, and at nearby Bitonto, General José Carrillo de Albornoz narrowly defeated Austrian forces under General Otto von Traun. Following the war, the Infanta received the Kingdom of the Two Sicilies as Charles III (25 May 1734).

Biyang I 563 BC I Wars of China's
Spring and Autumn Era

The small state of Biyang in southern Shan-dong, traditionally an ally of Chu, came under attack by Chu's enemy Jin (Chin), which at-tacked the capital to create it as a fief. After an unsuccessful siege by Jin commander Xun Ying, the feudal Lords of Jin's allies wanted to with-draw and return home. However, Xun Ying forced them to make a direct bloody assault, and Biyang fell by storm.

Bizani I 1913 I 1st Balkan War

When Greek General Constantine Sapoun-tzakis advanced into Turkish Macedonia to be-siege **Jannina**, he was blocked by surrounding fortresses, including the key position, 10 miles away at Bizani. A costly assault saw the Greeks driven off with very heavy losses, but Prince Constantine later regrouped his forces for the subsequent successful assault on Jannina (20–23 January 1913).

Bizerte I 1961 I Franco-Tunisian Crisis

With France at war in Algeria, Tunisia de-manded France abandon her last naval base, at Bizerte, and besieged the port. Over 10,000 paratroops, Legionnaires and marines, supported by naval bombardment, landed to break the blockade, and heavy fighting killed 1,370 Tu-nisians (including 700 civilians) and wounded over 2,000. France abandoned Bizerte in Octo-ber 1963 (19–21 July 1961).

Bizerte-Tunis I 1943 I World War II (Northern Africa)

Despite heavy reinforcements from Sicily, Axis forces in **Tunisia** were cornered in the north by Allied armies converging under British General Harold Alexander. In the final costly fighting, American troops took Bizerte and the British captured nearby Tunis, effectively ending the campaign. General Jürgen von Arnim surrendered 120,000 Italians and 130,000 Germans (6–7 May 1943).

Blaauwberg I 1806 I Napoleonic Wars (4th Coalition)
   See **Blueberg**

Black and Yellow Offensive I 1915 I World War I (Eastern Front)
   See **Lutsk**

Blackburn's Ford I 1861 I American Civil War (Eastern Theatre)

Sent west from Washington, D.C., against the Confederates concentrating around Manassas, Union General Irvin McDowell led a reconnaissance in force attempting to cross the Bull Run at Blackburn's Ford, Virginia, guarded by General Pierre G. T. Beauregard. Despite superior numbers, McDowell was driven off in a prelude to his disaster three days later at **Bull Run** (18 July 1861).

Blackheath I 1497 I Flammock's Rebellion

In protest against taxes for a Scottish War, Cornish rebels led by Thomas Flammock and Michael Joseph marched towards London, later joined as leader by James Touchet Baron Audley. The Royal army under Giles Lord Daubeney and John de Vere Earl of Oxford crushed the rebels at Deptford Strand, near Blackheath, and Audley, Flammock and Joseph were executed (22 June 1497).

Black Mango Tree I 1761 I Indian Campaigns of Ahmad Shah
   See **Panipat**

Black Mountain I 1794 I French Revolutionary Wars (1st Coalition)
   See **Figueras**

Black Point I 1835 I 2nd Seminole Indian War

While convoying a wagon train south of Newnansville, Florida, Colonel John Warren of the Florida militia was attacked by Seminole Indians at Black Point near Hogtown (later Gainesville). After the troops were driven off, with eight killed and eight wounded, the Indians looted and burned the wagon train, helping trigger the **Dade Massacre** and the Second Seminole War (18 December 1835).

Black Rock (1st) I 1813 I War of 1812

British Colonel Cecil Bisshop and 250 men raiding in force across the southern Niagara River into New York State attacked Black Rock, just north of **Buffalo**, on Lake Erie. They destroyed a barracks, a naval yard and a schooner, and captured valuable supplies. However, they suffered 40 casualties in a sharp American counter-attack and Bisshop was fatally wounded (11 July 1813).

Black Rock (2nd) I 1813 I War of 1812
   See **Buffalo**

Black Sea I 1993 I Somalian Civil War
   See **Mogadishu**

Blackstocks I 1780 I War of the American Revolution

Pursuing General Thomas Sumter after his defeat at **Fishing Creek** and **Fishdam Ford**, Tory cavalry leader Colonel Banastre Tarleton attacked Sumter's guerrillas at Blackstock's Plantation, south of Spartanburg, near Enoree, South Carolina. Tarleton's outnumbered force was mauled with greater losses, but Sumter was badly wounded and his force temporarily dispersed (20 November 1780).

Blackwater I 1598 I Tyrone Rebellion

Hugh O'Neill Earl of Tyrone renewed the rebellion of his uncle Shane O'Neill (crushed in 1567 at **Letterkenny**), and joined Hugh O'Donnell against the English at Yellow Ford on the Blackwater near Armargh. One of England's worst defeats in Ireland saw Lord Lieutenant Sir Henry Bagenal killed along with 2,000 of his men. O'Neill was beaten in December 1601 at **Kinsale** (14 August 1598).

Bladensburg ∎ 1814 ∎ War of 1812

Advancing up the Patuxent River against Washington, D.C., British forces under General Robert Ross were met just outside the capital at Bladensburg by mainly American militia under the incompetent General William Winders. Despite a courageous defence by Commodore Joshua Barney, the British entered and burned Washington, then sailed against **Baltimore** (24 August 1814).

Blair's Landing ∎ 1864 ∎ American Civil War (Trans-Mississippi)

Soon after action at **Pleasant Hill**, Louisiana, Confederate General Tom Green attacked the supporting Union flotilla to the east on the Red River at Blair's Landing. A well-managed defence by General Thomas Kilby Smith and Admiral David D. Porter saw the Confederates repulsed with Green killed. The Union army then withdrew through **Monett's Ferry** (12–13 April 1864).

Blakely ∎ 1865 ∎ American Civil War (Western Theatre)

On an expedition east from New Orleans, Union General Edward R. S. Canby led an assault on Mobile Bay and laid siege to Fort Blakely, Alabama, northeast of Mobile. With the fall of nearby **Spanish Fort**, Canby was able to concentrate his forces, and the following day garrison commander General St John R. Liddell surrendered 3,400 men and over 40 guns (2–9 April 1865).

Blanco Canyon ∎ 1871 ∎ Comanche Indian Wars

In warfare against Comanche in West Texas after the massacre at **Salt Creek** (17 May), Colonel Ranald Mackenzie reached the Blanco Canyon, near modern Crosbyton, where a detachment was ambushed by Quanah Parker. Mackenzie arrived to save his men, but heavy snow prevented pursuit. He was later wounded in skirmish (15 October) and the expedition withdrew (10 October 1871).

Blar-na-Leine ∎ 1544 ∎ Scottish Clan Wars

See **Shirts**

Bleichfeld ∎ 1796 ∎ French Revolutionary Wars (1st Coalition)

The French rearguard under General Paul Grenier withdrawing towards the Rhine after defeat at **Würzburg** attempted to stall General Paul Kray's victorious Austrians just to the southeast at Bleichfeld. The French division escaped under cover of dark after heavy losses in casualties and prisoners and commander General Jean-Baptiste Jourdan sought an armistice (3 September 1796).

Blenau ∎ 1652 ∎ War of the 2nd Fronde

Louis II de Bourbon Prince of Condé, leading a rebellion against Cardinal Jules Mazarin during the minority of Louis XIV, surprised and defeated part of the Royal army under Marshal Charles d'Hocquincourt at Blenau, near Gien on the Loire. However, Marshal Henri de Turenne rescued the Royal Court at Gien and within months defeated Condé at **Etampes** and **St Antoine** (7 April 1652).

Blenheim ∎ 1704 ∎ War of the Spanish Succession

After victory on the Danube at **Donauwörth** (2 July), Allied commander John Churchill Duke of Marlborough joined Prince Eugène of Savoy to attack Elector Maximilian Emanuel of Bavaria and Marshal Count Camille de Tallard at nearby Blenheim, east of Höchstädt. The Franco-Bavarian army was shattered, Vienna was saved, and France withdrew behind the Rhine (13 August 1704).

Block Island ∎ 1636 ∎ Pequot Indian War

When Pequot Indians murdered John Oldham near Block Island, off southern New England, Massachusetts Governor Sir Henry Vane sent Captains John Endecott and John Underhill with a punitive expedition against Block Island. There they massacred every male and destroyed the village, which proved to be Narragansett. The Pequot were routed the next year at **Mystic** (24 August 1636).

Bloemfontein I 1900 I 2nd Anglo-Boer War

See **Driefontein**

Blood River I 1838 I Boer-Zulu War

Boer leader Andries Pretorius recovered from loss at **Ethaleni** and **Tugela** and led 500 men against King Dingane. Intercepted at the Ncome, east of Dundee in northern Natal, the Boers inflicted a terrible and decisive defeat with perhaps 3,000 Zulus killed. The Ncome reportedly ran red and was renamed Blood River. Dingane was overthrown later two years at **Maqonqo** (16 December 1838).

Blood River Poort I 1901 I 2nd Anglo-Boer War

A guerrilla raid into Natal by Louis Botha was met at Blood River Poort, near the junction with the Buffalo, by a column from nearby Dundee under Major Hubert Gough. Botha attacked and routed Gough, inflicting 50 casualties and taking 240 prisoners, 180 rifles, 30,000 rounds and 200 horses. He then continued into Natal to attack the British position a week later at **Fort Itala** (17 September 1901).

Bloody Angle I 1864 I American Civil War (Eastern Theatre)

See **Spotsylvania Court House**

Bloody Bay I 1480 I MacDonald Rebellion

John MacDonald Lord of the Isles made peace with the government and relinquished his Earldom of Ross, but his illegitimate son Angus Og declared war on his father and the King. At Bloody Bay, off Mull, Angus defeated and captured his father, then attempted to continue the rebellion. However, he was murdered in 1490 and the title and Kingdom of the Isles was soon forfeited.

Bloody Brook I 1675 I King Philip's War

See **Deerfield**

Bloody Meadow I 1471 I Wars of the Roses

See **Tewkesbury**

Bloody Nose Ridge I 1944 I World War II (Pacific)

When Americans invaded **Peliliu**, brutal resistance at the Umurbrogol (Bloody Nose) Ridge cost Colonel Lewis "Chesty" Puller 56 percent of his marines in a week, America's highest ever regimental casualties. He was replaced by army units and the summit was seized, but Japanese Colonel Nunio Nagakawa fought on for months before committing suicide (15 September–25 November 1944).

Bloody Ridge, Guadalcanal I 1942 I World War II (Pacific)

Recovering from defeat at the **Tenaru**, Japanese forces on **Guadalcanal** were reinforced by General Kiyotake Kawaguchi, who attacked with 3,000 men south and east of Henderson Field, supported by heavy naval and aerial bombardment. Colonel Merritt Edson led a decisive defence on Bloody Ridge and Kawaguchi finally withdrew with 1,200 killed (12–14 September 1942).

Bloody Ridge, Korea I 1951 I Korean War

In the wake of failed truce talks, South Korean and United Nations forces launched a fresh offensive in the east, northeast of Yangu. Very heavy fighting around Bloody Ridge cost perhaps 3,000 Allied and 15,000 Communist casualties. The North Koreans eventually risked being outflanked and withdrew a few miles north to new positions on **Heartbreak Ridge** (18 August–5 September 1951).

Bloody River I 1944 I World War II (Southern Europe)

See **Rapido**

Bloody Run I 1763 I Pontiac's War

Captain James Dalyell reached besieged **Detroit** with 280 men and 22 barges of supplies, then led an impulsive night attack on Ottawa Chief Pontiac's nearby camp. Ambushed at Parent's Creek, in the war's fiercest action, Dalyell and 19 others were killed and 40 were wounded. However, supplies still got through and Pontiac later withdrew. The creek was re-named Bloody Run (31 July 1763).

Bloody Sunday **I** 1920 **I** Anglo-Irish War

One of the most notorious incidents of the largely guerrilla campaign against Britain in Ireland saw troops of the Royal Irish Constabulary (Black and Tans) open fire with machine-guns into a football crowd at Croke Park, Dublin (later claiming they were returning fire from Republicans). The incident left 12 dead and 60 wounded, and the bitter war continued until July 1921 (21 November 1920).

Bloody Swamp **I** 1742 **I** War of the Austrian Succession

Invading British colonial Georgia from Florida and Cuba, 3,000 Spanish troops under Antonio Anedondo and Governor de Montiano landed on St Simons Island, at the mouth of the Altamaha. The Spaniards were heavily repulsed in a fierce action at the nearby Bloody Swamp by James Oglethorpe, founder of the new colony, and re-embarked, securing the future of Georgia (June 1742).

Bloody Tanks **I** 1864 **I** Apache Indian Wars

When the Rancher King S. Woolsey set out with 30 Americans and 14 Maricopa and Pima Indians in pursuit of stolen cattle, he met about 250 Apache at Bloody Tanks, in the Aravaipa Canyon in southeast Arizona. With the Indians lured to a false parley, Woolsey opened fire and 24 died, including Chief Parramucca. Cyrus Lennon of Woolsey's party was also killed (24 January 1864).

Blore Heath **I** 1459 **I** Wars of the Roses

Richard Neville Earl of Salisbury was marching south from Yorkshire to join his son-in-law Richard Duke of York when he was intercepted in Shropshire by a larger Lancastrian force under James Baron Audley. At Blore Heath, three miles east of Market Drayton, Lord Audley was defeated and killed and his army was virtually destroyed, with perhaps 4,000 dead (3 September 1459).

Blouberg **I** 1806 **I** Napoleonic Wars (4th Coalition)

See **Blueberg**

Bloukranz **I** 1838 **I** Boer-Zulu War

At war with the Boers in Natal after ordering the **Retief Massacre**, Zulu King Dingane sent his forces against Trekkers encamped near the Tugela. In a night attack at Bloukranz, the entire camp was killed, but the Zulus were eventually driven off at nearby Saailaager, outside modern Estcourt. An attempted Boer counter-offensive was routed two months later at **Ethaleni** (17–18 February 1838).

Blountsville **I** 1863 **I** American Civil War (Western Theatre)

Campaigning in the far northeast of Tennessee, Union commander Ambrose Burnside sent Colonel John W. Foster, who captured Bristol, then attacked Blountsville on the Watauga, held by Colonel James E. Carter. After an artillery duel destroyed much of the town, Carter withdrew. The following month Foster supported an attack to the southwest at **Blue Springs** (22 September 1863).

Blueberg **I** 1806 **I** Napoleonic Wars (4th Coalition)

In response to renewed French occupation of Holland, Britain again sent a force to occupy the Dutch Cape of Good Hope, seized in 1795, and returned to Holland in 1803. General Sir David Baird landed a force on 5 January and, three days later at Blueberg, defeated Dutch General Jan Willem Janssens. Within ten days he had captured Capetown and the entire colony (8 January 1806).

Blue Licks **I** 1782 **I** War of the American Revolution

Simon Girty led Canadians and Indians into Kentucky against Bryan's (Bryants') Station and nearby Fort Lexington before withdrawing before pursuing militia under Colonel Daniel Boone and Major Hugh McGary. Forty miles away on the Licking at Blue Licks, in the "last battle of the war," the outnumbered militia rashly attacked and 70 died, including Boone's son Israel (19 August 1782).

Blue Mills Landing I 1861 I American Civil War (Trans-Mississippi)

With Confederate forces besieging **Lexington, Missouri**, "General" David R. Atchison moved south against a Union column under Colonel John Scott near the town of Liberty. Crossing the Missouri at Blue Mills Landing, Atchison marched towards Liberty and soon met Scott's approaching force, which was defeated and fled. Lexington surrendered three days later (17 September 1861).

Blue Mounds I 1832 I Black Hawk Indian War

See **Wisconsin Heights**

Blue Springs I 1863 I American Civil War (Western Theatre)

While campaigning in northeast Tennessee, Union forces captured **Blountsville**, and General Samuel P. Carter later advanced on Greeneville against Confederate General John S. Williams. Williams suffered heavy losses in battle just to the west at Blue Springs (modern Mosheim) and, threatened in the rear by General John W. Foster, he withdrew into Virginia (10 October 1863).

Blue Water I 1362 I Russian-Mongol Wars

See **Syni Vody**

Blue Water Massacre I 1855 I Sioux Indian Wars

See **Ash Hollow**

Blumenau I 1866 I Seven Weeks War

Prince Friedrich Karl of Prussia followed his great victory at **Königgratz** by sending Generals Eduard von Fransecky and Julius von Bose across the Main to prevent the Austrians reaching Vienna. Unaware an armistice was imminent, the Prussians attacked at Blumenau, northwest of Pressburg, and there was costly fighting before news of the armistice brought the battle to an end (22 July 1866).

Boadilla del Monte I 1936 I Spanish Civil War

As part of the major campaign against Madrid along the **Corunna Road**, severe fighting focussed on the small town of Boadilla del Monte, 20 miles west of the capital. Nationalists seized the town in heavy hand-to-hand fighting against International Brigades, lost it to Republican Regulars under Major Luis Barcelo, then took it again in a bloody counter-attack (14–19 December 1936).

Boa Ogoi Massacre I 1863 I Bear River Indian War

See **Bear River**

Bobe I 1906 I Bambatha Rebellion

Squeezed from their land, and with their crops and cattle decimated by pests, Zulus in Natal under the minor Chief Bambatha rebelled against a new poll tax and gathered in the Nkandla Forest. In the first major action of the rising, advancing government troops were ambushed near the Bobe Ridge by rebels under Sigananda. He was driven off and withdrew towards the **Mome** Gorge (5 May 1906).

Böblingen I 1525 I German Peasants' War

After victory at **Leipheim** (4 April), Georg Truchsess von Waldburg fought across Würtemberg against a combined peasant force under Matem Feuerbacker, Theus Gerber and Jaecklein Rohrbach. On marshy ground at Böblingen, southwest of Stuttgart, the peasant army was utterly routed. Rohrbach, who had instigated the massacre at **Weinsberg** in April, was captured and roasted alive (12 May 1525).

Bobruysk I 1944 I World War II (Eastern Front)

General Konstanin Rokossovsky on the left of the Russian offensive into **Belorussia** rapidly encircled five divisions of the German Ninth Army at Bobruysk on the main railway to Minsk. Aided by devastating air support, Rokossovsky rapidly crushed the pocket, with perhaps 30,000 Germans killed and 20,000 captured. The Russians then drove northwest towards **Minsk** (24–29 June 1944).

Bocairente I 1873 I 2nd Carlist War
Campaigning in Valenica, Spanish Republican General Valeriano Weyler was attacked at Bocairente, northwest of Alcoy, by a greatly superior Carlist force under General José Santés. Weyler was intially driven back, losing some of his guns. But a brilliant counter-attack turned defeat into victory. Santés was heavily repulsed and forced to withdraw (22 December 1873).

Bodegas I 1860 I Ecuadorian Civil Wars
In war between rival Presidents Guillermo Franco in Guayaquil and Gabriel García Moreno in Quito, the old hero General Juan José Flores returned from exile in Peru to support García Moreno and led his Conservative army to decisive victory at Bodegas on the Guayas. When Flores advanced on Guayaquil, Franco fled into exile and Ecuador was unified under García Moreno (7 August 1860).

Bodrum I 1824 I Greek War of Independence
As Turkish Admiral Khosrew Pasha and Egyptian Ibrahim Pasha assembled at Bodrum in Turkey, opposite Cos, Greek Admiral Andreas Miaoulis twice lured their fleet out to fight. After an initial indecisive action, the Greeks destroyed two Turkish vessels with fireships, forcing an Ottoman withdrawal. However, Miaoulis was unable to prevent the invasion of Crete (5 & 10 September 1824).

Boffalora I 1636 I Thirty Years War (Franco-Habsburg War)
See **Tornavento**

Bogesund I 1520 I Wars of the Kalmar Union
Opposed to the pro-Danish Stolle faction in Sweden, Regent Sten Sture the Younger repulsed Christian II of Denmark at **Brännkyrka**

in 1518, but was defeated and mortally wounded at Bogesund near Lake Asunden in southeast Sweden by Danish General Otte Krumpen. The subsequent suppression of the Sture party in the "Stockholm Bloodbath" led to the rise of Gustav Vasa (20 January 1520).

Bogotá I 1813 I Colombian War of Independence
See **Santa Fé de Bogotá**

Bogotá I 1814 I Colombian War of Independence
Entering Colombia to support the revolutionary government in Tunja, Simón Bolívar and a largely Venezuelan force besieged Bogotá, held by local Dictator Manuel Bernardo Alvarez and General José Ramón de Leiva against the new national union. The city fell by storm after two days, with much needless bloodshed, and Bolívar marched north against **Cartagena** (8–10 December 1814).

Bogotá I 1854 I Colombian Civil Wars
When General José Maria Melo seized power in a coup (17 April 1854), his forces met with initial success. But after defeat at Pamplona, Palmira and Bosa Bridge, Melo was finally defeated at Bogotá by forces of the legitimate government under General Pedro Alcántara Herrán. Melo fled into exile and was later killed in a Mexican rebellion (4 December 1854).

Bogotá I 1861 I Colombian Civil Wars
Former President General Tomás Cipriano de Mosquera resumed war against the government of Mariano Ospina, eventually advancing on the Colombian capital to win at nearby **Subachoque**. Mosquera then defeated General Ramón Espina at Bogotá itself to overthrow acting President Bartolomé Calvo. In 1863 he defended his country against Ecuador at **Cuaspud** (18 July 1861).

Bogowonto I 1751 I Later Dutch Wars in the East Indies
See **Jenar**

Bogue Forts (1st) ∎ 1841 ∎ 1st Opium War

In a fresh offensive against China, British Superintendent Captain Charles Elliot led an expeditionary force against the Bogue (Boca Tigris) Forts at the mouth of the Zhujiang River, supported by troops under Major Thomas Pratt. After Chuanbi and Taikok were captured in heavy fighting, Admiral Guan Tianpei was defeated and driven off in a naval action nearby (7 January 1841).

Bogue Forts (2nd) ∎ 1841 ∎ 1st Opium War

British Superintendent Captain Charles Elliot renewed his offensive against the Bogue Forts guarding the Zhujiang River, leading a larger force of 26 warships against Chinese commander Qishan. Forty war junks were routed, with Admiral Guan Tianpei killed. Wangtong and Anunghoy (Weiyuan) were taken, opening the river to advance on **Guangzhou** three months later (26 February 1841).

Bois le Duc ∎ 1629 ∎ Netherlands War of Independence
  See **Hertogenbosch**

Bois-le-Duc ∎ 1794 ∎ French Revolutionary Wars (1st Coalition)

As a French Republican army under General Charles Pichegru advanced into southern Holland, British and Dutch forces led by Prince Frederick Augustus Duke of York were defeated at Bois-le-Duc (Hertogenbosch or Den Bosch). York was forced to abandon the position and, after a failed counter-attack at **Boxtel** next day, he retreated back across the Meuse (14 September 1794).

Boju ∎ 506 BC ∎ Wars of China's Spring and Autumn Era

King He-lü built up the military power of Wu and, when Chu attacked the small state of Cai (Ts'ai), He-lü united with Cai and Tang to invade Chu. At Boju, on the Han, the Allies routed the Chu army of General Nang Wa and Marshal Shenyin Xu and advanced to briefly occupy the capital at Ying. But in the face of Qin (Ch'in) intervention and an attempted coup at home, He-lü withdrew to Wu.

Bokhara ∎ 1220 ∎ Conquests of Genghis Khan

Launching his western offensive against the Khwarezmian Empire, the Mongol Genghis Khan left his sons to besiege **Otrar** and continued west against Bokhara, defended by a Khwarezmian Turk garrison after Sultan Mohammad II fled. When Bokhara fell, it was destroyed. Thousands of prisoners were then used as a human shield for the advance east against **Samarkand** (February–March 1220).

Bokhara ∎ 1868 ∎ Russian Conquest of Central Asia

When Russian troops captured **Tashkent** in the Khanate of Bokhara, General Konstantin von Kaufmann took a fresh force against Bokhara itself, where Amir Muzaffar al Din's army was rapidly crushed. The Amir signed a peace treaty with von Kaufmann (18 June 1868), and within a few years the Russian commander turned his attention against the neighbouring Khanates of **Khiva** and **Khokand**.

Bolia ∎ 469 ∎ Goth Invasion of the Roman Empire

Campaigning in Pannonia, a Roman and tribal coalition under the Suevic King Hunimond, supported by Gepids and others, met the Ostrogoth Theodimer at the River Bolia (probably the Ipel, north of Budapest). When the Goths secured a decisive victory, an approaching Roman army under Aspar turned back, and Emperor Leo made peace with Theodoric of the Thracian Goths.

Bolimov ∎ 1915 ∎ World War I (Eastern Front)

German General August von Mackensen took the offensive in northern Poland with a winter advance southwest of Warsaw at Bolimov against General Vasili Gurko, including the first reported use of gas. While the German attack was driven off with about 20,000 casualties, it created a diversion from the main advance further north at the **Masurian Lakes** (31 January–2 February 1915).

Bolingbroke I 1643 I British Civil Wars
See **Winceby**

Bolkhov I 1608 I Russian Time of Troubles
Supported by a Polish-Cossack army, a pretender claiming to be Dimitri—murdered son of former Tsar Ivan IV—marched from Orel to Bolkhov and met the army of Tsar Basil Shuiski under his brother Prince Dimitri Shuiski. Led by Prince Roman Rozynski, the army of the "Second False Dimitri" achieved a remarkable victory, then advanced towards **Khodynka** near Moscow (24 April 1608).

Bologna I 1944 I World War II (Southern Europe)
Assaulting the **Gothic Line** across northern Italy, Americans attacked from the **Apennines** and the British from **Rimini**. Heaviest fighting was south of Bologna, where American General Mark Clark was halted by a counter-offensive under Field Marshal Albert Kesselring. The British took Ravenna, but the advance stalled until the attack into the **Po Valley** in April 1945 (19 October–7 December 1944).

Bolshoi-Stakhov I 1812 I Napoleonic Wars (Russian Campaign)
After Napoleon Bonaparte's disaster crossing the **Berezina** on his retreat from Moscow, Russian Admiral Paul Tchitchakov and cavalry of General Sergei Lanskoi tried to cut off the defeated French west of the Berezina at Bolshoi-Stakhov. Troops under Marshals Michel Ney and Nicolas Oudinot managed to repulse the attack, and the terrible withdrawal continued (29 November 1812).

Bolton I 1644 I British Civil Wars
As a Parliamentary outpost in Royalist Lancashire, Bolton withstood attacks in February 1643 and January 1644, before Prince Rupert and James Stanley Earl of Derby led a third massive assault. Following a brief siege, Colonel Alexander Rigby escaped when the city fell by storm, with up to 1,500 Puritans killed. Derby was later executed for the so-called Bolton Massacre (28 May 1644).

Bomarsund I 1854 I Crimean War
An Anglo-French expedition under Admiral Sir Charles Napier (1786–1860) attacked Russia in the Baltic, where they bombarded Bomarsund on the Aland Islands, at the mouth of the Gulf of Bothnia. French Marshal Achille Baraguay d'Hillier then landed a strong force, and the Russian garrison surrendered. Another Baltic diversion was attempted a year later at **Sveaborg** (7–16 August 1854).

Bombino I 1822 I Colombian War of Independence
See **Bomboná**

Bomboná I 1822 I Colombian War of Independence
Patriot leader Simón Bolívar marched into modern southwestern Colombia, advancing on Pasto, defended by Spanish Colonel Don Basilio García in mountains to the south at Bomboná. Bolívar lost very heavy casualties in a rash attack on entrenched positions and was forced to withdraw. However, Garcia surrendered Pasto after Patriot victory in Ecuador at **Pichincha** (7 April 1822).

Bomdila I 1962 I Sino-Indian War
Renewing their offensive in the border war in northeast India, Chinese forces took **Se La**, then drove south through Dirang Dzong towards the last major Indian position at Bomdila, where troops under General Anant Singh Pathania were badly beaten in a major defeat. China declared a unilateral ceasefire and partly withdrew, but retained some key strategic conquests (18–19 November 1962).

Bomischbrod I 1434 I Hussite Wars
See **Lipany**

Bone I 430–431 I Roman Vandal Wars
See **Hippo Regius**

Bonn I 1673 I 3rd Dutch War

After invading Alsace and Lorraine, Louis XIV of France faced increasingly united enemies, and Marshal Henri de Turenne was unable to prevent Imperial commander Count Raimondo Montecoccoli marching from Bohemia to join William of Orange besieging Bonn. The city fell to overwhelming forces and France's German allies were forced out of the war (7–12 November 1673).

Bonsaso I 1824 I 1st British-Ashanti War

Marching west of Accra, in Gold Coast (Ghana), to resist the Ashanti moving towards the coast, a small force of Royal African regulars and local militia led by General Sir Charles McCarthy crossed the Pra and were then surrounded at Bonsaso by a reputed 10,000 warriors. The British lost 178 men killed, including McCarthy, but the Ashanti were eventually repulsed in 1826 at **Dodowa** (21 January 1824).

Bon Son I 1966 I Vietnam War

Up to 20,000 Americans, South Vietnamese and South Koreans supported the coastal offensive at **Tuy Hoa** with a massive offensive further north in Bin Dinh to secure the rice bowl Bon Son Plain. The huge action—Operations Double Eagle and Masher (renamed White Wing)—saw severe losses on both sides before the Viet Cong and North Vietnamese regulars withdrew (24 January–6 March 1966).

Boomah Pass I 1850 I 8th Cape Frontier War

In renewed war against the Xhosa Chief Sandile, Colonel George Mackinnon took 700 regulars and Colonials from Fort Cox across the Wolf River towards the Amatola Mountains. Ambushed at Boomah Pass, near the Keiskamma River, they lost 23 killed and 23 wounded and withdrew to **Fort White**. An outlying picket of 15 men was killed next day (24 December 1850).

Boomplaats I 1848 I Orange Free State War

Resisting British annexation of the Orange River Valley, Boers under Andries Pretorius took up arms. When they attacked Bloemfontein, British General Sir Harry Smith marched north from Cape Colony and at Boomplaats, south of Hopetown, the Boers were defeated. A few years later, after defeat at **Viervoet** and **Berea**, the British withdrew from north of the Orange (29 August 1848).

Boonsboro I 1863 I American Civil War (Eastern Theatre)

As General Robert E. Lee's defeated Confederate army fell back to the Potomac after defeat at **Gettysburg**, cavalry under General James "Jeb" Stuart attempted to delay the pursuing Union army of General George G. Meade at Boonsboro, Maryland, west of South Mountain. Stuart fell back after inconclusive action and, a week later, Lee crossed into Virginia at **Williamsport** (8 July 1863).

Boonville I 1861 I American Civil War (Trans-Mississippi)

Determined to prevent Missouri joining the Confederacy, Union General Nathaniel Lyon secured Jefferson City, then pursued secessionist Governor Claiborne Price up the Missouri towards Boonville, where Lyon defeated Confederates led by Colonel John S. Marmaduke under General Sterling Price. Claiborne's forces were defeated again to the southwest at **Carthage** (17 June 1861).

Boquerón, Gran Chaco I 1932 I Chaco War

When war broke out between Paraguay and Bolivia in the Chaco Boreal over the incident at **Carlos Antonio López** in June, 8,000 Paraguayans under Colonel Carlos José Fernández besieged Boquerón. Outnumbered Bolivian Colonel Manuel Marzana was forced to surrender after three weeks' heavy fighting, but Bolivia soon attacked further south at **Nanawa** and **Gondra** (9–29 September 1932).

Boquerón, Nhembucu ∎ 1866 ∎ War of the Triple Alliance

A week after action at **Yataití-Corá**, Paraguayan President Francisco Solano López attacked Argentine General Venancio Flores and Brazilian Marshal Polidoro to the southwest at Boquerón, at the junction of the Paraguay and the Upper Parana. The Allies broke off the action after about 5,000 casualties—twice the Paraguayan losses—and López claimed a great victory (16–18 July 1866).

Bordeaux ∎ 732 ∎ Muslim Invasion of France

Abd-ar-Rahman, Umayyad Muslim Governor of Spain, crossed the Pyrenees into France and invaded Aquitaine to avenge the Arab defeat at **Toulouse** ten years earlier at the hands of Duke Eudo of Aquitaine. At Bordeaux, Eudo once again confronted the invaders and was heavily defeated. He then made peace with Charles Martel of the Franks and joined him for the decisive battle at **Tours**.

Bordeaux ∎ 1453 ∎ Hundred Years War

After destroying an English army at the siege of **Castillon** in July, French Master of Artillery, General Jean Bureau, marched west to besiege the remaining English garrison at Bordeaux. Cut off by a naval blockade of the River Gironde, the starving garrison surrendered, bringing the war to an end and leaving Calais as England's only remaining foothold in France (19 October 1453).

Bordeaux ∎ 1814 ∎ Napoleonic Wars (Peninsular Campaign)

Arthur Wellesley Lord Wellington defeated Marshal Nicolas Soult at **Orthez**, then ordered General Sir William Beresford north to capture the great French port of Bordeaux. The Bonapartist garrison fled after a military demonstration rather than a battle, and local Royalists surrendered the city. Beresford then returned southeast to support Wellington in battle at **Tarbes** (12 March 1814).

Borghetto ∎ 1796 ∎ French Revolutionary Wars (1st Coalition)

Two weeks after capturing Milan, Napoleon Bonaparte continued pursuing Austrian General Jean-Pierre de Beaulieu, who attempted to make a stand on the Mincio. Defending a partially demolished bridge at Borghetto, near Peschiera, the Austrians were again defeated and driven north into the Tyrol. Bonaparte meanwhile besieged the powerful fortified city of **Mantua** (30 May 1796).

Borghetto ∎ 1814 ∎ Napoleonic Wars (French Campaign)

In support of the campaign in France, Austrian forces in northern Italy under Count Heinrich von Bellegarde advanced from Borghetto across the Mincio. On the heights of nearby Vallegio, Prince Eugène de Beauharnais, supported by Generals Paul Grenier and Jean-Antoine Verdier, forced the Austrians back. He was later forced to sign an armistice, ending the war in Italy (8–10 February 1814).

Borgomanero ∎ 1449 ∎ Milanese War of Succession

Amid confusion following the death of Filippo Visconti Duke of Milan, his son-in-law Francesco Sforza secured Borgomanero, northwest of Milan, which was then attacked by his rival, Duke Ludovico of Savoy. In a famous defence by Bartolomeo Colleoni, the army of Savoy was badly beaten, and Ludovico had to withdraw. Sforza then besieged **Milan** and later became Duke (22 April 1449).

Borisov ∎ 1812 ∎ Napoleonic Wars (Russian Campaign)

As Napoleon Bonaparte's retreat from Moscow approached the **Berezina**, Polish forces under General Jean Henri Dombrowski fell back to Borisov to secure a bridgehead for the retreating army. Russian forces under General Karl de Lambert drove Dombrowski across the bridge with heavy losses, and that night Admiral Paul Tchitchakov had reached Borisov (21 November 1812).

Borneo I 1945 I World War II (Pacific)

Overshadowed by major campaigns in **Okinawa** and the **Philippines**, Australian forces under General Leslie Morshead attacked Japanese troops isolated in northern Borneo. Landings at **Tarakan**, **Brunei Bay** and **Balikpapan** saw over 600 Australians and about 4,500 Japanese killed in a campaign regarded by some as wholly unnecessary in the twilight of the war (1 May–15 August 1945).

Bornholm I 1535 I Danish Counts' War

When Count Christopher of Oldenberg intervened in the Danish succession, his army was beaten at **Oksnebjerg**, and at the same time his Lubeck navy was decisively defeated off Bornholm by a combined Danish-Swedish fleet under Peder Skram. A few days later, Skram defeated a smaller squadron off Svendborg, on Funen, then sailed to support the siege of **Copenhagen** (9 & 14 June 1535).

Bornholm I 1676 I Scania War
See **Oland**

Bornholm I 1789 I 2nd Russo-Swedish War

In war with Russia over Finland, Swedish naval forces withdrew to Sveaborg near Helsinki after battle near **Hogland** (July 1788). Swedish Admiral Karl Ehrensward broke Russia's blockade and met Admiral Paul Vasili Tchitchakov off southern Sweden near Bornholm. The Swedes were forced back to nearby Karlskrona, and a month later met the Russians again off **Oland** (26 June 1789).

Bornhoved I 1227 I Danish Wars of Expansion

Waldemar II of Denmark was ransomed from captivity in Schwerin and later took a large force to Schleswig Holstein to punish Heinrich of Schwerin and his allies Adolf of Holstein and Albert of Saxony. At Bornhoved, east of Neumunster, Waldemar lost heavily to the Germans, ending Danish dominance in northern Europe until 150 years later under Waldemar IV (22 July 1227).

Bornos I 1811 I Napoleonic Wars (Peninsular Campaign)

Marching out from Gibraltar, Spanish General Francisco Ballesteros surprised French forces under General Jean-Baptiste Semele, who had been campaigning northeast from Cadiz. Ballesteros attacked Semele near the Guadalete River at Bornos, but the outnumbered French cut their way through for the loss of about 100 prisoners and made it safely back to Cadiz (5 November 1811).

Bornos I 1812 I Napoleonic Wars (Peninsular Campaign)

Spanish General Francisco Ballesteros unwisely advanced from Gibraltar and took 8,000 men to attack General Baron Nicolas-Francois Conroux, who had occupied an entrenched position at Bornos, northeast of Cadiz. An unexpected sortie saw the French kill or capture 1,500 Spaniards, then drive Ballesteros back to San Roque (1 June 1812).

Borny I 1870 I Franco-Prussian War
See **Colombey**

Borodino I 1812 I Napoleonic Wars (Russian Campaign)

Advancing into Russia past **Smolensk**, Napoleon Bonaparte met Prince Mikhail Kutuzov at Borodino on the Moskva, west of Moscow. In one of his bloodiest battles, Bonaparte inflicted over 40,000 Russian casualties—including Prince Pyotr Bagration fatally wounded—then seized Moscow. Loss of up to 20,000 French soldiers was however a critical blow to his campaign (7 September 1812).

Boroughbridge I 1322 I Rebellion of the Marches

Threatened by rebellion among northern Barons led by Thomas Earl of Lancaster and Humphry de Bohun Earl of Hereford, King Edward II sent an army into Yorkshire under Sir Andrew Harclay. At Boroughbridge, on the Ure southeast of Ripon, the Lancastrians were defeated, with Hereford killed. Lancaster was captured and beheaded, while Harclay was created Earl of Carlisle (16 March 1322).

Borough Hill ∎ 1645 ∎ British Civil Wars

When **Leicester** fell to Charles I (31 May), General Sir Thomas Fairfax abandoned the Parliamentary siege of Oxford and pursued the King into Northamptonshire. Fairfax routed outlying Royalists units in a preliminary action near Kislingbury at Borough Hill, east of Daventry. Two days later his Ironsides destroyed the King's main army at **Naseby** (12 June 1645).

Boroughmuir ∎ 1335 ∎ Anglo-Scottish War of Succession

Pro-English Flemish mercenaries under Count Guy of Namur, who landed at Berwick and advanced on Edinburgh, were attacked at nearby Boroughmuir by Scottish Royalists led by John Randolph Earl of Moray, Sir Alexander Ramsay and Sir William Douglas of Liddesdale. The Flemings were heavily defeated, then escorted across the border to England (August 1335).

Borovitsa ∎ 1625 ∎ Cossack-Polish Wars

Polish commander Stanislas Koniecpolski beat Tatars in the southern Ukraine at **Martynow** (June 1624), then attacked unruly Cossacks further east at Borovitsa, near Chigirin, under Hetman Marko Zhmailo, but failed to secure victory. Poland made the compromise Peace of Kurukove with Zhmailo's successor Mikhail Doroshenko and Koniecpolski marched to Prussia to fight the Swedes.

Bor Pansky ∎ 1420 ∎ Hussite Wars

Continuing war against Sigismund of Hungary after victory at **Vitkov** (14 July), the Hussite Jan Zizka besieged Bor Pansky (modern Bor Maly) west of Strakonice, held for the Royalist Baron Ulrich of Rosenberg, who arrived too late to save the town. Rosenberg was defeated in battle nearby after heavy losses on both sides and was thus unable to support Sigismund at **Vysehrad** (12 October 1420).

Boshof ∎ 1900 ∎ 2nd Anglo-Boer War

While attacking Lord Paul Methuen's communications east of Kimberley, French commander Georges Henri Comte de Villebois-Mareuil and his pro-Boer foreign contingent were intercepted and surrounded by Methuen at Boshof near Tweefontein. Heavy shell-fire killed 10 (including Villebois-Mareuil) and wounded 11, and the 51 survivors surrendered (5 April 1900).

Bosra ∎ 634 ∎ Muslim Conquest of Syria

Soon after Khalid ibn al-Walid beat a Byzantine force east of Damascus at **Marj Rahit**, local Muslim commander Abu Ubayd sent Shurahbil against Bosra, south of Damascus. The garrison marched out, and fierce fighting ensued before Khalid arrived with reinforcements. The Byzantines withdrew under siege and Bosra soon surrendered, the first major Syrian town to fall to Islam (July 634).

Boston ∎ 1775–1776 ∎ War of the American Revolution

Withdrawing after skirmishes at **Lexington** and **Concord**, which triggered the war, British forces fell back on Boston, initially led by General Thomas Gage. After a long American siege, commanded by General Artemus Ward and later George Washington, and action at **Bunker Hill**, the British were eventually permitted to evacuate and sailed for Halifax (19 April 1775–17 May 1776).

Boston Harbour ∎ 1813 ∎ War of 1812

The American frigate *Chesapeake* (Captain James Lawrence) emerging from Boston was met by the British frigate *Shannon* (Captain Philip Broke). After a brief ship-to-ship action, *Chesapeake* was captured with heavy casualties and entered British service. The last words of the mortally wounded Lawrence—"Don't give up the ship"—became a rallying cry for the American cause (1 June 1813).

Bosworth Field ∎ 1485 ∎ Wars of the Roses

Henry Tudor invaded England against the Yorkist usurper Richard III and gathered

Lancastrian support. He marched to meet the King at Bosworth, west of Leicester and, when Henry Percy Earl of Northumberland deserted and Lord Thomas and Sir William Stanley charged sides, Richard was defeated and killed. The war ended and Tudor was crowned as Henry VII (22 August 1485).

Boteler's Ford | 1862 | American Civil War (Eastern Theatre)
See **Shepherdstown**

Bothaville | 1900 | 2nd Anglo-Boer War
In a remarkable coup, British General Charles Knox surprised a commando under General Christiaan de Wet at Bothaville, on the Valsch, west of Roodewal. Attacked at dawn, de Wet was routed and fled, along with Marthinus Steyn, President of the Orange Free State. A bloody rearguard action allowed the main force to escape, but the Boers lost all their field guns (6 November 1900).

Bothwell Bridge | 1679 | Scottish Covenanter Rebellion
Rising against Episcopalianism, non-conformist Covenanters repulsed a small government force at **Drumclog** (1 June), then soon faced an army under James Duke of Monmouth and John Graham of Claverhouse. At Bothwell Bridge, on the Clyde southeast of Glasgow, the rebels were crushed, with heavy losses. Two leaders were hanged and about 250 others were transported (22 June 1679).

Bou Denib | 1908 | French Colonial Wars in North Africa
Determined to avenge French losses on the western Algerian border at **El Menabba** in April, a punitive expedition under General Charles Vigy attacked more than 6,000 Moroccans further west at Bou Denib, just inside modern Morocco. Very heavy fighting saw the Moroccans defeated and a garrison was established. A Moroccan attack in September was repulsed at nearby **Djorf** (13 May 1908).

Boudicca | 61 | Roman Conquest of Britain
When King Prasutagus of the Iceni died, Rome tried to increase control, and his widow Queen Boudicca attacked Camulodunum (Colchester) and Londinium before her army was utterly defeated by Governor Suetonius Paulinus at an uncertain site, possibly near Verulamium (St Albans) or modern Towcester or perhaps Mancetter. Boudicca escaped the ensuing massacre and reputedly took poison.

Bougainville | 1943–1944 | World War II (Pacific)
Allied forces secured **Guadalcanal**, then attacked Bougainville, held by 35,000 under General Haruyoshi Hyakutake. Landing at **Empress Augusta Bay**, the marines defended their perimeter at **Piva Forks**, followed by months of Japanese counter-attacks. The final Japanese assault (8–25 March) was driven off with up to 5,000 killed, but Japanese resistance continued (1 November 1943–March 1944).

Bougie | 1510 | Spanish Colonial Wars in North Africa
A year after taking **Oran** in Algeria, Spanish commander Pedro Navarro led a fresh expedition against the once-powerful port of Bougie, 120 miles east of Algiers. The Spanish captured and fortified Bougie and held it against counter-attacks from Algiers by the Corsair Arudj in 1512 and 1515. In 1555, the port was retaken by Salah Rais, Pasha of Algiers, and soon fell into decay (January 1510).

Bougie | 1671 | Corsair Wars
Admiral Sir Edward Spragge continued war against the Barbary pirates, taking the English Mediterranean fleet against the Corsair anchorage at Bougie in northeast Algeria. Breaking the protective boom, he destroyed the entire pirate fleet, sinking seven ships and capturing three. The Algerians then killed their Dey and forced his successor to make peace (8 May 1671).

Boulay I 1635 I Thirty Years War (Franco-Habsburg War)

Withdrawing from **Mainz** on the Rhine, French under Louis de Nogaret Cardinal de la Valette and Bernard of Saxe-Weimar suffered heavy losses retreating southwest across the mountains, pursued by Imperial commander Count Matthias Gallas. Crossing the Saar at Wallerfangen, Bernard routed a rearguard attack at nearby Boulay and the French army safely reached Metz (September 1635).

Boulcott's Farm I 1846 I 1st New Zealand War

With Maori war parties raiding settlements outside Wellington, about 200 men under Topine Te Mamaku attacked Lieutenant George Page's remote British garrison at Boulcott's Farm, in the Hutt Valley. The Europeans lost eight killed before Te Mamaku was driven off and withdrew to **Wanganui**. Another action at **Horokiri** soon ended fighting around Wellington (16 May 1846).

Boulogne I 1544 I French War of Henry VIII

Henry VIII of England took a huge force to Calais in support of Emperor Charles V against Francis II of France. He then marched against Boulogne to assist the siege of the city by John Dudley Lord Lisle. Boulogne fell after two months, but within days the Emperor made a separate peace. Six years later, England sold the city back to France (19 July–14 September 1544).

Boulogne I 1801 I French Revolutionary Wars (2nd Coalition)

With France developing plans for a cross-channel invasion, English Admiral Horatio Nelson was sent to bombard the fleet of gunboats and barges assembling at Boulogne. Following a failed attempt (4 August), Nelson made a second larger-scale assault. With the port defended at sea by Admiral René La Touche-Treville, the attack was a complete failure (15–16 August 1801).

Boulogne I 1804 I Napoleonic Wars (3rd Coalition)

In a night attack against up to 150 French craft at Boulogne, English Admiral Sir George Keith Elphinstone sent four fireships and five explosive-packed floating torpedoes—which all exploded with minimal damage. French commander Admiral Jean Raimond Lacrosse drove off the attack at the cost of just 14 killed and Elphinstone withdrew without loss, but with nothing achieved (1–2 October 1804).

Boulogne I 1940 I World War II (Western Europe)

Leading a rapid Panzer advance through France from the **Ardennes**, General Heinz Guderian reached the coast at Abbeville (19 May), then raced north for the strategic port at Boulogne. After heavy fighting and German dive-bombing, some Allied troops were evacuated by sea before the citadel fell by storm. About 5,000 British and French surrendered and Guderian drove on for **Calais** (22–25 May 1940).

Boulou I 1794 I French Revolutionary Wars (1st Coalition)

When Spanish forces invaded the Rousillon in southeastern France, General Jacques Dugommier attacked his enemy's rear at Boulou, south of Perpignan, while Spanish commander General Amarillas Comte de la Union attempted to hold the bridge on the Tech at Céret. The Spanish were crushed, losing over 1,500 men and 150 guns, and fled across the border (30 April–1 May 1794).

Bou Nouala I 1908 I French Colonial Wars in North Africa

Soon after indecisive actions east of Casablanca at **Wadi M'Koun** and **R'Fakha**, French General Albert d'Amade marched south to attack the Moroccan army in camp at Bou Nouala. Offering no quarter in a virtual massacre, the French slaughtered the Moroccans with artillery then killed every man they found, effectively ending resistance in the Chaouia region (15 March 1908).

Bourbon | 1810 | Napoleonic Wars (5th Coalition)
See **Réunion**

Bourgtherolde | 1126 | Norman Dynastic Wars
Facing rebellion in France against Henry I, Royal forces under Ralph of Bayeaux, supported by Odo Borleng, attacked the rebels led by Amaury de Montfort near Bourgtherolde, southwest of Rouen. In a well-executed action, Ralph attacked with dismounted knights, supported by archers and a reserve of mounted cavalry, and the rebels were utterly routed (26 March 1126).

Bouvines | 1214 | Anglo-French Wars
King John of England took an army to France to recapture lost land from Philip II Augustus, and won support from Count Ferdinand of Flanders and German Emperor Otto IV. But at Bouvines, near Lille, Otto fled, and his allies were overwhelmed. The battle secured the French monarchy and prompted John's Barons into rebellion, leading to the eventual signing of Magna Carta (26 July 1214).

Bov | 1848 | 1st Schleswig-Holstein War
Encouraged by Prussia, the Duchies of Schleswig and Holstein rose against Frederick VII of Denmark, and Danish troops immediately marched into Schleswig. The poorly led rebels were heavily defeated just north of Flensburg at Bov, and Danish troops occupied Schleswig. Just weeks later they were driven out by Prussian intervention and defeat at the **Dannevirke** (9 April 1848).

Bovianum | 305 BC | 2nd Samnite War
Despite Etruscan defeat at **Lake Vadimo**, the Samnites of central Italy sustained resistance against Rome for five years, until a large force under Marcus Fulvius Paetinus and Lucius Postumius Megellus was sent to besiege the principal rebel fortress at Bovianum (modern Boiano), north of Caserta. A Samnite relief force under Statius Gellius was routed and Bovianum fell, effectively ending the war.

Bowers Hill | 1862 | American Civil War (Eastern Theatre)
See **Winchester, Virginia**

Bowling Alley | 1950 | Korean War
See **Naktong Bulge (1st)**

Boxtel | 1794 | French Revolutionary Wars (1st Coalition)
As French General Charles Pichegru advanced into southern Holland, British and Dutch forces led by Prince Frederick Augustus Duke of York were driven out of **Bois le Duc**, east of Tilburg. An attempted counter-attack next day by Lieutenant Colonel Arthur Wellesley was repulsed at nearby Boxtel. This is regarded as the later Duke of Wellington's first battle (15 September 1794).

Boyacá | 1819 | Colombian War of Independence
Republican leader Simón Bolívar advancing through western Colombia captured Tunja after action at **Pantano de Vargas**, then routed Spanish Colonel José María Barreiro at nearby Boyacá. Bolívar took 1,600 prisoners, including Barreiro and his staff (later executed). He then marched southwest to occupy Bogotá and establish a Republic with himself as President (7 August 1819).

Boydton Plank Road | 1864 | American Civil War (Eastern Theatre)
See **Hatcher's Run**

Boyne | 1690 | War of the Glorious Revolution
Invading Ireland to put down Catholic opposition, William III of England and Duke Friedrich of Schomberg led a 35,000-strong force towards Dublin and encountered the Jacobite army under James II and Comte Antonin de Lauson near Drogheda at the River Boyne. Although Schomberg was killed, William won a decisive victory and went on to capture Dublin and besiege **Limerick** (1 July 1690).

Boyuibé ▮ **1935** ▮ **Chaco War**

Paraguayan Colonel Eugenio Garay advanced north into the Chaco Boreal through victory at **Ybibobo** and crossed the Parapití to seize Charagua in southeastern Bolivia. But in a new Bolivian offensive, 15,000 men under General Arturo Guillén attacked and defeated the over-extended Paraguayans at Boyuibé. A final action further east at **Ingavi** soon ended the war (17 April 1935).

Braddock Down ▮ **1643** ▮ **British Civil Wars**

Royalist commander Sir Ralph Hopton rallied local forces in Cornwall and marched against Parliamentary Colonel William Ruthin, who had advanced to occupy Liskeard. Supported by infantry under Sir Bevil Grenville at nearby Braddock Down, east of Lostwithiel, Hopton defeated Ruthin, who withdrew from Cornwall after losing 1,200 prisoners and all his guns (19 January 1643).

Braddock's Defeat ▮ **1755** ▮ **Seven Years War (North America)**

See **Monongahela**

Bradford ▮ **652** ▮ **Anglo-Saxon Territorial Wars**

Attempting to expand the power of Wessex, King Cenwalh (Coenwalch), son of Cynegils, advanced west and defeated a force of Britons at Bradford on Avon, in Wiltshire, southeast of Bath. The victory secured land for Wessex as far as Malmesbury, and was followed by a further victory for Cenwalh over the Welsh in 658 at **Penselwood**.

Braga ▮ **1809** ▮ **Napoleonic Wars (Peninsular Campaign)**

French Marshal Nicolas Soult invaded Portugal from the north to capture **Chaves** (11 March), then advanced through Lanhozo to Braga, where he met a peasant army which had murdered its cowardly commander General Bernadim Freire. Fighting under Prussian Colonel Frederick Eben, the ill-armed Portuguese levies were destroyed, and Soult advanced towards **Oporto** (17–20 March 1809).

Bramham Moor ▮ **1408** ▮ **Percy's Rebellion**

Renewing rebellion against Henry IV after defeat at **Shrewsbury**, Henry Percy Earl of Northumberland marched into Yorkshire, aided by Scots under Lord Thomas Bardolph. On Bramham Moor near Tadcaster, they encountered a large force led by Sir Thomas Rokeby, Sheriff of Yorkshire, who defeated and killed both Percy and Bardolph, ending the rebellion (19 February 1408).

Bramham Moor ▮ **1643** ▮ **British Civil Wars**

See **Seacroft Moor**

Brandeis ▮ **1639** ▮ **Thirty Years War (Franco-Habsburg War)**

Swedish commander Johan Banér advancing towards Prague after his victory at **Chemnitz** (14 April) found himself being pursued by an Imperial force under Count Raimondo Montecuccoli. Turning on the Imperials at Brandeis, on the Elbe, 10 miles northeast of Prague, Banér routed his pursuers. Montecuccoli was captured and held prisoner for almost three years (19 May 1639).

Brandenburg ▮ **928** ▮ **German Imperial Wars**

See **Brennaburg**

Brander ▮ **1308** ▮ **Rise of Robert the Bruce**

Robert the Bruce secured his position with victory at **Loudon Hill** in 1307, then marched into Argyle, where the Pass at Brander was held for Edward II by John MacDougall of Lorne (who had defeated Bruce in 1306 at **Dalry**). Aided by a flank attack from the heights of Cruachan by Sir James "Black" Douglas, Bruce routed MacDougall and seized nearby Dunstaffnage Castle (August 1308).

Brandy Station ▮ **1863** ▮ **American Civil War (Eastern Theatre)**

As Confederate commander Robert E. Lee began to march north towards **Gettysburg**,

Union General Alfred Pleasonton crossed the Rappahannock and attacked Lee's screening forces under General James "Jeb" Stuart. On the railway east of Culpeper at Brandy Station, Virginia, in the war's largest cavalry action, Pleasonton was driven off, though Union cavalry was finally proved (9 June 1863).

Brandywine ∎ 1777 ∎ War of the American Revolution

On a fresh offensive into Pennsylvania, British General Sir William Howe advanced through **Cooch's Bridge** to the Brandywine, where General George Washington made a stand. With Generals Charles Earl Cornwallis and Wilhelm von Kniphausen, Howe secured a decisive victory in a large-scale action, and continued through **Paoli** toward Philadelphia (11 September 1777).

Brännkyrka ∎ 1518 ∎ Wars of the Kalmar Union

Campaigning against the rebellious Sten Sture the Younger, who had seized the Regency of Sweden from the pro-Danish Stolle faction, Christian II of Denmark landed near Stockholm. To the southwest at the Brännkyrka, he was heavily defeated by Sture and Gustav Vasa and was forced to withdraw. When Christian invaded again a year later, Sture was killed at **Bogesund** (22 July 1518).

Branxton ∎ 1513 ∎ Anglo-Scottish Royal Wars

See **Flodden**

Brasov ∎ 1603 ∎ Balkan National Wars

When Moise Székely seized part of Transylvania with the aid of Turkish and Tatar auxiliaries, Habsburg Emperor Rudolf II requested Radu Serban of Wallachia to put down the rebel. When Radu invaded Transylvania, many of the nobility sided with him against the excesses of the Ottoman-supported usurper, who was defeated in the northwest at Brasov (17 July 1603).

Bratislava ∎ 907 ∎ Magyar Invasion of Germany

See **Pressburg**

Brattonville ∎ 1780 ∎ War of the American Revolution

See **Williamson's Plantation**

Braunau ∎ 1743 ∎ War of the Austrian Succession

As part of the Austrian invasion of Bavaria, Count Ludwig Khevenhuller marched north from Salzburg and met a Franco-Bavarian army under Marshals Francois de Broglie and Count Friedrich von Seckendorf on the Inn at Braunau. The Allies fell back when the Austrians stormed entrenchments outside the city and Elector Karl Albrecht of Bavaria fled from Munich (9 May 1743).

Bravalla ∎ 735 ∎ Danish War of Succession

The Viking King Harold Hildetand of Denmark secured victories in Britain and the Baltic, then sailed to the Swedish coast of Skane, where he faced a large army at Bravalla under his ambitious nephew Sigurd Ring. In a massive semi-legendary engagement, both at sea and on land near Norrköping, Harold was defeated and killed and Sigurd took the Danish throne.

Brazito ∎ 1846 ∎ American-Mexican War

American Colonel Alexander Doniphan was marching south from Santa Fe when he was met on the Upper Rio Grande at Brazito, 30 miles from El Paso del Norte (Ciudad Juárez) by Mexican militia and Regular Lancers under Major Antonio Ponce de Léon, who was wounded. Captain Rafael Carabajal led the withdrawal, and Doniphan soon advanced to the **Sacramento** (25 December 1846).

Brechin ∎ 1452 ∎ Douglas Rebellion

After James II of Scotland murdered William Earl of Douglas, he sent Alexander Seton Earl of Huntly against the Douglas allies under Alexander Crawford Earl of Crawford. Huntly crushed the rebels on the South Esk at Brechin, though his brothers Sir William and Sir Henry Seton were killed. Crawford fled and Huntly devastated the Moray lands (18 May 1452).

Breda I 1590 I Netherlands War of Independence

With Alexander Farnese Duke of Parma occupied in France, Prince Maurice of Orange began an offensive along the Dutch coast and sent Charles de Heraugière and just 70 men to capture Breda. Hidden in peat-barges on the Mark, the Netherlanders penetrated the city's defences and led to its capture. This was followed by further Dutch success at Deventer and **Zutphen** (3 March 1590).

Breda I 1624–1625 I Netherlands War of Independence

In renewed warfare after the Twelve Years Truce, Spanish commander Ambrogio de Spinola besieged the powerful Netherlands fortress of Breda, and Maurice of Orange died while raising a relief army. His brother Frederick Henry of Orange could make no impact and, after eleven months of siege, their natural brother—Justin of Nassau—was forced to capitulate (28 August 1624–2 June 1625).

Breda I 1636–1637 I Netherlands War of Independence

Twelve years after failing to prevent Spanish capture of Breda, Frederick Henry of Orange besieged the fortress-city, held by Gomar Fourdin, flooding the surrounding country and driving off a relief attempt by Spanish Governor Cardinal Infante Ferdinand. The Dutch captured starving Breda after more than a year and gave the defeated garrison free passage (20 July 1636–10 October 1637).

Breed's Hill I 1775 I War of the American Revolution
    See **Bunker Hill**

Bregalnica I 1913 I 2nd Balkan (Inter-ally) War

Angry over division of Macedonia, Bulgaria turned on her former allies, and General Mikhail Savoff suddenly attacked along the Macedonian frontier, where his forces were met on the Bregalnica by Serbian commander Radomir Putnik. Bloody fighting forced the invaders to withdraw.

They were meantime also beaten by the Greeks around **Kilkis** to end the four-week war (30 June–9 July 1913).

Bregenz I 1408 I Habsburg-Swiss Wars

The people of Appenzell in northeast Switzerland rose against the Habsburg Abbot Cuno of St Gall and Duke Fredrick IV of Austria, and won valuable victories at **Speicher** (1403) and **Stoss** (1405). But when rebels attacked the loyal Imperial city of Bregenz, they were badly defeated. Appenzell was forced out of the Swiss League, although it remained a Confederate ally (13 January 1408).

Breisach I 1638 I Thirty Years War (Franco-Habsburg War)

After repulsing an Imperial army at **Wittenweier** in July, Bernard of Saxe-Weimar was joined by French forces under Jean-Baptiste Guébriant and Henri de Turenne besieging Breisach, on the Rhine near Freiburg. Another relief army was repulsed at **Sennheim**, and Baron Hans Heinrich von Reinach's starving garrison finally capitulated, giving Bernard all of Alsace (18 August–17 December 1638).

Breisach I 1703 I War of the Spanish Succession

As part of the French campaign to clear the Austrian and German allies from Bavaria, Marshal Count Camille de Tallard launched an offensive along the middle Rhine. The major fortified position on the east bank at Breisach was besieged by the great French engineer Marshal Sebastien Vauban, and its capture opened the way to Tallard's great victory in November at **Speyer** (6 September 1703).

Breisach I 1870 I Franco-Prussian War
    See **Neu-Breisach**

Breitenfeld I 1631 I Thirty Years War (Swedish War)

When Imperial commander Johan Tserclaes Count Tilly invaded Saxony and occupied Leipzig, Elector John George of Saxony joined Gustavus Adolphus of Sweden against the outnumbered Catholic army just north of Leipzig near Breitenfeld. Tilly and Gottfried zu Pappenheim were routed with massive losses and Gustavus occupied the Rhineland (17 September 1631).

Breitenfeld I 1642 I Thirty Years War (Franco-Habsburg War)

Swedish Marshal Lennart Torstensson withdrawing to Saxony from **Olmütz** in June besieged Leipzig, but was impetuously attacked at nearby Breitenfeld by the pursuing Imperial army of Archduke Leopold William and General Ottavio Piccolomini. Torstensson routed the Imperials in a brilliant action, inflicting up to 10,000 casualties, and the Archduke fled to Bohemia (2 November 1642).

Brema I 1638 I Thirty Years War (Franco-Habsburg War)

In a fresh offensive against the French, the Spanish Governor of Milan, Diego Felipe de Guzmán Marquis of Leganés, besieged the nearby fortress of Brema. French commander Marshal Charles de Crequi led a relief force from Turin, but while observing the Spanish siege lines, he was killed by a cannonball. His force withdrew in confusion and Brema capitulated (17 March 1638).

Bremberg I 1813 I Napoleonic Wars (War of Liberation)

See **Katzbach**

Bremgarten I 1712 I 2nd Villmergen War

Almost 60 years after Catholic victory in the First Villmergen War, religious conflict in Switzerland resumed, and the Bernese army defeated a much smaller Catholic force from Lucerne in the "Battle of the Shrubs" (Staudenschlach) on a wooded area west of Zurich near Bremgarten. The Protestants then captured Baden after a brief bombardment and soon secured victory at **Villmergen**.

Bremule I 1119 I Norman Dynastic Wars

See **Brenneville**

Brennaburg I 928 I German Imperial Wars

A determined offensive against the Pagan Wends of northern Germany saw Emperor Henry I lead a brilliant mid-winter attack on the Hevelli, a sub-tribe living near the River Havel. Camping his army on the frozen river, Henry besieged Brennaburg (modern Brandenburg) and starved the garrison into submission. The combined Wend tribes were finally defeated the following year at **Lenzen**.

Brenneville I 1119 I Norman Dynastic Wars

Henry I reunited England and Normandy with victory at **Tinchebrai** in 1106, then imprisoned his brother Robert, former Duke of Normandy. In support of Robert's disinherited son, William Clito, Louis VI of France took an army against Henry's Anglo-Norman knights at Brenneville, southeast of Rouen. Though casualties were light, Louis fled and abandoned Clito's cause (20 August 1119).

Brennkirk I 1518 I Wars of the Kalmar Union

See **Brännkyrka**

Brenta I 1917 I World War I (Italian Front)

See **Monte Grappa**

Brentford I 1642 I British Civil Wars

Advancing towards London after the indecisive engagement at **Edgehill** (23 October), Charles I sent Prince Rupert's cavalry ahead to Brentford, on the Thames west of the capital, strongly defended by Parliamentary General Denzil Holles. Holles withdrew after bitter street fighting and next day the King was confronted by London militia at **Turnham Green** (12 November 1642).

Brentwood I 1863 I American Civil War (Western Theatre)

Three weeks after the Union rout south of Nashville, Tennessee, at **Thompson's Station**, Confederate General Nathan B. Forrest attacked the railway closer to Nashville at Brentwood, where Colonel Edward Bloodgood was defeated and forced to surrender. General G. Clay Smith arrived to retake the station, but had to burn the recaptured wagons and fall back on **Franklin** (25 March 1863).

Brescia ❙ 1238 ❙ Imperial-Papal Wars

Following his great victory at **Cortenuova** against the Lombard League of Northern Italy (November 1237), Emperor Frederick II turned his army of Germans and Italian Guelphs against Brescia, one of the few cities which remained an ally of Milan. Frederick was forced to admit failure after a three-month siege and withdrew from Brescia to regroup his forces (August–October 1238).

Brescia ❙ 1401 ❙ Florentine-Milanese Wars

The city of Florence was threatened by the growing power of Gian Galeazzo Visconti Duke of Milan and sought help from the newly elected Rupert III of Germany, who had replaced Visconti's former ally, the deposed King Wenceslas. Rupert marched into Italy, but near Brescia he was heavily defeated by the Milanese and was forced back to Germany (14 October 1401).

Brescia ❙ 1426 ❙ Venetian-Milanese Wars

In renewed war by Venice and Florence against Milan, a major struggle developed around Brescia, defended by Francesco Sforza for Filippo Maria Duke of Milan. The former Milanese commander and soldier of fortune Francesco Bussone Count Carmagnola led a brutal assault, gradually capturing strongholds around Brescia until the city fell to Venice (April–November 1426).

Brescia ❙ 1849 ❙ 1st Italian War of Independence

On the same day that King Charles Albert of Sardinia was decisively defeated at **Novara**, the city of Brescia rose in support of the doomed Piedmontese revolt against Austria. A week later, Austrian Baron Julius von Haynau took Brescia by storm, crushing the revolt with hundreds of executions. Genoa then fell without a fight and the King abdicated in favour of his son Victor Emanuel II (31 March 1849).

Breskens ❙ 1944 ❙ World War II (Western Europe)

When Allied forces captured **Antwerp**, German General Gustav von Zangen was trapped against the coast. But Allied delay let more than 80,000 men and their equipment escape north through Breskens, downstream on the Scheldt. Another 10,000 under General Kurt Eberding then held Breskens against the intense Allied offensive on the **Scheldt Estuary** (6 October–2 November 1944).

Breslau ❙ 1757 ❙ Seven Years War (Europe)

While Frederick II of Prussia was defeating the Allies at **Rossbach** in Saxony, an Austrian army under Prince Charles of Lorraine and Marshal Leopold von Daun advanced into Silesia and, after victory at **Moys** and **Schweidnitz**, routed and captured Duke August Wilhelm of Bevern near Breslau (modern Wroclaw). Breslau was retaken by Prussia two weeks later after **Leuthen** (22 November 1757).

Breslau ❙ 1806–1807 ❙ Napoleonic Wars (4th Coalition)

As Napoleon Bonaparte marched into Poland, his brother Jerome on the right flank advanced with an army from Saxony into Silesia, and General Dominique Vandamme besieged Breslau (modern Wroclaw). The Russian-held fortress on the Oder drove off a costly assault (22–23 December) but eventually fell, securing the French position in the south (10 December 1806–7 January 1807).

Breslau ❙ 1945 ❙ World War II (Eastern Front)

The **Vistula-Oder** offensive across Poland bypassed the German city of Breslau (Wroclaw) on the Oder, which was encircled by Generals Vladimir Gluzdovksy and Aleksei Zhadov. A long siege saw very costly fighting and two-thirds of Breslau destroyed. Four days after the fall of **Berlin**, General Hermann Niehoff surrendered the city and it later became part of Poland (8 February–6 May 1945).

Brest I 1342 I Hundred Years War

Soon after the relief of **Hennebont**, Countess Jeanne of Montfort withdrew to Brest, where she was besieged by Charles of Blois on land and by 14 Genoese galleys under Carlo Grimaldi. An English relief fleet under William Bohun Earl of Northampton surprised Grimaldi, and only three Genoese ships escaped. The others were driven ashore and burned and Blois had to raise the siege (18 August 1342).

Brest I 1512 I War of the Holy League

Admiral Sir Edward Howard supported the alliance between Henry VIII of England and Spain by attacking the coast of France, where he fought an indecisive engagement off Brest with the French fleet of Jean de Thenouenal. Despite losing his two largest ships and Sir Thomas Knyvet killed in the ship *Regent*, Howard still claimed victory. He was killed off **Brest** a year later (10 August 1512).

Brest I 1513 I War of the Holy League

A year after his bloody but indecisive battle against the French navy off **Brest**, English Admiral Sir Edward Howard attempted a cutting-out action against French Admiral Pregent de Bidoux at anchor in Brest Harbour. Sir Edward was killed and his force was repulsed, but his brother Sir Thomas Howard later returned to Brest and captured several prizes (25 April 1513).

Brest I 1694 I War of the Grand Alliance

See **Camaret Bay**

Brest I 1944 I World War II (Western Europe)

When American forces seized **Avranches**, General Troy Middleton secured **St Malo**, then drove west into Brittany towards the great naval base at Brest, tenaciously held by General Her-

mann Ramcke. Brest fell after very heavy fighting, yielding 35,000 prisoners, but the Americans lost about 10,000 casualties. The port itself was completely wrecked (25 August–18 September 1944).

Brest-Litovsk I 1794 I War of the 2nd Polish Partition

Polish Nationalist General Karol Sierakovski withdrew from **Kruptchitsa**, and days later attempted to hold the Russian counter-offensive of Field Marshal Alexander Suvorov on the Bug at Brest. In a one-sided disaster, the Poles lost 20 guns and were utterly overwhelmed with terrible casualties. Sierakovski and his survivors fled west to defend **Warsaw** (19 September 1794).

Brest-Litovsk I 1915 I World War I (Eastern Front)

As part of Germany's new **Triple Offensive**, Austro-German commander August von Mackensen campaigned north from **Lemberg** through Lublin (30 July) and Chelm (31 July), then advanced on the important city of Brest-Litovsk, east of **Warsaw**. A determined delaying action was crushed by Mackensen's siege guns and the Russians withdrew further east (25 August 1915).

Briar Creek I 1779 I War of the American Revolution

Campaigning against Britain in Georgia, General Benjamin Lincoln sent Colonel John Ashe pursuing the British from Augusta, downstream towards **Savannah**. On Briar Creek, Ashe's militia were surprised by a much smaller British force under Colonel Mark Prevost and Major John McPherson. With 200 killed and 170 captured, the American counter-offensive failed (3 March 1779).

Brice's Cross Roads I 1864 I American Civil War (Western Theatre)

After attacking **Fort Pillow**, Tennessee, and widespread destruction of Union railroads, Confederate General Nathan B. Forrest was finally intercepted in Mississippi by a Union force sent from Memphis under General Samuel B. Sturgis. Forrest utterly defeated the much larger Union force at Brice's Cross Roads, near Guntown, and continued south to **Tupelo** (10 June 1864).

Bridge I 634 I Muslim Conquest of Iraq

Facing a Persian offensive in Mesopotamia to recover **Hira**, Muslim Generals Muthanna and Abu Ubayd won at **Babylon** and **Nimaraq**, then met Persian commander Bahman on the Euphrates. At the Battle of the Bridge, the Arabs were utterly routed with Abu Ubayd killed. Muthanna only just managed to extricate the survivors, then recovered to win in May 635 at **Buwayb** (26 November 634).

Bridge of Dee I 1639 I 1st Bishops' War
See **Dee**

Bridgewater, Florida I 1840 I 2nd Seminole Indian War

When an army patrol was attacked near Fort Micanopy, south of modern Gainesville, Florida, Lieutenant James Sanderson marched out with 18 men and was ambushed at nearby Bridgewater by Seminole under Halleck Tustenuggee. Sanderson and nine others were killed. Sergeant-Major Francis Carroll, who was wounded, later died in a similar ambush at nearby **Martin's Point** (19 May 1840).

Bridgnorth I 1102 I Norman Dynastic Wars

Henry I of England faced renewed rebellion by Robert of Beleme Earl of Salisbury, and captured the Norman's castle at **Arundel**, then besieged his powerful fortress of Bridgnorth, on the Severn west of Wolverhampton. Earl Robert could not send aid to his captains, who had to surrender. Henry then marched on Shrewsbury, where the Earl himself surrendered and withdrew to Normandy.

Bridgwater, England I 1645 I British Civil Wars

Days after defeat at **Langport** in Somerset, Royalist General George Lord Goring withdrew into Devon and Sir Thomas Fairfax took his victorious Ironsides against Bridgwater, on the Parrett, northeast of **Taunton**, defended by

Governor Sir Hugh Wyndham. Part of the burning town was taken by storm after a massive bombardment and Wyndham was forced to surrender (21–23 July 1645).

Brielle I 1572 I Netherlands War of Independence

Supported by William of Orange, Dutch privateers known as "Sea Beggars" attacked Spanish shipping. Their Admiral, Willem van Lumey Count of Marck, then joined with William of Blois Seigneur of Treslong to surprise the town of Brielle, west of Rotterdam. Brielle fell in a severe blow to Spanish prestige, encouraging rebellion by other towns in the Netherlands (1 April 1572).

Brienne I 1814 I Napoleonic Wars (French Campaign)

Napoleon Bonaparte marched east from Paris to prevent a junction of the invading Prussian and Austrian armies, moving first against General Gebhard von Blucher between the Aube and Marne at Brienne-le-Chateau. The Allies fell back after a bloody, indecisive struggle, and Bonaparte occupied Brienne and nearby **La Rothière**, where he faced a massive assault three days later (29 January 1814).

Brier Creek I 1779 I War of the American Revolution
See **Briar Creek**

Brignais I 1362 I Hundred Years War

During the course of the war, undisciplined bands of English, French, German and Spanish soldiers known as "routiers" formed freebooting companies which roamed much of France. A small French Royal army attempted to block one such company marching north along the Rhone valley from the Languedoc, but was utterly defeated at Brignais, southwest of Lyons (6 April 1362).

Brihuega I 1710 I War of the Spanish Succession

After capturing Madrid, an Anglo-Austrian army was driven out by French troops under

Louis Duke de Vendôme. Pursuing the Allies towards Aragon, Vendôme attacked the separated rearguard at Brihuega, northeast of Guadalajara, and forced surrender, including General James Stanhope captured. Another Allied defeat next day at **Villaviciosa** virtually ended the campaign (9 December 1710).

Brihuega ∎ 1937 ∎ Spanish Civil War
See **Guadalajara, Spain**

Bril ∎ 1572 ∎ Netherlands War of Independence
See **Brielle**

Brimstone Hill ∎ 1782 ∎ War of the American Revolution
See **St Kitts**

Brindisi ∎ 1156 ∎ 1st Byzantine-Sicilian War
When Byzantine Emperor Manuel I invaded southern Italy with Papal support against William I of Sicily, naval victory off **Apulia** gave him a foothold. But the following year a Byzantine army under Alexius Comnenus was defeated at Brindisi. When William marched on Benevento, Pope Hadrian IV had to recognise him, and two years later Manuel made peace and withdrew from Italy.

Bristoe Station ∎ 1863 ∎ American Civil War (Eastern Theatre)
Manoeuvring in Virginia months after defeat at **Gettysburg**, Confederate commander Robert E. Lee sent General Ambrose P. Hill against General George G. Meade's army marching towards Manassas. Hill was heavily repulsed at nearby Bristoe Station by Union General Gouverneur K. Warren. Lee's army continued south through further defeat at **Rappahannock Station** (14 October 1863).

Bristol ∎ 1643 ∎ British Civil Wars
Prince Rupert followed the decisive Royalist victory at **Roundway Down** (13 July) by marching to besiege Bristol, defended by a largely Cornish garrison under the Governor Nathaniel Fiennes.

With fresh reinforcements under his brother Prince Maurice, Rupert took Bristol by storm and the second most important port in England at the time was forced to capitulate (23–26 July 1643).

Bristol ∎ 1645 ∎ British Civil Wars
Within weeks of victory in the west at **Langport**, Parliamentary commander Sir Thomas Fairfax took **Bridgwater, England**, then turned to besiege Bristol, held by Prince Rupert. After preliminary bombardment and failed negotiations, Fairfax took the city by storm and Rupert withdrew to Bristol Castle. When the Prince surrendered, the King had him dismissed and exiled (21 August–11 September 1645).

Britain ∎ 1940 ∎ World War II (Western Europe)
When **France** fell, Marshal Herman Goering resolved to destroy the Royal Air Force before Hitler's planned invasion and was met by Air Vice Marshal Hugh Dowding's Fighter Command. The Battle of Britain over southern England saw perhaps 900 British and 1,600 German planes lost before the invasion was called off. Goering then turned to night bombing of cities (10 July–31 October 1940).

Brody ∎ 1916 ∎ World War I (Eastern Front)
In the second phase of the **Brusilov Offensive**, Russian General Platon Lechitsky swung north from **Czernowitz** and joined Vladimir Sakharov northeast of Lemberg (Lvov). Heavy fighting around Brody saw General Eduard Böhm-Ermolli forced back to the Zlota Lipa, where the Russian offensive petered out around **Brzezany** and also further north in front of **Kovel** (16–28 July 1916).

Brody ∎ 1917 ∎ World War I (Eastern Front)
See **Brzezany**

Brody ∎ 1944 ∎ World War II (Eastern Front)
See **Lvov**

Brody-Dubno ∎ 1941 ∎ World War II (Eastern Front)

Marshal Gerd von Rundstedt was driving deep into the Ukraine on the southern flank of the German invasion when Russian General Mikhail Kirponos attempted a major counter-attack around Brody. A very large-scale tank action saw General Ewald von Kleist, with air support, break up the delaying forces. Kirponos was forced to fall back on **Kiev**, where he was later killed (25–29 June 1941).

Broken Staves ∎ 1743 ∎ War of the Austrian Succession
 See **Dettingen**

Bronkhorstspruit ∎ 1880 ∎ 1st Anglo-Boer War

When Britain annexed the Transvaal in 1877, Boers under Paul Kruger rose in revolt, and the 94th British Regiment under Colonel Philip Anstruther was sent to march on Pretoria. Ambushed 38 miles east at Bronkhorstspruit by Boer commander Frans Joubert, the column lost 57 killed and 100 wounded out of 264 and the mortally wounded Anstruther surrendered (20 December 1880).

Bronnicy ∎ 1614 ∎ Russo-Swedish Wars
 See **Bronnitsa**

Bronnitsa ∎ 1614 ∎ Russo-Swedish Wars

Determined to secure Novgorod, Tsar Michael sent Dimitri Trubetskoi, who captured Gdov and Tichvin, then was intercepted and besieged east of Novgorod at Bronnitsa by Swedes under Jakob de la Gardie. The defeated Russians withdrew after a confused defence and the Swedes besieged **Gdov**. Novgorod was ceded to Russia by treaty after the siege of **Pskov** in 1616 (July 1614).

Bron yr Erw ∎ 1075 ∎ Welsh Dynastic War

Fighting off usurpers following the death of his father Cynan, Gruffydd of Gwynnedd (North Wales) was heavily defeated by Trahaiarn ap Caradog at Bron yr Erw (modern Bron-y-aur near Dolgellau) and was driven into exile with the Danes of Ireland. In 1081 he returned to kill Trahaiarn in battle at **Mynydd Carn** and thus regain the throne.

Broodseinde ∎ 1917 ∎ World War I (Western Front)

In his third successive attack from **Ypres** against General Friedrich von Arnim, General Sir Herbert Plumer followed success on the **Menin Road** and at **Polygon Wood** with an advance north on Broodseinde. Despite German use of mustard gas, British troops seized the town to effectively secure the key ridges east of Ypres and open the way north to **Passchendaele** (4 October 1917).

Brooklyn ∎ 1776 ∎ War of the American Revolution
 See **Long Island**

Broomhouse ∎ 1513 ∎ Anglo-Scottish Royal Wars

James IV of Scotland resolved to avenge defeat off the **Goodwin Sands** and sent Alexander Lord Home raiding across the border. But while returning, Lord Alexander was ambushed by English cavalry at Broomhouse, near Alnwick, suffering about 500 dead and 400 prisoners, including his brother Sir George Home. A full Scottish invasion led to disaster a month later at **Flodden** (13 August 1513).

Brown's Ferry ∎ 1863 ∎ American Civil War (Western Theatre)
 See **Wauhatchie Station**

Brownstown ∎ 1812 ∎ War of 1812

Attempting to escort supplies to **Detroit** on Lake St Clair, Ohio militia under Major Thomas van Horne were attacked on the American side of the Detroit River at Brownstown by British Captain Adam Muir and Indians led by Tecumseh. The Americans were dispersed, losing vital military mail, and a further escort was defeated four days later at **Magagua** (5 August 1812).

Bruderholz | 1499 | Swabian War

In their final struggle for freedom, the Swiss cantons marched against the Habsburg cities of the Swabian League and advanced to the Upper Rhine. A month after victory at **Hard**, a small force met over 3,000 infantry and knights who had invaded from Alsace and, at Bruderholz, south of Basle, defeated the Germans. In April the Swiss secured further victory at **Schwaderloch** (22 March 1499).

Bruges | 1302 | Franco-Flemish Wars

The Flemish rising against France—crushed at **Furnes**—was renewed five years later when weaver Peter de Conync roused the people of Bruges to massacre the French garrison. In a reprise of the more famous "Sicilian Vespers" 20 years earlier, over 3,000 soldiers were killed during the so-called Matins of Bruges. The Flemish artisan army went on to victory in July at **Courtrai** (19 May 1302).

Bruges | 1382 | Hundred Years War

Renewing popular rebellion against Louis II Count of Flanders, workers and tradesmen in Bruges armed themselves against Royalist forces. Led by Philip van Arteveldt—whose father led a similar rising 80 years before—the Flemish popular army defeated the French Count's forces and seized Bruges. However, they were destroyed six months later at **Roosebeke** (3 May 1382).

Brunanburh | 937 | Viking Wars in Britain

Aethelstan of Wessex attempted to recover Viking Northumbria, provoking a massive counter-attack up the Humber by the Dane Olaf Guthfrithson of Dublin, Constantine II of the Scots and his father-in-law Owain of Strathclyde. At Brunanburh, an uncertain site in the Midlands, Aethelstan inflicted a terrible defeat, breaking up the alliance, and assumed the title King of England.

Brunei | 1962 | Brunei Rebellion

In a failed coup against the Sultan of Brunei, Indonesian-backed rebels loyal to Sheik Azahari, led by Yassin Affendi, attacked Brunei Town (modern Bandar Seri Begauan). British Gurkhas airlifted from Singapore under Major Tony Lloyd-Williams retook the capital after a sharp action, with 24 rebels killed. Fighting then moved southwest to **Seria** and east to **Limbang** (8–9 December 1962).

Brunei Bay | 1945 | World War II (Pacific)

Australian General George Wootten captured **Tarakan**, off northeast **Borneo** (14 June), then landed at Labuan Island and Brunei Bay in the northwest. Brunei Town fell in three days, but there was severe fighting and further landings before Wootten secured Beaufort and Kuala Belait in Brunei. The Australians lost 114 killed and Japanese General Masao Baba about 1,200 (10–24 June 1945).

Brunete | 1937 | Spanish Civil War

With the Nationalists checked around Madrid at **Corunna Road, Jarama** and **Guadalajara**, Republican Generals Juan Modesto and Enrique Jurado led a large counter-offensive west towards Brunete. After initial success, the Republicans were driven back by General José Varela with massive losses in men, tanks and aircraft. Another offensive was later contained at **Teruel** (6–26 July 1937).

Bruneval | 1942 | World War II (Western Europe)

One of the most famous British commando raids on occupied Europe saw 200 airborne Special Forces attack the German radar station at Bruneval, near Le Mans in Normandy, which was taken after sharp fighting at the cost of three killed and seven wounded. The parachutists seized vital parts of the Würzburg fighter-control radar, which were taken for examination by scientists (27–28 February 1942).

Brunkeberg | 1471 | Wars of the Kalmar Union

Campaigning against Danish influence in Sweden, the nobleman Sten Sture marched against Christian I of Denmark, who was besieging Stockholm with about 5,000 mainly Scottish and German mercenaries. In decisive action at nearby Brunkeberg—joined from Stockholm by Knut Posse—the King was defeated and fled. Sture ruled as Chancellor until defeat at **Rotebro** in 1497 (10 October 1471).

Brusa I 1317–1326 I Byzantine-Ottoman Wars

Osman I expanded his power south of the Sea of Marmara, where he besieged Byzantine Brusa, near Mount Olympus. Osman's son Orkhan Gazi led the final assault after a nine-year siege and carried news of Brusa's fall to his dying father. Orkhan defeated a Greek counter-offensive at **Pelacanon** and the city of Brusa became Ottoman capital until the fall of **Adrianople** in 1362 (1317–6 April 1326).

Brusa I 1922 I 2nd Greco-Turkish War
See **Bursa**

Brushy Creek I 1839 I Comanche Indian Wars

During a broad offensive against Comanches in Williamson County, Texas, Captain Jacob Burleson and a small force attacked the Indians on Brushy Creek, near modern Taylor. Burleson was killed in a frontal attack before his outnumbered unit was rescued by his brother Edward. General Burleson then pursued the Comanche and drove them off with heavy losses (25 February 1839).

Brusilov Offensive I 1916 I World War I (Eastern Front)

Despite losses at **Lake Naroch**, Russian General Aleksei Brusilov led a stunning offensive to capture **Lutsk** and **Czernowitz**, then renewed his offensive towards **Baranovitchi** and **Brody**, and across the **Styr** and **Stochod**. German reinforcements finally checked the "Russian steamroller" around **Kovel** and **Brzezany** until the new **Kerensky Offensive** (4 June–20 September 1916).

Brussels I 1914 I World War I (Western Front)
See **Tirlement**

Brusthem I 1467 I Franco-Burgundian Wars

Encouraged by Louis XI of France following the death of Philip Duke of Burgundy, the people of Liège renewed their revolt against Burgundy, defeated in 1465 at **Montenaeken**. In battle at Brusthem, near St Trond, they were routed by the new Duke, Charles the Bold, fresh from his sack of the city of **Dinant**. The following year Charles stormed and destroyed **Liège** itself (28 October 1467).

Bryansk I 1941 I World War II (Eastern Front)

Soon after the fall of **Kiev**, Panzer General Heinz Guderian resumed the offensive southwest of Moscow, where he took Orel, then encircled three Soviet armies near Bryansk. The Bryansk Pocket was crushed, and, with the **Vyazma** Pocket further north, yielded 630,000 prisoners, 1,200 tanks and 5,400 guns. The Russians later counter-attacked west from **Moscow** (30 September–20 October 1941).

Bryan's Station I 1782 I War of the American Revolution
See **Blue Licks**

Bryn Derwyn I 1255 I War of Welsh Succession

The years of instability following the death of Welsh leader Llewellyn the Great in 1240 ended with a decisive battle between his grandsons David and Owain the Red on one side and Llewellyn ap Griffith. At Bryn Derwyn, near Caernarvon, Llewellyn defeated his brothers and led the last flowering of Welsh power. His eventual defeat at **Aber Edw** in 1282 saw the end of Welsh independence.

Brzezany I 1916 I World War I (Eastern Front)

As Russian forces advanced around **Brody** in July, Austrian General Felix von Bothmer fell back and attempted to hold the Zlota Lipa near Brzezany, southeast of Lemberg (Lvov). Russian General Dimitri Shcherbachov seized nearby heights, but was eventually repulsed by an Austrian counter-attack, effectively ending the **Brusilov Offensive** (29 August–4 September 1916).

Brzezany ∎ 1917 ∎ World War I (Eastern Front)

At the start of the **Kerensky Offensive**, Russian commander Aleksei Brusilov launched his main attack through Brody and advanced on Lemberg (Lvov) against General Felix von Bothmer's Austro-German army. After very heavy fighting further south near Brzezany, German reinforcements counter-attacked through **Tarnopol** and Russia's last offensive was utterly crushed (1–6 July 1917).

Bubiyan ∎ 1991 ∎ 1st Gulf War

When Iraqi missile boats and amphibious ships left naval bases at az-Zubayr and Umm Qasr, possibly to support Iraq's offensive towards **Khafji**, they were attacked off Bubiyan Island by US, British and Saudi jets and helicopters. Within days, Iraq's navy in the Gulf was effectively destroyed and only two badly damaged vessels reached safety in Iranian waters (29 January–2 February 1991).

Bucharest ∎ 1771 ∎ Catherine the Great's 1st Turkish War

Following success against the Turks on the **Pruth**, a northern tributary of the Danube (September 1770), Russian General Pyotr Rumyantsev launched a spring offensive west towards Bucharest, held by Turkish General Mousson Oglon. The city fell to Rumyantsev's troops after a sharp defence and was turned over to them for rape and destruction as the Turks fled south across the Danube.

Bucharest ∎ 1916 ∎ World War I (Balkan Front)

See **Arges**

Buck Head Creek ∎ 1864 ∎ American Civil War (Western Theatre)

Union commander William T. Sherman advanced through Georgia from Atlanta to **Savannah**, and General H. Judson Kilpatrick marched northeast against Confederate General Joseph Wheeler in the area around Waynesborough. Surprised at Buck Head Creek, Kilpatrick recovered to repulse Wheeler, and days later defeated him at nearby **Waynesborough** itself (28 November 1864).

Buckland Mills ∎ 1863 ∎ American Civil War (Eastern Theatre)

As Confederate commander Robert E. Lee withdrew through Virginia after defeat at **Bristoe Station** near Manassas, General James "Jeb" Stuart turned to meet a flank attack by cavalry from General George B. Meade's army under General H. Judson Kilpatrick. At Buckland Mills, Kilpatrick was routed, though Lee himself was defeated the next month at **Rappahannock Station** (19 October 1863).

Bucov ∎ 1600 ∎ Balkan National Wars

After Prince Michael of Wallachia lost Transylvania at **Mirischlau** (18 September), the Poles restored Jeremiah Movila in Moldavia (seized by Michael after **Khotin**), then entered Wallachia. Polish Chancellor Jan Zamoyski defeated Michael at Bucov, on the Teleajan near Ploesti, and Simeon Movila was put on the throne of Wallachia. Michael was defeated the next year at **Goraslau** (20 October 1600).

Buda ∎ 1529 ∎ Turkish-Habsburg Wars

When Habsburg forces recovered Hungary after victory at **Mohacs**, Ottoman Sultan Suleiman I led a fresh invasion to support his vassal John Zapolya, who had been defeated at **Tokay**. Together they laid siege to regain Buda, defended by Imperial General Támas Nádasdy. The garrison capitulated on terms of safe passage but was massacred, and Suleiman marched on to **Vienna** (3–8 September 1529).

Buda ∎ 1540 ∎ Turkish-Habsburg Wars

Following the death of John Zapolya of Hungary (July 1540), Ferdinand I of Austria soon made an attempt to recover Buda from nationalist supporters of the former King's infant son John Sigismund, led by Bishop Martinuzzi (Friar George Utiesenic). The ill-prepared

Habsburg army of General Lenart Fels was driven off and Martinuzzi sought Ottoman aid against the Emperor (October 1540).

Buda **|** 1541 **|** Turkish-Habsburg Wars

In a fresh attempt to recover Buda following the death of John Zapolya of Hungary, Ferdinand I of Austria sent Marshal Wilhelm Roggendorf against anti-Habsburg supporters of the infant John Sigismund, led by Bishop Martinuzzi (Friar George Utiesenic). Ottoman Sultan Suleiman I arrived to help defeat Roggendorf, then seized much of Hungary as a vassal state for his empire.

Buda **|** 1686 **|** Later Turkish-Habsburg Wars

Invading Turkish Hungary after victory at **Vienna** (1683), Charles V of Lorraine and Louis of Baden were heavily repulsed at Buda (1684) but in a second siege drove off a relief army under Grand Vizier Kara Ibrahim. They retook the city after 78 days, slaughtering most of the garrison including the heroic commander Abdi Pasha, ending almost 150 years of Turkish rule (17 June–2 September 1686).

Buda **|** 1849 **|** Hungarian Revolutionary War

Weeks after victory northwest of Budapest at **Nagy Sallo**, Hungarian Nationalist commander Artur Gorgey returned to the capital to besiege 4,000 Imperial troops under General Heinrich von Hentzi, holding out in the old fortress on the Danube at Buda. After several costly assaults, the fortress was taken by storm with heavy Austrian losses, including Hentzi mortally wounded (4–21 May 1849).

Budapest **|** 1919 **|** Hungarian-Romanian War

On a fresh offensive into Hungary, the Romanian army crossed the **Tisza** in July, then advanced on Budapest. Facing white counter-revolution, Hungary's Red Army declined to fight and Dictator Béla Kun fled to Vienna (he was later executed in a Stalinist Purge). Romanian forces captured Budapest to overthrow the

Soviet Republic and pillaged the capital before withdrawing (4 August 1919).

Budapest **|** 1921 **|** Hungarian Civil War

Former Austrian Emperor and King of Hungary Charles attempted to reclaim Hungary from Regent Miklos Horthy and advanced on Budapest. In the suburbs at Buda-Ors, Royalist Colonel Gyula Ostenburg was attacked and repulsed by Captain Gyula Gombos (later Prime Minister). Charles was arrested and exiled in Madeira, ending Habsburg claims on Hungary (23 October 1921).

Budapest **|** 1944–1945 **|** World War II (Eastern Front)

Soviet Marshals Rodion Malinovsky and Fedor Tolbukhin drove north from the **Balkans** and advanced on Budapest against strong resistance. Pest fell (18 January) with 35,000 Germans killed and 62,000 captured, and Buda a month later with 30,000 captured. A final breakout was crushed and SS General Karl von Pfeffer-Wildenbruch surrendered (26 December 1944–13 February 1945).

Bud Bagsak **|** 1913 **|** American-Moro Wars

Attempting to disarm the Muslim Moros of the southern Philippines, Colonel John Pershing attacked rebels on Jolo, who fortified the crater of the extinct volcano Bud Bagsak, near Bun Bun. Artillery bombardment and bayonet charges killed over 500 Moros, including their leader Amil and many women and children. Within months, resistance was crushed at **Mount Talipao** (11–15 June 1913).

Bud Dajo **|** 1906 **|** American-Moro Wars

Two years after Muslim Moros were routed at **Pangpang**, on Jolo in the southern Philippines, about 600 rebels took refuge in the crater of the extinct volcano of Bud Dajo. Attacked by Colonel Joseph Duncan, the ill-armed men, women and children were slaughtered, provoking public outrage in America. A similar massacre followed seven years later at **Bud Bagsak** (5–6 March 1906).

Budhayan I 1858 I Indian Mutiny

Campaigning in Oudh, General Thomas Franks seized **Chanda, Uttar Pradesh**, southeast of Sultanpur, when rebel leader Mehndi Husain arrived too late to save his key base. Later that day, Husain tried to block Franks at Hamirpur, near the fortress at Budhayan, but was heavily defeated and fled. Budhayan was occupied two days later, with Husain subsequently defeated again at **Badshahganj** (19 February 1858).

Budlee-ke-Serai I 1857 I Indian Mutiny
See **Badli-ki-Serai**

Budweis I 1742 I War of the Austrian Succession
See **Sahay**

Buenavista, Colombia I 1840 I Colombian War of Supreme Commanders
See **Culebrera**

Buenavista, Mexico I 1847 I American-Mexican War

American General Zachary Taylor faced a counter-offensive in northern Mexico, where he chose to defend the mountain pass at Angostura, south of Saltillo near Buenavista, against Mexican General Antonio de Santa Anna. Taylor eventually won a difficult victory after a complex two-day action and Santa Anna fled to Mexico City with 500 killed and 1,000 wounded (22–23 February 1847).

Buenos Aires I 1806 I Napoleonic Wars (4th Coalition)

When Britain received exaggerated reports of local dissatisfaction with Spanish rule in Argentina, an expedition under Admiral Sir Home Popham and General William Beresford took Buenos Aires by surprise with just 1,200 men. However, after Popham left, a local force under French General Jacques Liniers Bremont retook the city (12 August) and captured Beresford (27 June 1806).

Buenos Aires I 1807 I Napoleonic Wars (4th Coalition)

After British forces seized **Montevideo** in February, command passed to Sir John Whitelock, who led an ill-prepared expedition to recapture Spanish-held Buenos Aires, defended by French General Jacques Liniers Bremont. Following heavy losses, Whitelock surrendered, agreeing to evacuate not only Buenos Aires but also Montevideo. He was later court-martialled and cashiered (2–5 July 1807).

Buenza I 1813 I Napoleonic Wars (Peninsular Campaign)

Despite winning at **Lizasso**, French General Jean Baptiste d'Erlon had to retreat from the "Battles of the Pyrenees," and later the same day, General Sir Rowland Hill met his rearguard under General Louis Abbé in the Ulzema Valley near Buenza. Fighting along the ridge at Venta de Urroz, Hill's outnumbered force was driven off, opening d'Erlon's route to **Dona Maria** (30 July 1813).

Buerat I 1943 I World War II (Northern Africa)

British General Sir Bernard Montgomery pursued Field Marshal Erwin Rommel across Libya from **El Alamein** and broke the defensive line at **El Agheila**, then advanced on a strong rearguard at Buerta. In two days' fighting, the British outflanked the Axis position, then raced to occupy the capital Tripoli before entering Tunisia to defeat the Axis at **Médenine** and **Mareth Line** (15–16 January 1943).

Buesaco I 1839 I Colombian Civil Wars

When rebellion arose in southwest Colombia against the closing of four minor convents near Pasto, the government sent a force under General Pedro Alcántara Herrán, who met and defeated the rebels northeast of Pasto at Buesaco. Herrán eventually negotiated an armistice, but rebellion was renewed a year later as part of the War of the Supreme Commanders (31 August 1839).

Buesaco I 1851 I Colombian Civil Wars

Facing Conservative rebellion in southern Colombia, President José Hilario López sent

General Manuel María Franco against General Julio Arboleda, who had established a junta in Popayán. Northeast of Pasto at Buesaco, Arboleda was defeated and, in September, the government won again in the north at **Rionegro**. Arboleda fled into exile but returned ten years later as President (10 July 1851).

Buffalo ∎ 1813 ∎ War of 1812
On a large-scale raid across the Niagara River under General Sir Phineas Riall, 1,000 British regulars and militia and 400 Indians attacked the American city of Buffalo, defended by General Amos Hall. A spirited defence cost over 100 British casualties before Hall was forced to withdraw. Riall looted and torched Buffalo and also burned nearby Black Rock (30 December 1813).

Buffalo ∎ 1967 ∎ Vietnam War
See **Con Thien (1st)**

Buffalo Mountain ∎ 1861 ∎ American Civil War (Eastern Theatre)
See **Camp Allegheny**

Buffalo Wallow ∎ 1874 ∎ Red River Indian War
Sent to locate **Lyman's Wagon Train**, bringing supplies to Colonel A. Nelson in western Oklahoma, scouts Billy Dixon and Amos Chapman and four soldiers were surrounded by over 100 Kiowa in a shallow Buffalo Wallow near the Washita. After repulsing the Indians all day, they were relieved by Major William R. Price. The incident grew greatly in legend (12 September 1874).

Buffington Island ∎ 1863 ∎ American Civil War (Western Theatre)
On a raid into Kentucky and Ohio, Confederate General John H. Morgan captured **Corydon**, but was pursued by General Edward H. Hobson and attempted to cross the Ohio into West Virginia at Portland. Attacking at nearby Buffington Island, Union Generals Augustus V. Kautz and Henry M. Judah took about 500

prisoners. Morgan escaped north through **Salineville** (19 July 1863).

Bug ∎ 1018 ∎ Russian Dynastic Wars
Driven from the Kievan throne by his stepbrother Yaroslav after defeat at **Liubech** in 1016, Russian Prince Sviatopolk fled to his father-in-law Boleslaw of Poland, who led a large Polish army to help him regain the throne. Yaroslav was defeated in battle on the Bug, north of Lvov, and withdrew to Novgorod, while Sviatopolk secured Kiev. Yaroslav soon counter-attacked at the **Alta** (August 1018).

Builth ∎ 1282 ∎ English Conquest of Wales
See **Aber Edw**

Bukairiya ∎ 1904 ∎ Saudi-Rashidi Wars
Following bloody battle at **Unayzah** in June, the Rashid and their Turkish allies were routed in actions around Bukairiya by Emir Abd al-Aziz (Ibn Saud) of Riyadh. When the Turks abandoned the Rashid, Abd al-Aziz submitted to the Ottoman Sultan, who recognised him as ruler of the Nejd. He killed the Rashidi leader two years later at **Rawdhat al Muhanna** (August–September 1904).

Bukittingi ∎ 1958 ∎ Indonesian Civil Wars
Concerned by growing Javanese influence in government, dissident Indonesian politicians and army officers declared a rebel authority in Sumatra under Sjafruddin Prawiranegara. Following naval bombardment, government Colonel Ahmad Yanu landed at Padang (17 April) and advanced 45 miles north to take Bukittingi, the rebel capital, which was then moved to **Manado** in Sulawesi (5 May 1958).

Bukowa ∎ 1600 ∎ Balkan National Wars
See **Bucov**

Bulandshahr ∎ 1857 ∎ Indian Mutiny
Colonel Edward Greathed marched from **Delhi** towards besieged **Agra**, advancing through Sikandarabad to Bulandshahr, where Walidad Khan took a strong defensive position. Having endured heavy gunfire, the rebels were taken in

the rear by cavalry and fled, abandoning nearby Malaghur. Greathed destroyed its fortifications, then advanced on **Aligarh** (28 September 1857).

Bulawayo I 1893 I Matabele War
See **Bembesi**

Buleleng I 1846 I Dutch Conquest of Bali
See **Singaraja**

Bulge I 1944–1945 I World War II (Western Europe)
See **Ardennes**

Bulgnéville I 1431 I Hundred Years War
On the death of Charles of Lorraine, his son-in-law René of Anjou claimed the dukedom, but he was defeated and captured in battle at Bulgnéville by Antoine de Vaudement, nephew of Charles and an ally of Phillip of Burgundy. After his eventual release, René was defeated pursuing his claim to **Naples**. Burgundy was not finally repulsed from Lorraine until 1477 at **Nancy** (30 June 1431).

Bulla Regia I 533 I Vandal War in Africa
See **Tricameron**

Bull Run I 1861 I American Civil War (Eastern Theatre)
Sent to meet the Confederate army concentrating near Manassas to threaten Washington, D.C., General Irvin McDowell led about 30,000 men against Generals Joseph E. Johnston and Pierre G. T. Beauregard. McDowell lost perhaps 3,000 men in a bloody battle on the Bull Run and fled east towards the capital. He was quickly replaced by General George B. McClellan (21 July 1861).

Bull Run I 1862 I American Civil War (Eastern Theatre)
In the decisive battle of his northern Virginia offensive, Confederate commander Robert E. Lee, with Generals Thomas "Stonewall" Jackson and James Longstreet, smashed into General John Pope's Union army at Bull Run. After initial success, Pope was destroyed by a massive counter-attack. He fled towards Washington, D.C., via **Chantilly** and was relieved of command (29–30 August 1862).

Bull Run Bridge I 1862 I American Civil War (Eastern Theatre)
See **Kettle Run**

Bull's Gap I 1864 I American Civil War (Western Theatre)
General John C. Breckinridge led a Confederate expedition into eastern Tennessee, where he attacked Union General Alvan C. Gillem at Bull's Gap, just northeast of Morristown. Continuous assaults and a threat in the rear by General John C. Vaughan forced Gillem to withdraw. Terrible winter weather later made Breckinridge retire into Virginia (11–13 November 1864).

Buluan I 1905 I American-Moro Wars
See **Malala**

Bu Meliana I 1911 I Italo-Turkish Wars
See **Sidi Mesri**

Buna I 1942–1943 I World War II (Pacific)
Having driven the Japanese back to the north coast of **Papua**, Australian General George Vasey took **Gona**, then joined American General Robert Eichelberger against nearby Buna. After costly attacks, more tanks and artillery arrived and the well-defended village fell, with heavy losses on both sides. Attention then turned to **Sanananda** (19 November 1942–2 January 1943).

Bundelkhand I 800 I Later Indian Dynastic Wars
Govinda III of Rashtrakuta consolidated power in southern India, then took an expedition north against Nagabhata II of Pratihara, who had just won a decisive battle at **Monghyr**. At an uncertain site in Bundelkhand, Govinda crushed Nagabhata, who fled to Rajputana, his dreams of empire shattered. The rulers of Pala and Kanauj submitted to Govinda before he returned south (disputed date c 800).

Bunker Hill I 1775 I War of the American Revolution

When American Colonel William Prescott was sent to secure Bunker Hill, overlooking Boston harbour, he dug in instead on nearby Breed's Hill and was counter-attacked from besieged **Boston** by British General William Howe. Howe was reinforced by General Henry Clinton after two costly assaults and the Americans were driven off, but only after heavy British losses (17 June 1775).

Burdwan I 1747 I Later Mughal-Maratha Wars

When Marathas under Janoji Bhonsle invaded Orissa, Governor Mir Ja'far retreated before being reinforced to check the Marathas at Burdwan, northwest of Calcutta. Mughal Nawab Ali Vardi Khan dismissed Mir Ja'far and, with a much larger force, heavily defeated Janoji at Burdwan. However, four more years of war finally persuaded the Emperor to cede Orissa to the Marathas (January 1747).

Burford I 752 I Anglo-Saxon Territorial Wars

In an attempt to throw off the overlordship of Mercia, King Cuthred of Wessex defeated Aethelbald of Mercia at Burford, in Oxfordshire. The victory was due in part to the valour of the West Saxon Aethelhun the Proud, who is claimed to have defeated Aethelbald in single combat. Aethelbald fled and the independence of Wessex was secured.

Burgidiah I 1858 I Indian Mutiny

Pursuing Nana Sahib across the Gaghara, British commander Sir Colin Campbell and General Sir William Mansfield advanced through Bahraich and Napara towards the village of Burgidiah, held by about 4,000 men. Opening artillery fire at long range, Campbell sent his cavalry on a flanking movement and the rebels fled for the nearby fortress at **Musjidiah** (26 December 1858).

Burgos I 1589 I Anglo-Spanish Wars

A year after destruction of the **Spanish Armada**, English General Sir John Norris invaded northern Spain and burned part of Corunna. Marching east, he was eventually attacked by Rodrigo Conde de Altamira near Burgos, on the Arlanzon. Norris drove off the attack but withdrew and, after an abortive landing near Lisbon in Spanish-held Portugal, he returned to England with nothing achieved.

Burgos I 1808 I Napoleonic Wars (Peninsular Campaign)

See **Gamonal**

Burgos I 1812 I Napoleonic Wars (Peninsular Campaign)

Arthur Wellesley Lord Wellington advanced north from Madrid and attacked Burgos on the Arlanzon, defended by French General Jean Dubretonand. The outer defences quickly fell, but after a month of unsuccessful bombardment and costly assaults, a relief army under General Joseph Souham appeared and Wellington withdrew towards Portugal (19 September–21 October 1812).

Burkersdorf I 1762 I Seven Years War (Europe)

With Russia out of the war, Frederick II of Prussia turned against Austrian Marshal Leopold von Daun in Silesia. At Burkersdorf, southwest of Breslau—in a battle of manoeuvre with few casualties—the Austrians were driven from the field, helping secure Frederick's hold on Silesia when the war ended a few months later after further victories at **Reichenbach** and **Freiberg** (21 July 1762).

Burkersdorf I 1866 I Seven Weeks War

See **Soor**

Burlington Heights I 1813 I War of 1812

See **Dudley's Defeat**

Burma I 1942 I World War II (Burma-India)

As Japanese forces invaded Burma through **Kawkareik**, **Moulmein** and **Kuzeik**, the British began their longest retreat, across the **Bilin** and **Sittang** Rivers and through **Pegu** to Rangoon, which was abandoned on 7 March. They then withdrew north through **Prome**, **Yenangyaung** and **Shwegyin** to India, while the Chinese fell back through **Toungoo** and **Lashio** (20 January–11 May 1942).

Burmi I 1903 I British Conquest of Northern Nigeria

With his capital at **Sokoto** destroyed in March, Sultan Attahiru withdrew north to Burmi, near Gombe, and later came under attack by 30 officers and 500 Africans of the Royal West African Frontier Force. Very heavy fighting saw commander Major Francis Marsh killed, but the Sultan and hundreds of his followers fell. With them died the once great Fulani Empire of northern Nigeria (27 July 1903).

Burnham I 848 I Viking Raids on Britain

Five years after a second Saxon defeat at **Carhampton** in West Somerset, Ealdorman Earnwulf of Somerset and Ealdorman Osric of Dorset fought a Danish force about 20 miles further east at the mouth of the River Parrett near modern Burnham. The Vikings were driven off with heavy losses, but they continued to raid the southwestern coast of England.

Burnshill I 1846 I 7th Cape Frontier War

Determined to capture the Xhosa Chief Sandile, threatening Cape Colony, Colonel Henry Somerset led a large force towards the Amatolas, only to find Sandile's "Great Place" abandoned. The Xhosa meantime attacked Somerset's camp at nearby Burnshill, largely destroying his cumbersome supply train. The humiliated British had to retreat back across the Keiskamma (16–17 April 1846).

Burnt Corn I 1813 I Creek Indian War

With Creek Indians threatening to take advantage of America's war with Britain, 180 Mississippi militia under Colonel James Caller attacked Chief Jim Boy at Burnt Corn Creek, Escambia County, Alabama. The Indians lost trade goods and about ten killed, but drove the Americans from the field. While only a skirmish, it led directly to the Indian attack on **Fort Mims** in August (27 July 1813).

Bursa I 1317–1326 I Byzantine-Ottoman Wars

See **Brusa**

Bursa I 1922 I 2nd Greco-Turkish War

Determined to drive the Greek invaders out of Anatolia, Turkish commander Mustafa Kemal won at **Afyon** (30 August), then detached a large force north to recover Bursa (previously Brusa), which had fallen during the initial Greek offensive in July 1919. Heavy fighting saw the city near the Sea of Marmara fall to the Turks, who then rejoined the pursuit west towards **Smyrna** (5 September 1922).

Burtinah I 1839 I Russian Conquest of the Caucasus

Russian Baron Pavel Grabbe marched into Dagestan, west of the Caspian, where he was met on the Aghdash River at Burtinah by Imam Shamil of Dagestan. Although threatened by a flank attack, Grabbe immediately fell on the Muslims and inflicted a heavy defeat. He was checked a few days later at the village of Irghun, then continued his advance against Shamil at **Akhulgo** (5 June 1839).

Bushire I 1856 I Anglo-Persian War

In response to Persia's capture of **Herat** in Afghanistan in October, British Colonel Foster Stalker captured **Reshire** in the Persian Gulf, then drove the survivors north along the coast towards Bushire (modern Bushehr). Harried by British and Indian troops and shelled by warships, the Persians were heavily defeated next day and the Governor of Bushire surrendered the town (10 December 1856).

Bushy Run I 1763 I Pontiac's War

Advancing from Carlisle, Pennsylvania, to relieve besieged **Fort Pitt** (modern Pittsburgh), Scottish regulars under Swiss-born Colonel

Henry Bouquet were ambushed by Delaware and Shawnee, about 26 miles east near Edge Hill. Despite costly losses the following day at Bushy Run, a bloody bayonet charge secured victory and Fort Pitt was relieved four days later (5–6 August 1763).

Bussaco I 1810 I Napoleonic Wars (Peninsular Campaign)
French Marshals André Masséna and Michel Ney drove across central Portugal after capturing **Almeida** and attacked a strong Anglo-Portuguese position at Bussaco, north of Lisbon, held by Arthur Wellesley Lord Wellington. A bloody engagement saw Masséna driven back with four times the Allied losses, but he circled around Wellington and forced him back to **Torres Vedras** (27 September 1810).

Busta Gallorum I 552 I Gothic War in Italy
See **Taginae**

Buttar Dograndi I 1965 I 2nd Indo-Pakistan War
Following success at **Phillora**, north of Chawinda, Indian forces fatally delayed four days before resuming the offensive further west at Buttar Dograndi. The town changed hands several times, but in the face of heavy Pakistani artillery, the Indians were forced to withdraw with heavy losses, contributing to the subsequent failed final assault on **Chawinda** (16–17 September 1965).

Buttington I 894 I Viking Wars in Britain
Despite Viking defeat at **Farnham** in 893, Danish King Haesten took a large force up the Thames and Severn. But he was driven off and besieged on a Severn island at Buttington by Aethelred of Mercia and the West Saxon Ealdormen, Aethelhelm of Wiltshire and Aethelnoth of Somerset. The starving Danes counter-attacked after weeks of costly hard fighting and broke through to Essex.

Butui I 1865 I War of the Triple Alliance
See **Mbutuy**

Buwayb I 635 I Muslim Conquest of Iraq
Following Arab disaster in battle at the **Bridge** (November 634), Caliph Omar sent more troops to support Muthanna of the Bakr ibn Wail against Sassanian Persians on the Euphrates. The reinforced Arabs defeated the advancing Persian army at Buwayb, near Kufa, killing General Mirhan. However, it was only a tactical victory until fresh Arab forces soon resumed the offensive at **Qadisiyya** (April 635).

Buxar I 1539 I Mughal Conquest of Northern India
See **Chausa**

Buxar I 1764 I Bengal War
Mir Kassim, deposed Nawab of Bengal, secured an alliance with Mughal Emperor Shah Alam and Shuja-ud-Daula, Nawab of Oudh, against Britain's East India Company. Following British victory at **Patna** (3 May), a greatly outnumbered force under Major Hector Munro crushed the Indian allies at Buxar, west of Patna. The Emperor submitted next day and Britain secured Bengal (23 October 1764).

Buzakha I 632 I Muslim Civil Wars
After establishing his authority in Medina following the death of the Prophet Mohammed, the new Caliph Abu Bekr sent the warrior Khalid ibn al-Walid east through the Nejeb to spread the message. At Buzakha, Tulaiha of the powerful Beni Asad was routed when abandoned by his ally, the Ghatafan leader Uyaina. Tulaiha and the neighbouring tribes quickly rallied to Islam (September 632).

Buzancy I 1870 I Franco-Prussian War
As French Marshal Marie MacMahon manoeuvred west of the Meuse, elements of his cavalry encountered the advance guard of a Saxon cavalry division under General Friedrich Senfft von Pilsach at Buzancy, on the road west from Stenay to Vouziers. The French were dispersed after a costly action and MacMahon turned north through **Beaumont** and **Bazeilles** towards **Sedan** (27 August 1870).

Buzenval I 1871 I Franco-Prussian War
  See **Mont Valerian**

Byczyna I 1588 I Habsburg-Polish War
  When Stephen Bathory of Poland died, Habsburg Duke Maximilian (brother of Emperor Rudolf II) invaded to claim the crown, but was repulsed at Cracow by Jan Zamoyski, who brilliantly defended the city. The following year at Byczyna, east of Wroclaw, Maximilian was defeated by Zamoyski and was held prisoner until Austria abandoned its claim on Poland (24 January 1588).

Bydgoszcz I 1794 I War of the 2nd Polish Partition
  During the long siege of **Warsaw** by King Frederick William III of Prussia, Polish General Jan Henryk Dabrowski took a force from the capital to support Polish rebels in the western province of Wielkopolska. He defeated the Russians in northwest Poland at Bydgoszcz (Bromberg), then marched into Prussian Poznania to threaten Frederick's communications (July 1794).

Byland I 1322 I Rise of Robert the Bruce
  Edward II of England was preparing for yet another invasion of Scotland when he was surprised at Byland, near Newburgh in North Yorkshire, by Robert the Bruce, who routed the English and drove them back towards York. Edward only narrowly escaped capture and sought a truce which eventually led to formal recognition of Bruce as King of independent Scotland (14 October 1322).

Byram's Ford I 1864 I American Civil War (Trans-Mississippi)
  See **Big Blue River**

Bytham I 1221 I 1st English Barons' War
  Despite the end of the Barons' rebellion after **Lincoln** in 1217, the King's Justiciar Hubert de Burgh faced continued opposition by the "Foreign Party" of Earl William of Aumale and Falke de Breaute. De Burgh besieged and defeated Aumale in his castle at Bytham, Lincolnshire, forcing him to acknowledge Henry III, though rebellion flared again three years later at **Bedford** (8 February 1221).

Byzantium I 340 BC I 4th Sacred War
  See **Perinthus**

Byzantium I 193–196 I Wars of Emperor Severus
  When Emperor Septimius Severus marched east against Pescennius Niger, he left Marius Maximus to continue a siege of rebel Byzantium and pursued Niger into Asia. Following Niger's defeat at **Issus**, his severed head was sent to the besieged people of Byzantium as a warning, but resistance continued. When Byzantium fell by storm, public buildings and defences were destroyed as punishment.

Byzantium I 324 I Roman Wars of Succession
  See **Hellespont**

Bzura I 1914 I World War I (Eastern Front)
  See **Warsaw (2nd)**

Bzura I 1939 I World War II (Western Europe)
  As German forces swept deep into **Poland**, General Tadeusz Kutrzeba counter-attacked into the exposed left flank of General Johannes Blaskowitz's Eighth Army. Very heavy fighting west of Warsaw along the Bzura saw initial Polish success, but the Poznan Army was eventually surrounded and forced to surrender. Some survivors broke out to help defend **Warsaw** (9–20 September 1939).

C

Caaguazú ▌ 1841 ▌ Argentine Civil Wars

Having taken Entre Rios after victory at **Sauce Grande** in 1840, Federalist Governor Pascual Echague invaded Corrientes for Dictator Manuel de Rosas. South of Corrientes at Caaguazú, he was brilliantly defeated by Unitarist commander José María Paz. The victory avenged defeat at **Pago Largo** and secured Corrientes against Rosas until defeat in 1847 at **Rincón de Vences** (28 November 1841).

Caaibaté ▌ 1756 ▌ Guarani War

See **Caibaté**

Cabala ▌ 383 bc ▌ 3rd Dionysian War

When Dionysius, Tyrant of Syracuse, renewed his attempts to drive Carthage out of Sicily, Carthaginian leader Mago launched a fresh offensive to secure his Sicilian possessions. At Cabala, in the west near Palermo, the Syracusans achieved an overwhelming victory, and Mago was killed, along with much of his army. However, the Carthaginians were quickly avenged at **Cronium**.

Cabeira ▌ 72 bc ▌ 3rd Mithridatic War

See **Cabira**

Cabezon ▌ 1808 ▌ Napoleonic Wars (Peninsular Campaign)

At the start of Bonaparte's campaign in Spain, Marshal Jean-Baptiste Bessières sent General Antoine Lasalle against Spanish General Gregorio de la Cuesta, defending the bridge at Cabezon on the Pisuerga in the northwest. French cavalry routed the raw infantry and Bessières captured nearby Valladolid before inflicting an even worse defeat on Cuesta at **Medina del Rio Seco** (12 June 1808).

Cabin Creek ▌ 1863 ▌ American Civil War (Trans-Mississippi)

As Union Colonel James M. Williams led a supply train south through Indian Territory towards Fort Gibson, Oklahoma, he was met at Cabin Creek by Texans and American Indians under the Cherokee Colonel Stand Watie. With Confederate General William C. Cabell delayed by flooded rivers, Watie was driven off and the Union took the offensive days later at **Honey Springs** (1–2 July 1863).

Cabira ▌ 72 bc ▌ 3rd Mithridatic War

Roman General Lucius Licinius Lucullus defeated Mithridates VI of Pontus at **Cyzicus** (73 bc), then pursued him east to the Lycus (Kelkit) River in northern Turkey, where Mithridates was routed at Cabira (modern Sivas) and fled to his son-in-law, Tigranes of Armenia. Victory brought a temporary pause until Rome invaded Armenia itself for victory within four years at **Tigranocerta** and **Artaxata**.

Cabo de Gata ▌ 1643 ▌ Thirty Years War (Franco-Habsburg War)

When Spain sent Admiral Martin de Mencos and Flemish commander Josse Pieters with 25 ships to reinforce Cartagena, they were met off Cabo de Gata, near Almeria, by French Admiral Jean-Armande de Maillé-Brézé. After fierce fighting the Spanish flagship sank and others were damaged and driven ashore. The French suffered heavy damage but lost no ships (3 September 1643).

Cabo de Gata | 1815 | Algerine War

The United States was determined to finally defeat the Barbary pirates and declared war, then sent Captain Stephen Decatur, whose flagship *Guerrière* was supported by *Constellation* and *Epervier*. Off Cabo de Gata, the southeastern tip of Spain, Decatur captured the Algerine flagship *Mashuda* and 486 prisoners. The Dey of Algiers sued for peace and Tunis and Tripoli followed suit (17 June 1815).

Cabra | 1079 | Early Christian Reconquest of Spain

Amid the confused alliances of the Spanish War, the Muslim ruler Abd-allah of Granada, supported by Christian knights, marched against his Muslim rival al-Mutamid of Seville, whose army was led by Spaniard Rodrigo Diaz de Bivar—El Cid. Southeast of Cordova at Cabra, El Cid defeated the Granadans and took many prisoners, including the powerful Count Garcia Ordonez.

Cabrillas | 1808 | Napoleonic Wars (Peninsular Campaign)

French Marshal Bon Adrien Moncey was sent to suppress insurrection in Catalonia, where he met a large Spanish force at the Cabrillas in southern Guadalajara, led by Brigadier Marimón serving under General Pedro Adorno. A bold flank assault by General Jean Harispe secured victory, but Moncey was repulsed a few days later outside the walls of **Valencia** and withdrew to Madrid (23 June 1808).

Cabrita Point | 1705 | War of the Spanish Succession

See **Marbella**

Cacabellos | 1809 | Napoleonic Wars (Peninsular Campaign)

As Sir John Moore's British army retreated from **Benavente** towards **Corunna** in northwest

Spain, General Edward Paget made a stand at the bridge over the Coa at Cacabellos, just east of Villafranca. An impetuous attack by French cavalry General Jean-Baptise Colbert was repulsed, with Colbert killed, and Paget withdrew during the night towards Villafranca (3 January 1809).

Cacarajicara | 1896 | 2nd Cuban War of Independence

After taking command in Cuba, Spanish commander Valeriano Weyler sent General Julián Suárez Inclán southwest of Havana against insurgent leader Antonio Maceo. At Cacarajicara, Maceo and a small force attacked the Spanish column and took costly losses until Cuban reinforcements arrived under Colonel Juan E. Ducasse. Suárez Inclán then suffered a decisive defeat (30 April 1896).

Cache River | 1862 | American Civil War (Trans-Mississippi)

See **Hill's Plantation**

Cacheuta | 1817 | Chilean War of Independence

See **Potrerillos**

Cachirí | 1816 | Colombian War of Independence

Spanish Colonel Sebastián Calzada advanced through **Balaga** in Norte de Santander, marching against Patriot General Custodio García Rovira and Colonel Francisco Santander at Cachirí. A two-day action saw heavy losses before a Spanish attack with bayonet and cavalry secured decisive victory. The Patriots withdrew to Socorro and Calzada threatened Bogotá (21–22 February 1816).

Cadesia | 636 | Muslim Conquest of Iraq

See **Qadisiyya**

Cadiz | 1587 | Anglo-Spanish Wars

Sent to cruise off Spain, Sir Francis Drake took about 30 ships into the key port of Cadiz, where he destroyed a large number of Spanish vessels before escaping without loss. On the way home he captured the treasure galleon *St Philip*. Drake claimed to have "singed the King of Spain's beard" and the action reportedly delayed the Spanish **Armada** by up to a year (19 April 1587).

Cadiz I 1596 I Anglo-Spanish Wars

In a large-scale raid, Lord Howard of Effingham attacked Cadiz harbour, supported by Lord Thomas Howard, Robert Devereux Earl of Essex and Dutch Admiral Johan Duivenoorde. The Spanish fleet was destroyed and Essex took a landing force which captured and sacked Cadiz. Essex wanted to march into Andalusia, but the fleet returned home with its massive booty (21–22 June 1596).

Cadiz I 1625 I Anglo-Spanish Wars

Charles I of England resolved to make war on Catholic Spain and sent an ill-equipped fleet of 80 ships to Cadiz under the inexperienced Edward Cecil Lord Wimbledon. While troops under Sir John Burgh captured Fort Puntales, they later got drunk and were heavily repulsed. Wimbledon withdrew and, after the West Indies treasure fleet eluded him, he returned home in disgrace (23–29 October 1625).

Cadiz I 1656 I Anglo-Spanish Wars

English Admiral Richard Stayner intercepted a West Indies treasure fleet off Cadiz, attacking with just six frigates. A brilliant action saw only two Spanish ships escape while Stayner sank or burned two others, drove two ashore and captured two. He was knighted for his success, which yielded 600,000 sterling. He destroyed another fleet a year later at **Santa Cruz de Tenerife** (8 September 1656).

Cadiz I 1702 I War of the Spanish Succession

Leading a large Anglo-Dutch force, Admiral Sir George Rooke and James Butler Duke of Ormonde landed near Cadiz after a heavy bombardment. Although Ormonde captured Rota and Santa Maria, the siege failed and the fleet withdrew. On the return home, Rooke re-deemed himself at **Vigo Bay** and was cleared by a Parliamentary inquiry into the fiasco at Cadiz (15 August–15 September 1702).

Cadiz I 1808 I Napoleonic Wars (Peninsular Campaign)

In the wake of the French attack on Spain at the beginning of the Peninsular Campaign, Spain turned against the French fleet under Admiral Francois Rosily, which had been blockaded at Cadiz since the rout at **Trafalgar** in 1805. Rosily was forced to surrender after the Spanish blocked the harbour entrance and opened fire from shore batteries (14–15 June 1808).

Cadiz I 1810–1812 I Napoleonic Wars (Peninsular Campaign)

With France occupying Andalusia after victory at **Ocaña** in late 1809, Spanish forces withdrew to the fortified port of Cadiz, later reinforced by Anglo-Portuguese under General Thomas Graham. After more than two years tying down much of Marshal Nicolas Soult's available army, the siege was lifted when the French withdrew following defeat at **Salamanca** (5 February 1810–21 August 1812).

Cadiz I 1823 I Franco-Spanish War

See **Trocadera**

Cadore I 1508 I War of the League of Cambrai

As part of the League of Cambrai between Germany, France, Spain and the Papal states, Emperor Maximilian invaded Italy to capture Milan. His army under the Duke of Brunswick was routed in the Cadore by Venetian General Bartolomeo d'Alviano, and the Emperor withdrew across the Alps. He returned to attack **Padua** after the French beat d'Alviano in 1509 at **Agnadello** (2 March 1508).

Cadsand I 1337 I Hundred Years War

In support of a popular rising against Count Louis I of Flanders, led by Jacob van Artevelde of Ghent, Edward III of England sent Sir Walter Manny to raise the blockade by French and

Flemish nobles of the island of Cadsand, near Walcheren. The English expedition was victorious and Edward proclaimed himself King of France, triggering the Hundred Years War (10 November 1337).

Caen I 1346 I Hundred Years War

When French forces invaded Gascony, Edward III of England took a large army against Caen in Normandy, defended by Raoul II de Brienne Comte d'Eu and Jean de Melun Comte de Tancarville. Thomas Beauchamp Earl of Warwick took the city by storm, and Eu and Tancarville were among the 300 prisoners sent to England for ransom. Edward marched on to meet the French at **Crecy** (26 July 1346).

Caen I 1417 I Hundred Years War

During a fresh invasion of France after victory at **Agincourt** in 1415, Henry V of England and his brother Thomas Duke of Clarence marched to besiege Caen. Attacking after heavy bombardment, the King's troops were repulsed, but Clarence succeeded in forcing a breach and the city fell (4 September). The citadel held out for another two weeks before surrendering (14 August–20 September 1417).

Caen I 1450 I Hundred Years War

Following the English rout at **Formigny** in April, the incompetent Edmund Beaufort Duke of Somerset withdrew under siege to Caen. With no hope of relief, Somerset surrendered after three weeks to the huge French army of Count Arthur of Richemont and Count Charles of Clermont. The fall of Caen, followed by Cherbourg, ended English presence in Normandy (1 July 1450).

Caen I 1944 I World War II (Western Europe)

British commander Sir Bernard Montgomery successfully invaded **Normandy**, then faced a heavy counter-attack by German armour, which blocked repeated attempts to advance on Caen. After the costly Operation **Epsom**, a large-scale assault finally took Caen, following massive aerial bombardment. After Operation **Good-wood**, Montgomery stalled until the advance on **Falaise** (6 June–8 July 1944).

Caer Caradoc I 50 I Roman Conquest of Britain

In the aftermath of defeat at the **Medway** in Kent in 43, Caratacus of the Catuvellauni was driven into Wales, where he fought on against the Romans until Governor Ostorius Scapula mounted a major expedition to defeat him, traditionally at Caer Caradoc on the Clun and Teme in Shropshire. Caratacus was betrayed by Cartimandua, Queen of the Brigantes, and was taken in chains to Rome.

Caffa I 1296 I Venetian-Genoese Wars
See **Kaffa**

Caffa I 1475 I Genoese-Turkish War
See **Kaffa**

Cagancha I 1839 I Argentine Civil Wars

After losing to forces opposed to Dictator Manuel de Rosas in northern Argentine at **Yerua**, Federalist General Pascual Echague, Governor of Entre Rios, invaded Uruguay against Fructuoso Rivera. At Cagancha in San José, aided by French volunteers and anti-Rosas Argentine forces, Rivera defeated Echague, who returned to Entre Rios for victory at **Sauce Grande** (29 December 1839).

Cagancha I 1858 I Diaz Revolt in Uruguay

A Conservative rising against President Gabriel Periera saw General César Diaz fail in a siege of Montevideo before meeting a larger government force under Colonel Lucas Moreno at Cagancha. Although Diaz secured a decisive victory, he was pursued by General Anacleto Medina north to Paso de Quinteros and surrendered. Diaz and many others were shot on Pereira's orders (15 January 1858).

Cahul I 1574 I Moldavian Rebellion
See **Kagul Lagoon**

Caia ▍ 1709 ▍ War of the Spanish Succession
See **Val Gudina**

Caibaté ▍ 1756 ▍ Guarani War
When Spain ceded Portugal an area east of the Uruguay River in the south of modern Brazil, local Guarani Indians in Jesuit missions rose in rebellion. But in the decisive action at Caibaté, west of Santo Angelo, they were routed by the Portuguese, reportedly losing 1,300 dead for just four Europeans killed. Although the battle ended the war, Spain soon resumed control of the area (10 February 1756).

Cairo ▍ 1517 ▍ Ottoman-Mamluk War
See **Ridanieh**

Cairo ▍ 1772 ▍ Mamluk Wars
Mamluk General Abu'l-Dhahab captured Mecca and Jeddah in Arabia, and much of Ottoman Syria including **Damascus**, then returned to Egypt to attack his master, Sultan Ali Bey. Ali Bey was defeated in battle near Cairo and fled to Shayk Zahir al-Umar of Acre, supporting his siege of Ottoman **Jaffa**, before returning to Egypt and final defeat in May 1773 at **Salihiyya** (April 1772).

Cairo ▍ 1801 ▍ French Revolutionary Wars (Middle East)
Ottoman Vizier Yusuf Pasha supported the Allies at **Alexandria**, then advanced alone on Cairo, where French General Auguste Belliard marched out to meet him at El Hanka. The Turkish cavalry managed to repulse Belliard and, as General Sir John Hely-Hutchinson approached with the main force supported by Capitan Pasha, the French withdrew to the city and soon capitulated (27 June 1801).

Caishi ▍ 1161 ▍ Jin-Song Wars
Leading a massive assault on the Southern Song, Jin Emperor Wanyan Liang took a huge army to the Yangzi, southwest of Nanjing. Just days after his navy was routed at sea off **Chenjia**, he tried to cross the river at Caishi, where his ships and army were destroyed by

Song General Yu Yun Wen. The Emperor was soon assassinated by his generals, who made peace and withdrew (25–27 November 1161).

Caister Castle ▍ 1469 ▍ Wars of the Roses
Amid anarchy caused by war, private feuds flared and John Mowbray Duke of Norfolk besieged Caister Castle, just north of Yarmouth, where John Paston the Younger was forced to capitulate after a heavy bombardment. While Paston regained the castle during the brief Lancastrian restoration, he lost it again after **Barnet** (April 1471) and Norfolk held it until his death in 1476 (September 1469).

Caizhou ▍ 817 ▍ Later Tang Imperial Wars
In the face of recalcitrance by ambitious provincial military leaders, Chinese Emperor Xianzong determined to make an example of Huaixi in southern Henan. The largely volunteer and militia army of Huaixi fought on for more than two years until Imperial General Li Su led a bold surprise advance on the capital, Caizhou (Ts'ai-chou). Li won a decisive victory and Huaixi was dismembered.

Cajamarca ▍ 1532 ▍ Spanish Conquest of Peru
With the Inca Empire weakened by a bloody civil war at **Cuzco**, the Spanish Conquistador Francisco Pizarro met the new Emperor Atahualpa at nearby Cajamarca, where he seized the Inca and slaughtered his mainly unarmed supporters. Atahualpa paid a massive ransom, but he was executed in August 1533. An Inca revolt failed in 1535–1536 and the empire was effectively destroyed.

Cakranegara ▍ 1894 ▍ Dutch Conquest of Bali
To support Sasak Muslims against the Balinese rulers of Lombok, Dutch General Jacobus Vetter advanced on Cakranegara, where he was surprised and routed. The "Lombok Treachery" cost the Dutch almost 100 killed (including

General Petrus Van Ham) and 300 wounded. However, Vetter soon returned to burn Cakrenegara and defeat the Balinese outside nearby **Mataram** (26 August 1894).

Calabar ▌ 1967 ▌ Biafran War

While Nigerian Federal forces advanced on the Biafran capital at **Enugu**, further south the dynamic Colonel Benjamin Adekunle prepared an ambitious amphibious assault at Calabar. Attacking after a massive naval and aerial bombardment, 3,000 Federals stormed the city, which fell after vicious street fighting. Six months later, Adekunle advanced west towards **Port Harcourt** (17–19 October 1967).

Calabee Creek ▌ 1814 ▌ Creek Indian War

Soon after defeat at **Holy Ground**, Creeks led by Red Eagle (William Weatherford) ambushed 1,500 Georgia militia and 500 Indians under General John Floyd at Calabee Creek, near Tuskegee, Alabama. Floyd withdrew after losing about 20 killed and 150 wounded. Following Creek defeat at **Horseshoe Bend** in March, Weatherford surrendered to General Andrew Jackson (27 January 1814).

Calabozo ▌ 1818 ▌ Venezuelan War of Independence

Patriot leader Simón Bolívar renewed his advance from **Angostura** through **La Hogaza** (December 1817), attacking Spanish commander Pablo Morillo in camp on the Guárico near Calabozo. The outnumbered Royalists lost 300 killed and withdrew into the city, then escaped through Republican negligence towards Valencia, and checked Bolívar's pursuit at **Sombrero** (12 February 1818).

Calabria ▌ 1940 ▌ World War II (War at Sea)

The largest naval action in the Mediterranean took place off Calabria when British Admiral John Cunningham (one carrier, three battleships, five cruisers and 16 destroyers) met Italian Admiral Inigo Campioni (two battleships, 14 cruisers and 24 destroyers). Air support on both sides failed and the action was broken off after

damage to both fleets, though Britain claimed victory (9 July 1940).

Calafat ▌ 1854 ▌ Crimean War

Just weeks after a check at **Citate**, Russian forces on the Danube resumed their advance on Calafat, opposite Vidna, held by Ahmed Pasha. After a four-month siege, with heavy losses from disease and costly assaults, Russian General Iosif Romanovich Anrep withdrew his forces. At the same time, Russia's main army remained stalled on the lower Danube at **Silistria** (28 January–May 1854).

Calagurris ▌ 74 BC ▌ Sertorian War
See **Calahorra**

Calahorra ▌ 74 BC ▌ Sertorian War

Defeated at **Murviedro** in 75 BC, Rome's commander in Spain, Gnaeus Pompey, withdrew up the Ebro with Quintus Metellus Pius, and was later attacked and badly beaten at Calahorra, southeast of Logroño, by the rebel Quintus Sertorius. However, Sertorius began to lose support and was later killed by his lieutenant Marcus Perpenna. Pompey quickly defeated and executed Perpenna to end the war.

Calais ▌ 1346–1347 ▌ Hundred Years War

Edward III of England followed his decisive victory at **Crecy** (26 August) by marching north to invest Calais. When it became clear after almost a year under siege that Philip VI of France could not send relief, the starving city surrendered. England held Calais until 1558, by which time it was her last possession in France (4 September 1346–4 August 1347).

Calais ▌ 1558 ▌ 5th Habsburg-Valois War

When England supported a Spanish invasion of France, Henry II of France sent Francis Duke of Guise against English-held Calais, defended by Lord Thomas Wentworth. Following failure in mid-1557, a renewed attack captured the outlying forts of Nieullay and Rysbank and Calais was besieged. When the city capitulated, England lost her last territory in France (1–8 January 1558).

Calais ∎ 1596 ∎ 9th French War of Religion

During intermittent war between Henry IV of France and Phillip II of Spain, Spanish troops from the Netherlands marched into northwest France and captured a considerable amount of territory. A key action was the surprise attack and capture of Calais by Archduke Albert of Austria. The city was returned to France in 1598 by the treaty which ended the war (9 April 1596).

**Calais ∎ 1940 ∎ World War II
(Western Europe)**

During the German advance on the **Channel Ports**, Panzer General Heinz Guderian seized **Boulogne**, then drove north to attack Calais, tenaciously held by French and British under Brigadier Claude Nicholson. With evacuation by sea ruled out, Nicholson refused to surrender. The port finally fell by storm, but its resistance is claimed to have bought time for the defence of **Dunkirk** (24–27 May 1940).

Calakmul ∎ 695 ∎ "Star" Wars

Succeeding his father, killed at **Dos Pilas** (679), the energetic King Jasaw Chan K'awiil of Tikal determined to restore his Mayan Kingdom, in modern Guatemala. In a campaign planned by the position of the stars, he marched north against his arch-rival, the city of Calakmul. King Yich'ak K'ak of Calakmul was decisively defeated and executed and Tikal regained its pre-eminence (August 695).

Calama ∎ 109 BC ∎ Jugurthine War
See **Suthul**

**Calatafimi ∎ 1860 ∎ 2nd Italian War
of Independence**

After landing with "The Thousand" in western Sicily, Giuseppe Garibaldi rallied the local population to rise against the Bourbon Kingdom of Naples. Neapolitan Major Antonio Landi was decisively defeated in action at Calatafimi, near Alcamo, which cost over 100 lost on either side. It opened the way to Garibaldi's capture of **Palermo** and final victory in July at **Milazzo** (15 May 1860).

**Calatanazar ∎ 1002 ∎ Later
Christian-Muslim Wars in Spain**

Muslim Chief Minister Ibn Abi Amir al-Mansour advanced into Castile to meet the combined Christian armies of King Sancho III of Navarre, Count Sancho of Castile and Alfonso V of Leon. In a battle near Calatanazar, west of Soria in central Spain, the great Muslim warrior was routed and fatally wounded, leading directly to the fall of the Caliphate of Cordova.

**Calatayud ∎ 1811 ∎ Napoleonic Wars
(Peninsular Campaign)**

To divert French attention from the Allied offensive in Valencia, Spanish guerrilla leaders Juan Martin Diaz and José Duran captured Calatayud, southwest of Saragossa, and besieged the convent of La Merced. While explosive mines forced the garrison to surrender, the Spanish withdrew with their prisoners before a French relief force arrived next day (26 September–4 October 1811).

**Calavryta ∎ 1079 ∎ Byzantine Wars of
Succession**

When Nicephorus III Botaniates seized Constantinople's throne following victory at **Nicaea**, he sent General Alexius Comnenus against the rival Imperial claimant Nicephorus Briennes, Governor of Dyrrhachium. A cavalry action in Achaea at Calavryta (modern Kalavryta, Greece) saw Briennus defeated, then blinded, but Comnenus himself soon revolted and seized the throne as Alexius I.

**Calcinato ∎ 1706 ∎ War of the Spanish
Succession**

French commander Louis Duke de Vendôme launched a fresh offensive in northern Italy, where he defeated Austrian General Count Christian Reventlau at Calcinato, southeast of Brescia, driving the Imperial forces out of central Lombardy and forcing a withdrawal up the Trentino Valley. French troops then besieged **Turin**, but they were decisively defeated by Prince Eugène of Savoy (19 April 1706).

Calcutta I 1756 I Seven Years War (India)

In a pre-emptive move against the British in Bengal, the French-supported Nawab Siraj-ud-Daula attacked Calcutta, where most Europeans fled, leaving fewer than 200 to defend Fort William. The garrison surrendered after four days and only 23 of 146 survived overnight imprisonment in the "Black Hole of Calcutta." The city was retaken the following January (16–20 June 1756).

Calcutta I 1757 I Seven Years War (India)

At war with the French-supported Nawab Siraj-ud-Daula of Bengal, British Colonel Robert Clive recaptured Calcutta (taken the previous June), then a month later repulsed a massive counter-attack by a reputed 40,000 Indians. When Clive defeated the French at **Chandernagore** (24 March), Siraj made peace and withdrew until the decisive battle at **Plassey** in June (2 January & 5 February 1757).

Caldera Bay I 1891 I Chilean Civil War

Although war between Chile's Congress and President José Manuel Balmaceda was fought mainly on land, two government gunboats attacked the Congressional squadron in Caldera Bay. In a confused night action, the gunboat *Almirante Lynch* (Commander Alberto Funtes) sank the battleship *Blanco Encalada*, the first ironclad warship lost to a self-propelled torpedo (23 April 1891).

Calderón I 1811 I Mexican Wars of Independence

Two months after victory at **Guanajuato**, Mexican Royalist commander Félix María Calleja advanced on the main rebel army of Miguel Hidalgo at Guadalajara. Marching out to meet Calleja at the Bridge of Calderón, Hidalgo and his Generals Ignacio Allende and Juan Aldama suffered a terrible and decisive defeat. They were eventually captured and shot, and the rising was crushed (17 January 1811).

Calderón I 1860 I Mexican War of the Reform

Reversing previous Liberal defeats, new commander Jesús González Ortega captured **Guadalajara**, then met an approaching government relief force under General Leonardo Márquez at nearby Calderón. Márquez was heavily defeated, losing all his ammunition and baggage and more than 2,000 prisoners. Ortega soon also won the decisive battle at **Calpulalpam** (10 November 1860).

Caldiero I 1796 I French Revolutionary Wars (1st Coalition)

In yet another Austrian attempt to relieve the French siege of **Mantua**, Baron Josef Alvinzi forced Napoleon Bonaparte to split his forces between the siege and covering Verona. On the nearby heights of Caldiero, Bonaparte was repulsed attacking a strong Austrian position. He was forced back to Verona, but reversed his loss with a bloody victory a few days later at **Arcola** (12 November 1796).

Caldiero I 1805 I Napoleonic Wars (3rd Coalition)

While Napoleon Bonaparte was campaigning in Austria, the Austrians in northern Italy under Archduke Charles were attacked in a strong defensive position at Caldiero, east of Verona, by French Marshal André Masséna. Although Masséna was repulsed, both sides suffered heavy casualties and, following battle at the **Tagliamento**, Charles began his withdrawal across the Alps (30 October 1805).

Caliano I 1796 I French Revolutionary Wars (1st Coalition)
See **Calliano**

Calibee Creek I 1813 I Creek Indian War
See **Talladega**

Calibio I 1814 I Colombian War of Independence

When Spanish Royalists under Juan de Samano invaded southern Colombia, Republican General Antonio Nariño marched south from

Bogotá, and two weeks after victory at **Palacé**, he attacked Generals Juan de Samano and Ignacio Asín at Calibio, northeast of Popayán. Heavy fighting saw the Royalists repulsed at bayonet point with Asín killed. Nariño then retook Popayán (15 January 1814).

Calicut I 1500 I Early Portuguese Colonial Wars in Asia

Following the explorer Vasco da Gama, Portuguese Admiral Pedro Alvares Cabral was sent to establish a depot at Calicut, in southwest India. When Muslims induced local Indians to attack the depot, Cabral destroyed the Arab fleet, then bombarded Calicut and burned it. In 1502, the Raja of Calicut refused to expel the Muslims, and the city was burned again (16 December 1500).

Calicut I 1790 I 3rd British-Mysore War

When Tipu Sultan of Mysore renewed war against Britain, Colonel James Hartley advanced into southeast India to attack the port of Calicut, defended by Mysorean General Hussein Ali. Hartley inflicted heavy casualties in a one-sided rout and took many prisoners. Sir Robert Abercromby's main force then arrived and secured the whole province of Malabar (10 December 1790).

Callao I 1819 I Peruvian War of Independence

While privateers attacked Spanish ships off Chile, Lord Thomas Cochrane took the Chilean squadron from Valparaiso against Callao, the port outside Lima in Spanish Peru. With an inadequate force of just 400 marines under Major William Miller (who was badly wounded), and failure of his Congreve rockets, Cochrane was driven off, though succeeded against **Valdivia** (29 September 1819).

Callao I 1820–1821 I Peruvian War of Independence

Despite previous failure, Chilean Admiral Lord Thomas Cochrane and General José de San Martin blockaded Callao outside Lima. In a brilliant coup, Cochrane entered the harbour in boats and captured the Spanish frigate *Esmer-*

elda (5 November 1820). Lima later fell (6 July 1821), but garrison commander Colonel José de Lamar held out in the fortress (8 October 1820–21 September 1821).

Callao I 1824–1826 I Peruvian War of Independence

When Peru was liberated by victory at **Ayacucho**, Spanish General José Rodil held out in the fortress port of Callao, outside Lima, against Generals Simón Bolívar and Bartolomé Salóm. After 14 months, and heavy losses from starvation and disease, Rodil surrendered with the honours of war and Spain finally lost its last garrison on the South American continent (10 December 1824–23 January 1826).

Callao I 1866 I Peruvian-Spanish War

Commodore Casto Mendez-Nuñez attempting to recover Spanish influence in South America bombarded **Valparaiso** in Chile in March, then sailed against Calloa, near Lima, defended by Peruvian President Mariano Ignacio Prado. In a courageous action, with costly losses on both sides, shore batteries damaged and repulsed the Spanish ships. Hostilities ceased a week later (2 May 1866).

Calliano I 1796 I French Revolutionary Wars (1st Coalition)

A month after losing at **Castiglione**, Austrian General Dagobert Wurmser renewed his effort to relieve the French siege of **Mantua**, again ill-advisedly splitting his force. Having repulsed Austrian General Paul Davidovich at **Roveredo** in the Adige Valley, Napoleon Bonaparte smashed him next day at nearby Calliano. Bonaparte then turned to defeat Wurmser days later at **Bassano** (5 September 1796).

Callicinus I 171 BC I 3rd Macedonian War

The ambitious young King Perseus of Macedon was determined to attack Rome in Greece and led a force into Thessaly. At Callicinus, near Larissa, he defeated a large Roman army under Lucius Portius Licinius, supported by Licinius Crassus on the right wing. However, Perseus failed to follow up his victory and, two years later, his empire was destroyed by a Roman counter-offensive at **Pydna**.

Callinicum I 297 I Roman-Persian Wars

When Shah Narses of Persia invaded Roman Syria, Emperor Diocletian sent his son-in-law Galerius Maximus, who crossed the Euphrates, but was forced to withdraw towards Carrhae. Ambushed to the south at Callinicum (modern Rakka), Galerius suffered a terrible defeat, effectively losing Mesopotamia to Persia. The following year he defeated Narses at **Erzurum** and regained lost territory.

Callinicum I 531 I Byzantine-Persian Wars

A year after defeating the Sassanian Persians at **Dara** in northern Mesopotamia, Byzantine General Belisarius harassed a Persian army under Azareth, retreating down the west bank of the Euphrates. Belisarius attacked near the frontier at Callinicum (Rakka), but was heavily defeated and withdrew north of the river. Azareth also suffered heavy losses and the Persians decided to make peace.

Caloocan I 1899 I Philippine-American War

At the start of the war, American commander Arthur MacArthur advanced a few miles north of **Manila** against the key railway terminus at Caloocan. General Henry W. Lawton took the town by assault after a heavy naval bombardment in the first full-scale action of the war. However, Philippine General Antonio Luna eluded defeat and withdrew north through **Polo** to **Malolos** (10 February 1899).

Caloosahatchee I 1839 I 2nd Seminole Indian War

The so-called "Spanish" Seminole under Chakaika launched a night attack on the army camp at Caloosahatchee, in southwest Florida, east of Fort Myers, killing nine regulars and three civilians and looting the nearby trading post before Colonel William Harney rallied the survivors. Chakaika escaped with captured arms

and other booty and a year later he attacked peaceful **Indian Key** (23 July 1839).

Calpulalpam I 1860 I Mexican War of the Reform

In the wake of the terrible government defeat at **Calderón** (10 November), President Miguel Miramón took 8,000 troops northeast from Mexico City to meet Liberal commander Jesús González Ortega and perhaps 15,000 men on the heights of San Miguel Calpulalpam. Miramón was crushed and fled to Europe. The war ended, and Benito Juarez was installed as President (22 December 1860).

Calugareni I 1595 I Wallachian-Turkish War

Ottoman Grand Vizier Sinan Pasha advanced into Romania against Prince Michael the Brave of Wallachia and suffered a terrible defeat in the marshes of Calugareni, north of the Danube. However, the Turks went on to attack Bucharest and **Tirgovist** before being forced to withdraw. In October Sinan suffered another heavy loss on the Danube at **Giurgiu** (23 August 1595).

Calumpit I 1899 I Philippine-American War

Marching north from **Malolos** across the **Bagbag**, American commander Arthur MacArthur attacked Philippine General Antonio Luna at Calumpit on the Rio Grande. When General Frederick Funston's Kansans boldly swam the river under heavy fire to draw the boats across, MacArthur captured Calumpit. He later continued north to secure San Fernando (27 April 1899).

Calven I 1499 I Swabian War

In their final struggle for freedom, the Swiss cantons defeated the Habsburg cities of the Swabian League at **Schwaderloch** and **Frastenz**, then about 8,000 Swiss under Benedict Fontana attacked German entrenchments at Calven Gorge in the Munstertal. While Fontana was killed in the first assault, the position was taken at the cost of a reported 5,000 Habsburg casualties (22 May 1499).

Calvi I 1794 I French Revolutionary Wars (1st Coalition)

With Britain's navy forced out of **Toulon** (December 1793), Admiral Sir Samuel Hood (1724–1816) invaded Corsica and, after capturing **Bastia**, moved General Sir Charles Stuart west to besiege Calvi (where Captain Horatio Nelson lost his right eye). General Raphael de Casabianco surrendered after two months and British forces held Corsica until December 1796 (19 June–10 August 1794).

Camaret Bay I 1694 I War of the Grand Alliance

English Admiral Peregrine Osborne Marquis of Carmarthen led a misconceived expedition against Brest, where he bombarded nearby Fort Camaret while General Thomas Talmach tried to land about 800 troops. The bombardment failed, with one English ship sunk, and Talmach lost more than half his men killed or captured before being driven off. He died of wounds four days later (8 June 1694).

Camargo I 1866 I Mexican-French War
See **Santa Gertrudis**

Cambodia I 1970 I Vietnam War

When 20,000 American and South Vietnamese invaded Cambodia to destroy Communist bases, they captured massive quantities of weapons and food. While the Viet Cong and North Vietnamese attempted to avoid major battles, there was some intense fighting, with over 350 Americans and perhaps 4,000 Communists killed, before the controversial "incursion" came to an end (1 May–30 June 1970).

Cambrai I 1657 I Franco-Spanish War

Following an alliance between France and Cromwell's England against Spain in northern France, French Marshal Henri de Turenne besieged Spanish-held Cambrai. Louis II de Bourbon Prince of Condé, in Spanish service, inflicted a heavy defeat and drove off the siege, as at **Valenciennes** in 1656. His subsequent defeat at the **Dunes** in June 1658 effectively ended the war (30 May 1657).

Cambrai I 1794 I French Revolutionary Wars (1st Coalition)
See **Villers-en-Cauchies**

Cambrai I 1917 I World War I (Western Front)

General Julian Byng was determined to pierce the **Hindenburg Line**, sending 340 tanks against General Georg von de Marwitz, south of Cambrai. Advancing without bombardment, the first mass tank attack surprised and smashed through the defences. However, the tanks lacked infantry support, and a German counter-attack soon retook most of the lost ground (20 November–3 December 1917).

Cambrai-St Quentin I 1918 I World War I (Western Front)

While Allied forces attacked on the **Meuse** and advanced in **Flanders**, British commander Sir Douglas Haig launched his offensive between Cambrai and St Quentin against General Max von Boehn. Initial action at **Canal du Nord** and the **St Quentin Canal** broke through the **Hindenburg Line**, leading to the capture of Cambrai (9 October) and **Le Cateau** (27 September–10 October 1918).

Cambuskenneth I 1297 I William Wallace Revolt
See **Stirling**

Camden I 1780 I War of the American Revolution

When rebel militia attacked British outposts at **Rocky Mount** and **Hanging Rock** in early August, American General Horatia Gates advanced on the main British base at Camden, South Carolina, held by Colonel Lord Francis Rawdon, later reinforced by General Charles Earl Cornwallis. Gates was routed with terrible losses in a decisive defeat and fled to Hillsboro, North Carolina (16 August 1780).

Camden I 1864 I American Civil War (Trans-Mississippi)
See **Poison Spring**

Camel, England ❚ 721 ❚ Anglo-Saxon Territorial Wars

King Ine of Wessex was beaten by Mercia in the north at **Wodnesbeorg** in 715, and later tried to extend Saxon territory west into Cornwall, where he was heavily defeated near the Camel River. A few years later, he resigned the Kingship of the West Saxons, leaving the fierce Britons of Cornwall to maintain their independence from Wessex until defeat after a hundred years at nearby **Gafulford**.

Camel, Iraq ❚ 656 ❚ Muslim Civil Wars

Following the murder of Caliph Omar, Mohammed's son-in-law Ali was opposed by Omar's widow, Aisha, and the Generals Talha and Zubair. At Khoraiba, near Basra in Mesopotamia, the rebels were defeated and killed, securing Ali's caliphate. From the bloody battlefield defence of the camel pavilion carrying Aisha, this became known as the Battle of the Camel (9 December 656).

Camelodunum ❚ 43 ❚ Roman Conquest of Britain

See **Medway**

Camerinum ❚ 295 BC ❚ 3rd Samnite War

Determined on a final attempt to resist Rome in central Italy, Samnites under Gellius Egnatius, supported by Gauls, attacked advance Roman legions defending a pass near Camerinum, in the Apennines, 90 miles northeast of Rome. Although Roman commander Lucius Cornelius Scipio suffered a costly defeat, the main Roman force soon arrived and was avenged at nearby **Sentinum**.

Camerone ❚ 1863 ❚ Mexican-French War

In a celebrated French Foreign Legion episode, three officers and 62 men led by Captain Jean Danjou, sent to escort supplies from Veracruz to the siege of **Puebla**, were attacked by overwhelming Mexican forces, and determined to defend a farmhouse at Camerone. Swearing to fight to the death, Danjou and 21 others were killed, with all the remainder wounded or captured (30 April 1863).

Camerontown ❚ 1863 ❚ 2nd New Zealand War

As General Duncan Cameron advanced south from Auckland, about 100 Ngati Maniapoto attacked his lines at Camerontown, where five Europeans were killed and stores destroyed. When reinforcements arrived from Tuakau, the officers were killed and Sergeant Edward McKenna won the Victoria Cross for saving the survivors. Another attack followed at **Pukekohe East** (7 September 1863).

Camlann ❚ 515 ❚ Anglo-Saxon Conquest of Britain

About twenty years after victory over the Saxons at **Mons Badonicus**, the semi-mythical King Arthur of Britain found himself in conflict with his rebellious nephew Mordred. The two traditionally met in battle at Camlann, the location of which is shrouded in legend and greatly disputed, but possibly on Salisbury Plain. Mordred and Arthur were both killed (trad date c 515).

Campaldino ❚ 1289 ❚ Guelf-Ghibelline Wars

Amid continuing factional war in northern Italy, Guelf forces from Florence led by Amerigo di Nerbona, aided by Pistoians and Luchesse under Corso Donati, marched against the Ghibelline city of Arezzo. At Campaldino, near Poppi, Count Guido Novello of Arezzo fled and the warrior-Bishop Guiglielmino of Arezzo was routed and killed. Florence secured much of Tuscany (11 June 1289).

Camp Allegheny ❚ 1861 ❚ American Civil War (Eastern Theatre)

Union General Robert H. Milroy resumed the offensive in West Virginia after the costly action at **Greenbrier River** (3 October) and advanced southeast from Cheat Summit against Confederate Camp Allegheny on the Staunton turnpike, held by Colonel Edward "Allegheny" Johnson. Both sides lost about 140 men in inconclusive fighting and Milroy retreated to **Cheat Summit** (13 December 1861).

Camp Baldwin I 1861 I American Civil War (Eastern Theatre)
See **Camp Allegheny**

Campbell's Station I 1863 I American Civil War (Western Theatre)
While attempting to intercept Union General Ambrose E. Burnside south of Knoxville, Tennessee, Confederate General James Longstreet found himself blocked near the important railway junction at Campbell's Station. Burnside held off the Confederate attack in heavy fighting, then withdrew into Knoxville, securing a decisive victory two weeks later at **Fort Sanders** (16 November 1863).

Camperdown I 1797 I French Revolutionary Wars (Irish Rising)
Off the Dutch coast near Texel at Camperdown (Kamperduijn), British Admiral Adam Duncan attacked Dutch Admiral Jan de Winter attempting to take 13,000 Dutch troops and rebels under Wolfe Tone to join a French landing in Ireland. During a hard-fought engagement, with heavy casualties on both sides, Duncan took or destroyed nine Dutch vessels (11 October 1797).

Camp Grant I 1871 I Apache Indian Wars
When Apache under Eskiminzin approached Camp Grant, north of Tucson, Arizona, to seek peace, their camp was attacked at night while the warriors were away hunting, by about 150 whites, Mexicans and Indians under William S. Oury and Jesus Elias. About 140 Apache were killed in cold blood, mainly women and children, helping to escalate war with the Apache (30 April 1871).

Campi Cannini I 457 I Alemannic Invasion of Northern Italy
Taking advantage of confusion following the defeat of Emperor Avitus at **Placentia** (16 October 456), an invading army of Alemanni crossed the Rhaetian Alps from Switzerland into Italy and reached Lake Maggiore. At nearby Campi Cannini, they were defeated and repulsed by the Roman General Majorian, who was later established as Emperor with the aid of his Suevic ally Ricimer.

Campi Raudii I 101 BC I Rome's Gallic Wars
See **Vercellae**

Camp Izard I 1836 I 2nd Seminole Indian War
See **Withlacoochee**

Campo Grande, Boquerón I 1933 I Chaco War
See **Pampa Grande**

Campo Grande, Cordillera I 1869 I War of the Triple Alliance
See **Acosta-Ñu**

Campo Mayor I 1644 I Spanish-Portuguese Wars
See **Montijo**

Campo Mayor (1st) I 1811 I Napoleonic Wars (Peninsular Campaign)
French Marshal Édouard Mortier set out from **Badajoz** and crossed the Portuguese border to besiege the fortress at Campo Mayor, held by a scratch force of militia and a handful of regulars under the Portuguese Major Jose Joaquim Talaya. The fortress surrendered after an heroic defence against heavy bombardment and was later held against the Allies (14–21 March 1811).

Campo Mayor (2nd) I 1811 I Napoleonic Wars (Peninsular Campaign)
In a prelude to the Allied siege of **Badajoz**, an Anglo-Portuguese force under General Sir William Beresford attacked Campo Mayor, just inside Portugal. Withdrawing south in good order, General Marie Latour-Maubourg repulsed a badly handled Allied attack, and a sortie across the Guadiana from Badajoz by Marshal Édouard Mortier completed the French victory (25 March 1811).

Camposanto I 1743 I War of the Austrian Succession

Campaigning in northern Italy, Spanish commander Count Juan de Gages marched northwest from Bologna in an attempt to join forces with French Prince Louis-François of Conti. Crossing the Panaro, he attacked the Austro-Sardinian army of Marshal Otto von Traun at Camposanto, northwest of Modena. While both sides claimed victory, the Spanish withdrew towards Naples (8 February 1743).

Campo Vía I 1933 I Chaco War

Days after being driven back from **Alihuatá** in the Chaco Boreal, Bolivian commander General Hans Kundt was surrounded and defeated at Campo Vía, just west of Gondra, by Paraguayan Brigadier José Félix Estigarribia. Colonels Carlos Banzer and Emilio González Quint surrendered 8,000 men and Kundt was promptly dismissed, but Paraguay unwisely agreed to a truce (11 December 1933).

Campus Ardiensis I 317 I Roman Wars of Succession

Despite bloody action at **Cibalae** (October 316), Eastern Emperor Valerius Licinius continued the war against his rival Constantine, who took his army into Thrace and attacked at Campus Ardiensis near the Hebrus. Licinius lost half his troops and sued for peace, agreeing to give up Illyria and Greece though retaining his Asian possessions. Eight years later war resumed at **Adrianople** (January 317).

Campus Castorum I 69 I Vitellian Civil War
See **Bedriacum**

Campus Mardiensis I 317 I Roman Wars of Succession
See **Campus Ardiensis**

Campus Vocladensis I 507 I Visigothic-Frankish Wars
See **Vouillé**

Camp Wild Cat I 1861 I American Civil War (Western Theatre)

Confederate General Felix K. Zollicoffer advanced into southeastern Kentucky through **Barbourville**, and was blocked to the northwest on the Rockcastle River at Camp Wild Cat by Union forces under General Albin F. Schoepf and Colonel Theophilus T. Garrard. The Confederate attacks were repulsed in heavy fighting and Zollicoffer withdrew to Cumberland Ford (21 October 1861).

Cañada I 1847 I American-Mexican War
See **La Cañada**

Cañada el Carmen I 1934 I Chaco War

Despite a check at **Villazón**, Paraguayan commander General José Félix Estigarribia continued west towards the Bolivian Andes, and days later at Cañada el Carmen, Colonel Carlos José Fernández routed Bolivian Colonel Walter Méndez. Over 7,000 prisoners and massive military materials were captured and Paraguayan forces advanced on the nearby fortress of **Ballivian** (11–16 November 1934).

Cañada-Strongest I 1934 I Chaco War

Resuming the offensive in the Chaco Boreal five months after victory at **Campo Vía**, General José Félix Estigarribia's Paraguayans advanced west towards the Andes. Four of his regiments were attacked at Cañada-Strongest, near Cochabamba, where Bolivian Colonel Enrique Peñaranda captured 1,500 men and their arms. Bolivia was routed six months later at **Cañada el Carmen** (24 May 1934).

Cañada Tarija I 1934 I Chaco War

When Bolivian forces in the disputed Chaco Boreal concentrated near Picuiba under Colonel Francisco Peña, Paraguayan Colonel Frederico Smith advanced northwest from Camacho and encircled Colonel Angel Bavía at Cañada Tarija. Almost 1,200 Bolivians were forced to surrender, after which Bavía committed suicide and Peña was dismissed from command (26–27 March 1934).

Canal du Nord ∎ 1918 ∎ World War I (Western Front)

Near the start of the assault on the **Hindenburg Line**, British Generals Julian Byng and Henry Horne attacked across the heavily defended Canal du Nord, just west of **Cambrai**. Supported by artillery fire, Canadian forces stormed through the German defences, while two days later the offensive continued further south on the **St Quentin Canal** (27 September–1 October 1918).

Cancale ∎ 1758 ∎ Seven Years War (Europe)

Admiral Sir Edward Hawke and Commodore Richard Howe attacked the Brittany coast, where they landed 13,000 men under Charles Spencer Duke of Marlborough and Lord George Sackville in Cancale Bay, east of St Malo. The raiders damaged the small harbour of Servan, but realised they had insufficient forces to take St Malo and returned home with little achieved (2–12 June 1758).

Cancha Rayada ∎ 1813 ∎ Chilean War of Independence

While marching south from Santiago with 1,000 men against Talca, the Argentine Patriot Manuel Blanco Encalada was intercepted at Cancha Rayada by guerrilla leader Ildefonso Elorreaga. Although Encalada was heavily defeated, the Patriots recovered to repulse an advance on Santiago a week later by Spanish General Gabino Gainza, who retired to Talca (29 March 1813).

Cancha Rayada ∎ 1818 ∎ Chilean War of Independence

Attempting to restore Spanish authority in Chile after rebel victory at **Chacabuco** (13 February 1817), General Manuel Osorio invaded from Peru and surprised Patriot General José de San Martin at Cancha Rayada, near Talca. San Martin was defeated, losing 120 killed and all his guns, but Osorio also suffered heavy losses and was beaten the following month at the **Maipú** (19 March 1818).

Candelaria, Cuba ∎ 1896 ∎ 2nd Cuban War of Independence

Insurgent leader Antonio Maceo recovered from the bloody action in western Cuba at **Paso Real**, and soon attacked the fortified town of Candelaria on the railway southwest of Havana, held by Cuban negros supporting the Spanish. Threatened with death as traitors if captured, the defenders fought bravely for 24 hours until reinforced from **Artemisa**, and Maceo had to withdraw (January 1896).

Candelaria, Mexico ∎ 1864 ∎ Mexican-French War

On campaign southwest of Guadalajara in Jalisco, Liberal General Ignacio Ugalde tried to trap a larger French force under Colonel Jean-Francois Tourre in the defile at La Candelaria. Despite the superior Mexican position and almost 50 casualties, the French troops fought back courageously in intense heat, repulsing the attack. They then marched northwest to occupy Ayutla (1 August 1864).

Candia ∎ 1648–1669 ∎ Venetian-Turkish Wars

Supposedly responding to attacks by pirates, Sultan Ibrahim I sent a massive army against Venetian-held Crete, where the capital, Candia, held out under Captain-General Francesco Morosoni against one of history's longest sieges. Vizier Ahmed Fazili Koprulu forced the surrender after 21 years and massive casualties on both sides. He then seized most of Crete (1648–27 September 1669).

Candorcanqui ∎ 1824 ∎ Peruvian War of Independence
See **Ayacucho**

Canea ∎ 1645 ∎ Venetian-Turkish Wars
See **Khania**

Canea ∎ 1692 ∎ Venetian-Turkish Wars
See **Khania**

**Cane Hill | 1862 | American Civil War
(Trans-Mississippi)**

A month after victory at **Old Fort Wayne**, Union commander James G. Blunt marched east into northern Arkansas to intercept approaching Confederates under General John S. Marmaduke. The Confederate rearguard under General Joseph O. Shelby fought a bloody holding action at Cane Hill, southwest of Fayetteville, before withdrawing northeast to **Prairie Grove** (28 November 1862).

**Cangallo | 1814 | Peruvian War of
Independence**
  See **Apacheta**

**Canglor | 1488 | Scottish Barons'
Rebellion**
  See **Sauchieburn**

Cannae | 216 BC | 2nd Punic War

Facing crisis after defeat by Hannibal at **Lake Trasimene** (April 217 BC), fresh Roman legions met the Carthaginian invaders on the Plain of Cannae, at the Aufidus River, north of modern Bari. In the classic double-encirclement, the Romans were surrounded and massacred, with General Aemilius Paulus killed. Cannae is regarded as the most brilliant and brutal victory in ancient history (2 August 216 BC).

**Cannae | 1018 | Norman Conquest of
Southern Italy**

At the start of Norman military operations in Italy, Rainulf joined with Lombard noble Melo who had been exiled from Byzantine Bari. On the famous battlefield north of Bari at Cannae the Lombard-Norman force was routed by Byzantine General Basil Boioannes. Twenty years later, Rainulf (eventually Count of Aversa) supported Byzantium against Muslim Sicily at **Rometta** (October 1018).

**Canne | 1018 | Norman Conquest of
Southern Italy**
  See **Cannae**

**Cañón de Ugalde | 1790 | Mexican-
Apache Wars**

General Juan de Ugalde, Spanish Governor of Coahuila, had campaigned for several years against Indians in West Texas before taking a large force of troops and Indian allies against about 300 Apache at the Arroyo de la Soledad (Sabinal River Canyon), near the modern town of Utopia. The Apache suffered a decisive defeat and the battlefield was renamed Cañón de Ugalde (9 January 1790).

**Cantigny | 1918 | World War I
(Western Front)**

When American forces rushed to reinforce the French against the German offensive across the **Aisne**, General Robert Lee Bullard attacked the village of Cantigny, near Montdidier. Driving out Germans under General Oscar von Hutier, he then repulsed repeated counter-attacks, losing over 1,000 men. While only a limited action, it was the first American attack of the war (28 May 1918).

Canton | 879 | Huang Chao Rebellion
  See **Guangzhou**

Canton | 1841 | 1st Opium War
  See **Guangzhou**

Canton | 1857 | 2nd Opium War
  See **Guangzhou**

**Canton | 1927 | 2nd Chinese
Revolutionary Civil War**
  See **Guangzhou**

Canton | 1938 | Sino-Japanese War
  See **Guangzhou**

Canusium | 209 BC | 2nd Punic War
  See **Asculum, Apulia**

**Canyon Creek | 1877 | Nez Percé
Indian War**

Nez Percé Chief Joseph was leading his people's epic retreat across Montana from the **Big Hole River** when he was intercepted at Canyon

Creek by Colonel Samuel Sturgis and 350 troopers. Sturgis was heavily repulsed in a brilliant defensive action, but Joseph also suffered costly losses in men and horses and continued north across the Missouri to the **Bear Paw Mountains** (13 September 1877).

Canyon de Chelly ▪ 1864 ▪ Navajo Indian War

Colonel Kit Carson and New Mexico cavalry were sent against the Navajo in northeast Arizona, and eventually defeated them at their stronghold in Canyon de Chelly, north of Fort Defiance. Sixty warriors surrendered and, by the end of the year, 8,000 Navajo were removed to the Pecos River in eastern New Mexico. One quarter had died by the time they returned home in 1868 (January 1864).

Canyon of the Dead Sheep ▪ 1857 ▪ Apache Indian Wars

Supporting Colonel Benjamin Bonneville's expedition on the **Gila River**, Colonel William Wing Loring marched from Fort Union, New Mexico, against Mimbreno Apache under Cuchilla Negro stealing sheep along the Rio Grande. In the Canyon of the Dead Sheep, near the Arizona border, the Mimbreno Chief and several others were killed, temporarily halting these raids (25 May 1857).

Cao-Bang ▪ 1950 ▪ French Indo-China War

On a large offensive in northern Vietnam, General Vo Nguyen Giap overwhelmed **Dong-Khé**, isolating the garrison to the northwest at Cao-Bang, which withdrew towards a column advancing from That-Khé. Both French forces were destroyed with 4,000 men lost (mainly captured) plus huge quantities of equipment. Lang Son was abandoned and the French had lost northern Tonkin (3–7 October 1950).

Caohekou ▪ 1894 ▪ Sino-Japanese War

Japanese Marshal Aritomo Yamagata crossed the **Yalu** into southern Manchuria, where he advanced to secure Caohekou (Ts'ao-ho-kou), commanding the road between Motien Pass and Saimachi. Attacked by the Amur army of Tatar General Yiketang'a, Yamagata secured a bloody victory before extreme cold and over-extended supply lines made him retire on **Fenghuang-cheng** (25 November 1894).

Cape Bon ▪ 468 ▪ Roman-Vandal Wars

Leading a combined offensive against the Vandals in Carthage, Western Emperor Anthemius sent Marcellinus against Sardinia and Sicily, while Eastern Emperor Leo sent Heraclius of Edessa through Tripoli and Basiliscus commanded the combined fleet. After Gaiseric surprised and destroyed the fleet off Cape Bon in Tunisia, and Marcellinus was murdered, Leo agreed to make peace.

Cape Bon ▪ 1941 ▪ World War II (War at Sea)

With Axis forces in North Africa desperately short of fuel, Italian Admiral Antonio Toscano took the supply-laden light cruisers *Alberico da Barbiano* and *Alberto di Giussano* from Palermo. Tracked by ULTRA intelligence, he was ambushed off Cape Bon by four destroyers under Commander Graham Stokes. Both cruisers were sunk, with Toscano among over 900 men lost (13 December 1941).

Cape Carmel ▪ 1799 ▪ French Revolutionary Wars (Middle East)

While Napoleon Bonaparte besieged **Acre**, north of modern Haifa, British Captain Sir William Sidney Smith, providing support at sea, intercepted French Admiral Jean-Baptiste Perrée arriving with a siege train. In a sharp action off Cape Carmel, Smith captured all nine enemy ships, effectively ending French hopes of taking Acre. Within days Bonaparte abandoned the siege (18 May 1799).

Cape Cherchell ▪ 1937 ▪ Spanish Civil War

During the Nationalist blockade of southeastern Spain, the new cruiser *Balaeres* intercepted four freighters escorted by two Republican cruisers and seven destroyers off Cape Cherchell, west of Algiers. During heavy action in the morning, resumed that afternoon, *Balaeres* and the Republican cruiser *Libertad* were both hit, but the convoy was forced to divert to Port Cherchell (7 September 1937).

Cape Colony | 1795 | French Revolutionary Wars (1st Coalition)

When France invaded Holland, British General James Craig and Admiral Sir George Keith Elphinstone went to occupy the Dutch Cape of Good Hope. Craig repulsed Dutch regulars and militia at Wynberg (14 September), and a Dutch naval force was beaten a year later at **Saldanha Bay**. Britain held Cape Colony until it was returned to Holland in 1803 (12 June–17 September 1795).

Cape Colony | 1806 | Napoleonic Wars (4th Coalition)
See **Blueberg**

Cape Ecnomus | 256 BC | 1st Punic War
See **Ecnomus**

Cape Engaño | 1944 | World War II (Pacific)

Wrongly thinking he had repulsed the Japanese in the **Sibuyan Sea**, Admiral William Halsey raced north against a decoy force under Admiral Jizaburo Ozawa. Next day off Cape Engaño, the northeastern point of Luzon, American forces sank all four Japanese carriers and five other ships, but Halsey's action had left an under-strength force off **Samar** to defend **Leyte Gulf** (25 October 1944).

Cape Espartel | 1936 | Spanish Civil War

Captain Francisco Moreno was determined to break the Republican blockade of Morocco, and took two cruisers south from **El Ferrol** to surprise his opponents off Cape Espartel. A vital strategic action cost the Republicans one destroyer sunk and another damaged and the Nationalists won control of the Straits of Gibraltar. The Army of Africa was then able to cross into Spain (29 September 1936).

Cape Esperance | 1942 | World War II (Pacific)

When Admiral Aritomo Goto sailed for **Guadalcanal**, he was met by Admiral Norman Scott off Cape Esperance, where a confused night action saw a Japanese cruiser and two destroyers sunk while Scott had a destroyer sunk and two cruisers damaged. While Goto himself was killed, his ships bombarded Henderson Field and landed vitally needed troops and supplies (11–12 October 1942).

Cape Finisterre (1st) | 1747 | War of the Austrian Succession

British Admirals George Anson and Peter Warren led a brilliant action off northwest Spain, intercepting a French troop convoy near Cape Finisterre, escorted by Admiral Clement de Taffanel Marquis de la Jonquière. Without any loss, Anson captured all nine French warships and seized six merchantmen, yielding 3,000 prisoners. He was created a Peer and Warren was knighted (3 May 1747).

Cape Finisterre (2nd) | 1747 | War of the Austrian Succession

While escorting a large French convoy, Admiral Henri-Francois des Herbiers de l'Étenduère, with just eight warships, was intercepted off Cape Finisterre, in northwest Spain, by a much larger English fleet under Admiral Edward Hawke. In a courageous defence, l'Étenduère lost six ships and 2,500 prisoners, but his convoy escaped unscathed. Hawke received a knighthood (14 October 1747).

Cape Finisterre | 1780 | War of the American Revolution

Sailing from Plymouth with a large fleet to relieve besieged **Gibraltar**, British Admiral George Rodney encountered a small squadron under Spanish Admiral Don Juan de Yadri escorting a convoy to Cadiz. Rodney captured the entire convoy in a decisive action off Cape Finisterre, in northwest Spain. A week later he met a much larger Spanish force off **Cape St Vincent** (8 January 1780).

Cape Finisterre ▌ 1805 ▌ Napoleonic Wars (3rd Coalition)

The Franco-Spanish fleet of Admiral Pierre Villeneuve was driven back across the Atlantic from the West Indies and was met off Ferrol, near Cape Finisterre, the northwestern tip of Spain, by a British squadron under Admiral Sir Robert Calder. Villeneuve lost two ships captured before escaping to Cadiz. Three months later he was utterly defeated at **Trafalgar** (22 July 1805).

Cape Girardeau ▌ 1863 ▌ American Civil War (Trans-Mississippi)

On a second expedition into Missouri after his previous repulse in January at **Hartville**, Confederate General John S. Marmaduke attacked the important supply depot at Cape Girardeau on the Mississippi, recently reinforced by General John McNeil from Bloomington. After a costly assault and over 300 casualties, Marmaduke withdrew south across the St Francis at **Chalk Bluff** (26 April 1863).

Cape Gloucester ▌ 1943–1944 ▌ World War II (Pacific)

Aided by a diversionary landing at **Arawe**, Marine General William Rupertus landed at Cape Gloucester in western **New Britain**, fiercely defended by General Iwao Matsuda. The key airfield was quickly taken, though there was costly fighting and a further landing at Talasea (6 March) before the western end of the island was secured to isolate **Rabaul** (26 December 1943–April 1944).

Cape Henry ▌ 1781 ▌ War of the American Revolution

See **Chesapeake Capes**

Cape Kaliakra ▌ 1791 ▌ Catherine the Great's 2nd Turkish War

A few weeks after the great Russian land victory near the mouths of the Danube at **Matchin**, Russian Admiral Fedor Fedorovich Ushakov surprised a Turkish fleet under Algerian Admiral Seit-Ali off Cape Kaliakra, north of Varna, on the western shore of the Black Sea.

The Turkish ships were driven off and an armistice between Russia and Turkey was agreed the same day (31 July 1791).

Cape Matapan ▌ 1941 ▌ World War II (War at Sea)

Pursuing an Allied convoy, Italian Admiral Angelo Iachino, with a battleship, eight cruisers and destroyers, was surprised at night off Cape Matapan in southern Greece by Admiral John Cunningham, with three battleships, an aircraft carrier and destroyers. Attacking with torpedo aircraft and heavy guns, Cunningham sank three cruisers and two destroyers before the Italians withdrew (29 March 1941).

Cape of Good Hope ▌ 1795 ▌ French Revolutionary Wars (1st Coalition)

See **Cape Colony**

Cape Ortegal ▌ 1747 ▌ War of the Austrian Succession

See **Cape Finisterre (2nd)**

Cape Palos ▌ 1938 ▌ Spanish Civil War

A rare Republican success at sea saw two cruisers and five destroyers under Admiral González de Ubieta attack three Nationalist cruisers escorting a convoy off Cape Palos, in the Mediterranean, east of Cartagena. The new Nationalist cruiser *Balaeres* was sunk with over 700 men killed, including Admiral Manuel de Vierna, but the Republicans failed to follow up their victory (6 March 1938).

Cape Passaro ▌ 1718 ▌ War of the Quadruple Alliance

Spain was determined to regain losses from the War of the Spanish Succession and sent forces to reoccupy Sardinia and later Sicily, where English Admiral Sir George Byng met Admiral Antonio Castaneta off Cape Passaro, near Syracuse. Sixteen Spanish warships were taken or sunk in a disastrous defeat, with Castaneta fatally wounded. A year later, Byng blockaded **Messina** (11 August 1718).

Cape Passaro ▮ 1940 ▮ World War II (War at Sea)

Britain's Mediterranean fleet had escorted a convoy to **Malta**, when the cruiser *Ajax* (Captain Desmond McCarthy) was attacked off Cape Passaro, in southeast Sicily, by four Italian destroyers and three torpedo boats. Despite Italian numbers and aggression, *Ajax* sank two torpedo boats, and a damaged destroyer was sunk next day when the main British fleet arrived (11 October 1940).

Capes ▮ 1781 ▮ War of the American Revolution

See **Chesapeake Capes**

Cape Sarych ▮ 1914 ▮ World War I (War at Sea)

After the attack on **Sevastopol** by the German-manned Turkish cruisers *Goeben* (Yavuz) and *Breslau* (Midilli), Russian Admiral Andrei Ebergard took his obsolescent battle fleet and met the Turkish squadron off Cape Sarych, on the southern tip of the Crimea. Despite inflicting considerable damage, Admiral Wilhelm Souchon on *Goeben* was hit and broke off the action (18 November 1914).

Cape Spada ▮ 1940 ▮ World War II (War at Sea)

When two Italian light cruisers (Admiral Ferdinando Casardi) sailed from Tripoli for Leros, they were intercepted off Cape Spada, between Crete and Cerrigotto, by a British destroyer flotilla and the Australian cruiser *Sydney*. Intense gunfire saw the cruiser *Bartolomeo Colleone* sunk with 120 killed (including Captain Umberto Novaro) and the other cruiser fled to Benghazi (19 July 1940).

Cape Spartivento ▮ 1940 ▮ World War II (War at Sea)

Two weeks after success at **Taranto**, Admiral John Cunningham, on convoy escort, led a large fleet (including an aircraft carrier, a battleship and eight cruisers) against the main Italian battle fleet (Admiral Inigo Campioni) off Cape Spar-tivento in southern Sardinia. Both sides suffered damage before the Italians broke off. Cunningham was criticised for failure to pursue (27 November 1940).

Cape St George ▮ 1943 ▮ World War II (Pacific)

As Allied forces fought to secure **Bougainville**, an American destroyer squadron led by Captain Arleigh Burke intercepted Japanese destroyers under Captain Kiyoto Kagawa, off Cape St George, returning from Buka to Rabaul. The last surface action in the **Solomons** campaign saw three out of five Japanese destroyers sunk without American loss (25 November 1943).

Cape St Mathieu ▮ 1293 ▮ Anglo-French Wars

When a quarrel between crews of English and Norman ships in Brittany escalated into large-scale battle, Gascon forces supported the English and helped defeat 200 Norman and French ships off Cape St Mathieu near Brest. Philip IV of France then instigated full-scale war against Edward I of England, who invaded Gascony but was repulsed in 1297 at **Furnes** (15 May 1293).

Cape St Vincent ▮ 1606 ▮ Netherlands War of Independence

Dutch Admiral Willem Hultain was attempting to intercept the homeward bound Spanish silver fleet when he found himself heavily outnumbered in a clash off Cape St Vincent, the southwestern tip of Portugal. The Dutch were defeated and fled before the larger Spanish fleet, except for Vice Admiral Reinier Klaazoon, who fought to the last, then blew up his ship, along with his crew and himself.

Cape St Vincent ▮ 1693 ▮ War of the Grand Alliance

See **Lagos Bay**

Cape St Vincent ▮ 1780 ▮ War of the American Revolution

When he sailed from Plymouth with a large fleet to relieve besieged **Gibraltar**, British Admiral George Rodney met a much smaller Spanish force under Admiral Don Juan de Langara off Cape St Vincent, the southwestern point of Portugal. Rodney sank one Spanish ship and captured six others in a hard-fought night action before continuing on to Gibraltar (16 January 1780).

Cape St Vincent I 1797 I French Revolutionary Wars (1st Coalition)

Intercepting Admiral José de Cordova sailing from the Mediterranean to Brest, outnumbered British Admiral Sir John Jervis attacked the Spanish fleet off southern Portugal near Cape St Vincent. Cordova was routed in a brilliant one-sided victory—which marked out Commodore Horatio Nelson. The Spanish fleet ceased to be a threat, and Jervis was created Earl St Vincent (14 February 1797).

Cape St Vincent I 1833 I Miguelite Wars

In support of Maria da Gloria, legitimate heir to the throne of Portugal, England sent a fleet under Captain (later Admiral Sir) Charles Napier to assist the Regent Don Pedro against his brother, the usurper Miguel. Napier routed Miguel's fleet off Cape St Vincent, in southwestern Portugal and, three weeks later, the constitutional army seized Lisbon for the young Queen (5 July 1833).

Cape Styrsudden I 1790 I 2nd Russo-Swedish War
See **Kronstadt Bay**

Cape Teulada I 1940 I World War II (War at Sea)
See **Cape Spartivento**

Capetown I 1795 I French Revolutionary Wars (1st Coalition)
See **Cape Colony**

Capetown I 1806 I Napoleonic Wars (4th Coalition)
See **Blueberg**

Cape Trafalgar I 1805 I Napoleonic Wars (3rd Coalition)
See **Trafalgar**

Cap Francais I 1757 I Seven Years War (Caribbean)

A British naval squadron under Captain Arthur Forrest attempting to intercept a French convoy off northern Santo Domingo was attacked by Admiral Guy-Francois de Kersaint near Cap Francais (modern Cap Haitien). Both sides suffered heavy damage in a severe action and, when Forrest withdrew to Jamaica for repairs, the French convoy sailed safely for France (21 October 1757).

Cap Francais I 1803 I Napoleonic Wars (Santo Domingo Rising)
See **Vertieres**

Capharsalma I 161 BC I Maccabean War

The Seleucid General Nicanor, who had been defeated at **Emmaus** five years earlier, was sent to renew the campaign against the Hebrew Judas Maccabeus, and pursued the rebels into hills north of Jerusalem. Nicanor stumbled into an ambush at Capharsalma (modern Kfar Shalem) and was driven back to Jerusalem with heavy losses. He soon fought again and was killed at **Adasa**.

Caporetto I 1917 I World War I (Italian Front)

With Austrian resistance failing on the **Isonzo**, Germany sent reinforcements and General Otto von Below attacked in the north through Caporetto. Massive bombardment helped an Austro-German breakthrough, and Italian General Luigi Cadorna retreated to the **Piave** with shocking losses. He was dismissed and a year later Italy struck back at **Vittorio Veneto** (24 October–7 November 1917).

Cappel I 1531 I Swiss Religious Wars
See **Kappel**

Capua ∎ 212 BC ∎ 2nd Punic War

Having defeated Carthaginian General Hanno at **Beneventum** (212 BC), Roman Consuls Quintus Fulvius Flaccus and Appius Claudius moved west to besiege Capua, where Hanno's brother Hannibal arrived to defend the town. After fierce fighting, fresh Roman cavalry reinforcements forced Hannibal to withdraw. Later that year he defeated a Roman blocking force at the **Silarus**.

Capua ∎ 211 BC ∎ 2nd Punic War

Carthaginian General Hannibal launched a renewed attempt to relieve the Roman siege of Capua, approaching from Mt Tifata, while the garrison under Hanno attempted a massive sortie. Appius Claudius held the Capuans and Quintus Fulvius Flaccus turned on Hannibal, inflicting a decisive defeat. Hannibal then led a diversionary advance on Rome, but Capua was starved into surrender.

Capua ∎ 554 ∎ Gothic War in Italy
See **Casilinum**

Carabobo ∎ 1814 ∎ Venezuelan War of Independence

When Patriot leader Simón Bolívar withdrew west from **San Mateo** in northern Venezuela to Valencia, he gathered reinforcements under Colonel José Félix Ribas, then met approaching Royalists led by General Juan Manuel Cagigal outside Valencia on the Plain of Carabobo. Cagigal was defeated and fled south towards El Pao, but Bolívar was crushed two weeks later at **La Puerta** (28 May 1814).

Carabobo ∎ 1821 ∎ Venezuelan War of Independence

Having liberated Colombia in 1819 after **Boyacá**, Patriot Simón Bolívar returned to Venezuela and joined José Antonio Páez advancing on **Caracas**. On the Plain of Carabobo, east of Valencia, he was blocked by Royalist Generals Miguel de La Torre and Tomás Morales, who were routed and fled to Puerto Cabello. Bolívar then entered Caracas to assure Venezuelan independence (24 June 1821).

Caracas ∎ 1813 ∎ Venezuelan War of Independence
See **Taguanes**

Caracas ∎ 1821 ∎ Venezuelan War of Independence

While Patriot leader Simón Bolívar advanced through western Venezuela against Spanish commander Miguel de La Torre, other rebels under General José Bermúdez attacked from the east and seized Caracas. De La Torre had to send a large force under General Tomás Morales, who retook the city. However, the diversion contributed to the Royalist defeat at **Carabobo** (14 and 24 May 1821).

Caraguatay ∎ 1869 ∎ War of the Triple Alliance
See **Piribebuy**

Carandayty ∎ 1934 ∎ Chaco War
See **Yrendagüe**

Caravaggio ∎ 1448 ∎ Milanese War of Succession

Amid confusion after the death of Filippo Visconti Duke of Milan, his son-in-law Francesco Sforza met a Venetian offensive east of Milan at Caravaggio. Supported by Roberto Sanseverino, and Jacopo and Francesco Piccinino (sons of the famous Niccolo), Sforza won a decisive victory, which consolidated his position. He succeeded as Duke in 1450 after besieging **Milan** (15 September 1448).

Carberry Hill ∎ 1567 ∎ Uprising against Mary Queen of Scots

Led by Alexander Lord Home, Scottish nobles who objected to Mary Queen of Scots' marriage to James Hepburn Earl of Bothwell defeated and took her prisoner at Carberry Hill, near Musselburgh, east of Edinburgh. The Queen was forced to dismiss Bothwell, and abdicated in favour of her infant son James VI. Her attempt to regain the throne was defeated the following year at **Langside** (15 June 1567).

Carbiesdale I 1650 I British Civil Wars

Following the execution of Charles I, James Graham Marquis of Montrose returned from the Continent with Scottish and mercenary forces to support Charles II, and was opposed by Presbyterian extremist Remonstrants under Colonel Archibald Strachan. Montrose was heavily defeated in northern Scotland at Carbiesdale and fled abroad. On his return he was betrayed and executed (27 April 1650).

Carcassonne I 589 I Frankish Imperial Wars

In a decisive success over the Franks, Recared I, Gothic King of Spain, defeated an invasion of southern Gaul by Guntram, Frankish King of Burgundy. The massive victory at Carcassonne, just north of the Pyrenees, secured Recared's northern border for most of his reign, which was noted for his historic declaration of Catholicism as the Spanish religion of state.

Carcassonne I 1209 I Albigensian Crusade

Soon after the massacre of Albigensian heretics at **Beziers** in southern France, Anglo-Norman knight Simon de Montfort besieged nearby Carcassonne, where he offered safe conduct to Raymond Roger Viscount of Beziers and Caracassonne, and his supporters. However, he promptly seized them and the Viscount died in prison. De Montfort was granted Beziers and Carcassonne (1–15 August 1209).

Carchemish I 605 BC I Babylon's Wars of Conquest

Driven out of **Harran** in 610 BC, the remnants of the Assyrian army joined with Necho II of Egypt on the Euphrates at Carchemish, where they were attacked by Prince Nebuchadrezzar of Babylon, son of Nabopolassar. In a decisive action, the Babylonians won a brilliant victory, driving Egypt out of Syria and Palestine. The battle also represented the last death throes of the once-great Assyrian empire.

Cardedeu I 1808 I Napoleonic Wars (Peninsular Campaign)

General Laurent Gouvion Saint-Cyr advancing to relieve the siege of French-held Barcelona broke through at **Rosas**, then two weeks later smashed into a Spanish force under Generals Francois Vives and Teodoro Reding at Cardedeu, north of Barcelona. Driving off the Spanish, St-Cyr reached Barcelona next day and relieved the garrison of General Philibert Duhesme (16 December 1808).

Carenage Bay I 1778 I War of the American Revolution
   See **St Lucia**

Carham I 1018 I Danish Conquest of England

Eight years after defeating the Danes at **Mortlack**, Malcolm II of Scotland, supported by Owen of Strathclyde, advanced into Northumbria and heavily defeated Eadulf Cudel, the Danish Earl of Bernicia, on the River Tweed at Carham. The Lothian lowlands below the Firth of Forth became part of Scotland and King Knut recognised the Tweed as England's new northern border.

Carhampton I 835 I Viking Raids on Britain

Vikings who landed in Bridgwater Bay, West Somerset, immediately faced a force under King Egbert of Wessex just inland near Watchet. In battle at Carhampton, Egbert's West Saxons were driven off with heavy losses. The King was more successful in 837 against a subsequent large-scale Danish invasion of Cornwall at **Hingston Down**.

Carhampton I 843 I Viking Raids on Britain

After Egbert of Wessex was defeated by a Viking force at **Carhampton** (835), he won a great victory at **Hingston Down** in 837. A few years later his son King Aethelwulf met a fresh Viking landing in West Somerset, near Watchet, in the so-called Second Battle of Carhampton. Aethelwulf was heavily defeated and the Vikings continued to raid along the southwest coast of England.

Carigat ▌ 1791 ▌ 3rd British-Mysore War
See **Arikera**

Carillo ▌ 1813 ▌ Colombian War of Independence
Spanish Royalist Captain Bartolomé Lizón campaigning in northern Colombia attacked and bloodily defeated Republican commander Francisco de Paula Santander in the Cúcuta Valley at Carillo. Lizón then seized and butchered San José, and new Scots-born Republican commander Colonel Gregor MacGregor was unable to prevent Spanish capture of Pamplona (October 1813).

Carisbrook ▌ 530 ▌ Anglo-Saxon Conquest of Britain
Having established the Kingdom of Wessex in southern England, the great Saxon warrior Cerdic and his son Cynric invaded the offshore Isle of Wight, where they defeated the local Britons at a fortress on the site of modern Carisbrook. The island was then settled by Jute invaders, possibly Cerdic's nephews Stuf and Wihtgar.

Carlisle ▌ 1745 ▌ Jacobite Rebellion (The Forty-Five)
Charles Stuart—Bonnie Prince Charlie—invaded England and laid siege to Carlisle, where Colonel Durand surrendered after five days. Following his failed invasion, Charles withdrew north, pursued by Duke William of Cumberland, and left 400 men under John Hamilton to hold Carlisle. They surrendered after a bold defence and many were executed (9–15 September & 21–30 December 1745).

Carlos Antonio López ▌ 1932 ▌ Chaco War
As Paraguay and Bolivia advanced into the disputed Chaco Boreal, Bolivian Major Oscar Moscoso attacked the fortress of Carlos Antonio López on east shore of Lake Pitiantuta, killing a five-man Paraguayan unit led by Corporal Liborio Talavera. It was quickly retaken by Para-

guay, but Bolivia soon captured fortresses on the Pilcomayo at Corrales, Toledo and **Boquerón** (15 June 1932).

Carlow ▌ 1798 ▌ Irish Rebellion
At the start of the rebellion in Ireland, an estimated 1,200 insurgents under a cobbler named Michael Heydon attacked Colonel Stephen Mahon of the 9th dragoons and a force of about 500 on the River Barrow at Carlow. The rebels suffered very heavy losses, quickly followed by another costly repulse 15 miles further east at the small town of Hacketstown (25 May 1798).

Carmen, Cañada el ▌ 1934 ▌ Chaco War
See **Cañada el Carmen**

Carmen Alto ▌ 1844 ▌ Peruvian Civil Wars
During disorder in Peru following the death of President Agustín Gamarra at **Ingavi**, Manuel Ignacio de Vivanco seized the country as Dictator and overthrew the constitution. However, Constitutionalists under Ramón Castilla captured Lima, then defeated Vivanco's army near Arequipa at Carmen Alto. The Dictator fled into exile and Castilla secured the Presidency (17 July 1844).

Carnifex Ferry ▌ 1861 ▌ American Civil War (Eastern Theatre)
Confederate General John Floyd took the initiative in West Virginia at **Cross Lanes**, then withdrew to Carnifex Ferry, on the Gauley near Summerville, where he was later attacked by heavily reinforced Union troops under General William S. Rosecrans and Major Henry W. Benham. After several hours of fighting, the outnumbered Confederates withdrew south at night (10 September 1861).

Carpathian Passes ▌ 1241 ▌ Mongol Invasion of Europe
With his northern forces advancing through Poland towards **Liegnitz**, the Mongol Batu (grandson of Genghis Khan) and General Subetai marched west from **Kiev** to force the Carpathian Passes towards the Danube. Between Uzhgorod and Mukacehvo, a large Hungarian army sent to stop them suffered a massive defeat,

and Batu continued west to decisive battle at the **Sajo** (12 March 1241).

Carpathians I 1915 I World War I (Eastern Front)

While Germany attacked Russia at the **Masurian Lakes**, further south, Austrian Generals Karl von Pflanzer-Baltin and Alexander von Linsingen advanced through the Carpathians into Bukowina against General Platon Lechitsky. Czernowitz fell, but a Russian counterattack seized **Przemysl** and halted the advance until the spring offensive at **Gorlice-Tarnow** (23 January–10 April 1915).

Carpi I 1701 I War of the Spanish Succession

Commanding French forces in Lombardy, the elderly Marshal Nicolas Catinat faced an offensive by Austria's Prince Eugène of Savoy, who crossed the Alps then advanced to Carpi, on the Adige near Legnago. Catinat was completely outmanoeuvered and defeated. He withdrew behind the Minco, then the Oglio, and was replaced by Francois de Neufville Marshal Villeroi (9 July 1701).

Carpinteria I 1836 I Uruguayan Civil War

Former Uruguayan President Fructuoso Rivera led a rising against his successor Manuel Oribe and met a large government force under Oribe's brother Ignacio and Juan Antonio Lavalleja at Arroyo de la Carpinteria, north of Durazno. Rivera was badly beaten but escaped to rebuild his forces. He defeated Oribe two years later at **Palmar** to regain the Presidency (19 September 1836).

Carpio de Azaba I 1811 I Napoleonic Wars (Peninsular Campaign)

As French forces advanced to relieve the Anglo-Portuguese blockade of **Ciudad Rodrigo**, troops under General Thomas Graham met General Pierre Watier southwest near the Azaba at Carpio. Although Watier took the town and crossed the river, he was driven back after a feeble action. Meanwhile, a fierce battle was

being fought only ten miles away at **El Bodon** (25 September 1811).

Carrhae I 610 BC I Babylon's Wars of Conquest
See **Harran**

Carrhae I 53 BC I Roman-Parthian Wars

Roman Consul Marcus Licinius Crassus, trying to match his rivals Pompey and Caesar, rashly crossed the Euphrates to attack Parthia. At Carrhae (modern Harran), he was attacked by Parthian General Surenas and his Legions were caught in the open desert after his cavalry were destroyed. The Romans were annihilated in one of their worst defeats and Crassus himself was killed after surrendering.

Carrhae I 297 I Roman-Persian Wars
See **Callinicum**

Carrhae I 1104 I Crusader-Muslim Wars
See **Harran**

Carrick I 1922 I Irish Civil War
See **Clonmel**

Carrickfergus I 1760 I Seven Years War (Europe)

In a futile invasion of Ireland, French privateer Francois Thurot landed at Carrickfergus, northeast of Belfast, after a storm dispersed half his fleet. The town surrendered following a brief siege, but Thurot had insufficient forces and re-embarked. When two of his three remaining ships became separated in another storm, Thurot was attacked and killed by a British squadron (10–20 January 1760).

Carrickfergus I 1778 I War of the American Revolution

The day after raiding **Whitehaven** in England, American John Paul Jones in the sloop *Ranger* sailed to Ireland, where he met the sloop *Drake* off Carrickfergus, near Belfast. *Drake* was captured after a fierce action in which British Captain Gordon Burdon was killed. While not the first British prize taken, it was reputedly the first major ship-to-ship action between the two navies (24 April 1778).

Carrick's Ford ▪ 1861 ▪ American Civil War (Eastern Theatre)
  See **Rich Mountain**

Carrignagat ▪ 1798 ▪ French Revolutionary Wars (Irish Rising)
  See **Collooney**

Carrion ▪ 1037 ▪ Spanish Territorial Wars
  See **Tamaron**

Carrion ▪ 1812 ▪ Napoleonic Wars (Peninsular Campaign)
  See **Villa Muriel**

Carrizal ▪ 1916 ▪ United States' Expedition against Villa
  Following the raid on **Columbus**, New Mexico, in March by Francisco (Pancho) Villa, General John Pershing invaded northern Mexico. He failed to locate the rebel but, at Carrizal, Captain Charles Boyd met Federal troops under General Felix Gómez. After heavy Mexican losses, and the opposing leaders both killed, the American patrol had to retreat and the expedition later withdrew (21 June 1916).

Cartagena, Colombia ▪ 1586 ▪ Drake's Caribbean Raid
  A large-scale raid against Spain in the Caribbean saw an English fleet of about 30 ships under Sir Francis Drake sack **Santo Domingo** in January, then attack the rich city of Cartagena, in modern Colombia. After Drake seized the port in sharp fighting, the residents paid a massive ransom (said to be 100,000 ducats or ten million pesos) and he sailed north against **St Augustine** (9 February 1586).

Cartagena, Colombia ▪ 1697 ▪ War of the Grand Alliance
  Near the end of the war, French Admiral Jean-Bernard Desjeans Baron de Pointis left Brest for Santo Domingo and took a mixed fleet against Spanish Cartagena. The city, in modern Colombia, was taken by storm after a brief siege and De Pointis seized a massive treasure. However, when sickness struck his men, he destroyed Cartagena's fortifications and withdrew (12 April–2 May 1697).

Cartagena, Colombia ▪ 1702 ▪ War of the Spanish Succession
  See **Santa Marta**

Cartagena, Colombia ▪ 1708 ▪ War of the Spanish Succession
  British Commodore Charles Wager, commanding just three ships, attacked 17 heavily armed Spanish treasure ships off Cartagena, Colombia. While the Spanish flagship blew up with 700 men lost, Wager's ship was badly damaged and his other two captains gave only half-hearted pursuit. They were later tried and dismissed, while Wager was knighted for his exploit (28 May 1708).

Cartagena, Colombia ▪ 1741 ▪ War of the Austrian Succession
  After seizing **Porto Bello** (November 1739), English Admiral Edward Vernon led an expedition against Cartagena, fiercely defended by General Blas de Lezo and Governor Sebatián de Eslava. Despite a large fleet and over 8,000 troops under General Thomas Wentworth, the English attack foundered in swamps and was driven off. Vernon withdrew and later attacked **Santiago** (3 March–17 April 1741).

Cartagena, Colombia ▪ 1815 ▪ Colombian War of Independence
  In support of revolution in Colombia, Simón Bolívar secured **Bogotá**, then besieged dissident Cartagena, held by General Manuel de Castillo. When a large Spanish army under General Pablo Morillo landed at nearby Santa Marta, Bolívar was driven off and he fled to Jamaica (26 March–10 May 1815). Morillo captured Cartagena after a long siege (6 December 1815) and later retook Bogotá.

Cartagena, Colombia I 1820–1821 I
Colombian War of Independence

Although Colombian independence was assured by the decisive action at **Boyacá** in August 1819, Spanish Brigadier Gabriel de Torres held out at Cartagena against Colonel Mariano Montilla, supported at sea by commander José Padilla. Torres accepted generous terms after more than a year and South America's greatest fort surrendered to the cause of liberation (10 July 1820–10 October 1821).

Cartagena, Spain I 209 BC I 2nd
Punic War

See **New Carthage**

Cartagena, Spain I 460 I Roman-Vandal
Wars

When the Western Emperor Majorian assembled 300 ships in Spain to attack the Vandals of North Africa, Gaiseric led a brilliant pre-emptive attack on the Romans at Cartagena. The Vandals surprised and captured or sank virtually the entire fleet, dealing Majorian's prestige such a blow that he was soon overthrown. It was eight years before a new expedition was sent against **Carthage** (May 460).

Cartagena, Spain I 1706 I War
of the Spanish Succession

Admiral Sir John Leake led an Anglo-Dutch fleet to Cartagena, where he landed marines under Major Richard Hedges, who forced the city's surrender before General Daniel O'Mahony could bring aid. Leake then captured **Alicante** (29 July), but Cartagena was soon besieged and recaptured by Franco-Spanish commander Marshal James Duke of Berwick (4–13 June & 11–17 November 1706).

Cartago I 1842 I Central American
National Wars

In a last attempt to restore the Central American Federation, exiled Francisco Morazán of Salvador entered Costa Rica and, aided by defecting army commander Vicente Villaseñor, overthrew Dictator Braulio Carrillo. Morazán

soon faced rebellion by Antonio Pinto Suárez, who ousted him after heavy fighting at Cartago. Morazán and Villaseñor were both executed (12 September 1842).

Cartago I 1948 I Costa Rican Civil War
See **Ochomogo**

Carthage, Missouri I 1861 I American
Civil War (Trans-Mississippi)

Secessionist Governor Claiborne Price lost at **Boonville**, Missouri, in June, and withdrew southwest, then turned on a pursuing Union force under Colonel Franz Sigel at Carthage, west of Springfield. Outnumbered three to one, Sigel fought a brief action, then withdrew southeast through Sarcoxie. A decisive Confederate victory followed further east at **Wilson's Creek** (5 July 1861).

Carthage, Tunisia I 310–307 BC I
Agathoclean War

Besieged by Carthaginian forces in Sicily at **Syracuse**, the Tyrant Agathocles led a counter-invasion against Carthage itself, where he defeated and killed Hanno. When he returned to Sicily, his son Achagethus was driven off from Carthage by Himilco and was later killed by mutinous troops. Agathocles went back with a large mercenary force, but he was also defeated and soon made peace.

Carthage, Tunisia I 255 BC I 1st
Punic War
See **Tunis**

Carthage, Tunisia I 148–146 BC I 3rd
Punic War

In the last terrible act of the wars between Rome and Carthage, Publius Scipio Aemilianus besieged Carthage, which held out for two years under the leadership of Hasdrubal against starvation and disease. After the final successful assault and a six-day rampage of destruction, the surviving population was sold into slavery and the city was razed to the ground.

Carthage, Tunisia I 238 I Roman Military Civil Wars

When Maximinus in Germany was proclaimed Emperor by his soldiers, Legions in Africa proclaimed the octogenerian Gordian I as a rival. But at Carthage, his son and co-Emperor Gordian II was defeated and killed by veterans loyal to Maximinus under Cappellianus, Governor of Numidia. Gordian I committed suicide, while Maximinus was killed by his own troops at **Aquileia** two years later.

Carthage, Tunisia I 439 I Roman-Vandal Wars

The Vandal Gaiseric and his followers invaded North Africa and seized **Hippo Regius** in 431, gradually establishing an independent kingdom at uncertain peace with Rome. But within a few years, Gaiseric surprised and captured the key city of Carthage and put it to the sack. Carthage remained capital for the Vandals until their defeat a hundred years later at **Tricameron** (19 October 439).

Carthage, Tunisia I 468 I Roman-Vandal Wars

See **Cape Bon**

Carthage, Tunisia I 533 I Vandal War in Africa

See **Ad Decimum**

Carthage, Tunisia I 697–698 I Muslim Conquest of North Africa

During continuing Muslim civil war, Byzantine troops recovered coastal Tripoli before the Arab General Hassan ibn Noman invaded with a large army and stormed and sacked Carthage. In 697 a powerful Byzantine fleet then drove the Arabs out, but the following year massive reinforcements again enabled them to recapture the city, virtually ending the Byzantine presence in North Africa.

Carthage, Tunisia I 1270 I 8th Crusade

Two years after the fall of **Antioch, Syria**, King Louis IX of France launched his second Crusade, attempting to capture Carthage as a base in North Africa. After seizing the harbour, his army had to besiege the walled city in extremely hot and pestilential conditions. When the King died of fever, his brother Charles negotiated a cash indemnity to abandon the siege and go home (July–August 1270).

Casa-al-Secco I 1427 I Venetian-Milanese Wars

Filippo Maria Visconti Duke of Milan defended the city of **Cremona**, against attack by a large Venetian-Florentine army under Francesco Bussone Count Carmagnola. A day-long battle at the nearby pass of Casa-al-Secco saw the Milanese led by Agnolo della Pergola cut down by Allied crossbowmen. Despite heavy losses on both sides, it was a bloody victory for Carmagnola (July 1427).

Casablanca I 1907 I French Colonial Wars in North Africa

Responding to the murder of some Europeans working on the new harbour at Casablanca, French forces bombarded, then seized, the city (4 August). However, Casablanca was soon besieged by Moroccan Chief Madoni el Glaoui until he was driven off at nearby **Taddert**. Morocco was eventually declared a French Protectorate in 1912 after the second siege of **Fez** (18 August–12 September 1907).

Casablanca I 1942 I World War II (Northern Africa)

As part of the **Torch** operations in French Northwest Africa, 34,000 Americans under General George Patton landed in Morocco near Casablanca. There was resistance ashore under Vichy General Charles Nogùes, and Admiral Gervais de Lafond suffered costly losses in ships and men. Threatened with assault on Casablanca itself, Admiral Francois Darlan surrendered (8–10 November 1942).

Casa de Salinas I 1809 I Napoleonic Wars (Peninsular Campaign)

British General Sir Arthur Wellesley was advancing east along the Tagus towards Talavera, southwest of Madrid, when Marshal Claude

Victor sent Generals Pierre Lapisse and Francois Ruffin across the shallow Alberche, where they surprised and nearly captured Wellesley at Casa de Salinas. In a costly action, Wellesley finally checked the French then won at **Talavera de la Reina** next day (27 July 1809).

Casale I 1628–1629 I Thirty Years War (Mantuan War)

During a disputed succession in Mantua and Montferrat, Gonzalo Fernández de Cordoba, Spanish Governor of Milan, laid siege to Casale, east of Turin, held for the French-born heir Charles di Gonzaga Duke of Nevers. When Louis XIII crossed the Alps and defeated a Savoyard army at Susa, Cordoba raised the siege, but it was resumed a few months later (1628– March 1629).

Casale I 1629–1630 I Thirty Years War (Mantuan War)

In the breakdown of negotations over the succession of **Mantua** and Montferrat, Spain sent the veteran Ambrogio de Spinola to renew the siege of Casale, east of Turin. The city fell, but the citadel held out. Spinola died during negotiations and, in the peace which followed, the French-born heir Charles di Gonzaga Duke of Nevers received his inheritance (September 1629–October 1630).

Casale I 1640 I Thirty Years War (Franco-Habsburg War)

After victory in northern Italy at **Chieri** (November 1639), French commander Henri Comte d'Harcourt and Henri de Turenne made a second advance on Casale, on the Po, 40 miles east of Turin. Despite having twice as many troops, Spanish General Diego Felipe de Guzmán Marquis of Leganés suffered a decisive defeat and the French advanced on **Turin** (29 April 1640).

Casalechio I 1511 I War of the Holy League

Following breakup of the League of Cambrai, Pope Julius II formed a new alliance with Venice against France in northern Italy. At Casalechio,

Papal commander Francesco Maria della Rovere Duke of Urbino was routed by the French under Gian Giacomo Trivulzio of Milan, who then captured nearby Bologna. The Pope retired to **Ravenna**, where he was defeated 12 months later (21 May 1511).

Casal Novo I 1811 I Napoleonic Wars (Peninsular Campaign)
See **Cazal Novo**

Casas Grandes I 1911 I Mexican Revolution

At the start of Mexico's Revolution, Francisco Madero crossed from Texas and, after initial success, led an ambitious dawn attack on Casas Grandes, in Chihuahua. In the first pitched battle of the Revolution, his 600 ill-armed men were decisively defeated when Federal cavalry reinforcements drove them from the field. Madero soon regained the initiative at **Ciudad Juárez** (6 March 1911).

Casco Bay I 1690 I King William's War
See **Fort Loyal**

Caseros I 1852 I Argentine Civil Wars

Opposing the costly intervention in Uruguay by Argentine Dictator Juan Manuel de Rosas, rebel General Justo José de Urquiza raised the siege of **Montevideo**, then met Rosas at Monte Caseros, west of Buenos Aires. Supported by Brazilians and Uruguayans, Urquiza secured a decisive victory. The Dictator then fled into exile and Urquiza became President (3 February 1852).

Casilinum I 214 BC I 2nd Punic War

Soon after Hannibal withdrew to Apulia from his third failed attempt on **Nola**, Marcus Claudius Marcellus and Fabius Cunctator attacked Casilinum, just west of Capua, held by Carthaginians and Capuans under Status Metius. Following a heavy assault, the garrison surrendered to Fabius in return for free passage to **Capua**. Marcellus, claiming ignorance, attacked and destroyed the withdrawing column.

Casilinum | 554 | Gothic War in Italy

The Romano-Byzantine General Narses was campaigning in Italy against the Goths when a Frankish army under the brothers Buccelin and Lothair invaded from Germany. Part of the army under Buccelin met Narses on the Volturno River at Casilinum, just west of Capua, and was destroyed. Buccelin was killed, and the Frankish offensive into Italy was virtually over.

Caspe | 1874 | 2nd Carlist War

Campaigning on the Ebro in Aragon for the Spanish Republican government, Colonel Eulogio Despujol surprised a Carlist force under Manuel Marco de Bello at Caspe, northeast of Alcañiz. The Carlists were routed in a brilliant action, losing 200 prisoners and 80 horses. Despujol was promoted to Brigadier and became Conde de Caspe (23 February 1874).

Cassano | 1158 | Frederick's 2nd Expedition to Italy

German Emperor Frederick Barbarossa crossed the Alps into northern Italy, where he marched against the Milanese, who had campaigned against his feudatory lord, Otto von Wittelsbach (later Duke Otto I of Bavaria). The Emperor defeated the Italians on the Adda River at Cassano, then marched west in August to besiege **Milan**.

Cassano | 1259 | Guelf-Ghibelline Wars

With the death of Frederick II, the Imperial cause in northern Italy was sustained by the cruel Ghibelline despot Ezelino III da Romana. Pro-Papal Guelfs gradually recovered territory and at Cassano, east of Milan, Ezelino was defeated and died of wounds a prisoner. The Guelfs butchered many Ghibelline leaders but were defeated the following year at **Montaperti** (27 September 1259).

Cassano | 1705 | War of the Spanish Succession

Returning to Italy to meet a new French offensive, Prince Eugène of Savoy joined Victor Amadeus II of Savoy (now an Imperial ally) attacking the French at Cassano, on the Adda, east of Milan. French commander Philippe de Vendôme failed until reinforced by his brother Louis Duke de Vendôme. Eugène withdrew, returning next year for his great victory at **Turin** (16 August 1705).

Cassano | 1799 | French Revolutionary Wars (2nd Coalition)

Three weeks after their victory at **Magnano**, the Austrians of General Paul Kray were joined by Russians under General Alexander Suvorov and attacked the demoralised French on the Adda at Cassano, east of Milan. Despite the inspired leadership of newly appointed commander Jean Victor Moreau, the French were again defeated and the Allies seized Milan (27 April 1799).

Cassel | 1071 | Franco-Frisian War

When he became King of France, Philip I took an army to protect Flanders on behalf of his aunt Adela—sister of Henry I of England and widow of his former Regent, Baldwin V—against attack by Count Robert of Frisia. Philip was heavily defeated at Cassel, inland from Dunkirk, and Count Robert continued his struggle against the King for five years before eventually swearing allegiance.

Cassel | 1328 | Franco-Flemish Wars

Soon after being crowned, Philip VI of France determined on a fresh expedition to secure control of Flanders. At Cassel, east of Saint-Omer, Flemish leader Nicolas Zannequin led a doomed force of infantry and pikemen, who were ridden down and destroyed by French cavalry. Philip, first of the House of Valois, then sacked Bruges and seized most of Flanders (23 August 1328).

Cassel | 1677 | 3rd Dutch War

Louis XIV of France launched a fresh offensive in the Netherlands to capture Valenciennes, then besieged St Omer, with the support of Marshal Sebastien Vauban and Duke Francois Henri of Luxembourg. A relief army under William of Orange was defeated at nearby Cassel by Luxembourg and the King's brother,

Duke Philippe d'Orleans. St Omer soon surrendered (11 April 1677).

Cassel I 1813 I Napoleonic Wars (War of Liberation)

As Napoleon Bonaparte returned west of the Elbe, former French Marshal Jean Baptiste Bernadotte sent a Cossack force under Prince Alexander Tchernitcheff against Cassel, the capital of Jerome Bonaparte's Kingdom of Westphalia. Jerome quickly fled and the Russians inflicted a heavy defeat, capturing nine French guns and declaring Jerome's kingdom at an end (28 September 1813).

Cassina Grossa I 1799 I French Revolutionary Wars (2nd Coalition)
See **Alessandria**

Cassino I 1944 I World War II (Southern Europe)
See **Monte Cassino**

Cassiope I 1084 I 1st Byzantine-Norman War
See **Corfu**

Cassville I 1864 I American Civil War (Western Theatre)
See **Adairsville**

Castagnaro I 1387 I Padua-Verona War

Attacking Verona, Francesco de Carrara of Padua sent a large mercenary army under Englishman Sir John Hawkwood (Giovanni Acuto), who met Giovanni dei Ordelaffi at Castagnaro. Despite inferiority in men and guns, Hawkwood secured a brilliant tactical victory, taking almost 5,000 prisoners (including Ordelaffi) and most of the Veronese artillery (11 March 1387).

Castalla I 1812 I Napoleonic Wars (Peninsular Campaign)

In an unwise advance from Alicante, Spanish General José O'Donnell (brother of Henry) marched north towards Castalla to try and surprise General Jean-Isidore Harispe. However, the outnumbered French routed the Murcian army, with about 3,000 Spanish lost for 200 French casualties. O'Donnell's survivors fled back to Alicante (21 July 1812).

Castalla I 1813 I Napoleonic Wars (Peninsular Campaign)

Leading a new offensive in Valencia, French Marshal Louis Suchet beat Allied forces at **Yecla** and **Biar** before meeting a mixed army under the incompetent leadership of General Sir John Murray in hills west of Castalla. Despite a poorly managed battle, Murray's subordinates won a remarkable victory and Suchet withdrew. Murray did not pursue and remained on the defensive (13 April 1813).

Casteel Zeelandia I 1661–1662 I Chinese Conquest of Taiwan
See **Fort Zeelandia**

Casteggio I 1800 I French Revolutionary Wars (2nd Coalition)
See **Montebello**

Castelfidardo I 1860 I 2nd Italian War of Independence

With the Kingdom of Naples under attack by Giuseppe Garibaldi, Count Camillo Cavour of Piedmont sent General Enrico Cialdini into the Papal states against Pope Pius IX's army. French General Léon Louis Lamoricière was decisively defeated at Castelfidardo and fell back on nearby **Ancona**, while Cialdini marched south to join Garibaldi at the **Volturno** (18 September 1860).

Castellazzo I 1391 I Florentine-Milanese Wars

When Gian Galeazzo Visconti of Milan sent Jacopo Dal Verme against Florence and Bologna, he was met at Castellazzo, near Alessandria, by English mercenary Sir John Hawkwood and Jean III Count of Armagnac, who crossed the alps to aid his allies. The massive French army was routed, with Armagnac killed, and the Visconti family effectively secured most of northern Italy (25 July 1391).

Castellfullit de la Roca I 1874 I 2nd Carlist War

General Ramón Nouvilas was appointed to command the Spanish Republican army in the north and attempted to relieve the Carlist siege of Olot in Gerona. However, at Castellfullit de la Roca, in one of the government's worst defeats, Nouvilas was routed by Carlist General Francisco Savalls. He was captured along with about 2,000 of his men, and Olot capitulated two days later (14 March 1874).

Castellón de la Plana I 1938 I Spanish Civil War

Expanding the offensive on the Ebro, which began at **Belchite**, the Nationalist army of General Fidel Dávila seized the coastal city of **Vinaroz** in April, then resumed the offensive south towards the key city of Castellón de la Plana. Heavy fighting saw Castellón fall to General Antonio Aranda's corps, and the Nationalists then continued south along the coast towards **Valencia** (14 June 1938).

Castelnaudary I 1632 I French Civil War

Rebelling against Louis XIII and his Minister Cardinal Richelieu, the King's brother Duke Gaston of Orleans was supported by the great Henry Duke of Montmorency and nobles of the Languedoc. The rebel army was crushed at Castelnaudary, south of Toulouse, by Marshal Henry of Schomberg. Montmorency was executed and Gaston fled into exile (1 September 1632).

Castelnuovo, Albania I 1538–1539 I Later Venetian-Turkish War

Venetian Admiral Andrea Doria recovered from failure at **Preveza** in September 1538 and, with Ferrante Gonzaga, captured the Albanian fortress of Castelnuovo (24 October). The following summer Turkish Admiral Khair-ed-Din Barbarossa led a costly siege which eventually recovered the port (modern Herceg Novi), and a truce soon ended the war with Venice (13 July–10 August 1539).

Castelnuovo, Albania I 1687 I Venetian-Turkish Wars

Campaigning against the Turkish Corsairs of Dalmatia, Venetian Captain-General at Sea, Girolamo Cornaro, in alliance with Montenegrans under Vuceta Bogdanovic, won a great victory over the Turks near Castelnuovo (modern Herceg Novi). The fortress became part of Venetian Albania and Cornaro went on to besiege **Monemvasia** (30 September 1687).

Castelnuovo, Albania I 1806 I Napoleonic Wars (4th Coalition)

On a fresh offensive in Dalmatia, French forces under General Auguste Marmont advanced from Dubrovnik towards Castlenuovo (modern Herceg Novi) against a large force of Russians and Montenegrans. Marmont secured a decisive victory in a night-time attack outside Castlenuovo, completed next day when he destroyed a Montenegran counter-attack (29–30 September 1806).

Castelnuovo, Italy I 1796 I French Revolutionary Wars (1st Coalition)

Responding to the French check at **Caldiero**, Austrian General Paul Davidovich advanced down the Adige Valley towards Verona. North of Castelnuovo, he faced a large force under General Barthélemy Joubert, while General Pierre Augereau had advanced upriver to cut him off at Peri. After heavy losses in men and supplies, Davidovich broke through to withdraw north (21 November 1796).

Castelo Branco I 1704 I War of the Spanish Succession

Franco-Spanish commander James Fitz-James Duke of Berwick advanced into Portugal and fell on a Dutch-Portuguese force under Baron Nicolas Fagel near the frontier fortress of Castelo Branco. Fagel's outnumbered troops were heavily defeated, with most killed or captured. He managed to escape southwest towards Abrantes, while Berwick marched south to capture Portalegre (May 1704).

Castiglione | 1796 | French Revolutionary Wars (1st Coalition)

Marching to relieve the French siege of **Mantua**, Austrian commander Dagobert Wurmser unwisely divided his fresh army down both sides of Lake Garda. Two days after defeating an Austrian force at **Lonato**, Napoleon Bonaparte routed Wurmser near Castiglione delle Stiviere, north of Medole. Wurmser withdrew and Bonaparte renewed the siege of Mantua (5 August 1796).

Castillejos, Morocco | 1860 | Spanish-Moroccan War

When Moroccan forces raided Spanish possessions in North Africa, a large invasion force landed and, in the first major action of the war, General Juan Prim y Prats met the Moors at Castillejos (Fnideq), just south of Ceuta. The Moors were defeated in very heavy fighting, permitting a Spanish advance south towards victory at **Tetuán**. Prim was created Marques de Castillejos (1 January 1860).

Castillejos, Spain | 1811 | Napoleonic Wars (Peninsular Campaign)

During the siege of **Olivenza**, in central Spain, south of Badajoz, Spanish General Francisco Ballesteros advanced south towards Niebla, but was pursued by General Honoré Gazan and turned to fight at Villaneuva de los Castillejos. Ballesteros was heavily defeated, losing 1,500 prisoners as well as numerous casualties, and was driven over the Guadiana into Portugal (24 January 1811).

Castillon | 1453 | Hundred Years War

England lost Normandy at **Formigny** in 1450, and John Talbot Earl of Shrewsbury landed with a fresh army at **Bordeaux** (23 October 1452). Ill-advisedly marching east to relieve Castillon, besieged by French General Jean Bureau, the 80-year-old Earl was defeated and killed. The fortress surrendered three days later and the defeat cost England the southwest (17 July 1453).

Castine | 1814 | War of 1812

See **Hampden**

Castlebar | 1798 | French Revolutionary Wars (Irish Rising)

French General Joseph Humbert advanced south from **Killala** to attack a strong defensive position at Barnageerah Pass near Castlebar, County Mayo. Loyalist General Gerard Lake had only just taken command from General John Hely-Hutchinson, and his defeated garrison of about 1,500 fencibles and militia fled in a disgraceful rout known as the "Castlebar Races" (27 August 1798).

Castleford | 948 | Viking Wars in Britain

During the confused struggle for Northumbria following Viking defeat in 937 at **Brunanburh**, the Saxon Eadred marched against Erik Blood-axe, the exiled Norwegian who claimed northern England. Returning south after burning the city of Ripon, Eadred's rearguard was ambushed at Castleford on the River Aire. The Saxons suffered terrible losses, and Eadred turned back and overthrew Erik.

Castle Hill | 1849 | Hungarian Revolutionary War

See **Buda**

Castrejon | 1812 | Napoleonic Wars (Peninsular Campaign)

Marshal Auguste Marmont led a counteroffensive south of the Duoro through Tedula towards **Salamanca**, and attacked General Sir Stapleton Cotton, defending a line on the Tarabancos at Castrejon, west of Medina del Campo. Though Cotton resisted heavy artillery fire, when the French threatened to turn his position, he fell back west to **Castrillo** on the Guarena (18 July 1812).

Castricum | 1799 | French Revolutionary Wars (2nd Coalition)

Four days after success at **Alkmaar** in northern Holland, Frederick Augustus Duke of York and his Russian ally General Ivan Hermann advanced on French entrenchments among coastal dunes near Castricum, southwest of **Bergen-aan-Zee**. However, General Guil-laume Brune drove them back with heavy losses in men and guns. York quickly made peace and returned home (6 October 1799).

Castrillo | 1812 | Napoleonic Wars (Peninsular Campaign)

Advancing northeast after taking **Salamanca** (27 June), Arthur Wellesley Lord Wellington was surprised by a counter-offensive through **Castrejon** by French Marshal Auguste Marmont. In a defensive position further west on the Guarena at Castrillo, British-German troops under General Victor Alten repulsed General Bertrand Clausel and Wellington withdrew to Salamanca (18 July 1812).

Castrogiovanni | 859 | Byzantine-Muslim Wars

With the fall of **Palermo** in 831, the key to the Byzantine defence of central Sicily became the heavily fortified city of Castrogiovanni (modern Enna), held in the final months by a force under Theodotus. Following several failed assaults, the city was eventually stormed by Emir Abbas ibn Fadl, giving Arabs the "navel of Sicily" and leaving the Byzantines little else but **Syracuse** (24 January 859).

Castro Urdiales | 1812 | Napoleonic Wars (Peninsular Campaign)

British Admiral Sir Home Popham led an offensive on the northern coast of Spain to relieve pressure on the Allied campaign around **Salamanca**, attacking **Lequeitio** and **Guetaria**. He soon joined with Spanish troops under Colonel Francisco Longa to capture the fortress at Castro Urdiales, northwest of Bilbao. A few days later, Popham marched southeast against **Portugalete** (6–8 July 1812).

Castro Urdiales | 1813 | Napoleonic Wars (Peninsular Campaign)

Campaigning on the Biscay Coast, French General Maximilien Foy besieged Castro Urdiales, northwest of Bilbao, captured by the British the previous July and held by Spanish Colonel Pedro Alvarez. A relief force under

General Gabriel Mendizibal was driven off (29 April) and, despite British naval support, Foy took the port by storm (25 April–11 May 1813).

Catalaunian Plain | 451 | Hun Invasion of the Roman Empire
See **Chalons**

Catalca | 1912 | 1st Balkan War
See **Chataldja**

Catambuco | 1823 | Colombian Civil Wars

Royalist rebels under Colonel Agustín Agualongo rose in support of Ferdinand VII and seized Pasto, but it was retaken by Colonel Bartolomé Salom. Returning after defeat at **Ibarra** in July, the rebels besieged the city. Salom marched out to inflict a terrible defeat at nearby Catambuco and the rising was suppressed until the final Royalist defeat in June 1824 at **Barbacoas** (13 September 1823).

Catania | 1849 | 1st Italian War of Independence

Following the bombardment of Messina, and truce in 1848, Sicily renewed her uprising against Ferdinand II of Naples, aided by foreigners including the Pole Ludwig Mieroslawski. In eastern Sicily at Catania the rebels were defeated in a decisive battle by General Carlo Filangieri and Swiss mercenaries. Filangieri became Governor of Sicily as the Duke of Taormina (6 April 1849).

Catania | 1943 | World War II (Southern Europe)

British General Sir Bernard Montgomery opened the Allied invasion of **Sicily**, landing in the southeast, where he captured Syracuse (10 July). However, he stalled on the Plain of Catania, with costly losses while attempting to secure the Primosole Bridge over the Simeto. Montgomery then diverted inland towards Adrano and the Germans held Catania until they withdrew on 4 August (12–17 July 1943).

Catawba Ford I 1780 I War of the American Revolution
See **Fishing Creek**

Cateau Cambresis I 1794 I French Revolutionary Wars (1st Coalition)
See **Beaumont-en-Cambresis**

Cathraeth I 598 I Anglo-Saxon Territorial Wars
Marching into northern Northumbria against King Aethelfrith, the Scottish Princes Mynydawc and Cynan of Edinburgh were met in battle on the Swale at Cathraeth (modern Catterick). While Aethelfrith's Bernicians suffered heavy losses, the army of Edinburgh was destroyed. A further victory at **Daegsaston** in 603 secured Aethelfrith's northern border against the Scots.

Catlett's Station I 1863 I American Civil War (Eastern Theatre)
See **Auburn**

Cattaro I 1690 I Venetian-Turkish Wars
While Venice besieged the Turkish fortress at **Monemvasia** in southern Greece, other Venetian forces on the Dalmatian coast marched against Zin Ali Pasha of Herzogovina, who was reinforced by cavalry from the Pasha of Bosnia. In a decisive defeat near Cattaro (modern Kotor), south of Dubrovnik, Zin Ali was captured and lost 700 men out of his army of 3,500 (30 April 1690).

Cattaro I 1813–1814 I Napoleonic Wars (War of Liberation)
Following French defeats in Germany, Peter I of Montenegro besieged the Adriatic port of Cattaro (Kotor), south of Dubrovnik, defended by French General Jean-Joseph Gauthier. Aided by Captain William Hoste in the frigate *Bacchante*, the Montenegrans forced Gauthier to surrender. The Congress of Vienna in 1815 made them return Cattaro to Austria (14 October 1813–3 January 1814).

Caucasus I 1942–1943 I World War II (Eastern Front)
To secure Caucasus oil, German Army Group A under Marshal Wilhelm List (later, General Ewald von Kliest) drove south from **Rostov** and took Maikop (9 August). Russian counterattacks then stopped the Germans crossing the Caucasus Mountains towards Grozny and Baku. Threatened in the rear by the fall of **Stalingrad**, the Germans were forced to withdraw (29 July 1942–14 February 1943).

Caudebec I 1592 I 9th French War of Religion
The Catholic forces of Alessandro Farnese Duke of Parma relieved **Rouen** (21 April) then marched west and captured the town of Caudebec on the Seine, where they found themselves trapped by the massively reinforced Royalist army of Henry of Navarre. In a brilliant manoeuvre, Parma led his 15,000 men across the river in a single night to escape to the south (24 April–21 May 1592).

Caudine Forks I 321 BC I 2nd Samnite War
Determined to conquer central Italy after victory at **Suessa** in 339 BC, Rome renewed war against the Samnites. After initial success, Consuls Titus Veturius Calvinus and Spurius Postumius Albinus were routed by Caius Pontius on the Plain of Caudium at the Caudine Forks, and surrendered. Rome accepted a harsh truce and, when war resumed, she was defeated again in 315 BC at **Lautulae**.

Caudium I 321 BC I 2nd Samnite War
See **Caudine Forks**

Cau Giay I 1883 I Sino-French War
See **Hanoi**

Cauldron I 1942 I World War II (Northern Africa)
Axis commander Erwin Rommel turned the British line at **Gazala**, then concentrated his tanks in a defensive position in the Allied rear known as the Cauldron. Rommel drew in and

destroyed British armour and, with the fall of **Bir Hacheim** (11 June), the British retreated into Egypt through **Mersah Matruh** to **El Alamein**, while Rommel turned northeast on **Tobruk** (30 May–4 June 1942).

Caulk's Field | 1814 | War of 1812

As a diversion from the advance on **Baltimore**, Captain Sir Peter Parker (HMS *Menelaus*) took 260 men against the eastern shore of Chesapeake Bay to attack about 175 Americans under Colonel Phillip Reed in camp west of Chestertown. Landing at night without the element of surprise, the British were badly beaten at Caulk's Field with 17 killed, including Parker fatally wounded (31 August 1814).

Caurières | 1916 | World War I (Western Front)
    See **Louvement**

Caversham Bridge | 1643 | British Civil Wars
    See **Reading**

Caving Banks | 1861 | American Civil War (Trans-Mississippi)
    See **Bird Creek**

Cawnpore (1st) | 1857 | Indian Mutiny

Near the start of the mutiny, rebel leader Nana Sahib laid siege to Cawnpore (modern Kanpur), held by a small garrison under General Sir Hugh Wheeler. Three weeks of bombardment forced the starving garrison to surrender in return for safe passage to Allahabad. But as they left, Wheeler and most of the men were killed. The women and children were taken and later murdered (6–26 June 1857).

Cawnpore (2nd) | 1857 | Indian Mutiny

Advancing from Allahabad to recapture Cawnpore (modern Kanpur), Sir Henry Havelock beat rebel forces at **Fatehpur**, **Aong** and **Pandu Nadi**, yet arrived too late to prevent the murder of European women and children by Nana Sahib. Just outside the city at Maharajpur,

Nana Sahib was routed and fled. British forces then entered Cawnpore and exacted terrible retribution (16 July 1857).

Cawnpore (3rd) | 1857 | Indian Mutiny

As General Sir Colin Campbell marched south from **Lucknow**, General Charles Windham marched out of Cawnpore (modern Kanpur) against approaching rebels from Gwalior under Tantia Topi. Heavily outnumbered Windham was routed and driven back to his entrenchments. The rebels seized the city before Campbell arrived to stabilise the situation (27–28 November 1857).

Cawnpore (4th) | 1857 | Indian Mutiny

Securing the British entrenchments at Cawnpore (modern Kanpur) after General Charles Windham's defeat, General Sir Colin Campbell attacked the rebels outside the city under Tantia Topi. In a vital strategic defeat, despite massive numerical superiority, the rebels were driven out with heavy losses in men and guns, saving Cawnpore. Campbell then prepared to retake **Lucknow** (6 December 1857).

Cayenne | 1809 | Napoleonic Wars (5th Coalition)

British Admiral Sir Sydney Smith supported Portuguese Brazil against French Guyana, sending Captain James Yeo in the sloop *Confiance* with Colonel Manoel Marques to take Cayenne. Five weeks after the combined force landed near Cayenne and captured Fort Diamant, French General Victor Hugues surrendered. Guyana remained Portuguese until 1814 (January–February 1809).

Cazal Novo | 1811 | Napoleonic Wars (Peninsular Campaign)

While retreating from the failed French invasion of Portugal, part of Marshal Michel Ney's rearguard under General Jean-Gabriel Marchand took a strong position at Cazal Novo, southeast of Coimbra. There they inflicted heavy losses on the Light Division under General Sir William Erskine before continuing the French withdrawal east through Miranda do Corvo (14 March 1811).

Cecora | 1620 | Polish-Turkish Wars

After victory at **Jassy** in support of Moldavian intrigue, Polish Hetman Stanislas Zolkiewski was abandoned by local allies and retreated north before a large Ottoman army under Sultan Osman II. On the Dniester at Cecora, near Mogilev-Podolski, the 73-year-old Polish General was killed and his army was annihilated. The Turks were stopped in 1621 at **Khotin** (September–6 October 1620).

Cedar Canyon | 1864 | Cheyenne-Arapaho Indian War

In response to Indian attacks in northern Colorado, Major Jacob Downing took a force against a Cheyenne village at Cedar Canyon, north of the South Platte. Downing claimed he killed 26, wounded 30 and captured 100 horses in a dawn attack. While he was unable to pursue because he had run out of ammunition, this was the first major action on the Platte (May 1864).

Cedar Creek | 1864 | American Civil War (Eastern Theatre)

Despite defeat at **Fisher's Hill** and **Tom's Brook**, Confederate commander Jubal A. Early boldly attacked Union General Horatio G. Wright at Cedar Creek, just northeast of Strasburg, Virginia. Early secured the initial advantage, but Union commander Philip Sheridan arrived to turn certain defeat into brilliant triumph, and he finally defeated Early in March 1865 at **Waynesboro** (19 October 1864).

Cedar Falls | 1967 | Vietnam War

See **Iron Triangle**

Cedar Mountain | 1862 | American Civil War (Eastern Theatre)

A month after saving Richmond in the **Seven Days' Battles**, Confederate commander Robert E. Lee sent Generals Thomas "Stonewall" Jackson and Ambrose P. Hill into northern Virginia, where part of General John Pope's army under General Nathaniel Banks was defeated at Cedar Mountain, near Culpeper. Jackson soon continued the offensive along the **Rappahannock** (9 August 1862).

Cedarville | 1862 | American Civil War (Eastern Theatre)

See **Front Royal**

Cedarville | 1864 | American Civil War (Eastern Theatre)

Sent from Petersburg to reinforce the Confederates in the Shenandoah Valley, General Richard H. Anderson was intercepted on the Shenandoah in Virginia, just north of Front Royal at Cedarville, by Union General Wesley Merritt. The Union forces withdrew north after an inconclusive action, and Anderson supported the attack further north at **Summit Point** five days later (16 August 1864).

Cedynia | 972 | Polish-German Wars

Mieszko I of Poland expanded into eastern Pomerania, where he met a force under Margrave Hodo of the Eastern March at Cedynia, just inside the modern Polish border northeast of Berlin. Driven onto swampy ground, the German knights were badly defeated and, after repulsing an attempt by Emperor Otto II to regain the area in 976, Mieszko was confirmed as Count of the March (24 June 972).

Cefn Carnedd | 50 | Roman Conquest of Britain

See **Caer Caradoc**

Celaya | 1859 | Mexican War of the Reform

See **La Estancia**

Celaya | 1915 | Mexican Revolution

After supporting Venustiano Carranza to overthrow President Victoriano Huerta, rebel leader Francisco (Pancho) Villa fell out with his former ally and, at Celaya, west of Querétaro, attacked a large government army under General Álvaro Obregón. Villa suffered massive losses in two battles—among the bloodiest in Mexican history—and fell back on **Trinidad** (6–7 & 13–15 April 1915).

Cempoala I 1520 I Spanish Conquest of Mexico

Conquistador Hernán Cortés destroyed **Cholula** and arrived at the Aztec capital, Tenochtitlan (November 1519), before Pánfilo de Narváez left Cuba with 1,000 men to remove him from command. Leaving Pedro de Alvarado in charge, Cortés marched to Cempoala on the coast and beat Narváez, enlisting his men. Cortés returned to **Tenochtitlan**, where fierce resistance had begun (May 1520).

Central Henan I 1944 I World War II (China)

In the opening Kogo phase of the **Ichigo** offensive, General Eitaro Uchiyama advanced south to clear the Beijing-Hankou Railway. Storming across Central Henan, the Japanese secured massive territory including Zhengzhou (22 April) and Luoyang (24 May). Army commander Shunroku Hata then moved his field headquarters to Hankou to prepare the next phase towards **Changsha** (18 April–25 May 1944).

Cepeda I 1820 I Argentine Civil Wars

On campaign against the Unitarians of Buenos Aires, Argentine Federalist forces under Estanislao López of Sante Fe and Francisco Ramirez of Entre Ríos attacked and defeated General José Rondeau of Río de la Plata at Cepeda, northwest of Buenos Aires. However, the struggle between the provinces and Buenos Aires continued for 40 years until a second action at Cepeda (1 February 1820).

Cepeda I 1859 I Argentine Civil Wars

Concluding protracted conflict between the warring provinces of Argentina, President Justo José de Urquiza at Paraná took an army against the Porteño forces of Buenos Aires, led by General Bartolomé Mitre. In battle northwest of Buenos Aires at Cepeda, Mitre was defeated, and Buenos Aires agreed to join the Confederation, though fighting resumed two years later at **Pavón** (23 October 1859).

Cephisus I 1311 I Wars of the Catalan Company

The Spanish mercenary army known as the Catalan Grand Company turned against their former Byzantine allies at **Aprus** (1305) and descended into Greece, to be confronted at the River Cephisus by Walter de Brienne Duke of Athens. Luring the French knights onto marshy ground, the Catalans utterly crushed them, killing Walter. They then established themselves as rulers of Athens (15 March 1311).

Cer I 1914 I World War I (Balkan Front)

Near the start of the war, Austrian Generals Liborius von Frank and Oskar Potiorek invaded Serbia and were met in the Cer Mountains west of Belgrade by Serbian Generals Stepa Stepanovic and Zivojin Misic. Despite costly Serbian losses, this first Allied victory saw the Austrians driven out of the mountains, and they fell back across the Drina to the city of **Sabac** (12–20 August 1914).

Cerami I 1063 I Norman Conquest of Southern Italy

Two years after seizing **Messina** in Sicily, Roger d'Hauteville marched inland to capture Troina, then met a large Muslim army in the mountains at Cerami. The Muslims suffered massive casualties, including a leading general identified as Arcadius of Palermo said to have been killed by Roger himself. Victory secured the Normans northeast Sicily, and Roger soon won again at **Misilmeri**.

Ceresole I 1544 I 4th Habsburg-Valois War

When a French-Swiss force under Francis de Bourbon Prince of Enghien besieged Carignano, south of Turin, they faced the large Spanish-Italian force of Alfonso d'Avalos Marquis del Vasto, reinforced by 7,000 Landsknechts. The Germans were virtually annihilated in a bloody action to the southeast at Ceresole and del Vasto withdrew with 9,000 killed or captured (14 April 1544).

Céret | 1794 | French Revolutionary Wars (1st Coalition)
See **Boulou**

Cerignola | 1503 | Italian War of Louis XII
In resumed war between France and Spain over Naples, Spanish General Gonsalvo de Cordoba was forced back to an eight-month siege at the port of **Barletta**. However, when reinforcements arrived by sea, Cordoba marched west to Cerignola and inflicted a terrible defeat, killing French commander Louis d'Armagnac Duke of Nemours and securing Naples for Spain (28 April 1503).

Cerigotto | 1940 | World War II (War at Sea)
See **Cape Spada**

Cerisole | 1544 | 4th Habsburg-Valois War
See **Ceresole**

Cernay | 58 BC | Rome's Later Gallic Wars
See **Mühlhausen**

Cernomen | 1371 | Ottoman Conquest of the Balkans
See **Maritza**

Cerquin | 1539 | Spanish Conquest of Honduras
As Spain tried to secure Honduras, the Lenca Chief Lampira raised powerful resistance in the mountains, where he held out in his stronghold at Cerquin against a force under Alonso de Cáceres, sent by Governor Francisco de Montejo. After six months' failed siege, Lampira was lured to peace talks and killed. Resistance was soon crushed. The modern Honduran national currency is named in his honour.

Cerrito | 1812 | Argentine War of Independence
Spanish Viceroy Gaspar Vigodet led an offensive from Montevideo which was met at nearby Cerrito by a makeshift force under the Argentine General José Rondeau. With brilliant tactics, Rondeau secured a decisive Patriot victory and succeeded San Martin to command the Patriot Army of the North. Vigodet meanwhile withdrew to eventual siege at **Montevideo** (31 December 1812).

Cerro Corá | 1870 | War of the Triple Alliance
Despite defeat at **Piribebuy** and **Acosta-Ñu** in August 1869, Paraguayan Dictator Francisco Solano López continued fighting until cornered at Cerro Corá, near the Aquidaban in northeast Paraguay, by Brazilian commander Gaston d'Orleans Comte d'Eu. Attacked by General José Antonio Câmara, López and most of his men were killed, ending Latin America's bloodiest war (1 March 1870).

Cerro del Borrego | 1862 | Mexican-French War
See **Orizaba**

Cerro de Pasco | 1820 | Peruvian War of Independence
While Patriot commander José de San Martin besieged **Callao**, he sent General Juan Antonio Alvarez de Arenales inland to raise support, where he was met at Cerro de Pasco by a Royalist force under General Diego O'Reilly. A decisive action saw the Royalists lose 70 casualties and 350 captured, including O'Reilly, and Arenales captured vital Spanish military equipment (6 December 1820).

Cerro Gordo | 1847 | American-Mexican War
General Winfield Scott's expeditionary force advancing inland from **Veracruz** towards **Mexico City** met Mexican commander Antonio de Santa Anna at Cerro Gordo, a mountain pass near Plan del Rio. After a premature assault by General David Twiggs, Scott's main force attacked next day and the Mexicans fled with heavy casualties and prisoners (17–18 April 1847).

Cerro Grande I 1859 I 2nd Chilean Liberal Revolt

Faced by a widespread Liberal army rising and defeat at **Loros** in March, Conservative Chilean President Manuel Montt Torres sent General Juan Viduarra Leal against rebel leader Pedro León Gallo and over 2,000 men at Cerro Grande, near La Serena. Gallo was defeated by the smaller government force when some commanders changed sides and the rising was bloodily crushed (29 April 1859).

Cerro Porteño I 1811 I Argentine War of Independence

Near the start of her war against Spain, Argentina sent General Manuel Belgrano to incorporate Paraguay under the authority of Buenos Aires. At Cerro Porteño, southeast of Asunción near Paraguarí, Spanish Governor Bernardo de Velazco fled the field. However, militia commander Colonel Manuel Atanasio Cavañas secured a decisive victory and soon won again at **Tacauri** (15 January 1811).

Cerros de San Francisco I 1879 I War of the Pacific

See **San Francisco, Chile**

Cesis I 1577 I Livonian War

See **Wenden**

Cesis I 1919 I Estonian War of Independence

When a counter-offensive at **Tallinn** drove the Red Army out of Estonia, Estonian General Johan Laidoner marched into northern Latvia to meet a German offensive from **Riga**. With Latvian aid, Laidoner decisively defeated General Rudiger von der Goltz near Cesis (Vönnu)—celebrated in Estonia by Victory Day—and checked Russia later that year at the **Narva** (19–23 June 1919).

Cesky Brod I 1434 I Hussite Wars

See **Lipany**

Cesme I 1770 I Catherine the Great's 1st Turkish War

See **Chesme**

Ceuta I 1415 I Portuguese Colonial Wars in North Africa

King John I of Portugal was urged on by his glory-hunting sons to attack the Muslim fortress of Ceuta (modern Sabta), south of the Strait of Gibraltar. The city fell with heavy Arab losses after a ferocious defence by Governor Salat ben Salat. Portugal's first overseas colony was given to Dom Pedro de Menezes, who held it against repeated attacks, including a major siege in 1419 (21 August 1415).

Ceuta I 1720 I Spanish-Moroccan Wars

Determined to save Ceuta (Sabta) from constant Moroccan attack, Philip V sent about 16,000 men under Jean de Bette Marquis de Lede and, following a naval bombardment, a successful Spanish offensive inflicted over 500 casualties and captured 29 cannon. Although de Lede was soon driven back and later withdrew, the blockade continued for many years (15 November 1720–February 1721).

Ceva I 1796 I French Revolutionary Wars (1st Coalition)

Just days after defeat at **Millessimo**, in northwest Italy, Austrian Baron Michael Colli took a defensive position west of **Dego** at Ceva and inflicted a costly repulse on French General Pierre Augereau. The French withdrew and gathered a large force to attack next day. Colli skillfully slipped away in the night and withdrew to **Mondovi**, where he was quickly defeated (16–17 April 1796).

Cevo I 1768 I Ottoman Invasions of Montenegro

Abandoned by Venice, Montenegro faced separate Ottoman armies invading from Rumelia and Bosnia. The two forces united, but near Cevo, just west of Danilograd, they were beaten by the much smaller Montenegran army in the "Marathon of Montenegro." Three days later, a lightning storm reputedly destroyed the Turks' gunpowder supply, and they had to withdraw (28 October 1768).

Ceylon I 1942 I World War II (Indian Ocean)

Admiral Chuichi Nagumo in command of a large Japanese fleet bombed key naval ports at **Colombo** and **Trincomalee** in Ceylon and sank an aircraft carrier, two cruisers, two destroyers and five other ships at the cost of just 36 aircraft lost. A supporting force under Admiral Jizaburo Ozawa sank 18 merchant ships in the Bay of Bengal before they both withdrew (5–9 April 1942).

Ceza I 1888 I Zulu Rebellion

When Britain annexed the last of Zululand and imposed a new hut tax, Zululand Police and Imperial troops supported Magistrate Dick Addison going to arrest uSuthu Chief Dinuzulu. Attacked by the Zulus at Ceza, on the border of the Boer New Republic, the British turned and fled. Losses were minimal, but this blow to British prestige was followed by another at **Ivuna** (1 June 1888).

Chabreiss I 1798 I French Revolutionary Wars (Middle East)

See **Shubra Khit**

Chacabuco I 1817 I Chilean War of Independence

Recovering from rebel defeat at **Rancagua** in 1814, General José de San Martin crossed the Andes and joined Bernardo O'Higgins against outnumbered Royalists under Brigadier Rafael Maroto, north of Santiago at Chacabuco. Maroto was routed, losing 500 killed, 600 captured and all his guns. Santiago fell two days later and O'Higgins proclaimed independence for Chile (12–13 February 1817).

Chacaltaya I 1814 I Peruvian War of Independence

José Pinelo captured La Paz, in modern Bolivia, in support of Indian Chief Mateo Pumacahua then faced 1,200 Royalists from Oruro under General Juan Ramirez de Orosco. Pinelo

was defeated northeast of La Paz at Chacaltaya, and Ramirez occupied the city. He then marched into Peru and drove Pumacahua out of Arequipa (9 December), seized after victory at **Apacheta** (2 November 1814).

Chaeronea I 338 BC I 4th Sacred War

A decade after success at **Pagasae** and **Olynthus**, Philip II of Macedon took a large army into central Greece and at Chaeronea in Boeotia, met Athenians under Chares and Thebans led by Theagenes. In a brutal action, with terrible losses including the entire Theban "Sacred Band," Philip secured victory, ensuring Macedonian dominance over Greece. He was assassinated two years later (August 338 BC).

Chaeronea I 86 BC I 1st Mithridatic War

Driven out of **Piraeus**, the Pontic General Archelaus, commanding the army of Mithridates VI in Greece, quickly occupied Chareonea in Boeotia, where he came under attack by Roman commander Lucius Sulla. Archelaus was decisively defeated in a large-scale action outside Chaeronea, but escaped with 10,000 men to Chalcis. He soon returned to Boeotia to fight again further east at **Orchomenus**.

Chaffin's Bluff I 1864 I American Civil War (Eastern Theatre)

See **New Market Heights**

Chahar Mahall I 1751 I Persian Wars of Succession

In the struggle for control of Persia after the assassination of Nadir Shah, the Zand Chieftain Karim Khan and his brother Sadeq Khan seized Isfahan (January 1751), then turned against their former ally, the Bakhtiyari Ali Mardan Khan. In battle southwest of Isfahan in the Chahar Mahall, Ali Mardan was defeated and fled. Karim seized power as Regent for the boy-Shah Ismail III.

Chaidari I 1826 I Greek War of Independence

During the Ottoman siege of the **Acropolis**, a relief force under Georgios Karaiskakis and

French Colonel Charles Nicolas Baron Fabvier approached as far as Chaidari, where they came under heavy attack and were routed. Although Fabvier blamed the loss on Karaiskakis withdrawing prematurely, Karaiskakis redeemed his reputation four months later at **Arachova** (20 August 1826).

Chains I 633 I Muslim Conquest of Iraq
See **Hafir, Iraq**

Chakan I 1660 I Mughal-Maratha Wars
With Maratha commander Shivaji besieged near Kolhapur at **Panhala**, further north, Mughal General Shaista Khan besieged the fortress of Chakan, near Poona, held for Shivaji by Phirangoji Narsala. When a powerful mine destroyed part of the wall, Chakan fell in a bloody two-day assault with most of the garrison slaughtered and Phirangoji surrendered (21 June–15 August 1660).

Chaksana I 1788 I Mughal-Maratha War of Ismail Beg
When Mahadji Sindhia sent Rana Khan and Benoit de Boigne to relieve **Agra**, renegade Mughal leader Ismail Beg and Rohilla Chief Ghulam Kadir raised their siege and met Mahadji's army at Chaksana, eight miles from Bharatpur. The Marathas quit the field early after terrible losses on both sides, but de Boigne also had to withdraw. They met again in June at **Bagh Dera** (22 April 1788).

Chalcedon I 74 BC I 3rd Mithridatic War
War resumed between Rome and Mithridates VI of Pontus, and Consul Marcus Aurelius Cotta sailed to the Bosphorus, where he was heavily defeated outside Chalcedon and had to retire into the city. Pontic ships then forced their way into the harbour and destroyed or captured the Roman fleet. The following year, Mithridates moved west along the Sea of Marmara against **Cyzicus**.

Chalchuapa I 1885 I Central American National Wars
President Justo Rufino Barrios of Guatemala was determined to reimpose a Central American

Confederation and, aided by Honduras, invaded western El Salvador against President Rafael Zaldívar. His army stormed the fortress of Santa Ana, but just to the west, at Chalchuapa, Barrios was killed in further fighting. His defeated army fled, ending the dream of Guatemalan dominance (2 April 1885).

Chalcis I 429 BC I Great Peloponnesian War
See **Patras**

Chaldiran I 1514 I Turko-Persian War in Anatolia
Invading Shi'ite Persia, Turkish Sultan Selim I took about 60,000 men across the Upper Euphrates and, northeast of Lake Van, met Shah Ismail I with a reported 50,000 horsemen on the Plain of Chaldiran. Utilising newly introduced artillery, the Ottomans routed the Persians, and Selim inflicted a further defeat at **Turna Dag** before turning against Syria in 1516 at **Marj-Dabik** (23 August 1514).

Chalgrove Field I 1643 I British Civil Wars
After a failed attempt to intercept a Parliamentary pay convoy near Oxford, a strong Royalist force under Prince Rupert were themselves intercepted on the Thame, southeast of Oxford. The Prince cut his way through to Oxford after a sharp action on Chalgrove Field, near Chiselhampton, although Parliamentary Colonel John Hampden was fatally wounded (18 June 1643).

Chalibee I 1814 I Creek Indian War
See **Calabee Creek**

Chalk Bluff I 1863 I American Civil War (Trans-Mississippi)
Repulsed on the Mississippi at **Cape Girardeau** (26 April), Confederate General John S. Marmaduke's expedition into Missouri retreated southwest, pursued by General William Vandever, who had arrived to take command from General John McNeil. At Chalk Bluff, on the St Francis River north of Kennet, Marmaduke's

rearguard fought a bloody action as he escaped into Arkansas (1–2 May 1863).

Chalmette | 1815 | War of 1812
See **New Orleans**

Chalons | 273 | Roman Military Civil Wars

When military Governor Gaius Tetricus was proclaimed Emperor in Gaul, the legitimate Emperor Aurelian, returning from victory in the east, marched into Gaul against the usurper. The Gallic force was decisively defeated in battle near Chalons-sur-Marne after Tetricus deserted, reputedly by prior agreement. Tetricus was subsequently pardoned by Aurelian.

Chalons | 366 | Alemannic Invasion of Roman Gaul

Soon after appointing his brother Valens co-Emperor in the East, Roman Emperor Valentinian I moved to Paris to better combat fresh barbarian incursions. Building up a substantial military presence, he sent General Jovinus against barbarian Alemanni, who had crossed the frozen Rhine. Jovinus defeated the Alemanni at Chalons-sur-Marne, reputedly killing more than 6,000 (January 366).

Chalons | 451 | Hun Invasion of the Roman Empire

Attila the Hun overran much of the Balkans, then led a reported 40,000 men into Gaul and besieged Orleans. In one of history's decisive battles, on the Catalaunian Plain between Chalons and Troyes, Attila was defeated by Roman commander Aetius and Theodoric the Visigoth (who was killed). Attila had to withdraw across the Rhine, but he invaded Italy the next year to sack **Aquileia**.

Chalus | 1199 | French War of Richard I

In a pointless dispute over ownership of some supposed treasure, Richard I—the Lion Heart—besieged one of his own Barons, Viscount Ademar, at the castle of Chalus, southwest of Limoges. An otherwise insignificant action saw the English King hit by a crossbow bolt and he died ten days later. The Viscount was later murdered in revenge by Richard's illegitimate son Philip (26 March 1199).

Chambly | 1775 | War of the American Revolution

Attempting to support besieged **St Johns**, southeast of Montreal, British General Sir Guy Carleton reinforced Chambly, ten miles further north, held by Major Joseph Stopford. Surrounded by Canadian Colonel James Livingston and American Major John Brown, Stopford prematurely surrendered, yielding vital military supplies, which hastened the fall of St Johns (18 October 1775).

Chamkaur (1st) | 1704 | Mughal-Sikh Wars

Amid renewed war against Sikh Guru Gobind Singh in the Upper Punjab, suspended after defeat at **Basoli** in 1702, Raja Ajmer Chand of Kahlur sought aid from an Imperial force under Generals Saiyad Beg and Alif Khan. In battle at Chamkaur, southwest of Rupar, Saiyad Beg changed sides—reportedly won over to the Sikh cause—and Alif Khan was forced to withdraw to Delhi.

Chamkaur (2nd) | 1704 | Mughal-Sikh Wars

Despite being promised safe passage after the siege of **Anandpur** in the Upper Punjab, Sikh Guru Gobind Singh was defeated at the **Sarsa**, and was routed next day at nearby Chamkaur by Mughal Generals Khwaja Mohammad and Nahar Khan. The Guru's sons Ajit and Jujhar were killed in this final stand, while Gobind Singh and a handful of survivors escaped (22 December 1704).

Chamorlu | 1413 | Ottoman Civil Wars

Ottoman Sultan Mehmed II resolved to put an end to rebellion by his brother Musa Celebi and took a large force into Serbia, where he was supported by the Serbian Despot George Brankovic. In battle at Chamorlu, near Samokov, Brankovic helped defeat Musa, who was later captured and killed. As a reward the Despot secured Serbia's freedom from Ottoman assault (5 July 1413).

Champa ∎ 1281–1283 ∎ Mongol Wars of Kubilai Khan

When Kubilai Khan sent General Sodu and a small force against King Jaya Indravarman VI of Champa (in southern Vietnam), they captured his capital Vijaya (near modern Quy Nhon). Despite reinforcements, the Mongols could not secure decisive victory and Kubilai then sent his son Toghon. But war with **Annam** intervened and Champa remained undefeated, though later agreed to pay tribute.

Champagne ∎ 1914–1915 ∎ World War I (Western Front)

Despite bloody stalemate in Flanders around **Ypres**, French commander Joseph Joffre determined to resume the offensive and attacked German positions in Champagne around Perthes. Fighting in bad winter conditions, bold French assaults against entrenched machine-guns eventually failed and both sides settled in to stubborn trench warfare (20 December 1914–17 March 1915).

Champagne ∎ 1915 ∎ World War I (Western Front)

Coinciding with the Allied offensive in **Artois**, Generals Henri Pétain and Fernande de Langle de Cary led a massive French advance in Champagne between Rheims and the Argonne, against General Karl von Einem and Crown Prince Wilhelm. The French took ground, prisoners and guns, but were finally checked with about 145,000 casualties (25 September–6 November 1915).

Champaner ∎ 1535 ∎ Mughal Conquest of Northern India

Emperor Humayun expanded the Mughal Empire into central India, where he captured **Mandu** from Sultan Bahadur Shah of Gujarat, then pursued him to the supposedly impregnable fortress of Champaner, 20 miles south of Godhra. Humayun led a brilliant night-time escalade of the massive walls after the Sultan fled to Diu

and General Ikhtiyar Khan surrendered the fortress (9 August 1535).

Champaubert ∎ 1814 ∎ Napoleonic Wars (French Campaign)

In a brilliant campaign east of Paris against the invading Prussian-Russian army of General Gebhard von Blucher, Napoleon Bonaparte attacked part of Blucher's force under Generals Zacharii Olssusiev and Konstantin Poltoratski at Baye, outside Champaubert. He captured both Generals and destroyed their force, then achieved another victory next day at **Montmirail** (10 February 1814).

Champ Blanc ∎ 1650 ∎ War of the 2nd Fronde

Rebelling against the power of Cardinal Jules Mazarin during the minority of Louis XIV, French nobleman Viscount Henri de Turenne led a force with Spanish support to relieve the so-called Frondeurs besieged at Rethel, north of Rheims. The rebels were routed by a Royal army under Marshal Cesar de Choiseul at nearby Champ Blanc and Turenne later changed sides (15 December 1650).

Champion Hill ∎ 1863 ∎ American Civil War (Western Theatre)

Confederate General John C. Pemberton attempting to defend besieged **Vicksburg**, on the Mississippi, marched east against the Union army, which had just captured **Jackson**. At Champion Hill, Mississippi, some of the campaign's hardest fighting saw Pemberton finally defeated by General John A. McClernand and he withdrew towards Vicksburg across the **Big Black River** (16 May 1863).

Champions ∎ 547 BC ∎ Spartan-Argive Wars

In a dispute over Cynuria, a strategic strip of coast between Argos and Laconia, the Argives demanded the matter be settled by 300 champions from either side. It is claimed that only two Argives and one Spartan survived the semi-legendary Battle of Champions, but the Spartan remain on the battlefield to claim victory. Sparta won the ensuing general engagement and annexed Cynuria.

Champotón I 1517 I Spanish Conquest of Yucatan

Three ships under Francisco Hernandez de Cordoba sailed from Cuba to the west coast of the Yucatan Peninsula, where they were driven off from the Mayan city of Campeche. They then attempted to land further south at the fortified town of Champotón, where an armed party found itself in a fierce battle and withdrew with heavy losses. Hernandez returned to Cuba, where he later died of wounds.

Chancellorsville I 1863 I American Civil War (Eastern Theatre)

Crossing the Rappahannock at **Fredericksburg**, Virginia, Union commander Joseph Hooker marched towards Chancellorsville against Confederate General Robert E. Lee. Despite heavy losses, including General Thomas "Stonewall" Jackson killed, Lee won perhaps his greatest victory, while Hooker, with his reinforcements repulsed at **Salem Church**, withdrew across the river (1–4 May 1863).

Chanda, Maharashtra I 1818 I 3rd British-Maratha War

As victorious British forces moved to capture remaining Maratha fortresses to end the war, Colonel Sir John Worthington Adams marched against Chanda (modern Chandrapur, south of Nagpur), stubbornly defended by troops of the Raja of Nagpur. Chanda was taken by storm after two days' bombardment, and the subsequent fall of **Malegaon** virtually ended the war (19–21 May 1818).

Chanda, Uttar Pradesh I 1857 I Indian Mutiny

Following Gurkha success at **Manduri** (19 September), British Colonel Frederick Wroughton sent 1,100 of the Nepalese soldiers under Dhir Shamshar Rana against rebel forces gathering at Chanda, in the Jaunpur district, southeast of Sultanpur. After marching ten miles, the Gurkhas met a rival force of about 5,000, but savage fighting dispersed the rebels, who lost perhaps 300 dead (31 October 1857).

Chanda, Uttar Pradesh I 1858 I Indian Mutiny

General Thomas Franks campaigned against Mehndi Husain in Oudh, where he defeated rebel lieutenants Fazil Azim at Saraun (21 January) and Beni Bahadur at Nasratpur (23 January). Franks then attacked Chanda, 20 miles southeast of Sultanpur, held by Banda Husain. The rebels were routed in fierce fighting and Franks met Mehndi himself the same day near **Budhayan** (19 February 1858).

Chandax I 961 I Later Byzantine-Muslim Wars

See **Crete**

Chanderi I 1858 I Indian Mutiny

While General Sir Hugh Rose advanced on **Jhansi**, further west, Brigadier Charles Stuart attacked rebel forces in the powerful hilltop fortress at Chanderi. Stuart breached the walls with artillery fire, then sent in a storming party under Major Richard Keatinge, who was severely wounded. Although most of the rebels escaped, Stuart captured the fort and all its guns (13–17 March 1858).

Chandernagore I 1757 I Seven Years War (India)

With **Calcutta** retaken in January from French-supported Nawab Siraj-ud-Daula of Bengal, British Colonel Robert Clive advanced up the Hooghly against the French base at Chandernagore. Supported by Admiral Charles Watson on the river, Clive bombarded the town until commander Pierre Renault surrendered, effectively ending the French presence in Bengal (14–24 March 1757).

Chandwar I 1194 I Later Muslim Conquest of Northern India

The great Muslim conqueror Muhammad of Ghor secured Delhi following victory at **Taraori**, then turned against the Kingdom of Kanauj under Raja Jaichand. In a terrible rout near the Jumna at

Chandwar (modern Ferozabad), the elephant-based army of Kanauj was routed by horse archers. Jaichand was killed, his capital at Benares was sacked and his kingdom was virtually destroyed.

Chang'an ▮ 316 ▮ Wars of the Sixteen Kingdoms Era

With the dramatic fall of the Jin capital at **Luoyang** (311), new Emperor Min moved his court to Chang'an. But Jin military power had been fatally weakened and Chang'an (Xi'an) fell by storm to a Xiongnu army under General Liu Yao. Like his predecessor, Min was captured and later executed. The rump of the Jin Dynasty survived only in southern China as the Eastern Jin, with their capital at Nanjing.

Chang'an ▮ 756 ▮ An Lushan Rebellion

The rebel An Lushan was advancing through **Luoyang** towards the Tang Imperial capital at Chang'an, when he was checked to the west at Tongguan by Tang General Feng Chang Qing. However, Emperor Xuan Zong had Feng executed for failure, and ordered General Geshu Han on a doomed offensive. The Tang army was destroyed and the Emperor abandoned Chang'an (January–July 756).

Chang'an ▮ 763 ▮ Later Tang Imperial Wars

Tang Emperor Daizong had recently defeated An Lushan rebels at **Luoyang**, when he faced a new threat with King Khri-srong-lde-brtsan of Tibet advancing on Chang'an (modern Xi'an). The Emperor fled east and General Guo Ziyi was defeated trying to hold the capital. After a brief occupation the Tibetans withdrew with their loot. Intermittent war continued for 60 years (12–30 November 763).

Changban ▮ 208 ▮ Wars of the Three Kingdoms

The great Han General and warlord Cao Cao (Ts'ao Ts'ao) secured most of northern China, then turned south against his rivals and attacked Liu Bei of Shu at Changban, near modern Yichang in Hubei. In a much mythologised battle, Liu Bei and his General Zhao Yun were pursued

and defeated. Liu Bei then formed an alliance with Sun Quan of Wu to meet Cao Cao on the Yangzi at **Red Cliffs**.

Chang-chou ▮ 1863–1864 ▮ Taiping Rebellion
See **Changzhou**

Changchun ▮ 1946 ▮ 3rd Chinese Revolutionary Civil War

As Soviet forces evacuated Manchuria, 4,000 Nationalist Chinese airlifted to the capital Changchun were attacked by a much larger Communist force under General Lin Biao. Severe street fighting forced General Chen Jicheng to surrender the city, but with the loss of **Siping** (Szepingkau) further south, Lin abandoned Changchun (22 May) and withdrew to Harbin (15–17 April 1946).

Changchun ▮ 1948 ▮ 3rd Chinese Revolutionary Civil War

At the start of the **Liaoshen** offensive in Manchuria, Communist General Lin Biao sent about 65,000 men to capture the northernmost Nationalist bridgehead at Changchun, isolated since the fall (13 March) of **Siping** (Szepingkau). Promised air drops failed to supply the city and, when some defenders changed sides, Zheng Dongguo surrendered his starving garrison (September–21 October 1948).

Changde ▮ 1943 ▮ World War II (China)

Regrouping after failure in **Western Hubei**, General Isamu Yokoyama led 100,000 Japanese into Hunan and captured Changde after heavy street fighting (3 December). Supported by American bombers, Generals Xue Yue and Sun Lianzhong retook Changde six days later after heavy losses on both sides, then drove the invaders back across the Li and Yuan (2 November–30 December 1943).

Changfukeng ▮ 1938 ▮ Russo-Japanese Border Wars

When Russians occupied Changfukeng Hill, close to Lake Khasan on the Tumen, General Kamezo Suetaka from Japanese-occupied

Manchukuo retook the border position, then faced an overwhelming air and land offensive under General Grigorii Shtern. After about 1,400 Japanese and 3,200 Russians casualties, a cease-fire was agreed, and Japan withdrew (6 July–11 August 1938).

Changjin I 1950 I Korean War
See **Chosin**

Changlu I 29 I Wars of the Later Han
With the Later Han Dynasty established after victory at Kunyang (23), Emperor Guangwu sent a large army against the warlords of the north China plain. Some pledged allegiance but others determined to fight and, at Changlu in modern Shandung, the Han army secured a decisive victory, including Liu Yu killed. Success enabled Guangwu to unify eastern China and he later turned west against **Chengdu**.

Changping I 260 BC I China's Era of the Warring States
During a period of struggle between states in eastern China, Qin (Ch'in) General Bai Qi launched a massive offensive against the Kingdom of Zhao. At Changping, he inflicted a crushing defeat on General Zhao Kuo, then massacred a claimed (but unlikely) 400,000 prisoners. Bai Qi then led his forces to besiege the Zhao capital of **Handan**, where he eventually committed suicide.

Changsha I 1852 I Taiping Rebellion
After campaigning in southern Hunan and gathering recruits, Taiping Western King Xiao Chaogui tried to surprise Changsha, held by Imperial Governor Luo Bingzhang. Xiao was killed leading the assault and, despite massive reinforcements under Heavenly King Hong Xiuquan, the city held out and the Taiping withdrew north towards **Hankou** (11 September–30 November 1852).

Changsha I 1926 I 1st Chinese Revolutionary Civil War
At the start of the Nationalist offensive against the warlords of northern China, Chiang Kai-shek's frontline commander Tang Shengzhi entered Hunan in force and advanced on General Ye Kaixin at Changsha. The city fell by storm and Chiang soon continued the advance north through **Pingjiang** and **Tingsiqiao** towards **Wuchang** (5–10 July 1926).

Changsha I 1930 I 2nd Chinese Revolutionary Civil War
When Li Lisan attempted a Communist rising in Jiangxi and Fujian, his General Peng Dehuai took Yochow (modern Yueyang) followed by Changsha. Driven out after ten days by Nationalist General He Yingqin, the Communists were then ordered to retake Changsha. However, they suffered further bloody losses and withdrew and Li was recalled to Moscow (28 July–September 1930).

Changsha I 1939 I Sino-Japanese War
General Yasuji Okamaru took and held **Nanchang** (18 March–8 May), then stormed the Xin Jiang River to advance on Changsha, in Hunan. To the northeast he captured Ganfang, then faced a huge Chinese counter-offensive under General Chen Cheng. Ganfang was retaken and, after very heavy fighting, the Japanese retreated behind the Xin Jiang to Yueyang (17–30 September 1939).

Changsha I 1941–1942 I World War II (China)
Renewing the offensive in Hunan, Japanese forces under General Anan Tadaki again advanced on Changsha and reached the outskirts (1 January), before General Xue Yeu inflicted massive casualties driving them back across the Xin Jiang. The so-called Third Battle of Changsha has been claimed as the first major Allied victory of the war (24 December 1941–15 January 1942).

Changsha I 1944 I World War II (China)
Continuing Japan's massive **Ichigo** offensive in eastern China from **Central Henan**, General Isamu Yokoyama led three columns into southern Hunan to neutralise Allied air bases. Chinese General Xue Yue was forced back with heavy losses, and the Japanese seized the much-disputed city of Changsha. The offensive

then turned south towards **Hengyang** and **Guilin** (26 May–19 June 1944).

Changshu ∣ 1856 ∣ Taiping Rebellion

Taiping leader Shi Dakai led a new offensive in Jiangxi, where he threatened Zeng Guofan at Nanchang by besieging Changshu (modern Qingjiang), just to the northwest. Zeng Guofan ordered his forces to abandon the siege of **Jiujiang** and sent a large force under Zhou Fengshan, who was routed in a massive battle. Shi was then inexplicably recalled to **Nanjing**, saving Nanchang (20–24 March 1856).

Changsintien ∣ 1922 ∣ 1st Zhili-Fengtian War

See **Changxindian**

Changteh ∣ 1943 ∣ World War II (China)
See **Changde**

Changxindian ∣ 1922 ∣ 1st Zhili-Fengtian War

Two years after Manchurian warlord Zhang Zuolin joined Kao Kun's Zhili faction at **Zhuozhou**, the allies fell out and Zhang marched on Beijing. Southwest of the capital at Changxindian, Zhili General Wu Beifu beat Fengtian General Zhang Jinghui, but heavy losses prevented Wu from pursuing into Manchuria. In October 1924 Zhang Zuolin won at **Shanhaiguan** (28 April–4 May 1922).

Changzhou ∣ 1863–1864 ∣ Taiping Rebellion

Following the fall of **Suzhou** (6 December), Imperial commander Li Hongzhang sent Liu Mingquan northwest of **Shanghai** to besiege Changzhou, held by the Taiping veteran Chen Kunshu (who later fought General Charles Gordon in nearby towns). When Li himself arrived to lead a massive assault, Chen was defeated and captured, further isolating **Nanjing** (19 December 1863–11 May 1864).

Chania ∣ 1645 ∣ Venetian-Turkish Wars
See **Khania**

Channel Dash ∣ 1942 ∣ World War II (War at Sea)

In a famous blow to British prestige, the German cruisers *Prince Eugen, Scharnhorst* and *Gneisenau* under Admiral Otto Ciliax raced through the English Channel from Brest to Wilhelmshaven, with heavy air and surface escort. While six British torpedo aircraft were shot down, and bomber and destroyer attacks failed, two of the German cruisers were damaged by mines (11–12 February 1942).

Channel Ports ∣ 1940 ∣ World War II (Western Europe)

As German forces stormed into France through the **Ardennes**, General Paul von Kleist's Panzer Group raced west towards the three great Channel Ports—Boulogne, Calais and Dunkirk. Frontline tank commander General Heinz Guderian reached the coast at Abbeville (19 May), then drove north through **Boulogne** and **Calais**, while other units closed in on **Dunkirk** (22 May–4 June 1940).

Chantilly ∣ 1862 ∣ American Civil War (Eastern Theatre)

Confederate commander Robert E. Lee pursued General John Pope's Union army from defeat at **Bull Run**, sending General Thomas "Stonewall" Jackson on a flank attack at Chantilly, northeast of Centreville, Virginia. Leading Union Generals Philip Kearny and Isaac I. Stevens were killed in a brief but bloody action and Pope continued falling back towards Washington, D.C. (1 September 1862).

Chaouen ∣ 1924 ∣ Spanish-Rif War

During a strategic withdrawal to the coast of Morocco, General Luis Aizpuru reached the garrison at Chaouen, 40 miles south of Tetuán, and more than 40,000 troops began the evacuation. Attacked by 7,000 Rif under Mhamed Abd el Krim (brother of the Chief), the disastrous trek cost up to 18,000 Spanish lives before the survivors reached Tetuán (15 November–13 December 1924).

Chapinería | 1936 | Spanish Civil War

As Nationalists advanced through **Talavera de la Reina** towards **Madrid**, the Republican army attempted to hold a line west of the capital at Chapinería. A government counter-attack met with initial success, but Nationalist commander Major Antonio Castejón broke through in heavy fighting. Another defensive effort a few days later failed to the southeast at **Navalcarnero** (18–19 October 1936).

Chaplin Hills | 1862 | American Civil War (Western Theatre)

See **Perryville**

Chapu | 1842 | 1st Opium War

See **Zhapu**

Chapultepec | 1847 | American-Mexican War

In his final advance on Mexico City following the costly diversion at **Molino del Rey**, American General Winfield Scott quickly attacked the fortress of Chapultepec, just west of the capital. After heavy fighting, with almost 2,000 Mexican casualties, Scott entered Mexico City the next day and army commander General Antonio de Santa Anna withdrew towards **Puebla** (12 September 1847).

Chapultepec | 1859 | Mexican War of the Reform

See **Tacubaya**

Charasia | 1879 | 2nd British-Afghan War

In response to the murder of Sir Louis Cavagnari, British Envoy to Afghanistan, General Sir Frederick Roberts was despatched to again occupy **Kabul**. Twelve miles south at Charasia, Roberts met a large Afghan force and defeated them with heavy losses. Four days later he reached Kabul and Amir Yakub Khan abdicated, retiring to British protection in India (6 October 1879).

Chardak Pass | 1176 | Byzantine-Turkish Wars

See **Myriocephalum**

Charenton | 1649 | War of the 1st Fronde

When the Paris Parlement rebelled against taxes and Cardinal Jules Mazarin, during the minority of Louis XIV, the royal family was forced to flee. Louis II de Bourbon Prince of Condé took an 8,000-strong Royal army against the rebels, and in heavy fighting seized the fortress of Charenton outside Paris. The Parlement sued for peace, but a fresh war began the following year (8 February 1649).

Charford | 508 | Anglo-Saxon Conquest of Britain

Ten years after victory over Arthur at **Badon**, the Saxon warrior Cerdic and his son Cynric met the British leader Natanleod on the Avon, at a site near modern Charford (later known as Cerdicesford for the King). The invaders reputedly killed 5,000 Britons and, after Cerdic received further Saxon reinforcements, he defeated the Britons again ten years later at the same site.

Charford | 519 | Anglo-Saxon Conquest of Britain

The Saxon warrior Cerdic was reinforced by a fresh migration of his countrymen and met a force of Britons on the Avon, at a site near modern Charford (later known as Cerdicesford for the King). As in battle at the same site ten years earlier, Cerdic defeated the Britons. Shortly afterwards he took the title of King of the West Saxons, consolidating establishment of the Kingdom of Wessex.

Charikar | 1841 | 1st British-Afghan War

Besieged by rebel tribesmen at Charikar, 35 miles north of Kabul, the Gurkha garrison under Lieutenant John Haughton decided to evacuate, leaving their wounded and families. In the so-called Massacre of Charikar, only the badly wounded Haughton, the political agent Major Eldred Pottinger and a handful of others out of

200 survived the march to **Kabul** (5–14 November 1841).

Charjui I 1740 I Persian-Uzbek Wars

Nadir Shah of Persia defeated Mughal India at **Karnal** (February 1739), then resolved to punish the Uzbeks for raiding his northern province of Khorasan. Marching northwest along the Oxus (Amy Darya), he beat Abdul Fayz Khan, King of Bokhara at Charjui (modern Chardzhou), southwest of Bokhara. Abdul Fayz surrendered and Nadir soon defeated the Uzbeks of **Khiva** (September 1740).

Charleroi I 1672 I 3rd Dutch War

As Louis XIV of France dispersed his army across a number of fronts in Holland, William of Orange attempted a bold attack on Charleroi, in modern Belgium. The Dutch Prince besieged the city, but facing severe winter conditions and with insufficient resources, he was driven off by a French and Flemish relief force under Louis II de Bourbon Prince of Condé (15 December 1672).

Charleroi I 1693 I War of the Grand Alliance

After victory at **Neerwinden** in July, French Marshal Duke Francois Henri of Luxembourg advanced on Charleroi, strongly defended by Francisco de Castillo Marquis of Villaderias. Francois de Neufville Marshal Villeroi and Marshal Sebastien Vauban then besieged Charleroi and, after suffering costly losses in heavy fighting, they took the city by storm (5 September–1 October 1693).

Charleroi I 1794 I French Revolutionary Wars (1st Coalition)

French General Jean-Baptiste Jourdan marched north into the Netherlands, where he besieged Charleroi, then sent forces to defeat the Austrians in the field at **Hooglede**. Threatened by the approaching Allied relief army of Friedrich Josias Prince of Saxe-Coburg, Jourdan shelled Charleroi and forced its surrender. Saxe-Coburg arrived too late and lost next day at **Fleurus** (12–25 June 1794).

Charleroi I 1914 I World War I (Western Front)

Turning north from the **Ardennes** to face the unexpected German invasion through Belgium, French commander Joseph Joffre sent Charles Lanzerac to meet Generals Karl von Bulow and Max von Hausen on the Sambre. After heavy fighting around Charleroi, the Belgians abandoned nearby **Namur**, and the French withdrew, exposing the late-arriving British at **Mons** (21–23 August 1914).

Charleston, Massachusetts I 1776 I War of the American Revolution

During the prolonged American siege of **Boston**, Major Thomas Knowlton led a daring raid on the British headquarters at Charleston, close to Bunker Hill on the Charleston Peninsula. Knowlton destroyed some barracks and took a handful of prisoners, but his raid had little strategic significance. He was killed later that year in a skirmish at **Harlem Heights** (8 January 1776).

Charleston, South Carolina I 1706 I Queen Anne's War

On the offensive in North America, a French squadron from Havana supported by Spanish troops attacked Charleston, South Carolina, which was suffering yellow fever. A courageous defence by Governor Sir Nathaniel Johnson and Colonel William Rhett saw one ship taken and the landing repulsed, with about 300 out of 800 killed or captured (27 August–2 September 1706).

Charleston, South Carolina I 1776 I War of the American Revolution
See **Fort Sullivan**

Charleston, South Carolina I 1779 I War of the American Revolution

Three months after a check at **Beaufort**, British commander General Augustine Prevost advanced from the Savannah to Charleston, South Carolina, defended by Colonel William Moultrie. Having insufficient forces for an assault, Prevost attempted to negotiate surrender. However, he withdrew when American reinforcements approached, leaving a rearguard at **Stono Ferry** (11–12 May 1779).

Charleston, South Carolina ▍ 1780 ▍ War of the American Revolution

British commander Sir Henry Clinton was encouraged by success at **Savannah** in October and took about 14,000 men from New York against Charleston, South Carolina, held by General Benjamin Lincoln. After Clinton invested the city (10 April), heavy fighting and bombardment forced Lincoln to surrender. Over 5,000 men were captured in one of America's worst defeats (29 March–12 May 1780).

Charleston, South Carolina ▍ 1781 ▍ War of the American Revolution

Despite surrender at **Yorktown** (October 1781), the British held on in the south at Savannah, Georgia, and at Charleston, South Carolina, besieged by General Nathanael Greene. Savannah surrendered to General Anthony Wayne (11 July 1782), but it was many more months before General Alexander Leslie evacuated Charleston and fighting ended (December 1781–14 December 1782).

Charleston Harbour (1st) ▍ 1863 ▍ American Civil War (Lower Seaboard)

The Union's South Atlantic Squadron attempted to force Charleston Harbour, South Carolina, by naval action, where Admiral Samuel F. Du Pont took nine ships to bombard Fort Sumter, held by General Pierre G. T. Beauregard. The Union squadron was repulsed with heavy damage in the face of accurate artillery fire, and one ship sank the following day (7 April 1863).

Charleston Harbour (2nd) ▍ 1863 ▍ American Civil War (Lower Seaboard)

While besieging **Fort Wagner**, at the entrance to Charleston Harbour, South Carolina, Union General Quincy A. Gillmore opened fire on nearby Fort Sumter, defended by General Pierre G. T. Beauregard. After three weeks' bombardment, a storming party under John A. Dahlgren was repulsed, and Charleston held out

until it fell to land assault in February 1865 (17 August–8 September 1863).

Charlestown, West Virginia ▍ 1864 ▍ American Civil War (Eastern Theatre)
See **Summit Point**

Charlotte ▍ 1780 ▍ War of the American Revolution

With British General Charles Earl Cornwallis marching north from victory at **Camden** in August, his advance cavalry led by Major George Hanger was delayed at the town of Charlotte, North Carolina, by a militia rearguard under Colonel William Davie. The rebels were driven back in a brisk action, but news of defeat at **King's Mountain** persuaded Cornwallis to withdraw (26 September 1780).

Charouine ▍ 1901 ▍ French Colonial Wars in North Africa

A force of Moroccan Berbers withdrawing from a costly assault on **Timimoun** in western Algeria was intercepted 30 miles to the southwest at Charouine by General Armand Servière and Captain Theodore Pein. A badly handled and dilatory action saw the French lose 27 killed and 41 wounded before the Moroccans withdrew west into the Tafilalet (28 February–3 March 1901).

Chascomús ▍ 1839 ▍ Argentine Civil Wars

Argentine Dictator Manuel de Rosas won in the north at **Yerua** in September, then sent his brother Prudencia against Unitarist rebels south of Buenos Aires at Chascomús, where he imposed a crushing defeat. Ambrosio Crámer was killed in the battle, with Pedro Castelli and Manuel Leonico Rico captured and executed, enabling Rosas to concentrate his effort in the north (7 November 1839).

Chashniki ▍ 1564 ▍ Livonian War

A year after Muscovites took the Lithuanian-held city of **Polotsk**, a Russian army of perhaps 30,000 men under Pyotr Shuiski was attacked further south at Chashniki, on the Ulla River, by a smaller Polish-Lithuanian force led by Prince

Nikolai "The Black" Radziwill. A terrible rout
saw Shuiski defeated and killed and the Russians
soon lost again northwest of Polotsk at **Nevel**
(January 1564).

Chataldja I 1912 I 1st Balkan War

Turkish forces were crushed by Bulgaria at
Kirk Kilissa and **Lüleburgaz** in October and
fled to the defensive lines at Chataldja, about
25 miles from Constantinople. Cholera and repeated attacks by General Radko Dimitriev cost
both sides terrible losses before an armistice saw
the Bulgarians fell back exhausted. Enver Bey
successfully defended the lines until the end of
the war (17–18 November 1912).

Chateaudun I 1870 I Franco-Prussian War

German General Friedrich Wilhelm Ludwig
von Wittich was sent northwest from **Orleans**,
where he attacked Chateaudun on the Loire, held
by 2,500 French irregulars led by the Pole Joseph de Lipowski. Chateaudun was captured and
largely destroyed after savage street fighting and
nearby Chartres quickly surrendered. Chateaudun was retaken by the French on 6 November
(18 October 1870).

Chateau Gaillard I 1203–1204 I Anglo-French Wars

In resumed war with King John of England,
Philip II Augustus of France besieged the powerful castle of Chateau Gaillard, built on the Seine
at Andelys by Richard I. While a relief force under
William Marshal Earl of Pembroke was driven off
in September, the eventual fall of Roger de Lacy's
garrison led to England's loss of Normandy and
Anjou (August 1203–6 March 1204).

Chateaugay I 1813 I War of 1812

Invading Canada from Lake Champlain,
American General Wayne Hampton advanced
down the Chateaugay River against defences
established by Sir George Prevost. An American
detachment under Colonel Robert Purdy was
sharply repulsed by Canadian militia led by
Colonel Charles-Michel Salaberry and Hampton
was forced to withdraw. He later resigned (26
October 1813).

Chateauneuf-de-Randon I 1380 I Hundred Years War

With Edward III of England in the ascendant
following victory near **Poitiers** in 1356, French
hopes focussed on Betrand de Guesclin, who
fought a guerrilla-style war before besieging the
fortress at Chateauneuf-de-Randon, near Mende.
The elderly warrior eventually forced the English garrison to surrender, but he died exhausted
a week later and France agreed to a lengthy truce
(May–4 July 1380).

Chateau-Thierry I 1814 I Napoleonic Wars (French Campaign)

In a brilliant campaign east of Paris against the
Prussian-Russian army of General Gebhard von
Blucher, Napoleon Bonaparte repulsed his enemy
at **Champaubert** and **Montmirail**. On the third
day, Bonaparte drove a large force under General
Hans Yorck at Chateau-Thierry back across the
Marne, then turned against Blucher himself at
Vauchamps (12 February 1814).

Chateau-Thierry I 1918 I World War I (Western Front)

Having smashed through the Anglo-French
Allies along the **Aisne**, the offensive by Generals Bruno von Mudra and Max von Boehn was
met on the Marne at Chateau-Thierry by newly
arrived Americans under General John Dick-
man. The German offensive was halted and
driven back across the river and days later the
Americans counter-attacked further west at
Belleau Wood (3–4 June 1918).

Chatham I 1667 I 2nd Dutch War
See **Medway**

Chatham I 1813 I War of 1812
See **Thames**

Chatillon-le-Duc I 1870 I Franco-Prussian War

German General Karl August Werder and
Baron Kolmar von der Goltz advanced southwest from the capture of **Strasbourg** in September, crossing the Vosges to attack General
Albert Cambriels at Chatillon-le-Duc, northwest

of Besançon. The commander of the French army in the east was heavily defeated in heavy fighting along the Ognon and fell back on Besancon (22 October 1870).

Chatillon-sous-Bagneux I 1870 I Franco-Prussian War

As German forces encircled Paris, General Auguste Alexandre Ducrot attempted to hold the Chatillon Heights to the southwest. Despite a courageous defence against heavy shell-fire from General Jakob von Hartmann's Bavarians advancing through Sceaux towards Versailles, Ducrot was forced back to **Paris** and the Germans occupied the redoubt at Moulin de la Tour (19 September 1870).

Chatillon-sur-Seine I 1870 I Franco-Prussian War

When Italian Liberator Giuseppe Garibaldi intervened to support France, his son Ricciotti and the 4th Brigade attacked 800 Germans at Chatillon-sur-Seine, 40 miles north of Dijon, where the Germans lost 120 killed and 165 prisoners. Although Chatillon was quickly retaken, this modest victory encouraged Garibaldi to launch an ambitious assault on **Dijon** (19 November 1870).

Chatillon-sur-Sevre I 1793 I French Revolutionary Wars (Vendée War)

Following early victories, the Royalist counter-revolution in western France met with considerable success until Republican General Jean-Baptiste Kléber arrived from Mainz with a veteran army to suppress the rising. Kléber routed the rebels at Chatillon-sur-Sevre, southeast of Cholet, then wore them down with successive defeats at **Cholet**, **Le Mans** and **Savenay** (3 July 1793).

Chatra I 1857 I Indian Mutiny

Campaigning against rebels in Chota Nagpur in western Bihar, Major Frederick English took just 350 men and two guns and, having secured Doranda, marched north against an estimated 3,000 Ramgarh rebels at Chatra, in the Hazaribagh district, south of Gaya. The rebels were defeated and

fled after a sharp action, abandoning a massive amount of military stores (2 October 1857).

Chattanooga I 1862 I American Civil War (Western Theatre)

On a bold offensive into eastern Tennessee, Union commander Ormsby M. Mitchel sent General James Negley's division against the strategic Confederate city of Chattanooga. Two days of bombardment across the Tennessee River caused heavy damage, but when Confederate General Edmund Kirby Smith arrived in the area, Negley withdrew west across the mountains (7–8 June 1862).

Chattanooga (1st) I 1863 I American Civil War (Western Theatre)

Union commander William S. Rosecrans, opening his campaign against Chattanooga, Tennessee, ordered Colonel John T. Wilder on a diversion northeast of the city, where he launched a heavy artillery bombardment from heights above the Tennessee River. Meanwhile, Rosecrans was able to advance in the southwest, though he was defeated next month at **Chickamauga** (21 August 1863).

Chattanooga (2nd) I 1863 I American Civil War (Western Theatre)

Besieged in Chattanooga, Tennessee, after defeat at **Chickamauga** (September 1863), Union commander William S. Rosecrans was replaced by General George H. Thomas, who was reinforced and led a fresh offensive to the northeast at Missionary Ridge. Confederate General Braxton Bragg was heavily defeated and began withdrawing south through **Ringgold Gap** (23–25 November 1863).

Chauca I 1528 I Spanish Conquest of Yucatan

See Aké

Chaul I 1508 I Early Portuguese Colonial Wars in Asia

Attempting to expand Portuguese influence in India, Lorenzo de Almeida, son of the Viceroy, engaged a large fleet sent to northwest India by

Sultan Kansu al-Ghuri of Egypt supporting Sultan Mahmud Shah of Gujarat. Trapped by a river bar off Dabhol, near Chaul, Almeida was defeated and died after a cannonball shattered his legs. A year later his father was avenged off **Diu** (January 1508).

Chau Nhai ▮ 1966 ▮ Vietnam War

Americans and South Vietnamese, attacking south of **Chu Lai**, landed near Chau Nhai, northwest of Quang Ngai City (Operation Utah), and came under heavy fire from Viet Cong and North Vietnamese regulars. After costly assaults against strong positions, the Allies withdrew to a defensive perimeter and intense air and artillery attack finally forced the Communists to retire (4–7 March 1966).

Chausa ▮ 1539 ▮ Mughal Conquest of Northern India

Leading Indian-Muslim forces against the Mughal Humayun, the Afghan-Turk rebel Sher Khan overthrew the Sultan of Bengal, then defeated the Imperial army at Chausa on the Ganges near Buxar. The Mughals retreated up the Ganges Valley and, after a further defeat at **Kanauj** in 1540, Humayun fled to Persia. Sher Khan (later Sher Shah) became Sultan of Delhi and, effectively, ruler of the empire (26 June 1539).

Chaves ▮ 1809 ▮ Napoleonic Wars (Peninsular Campaign)

French Marshal Nicolas Soult, invading Portugal from the north, crossed the border near Chaves and defeated a poorly armed peasant force under Brigadier Francisco Silveira. The town of Chaves surrendered next day, and Soult continued on towards **Oporto**. However, Chaves was retaken by Silveira later the same month, its capture having yielded little strategic importance (11 March 1809).

Chawinda ▮ 1965 ▮ 2nd Indo-Pakistan War

As part of India's offensive into Pakistan towards **Sialkot**, a fierce tank battle developed to the southeast around the key city of Chawinda.

Following Indian attacks to the north at **Phillora** and west at **Buttar Dograndi**, a final night assault (18–19 September) reached Chawinda, but was thrown back. Facing a bloody battle of attrition, the enemies brought the war to an end (8–20 September 1965).

Cheat Summit ▮ 1861 ▮ American Civil War (Eastern Theatre)

On his first offensive, Confederate General Robert E. Lee, with Colonel Albert Rust, advanced on General Joseph Reynolds at Cheat Summit, southeast of Huttonsville, West Virginia, and to the west near Elkwater. Lee withdrew after a poorly co-ordinated attack against stubborn resistance and a month later Reynolds counter-attacked 12 miles further east at **Greenbrier River** (12 September 1861).

Chekiang-Kiangsi ▮ 1942 ▮ World War II (China)

See **Zhejiang-Jiangxi**

Chelambram ▮ 1781 ▮ 2nd British-Mysore War

See **Porto Novo**

Chelmno ▮ 1794 ▮ War of the 2nd Polish Partition

Three days after the disastrous Polish defeat at **Szczekociny**, a separate insurgent force under General Josef Zajaczek was brought to battle on the Vistula at Chelmno (Kulm) near **Bydgoszcz** in northwest Poland. Prussians under the personal command of King Frederick William III inflicted another decisive defeat and continued marching east to besiege **Warsaw** (9 June 1794).

Chelyabinsk ▮ 1918 ▮ Russian Civil War

When the Treaty of Brest-Litovsk ended Russia's war with Germany, 40,000 Czech and Slovak prisoners of war were released by the Bolsheviks and sent east to safety along the Trans-Siberian Railway. At Chelyabinsk, they rioted against Hungarian Communists and took the city a week later. They then seized the railway and beat the Bolsheviks at **Ekaterinburg** (14–17 May 1918).

Chelyabinsk I 1919 I Russian Civil War

Mikhail Tukhachevski's Red Army took **Ekaterinburg** (15 July) as part of a massive counter-offensive into the Urals, while further south they stormed east through **Zlatoust** (13 July) and General Mikhail Frunze advanced on Chelyabinsk. The Whites were badly beaten for a third time, driving them out of the southern Urals, and Admiral Aleksandr Kolchak withdrew to the **Tobol** (25 July 1919).

Chemille I 1793 I French Revolutionary Wars (Vendée War)

Near the start of the Royalist rebellion in western France, Vendéean leader Maurice d'Elbée advancing south of the Loire captured Chemille, then faced a counter-attack by Republican General Jean-Francois Berruyer. Berruyer withdrew after a confused battle, but d'Elbée had lost his guns and lacked ammunition, so he also withdrew, falling back on **Cholet** (11 April 1793).

Chemin des Dames I 1918 I World War I (Western Front)

See **Aisne**

Chemnitz I 1639 I Thirty Years War (Franco-Habsburg War)

Swedish commander Johan Banér advanced into Saxony, where he scattered the Imperial forces of Count Matthias Gallas then, at Chemnitz, 40 miles southwest of Dresden, met a Saxon-Austrian army under John George of Saxony and Archduke Leopold William. Banér secured a brilliant tactical victory and advanced into Bohemia as far as Prague, routing his pursuers at **Brandeis** (14 April 1639).

Chemulpo I 1904 I Russo-Japanese War

On the first day of the war, the Russian gunboat *Koreetz* exchanged fire with Japanese Admiral Sotokichi Uriu approaching Chemulpo (modern Inchon, Korea). The following day, at the same time as a surprise Japanese attack on **Port Arthur** (modern Lüshun), *Koreetz* and the cruiser *Varyag* were damaged by shellfire outside the harbour and returned to scuttle themselves (8–9 February 1904).

Ch'en-chia I 1161 I Jin-Song Wars

See **Chenjia**

Chengam I 1767 I 1st British-Mysore War

When Haidar Ali of Mysore established an alliance with the treacherous Nizam Ali of Hyderabad, British Colonel Joseph Smith tried to block their advance in central Madras at the Pass of Chengam. However, Smith was defeated and driven back to **Trinomalee**, 20 miles to the southeast where, three weeks later, the British inflicted a severe defeat on the Indian allies (3 September 1767).

Chengdu I 36 I Wars of the Later Han

After defeating the warlords of the north China plain at **Changlu** (29), Emperor Guangwu sent an army under Wu Han west against Gongsun Shu in his capital at Chengdu, in modern Sichuan. Guangwu's last remaining major rival was drawn out on a rash sortie and was defeated and killed. The city then surrendered and was sacked by the Han army, effectively ending resistance.

Chenggao I 204 BC I Chu-Han War

Driven out of Yingyang, Han warlord Liu Bang struck back at rival Xiang Yu and beat a Chu army at Chenggao. Later that year, Xiang Yu returned with his main force and another battle at Chenggao saw Liu Bang heavily defeated. The rivals soon made peace and Liu Bang regained his wife and father, taken hostage at **Pengcheng**. Liu Bang eventually broke the truce and secured final victory at **Gaixia**.

Cheng-Jung I 404 I Wars of the Sixteen Kingdoms Era

See **Zhengrong**

Chengpu I 632 BC I Wars of China's Spring and Autumn Era

When the southern state of Chu expanded north across the Yellow River, the state of Jin and its northern allies joined forces under the great Duke Wen of Jin. In a massive battle at Chengpu, the Jin smashed into the enemy right wing, crushing their weak Che and Cai auxiliaries. Chu commander Ziyu was then routed, and he later committed suicide. The defeat decisively checked Chu territorial ambition.

Chenguanzhuang ▪ 1949 ▪ 3rd Chinese Revolutionary Civil War

Facing the **Huaihai** offensive, Nationalist General Du Yuming abandoned Xuzhou and, after failing to relieve **Shuangduiji**, was surrounded to the southwest at Chenguanzhuang, near Yungchen (6 December 1948). When Communist Generals Chen Yi and Liu Bocheng launched the final assault, Du was captured, along with 200,000 men and all their tanks and arms (6–10 January 1949).

Chenjia ▪ 1161 ▪ Jin-Song Wars

During a huge Jin assault on southern China, an armada claimed to comprise 600 ships and 100,000 men was intercepted off Chenjia Island, south of modern Qingdao, by a much smaller Song force under veteran commander Li Bao. The inexperienced Jin fleet was virtually annihilated and, a few days later, the main Jin invasion army was routed trying to cross the Yangzi at **Caishi** (16 November 1161).

Chenkiang ▪ 1842 ▪ 1st Opium War
See **Zhenjiang**

Chenkiang ▪ 1856 ▪ Taiping Rebellion
See **Zhenjiang**

Chenzhou ▪ 883–884 ▪ Huang Chao Rebellion

After defeat at **Liangtian**, warlord Huang Chao abandoned Chang'an and moved east, where his ally Meng Kai seized Caizhou but was defeated and killed attacking Chenzhou. Huang launched a full-scale siege of the city, which held out under prefect Zhao Chou. The failed year-long siege enabled loyalist forces to regroup and Huang withdrew to Shandong, where he was cornered and killed himself.

Cherbourg ▪ 1758 ▪ Seven Years War (Europe)

Despite the failed assault at **Cancale** in June, a second British expedition under Commodore Sir Richard Howe and General Thomas Bligh landed at Marais Bay, just east of Cherbourg. The French withdrew, and Bligh's force destroyed the harbour works and many ships, as well as capturing 200 guns, before re-embarking. They returned to Brittany a month later, at **St Cast** (7–16 August 1758).

Cherbourg ▪ 1864 ▪ American Civil War (High Seas)

At the end of a very successful cruise, the Confederate raider *Alabama* (Commander Raphael Semmes) was met in the English Channel off Cherbourg by the Union ship *Kearsage* (Captain John A. Winslow) and sunk by gunfire. For her failure to detain the British-built *Alabama*, Britain was later ordered to pay the United States compensation for damage caused (19 June 1864).

Cherbourg ▪ 1944 ▪ World War II (Western Europe)

After the great Allied landing in **Normandy**, American General Lawton Collins swung west to cut off the Cotentin Peninsula and the key port of Cherbourg. Facing tenacious German defence, the assault went in after heavy air attack and naval bombardment. Cherbourg finally surrendered, yielding about 35,000 prisoners, but extensive demolition delayed its use as a supply port (21–29 June 1944).

Cheriton ▪ 1644 ▪ British Civil Wars
See **Alresford**

Cherkassy ▪ 1944 ▪ World War II (Eastern Front)
See **Korsun**

Chernaya ▪ 1855 ▪ Crimean War

In a last attempt to break the Allied siege of **Sevastopol**, Russian commander Prince Mikhail Gorchakov sent a force towards Traktir Bridge on the nearby Chernaya River, defended by French and Sardinians under General Alfonso Ferrero Marquis di La Marmora. The Russians were driven back with heavy losses in hard fighting and a few weeks later Sevastopol finally fell (16 August 1855).

Chernigov ∎ 1078 ∎ Russian Dynastic Wars

See **Nezhatina Niva**

Chernigov ∎ 1094 ∎ Russian Dynastic Wars

Oleg Sviatoslavich returned from 15 years' exile, after defeat at **Nezhatina Niva**, seeking aid from the Kipchak Turks (fresh from victory over Kiev at **Tripole**) to regain the throne of Chernigov from his cousin Vladimir Monomakh. Vladimir was defeated and fled after an eight-day siege, but two years later, he returned to depose Oleg and eventually became Grand Prince of Kiev (16–24 July 1094).

Chernigovka ∎ 1941 ∎ World War II (Eastern Front)

With the fall of **Kiev**, Panzer General Ewald von Kleist raced south towards the Sea of Azov, cutting off two Russian armies around Chernigovka. The Soviet Eighteenth Army was destroyed, with General Andrei Smirnov killed, and the Ninth Army was badly battered. The pocket yielded 100,000 Russian prisoners, 200 tanks and 500 guns, and the survivors fell back on **Rostov** (5–10 October 1941).

Cherry Valley ∎ 1778 ∎ War of the American Revolution

Following the **Wyoming Massacre** at the hands of British Major John Butler, his son Captain Mark Butler attacked pro-rebel settlers in the Cherry Valley, New York, on the upper Susquehanna. In a brutal assault, supported by Indian Chief Joseph Brant, the settlement was destroyed, with many killed, including women and children. Retaliation came in August 1779 at **Newtown** (11 November 1778).

Chersonesus ∎ 443 ∎ Hun Invasion of the Roman Empire

Attila the Hun renewed his invasion of the Eastern Empire after destroying **Sirmium** in 441, defeating the Imperial army under Flavius Aspar the Alan outside **Constantinople**. He then pursued them into the Chersonesus, the Gallipoli Peninsula on the European side of the Dardanelles. Aspar suffered a decisive defeat and Emperor Theodosius was forced to sue for peace with the Huns.

Chesapeake Capes (1st) ∎ 1781 ∎ War of the American Revolution

Sailing from Newport to support the rebels in Virginia, French Commodore Sochet Destouches was met off Chesapeake Bay by a similar-sized British squadron under Admiral Marriott Arbuthnot. While Arbuthnot was outmanoeuvred in an indecisive action with three ships badly damaged, Destouches decided to return to Newport. Arbuthnot was replaced soon afterwards (16 March 1781).

Chesapeake Capes (2nd) ∎ 1781 ∎ War of the American Revolution

Reinforced by Britain's West Indian fleet, Admiral Thomas Graves sailed from New York to Chesapeake Bay to support the army in Virginia, where he was met by French Admiral Francois Comte de Grasse. The poorly handled British ships returned to New York after an indecisive action, and weeks later the army surrendered at **Yorktown**, effectively deciding the war (5–9 September 1781).

***Chesapeake* vs *Shannon* ∎ 1813 ∎ War of 1812**

See **Boston Harbour**

Chesme ∎ 1770 ∎ Catherine the Great's 1st Turkish War

Russian Admiral Alexei Orlov sailed from the Baltic to the Mediterranean, where he attacked Admiral Husam ul-Din Pasha off the Turkish coast near **Chios** and drove him into nearby Chesme Bay, where Scots-born Vice Admiral

John Elphinston attacked the following night with fire ships. One Turkish ship was captured and the rest were burned, with losses estimated at 9,000 men (7–8 July 1770).

Chester I 615 I Anglo-Saxon Territorial Wars

Turning south after victory over the Scots at **Daegsaston** in 603, King Aethelfrith of Northumbria marched on Chester, where he inflicted a terrible defeat on the Welsh of Powys. He then seized Chester and razed Bangor, the victory dividing the northern and southern Welsh forces and giving Aethelfrith strategic access to the Irish Sea. He was defeated and killed two years later at the **Idle**.

Chester I 1645 I British Civil Wars
See **Rowton Heath**

Chesterfield I 1266 I 2nd English Barons' War

With Simon de Montfort Earl of Leicester killed at **Evesham** (August 1265), remaining rebel Barons led by Robert de Ferrers Earl of Derby gathered a force in Derbyshire. At Chesterfield, in the last pitched battle of the war, the rebel Barons were defeated by Henry III's nephew Henry of Almaine. Remaining resistance to the King was largely confined to the Fens around **Ely** (15 May 1266).

Chester Station I 1864 I American Civil War (Eastern Theatre)

On an offensive against the railway north of Confederate Petersburg, Virginia, General Benjamin F. Butler attacked **Port Walthall Junction** (7 May), then marched northwest to destroy track at Chester Station. There he came under attack by General Robert Ransom's division of General Pierre G. T. Beauregard's Confederate army and retired east to the Bermuda Hundred lines (10 May 1864).

Chestnut Hill I 1777 I War of the American Revolution
See **White Marsh**

Chetate I 1854 I Crimean War
See **Citate**

Chevelon Fork I 1882 I Apache Indian Wars
See **Big Dry Wash**

Chevelu I 218 BC I 2nd Punic War

Marching into the Alps from Gaul, Carthaginian General Hannibal Barca was blocked at the Chevelu Pass, west of Lake du Bourget, by a large tribal force of Allobroges. Hannibal routed the tribesmen with massive losses with a surprise night attack. He then captured their capital further south at Chambéry before advancing through the Isère Valley past the **White Rock** (October 218 BC).

Chevilly I 1870 I Franco-Prussian War

General Joseph Vinoy led a reconnaissance in force south from besieged **Paris**, taking 20,000 men along the left bank of the Seine towards the villages of L'Hay and Chevilly. However, he was heavily repulsed by General Wilhelm von Tumpling and fell back with the loss of more than 2,000 men. A second sortie by Vinoy two weeks later at **Bagneux** was also repulsed (30 September 1870).

Chevy Chase I 1388 I Anglo-Scottish Border Wars
See **Otterburn**

Chhamb I 1965 I 2nd Indo-Pakistan War

Driven back in the north around **Haji Pir** (28 August), Pakistani forces in the southwest under General Akhtar Malik (later General Yayha Khan) crossed into Indian Kashmir with about 100 tanks and seized Chhamb. However, the Pakistani invasion stalled against stubborn defence and Chhamb was retaken at the start of India's counter-offensive towards **Lahore** (1–4 September 1965).

Chhamb I 1971 I 3rd Indo-Pakistan War

When India supported rebels in East Pakistan, Pakistan bombed Indian airfields, and General Iftikhar Khan Janjua advanced from Sialkot against Chhamb. Indian General Sartaj Singh was forced to withdraw, but a large-scale armoured action saw the pursuing Pakistanis heavily defeated, with massive losses in men and tanks. Pakistan soon lost again further south at **Shakargarh** (3–10 December 1971).

Chiang-kou ∎ 1851 ∎ Taiping Rebellion
See **Jiangkou**

Chiang-ling ∎ 1236 ∎ Mongol Conquest of China
See **Jiangling**

Chiari ∎ 1701 ∎ War of the Spanish Succession

Francois de Neufville Marshal Villeroi was appointed to French command in Lombardy after the defeat in July at **Carpi**, and attempted an offensive across the Oglio against the Austrian army of Prince Eugène of Savoy. At Chiari, west of Brescia, Villeroi was repulsed by Eugène with heavy losses. He then withdrew to **Cremona**, while Eugène blockaded the French at Mantua (1 September 1701).

Chibi ∎ 208 ∎ Wars of the Three Kingdoms
See **Red Cliffs**

Chichén Itzá ∎ 1531 ∎ Spanish Conquest of Yucatan

After a previous unsuccessful attempt to seize Yucatan, Francisco de Monteja led a fresh expedition, which secured Campeche in the west. His son Francisco then advanced inland to establish a capital at Chichén Itzá (southeast of modern Merida). But after continuous heavy attack by the Maya, the younger Montejo abandoned his settlement. All Spanish forces soon withdrew to Mexico.

Chickahominy ∎ 1864 ∎ American Civil War (Eastern Theatre)
See **Cold Harbour**

Chickamauga ∎ 1863 ∎ American Civil War (Western Theatre)

After securing the key city of Chattanooga, Tennessee, Union commander William S. Rosecrans marched southeast against the Confederate army at Chickamauga. In some of the war's bloodiest fighting, Confederate commander Braxton Bragg, supported by General James Longstreet, secured a costly victory and Rosecrans withdrew under siege to **Chattanooga** (18–20 September 1863).

Chickasaw Bluffs ∎ 1862 ∎ American Civil War (Western Theatre)

Union forces under General William T. Sherman advancing south against **Vicksburg** on the Mississippi attempted to force through the Confederate defences to the north at Chickasaw Bluffs, Mississippi, held by General John C. Pemberton. Sherman lost almost 2,000 men in a failed frontal assault and was forced to withdraw upstream to **Milliken's Bend** (26–29 December 1862).

Chiclana ∎ 1811 ∎ Napoleonic Wars (Peninsular Campaign)
See **Barrosa**

Chien-k'ang ∎ 548–549 ∎ Wars of the Six Dynasties
See **Jiankang**

Chien-k'ang ∎ 589 ∎ Wars of the Six Dynasties
See **Jiankang**

Ch'ien-shui-yuan ∎ 618 ∎ Rise of the Tang Dynasty
See **Qianshuiyuan**

Chieri ∎ 1639 ∎ Thirty Years War (Franco-Habsburg War)

While campaigning in northern Italy, French commander Henri Comte d'Harcourt and Henri de Turenne advanced to resupply Casale, east of Turin. At nearby Chieri, with just 8,000 men, Harcourt defeated an Imperial-Savoyard army of 20,000, inflicting almost 4,000 casualties and prisoners. **Casale** was relieved and the Spanish were defeated there again a year later (20 November 1639).

Chieveley ┃ 1899 ┃ 2nd Anglo-Boer War

On a reconnaisance south of besieged **Ladysmith**, Captain James A. L. Haldane led an armoured train north from Estcourt. Just past Frere at Chieveley, the train was ambushed and derailed by Boers under Commandant B. van der Merwe. The British lost five killed, 45 wounded and 70 captured, including Haldane and Winston Churchill, who both later escaped (15 November 1899).

Chigirin ┃ 1677 ┃ Turkish Invasion of the Ukraine

A renewed Turkish attempt on the Ukraine following defeat at **Zurawno** (1676) saw Kara Ibrahim Pasha and 100,000 men cross the Dneiper and besiege Chigirin, held by 32,000 Russians under Grigori Romodanovski and 25,000 Cossacks led by Ivan Samoilovych. Ibrahim withdrew after stubborn defence and was dismissed, but **Chigirin** fell the next year to a fresh assault (July–August 1677).

Chigirin ┃ 1678 ┃ Turkish Invasion of the Ukraine

Despite previous failure, Grand Vizier Kara Mustafa himself led 100,000 Turks and Tatars against Chigirin on the Dnieper, held by 80,000 Russians and Cossacks under Grigori Romodanovski and Ivan Samoilovych, and Scottish General Patrick Gordon. The city was stormed and burned but, three years later, the Turks withdrew from the Ukraine and made peace with Russia (August 1678).

Chihaya ┃ 1333 ┃ Genko War

With western Japan rising for Emperor Go-Daigo against Regent Hojo Takatoki, Kusunoki Masashige escaped from **Akasaka** (1331) and took a defensive position at the mountain fortress of Chihaya near Nara. A legendary defence saw the Shogun's besieging army driven off with terrible losses, greatly enhancing the Imperial cause and leading to offensives against **Kyoto** and **Kamakura**.

Chihchiang ┃ 1945 ┃ World War II (China)

See **Zhijiang**

Chi Hoa ┃ 1860–1861 ┃ French Conquest of Indo-China

French forces seized **Saigon** in 1859, which soon came under siege by the veteran Vietnamese Marshal Nguyen Tri Phoung, fresh from driving their opponents out of **Danang**. Almost a year later, a French relief force under Admiral Léonard Charner defeated the besieging force at nearby Chi Hoa. Emperor Tu Duc eventually sued for peace, ceding southern Vietnam (March 1860–25 February 1861).

Chihuahua ┃ 1847 ┃ American-Mexican War

See **Sacramento River**

Chihuahua ┃ 1913 ┃ Mexican Revolution

Francisco (Pancho) Villa captured **Torréon** in central Mexico, then took his revolutionary army against Chihuahua. After five days of heavy fighting he withdrew, and the Federals claimed victory. However, after Villa took **Ciudad Juárez**, then defeated the Federal army at **Tierra Blanca**, Chihuahua was evacuated (29 November). He entered the city a week later (5–10 November 1913).

Chikou ┃ 1937 ┃ Sino-Japanese War

See **Taiyuan**

Chiksan ┃ 1597 ┃ Japanese Invasion of Korea

Advancing on Seoul through **Namwon**, the Japanese army was blocked to the southeast at Chiksan by a Chinese-Korean garrison under Ma Gui. Desperate to hold the town, reinforcements were poured in and, soon after naval defeat at **Myongyang**, the Japanese were forced to withdraw—Kato Kiyomasa to **Ulsan**, Konishi Yukinaga to **Sunchon** and Shimazu Yoshihiro to **Sachon** (October 1597).

Chi Lang Pass ❙ 1427 ❙ Sino-Vietnamese War

While Le Loi and General Nguyen Trai besieged **Dong-do** (later Hanoi) to end Chinese overlordship, a claimed 100,000 Ming reinforcements under Liu Sheng were ambushed and routed to the northwest near Lang Son at Chi Lang Pass, with up to 70,000 lost. When China then abandoned Dong-do and withdrew from Vietnam, Le Loi founded the 350-year Le Dynasty (October 1427).

Chilchon ❙ 1597 ❙ Japanese Invasion of Korea
   See **Kyo Chong**

Chilianwallah ❙ 1849 ❙ 2nd British-Sikh War

With British forces besieging the Sikhs at **Multan**, northwest of Lahore, General Sir Hugh Gough advanced alone against a powerful Sikh position on the Jhelam at Chilianwallah. Terrible fighting saw Gough drive commander Sher Singh from the field. However, his own very heavy losses forced Gough to withdraw until reinforcements arrived to help him win at **Gujrat** (13 January 1849).

Chillicothe ❙ 1780 ❙ War of the American Revolution
   See **Piqua**

Chiloé ❙ 1826 ❙ Chilean War of Independence

Despite the decisive Spanish defeat at **Ayacucho** in 1824, 2,000 Royalists under Antonio Quintanilla held out on the island of Chiloé, in the Los Lagos region off the coast of southern Chile, which Quintanilla had defended in 1820. Facing renewed attack by a Chilean Patriot force under Ramón Freire, the garrison was forced to surrender and Spain lost her last foothold in Chile (15 January 1826).

Chilung ❙ 1884 ❙ Sino-French War

Supporting war against China in Vietnam, Admiral Sébastien Lespès took two ships and bombarded the port of Chilung (Keelung) in northern Taiwan. Troops landed to secure the port but were insufficient to hold it, and the French withdrew to establish a blockade. In October, an attack on nearby **Tanshui** and further bombardment persuaded Chilung to surrender in March 1885 (5 August 1884).

Chi-mo ❙ 279 BC ❙ China's Era of the Warring States
   See **Jimo**

Chinchow ❙ 1904 ❙ Russo-Japanese War
   See **Nanshan**

Chinchow ❙ 1948 ❙ 3rd Chinese Revolutionary Civil War
   See **Jinzhou**

Chinese Farm ❙ 1973 ❙ Arab-Israeli Yom Kippur War

At the start of Israel's counter-offensive to retake the Sinai Peninsula, advanced units became isolated by the Second Egyptian Army around fortifications at Chinese Farm, near Matzmed, north of the Great Bitter Lake. After intense and costly fighting, Israeli Generals Ariel Sharon and Avraham Adan relieved their hard-pressed forces, then swept west across the **Suez Canal** (16–18 October 1973).

Ching-hsing ❙ 205 BC ❙ Chu-Han War
   See **Jingxing**

Chingleput ❙ 1752 ❙ 2nd Carnatic War

Following French defeat at **Trichinopoly** (10 April), Robert Clive marched south from Madras against the remaining French fortresses. Having captured the coastal fortress of **Covelung**, Clive took his mixed British-Sepoy force inland to Chingleput on the Palar River, defended by a mainly native garrison. The French commander surrendered after four days' bombardment (13 October 1752).

Ching-lu-chen ❙ 1410 ❙ Ming Imperial Wars
   See **Jing Luzhen**

Chinhae Bay ∎ 1598 ∎ Japanese Invasion of Korea
See **Noryang**

Chinhai ∎ 1841 ∎ 1st Opium War
See **Zhenhai**

Chinhat ∎ 1857 ∎ Indian Mutiny
With rebel forces approaching the key city of Lucknow, General Sir Henry Lawrence unwisely took 300 British and 400 Indian troops eight miles to the northeast to Chinhat, where they met over 5,000 Sepoys under Barkat Ahmad. Lawrence retreated after a heavy defeat cost him four precious guns as well as many men lost, and the following day **Lucknow** was besieged (30 June 1857).

Chinkurli ∎ 1771 ∎ Maratha-Mysore Wars
On his final campaign, Maratha Peshwa Madhav Rao marched into the Carnatic in southeast India against his perennial enemy, Haidar Ali of Mysore. The Peshwa ravaged Mysore then fell fatally ill. His General, Trimbak Rao Pethe, concluded the campaign with decisive victory at Chinkurli near Seringapatam. It was Haidar Ali's worst defeat and he soon sued for peace (5 March 1771).

Chinsura ∎ 1759 ∎ Seven Years War (India)
Although Britain and Holland were not at war, Dutch in Java sent 1,400 men to support Nawab Mir Jafar of Bengal, plotting against the British who had put him on the throne after **Plassey**. With the concurrence of Governor Robert Clive, Colonel Francis Forde attacked the invaders on the Hooghly between Chinsura and Chandrenagore, capturing all seven Dutch ships (25 November 1759).

Chin-Tien ∎ 1851 ∎ Taiping Rebellion
See **Jintian**

Chioggia ∎ 1379–1380 ∎ War of Chioggia
Admiral Pietro Doria followed Genoese naval victory off **Pula** (May 1379) by seizing Chioggia to blockade nearby Venice and Venetian

Admiral Vittore Pisani, imprisoned after Pula, was released to counter-blockade the attackers. The Genoese surrendered Chioggia after months of assault (Doria was killed on 3 February) and Venetian primacy in the Adriatic was restored (December 1379–24 June 1380).

Chios ∎ 412 BC ∎ Great Peloponnesian War
The Spartan Chalcideus and renegade Athenian Alcibiades took a fleet across the Aegean to attack Athenian settlements in Ionia and assaulted Chios, one of the wealthiest Greek colonies in the eastern Aegean. They seized the city after defeating the pro-Athenian faction and immediately used the island as a base to attack **Miletus** and other Athenian allies on the Greek mainland of Asia Minor.

Chios ∎ 357 BC ∎ 1st Greek Social War
In a revolt against Athens, Chios and Rhodes were joined by Mausolos of Caria, and their combined fleet met Athenian Admiral Chabrias off Chios, where Athenian mercenaries under Chares had also landed. Chabrias was defeated and killed in a decisive naval action. The mercenaries were re-embarked and withdrew. Athens was defeated again a year later off **Embata**.

Chios ∎ 201 BC ∎ 2nd Macedonian War
While campaigning in Asia Minor, Philip V of Macedon seized Samos then besieged Chios, where he was attacked by Attalus of Pergamum, aided by Admiral Theophiliscus of Rhodes. Despite the death of the Rhodian Admiral, his ships prevailed, but on the other wing Attalus was forced to withdraw, allowing Philip to capture Chios. The Macedonians then sailed south to meet the Rhodian fleet at **Lade**.

Chios ∎ 1694 ∎ Venetian-Turkish Wars
Two years after Venetian defeat at **Canea**, Captain-General Antonio Zeno attacked Hassan Pasha's 3,000-strong garrison on Chios. After bombarding and mining breached the walls, the fortress surrendered and the Turks were allowed to withdraw to Chesme. While Zeno captured massive booty, including ships and 200 cannon,

he was soon defeated off nearby **Spalmadori** (7–15 September 1694).

Chios ∎ 1770 ∎ Catherine the Great's 1st Turkish War

The Russian Baltic fleet sailed to the Mediterranean under Admiral Alexei Orlov and attacked Turkish Admiral Hassan ul-Din Pasha in the narrow channel between Chios and the Anatolian coast. Russian Admiral Girgori Spiridov in the van bore the brunt of battle and, after both flagships blew up, the Turks cut their cables during the night and fled south to nearby **Chesme** (6 July 1770).

Chios ∎ 1822 ∎ Greek War of Independence

While Turkish forces attempted to suppress the strategic island of Chios, Greek Admiral Konstantinos Kanaris led a daring raid on the rival fleet. Using fireships, he inflicted heavy damage, including the flagship *Maizural-Livo* lost with Turkish Admiral Kara Ali and virtually his entire crew. The raid helped trigger Turkish reprisals, which completed the "massacre of Chios" (18–19 June 1822).

Chippenham ∎ 878 ∎ Viking Wars in Britain

Danish King Guthrum ended a five-year truce (concluded after Viking victory at **Wilton**) by seizing Saxon Mercia. He then led a mid-winter attack on King Alfred of Wessex at Chippenham, east of Bath. Surprised and defeated, Alfred fled to the marshes of Somerset, leaving the Vikings to overrun Wessex. However, he was able to rally his forces for battle in May at **Edington** (6 January 878).

Chippewa ∎ 1814 ∎ War of 1812

In a fresh American offensive across the Niagara River, commander Jacob Brown sent General Winfield Scott north along the Canadian shore to Chippewa against British forces under General Sir Phineas Riall. Unexpectedly finding himself facing American regulars, Riall fought bravely but, after heavy losses on both sides, he withdrew north towards **Lundy's Lane** (5 July 1814).

Chipyong ∎ 1951 ∎ Korean War

Renewing the offensive east of Seoul, 135,000 Chinese and North Koreans crushed the South Koreans at Hoengsong, then surrounded 5,000 Americans and French further west at Chipyong under Colonel Paul Freeman. After courageous defence, the siege was broken to produce the first Chinese defeat since their intervention. The Allies then struck back towards **Seoul** (13–15 February 1951).

Chire ∎ 1815 ∎ Colombian War of Independence

In action against Patriot commander Joaquín Ricaurte in Santander, Spanish Colonel Sebastián Calzada was attacked and heavily defeated at Chire, southeast of Barrancabermeja, losing 250 casualties and 150 prisoners as well as large quantities of equipment. Calzada then withdrew through Chita towards Pamplona and Cúcuta, but soon secured victory at **Balaga** (31 October 1815).

Chiricahua Pass ∎ 1869 ∎ Apache Indian Wars

Captain Reuben F. Bernard campaigned against Cochise in southeast Arizona, marching south from Camp Bowie to meet about 250 Apache at Chiricahua Pass, close to the Mexican border. Despite an indecisive daylong action—with two killed and two wounded—Bernard could not dislodge the Indians. He prudently withdrew at nightfall, claiming to have killed 18 Apache (19 October 1869).

Chita ∎ 1920 ∎ Russian Civil War

In the final stages of the war, Bolshevik forces of the Far Eastern Republic attacked Chita, east of Lake Baikal. The White forces had repulsed earlier assaults, but with Japanese support now withdrawn, they could not resist the attack by 30,000 men and two armoured trains. Some survivors fled into Manchuria, and the Trans-Baikal region was effectively secured (16–21 October 1920).

Chitaldrug ▌ 1695 ▌ Mughal-Maratha Wars

Campaigning in central India, Mughal Emperor Aurangzeb sent General Quasim Khan to intercept the Maratha warlord Santaji Ghorpade, reportedly transporting plunder to his base in Mysore. The Imperial army was destroyed in a disastrous defeat at Chitaldrug in northern Mysore and Quasim Khan committed suicide. The survivors were released for a massive ransom (November 1695).

Chitor ▌ 1534–1535 ▌ Mughal Conquest of Northern India

After a long siege of the famous Rajput fortress of Chitor, northeast of Udaipur, Sultan Bahadur Shah of Gujarat redoubled his efforts as a Mughal army approached. When he launched his final assault, the women of the fortress burned themselves to death and the men made a suicidal last sortie. Just as the fortress fell, Emperor Humayun arrived and Bahadur Shah fled to **Mandu**.

Chitor ▌ 1567–1568 ▌ Mughal Conquest of Northern India

In his most famous siege, Mughal Emperor Akbar attacked the powerful Rajput fortress of Chitor, using enormous mines to blow up the defences. However, after sniper fire killed commander Jai Mal, the defenders died in a final assault and Akbar massacred 30,000 local peasants. The subsequent capture of Ranthambhor gave Akbar control of Rajputana (20 October 1567–23 February 1568).

Chitral ▌ 1895 ▌ Chitral Campaign

A small British-Sepoy force under Major George Robertson, which intervened in a disputed succession in the tiny Kashmir kingdom of Chitral, was besieged in the fort at Chitral by Sher Afzul and Umra Khan. A relief force from Gilgit under Colonel James Kelly drove off the besiegers just before General Sir Robert Low's main force arrived from Peshawar (4 March–17 April 1895).

Chivington Massacre ▌ 1864 ▌ Cheyenne-Arapaho Indian War
See **Sand Creek**

Chize ▌ 1373 ▌ Hundred Years War

Following his naval defeat off **La Rochelle** (June 1372), Edward III of England was prevented from assisting his French allies, and La Rochelle, Poitiers and Surgeres soon fell. A small English-Poitevin force was then defeated outside Chize, east of Surgeres, by Bertrand du Guesclin, Constable of France. This final action ended English resistance, and Poitou was permanently restored to France.

Chmielnik ▌ 1241 ▌ Mongol Conquest of Europe
See **Cracow**

Chochiwon ▌ 1950 ▌ Korean War

American forces retreating from disaster at **Osan**, south of **Seoul**, were driven out of Chonan (8 July) and then Chonui (10 July), despite air-strikes destroying North Korean armour. Heaviest fighting was further south at Chochiwon, where the American 21st Infantry tried to slow the advance and lost over 400 men. The survivors fell back ten miles to the new line on the **Kum** (8–12 July 1950).

Chochow ▌ 1920 ▌ Anhui-Zhili War
See **Zhuozhou**

Chocim ▌ 1600 ▌ Balkan National Wars
See **Khotin**

Chocim ▌ 1621 ▌ Polish-Turkish Wars
See **Khotin**

Chocim ▌ 1673 ▌ Turkish Invasion of the Ukraine
See **Khotin**

Chocim ▌ 1769 ▌ Catherine the Great's 1st Turkish War
See **Khotin**

**Chocim I 1788 I Catherine the Great's
2nd Turkish War**
   See **Khotin**

Chojnice I 1454 I Thirteen Years War
   In a rising against the ruling Teutonic knights, Poles in Prussia sought aid from Casimir IV of Poland, who claimed sovereignty and declared war on the knights. At Chojnice, about 60 miles southwest of Gdansk, the disunited Royal army was brutally defeated by a small Teutonic force. The Poles recovered to seize Marienburg, then in 1462 defeated the Order at **Puck** (18 September 1454).

**Chokjinpo I 1592 I Japanese Invasion
of Korea**
   See **Okpo**

**Chokoho Incident I 1938 I Russo-
Japanese Border Wars**
   See **Changfukeng**

**Cholet I 1793 I French Revolutionary
Wars (Vendée War)**
   Despite defeat at **Torfou**, south of the Loire, Republican General Jean-Baptiste Kléber and his veteran army launched a fresh offensive south from Nantes and crushed the Royalist rebels at their headquarters in Cholet. Rebel leaders Maurice d'Elbée and Charles Bonchamp were badly wounded (Bonchamp fatally), and the Vendéean army fled northeast across the Loire (17–18 October 1793).

**Cholula I 1519 I Spanish Conquest of
Mexico**
   Conquistador Hernán Cortés landed in Mexico and overcame the Tlaxacans, who then joined him against their rivals at Cholula, near modern Puebla. After entering Cholula in peace, the Spaniards and their Tlaxacan allies launched a bloody massacre which saw perhaps 3,000 Cholulans killed and the temple of Quetzalcoatl destroyed. Cortés then marched towards **Tenochtitlan** (October 1519).

**Choluteca I 1894 I Central American
National Wars**
   When President José Santos Zelaya of Nicaragua aided rebels in Honduras, President Domingo Vásquez of Honduras declared war, then faced an invasion by Nicaraguan troops and Honduran rebels under the Liberal leader Policarpo Bonilla (13 December 1893). President Vásquez was routed at Choluteca and fell back 50 miles north on his capital, **Tegucicalpa** (6 January 1894).

Chonan I 1950 I Korean War
   See **Chochiwon**

Chongchon I 1950 I Korean War
   General Walton Walker recovered from defeat at **Unsan** (6 November) and attacked north from the Chongchon before a Chinese counteroffensive smashed through South Koreans on his right. With shocking losses in men and equipment, and facing another offensive to the east at **Chosin**, the Allies retreated south of the pre-war border and in March abandoned **Seoul** (24–28 November 1950).

**Chongju I 1592 I Japanese Invasion of
Korea**
   As Japanese General Konishi Yukinaga advanced from **Pusan** through **Sangju**, he was joined by Kato Kiyomasa just northwest of Chongju, where Korean General Shin Ip determined to halt them at the Tangumdae. After heavy losses on both sides, Shin and many officers threw themselves in the river to die. Seoul fell a few days later and King Songju fled north across the **Imjin** (7 June 1592).

Chongju I 1904 I Russo-Japanese War
   Advancing into Korea after a Japanese landing at **Chemulpo** (9 February), General Tamemoto Kuroki gathered further forces which had landed near Pyongyang and encountered General Pavel Ivanovich Mischenko's Cossacks at Chongju. In the reputed first land action of the war, the Russians were driven out of the town, and Kuroki's First Army continued on to the **Yalu** (28 March 1904).

Chonui ∎ 1950 ∎ Korean War
See **Chochiwon**

Chorokh ∎ 1854 ∎ Crimean War
Russian Prince Ivan Malkhazovich Andronikov on campaign in eastern Turkey following
victory at **Akhaltsikhe** (November 1853) met a
force of 34,000 Turks on the River Chorokh
(Turkish Coruh) near Batum. Andronikov attacked with a detachment of just 13,000 men and
gained a decisive victory, after which Russian
forces turned their attention south to **Bayazid**
and **Kars** (4 June 1854).

Chorrillos ∎ 1881 ∎ War of the Pacific
Negotiations after victory at **Arica** in June
1880 failed and Chile resumed the offensive
against Peru. General Manuel Baquedano advanced on Lima, attacking the defensive line at
Chorrillos, held by General Andrés Avelino
Cáceres. The Chileans captured the line in a
dawn attack at the cost of perhaps 2,000 casualties and two days later took the position at
Miraflores (13 January 1881).

Chosin ∎ 1950 ∎ Korean War
South Koreans and American marines drove
deep into northeast Korea, destroying a Chinese army in extreme cold around the Chosin
(Changjin) Reservoir. Chinese General Song
Shilun was however reinforced, and launched a
new offensive (27 November). After severe
losses on both sides, the defeated Allies were
forced to withdraw south towards **Koto-ri** (25
October–29 November 1950).

Chotin ∎ 1600 ∎ Balkan National Wars
See **Khotin**

Chotin ∎ 1621 ∎ Polish-Turkish Wars
See **Khotin**

**Chotin ∎ 1673 ∎ Turkish Invasion of the
Ukraine**
See **Khotin**

**Chotin ∎ 1739 ∎ Austro-Russian-Turkish
War**
See **Stavuchany**

**Chotin ∎ 1769 ∎ Catherine the Great's
First Turkish War**
See **Khotin**

**Chotin ∎ 1788 ∎ Catherine the Great's
2nd Turkish War**
See **Khotin**

**Chotusitz ∎ 1742 ∎ War of the Austrian
Succession**
Prince Charles of Lorraine led an Austrian
counter-offensive against the Prussian invasion
of Silesia, attacking Frederick II of Prussia
and Leopold the Younger of Anhalt-Dessau at
Chotusitz, east of Prague. Frederick suffered
more casualties in the bloody fighting, though
the Austrians also lost their guns and many
prisoners and withdrew. Empress Maria Theresa
then made peace (17 May 1742).

**Chra River ∎ 1914 ∎ World War I
(African Colonial Theatre)**
See **Kamina**

**Christmas Hill ∎ 1942 ∎ World War II
(Northern Africa)**
See **Longstop Hill**

Chrysler's Farm ∎ 1813 ∎ War of 1812
Advancing down the St Lawrence from Lake
Ontario, American General James Wilkinson
attacked the British under Colonel Joseph Mor-
rison on the Canadian shore at Chrysler's Farm.
After heavy losses on both sides, General John
Boyd was driven from the field (Wilkinson was
ill), but the American gunboats had passed the
rapids and wintered at French Mills (11 November 1813).

**Chrysopolis ∎ 324 ∎ Roman Wars of
Succession**
Constantine built on victory in 324 at **Adrianople** and on the **Hellespont**, pursuing his rival
Valerius Licinius across the Bosphorus to the
Asian shore, where he was in camp at Chrysopolis (modern Scutari). Licinius was disastrously
defeated and later executed, while Constantine
became sole Emperor at last and built his new

capital—Constantinople—at Byzantium (18 September 324).

Chuanbi | 1839 | 1st Opium War

Two months after an attack on British merchants off **Kowloon**, Captain Henry Smith and the frigates *Volage* (28) and *Hyacinth* (18) attacked a fleet of 29 war junks under Admiral Guan Tianpei at Chuanbi (Chuenpi) on the Zhujiang River. A brief action saw the junks destroyed and dispersed. Britain formally declared war in January 1840 and sent a fleet which captured **Dinghai** (4 November 1839).

Ch'uan-chou | 1852 | Taiping Rebellion
See **Quanzhou**

Chucalissa | 1736 | Chickasaw-French War

Marching from Illinois with French troops and Indian allies against the Chickasaw blocking trade in the Mississippi Valley, Major Pierre d'Artaguiette unwisely attacked Chucalissa village, near modern Memphis, and was heavily defeated and captured. When a large French force later advanced from the south towards **Ackia**, Artaguiette and other prisoners were tortured to death (25 March 1736).

Chu Dien | 547 | Sino-Vietnamese Wars

In a rising in northern Vietnam (then Annam), national hero Ly Bon (Ly Bi) expelled the local Governor and subsequently proclaimed himself Emperor. He then faced a massive counter-offensive by troops of the southern Chinese Liang Dynasty. At the village of Chu Dien, near Hanoi, Ly Bon was defeated and fled. His infant Van Xuan Kingdom was crushed, and he was later captured and killed.

Chudnov | 1660 | Russo-Polish Wars

Defeated in the Ukraine at **Liubar** in August, Russian commander Vasili P. Sheremetev withdrew to nearby Chudnov, while his Cossack ally, Yuri Chmielnicki, was defeated then defected at **Slobodyszcze**. Surrounded by Polish-Tatar forces under Jerzy Lubomirski and Stefan Czarniecki, Sheremetev was defeated and sur-

rendered. He died after 22 years in Tatar captivity (23 October 1660).

Chuenpi | 1839 | 1st Opium War
See **Chuanbi**

Chu Lai | 1965 | Vietnam War

In the first major American operation of the war, Marine General Lewis Walt launched a pre-emptive offensive south of his base at Chu Lai against Viet Cong commander Nguyen Dinh Trong readying his forces near Van Truong. Landing by air and sea, the Marines secured victory with only 45 killed against over 600 Communists dead. The Viet Cong later reoccupied the area (18–24 August 1965).

Chü-lu | 207 BC | Fall of the Qin Dynasty
See **Julu**

Chumatien | 1927 | 1st Chinese Revolutionary Civil War
See **Zhumadian**

Chunchon | 1950 | Korean War

At the start of the war, North Korean forces stormed across the border towards **Seoul** in the west, while further east, about 11,000 invaders without tanks were unexpectedly blocked by courageous South Korean defence at Chunchon. Diverting armour from other sectors, the North Koreans took the city after heavy losses on both sides, then advanced south towards **Wonju** (25–28 June 1950).

Chungtu | 1214–1215 | Conquests of Genghis Khan
See **Beijing**

Chunuk Bair | 1915 | World War I (Gallipoli)

As part of the Allied offensive against the **Sari Bair** Ridge, Australians and New Zealanders under General Alexander Godley (later reinforced by other British and Indian troops) seized Chunuk Bair, northeast of **Anzac**. In the purported turning point of the Gallipoli campaign, reinforced Turkish units counter-attacked and the Allies were driven back with shocking losses (8–10 August 1915).

Chupas | 1542 | Spanish Civil War in Peru

Four years after Diego del Almagro was killed at **Salinas**, his successor Francisco Pizarro was assassinated (26 June 1541) by supporters of Diego del Almagro the Younger, who was proclaimed Governor. In a bloody action at Chupas, near Huamanga (Ayacucho), Almagro was defeated by Viceroy Cristoval Vaca de Castro and Pizarrist Alonzo de Alvarado. He was later executed (16 September 1542).

Chu Pong | 1965 | Vietnam War
See **Ia Drang**

Chuquinga | 1554 | Spanish Civil War in Peru

Despite the execution of anti-Royalist leader Gonzalo Pizarro after defeat at **Xaquixaguana** (April 1548), war continued between rival Spanish factions in Peru, and Francisco Hernandez Giron led a fresh revolt at Cuzco. At Chuquinga, near Abancay in southern Peru, Giron defeated Royalists under Alonzo de Alvarado. However, Giron himself was later captured and beheaded (21 May 1554).

Churubusco | 1847 | American-Mexican War

American General Winfield Scott reached the southern approaches to Mexico City, where he drove the Mexicans out of **Contreras**, and later the same day his main army attacked Churubusco, held by General Antonio de Santa Anna. After a dispersed and confused action, with very heavy Mexican losses in killed and wounded, Santa Anna fled to **Mexico City** and sued for a truce (20 August 1847).

Chustenalah | 1861 | American Civil War (Trans-Mississippi)
See **Shoal Creek**

Chusto-Talasah | 1861 | American Civil War (Trans-Mississippi)
See **Bird Creek**

Chyhyryn | 1677 | Turkish Invasion of the Ukraine
See **Chigirin**

Cibalae | 316 | Roman Wars of Succession

Having disposed of all but one co-Emperor, Constantine turned against his former ally Valerius Licinius, Emperor in the East. At Cibalae (probably Vinkovce between the Drava and Sava Rivers in modern Croatia), the two rivals fought to exhaustion until Licinius broke off the battle to avoid further casualties. They met again the following January at **Campus Ardiensis** (8 October 316).

Cibecue Creek | 1881 | Apache Indian Wars

Preaching a revivalist mysticism, Apache medicine man Nokaidelklini and his supporters were attacked by Colonel Eugene Carr from Fort Apache, Arizona. The Apache suffered a terrible defeat at Cibecue Creek, near the San Cralos Agency northeast of Phoenix, and the mystic was killed. Geronimo then resumed the warpath but was eventually hunted down and surrendered (30 August 1881).

Cibik Ridge | 1943 | World War II (Pacific)
See **Piva Forks**

Cibotus | 1096 | 1st Crusade
See **Civetot**

Ciecierzyn | 1654 | Russo-Polish Wars
See **Szepiele**

Cieneguilla | 1854 | Apache Indian Wars

With Jicarilla Apache raiding south of Taos in northern New Mexico, Major George Blake sent 60 men under Lieutenant John Davidson into the Embudos Mountains, where they were ambushed at Cieneguilla by Chacon. With every man save two hit and 22 killed, Davidson led the survivors back to Taos. Chacon failed with a similar ambush a week later at **Rio Caliente** (30 March 1854).

Cienfuegos I 1898 I Spanish-American War

In a remarkable raid on Cuba at the start of the war, American Captain Bowman H. McCalla in the warship *Marblehead*, with *Nashville* in support, attacked the cable station at Cienfuegos. Landing under severe fire, a launch party cut the cables, severing telegraph communication between Havana and Spain. Forty-nine of the men involved received the Congressional Medal of Honour (11 May 1898).

Cienfuegos I 1957 I Cuban Revolution

During the mainly guerrilla war against President Fulgencio Batista, mutineers led by Dionisio San Román seized the naval base at Cienfuegos and were joined by civilian insurgents. In one of the largest-scale actions of the revolution, Batista units attacked in force, supported by tanks and bombers. Perhaps 300 rebels were killed and a subsequent general strike was also crushed (5 September 1957).

Cieszyn I 1919 I Polish-Czech War
See **Teschen**

Cinco de Mayo I 1862 I Mexican-French War
See **Puebla**

Cirencester I 628 I Anglo-Saxon Territorial Wars

Penda of Mercia began his campaign to expand the power of his kingdom by invading Wessex, where he attacked Cynegils and his son Cwichelm, joint Kings of the West Saxon Hwicce people. An indecisive daylong battle at Cirencester was followed by a peace by which Penda apparently secured land as far as the Avon. He subsequently married his sister to Cynegils' son, Cenwalh.

Cirta I 106 BC I Jugurthine War

Determined to end the war in Numidia after victory at **Thala**, new Roman commander Gaius Marius, with Lucius Cornelius Sulla, advanced on King Jugurtha and his father-in-law, King Bocchus of Mauretania, at Cirta (modern Constantine, Algeria). In battle outside the city, the Numidian army was defeated when Bocchus fled. He later betrayed Jugurtha, who was taken to Rome and executed.

Ciskei I 1834–1835 I 6th Cape Frontier War

When Xhosa under Maqoma entered Cape Province, they were checked by Piet Retief, then defeated in the Ciskei over several months by Colonel Harry Smith. When their presumed leader Hintsa was murdered, Governor Sir Benjamin D'Urban annexed the area between the Keiskamma and Kei as Queen Adelaide Province, but it was soon returned to the Xhosa (December 1834–June 1835).

Cissus I 191 BC I Roman-Syrian War
See **Corycus**

Citate I 1854 I Crimean War

After Turkey crossed the Lower Danube for victory at **Oltenitza** (November 1853), General Mikhail Gorchakov counter-attacked upstream in Wallachia, advancing on **Calafat**. Turkish commander Ahmed Pasha then attacked the Russian garrison of Colonel Alexander Baumgarten at nearby Citate. The main Russian army arrived after four days' fighting, and the Turks fell back (6–9 January 1854).

Citium I 450 BC I Greco-Persian Wars
See **Salamis, Cyprus**

Ciudad Bolívar I 1903 I Venezuelan Civil Wars

General Antonio Matos recovered from **La Victoria** (November 1902) and returned to Venezuela to resume resistance to President Cipriano Castro. After repulsing an advance on Caracas, Government General Juan Gomez sailed to the Orinoco to attack General Nicolás Rolando and 3,000 men at Cuidad Bolívar. Rolando was routed and captured, effectively ending the war (19–21 July 1903).

Ciudad Juárez ▮ 1911 ▮ Mexican Revolution

Near the start of Mexico's Revolution, Francisco Madero sent Pascual Orozco and Francisco (Pancho) Villa from El Paso, Texas, against the border city of Ciudad Juárez. In a remarkable victory of ill-trained fighters over professional troops, General Juan J. Navarro was forced to surrender. Subsequent Federal defeat in the south at **Cuautla** led to the fall of the government (10 May 1911).

Ciudad Juárez ▮ 1913 ▮ Mexican Revolution

Days after his failed attack on **Chihuahua**, in northern Mexico, Francisco (Pancho) Villa led a brilliant coup north against Ciudad Juárez. Riding a captured train into the city at night, he surprised the Federal garrison and, by morning Ciudad Juárez was in his hands. He then left General Juan Medina in command and marched south towards victory at **Tierra Blanca** (15 November 1913).

Ciudad Real ▮ 1809 ▮ Napoleonic Wars (Peninsular Campaign)

Following defeat of the Spanish Army of the Centre in January at **Uclés**, General Don José Urbina Count Cartaojal marched south to campaign on the Gaudiana between Manzanares and Ciudad Real. Forcing the river at Peralvillo near Ciudad Real, French General Francois Sébastiani routed Cartaojal, with a further Spanish loss two days later downstream at **Medellin** (26 March 1809).

Ciudad Rodrigo ▮ 1810 ▮ Napoleonic Wars (Peninsular Campaign)

In a renewed French attack towards central Portugal, Marshal André Masséna besieged the medieval fortress of Ciudad Rodrigo on the Agueda. Defended by Spanish militia under General Andreas Herrasti, the garrison held out against massive attack. However, terrible bombardment and losses made Herrasti surrender, and the French moved against **Almeida** (30 May–9 July 1810).

Ciudad Rodrigo ▮ 1812 ▮ Napoleonic Wars (Peninsular Campaign)

Arthur Wellesley Lord Wellington opened his rapid advance into Spain by besieging Ciudad Rodrigo, defended by General Jean-Leonard Barrié. Storming the fortress 12 days later, he captured the French siege train and massive supplies, opening the way to **Badajoz**. However, victory cost heavy British losses, including Generals Robert Craufurd and Henry McKinnon killed (8–19 January 1812).

Civetot ▮ 1096 ▮ 1st Crusade

Preceding the First Crusade, pilgrims of the so-called "People's Crusade" reached Civetot, east of Constantinople, and began an ill-advised advance towards **Nicaea**. Ambushed by Turks, they were driven back to Civetot with terrible losses including many German knights and thousands of women and children. The battle and massacre ended the disastrous People's Crusade (21 October 1096).

Civita Castelana ▮ 1798 ▮ French Revolutionary Wars (1st Coalition)

Encouraged by Britain, King Ferdinand IV of Naples sent Austrian General Karl Mack von Leiberich to occupy Rome. French General Jean-Étienne Championnet temporarily withdrew to gather his forces, then at Civita Castelana, east of Viterbo, crushed the Neapolitan army. Ferdinand fled to the British and, six weeks later, Championnet captured **Naples** (5–6 December 1798).

Civitate ▮ 1053 ▮ Norman Conquest of Southern Italy

Pope Leo IX resolved to subdue the Normans in Apulia and led a mixed army of Romans, Germans and Byzantine Greeks. At Civitate (San Paolo di Civitate), on the Fortore, he was thoroughly defeated by a small yet disciplined Norman force under Robert and Humphry Guiscard and Count Richard of Aversa. The Pope was captured and held as an honoured prisoner (16 June 1053).

Civitella I 1053 I Norman Conquest of Southern Italy
See **Civitate**

Clans I 1396 I Scottish Clan Wars
See **North Inch**

Clark's Mill I 1862 I American Civil War (Trans-Mississippi)
Campaigning in southwestern Missouri, a 1,000-strong Confederate force under Colonels John Q. Burbridge and Colton Greene attacked the Union Fort at Clark's Mill, near Vera Cruz, north of Gainesville. Captain Hiram E. Barstow and only 100 men withstood a five-hour attack before surrendering and the Confederates burned the blockhouse and other buildings (7 November 1862).

Clashmealcon Caves I 1923 I Irish Civil War
A famous incident of the guerrilla phase of the war saw Republican Timothy "Aero" Lyons and six others besieged by government troops for three days in Clashmealcon Caves at Kerry Head. After surviving firebombs and grenades, two drowned and Lyons was fatally wounded trying to scale the cliff. The others surrendered and three were executed. War ended a month later (April 1923).

Clastidium I 222 BC I Gallic Wars in Italy
Driven back from central Italy at the **Telamon** (225 BC), Insubre Gauls of the north were defeated at the **Adda**, then at Clastidium (modern Casteggio), south of Pavia. Marcus Claudius Marcellus defeated and killed their Chief Viridomarus (Britomatus), reputedly in single combat, and the Gauls were subjugated until Hannibal crossed the Alps four years later and induced them to rise against Rome.

Clear Lake I 1850 I Pit River Indian War
When surveyor Captain William Warner and two white settlers were murdered by Pit River Indians in northern California, Captain Nathaniel Lyon took a punitive expedition northwest through Benicia to Clear Lake. The soldiers killed about 160 warriors in a brutal bayonet assault, then massacred the women and children. Days later Lyon attacked again at the **Russian River** (15 May 1850).

Clearwater I 1877 I Nez Percé Indian War
One month after victory at **White Bird Canyon**, Nez Percé Chief Joseph was joined by Chief Looking Glass on the Clearwater River in central Idaho against a much larger force under General Oliver Howard. Joseph courageously repulsed the troopers with costly losses on both sides, then started an epic retreat east across the Bitterroot Mountains towards the **Big Hole River** (11–12 July 1877).

Cleidon Pass I 1014 I Byzantine Wars of Tsar Samuel
See **Balathista**

Clifton Moor I 1745 I Jacobite Rebellion (The Forty-Five)
Advancing into England soon after victory at **Prestonpans**, Scottish rebels under Charles Stuart—Bonnie Prince Charlie—finally turned back, and a mid-winter rearguard action on Clifton Moor, near Penrith, saw Jacobite commander Lord George Murray defeat the pursuing army of Duke William of Cumberland. The rebels then crossed into Scotland and besieged **Stirling** (18 December 1745).

Clissau I 1702 I 2nd "Great" Northern War
See **Kliszow**

Clitheroe I 1138 I Anglo-Scottish Territorial Wars
David I of Scotland took advantage of a period of instability in England and crossed the border to capture some key cities from King Stephen. He then sent his nephew William FitzDuncan against an English force at Clitheroe, Lancashire, where the Scots inflicted a sharp defeat. However, David was comprehensively defeated

a few months later at the Battle of the **Standard** (10 June 1138).

Clonmel ∎ 1650 ∎ British Civil Wars

Oliver Cromwell renewed his campaign against Catholic-Royalist Ireland after the destruction of **Drogheda** and **Wexford** in late 1649, besieging Clonmel on the Suir. Cromwell suffered heavy losses in an unexpected check, but a second attack succeeded. Hugh O'Neill and his garrison had escaped to **Limerick** and Cromwell promptly returned to England (21 April–10 May 1650).

Clonmel ∎ 1922 ∎ Irish Civil War

Government troops under the command of General John Prout, advancing through **Waterford** and **Tipperary**, converged on Clonmel and attacked the Republican forces of Dinny Lacey and Dan Breen attempting to hold the nearby town of Carrick-on-Suir. Carrick fell after four days' heavy fighting and further costly action eventually saw Prout secure Clonmel (31 July–10 August 1922).

Clontarf ∎ 1014 ∎ Later Viking Raids on Britain

In an attempt to reinforce the Viking presence in Ireland, fresh forces from the Orkneys invaded to support a Danish uprising in Dublin. At nearby Clontarf, the army of Irish King Brian Boru, led by his son Murchadh, utterly destroyed the Danes with 6,000 reported dead, though Brian himself was killed in his tent nearby. Thereafter, the Danes turned to the conquest of England (23 April 1014).

Clontibret ∎ 1595 ∎ Tyrone Rebellion

When Hugh O'Neill Earl of Tyrone renewed the rebellion of his uncle Shane O'Neill (which had been crushed at **Letterkenny** in 1567), the Lord Lieutenant in Ireland, Sir Henry Bagenal, marched from Dundalk to secure Monaghan. As the English withdrew southeast towards Dundalk, Hugh O'Neill attacked them on the march near Clontibret and Bagenal was utterly defeated (27 May 1595).

Clouds ∎ 1899 ∎ Philippine-American War
See **Tirad Pass**

Cloyd's Mountain ∎ 1864 ∎ American Civil War (Eastern Theatre)

Raiding against railways in southwestern Virginia, Union General George Crook attacked a dispersed Confederate force at Cloyd's Mountain, in Pulaski County near Dublin. The Confederates were defeated in a bloody action and commander General Albert G. Jenkins was captured and died of wounds. Another action was fought next day further west at **Cove Mountain** (9 May 1864).

Clusium ∎ 225 BC ∎ Gallic Wars in Italy
See **Faesulae**

Cnidus ∎ 394 BC ∎ Corinthian War

When King Agesilaus of Sparta returned from Asia Minor to attack Athens at **Coronea**, his brother-in-law Pisander led the Spartan navy against the Persian fleet under Conon of Athens and the Satrap Pharnabazus. Pisander was killed and the Spartan fleet was destroyed in a decisive action off Cnidus, near Rhodes, restoring Persian power in Asia Minor (August 394 BC).

Coa ∎ 1810 ∎ Napoleonic Wars (Peninsular Campaign)

Marshal André Masséna advanced into Portugal after capturing **Ciudad Rodrigo** (9 July) and sent Marshal Michel Ney against an Anglo-Portuguese force on the River Coa outside the border fortress of Almeida. A courageous defence by General Robert "Black Bob" Craufurd cost heavy French losses, yet the Allies were driven off and Masséna began his siege of **Almeida** (24 July 1810).

Coamo ∎ 1898 ∎ Spanish-American War

While American forces in southern Puerto Rico secured **Guánica** (25 July), another division further to the east under Generals James H. Wilson and Oswald H. Ernst attacked Coamo to cut Spanish communication north to San Juan. The town surrendered after a brief action with 40 American casualties. Within days the war ended and the United States gained Puerto Rico (9 August 1898).

Coatepeque I 1863 I Central American National Wars

When Honduras and El Salvador formed a Liberal alliance against Guatemala and Nicaragua, President José Rafael Carrera of Guatemala invaded El Salvador against Gerardo Barrios and captured Santa Ana. At nearby Coatepeque, he suffered a costly defeat and withdrew. President Barrios later lost in Nicaragua at **San Felipe** and Carrera returned to take **San Salvador** (23–24 February 1863).

Coatit I 1895 I 1st Italo-Ethiopian War

Weeks after crushing Okulé-Kusai rebellion in northern Ethiopia at **Halai**, Italian General Oreste Baratieri turned against rebel leader Ras Mangasha of Tigre. The Italians and native askaris attacked Ras Mangasha northeast of Adowa at Coatit, where badly armed Tigreans fought a brave draw, then withdrew. The Ethiopian Imperial army routed Baratieri in 1896 at **Adowa** (13 January 1895).

Cocboy I 641 I Anglo-Saxon Territorial Wars

See **Maserfield**

Cocherel I 1364 I Hundred Years War

With the accession of Charles V of France, Charles of Navarre attempted to recover land in Normandy and was opposed by the great Royalist warrior Bertrand du Guesclin. The Navarrese army, supported by English mercenaries, was attacked and destroyed west of Paris at Cocherel, near Mantes, and Navarrese leader Jean de Grailly Captal du Buch was captured (16 May 1364).

Cochin I 1506 I Early Portuguese Colonial Wars in Asia

When Portugal sent Duarte Pacheco to Cochin in southwest India to assist the Raja against **Calicut**, Pacheco was driven out by overwhelming forces before recapturing the city and restoring the Prince. Pacheco then resisted a massive siege by the Raja of Calicut. The Raja

was defeated and killed after a five-month assault and Cochin became Portuguese until Dutch conquest in 1663.

Cockpit Point I 1862 I American Civil War (Eastern Theatre)

Determined to blockade Washington, D.C. after victory at **Bull Run**, Confederate General Samuel G. French established batteries on the Potomac, where Cockpit Point, near Dumfries, Virginia, was shelled and heavily damaged by two gunboats under Lieutenant Robert H. Wyman. A few weeks later, the batteries were abandoned and the Confederates withdrew towards Richmond (3 January 1862).

Cogorderos I 1811 I Napoleonic Wars (Peninsular Campaign)

See **Benavides**

Coimbra, Brazil I 1864 I War of the Triple Alliance

In a pre-emptive attack on Brazil, Paraguayan Dictator Francisco Solano López sent 6,000 men under Colonels Vicente Barrios and Francisco Isidro Resquin on a brilliant lightning attack into the Mato Grosso. There they captured Coimbra, held by Colonel Hermenegildo de Albuquerque Porto Carrero, and also Corumbá, to hold the border province for the rest of the war (26–28 December 1864).

Coimbra, Portugal I 1064 I Early Christian Reconquest of Spain

King Ferdinand I won a civil war to unite the kingdoms of Castile, Leon and Galicia, then turned against the Muslims of Aragon and Valencia. Concluding a successful campaign, he besieged the city of Coimbra, south of Viseu, now in Portugal. Coimbra fell after six months with more than 5,000 Muslim prisoners taken, but Ferdinand died soon afterwards, and Spain reverted to civil war.

Coimbra, Portugal I 1811 I Napoleonic Wars (Peninsular Campaign)

While retreating from the failed invasion of Portugal, a French attempt to secure a crossing of the Mondego River was blocked at Coimbra by Portuguese militia under General Nicholas Trant, who had occupied the city. General Louis Montbrun failed in a three-day attempt to capture Coimbra and, after French defeat at **Condeixa**, his cavalry joined the general retreat (10–13 March 1811).

Coimbra, Portugal I 1828 I Miguelite Wars

During the disputed succession following the death of John VI of Portugal, his son Miguel attempted to seize the kingdom against the interests of his own niece Maria Da Gloria. Miguel's General, Alvaro Povoas, defeated the constitutional army of General John Carlos de Saldanha, near Coimbra in central Portugal. Two weeks later, Miguel usurped the throne (24 June 1828).

Coire I 1799 I French Revolutionary Wars (2nd Coalition)

French General André Masséna responded to an Austrian advance over the Lech by crossing the Rhine and marching south along the right bank of the river. He crushed an Austrian force under General Franz von Auffenberg at Coire (Chur) in eastern Switzerland, where he took over 3,000 prisoners before continuing his advance (7 March 1799).

Coixtlahuaca I 1458 I Aztec Wars of Conquest

During expansion under the powerful ruler Motecuhzoma I, Aztec forces moved southeast into the Gulf Lowlands to secure Tochtepec and Cotaxtla, then further south against the powerful trading city of Coixtlahuaca, on the Mixteca Alta, where merchants had supposedly been murdered. A very large army marched on Coixtlahuaca, and the city was crushed, consolidating Aztec power in the south.

Colberg Heath I 1644 I Thirty Years War (Franco-Habsburg War)

See **Kolberg Heath**

Colby Moor I 1645 I British Civil Wars

On a fresh offensive in southwest Wales following Royalist disaster at **Naseby** (14 June), General Rowland Laugharne, Parliamentary Governor of Pembroke, marched against local Royalists under Sir Edward Stradling. Supported by naval forces landing in Milford Haven near Carnaston Bridge, Laugharne crushed Stradling on Colby Moor and secured all of Pembrokeshire (30 July 1645).

Colchester I 1648 I British Civil Wars

With Kentish rebels under George Goring Earl of Norwich dispersed at **Maidstone** (1 June), Norwich joined Royalists led by Arthur Lord Capel and Sir Charles Lucas under siege at Colchester, Essex, which was starved into surrender by Parliamentarian Sir Thomas Fairfax. Lucas and Sir George Lisle were shot next day and the war was effectively over (12 June–27 August 1648).

Cold Harbour I 1862 I American Civil War (Eastern Theatre)

See **Gaines' Mill**

Cold Harbour I 1864 I American Civil War (Eastern Theatre)

As Union commander Ulysses S. Grant advanced through Virginia across the **Totopotomoy Creek** towards Richmond, he met General Robert E. Lee again at Cold Harbour, just west of the Confederate Capital. In what has been called Lee's last great victory, repeated Union attacks were repulsed with about 12,000 men lost. Grant then turned south against **Petersburg** (31 May–12 June 1864).

Colditz I 1813 I Napoleonic Wars (War of Liberation)

Advancing east following Napoleon Bonaparte's victory at **Lützen**, French forces led by Prince Eugène de Beauharnais caught up with the Russian rearguard under General Mikhail Miloradovich three days later at Colditz, southeast of Leipzig. Miloradovich was badly mauled but fought an effective delaying action as the Allies continued towards the Elbe (5 May 1813).

Colenso I 1899 I 2nd Anglo-Boer War

In a first attempt to relieve **Ladysmith**, British General Sir Redvers Buller led 21,000 men against the left flank of Boer leader Louis Botha on the Tugela, south of Ladysmith, at Colenso. Buller lost over 1,000 men in a failed, bloody frontal assault, and—with the third defeat of "Black Week" after **Stormberg** and **Magersfontein**—he was relieved of overall command (15 December 1899).

Coleraine I 1564 I O'Neill Rebellion

Campaigning against Anglo-Scots colonisation of Ulster, Shane O'Neill Lord of Tyrone met his Protestant rivals under Sorley Boy MacDonnell, near Coleraine in County Londonderry. The engagement was indecisive, but the following year O'Neill resoundingly defeated MacDonnell at **Ballycastle** and held him prisoner until his own defeat in 1567 at **Letterkenny**.

Coleroon I 1782 I 2nd British-Mysore War

See **Kumbakonam**

Coleshill I 1157 I Anglo-Welsh Wars

Shortly after succeeding to the English throne, Henry II led a force against Wales, where some districts had been lost during the anarchic reign of his predecessor Stephen. In the Coleshill Forest in North Flintshire, Henry was surprised and defeated with heavy losses by Welsh Chief Owen ap Gruffydd. However, the King resumed the campaign and gradually reasserted English authority.

Coleto Creek I 1836 I Texan Wars of Independence

Mexican General José Urrea invaded Texas through **San Patricio** and advanced against **Goliad**, southeast of the **Alamo**, held by Colonel James Fannin. Fatally delaying his withdrawal, Fannin was beaten at nearby Coleto Creek and surrendered after heavy losses. A week later (27 March), he and 400 other prisoners were executed, but the Texans were soon avenged at **San Jacinto** (20 March 1836).

Colima I 1859 I Mexican War of the Reform

Reactionary President Miguel Miramón secured decisive victory at **La Estancia** in November, then took 3,000 men against the west coast city of Colima, held by 5,000 Liberals under Generals Pedro Ogazón and Antonio Rojas. Miramón repulsed Rojas on the Tuxpan, then defeated the Liberals on the nearby heights of Tonila to secure Colima before returning to Mexico City (21–24 December 1859).

Coliseo I 1895 I 2nd Cuban War of Independence

Days after bloody victory in western Cuba at **Mal Tiempo**, insurgent leader Máximo Gómez entered Matanzas Province, where he met Spanish commander General Arsenio Martínez Campos at Coliseo, near Cárdenas. Gómez had to withdraw after heavy losses, but Martínez Campos failed to pursue and fell back towards Havana, where he was replaced in command (23 December 1895).

Collierville I 1863 I American Civil War (Western Theatre)

Confederate General James R. Chalmers attacking the railroad just east of Memphis, Tennessee, advanced on the small town of Collierville, courageously defended by Colonel Edward Hatch. Surprised by a Union counter-attack, Chalmers' much larger force was routed and fled across the Coldwater, leaving 50 prisoners including militia General James Z. George (3 November 1863).

Colline Gate I 82 BC I Sullan Civil War

Within months of victory at **Sacriportus** and **Faventia**, Lucius Cornelius Sulla virtually ended the civil war by destroying the army of Gaius Marius the Younger, led by Pontius Telesinas, just outside Rome at the Colline Gate. Sulla executed thousands of prisoners, including Telesinas, and when Marius committed suicide in the fall of Praeneste, Sulla made himself Dictator (1 November 82 BC).

Collooney ∎ 1798 ∎ French Revolutionary Wars (Irish Rising)

A week after victory at **Castlebar**, French General Joseph Humbert and a 1,600-strong French-Irish force were met five miles from Sligo near Collooney by a garrison of 300 Limerick militia under Colonel Charles Vereker. About 50 men were lost on either side in sharp fighting before Vereker surrendered. He and his men were released on parole to return to Sligo (5 September 1798).

Colmar ∎ 1675 ∎ 3rd Dutch War
See **Turckheim**

Colmar ∎ 1945 ∎ World War II (Western Europe)

Supporting the German offensive into **Alsace**, forces south of Strasbourg around Colmar broke out to the north, then faced stiff resistance under French commander Jean de Lattre de Tasigny, supported by American General Frank Milburn. The Colmar Pocket was finally eliminated with heavy losses on both sides, ending the last German presence on French soil (5 January–9 February 1945).

Colombey ∎ 1870 ∎ Franco-Prussian War

French Marshal Francois-Achille Bazaine, falling back after defeat at **Wörth**, was attacked east of **Metz** at Colombey by German forward units under Baron Kolmar von der Goltz. Both sides claimed victory after heavy losses—including French General Claude-Théodore Decaen killed—but the French were able to continue withdrawing across the Moselle towards **Mars-la-Tour** (14 August 1870).

Colombo ∎ 1587–1588 ∎ Portuguese Colonial Wars in Asia

In his war against the Portuguese in western Ceylon, the heroic King Rajasinha I of Sitavaka led a final massive siege of the key city of Colombo. However, his navy failed to prevent Portuguese reinforcements. Rajasinha was eventually forced to withdraw with heavy losses and,

within a few years, the Kingdom of Sitavaka had been destroyed (May 1587–February 1588).

Colombo ∎ 1655–1656 ∎ Later Portuguese Colonial Wars in Asia

After capturing Portuguese **Trincomalee** in 1639, Dutch forces joined with King Rajasinha II of Kandy, in central Ceylon, to attack Colombo. Following a seven-month siege, with shocking cruelty on both sides, the starving Portuguese garrison surrendered. With the subsequent fall of Jaffna, the Dutch ruled coastal Ceylon until British invasion in 1796 (November 1655–12 May 1656).

Colombo ∎ 1796 ∎ French Revolutionary Wars (1st Coalition)

Landing on Dutch Ceylon (modern Sri Lanka), British Admiral Peter Rainier and Colonel James Stuart (1741–1815) captured **Trincomalee**, then sailed to attack the capital, Colombo, which was surrendered by Governor Johan Gerard van Angelbeek after a sharp fight. Unlike other Dutch possessions, the island was not returned to Holland under treaty in 1802, and remained a British territory (15 February 1796).

Colombo ∎ 1942 ∎ World War II (Indian Ocean)

Admiral Chuichi Nagumo entered the Indian Ocean with a large fleet and launched a heavy carrier air-raid against the naval docks at Colombo in **Ceylon** (modern Sri Lanka). The British lost an armed merchant cruiser and destroyer sunk, and 25 fighters, for 21 Japanese planes shot down. Nagumo's aircraft also sank the heavy cruisers *Dorsetshire* and *Cornwall* south of Ceylon (5 April 1942).

Colorado ∎ 1840 ∎ Comanche Indian Wars

Pursuing Comanche survivors of defeat in August at **Plum Creek** in southern Texas, Colonel John Moore and 100 Texan militia marched north across the Concho for a dawn attack on the Comanche camp on the Colorado, near modern Ballinger, south of Abilene. The Indians lost

50 killed and a further 80 drowned in the river before Moore withdrew with 500 captured ponies (14 October 1840).

Columbia I 1864 I American Civil War (Western Theatre)

As Confederate commander John B. Hood advanced north across Tennessee from Florence, he was intercepted on the Duck River at Columbia, south of **Nashville**, by Union General John M. Schofield, marching north from Pulaski. Although the action was indecisive, Schofield was in danger of being cut off and withdrew north through **Spring Hill** to **Franklin** (24–29 November 1864).

Columbus I 1916 I Villa's Raids

Two months after his supporters murdered Americans in northern Mexico at **Santa Isabel, Sonora**, rebel leader Francisco (Pancho) Villa took more than 500 men across the border and burned the town of Columbus, New Mexico, killing 15 soldiers and civilians before being driven off with heavy losses. The raid led to the punitive expedition of General John Pershing and action at **Carrizal** (8–9 March 1916).

Comayagua I 1827 I Central American National Wars

President Manuel José Arce of the Central American Federation faced Liberal opposition in Honduras and El Salvador and sent General José Justo Milla against Hondura's capital, Comayagua. President Dionisio Herrera was deposed after a month besieged. Herrera's nephew Francisco Morazán soon beat Milla at **La Trinidad** and freed his uncle in 1829 in **Guatemala City** (10 May 1827).

Comayagua I 1845 I Central American National Wars

When Honduras supported efforts to restore President Francisco Malespín of El Salvador, overthrown after **Jutiapa**, Salvadoran General José Trinidad Cabañas led an army into Honduras. He was heavily defeated at Comayagua

and, after a further loss at Sensenti (10 June), he withdrew into El Salvador, pursued by a Honduran army which was eventually checked at **Obrajuela** (2 June 1845).

Comayagua I 1872 I Central American National Wars

Twelve months after seizing power in El Salvador at **Santa Ana**, President Santiago Gonzáles formed a Liberal alliance with President Miguel García Gránados of Guatemala and personally led an invasion against President José María Medina of Honduras. In a sharp two-month campaign, Gonzáles captured Comayagua and replaced Medina with the more Liberal Carlos Céleo Arias (May 1872).

Comayagua I 1874 I Central American National Wars

When Liberal President Miguel García Gránados of Guatemala was replaced by the more Conservative Justo Ruffino Barrios, the new government withdrew Guatemalan support for President Carlos Céleo Arias of Honduras and invaded in support of his opponent Ponciano Levía. The brief war ended with the fall of Comayagua and the installation of Levía as President (13 January 1874).

Combat de Trente I 1351 I Hundred Years War

See **Thirty**

Combolchia I 1941 I World War II (Northern Africa)

See **Dessie**

Como I 1964 I Guinea-Bissau War

At the start of the war for Portuguese Guinea, independence forces loyal to Amilcar Cabal, who had seized the coastal island of Como, faced a full-scale counter-offensive by up to 3,000 Portuguese regulars. Two months of intense fighting saw perhaps 600 Portuguese killed, and the much-mythologised rebel victory greatly increased support for what became a ten-year war (January–February 1964).

Compiègne ▌ 1430 ▌ Hundred Years War

In an attempt to counter the French military resurgence inspired by Jeanne d'Arc, Duke Philip of Burgundy joined the English in besieging Compiègne, north of Paris. A relief army sent by Charles VII of France eventually broke the siege, but Jeanne (Joan of Arc) was captured (23 May). She was later sold to the English for trial and execution at the stake (May–November 1430).

Comum ▌ 196 BC ▌ Gallic Wars in Italy
See **Lake Como**

Concepción, Peru ▌ 1882 ▌ War of the Pacific

Peruvian General Andrés Avelino Cáceres advanced against an isolated Chilean outpost in central Peru, where he sent 400 men under Colonel Juan Gastó against just 77 men holding out at the pueblo of Concepción, in Junin Province, northwest of Huancayo. In one of the heroic actions of the war, the Chileans fought bravely for about 18 hours before all were eventually killed (9–10 July 1882).

Concepcion, Texas ▌ 1835 ▌ Texan Wars of Independence

Following the skirmish at **Gonzales**, Stephen Austin's Texan army advanced on San Antonio, where General Martin de Cos sent a force against James Bowie and James Fannin in camp at nearby Concepcion. Colonels Domingo de Ugartechea and José María Mendoza were driven off with 14 killed and 39 wounded and the Texans moved closer to besiege **San Antonio** (28 October 1835).

Concón ▌ 1891 ▌ Chilean Civil War

With northern Chile seized from President José Manuel Balmaceda after victory in March at **Pozo Almonte**, Congressist Colonel Estanislao del Canto Arteaga landed 9,000 men north of Valparaiso and advanced against Colonel Orozimbo Barbosa Puga and 8,000 Loyalists entrenched at nearby Concón. Barbosa was driven out with over 2,000 casualties and lost again at **Placilla** (21 August 1891).

Concord ▌ 1775 ▌ War of the American Revolution

Determined to seize arms held by American patriots, British forces from Boston under Colonel Francis Smith and Major John Pitcairn dispersed rebels at **Lexington**, then continued west the same day against Concord. After a skirmish with militia under Colonel James Barrett, Smith headed back to **Boston**, reinforced by Lord Hugh Percy, with costly losses to both sides all the way (19 April 1775).

Condeixa ▌ 1811 ▌ Napoleonic Wars (Peninsular Campaign)

Marshal Michel Ney retreated from the failed French invasion of Portugal, fighting a series of remarkable rearguard actions against the cautious Allied pursuit led by Arthur Wellesley Lord Wellington. Forced back at **Redhina**, General Louis Montbrun turned on the Allies on the Mondego River at Condeixa, delaying their advance as the French fell back on **Cazal Novo** (13 March 1811).

Condé-sur-l'Escaut ▌ 1793 ▌ French Revolutionary Wars (1st Coalition)

While besieging Condé, east of St Amand, Friedrich Josias Prince of Saxe-Coburg and Frederick Augustus Duke of York were attacked in a strong defensive position by the new French commander August Picot Marquis Dampierre. Following repeated failed attacks, Dampierre was killed by a cannonball and his force withdrew. Condé fell to Saxe-Coburg in mid-July (8 May 1793).

Condore ▌ 1758 ▌ Seven Years War (India)
See **Rajahmundry**

Congella ▌ 1842 ▌ Natal War

In order to occupy Natal, Captain Thomas C. Smith secured Port Natal, then attacked the Boer camp at Congella, just outside Durban, held by Andreis Pretorius. The British column was driven off with 17 killed and 32 wounded and was then besieged in camp. Relieved by Colonel Abraham Cloete, they withdrew to Cape

Colony, though within a year Britain had secured Natal (23 May 1842).

Conjeeveram | 1692 | Mughal-Maratha Wars
See **Kanchi**

Conjeeveram | 1751 | 2nd Carnatic War
Days after victory at **Arni** over Raza Sahib (son of French-appointed Nawab Chanda Sahib), Robert Clive marched against the southeast Indian town of Conjeeveram (modern Kanchipuram), held by a French garrison under Portuguese soldier of fortune La Volonté. Two days of bombardment drove the garrison out and Clive pursued Raza Sahib to battle at **Kaveripak** (16–18 December 1751).

Conjeeveram | 1780 | 2nd British-Mysore War
See **Perambakam**

Connecticut | 1815 | War of 1812
Unaware that peace had been signed in Europe, the American frigate *President* (Captain Stephen Decatur) attempted to break out of the British blockade of New York. In a bloody action off Connecticut, the British frigate *Endymion* (Captain Henry Hope) was eventually disabled, but the frigates *Pomone* and *Tenedos* arrived, and the badly damaged *President* surrendered (15 January 1815).

Consarbruck | 1675 | 3rd Dutch War
With Marshal Henri de Turenne killed at **Sasbach** (27 July) Imperial forces advanced into Lorraine, and French Marshal Francois de Crequi was sent to drive off Duke Charles of Lorraine's siege of Trier. Crequi was defeated at nearby Consarbruck (modern Konz) and captured in the fall of Trier, leaving Louis II de Bourbon Prince of Condé to stem the threatened Imperial invasion (11 August 1675).

Constanta | 1916 | World War I (Balkan Front)
General August von Mackensen seized the Romanian Danube cities of **Tutrakan** and Si-listria, then took his German-Bulgarian-Turkish force east to attack the Black Sea port of Constanta, defended by Romanians and Russians under Andrei Zayonchovsky. Initially repulsed, Mackensen's second attack took the city by storm. He then turned west against **Bucharest** (22 October 1916).

Constantine | 1836–1837 | French Conquest of Algeria
Campaigning to complete the conquest of eastern Algeria, France faced continued resistance by the Bey of Constantine, who repulsed an attack by Marshal Bertrand Clausel (21 November 1836). Clausel was recalled and, in a hard-fought siege the next year, a larger force under Marshal Charles Damremont captured Constantine, though Damremont was killed by a sniper (6–13 October 1837).

Constantinople | 443 | Hun Invasion of the Roman Empire
Attila renewed his invasion of the Eastern Empire after destroying **Sirmium** in 441, capturing Naissus (Nis), Serdica (Sofia) and Arcadiopolis, then advancing on Constantinople, defended by Flavius Zeno. Outside the city, he defeated the Imperial army under Aspar the Alan and the Germans Areobindus and Arnegisclus, but lacked resources for a siege and pursued the Roman army to the **Chersonesus**.

Constantinople | 532 | Nika Insurrection
A riot by Hippodome factions in Constantinople shouting Nika (victory) became a revolt against Emperor Justinian. They proclaimed Hypatius (a nephew of Anastasius) as Emperor and six days of riot saw much of the city burned. Troops under Belisarius and Narses crushed the rising, with perhaps 30,000 killed. Hypatius and his brother Pompeius were arrested and executed (12–18 January 532).

Constantinople | 626 | Byzantine-Balkan Wars
While Emperor Heraclius was fighting the Persians in Asia Minor at the **Sarus**, the Avar Khan Baian advanced through Bulgaria to

besiege Constantinople, defended by the Patriarch Sergius and the Emperor's son Constantine. Advancing Persians under Shahbaraz were intercepted and destroyed on the Bosphorus, and the Avars were defeated trying to storm the city (29 June–10 August 626).

Constantinople ∎ 672–677 ∎ Early Byzantine-Muslim Wars
See **Syllaeum**

Constantinople ∎ 717–718 ∎ Early Byzantine-Muslim Wars
One of the most costly Saracen attacks on Constantinople saw Muslim General Maslama lead a huge army, supported by a very large fleet under Suleiman. During a year-long siege, the Emperor Leo III inflicted massive Muslim losses on land and at sea—claimed to be over 100,000 men. Maslama was eventually defeated by an advancing Bulgarian relief army at **Adrianople**, and withdrew.

Constantinople ∎ 1047 ∎ Later Byzantine Military Rebellions
In a rising against his uncle, Emperor Constantine IX, Leo Tornikios (Tornices) gathered backing in Macedonia and marched on the capital, supported by General John Vatatzes. Tornikios very nearly succeeded attacking Constantinople itself, but when he hesitated, reinforcements arrived and drove him off. The rebels were defeated and Tornikios and Vatatzes were captured and blinded.

Constantinople ∎ 1187 ∎ Branas Rebellion
Two years after defeating Norman Sicily at the **Strymon** and **Demetritsa**, the Byzantine Admiral-General Alexius Branas rose in revolt against Emperor Isaac II and marched against the Byzantine capital. Outside the walls of Constantinople, Branas was met by an army under the Emperor's new brother-in-law, Conrad of Montferrat, and the rebel was defeated and killed.

Constantinople ∎ 1203–1204 ∎ 4th Crusade
When Crusaders supported Venice in attacking Constantinople, supposedly in support of the deposed Isaac II and his son Alexius, they helped capture it on 17 July 1203. However, the restored Byzantines rose against the Crusaders and a second attack took place. The city fell amid violent assault and deliberate destruction and Baldwin was established as the first Latin Emperor (11–13 April 1204).

Constantinople ∎ 1236 ∎ 2nd Latin-Byzantine Imperial War
The Byzantine John III Vatatzes of Nicaea renewed warfare against the Latin Emperors in Constantinople, establishing an alliance with Ivan Asen II of Bulgaria. Together they laid siege to the capital by land and sea, but with the support of newly arrived Venetian ships, the great Latin warrior John of Brienne led a brilliant counter-offensive to repulse the allies and break the siege.

Constantinople ∎ 1261 ∎ 3rd Latin-Byzantine Imperial War
From his base in Nicaea, the Byzantine Emperor Michael VIII Paleologus sent General Alexius Strategopoulos to attack Constantinople. With the Venetian navy and the best French knights away campaigning on the Black Sea, the city was captured with little fighting. Its fall marked the end of the Latin Crusader Emperors and the restoration of the Greek Empire (25 July 1261).

Constantinople ∎ 1352 ∎ Venetian-Genoese Wars
During a threatened trade war with Byzantium, Genoese Admiral Peganino Doria took his fleet right to the walls of Constantinople. Emperor John VI Cantacuzenus brought in Venetian ships under Niccolo Pisani to reinforce his own fleet led by Constantine Tarchaniotes. However, they were driven off in an indecisive action and John was forced to make peace with Genoa (13 February 1352).

Constantinople ∎ 1422 ∎ Byzantine-Ottoman Wars
Ending some years of peace between the Turks and the declining Greek Byzantine Empire,

Emperor Manuel II Palaeologus supported a usurper against Ottoman Sultan Murad II, who responded by attacking Constantinople itself. Murad's siege was driven off with severe losses and he made peace with Manuel, who agreed to pay a heavy annual tribute (June 1422).

Constantinople ▎ 1453 ▎ Byzantine-Ottoman Wars

Sultan Mehmed II's decisive offensive saw him take a massive force against Constantinople, defended by Emperor Constantine XI and General John Giustiniani. The city fell by storm after a devastating siege and one of the heaviest bombardments then recorded. The 1,000-year Byzantine Empire ended in slaughter with Constantine and Giustiniani both killed (February–29 May 1453).

Constantinople ▎ 1807 ▎ Napoleonic Wars (4th Coalition)

In a large-scale military demonstration, British Admiral Sir John Duckworth appeared before Constantinople with eight ships of the line, demanding surrender of the Turkish fleet. With support from French General Francois Sébastiani, Sultan Selim II strengthened his resistance and Duckworth withdrew through the Dardanelles, suffering heavy damage (19 February–3 March 1807).

Constantinople ▎ 1912 ▎ 1st Balkan War
See **Chataldja**

Constellation vs *Insurgente* ▎ 1799 ▎ Franco-American Quasi War
See **Nevis**

Constellation vs *Vengeance* ▎ 1800 ▎ Franco-American Quasi War
See **Guadeloupe**

Constitution vs *Cyane* ▎ 1815 ▎ War of 1812
See **Madeira**

Constitution vs *Guerrière* ▎ 1812 ▎ War of 1812
See **Newfoundland**

Constitution vs *Java* ▎ 1812 ▎ War of 1812
See **Bahia**

Con Thien (1st) ▎ 1967 ▎ Vietnam War

Despite costly failure at **Khe Sanh** (April–May), North Vietnamese regulars attempted a large-scale offensive further east across the DMZ into Quang Tri. Badly outnumbered US Marines around the small base at Con Thien suffered bloody losses, but heavy reinforcements, artillery and air-strikes (Operation Buffalo) finally repulsed the invaders with high casualties on both sides (2–14 July 1967).

Con Thien (2nd) ▎ 1967 ▎ Vietnam War

As a prelude to the **Tet Offensive**, North Vietnamese troops again tried to seize Quang Tri, unleashing one of their heaviest bombardments of the war against the hilltop base at Con Thien. American forces responded with a massive counter-bombardment by artillery, air-strikes and naval guns, and the Communists were driven off with perhaps 2,000 killed (11 September–31 October 1967).

Contreras ▎ 1847 ▎ American-Mexican War

Nearing **Mexico City** after victory at **Cerro Gordo** (18 April), American General Winfield Scott split his force and sent General Persifor Smith west against General Gabriel Valencia in Contreras. Despite being initially repulsed, an American dawn attack with the bayonet drove the Mexicans out with heavy losses. Scott advanced later that day north through **Churubusco** (19–20 August 1847).

Convoy Pedestal ▎ 1942 ▎ World War II (War at Sea)

Determined to relieve besieged **Malta**, Allied Convoy Pedestal sailed from Gibraltar with a heavy escort. One of the war's most famous convoy battles saw Axis aircraft, submarines and surface ships sink an aircraft carrier, a cruiser, a destroyer and nine freighters. However, five merchant ships, including the tanker *Ohio*, reached Malta to prevent starvation and capitulation (10–15 August 1942).

Convoy PQ17 ▮ 1942 ▮ World War II (War at Sea)

One of the costliest convoy actions of the war saw Allied convoy PQ17 to Russia attacked by German aircraft and U-boats near Bear Island. Four German heavy ships in the area played no active part, but their threat led to a decision to scatter the convoy. Only 13 of 34 merchantmen reached Archangel. Later convoys to Russia were kept smaller for easier defence (27 June–8 July 1942).

Conwy ▮ 1295 ▮ English Conquest of Wales

Taking advantage of England's war in Gascony, Welsh nobles renewed the nationalist cause which had been crushed at **Aber Edw** in 1282. Edward I's advance into northern Wales was challenged at Conwy, south of Llandudno, where his archers and crossbowmen under William de Beauchamp Earl of Warwick destroyed the Welsh spearmen and Wales was occupied (January 1295).

Cooch's Bridge ▮ 1777 ▮ War of the American Revolution

As British General Sir William Howe marched towards Philadelphia, American commander General George Washington sent an inadequate force under General William Maxwell to halt the invaders. At Cooch's Bridge, on the Christiana northeast of Elkton, Delaware, Maxwell was repulsed by General Charles Earl Cornwallis and Howe advanced to victory at **Brandywine** (3 September 1777).

Cool Springs ▮ 1864 ▮ American Civil War (Eastern Theatre)

See **Snicker's Ferry**

Copenhagen ▮ 1362 ▮ Wars of the Hanseatic League

Waldemar IV Atterdag expanded the power of Denmark, capturing **Visby** on the Baltic island of Gotland (July 1361). As a result, he found himself at war with the cities of the Hanseatic League allied with Sweden and Norway. The Allied fleet under John Wittenborg of Lubeck entered the Sound and sacked Copenhagen. However, the League's ships were defeated later that year off **Helsingborg**.

Copenhagen ▮ 1523–1524 ▮ Wars of the Kalmar Union

After being deposed in Sweden by Gustav Vasa, the unpopular Christian II of Denmark faced rebellion in Jutland led by his uncle Duke Frederick of Holstein. Copenhagen was besieged by Frederick's General Johan Rantzau and, after the fall of the capital followed by capture of Malmo, the Duke became King of Denmark and Norway as Frederick I.

Copenhagen ▮ 1535–1536 ▮ Danish Counts' War

With Hanseatic forces destroyed at **Oksnebjerg** and **Bornholm** in June 1535, Lutheran Duke Christian of Schleswig and General Johan Rantzau besieged Copenhagen, which sided with Lubeck in favour of former King Christian II. Count Christopher of Oldenberg surrendered Copenhagen after 12 months of siege and the Duke entered the city in triumph as Christian III (24 July 1535–29 July 1536).

Copenhagen ▮ 1658 ▮ 1st Northern War

See **Sound**

Copenhagen ▮ 1700 ▮ 2nd "Great" Northern War

Attacked in Schleswig by Frederick IV of Denmark, 17-year-old Charles XII of Sweden boldly sailed against Copenhagen itself, repulsing the Danish fleet before landing under fire to seize nearby entrenchments. Copenhagen paid a massive indemnity to avoid siege, and Frederick was forced to make peace, freeing Charles to relieve the Russian siege of **Narva** (August 1700).

Copenhagen ▮ 1801 ▮ French Revolutionary Wars (2nd Coalition)

When Denmark joined Russia, Prussia and Sweden against the British navy's Continental blockade, Britain sent a large naval squadron to the Baltic to neutralise the Danish fleet. Admiral Sir Hyde Parker opened a hard-fought action in Copenhagen harbour and, after his second-in-command Admiral Sir Horatio Nelson ignored a signal to withdraw, the Danish fleet was destroyed (2 April 1801).

Copenhagen | 1807 | Napoleonic Wars (4th Coalition)

Concerned that Denmark might join the alliance between France and Prussia, British and Hanoverian troops led by General William Cathcart besieged Copenhagen, supported by warships under Admiral James Gambier. When negotiations failed, Copenhagen was bombarded for four days and capitulated, denying Napoleon Bonaparte the remaining Danish fleet (2–7 September 1807).

Cople | 1860 | Venezuelan Federalist Revolt

During a chaotic presidential succession, Federalist officers defeated the government at **Santa Inés**, yet, two months later, General León de Febres Cardero beat Federalist commanders Juan Crisótomo Falcón and Juan Antonio Sotillo near the Apure at Cople. Falcón fled to Colombia but, after years of costly war, he returned as President and oversaw decentralisation of authority (17 February 1860).

Coral Sea | 1942 | World War II (Pacific)

When Admiral Shigeyoshi Inoue took a large invasion force against Port Moresby in **Papua**, he was met in the nearby Coral Sea by Admiral Frank Fletcher. The first naval battle fought beyond the horizon saw greater losses in American ships, but the invasion was cancelled. Japanese losses, including a carrier sunk and another damaged, weakened them a month later at **Midway** (7–8 May 1942).

Corbach | 1760 | Seven Years War (Europe)

See **Korbach**

Corbie | 1636 | Thirty Years War (Franco-Habsburg War)

In a fresh invasion of France, General Johann von Werth and Ferdinand Cardinal-Infante of Spain invaded Picardy and captured Corbie, east of Amiens, while other Imperial forces in the south besieged **St Jean de Losne**. However, Louis XIII sent reinforcements to his brother Louis de Bourbon Count of Soissons, who recaptured Corbie and drove back the invasion (July–August 1636).

Corbridge | 914 | Viking Wars in Britain

The Viking Ragnall rallied the Danes of York and defeated the Bernician noble Ealdred Lord of Bamburgh at Corbridge-on-Tyne, just east of Hexham. Ealdred was driven out of northern Northumberland and sought refuge with King Constantine II of Scotland, who supported him four years later in another battle at the same site. (Some historians believe there was only one battle, in 918.)

Corbridge | 918 | Viking Wars in Britain

Supported by Constantine II of Scotland, Ealdred Lord of Bamburgh attempted to recover Bernica in northern Northumberland from the Danish Viking Ragnall, who had previously defeated him on the same site at Corbridge-on-Tyne, near Hexham (914). Although both sides claimed victory, Ragnall held part of Bernicia, while the Danes were kept out of Scotland.

Corcyra | 427 BC | Great Peloponnesian War

Despite Spartan Admiral Alcidas failing to aid a rising against Athens in **Mytilene**, he was sent to support a similar insurrection on Corcyra (modern Corfu), off northwest Greece. A small Athenian force led by Nicostratus was driven off, but next day, a large Athenian fleet arrived under Eurymedon. The Peloponnesians withdrew and the rising was bloodily suppressed (August 427 BC).

Corcyra | 1084 | 1st Byzantine-Norman War

See **Corfu**

Cordova I 1236 I Early Christian Reconquest of Spain

King Ferdinand III of Castile launched a brilliant offensive into Moorish Andalusia, where he besieged the Arab capital of Cordova, probably the greatest Muslim city in the West. While Cordova prepared for a lengthy resistance, the Emir Ibn Hud was assassinated and the city fell, leaving Ferdinand to advance down the Guadalquivir on a fresh expedition twelve years later to attack **Seville**.

Cordova I 1808 I Napoleonic Wars (Peninsular Campaign)

See **Alcolea**

Corfu I 1084 I 1st Byzantine-Norman War

Leading Norman forces against the Greek Empire, a year after victory at **Dyrrhachium**, Robert Guiscard took a large fleet to raise the naval blockade of Corcyra (modern Corfu), which the Normans had first captured in 1081. After twice being defeated by a Byzantine-Venetian fleet off Cassiope, south of Corfu, Guiscard won the third and decisive engagement off Corfu to regain the island.

Corfu I 1537 I Later Venetian-Turkish War

Sultan Suleiman turned against his former Venetian allies and besieged Corfu, off the coast of Albania, with massive assaults on the Venetian fortress. When an approaching fleet under Andrea Doria threatened to cut off his forces, Suleiman withdrew. However, the Turks were soon avenged at **Valpovo**, and Doria was defeated again a year later at **Preveza** (18 August–6 September 1637).

Corfu I 1810 I Napoleonic Wars (5th Coalition)

See **Ionian Islands**

Corfu I 1798 I French Revolutionary Wars (1st Coalition)

While Napoleon Bonaparte was campaigning in Egypt, the French-held **Ionian Islands** off Greece were attacked by a combined Turkish-Russian fleet under Admirals Kadir Bey and Fedor Ushakov. Most of the islands fell quickly, but Corfu, defended by General Louis Chabot, held out for four months and surrendered only after nearby Vido fell by storm (November 1798–March 1799).

Corfu I 1923 I Corfu Incident

When General Enrico Tellini and three other Italian members of a Boundary Commission were assassinated in Greece, Benito Mussolini sent his navy to bombard and occupy Corfu, with needless civilian losses. Greece was forced to apologise and pay a 50-million lire indemnity before the Italians withdrew, enhancing the reputation of Mussolini, who then annexed **Fiume** (27 August 1923).

Corinth, Greece I 394–392 BC I Corinthian War

Withdrawing from Boeotia after costly victory at **Coronea** and naval defeat at **Cnidus** (394 BC), King Agesilaus of Sparta laid siege to Corinth, which was later reinforced by troops from Argos. The city was eventually relieved by a column from Athens under Iphicrates. The Spartans later resumed the blockade of Corinth (390 BC) until defeat by Iphicrates at **Lechaeum**.

Corinth, Greece I 265 BC I Chremonidian War

In revolt against Antigonus II Gonatus of Macedonia, Athenians led by Chremonides and his brother Glaucon formed an alliance with Sparta and Egypt, and Antigonus led an army into the Peloponnese. King Areus of Sparta was defeated and killed in terrible fighting outside Corinth and the alliance broke up, freeing Antigonus to turn his force against **Athens** the following year.

Corinth, Greece I 243 BC I Wars of the Achaean League

During the formation of the Achaean League—a confederation of Greek city-states—the leading founder was Aratus of Sicyon. His first great exploit was seizing Corinth from its Macedonian garrison by a small force which broke into the city at night. The fall of Corinth was instrumental in inducing other cities to join the Achaean League and, in 241 BC, Aratus seized the neighbouring city-state of **Pellene**.

Corinth, Greece I 146 BC I Roman-Achaean War

Driven back from a failed invasion of Roman northern Greece at **Scarpheia**, the Achaean army of Diaeus was routed later that year outside Corinth by a large Roman force under Lucius Mummius, with strong naval support. Mummius then destroyed Corinth and slaughtered its inhabitants, putting an end to the Achaean League of city-states and establishing Roman control over Greece.

Corinth, Mississippi (1st) I 1862 I American Civil War (Western Theatre)

General Henry Halleck, advancing from the bloody Union victory at **Shiloh**, Tennessee, marched slowly south into Mississippi to besiege the defeated Confederate army of General Pierre G. T. Beauregard in the railroad centre at Corinth. Beauregard evacuated the town after a preliminary bombardment and most of his army escaped south to Tupelo (29 April–30 May 1862).

Corinth, Mississippi (2nd) I 1862 I American Civil War (Western Theatre)

Three weeks after eluding destruction at **Iuka**, Mississippi, Confederate General Sterling Price joined commander Earl Van Dorn attacking Union General William S. Rosecrans to the northwest at Corinth. The Confederates were eventually driven off with about 5,000 casualties, though a hesitant pursuit by Rosecrans failed to destroy Van Dorn next day at **Hatchie Bridge** (3–4 October 1862).

Cork I 1920 I Anglo-Irish War

Determined to crush Republican Cork City—where Lord Mayor Thomas MacCurtain was assassinated (20 March 1920) and his successor Terence MacSwiney died on hunger strike (25 October)—the Royal Irish Constabulary (Black

and Tans) attacked the city. Public buildings and the city centre were destroyed and the bitter war continued until July 1921 (11–12 December 1920).

Cork I 1922 I Irish Civil War

When government forces broke the line from **Limerick** to **Waterford**, the Republicans destroyed roads, bridges and railways to defend Cork City. However, General Emmet Dalton led an attack from the sea and 500 government troops sailed upriver towards the city. The Irregulars fled Cork after three days of heavy attack, virtually ending full-scale fighting in the field (7–10 August 1922).

Corona I 1797 I French Revolutionary Wars (1st Coalition)

See **La Corona**

Coronea I 447 BC I 1st Peloponnesian War

Ten years after securing central Greece at **Oenophyta**, Athens faced insurrection encouraged by Thebes and sent only about 1,000 men under Tolmides to support their Boeotian allies. The Athenians took Chaeronea but had to withdraw, and were attacked at Coronea, north of Mt Helicon. Tolmides was killed and much of his force was captured in a disastrous defeat. Athens then abandoned Boeotia.

Coronea I 394 BC I Corinthian War

Determined to avenge recent Spartan defeat at **Haliartus**, King Agesilaus returned to Greece from Asia Minor and advanced into Boeotia against Athens, Argos, Thebes and Corinth. Despite brilliant defence by the Thebans, Agesilaus finally secured victory in a hard-fought costly action at Coronea, but continued his return march to Sparta. He then laid siege to **Corinth** (August 394 BC).

Coronel I 1914 I World War I (War at Sea)

Five cruisers of the German Far East Squadron led by Admiral Maximilian von Spee, trying to return home via Cape Horn, met three British cruisers under Admiral Sir Christopher Cradock off Coronel, Chile. Two of the outgunned British vessels were sunk, with Cradock lost. The following month a fresh British force destroyed von Spee off the **Falkland Islands** (1 November 1914).

Corrales ∎ 1866 ∎ War of the Triple Alliance

In a surprise attack across the Upper Parana at Paso de Patria, Paraguayan General José Eduvigis Díaz attacked Argentine Colonel Emilio Coneza and cavalry led by Colonel Manuel Hornos. Díaz withdrew into Paraguay after heavy fighting at Corrales, but the Argentines had suffered very costly losses and Paraguayan President Francisco Solano López claimed victory (30 January 1866).

Corregidor ∎ 1942 ∎ World War II (Pacific)

When General Masaharu Homma invaded the **Philippines**, General Douglas MacArthur, President Manuel Quezon and 40,000 men withdrew to Corregidor Island, off Bataan. MacArthur escaped to Australia (12 March) and General Jonathon Wainwright withstood massive bombardment before surrendering. Resistance in the Philippines ended 18 May at Panay (7 January–6 May 1942).

Corregidor ∎ 1945 ∎ World War II (Pacific)

While securing **Bataan** in southwest **Luzon**, American General Charles Hall sent an amphibious force against nearby Corregidor, supported by a simultaneous paratroop landing. The Japanese garrison fought a tenacious defence, and many died when stored munitions were destroyed underground. Capture of the fortress island secured the entrance to Manila Bay (16–26 February 1945).

Corrichie ∎ 1562 ∎ Huntly Rebellion

Mary Queen of Scots undermined the powerful Gordons by giving land belonging to George Gordon Earl of Huntly to her half-brother James Stewart. Huntly marched on Aberdeen but was defeated by Stewart at nearby Corrichie and died after capture of apoplexy. Although his son Sir John was executed, their cause was renewed in 1571 at **Tillyangus** and in 1594 at **Glenlivet** (28 October 1562).

Corrick's Ford ∎ 1861 ∎ American Civil War (Eastern Theatre)

See **Rich Mountain**

Corrientes (1st) ∎ 1865 ∎ War of the Triple Alliance

After success against Brazil at **Coimbra** (December 1864), Paraguayan dictator Francisco Solano López sent a flotilla against Corrientes, on the Argentine shore of the Parana River. A sharp surprise attack saw the garrison defeated and two Argentine ships captured. Next day, Paraguayan General Wenceslao Robles landed with 3,000 men to briefly occupy the city (13 April 1865).

Corrientes (2nd) ∎ 1865 ∎ War of the Triple Alliance

Responding to Paraguay's capture of Corrientes in northern Argentina on the Parana, General Wenceslao Paunero counter-attacked with 2,000 men, including 350 Brazilians, while Paraguayan commander Wenceslao Robles was campaigning to the south. The garrison of 1,600 under Major Martinez was routed with 400 killed, but the Allies soon re-embarked (25 May 1865).

Corsica ∎ 456 ∎ Roman-Vandal Wars

When a fleet of 60 Vandal ships from Carthage sailed to Corsica, threatening both Gaul and Italy, they were surprised at anchor by the Suevic warrior Ricimer, acting for the Emperor Avitus. Ricimer overcame the Vandals—either in battle at sea or while they were dispersed ashore—and returned to Italy a hero. However, he soon rebelled against Avitus and defeated him at **Placentia**.

Cortenuova ∎ 1237 ∎ Imperial-Papal Wars

In renewed warfare against the Lombard League of northern Italy, Emperor Frederick II led a large army of Germans and Italians against Milan and its allies. Frederick eventually secured the victory in a protracted battle at Cortenuova, near Crema, with heavy losses on both sides. This convinced some Lombard cities to detach themselves from Milan (27 November 1237).

Corunna **I** 1809 **I** Napoleonic Wars (Peninsular Campaign)

Retreating into northwest Spain after an unsuccessful invasion of Portugal, Sir John Moore's British army arrived at the small port of Corunna. In a remarkable defensive battle four days later, Marshal Nicolas Soult's pursuing French army was defeated, enabling most of the British force to be evacuated. However, Moore was killed by a cannonball just as the battle ended (16 January 1809).

Corunna Road **I** 1936–1937 **I** Spanish Civil War

When Nationalists failed in a frontal assault on **Madrid**, General José Varela attacked to the north along the Corunna Road, where he was checked and wounded in a week of bloody fighting. General Luis Orgaz then resumed the offensive but suffered further heavy losses before both sides dug in. Orgaz later attacked southeast of the city at **Jarama** (13–20 December 1936 & 3–15 January 1937).

Corupedion **I** 281 BC **I** Wars of the Diadochi

War between Alexander's successors ended when Lysimachus of Thrace marched south to repulse an invasion by Seleucus of Syria. The septuagenarian warriors—who had fought together twenty years earlier at **Ipsus**—met at Corupedion, near the coast of Asia Minor, where Lysimachus was defeated and killed. Seleucus styled himself "Conqueror of the Conquerors," but he was soon assassinated.

Corus **I** 281 BC **I** Wars of the Diadochi
See **Corupedion**

Corycus **I** 191 BC **I** Roman-Syrian War
Driven from Greece at **Thermopylae**, Antiochus of Syria sent his fleet from Ephesus under

Polyxenidas against the Roman Gaius Livius Salinator. Though heavily outnumbered, Polyxenidas attacked off Corycus, the port of Seleucia on the Ionian Peninsula. He was defeated, losing 23 ships. Both fleets withdrew and fought again the following year at nearby **Myonnesus** (September 191 BC).

Corydon **I** 1863 **I** American Civil War (Western Theatre)

On a raid against Union communications in Kentucky, Confederate General John H. Morgan captured Lebanon, then crossed the Ohio and was met by militia under Colonel Lewis Jordan at Corydon, Indiana, just west of Louisville. Morgan secured a sharp victory at little cost, then continued his destructive raid along the Ohio until he was trapped at **Buffington Island** (9 July 1863).

Cos **I** 254 BC **I** Macedonian-Egyptian Wars

Antigonus II of Macedonia secured the Peloponnese in battle at **Corinth** (265 BC) and **Athens** (262 BC), then joined with Antiochus II of Syria against Ptolemy III of Egypt, who had supported Athens and Sparta. Aided by Rhodian ships, Antigonus personally met the Egyptian fleet off Cos and secured a decisive victory. With Egypt's role in the Aegean curtailed, Ptolemy soon made peace.

Cos **I** 1943 **I** World War II (Southern Europe)
See **Kos**

Cosmin **I** 1497 **I** Turkish Imperial Wars

In a breakdown of relations with Romania, John I Albert of Poland attacked his former ally Stephen of Moldavia, who had been promised Ottoman support. The Turks marched into Bukovina and, in the beech forests at Cosmin (modern Kitsman), near Chernovtsy, Albert was heavily defeated and sued for peace. Stephen also submitted, ending independent Romania (26 October 1497).

Cosseria I 1796 I French Revolutionary Wars (1st Coalition)

Having defeated the Austrians at **Montenotte**, west of Genoa, French General Pierre Augereau advanced next day on the Piedmontese at **Millesimo** and was blocked by Austrian General Giovanni Provera at nearby Cosseria. After being delayed 24 hours with heavy casualties, Napoleon Bonaparte ordered Augereau forward to the victory at **Dego** and Cosseria fell next day (13–14 April 1796).

Cotagaita I 1810 I Argentine War of Independence

In an early attack on Royalist forces in the southwest of modern Bolivia, Argentine Patriots under General Antonio González Balcarce advanced against an entrenched position at Cotagaita, southeast of Lake Poopo, held by Spanish General José de Cordoba. The Patriots suffered a costly reverse yet had their revenge ten days later further south at **Suipacha** (27 October 1810).

Cotechna I 1712 I Tuscarora Indian War

After Tuscarora Indians attacked Roanoke, North Carolina sought aid from South Carolina, and Colonel John Barnwell led 60 militia and 500 Indians against the main Tuscarora village at Cotechna, near modern Grifton. Barnwell inflicted heavy losses but was twice repulsed. Fearing for the lives of white hostages, he agreed to a short-lived truce with King Hancock (January 1712).

Cotiaeum I 491 I Later Roman Wars of Succession

See **Cotyaeum**

Cotonou I 1890 I 1st Franco-Dahomean War

When King Behanzin of Dahomey (modern Benin) attempted to regain land ceded by his predecessor, war broke out and his forces attacked the small French contingent near Cotonou under Colonel Sébastien Terrillon. The French suffered costly losses in two actions near the town before the Dahomeans were repulsed. Terrillon was soon defeated at **Atchoupa** (1 & 4 March 1890).

Cotrone I 204 BC I 2nd Punic War

See **Crotona**

Cotrone I 982 I Later German Imperial Wars

Emperor Otto II secured northern Italy, then attempted an offensive in the Byzantine south, where Abu Kasim, the Muslim Emir of Sicily, was also campaigning. Otto took Naples and Taranto, then faced an Arab-Byzantine alliance on the east coast near Cotrone (modern Crotone). Although Kasim was killed, Otto was routed and soon afterwards died in Rome, planning another offensive (July 982).

Cotyaeum I 491 I Later Roman Wars of Succession

After Anastasius was acclaimed Emperor on the death of Zeno, the former Emperor's brother Longinus of Cardala raised rebellion in Isauria. In battle at Cotyaeum (modern Kütahya), in west central Turkey, the Imperial army under John the Scythian and John the Hunchback secured decisive victory. Pockets of rebellion in Isauria persisted until resistance was finally suppressed in 498.

Cotyaeum I 1113 I Byzantine-Turkish Wars

When Malik Shah, son of the late Kilij Arslan, Seljuk Sultan of Rum, attempted to recover territory in Anatolia lost at the time of the 1st Crusade, he met with some early success before being challenged by Emperor Alexius I himself at Cotyaeum, south of Dorylaeum. In a major setback to his campaign, Malik Shah was heavily defeated and was beaten again in 1116 at **Philomelion**.

Coullioure I 1794 I French Revolutionary Wars (1st Coalition)

Following his victory at **Boulou** (1 May), French General Jacques Dugommier continued his offensive against the Spanish invasion of the Rousillon by besieging the coastal fortress of

Coullioure, supported by General Claude Victor. After a powerful sortie was repulsed (16 May), the garrison of 7,000 surrendered and the last coastal works were returned to French hands (26 May 1794).

Coulmiers I 1870 I Franco-Prussian War

In a French offensive towards Orleans, General Louis Jean-Baptiste d'Aurelle led 70,000 men against Baron Ludwig von der Tann and defeated a patrol in the nearby forest of Marchénoir. Von der Tann's heavily outnumbered Bavarians withdrew northwest to Coulmiers and fell back on Artenay after fierce fighting. The French occupied **Orleans**, claiming a great victory (9 November 1870).

Council House Affair I 1840 I Comanche Indian Wars

During peace talks between Comanche Indians and Texas officials at the Council House in San Antonio, shooting broke out in a dispute over the release of white prisoners. Of 65 Indians present, 33 were killed and the rest were captured, while seven whites died, including two judges. This treachery led to a vicious war with the Comanche, culminating in battle at **Plum Creek** (19 March 1840).

Countisbury Hill I 878 I Viking Wars in Britain

King Alfred of Wessex had fled after the surprise Viking attack at **Chippenham** in January, yet managed to raise a Saxon force against a landing in northern Devon by 1,200 Danes under Ubba, brother of the great Halfdan. At Easter, Ubba was defeated and killed at Countisbury Hill, along with up to 800 of his men, winning Alfred increasing support for his imminent showdown at **Edington**.

Courtrai I 1302 I Franco-Flemish Wars

When Flanders revolted against Philip IV of France, the King's army under Count Robert of Artois was slaughtered at Courtrai, near Lille, after becoming bogged in soft ground. In the so-called Battle of the Spurs, Guy de Namur's Flemish infantry succeeded against mounted knights. Cour-

trai Cathedral was decorated with hundreds of spurs from the French dead (11 July 1302).

Courtrai I 1794 I French Revolutionary Wars (1st Coalition)

Two weeks after French defeat at **Landrécies**, the French offensive was renewed as the left wing under Generals Jean Victor Moreau and Joseph Souham attempted a flanking movement around the Lys at Courtrai. Austrian Count Charles von Clerfayt was defeated trying to hold the advance and the French soon moved forward through Ghent to their decisive victory at **Tourcoing** (11 May 1794).

Courtrai I 1918 I World War I (Western Front)

In the second-phase offensive through **Flanders** against the northern **Hindenburg Line**, Belgian, British and French under King Albert of Belgium advanced on Courtrai and captured the key city. Further heavy fighting forced the Germans to evacuate Lille, and the Allies secured the strategic Belgian ports, then linked up with the main action on the **Selle** (14–19 October 1918).

Coutras I 1587 I 8th French War of Religion

In the War of the Three Henrys—King Henry III of France, Protestant King Henry of Navarre and Catholic Duke Henry of Guise—the principal battle was at Coutras, northeast of Bordeaux, where Henry of Navarre routed and killed Catholic commander Duke Anne of Joyeuse. Henry of Navarre gained southwest France and later took the throne as Henry IV (20 October 1587).

Covadonga I 718 I Muslim Conquest of Spain

Despite Muslim invaders driving the Visigoths out of Spain in 713 at **Merida** and **Segoyuela**, Don Pelayo, Christian king of Asturias in the northwest, led a revolt against Berber Governor Munuza, who sent an army under 'Alkama. A semi-legendary action at Covadonga, near Oveida, saw 'Alkama defeated and killed, traditionally marking the start of Christian Reconquest of Spain (trad date c 718).

Covelung ❙ 1752 ❙ 2nd Carnatic War

With the French defeated at **Trichinopoly** in April, Robert Clive and a mixed British-Sepoy force marched south from Madras against the remaining French fortresses. The coastal fortress of Covelung surrendered after a steady bombardment, yielding 50 British guns captured at Madras. Having repulsed a relief column next day, Clive then marched inland against **Chingleput** (16 September 1752).

Cove Mountain ❙ 1864 ❙ American Civil War (Eastern Theatre)

Raiding railways in southwest Virginia following Union victory at **Cloyd's Mountain**, Union General William W. Averell met a Confederate brigade under General William E. Jones further west at Cove Mountain, just northeast of Wytheville. Jones fell back after an inconclusive action and Averell burned the New River Bridge before continuing north to Meadow Bluff (10 May 1864).

Cowan's Ford ❙ 1781 ❙ War of the American Revolution

British commander Charles Earl Cornwallis crossed from South Carolina to attack North Carolina militia under General William Davidson at Cowan's Ford on the Catawba, west of Charlotte. Davidson was killed in a decisive action and his force scattered. Earl Cornwallis sent his cavalry forward the same day against other rebel forces at nearby **Tarrant's Tavern** (1 February 1781).

Cow Creek ❙ 1855 ❙ Rogue River War
See **Hungry Hill**

Cowpens ❙ 1781 ❙ War of the American Revolution

On a new rebel offensive in South Carolina, General Daniel Morgan advanced into the British rear, where he was pursued by Tory cavalry Colonel Banastre Tarleton. At Cowpens, near the Broad River, Tarleton was brilliantly outmanoeuvred and decisively defeated, reputedly escaping with only 200 men out of 1,100. Two weeks later he struck back at **Tarrant's Tavern** (17 January 1781).

Cox's Plantation ❙ 1863 ❙ American Civil War (Lower Seaboard)

Following victory on the Mississippi at **Donaldsonville**, Louisiana, Union forces under Generals Godfrey Weitzel and Cuvier Grover marched down the Lafourche and, six miles away at Cox's Plantation, were met by Confederate General Thomas Green. The Union forces were driven back with over 400 casualties and Green soon attacked again at **Stirling's Plantation** (12–13 July 1863).

Cracow ❙ 1241 ❙ Mongol Conquest of Europe

As the renewed Mongol invasion of Europe swept west after the destruction of **Kiev** (1240), Batu (grandson of Genghis Khan) sent his cousins Kaidu and Baidar into southern Poland against the strategic city of Cracow. The Polish army of Boleslav V was completely crushed to the northeast near Chmielnik and Kaidu continued west towards his decisive victory at **Liegnitz** (3 March 1241).

Cracow ❙ 1655 ❙ 1st Northern War

The Swedish army of Charles X took Warsaw and beat King John II Casimir at **Czarnowo**, then advanced south on Cracow, bravely defended by Hetman Stefan Czarniecki. However, with Polish defeat to the east at **Wojnicz**, Czarniecki had to evacuate Cracow. The Swedes were eventually checked at **Jasna Gora**, and Czarniecki briefly enjoyed victory in March 1656 at **Warka** (8 October 1655).

Cracow ❙ 1772 ❙ Polish Rebellion

In support of Polish Nationalists, French forces under Brigadier Claude-Gabriel Choisi took Cracow Castle by surprise but were quickly besieged by Russian Colonel Alexander Suvorov. A frontal assault was bloodily repulsed

(18 February) and, after a Polish relief force was defeated (28 February), the starving garrison finally surrendered, virtually ending the war (January–15 April 1772).

Cracow ∎ 1914 ∎ World War I (Eastern Front)
See **Limanowa**

Crag Picquet ∎ 1863 ∎ Pathan Rising
See **Ambela**

Craibstane ∎ 1571 ∎ Huntly Rebellion
Sir Adam Gordon, brother of George Earl of Huntly, renewed Catholic rebellion following abdication by Mary Queen of Scots and defeated the Forbes clan at **Tillyangus** in October, then faced a government force sent from Stirling under Lord William Master of Forbes. While Gordon won again at Craibstane, outside Aberdeen, Earl Huntly later submitted to the government (20 November 1571).

Crampton's Gap ∎ 1862 ∎ American Civil War (Eastern Theatre)
See **South Mountain**

Craney Island ∎ 1813 ∎ War of 1812
When a British naval squadron blockaded Norfolk to try and capture the frigate *Constellation*, about 500 Americans under Colonel Henry Beatty determined to block them at Craney Island, guarding the Elizabeth River. Approaching in 15 boats, Captain Samuel Pechell's landing party of about 700 was devastated by American artillery, losing almost 100 men, and Norfolk was saved (22 June 1813).

Crannon ∎ 322 BC ∎ Lamian War
Athens and other Greek cities rebelled after the death of Alexander the Great and Antipater, Regent of Macedonia, was besieged at **Lamia**, trying to reassert control. His son-in-law, Craterus, invaded Greece with a large Persian army, and at Crannon, in Thessaly, Greek commanders Antiphilus and Menon were crushed. After

Athens' fleet was destroyed off **Amorgos** the Greek revolt was over.

Craonne ∎ 1814 ∎ Napoleonic Wars (French Campaign)
Napoleon Bonaparte marched north from victory at **Montereau** (18 February), pursuing the Prussian-Russian army of General Gebhard von Blucher threatening **Paris**. To the northeast at Craonne, Marshals Michel Ney and Claude Victor defeated Blucher's rearguard under Baron Ferdinand von Winzingerode. However, the Allied army managed to escape and fell back to **Laon** (7 March 1814).

Crasus ∎ 805 ∎ Byzantine-Muslim Wars
When Nicephorus deposed the Empress Irene and withheld tribute due to Harun al-Rashid in Baghdad, the Caliph led a Muslim army into Phrygia (west central Anatolia) and defeated the Byzantine army several times, most notably at Crasus. The following year, Harun assembled an even larger army and secured decisive victory over the Emperor at **Heraclea**.

Crater ∎ 1864 ∎ American Civil War (Eastern Theatre)
During the Union siege of **Petersburg**, Virginia, by General Ambrose E. Burnside, a massive mine was successfully exploded under the Confederates' defensive line to the southeast. But as Union soldiers advanced through the resulting crater, they were massacred in a counter-attack by General William Mahone. It was terrible, costly failure, and Burnside was relieved of command (30 July 1864).

Cravant ∎ 1423 ∎ Hundred Years War
Following the death of Charles VI of France and his appointed heir, Henry V of England, war continued between the Dauphin Charles VII and English forces on behalf of the infant Henry VI. Attempting to seize Cravant, near Auxerre, the Dauphin's Franco-Scottish army was heavily defeated by an English-Burgundian relief force under Thomas Montacute Earl of Salisbury (30 July 1423).

Crayford | 457 | Anglo-Saxon Conquest of Britain

See **Creccanford**

Crazy Woman Creek | 1876 | Sioux Indian Wars

General George Crook pursued the Sioux after defeat at **Little Big Horn** (26 June) to win at **Slim Buttes**, then sent Colonel Ranald Mackenzie against the Cheyenne in the Big Horn Mountains. At Crazy Woman Creek, south of Sheridan, Wyoming, Mackenzie's attack destroyed Dull Knife's camp and pony herd. Crazy Horse himself was beaten at **Wolf Mountain** six weeks later (25 November 1876).

Creazzo | 1513 | War of the Holy League

See **Vicenza**

Creccanford | 457 | Anglo-Saxon Conquest of Britain

A year after defeating their former ally Vortigern King of the Britons at **Aegelsthrep**, the semi-legendary Jute warrior Hengist and his son Aesc achieved a further victory over the British leader on the banks of the Cray at Creccanford (modern Crayford), near Dartford. Another victory at **Wippedesfleet** in 465 gave this first Anglo-Saxon a kingdom in southeast England.

Crecy | 1346 | Hundred Years War

Following a French invasion of Gascony, Edward III of England took a large army which captured **Caen**, then met a French force almost three times as large at Crecy-en-Ponthieu, north of Abbeville. Repeated assaults by Philip VI's cavalry were destroyed by devastating fire from English longbows in one of the worst defeats ever inflicted by infantry on mounted knights (26 August 1346).

Cree | 1308 | Rise of Robert the Bruce

While Robert the Bruce was campaigning in Argyle, his brother Edward marched into Galloway against local lords led by Sir Ingram de Umfraville and Sir John de St John. Bruce defeated the Galwegians on the banks of the Cree, between the counties of Kircudbright and Wigtown and, after a further victory at the **Dee** in June, went on to occupy Galloway.

Crefeld | 1758 | Seven Years War (Europe)

As Frederick II of Prussia fought Austrians in Moravia at **Olmütz**, he sent Hanoverians, Hessians and Brunswickers led by Duke Ferdinand of Brunswick to drive the French across the Rhine. Louis de Bourbon-Condé Comte de Clermont made a stand at Crefeld, but his numerically superior force was heavily defeated and he continued withdrawing towards Cologne (23 June 1758).

Crema | 1159–1160 | Frederick's 2nd Expedition to Italy

Emperor Frederick Barbarossa took **Milan** (September 1158), then continued his campaign in Lombardy by marching east to besiege the heavily fortified small city of Crema. With the Emperor personally in command, the siege was pressed with extraordinary brutality. When Crema fell after six months, it was evacuated and razed to the ground (4 July 1159–27 January 1160).

Cremaste | 388 BC | Corinthian War

Two years after defeating Sparta outside Corinth at **Lechaeum**, the Athenian Iphicrates sailed to the Dardanelles to attack the Spartan Anaxibius at Abydos. Anaxibius was ambushed and badly defeated on the nearby Plain of Cremaste, but the Athenian fleet was cut off by Spartan, Persian and Syracusan ships under Antalcidas. Athens was forced to accept the "King's Peace," which ended the war.

Cremera | 477 BC | Early Roman-Etruscan Wars

In the war for control of the Lower Tiber, Romans under Marcus Fabius advanced against the Etruscans of Veii and fortified a camp on the Cremera, where it joins the Tiber near Fidenae. Disastrous defeat saw the Fabii virtually annihilated, with a claimed 300 of their patricians killed, along with other allies. Within a few years Rome had established temporary peace with the Etruscans (18 July 477).

Cremona I 200 BC I Gallic Wars in Italy

Boii, Insubres and Cenomani Gauls of northern Italy, commanded by the Carthaginian General Hamilcar, sacked **Placentia**, then quickly turned east against Cremona. However, the city held out under siege until Praetor Lucius Furius Purpureo arrived from Ariminum. The Gauls suffered a decisive defeat, with perhaps 35,000 killed. Three years later the Insubres were beaten at the **Mincio**.

Cremona I 69 I Vitellian Civil War
See **Bedriacum**

Cremona I 1431 I Venetian-Milanese Wars

A large-scale naval battle on the River Po near Cremona saw the Venetian fleet under Admiral Niccolo Trevigiano and the soldier of fortune Francesco Bussone Count Carmagnola defeated by the Duke of Milan's Generals, Niccolo Piccinino and Francesco Sforza. However, Milan eventually sued for peace. Carmagnola was later executed by Venice for alleged disloyalty (June 1431).

Cremona I 1648 I Thirty Years War (Franco-Habsburg War)
See **Trancheron**

Cremona I 1702 I War of the Spanish Succession

In a brilliant coup against the French in Lombardy, Prince Eugène of Savoy led a surprise night attack on Cremona, causing heavy damage and casualties and capturing French officers, including commander Francois de Neufville Marshal Villeroi. However, the citadel held out and Eugène withdrew when a relief army approached under Charles Henri Prince de Vaudemont (1 February 1702).

Cresson I 1187 I 3rd Crusade

Prior to Saladin's invasion of Palestine, a large Muslim reconnaissance force crossing Galilee under treaty was recklessly attacked at the Springs of Cresson, near Nazareth, by only about 140 knights of the military orders. Hospitallier Grandmaster Roger de les Moulins was killed in the ensuing disaster and Templar Grandmaster Gerard of Ridfort was among just a handful of survivors (1 May 1187).

Crete I 960–961 I Later Byzantine-Muslim Wars

Following decades of failed Byzantine campaigns against Muslim Andalusians in Crete, Emperor Romanos II sent a massive fleet and army under Nicephorus Phocas, who landed to attack the principal fortress of Chandax (modern Khania), defended by the Emir Kouroupas. Chandax was taken by storm after a long winter siege, effectively securing the whole of Crete (July 960–6 March 961).

Crete I 1941 I World War II (Southern Europe)

When **Greece** fell, British forces under General Bernard Freyberg withdrew to Crete, where General Kurt Student launched a bold assault with gliders and paratroops. A supporting seaborne assault was driven off at the cost of heavy losses to the Royal Navy, but after success at **Maleme** and elsewhere, the Germans captured Crete, along with over 11,000 prisoners (20 May–1 June 1941).

Crête-à-Perriot I 1802 I Napoleonic Wars (Santo Domingo Rising)

Napoleon Bonaparte's brother-in-law General Charles Leclerc, sent to suppress a rising in **Santo Domingo** by black leader Francois Toussaint l'Ouverture, besieged Fort Crête-à-Perriot inland from St Marc, held by troops of Jean Jacques Dessalines under Louis Lamartiniere. The rebels held out for three weeks and inflicted 2,000 French casualties before they slipped away (4–24 March 1802).

Creussen I 1003 I German War of Succession

Amid disputed succession for the German crown following the death of the childless young

Otto III, the new Emperor Henry II faced a rebellion by the Margrave Henry of Schweinfort,
Ernest of Babenburg and his own brother Bruno.
Inconclusive warfare ended when the rebels
were decisively defeated at the siege of Creussen, on the River Main, and Henry's succession
was assured.

Crichton I 1337 I Anglo-Scottish War of Succession

During the Scottish Royalist war against the
English-backed claimant Edward Baliol, Sir Andrew Moray, Regent for the boy-King David II of
Scotland, and Sir William Douglas of Liddesdale
laid siege to English-held Edinburgh. Southeast at
Crichton, they were attacked by an English relief
force. While Moray claimed the victory, Douglas
was severely wounded and the siege was lifted.

Crimea I 1771 I Catherine the Great's 1st Turkish War

See **Perekop**

Crimisus I 340 BC I Timoleon's War

Four years after securing Syracuse in eastern
Sicily with victory at **Adranum**, Timoleon of
Corinth was threatened by a fresh Carthaginian
invasion under Hamilcar and Hasdrubal. Marching northwest, he surprised the Punic army
crossing the Crimisus, near Segesta. The Carthaginians retreated under siege to Lilybaeum
with a reported 10,000 killed and 15,000 captured, and Timoleon withdrew.

Crisa I 590 BC I 1st Sacred War

The Phocian city of Crisa demanded tolls from
pilgrims travelling to Delphi, which sought aid
from the Sacred League of northern and central
Greece. Thessaly sent an army under Eurylochus,
who besieged the city, aided by troops from
Athens, while Cleisthenes of Sicyon sent ships for
a blockade. Crisa surrendered and was destroyed,
and Delphi became the seat of the Sacred League.

Crnomen I 1371 I Ottoman Conquest of the Balkans

See **Maritza**

Crocus Field I 352 BC I 3rd Sacred War

See **Pagasae**

Croia I 1466–1467 I Venetian-Turkish Wars

See **Krujë, Albania**

Croix d'Orade I 1814 I Napoleonic Wars (Peninsular Campaign)

As Arthur Wellesley Lord Wellington closed
in to besiege **Toulouse**, British forces under
General Sir Richard Vivian advanced in the
northeast to capture the key bridge at Croix
d'Orade on the River Hers, defended by General
Jacques Vial. Although a relatively minor action, in which Vivian was wounded, the bridge
was taken, securing strategic passage for Wellington's army (8 April 1814).

Cromdale I 1690 I First Jacobite Rebellion

In the last armed Scottish resistance to the
accession of William III after defeat at **Dunkeld**
(21 August 1689), Highland forces loyal to
James II rose in rebellion, led by General Thomas Buchan. Camped at Cromdale, east of
Grantown in Moray, the Jacobites were attacked
and routed by Royalist forces under Sir Thomas Livingstone, ending the rising (1 May
1690).

Cronion I 383 BC I 3rd Dionysian War

See **Cronium**

Cronium I 383 BC I 3rd Dionysian War

When Carthaginian leader Mago died at **Cabala** in Sicily, his son, also Mago, took command and later that year continued the offensive
against Dionysius, Tyrant of Syracuse. The
Syracusans suffered severe losses in a decisive
battle at Cronium, near Palermo, including
General Leptines, brother of Dionysius, killed.
The Tyrant sued for peace and Carthage secured
most of western Sicily.

Crooked Creek I 1859 I Comanche Indian Wars

Leading a new campaign against the Comanche following success at **Rush Springs**, Oklahoma (October 1858), Major Earl van Dorn took 500 men into Kansas and trapped about 90 Comanche in a deep ravine at Crooked Creek, north of the Canadian River. Not one escaped, with 49 warriors killed and five wounded and 37 prisoners, mainly women. Van Dorn lost six killed (13 May 1859).

Cropredy Bridge I 1644 I British Civil Wars

King Charles I attempted to concentrate his forces at Worcester but was blocked by Sir William Waller north of Banbury at Cropredy, where General John Middleton held the bridge over the River Cherwell. Waller was heavily repulsed at nearby Slat Mill after Royalist troops cleared the bridge, and the Parliamentary troops dispersed, abandoning their guns (29 June 1644).

Cross Keys I 1862 I American Civil War (Eastern Theatre)

Two weeks after supporting Confederate victory at **Winchester**, in the northern Shenandoah, General Richard S. Ewell was attacked by Union commander General John C. Frémont at Cross Keys, near Harrisonburg, Virginia. Ewell routed part of Frémont's army under General Julius Stahel, then marched south to support General Thomas "Stonewall" Jackson at **Port Republic** (8 June 1862).

Cross Lanes I 1861 I American Civil War (Eastern Theatre)

Confederate General John Floyd took the initiative in West Virginia, leading his brigade across the Gauley to surprise Colonel Erastus B. Tyler in camp at Kessler's Cross Lanes, just south of Summersville. The Union force was heavily defeated, losing almost 300 men, including many captured. Floyd withdrew south to the river, and next month met an attack at **Carnifex Ferry** (26 August 1861).

Crotona I 204 BC I 2nd Punic War

On the defensive in the "toe" of Italy after the defeat of reinforcements in the north in **Liguria** (16 June), Carthaginian General Hannibal defeated an approaching army under Publius Sempronius outside Crotona (modern Crotone). Reinforced by Licinius, Sempronius renewed his attack. Hannibal suffered greater losses in a drawn action, yet the Romans fell back and he was able to withdraw through Bruttium.

Crouy I 1814 I Napoleonic Wars (French Campaign)
See **Ourcq**

Crown Point (1st) I 1775 I War of the American Revolution

Two days after capturing **Fort Ticonderoga** on the western shore of Lake Champlain, American Major Ethen Allen sent Seth Warner and a company of the Green Mountain Boys ten miles north against Crown Point. The small isolated fort surrendered with little resistance, but was later reoccupied by the British after the failed American invasion of Canada (12 May 1775).

Crown Point (2nd) I 1755 I Seven Years War (North America)
See **Lake George**

Cruachan Ben I 1308 I Rise of Robert the Bruce
See **Brander**

Crusader I 1941 I World War II (Northern Africa)
See **Sidi Rezegh**

Császáhalom I 1441 I Turkish-Hungarian Wars

After rebuilding the fortifications of **Belgrade** following the previous year's failed Ottoman siege, Hungarian General Janos Hunyadi raided south against Ishak Bey, Ottoman Governor of Semendria (modern Smederevo). The forces met at nearby Császáhalom in a relatively minor battle. However, the Turks suffered a decisive defeat and were driven back to the fortress at Semendria.

Ctesiphon I 198 I Wars of Emperor Severus

Emperor Septimius Severus secured western Europe at **Lugdunum** (197), then led a major offensive through Mesopotamia, where he sacked Seleucia and Babylon, then advanced on Ctesiphon, southeast of modern Baghdad. Vologases V of Parthia was defeated and fled after a decisive action and Severus styled himself Parthicus Maximus. He was checked at **Atra** the following year (January 198).

Ctesiphon I 363 I Later Roman-Persian Wars

On campaign against the Sassanid Shapur II, Emperor Julian advanced down the Euphrates to destroy **Pirisabora** and **Maiozamalcha**, then moved east against Ctesiphon, on the Tigris. Lacking confidence to besiege a major city Julian declined a siege and ten days later he died in a skirmish. New Emperor Jovian sued for peace and surrendered Nisibis and Roman territory east of the Tigris (June 363).

Ctesiphon I 637 I Muslim Conquest of Iraq

See **Madain**

Ctesiphon I 1915 I World War I (Mesopotamia)

Anglo-Indian General Charles Townshend, advancing up the Tigris through **Kut-al-Amara**, attacked General Nur-ud-Din, who held two strongly defended lines at Ctesiphon, just 16 miles from Baghdad. The British seized the first line, but heavy losses and Turkish reinforcements forced them to withdraw through **Umm-at-Tubal** to the terrible siege at Kut (22–25 November 1915).

Cuarte I 1094 I Early Christian Reconquest of Spain

After the capture of **Valencia** by Rodrigo Diaz de Bivar—El Cid—Yusuf ibn Tashfin, King of the Almoravids, sent his nephew Mohammed against the city. The large Berber and Almoravid army camped at nearby Cuarte, and after they spent ten days demonstrating around the defences, El Cid counter-attacked in force, routing the Muslims and seizing a huge amount of booty (June 1094).

Cuaspud I 1863 I Ecuador-Colombia War

When President Tomás Cipriano de Mosquera of Colombia sent aid to rebels against President Gabriel García Moreno of Ecuador, General Juan José Flores took a large force into southern Colombia. In a disastrous defeat for Ecuador at Cuaspud, Flores was routed by a smaller Colombian army, losing 1,500 casualties and 2,000 captured, and the war quickly ended (6 December 1863).

Cuautla I 1812 I Mexican Wars of Independence

General Félix María Calleja captured **Zitácuaro**, then attacked Cuautla, southeast of Mexico City, held by Mexican rebels José María Morelos and Ermengildo Galeana. Ciriaco de Llano arrived with siege reinforcements and, after months of bombardment and assault with heavy losses on both sides, Morelos evacuated. In December 1813, he was beaten at **Valladolid** (18 February–2 May 1812).

Cuautla I 1911 I Mexican Revolution

Following victory for Francisco Madero in the north at **Ciudad Juárez** (10 May), Emiliano Zapata attacked Cuautla, southeast of Mexico City, where General Felipe Meri took the Convent of San Diego by storm. Zapata captured Cuautla next day, then took nearby Cuernavaca without a fight. President Porfirio Diaz resigned six days later and Madero formed a new government (20 May 1911).

Cuchilla del Tambo I 1816 I Colombian War of Independence

See **El Tambo**

Cuddalore I 1748 I 1st Carnatic War

During his unsuccessful siege of British **Fort St David**, south of Pondicherry, French Governor General in India, Marquis Joseph Dupleix, marched against nearby Cuddalore, defended by Major Stringer Lawrence and about 1,000 men. The superior French force was dispersed with heavy gunfire in a disorganised night-time assault and they returned to **Pondicherry** (27–28 June 1748).

Cuddalore I 1758 I Seven Years War (India)

In resumed warfare against Britain in India, French Admiral Comte Ann-Antoine d'Aché arrived on the southeast coast of India in support of new Governor General Comte Thomas Lally. During an indecisive naval action off Cuddalore, d'Aché was repulsed by Admiral Sir George Pocock and retired to Pondicherry. Cuddalore surrendered to Lally a week later (29 April 1758).

Cuddalore I 1782 I 2nd British-Mysore War

Encouraged by his overwhelming defeat in February of a small British force in southeast India at **Kumbakonam**, Tipu Sultan, heir to the ruler of Mysore, advanced with his French allies against the key seaport of Cuddalore, south of Pondicherry. Aided at sea by Admiral Pierre André Suffren, Tipu overwhelmed the garrison of 400 and the port became a key base against the British (April 1782).

Cuddalore (1st) I 1783 I War of the American Revolution

General James Stuart (1735–1793) led a British expedition from Madras and laid siege to Cuddalore, south of Pondicherry, garrisoned by the Marquis Charles de Bussy. While the French were driven from their trenches in heavy fighting, Stuart's force was demoralised by the defeat of the naval blockade off Cuddalore. De Bussy held out until peace in Europe ended the war (13 June 1783).

Cuddalore (2nd) I 1783 I War of the American Revolution

In the last of five indecisive naval actions off the east coast of India, French Admiral Pierre

André Suffren slipped into besieged Cuddalore for new crew, then attacked the blockade of British ships under British Admiral Edward Hughes. Despite the French captains failing to press their advantage, Hughes was forced to abandon his blockade, though the siege continued (20 June 1783).

Cuenca I 1874 I 2nd Carlist War

Soon after Carlist forces successfully defended **Estella**, Don Alfonso de Bourbon, brother of the Don Carlos VII, led 14,000 partisans south to attack Cuenca, bravely held by Republicans under Don Hilario Lozano. The outnumbered garrison capitulated after two days, but Don Alfonso permitted a terrible slaughter. He was then gradually driven back and left Spain three months later (July 1874).

Cuevas I 1865 I War of the Triple Alliance
See **Paso de Ceuvas**

Cuito Cuanavale I 1987–1988 I Angolan War

The decisive action in the long struggle for Namibia was fought in Angola at Cuito Cuanavale between Angola's Cuban-backed government (MLPA) and South African forces supporting the local opposition (UNITA). The largest battle in Africa since WW II saw very heavy losses in men and armour. Cuba and SADF withdrew and Namibia secured independence (September 1987–April 1988).

Culblean I 1335 I Anglo-Scottish War of Succession
See **Kilblain**

Culebrera I 1840 I Colombian War of Supreme Commanders

Rebel Colonel Manuel Gonzáles won in the north at **La Polonia** (29 September), then marched south towards Bogotá. In two actions on the same day to the northwest at Buenavista and Culebrera, the rebels were defeated by government forces under Colonels Juan José Neira and José Vargas Paris. Bogotá was saved and in early 1841 González was routed at **Aratoca** (28 October 1840).

Cullera | 1129 | Early Christian Reconquest of Spain

Despite his victories at **Saragossa** (1118) and **Cutanda** (1120), King Alfonso I of Aragon—El Batallador, the fighter—faced a fresh Muslim offensive into Christian Valencia by the powerful Emir Ali Ibn Yusuf. At Cullera, on the Jucar, south of Valencia, Alfonso inflicted a heavy defeat on the invaders with huge losses in men and stores. But he was unable to halt the Muslim advance (May 1129).

Culloden | 1746 | Jacobite Rebellion (The Forty-Five)

Standing with his outnumbered supporters on Culloden Moor, east of Inverness, Charles Stuart—Bonnie Prince Charlie—faced the well-equipped Hanoverian army of Duke William of Cumberland. Over 1,000 Highlanders died in a terrible rout, with many more killed in the subsequent pursuit and persecution. Charles fled to France and the rebellion was brutally crushed (16 April 1746).

Culp's Farm | 1864 | American Civil War (Western Theatre)

See **Kolb's Farm**

Cumae | 474 BC | Syracusan-Etruscan War

With Syracuse supreme in Sicily after victory at **Himera** (480 BC), the Tyrant Hiero sailed to the west coast of the Italian mainland to meet Etruscan forces advancing into Campania to threaten the Greek colony at Cumae, just west of Naples. Leading the Syracusan fleet into the Bay of Naples, Hiero secured a great naval victory, confirming Syracusan influence in southern Italy.

Cumae | 38 BC | Wars of the Second Triumvirate

Octavian planned to invade Sicily and prepared a large fleet under Caius Sabinius Calvisius and Mendorus, which was attacked in the Bay of Cumae, near Naples, by the fleet of Sextus Pompeius (Pompey the Younger) under Menecrates. While Menecrates was killed, Octavian's fleet suffered a heavy defeat and, after further ships were lost in a storm, he postponed his expedition against Pompey.

Cumberland | 1864 | American Civil War (Eastern Theatre)

Confederate General Jubal A. Early pursued Union forces across the Potomac after victory at **Kernstown** (24 July), sending General John McCausland to burn Chambersburg, Pennsylvania. McCausland was ambushed by General Benjamin Kelley two days later near Cumberland, Maryland, and he was soon defeated in West Virginia by pursuing Union cavalry at **Moorefield** (1 August 1864).

Cumberland Church | 1865 | American Civil War (Eastern Theatre)

See **Farmville**

Cunaxa | 401 BC | Persian Civil War

When young Prince Cyrus attempted to seize the throne of Persia from his elder brother Artaxerxes, his large force, including 13,000 Greek mercenaries, met Artaxerxes at Cunaxa, north of Babylon. When Cyrus himself was killed in the fighting, his Persian supporters fled, and the surviving Greeks, under Clearchus and later Xenophon, began the famous March of the 10,000 to the Black Sea.

Cuneo | 1744 | War of the Austrian Succession

Louis-Francois de Bourbon Prince of Conti led a French offensive which took Villefranche and other towns in northern Italy, before being stalled by the stubborn fortress of Cuneo, west of Turin, held by Baron Friedrich von Leutrum. Conti repulsed a relief force at nearby **Madonna del Olmo**, before heavy losses to casualties and disease made him raise the siege (September–22 October 1744).

Curalaba I 1598 I Spanish Conquest of Chile

Governor Martin García Oñez de Loyola of Chile renewed expansion to the south, provoking united opposition under the Araucanian leader Pelantaro. In a disastrous defeat at Curalaba, Loyola was killed, along with perhaps 150 Spaniards and 250 Indian auxiliaries. Pelantaro then destroyed colonial outposts and Spain withdrew, accepting the Bio Bio as their de facto border (23 December 1598).

Curicta I 49 BC I Wars of the First Triumvirate

Attempting to protect Illyricum against Pompey, Publius Cornelius Dolabella took a fleet across the Adriatic, but off the Dalmatian island of Curicta (modern Krk), he was heavily defeated by the Pompeian Admirals Marcus Octavius and Lucius Scribinius Libo. Dolabella withdrew with 40 ships lost, and the Caesarian garrison of Curicta under Gaius Antonius was starved into surrender.

Curtatone I 1848 I 1st Italian War of Independence

King Charles Albert of Sardinia joined the war against Austria, but he was defeated at **Santa Lucia** (6 May) and withdrew the Italian allies behind well-established entrenchments at Curtatone, just west of Mantua. Austrian Marshal Josef Radetzky, with Baron Heinrich von Hesse as Chief of Staff, stormed the defences, taking numerous prisoners, then won again at **Custozza** (29 May 1848).

Curupaíty I 1866 I War of the Triple Alliance

The Argentine, Brazilian and Uruguayan allies under Generals Bartolomé Mitre and Venancio Flores advanced into southwest Paraguay near **Curuzú** and attacked Paraguayan General José Eduvigis Diaz entrenched at Curupaíty, south of **Humaitá**. A disastrous reversal cost Mitre about half his army—9,000 casualties—while Diaz claimed to have lost fewer than 100 men (22 September 1866).

Curuzú I 1866 I War of the Triple Alliance

On the offensive in southwest Paraguay against Dictator Francisco Solano López, the Argentine, Brazilian and Uruguayan allies under General Venancio Flores attacked and overran advanced Paraguayan positions on the Paraguay at Curuzú. The victory encouraged the Allied advance, which was however broken against entrenched positions further north at **Curupaíty** (3 September 1866).

Curzola I 1298 I Venetian-Genoese Wars

Ending the long war between Genoa and Venice, Genoese Admiral Lamba Doria met the much larger Venetian fleet of Admiral Andrea Dandola near Curzola Island in the eastern Adriatic. The Venetian ships were virtually all sunk or captured, with massive casualties in killed or captured, and Genoa remained Italy's greatest maritime power for the next 80 years (7 September 1298).

Custer's Last Stand I 1876 I Sioux Indian Wars

See **Little Big Horn**

Custozza I 1848 I 1st Italian War of Independence

Defeated by Austria at **Curtatone** (29 May), King Charles Albert of Sardinia led an army against Marshal Josef Radetzky, covering Verona. A hard action to the southwest at Custozza saw Piedmontese forces defeated, and Radetzky crossed the Minco at Volta (27 July) to retake Milan. There was a brief armistice before fighting resumed in March 1849 at **Mortara** and **Novara** (24–25 July 1848).

Custozza I 1866 I 3rd Italian War of Independence

With Austria under attack by Prussia in Bohemia, Italy declared war (18 June), and King Victor Emmanuel sent a large army under Alfonso Ferrero Marquis di la Mamora against Archduke Albert of Austria. The Italians were utterly defeated at Custozza, southwest of Verona, but after Austrian disaster a week later at

Königgratz, Albert was withdrawn and Venetia was ceded to Italy (24 June 1866).

Cutanda I 1120 I Early Christian Reconquest of Spain

Capture of the key Muslim city of **Saragossa** in December 1118 by Alfonso I of Aragon—El Batallador, the fighter—provoked renewed Muslim resistance. However, the large-scale Almoravid counter-attack was heavily defeated at Cutanda. The Christian victory led directly to Alfonso's capture of nearby Daroca, Calatayud and other territory formerly under Muslim Saragossa (17 June 1120).

Cut Knife Creek I 1885 I 2nd Riel Rebellion

A week after relieving **Battleford**, in northwest Saskatchewan, Colonel William Otter advanced west against the Canadian Cree Poundmaker (Pitikwahanapiwiyin) in camp at Cut Knife Creek. Otter was driven back to Battleford with 23 casualties after seven hours and Poundmaker's band marched east to support the rebels at **Batoche**, intercepting Otter's supplies at **Eagle Hills** (2 May 1885).

Cutton Moor I 1138 I Anglo-Scottish Territorial Wars

See **Standard**

Cuzco I 1532 I Inca War of Succession

Following the death of the Inca Emperor Huayna Capac (1527), bloody war broke out between his successor Huascar and his younger son Atahualpa. The war reached its climax at the Inca capital Cuzco (in modern Peru), where Huascar was defeated and overthrown, followed by bloody reprisals. After Atahualpa was seized by the Spanish at nearby **Cajamarca** (1532) he ordered his brother Huascar's execution.

Cuzco I 1535–1536 I Inca Revolt

After Francisco Pizarro seized Peru at **Cajamarca**, the Inca Manco Capac took advantage of his absence to raise revolt, which saw initial success. Manco besieged Cuzco, where garrison commander Juan Pizarro was killed. Spanish forces captured Quito in the north, then drove off the ten-month siege of Cuzco in heavy fighting. The Inca withdrew into the mountains and Spanish civil war broke out.

Cuzco I 1538 I Spanish Civil War in Peru

See **Salinas, Peru**

Cuzco Hills I 1898 I Spanish-American War

American commander Bowman H. McCalla secured Fisherman's Point in **Guantánamo Bay**, Cuba, and a few days later 160 marines under Captain George F. Elliot and 50 Cubans led by Colonel Enrique Thomas attacked the Spanish on the nearby Cuzco Hills. Supported by naval shelling, the marines won a costly action and the Spanish troops fled towards Guantánamo City (14 June 1898).

Cyme I 474 BC I Syracusan-Etruscan War

See **Cumae**

Cymensore I 477 I Anglo-Saxon Conquest of Britain

Landing on the west Sussex coast with his sons Cymen, Wlencing and Cissa, the Saxon adventurer Aella defeated the Britons at a site traditionally known as Cymensore (named for his son), probably near Selsey, west of modern Portsmouth. Aella drove the Britons into the Andredsweald and, after victory at **Mearcredesburn** (485) and **Anderida** (491), he became King of the South Saxons.

Cynoscephalae I 364 BC I Wars of the Greek City-States

When several cities in Thessaly sought aid from Thebes against Alexander, Despot of Pherae, an expedition was sent under the powerful General Pelopidas, who was taken prisoner (368 BC). After being rescued by Epaminondas, Pelopidas defeated Alexander at Cynoscephalae, south of Larissa near Skotoussa, but was killed in action. The Tyrant was forced to acknowledge Theban hegemony.

Cynoscephalae I 197 BC I 2nd Macedonian War

After defeating Philip V of Macedonia in northwest Greece at the **Aous** (198 BC), Roman commander Titus Quinctius Flamininus advanced southeast into Thessaly and met the Greeks at Cynoscephalae, south of Larissa. The Macedonian phalanx was routed by Roman Legions in a decisive action, with perhaps 13,000 killed. Philip sued for peace, yielding all claim to Greece (June 197 BC).

Cynossema I 411 BC I Great Peloponnesian War

Recovering from disaster at **Syracuse** (413 BC), the Athenian navy was rebuilt and sailed to defend the Hellespont access to the Black Sea, where it faced an attack by Spartan Admiral Mindarus. Off Cynossema, near Abydos in the narrows, the Athenians secured a close victory. The following year they attacked and defeated Mindarus further east at **Cyzicus** (September 411 BC).

Cynthiana I 1864 I American Civil War (Western Theatre)

Confederate General John H. Morgan escaped from prison after surrender near **Salineville** (July 1863) and once again led a raid into Kentucky, where he captured General Edward Hobson's garrison at Cynthiana, northeast of Lexington. Morgan was attacked and driven out next day by fresh Union troops under General Stephen G. Burbridge and was forced to flee (11–12 June 1864).

Cypress Hills I 1873 I 2nd Riel Rebellion

Angry over alleged horse-theft, American wolfers attacked the Assiniboine village at Cypress Hills, in southwestern Saskatchewan, near the Montana border, and killed 30 Indians. Following the massacre, the newly formed Northwest Mounted Police built Fort Walsh nearby and restored peace. But it was a prelude to renewed rebellion which began with the attack at **Duck Lake** in 1885 (May 1873).

Cyrrhestica I 38 BC I Roman-Parthian Wars

See **Gindarus**

Cyzicus I 410 BC I Great Peloponnesian War

Despite defeat off **Cynossema** (411 BC), Spartan Admiral Mindarus, aided by the Persian Pharnabazus, captured Cyzicus on the southern shore of the Sea of Marmara. Attacked by a reinforced Athenian fleet under Alcibiades, Mindarus was killed in a decisive action. The Spartan fleet was burned or captured, yielding Athens command of the sea until 406 BC at **Notium** (April 410 BC).

Cyzicus I 73 BC I 3rd Mithridatic War

Determined to relieve Marcus Aurelius Cotta, blockaded after **Chalcedon**, Roman commander Lucius Licinius Lucullus entered the Sea of Marmara after victory off **Lemnos** and attacked Mithridates VI of Pontus besieging Cyzicus. Caught between two Roman armies, Mithridates suffered terrible losses and withdrew east into northern Turkey, where he was defeated the following year at **Cabira**.

Cyzicus I 194 I Wars of Emperor Severus

Emperor Septimius Severus took power in Rome (April 193), then marched against Pescennius Niger, ruler of Roman Asia. Recovering from defeat at **Perinthus** (191), Severus besieged **Byzantium** and sent General Tiberius Claudius Candidus across the Bosphorus against Niger's proconsul, Asellius Aemilianus. At Cyzicus, south of the Sea of Marmara, Aemilianus was defeated and executed.

Czarnowo, Lodzkie I 1655 I 1st Northern War

See **Opoczno**

**Czarnowo, Mazowieckie I 1806 I
Napoleonic Wars (4th Coalition)**

Having destroyed the Prussians at **Jena** and **Auerstadt** in October, Napoleon Bonaparte invaded Poland and captured Warsaw. Marching north across the Wkra, Marshal Louis Davout defeated the heavily outnumbered Russian General Count Alexander Ostermann-Tolstoy at Czarnowo. After further victories at **Pultusk** and **Golymin**, Bonaparte withdrew to winter quarters (23 December 1806).

**Czaslau I 1742 I War of the Austrian
Succession**

See **Chotusitz**

**Czernowitz I 1916 I World War I
(Eastern Front)**

As part of the brilliant **Brusilov Offensive**, Russian General Platon Lechitsky in the south stormed into Bukowina against General Karl von Pflanzer-Baltin. A stunning victory saw Lechitsky take Czernowitz and virtually destroy the Austrian Seventh Army. German reinforcements eventually stabilised the front and Czernowitz was lost a year later after **Stanislau** (4–17 June 1916).

**Czestochowa I 1655 I 1st Northern
War**

See **Jasna Gora**

D

Dabhoi ❘ 1731 ❘ Maratha Rebellions

When Maratha Senapati Trimbak Rao Dabhade rebelled and threatened to join forces with Nizam-ul-Mulk of Hyderabad, Peshwa Baji Rao I and his brother Chimnaji Appa intercepted the rebels at Dabhoi, southeast of Baroda in Gujarat. A fierce action saw Trimbak Rao defeated and killed and Baji Rao established as undisputed leader of the Maratha state (1 April 1731).

Dabik ❘ 1516 ❘ Ottoman-Mamluk War
See **Marj-Dabik**

Dabney's Mill ❘ 1865 ❘ American Civil War (Eastern Theatre)
See **Hatcher's Run**

Dabul ❘ 1508 ❘ Early Portuguese Colonial Wars in Asia
See **Chaul**

Dabusiyya ❘ 1032 ❘ Eastern Muslim Dynastic Wars

After Ilek Khan Ali Tegin invaded Khwarezm and captured Samarkand and Bokhara, Masud of Ghazni sent the Khwarezmshah Altuntash, who retook both cities, then defeated the Seljuk Turks near Samarkand at Dabusiyya. However, Altuntash was severely wounded in the battle and died a few days later. In the peace which followed, Ali Tegin retained Samarkand and Masud kept Bokhara.

Dacca ❘ 1971 ❘ Bangladesh War of Independence

In response to a popular uprising in East Pakistan, a major offensive by Pakistani forces under General Tikka Khan began with the arrest of Bengali leader Sheikh Mujibur Rahman. Within five days the city of Dacca was secured and by mid-April most resistance elsewhere was brutally crushed. Pakistan's subsequent defeat by India created independent Bangladesh (25–30 March 1971).

Dacca ❘ 1971 ❘ 3rd Indo-Pakistan War

When Pakistan invaded India in the west at **Chhamb**, Indian General Jagjit Singh Aurora launched a massive invasion of East Pakistan in support of Bengali independence (4 December) and advanced on Dacca. After heavy action, Pakistani General Amir Abdullah Khan Niazi surrendered the city and all of East Pakistan, which became independent Bangladesh (14–16 December 1971).

Dade Massacre ❘ 1835 ❘ 2nd Seminole Indian War

Major Francis Dade marching north from Tampa to reinforce Fort King was ambushed by about 280 Seminoles under Miconapy and Jumper in Florida's Wahoo Swamp, near Bushnell, north of modern Dade City. Terrible fighting saw only three out of 80 soldiers escape alive. Another force advancing south was attacked three days later, 30 miles down the **Withlacoochee** (28 December 1835).

Dadong Mountains I 1852 I Taiping Rebellion

After boldly defending **Yung'an** in Guangxi (Kwangsi), the Taiping army withdrew and pursuing General Wulantai attacked and killed about 2,000 stragglers and wounded at nearby Gusu. Next day the Imperial army was ambushed in the Dadong Mountains, losing over 2,000 men, as well as arms and supplies. The Taiping then fell back through the mountains to **Guilin** (8 April 1852).

Daegsaston I 603 I Anglo-Saxon Territorial Wars

Threatened by Scots under King Aidan, recovered from their defeat at **Cathraeth** in 598, Aethelfrith of Northumbria met the invaders at Daegsaston, in the Liddesdale Valley, northeast of Dumfries. While Aethelfrith's brother Theodbald was killed, Aidan's Scots and Picts were destroyed. Having secured the Kingdom of Northumbria in the north, Aethelfrith turned south towards **Chester**.

Dafeichuan I 670 I Tang Imperial Wars

When Tibet launched a major offensive north to seize Chinese-held towns in the Tarim Basin, in modern Xinjiang, China, General Xue Rengui led a large Tang army to restore control. The expedition established a base at Dafeichuan, where they were attacked by a massive Tibetan force under Mgar Khri'brin. The Imperial army suffered a devastating defeat and China had to withdraw.

Dagu Forts I 1858 I 2nd Opium War

Determined to open China to trade, Anglo-French forces captured **Guangzhou** in late 1857, before Admirals Sir Michael Seymour and Charles Rigault de Genouilly attacked the Dagu (Taku) Forts guarding the Bei He. After exchanging fire the Allies secured the forts, then advanced to Tianjin, where British Plenipotentiary James Lord Elgin imposed a truce opening more ports to trade (20 May 1858).

Dagu Forts I 1859 I 2nd Opium War

When war resumed with China over trade concessions, British General Sir James Hope Grant (with Chinese and French allies) attacked the Dagu Forts at the mouth of the Bei He, now strongly held by Prince Senggelinqin (Sang-ko-lin-chin). A bloody action saw Hope Grant with his landing party stuck in mud then forced to withdraw, with 90 killed, 300 wounded and three gunboats lost (25 June 1859).

Dagu Forts I 1860 I 2nd Opium War

In a renewed assault on the Dagu Forts on the Bei He, 11,000 British under General Sir James Hope Grant and 6,000 French led by General Charles Cousin-Montauban landed at Beicang to attack from the landward side, supported by ships on the river. Prince Senggelinqin (Sang-ko-lin-chin) fled after very heavy Chinese losses and the Allies advanced on Beijing through **Baliqiao** (21 August 1860).

Dagu Forts I 1900 I Boxer Rebellion

With an international relief force for **Beijing** blocked at **Langfang**, nine British, French, German and Russian warships demanded the surrender of the Dagu (Taku) Forts at the mouth of the Bei He. After fort commander Luo Rongguang opened fire, the Allies bombarded and seized the forts, ensuring Imperial support for the anti-foreign Boxers, who then besieged nearby **Tianjin** (17 June 1900).

Dahlenkirchen I 1812 I Napoleonic Wars (Russian Campaign)

As Napoleon Bonaparte invaded Russia, Prussian forces besieged the Baltic port of Riga after victory at **Eckau**. To cover a naval landing further west at Schlock, Russian commander General Jean Henri Essen sent General Ivan Alexandrovich Vilyaminov, who overran the siege lines outside Riga at Dahlenkirchen. Prussian General Julius Grawert withdrew to Mitau (22 August 1812).

Dai Do I 1968 I Vietnam War

See **Dong Ha**

Dail Righ I 1306 I Rise of Robert the Bruce

See **Dalry**

**Dakar I 1940 I World War II
(Northern Africa)**

An attempt to secure Vichy French West Africa, under Governor Pierre Boisson, saw Britain send a large naval force to Dakar, led by Admiral John Cunningham, with British and Free French troops under Generals Noel Irwin and Charles de Gaulle. After a failed landing and heavy damage by shellfire to warships on both sides, the expedition was abandoned (23–25 September 1940).

Dakhila I 1898 I British-Sudan Wars

Mahdist commander Ahmed Fedil was pursued to the Upper Blue Nile after defeat at **Omdurman** and lost at **Gedaref** before being brought to battle just south of Rosaires near Dakhila by a British-Sudanese force under Colonel David (Taffy) Lewis. The Dervishes suffered heavy losses, including Emir Saadallah killed, but fought again a year later at **Um Diwaykarat** (26 December 1898).

Dakka I 1919 I 3rd British-Afghan War

When Amir Amanullah of Afghanistan sent General Saleh Mohammad into India against the border village of **Bagh**, it was retaken by British General George Crocker (11 May), who then marched five miles northwest against the large village of Dakka. Following ineffectual aerial bombing, the Afghans were driven out after heavy ground-fighting and costly losses on both sides (13–17 May 1919).

Dak To I 1967 I Vietnam War

As further diversion from the planned **Tet Offensive** after action in the north at **Con Thien** and in the south at **Loc Ninh**, North Vietnamese regulars attacked American forces in the central highlands around Dak To. Intense fighting, supported by heavy US bombing and artillery, made the NVA withdraw with perhaps 1,500 dead, while the US lost almost 300 killed (3–22 November 1967).

Dalahican I 1896 I Philippines War of Independence

See **Binakayan**

Dalinghe I 1631 I Manchu Conquest of China

A major offensive into Manchuria saw Abahai (Hong Taiji) take 20,000 Manchu, Mongol and Han troops against the powerful Ming fortress city of Dalinghe (Ta-ling-ho), northeast of Jinzhou. Heavy fighting secured outlying fortified villages and, after a relief army was defeated at the **Xiaoling**, Ming commander Zu Dashou surrendered the starving city (1 September–21 November 1631).

Dalippur I 1858 I Indian Mutiny

General Sir Edward Lugard and Brigadier Claude Douglas captured **Jagdispur** (9 May), then pursued Amar Singh through jungle to the south and west, inflicting losses at Hetampur, Piru and Metahi before meeting the main force at Dalippur. Amar Singh's rebels were decisively beaten, losing the two guns taken from Le Grand at **Jagdispur** and withdrew west towards Ghazipur (27 May 1858).

**Dallas I 1864 I American Civil War
(Western Theatre)**

As General William T. Sherman's Union army advanced through Georgia, Confederate commander Joseph E. Johnston repulsed two flanking attempts southwest of Allatoona at **New Hope Church** and **Pickett's Mill**. Confederate General William J. Hardee then counter-attacked at nearby Dallas but suffered a costly defeat and Johnston withdrew east towards **Marietta** (27 May 1864).

Dalmanutha I 1900 I 2nd Anglo-Boer War

See **Belfast**

Dalry I 1306 I Rise of Robert the Bruce

Two months after defeat at **Methven**, Robert the Bruce of Scotland was attacked at Dalry, Ayrshire, by John MacDougall of Lorne, an English ally and kinsman of John Comyn, whom Bruce had murdered to claim the crown. Bruce's battered force lost again and he continued into hiding until he could raise a fresh army for victory in May 1307 at **Loudon Hill** (11 August 1306).

Dalton (1st) ▮ 1864 ▮ American Civil War (Western Theatre)

While Union commander William T. Sherman advanced east on **Meridian**, Mississippi, Union General George H. Thomas marched into northern Georgia to threaten the Confederate rear at Dalton. Thomas reached within three miles of Dalton before being blocked by the much larger Confederate army of General Joseph E. Johnston. He then returned to Chattanooga (22–27 February 1864).

Dalton (2nd) ▮ 1864 ▮ American Civil War (Western Theatre)

Confederate cavalry under General Joseph Wheeler raiding deep into the rear of the Union army besieging **Atlanta**, Georgia, attempted to seize Dalton, in the north of the state, held by Colonel Bernard Laibolt. After a failed assault, Wheeler came under attack by an approaching Union relief column led by General James B. Steedman and was forced to withdraw (14–15 August 1864).

Damalcherry Pass ▮ 1740 ▮ Later Mughal-Maratha Wars

When Maratha forces invaded the Carnatic in southeast India, Dost Ali Khan, Nawab of Arcot, took a defensive position at Damalcherry Pass, 30 miles north of Ambur. In a terrible rout, Maratha General Raghuji Bhonsle took them in the rear and Dost Ali and his son Hassan Ali were defeated and killed. Bhonsle occupied Arcot, then besieged and captured **Trichinopoly** (31 May 1740).

Damascus ▮ 635 ▮ Muslim Conquest of Syria

Muslim conqueror Khalid ibn al-Walid was besieging Damascus after victory in February at **Marj as-Suffar**, when Emperor Heraclius at Antioch is claimed to have sent a massive relief force under General Werban. Khalid supposedly raised the siege to destroy the approaching Christian army. He then returned to the siege. Part of Damascus fell by storm and the rest quickly surrendered (August 635).

Damascus ▮ 1148 ▮ 2nd Crusade

Despite suffering severe losses reaching Palestine, Emperor Conrad III of Germany and King Louis VII of France joined Baldwin III of Jerusalem in a mismanaged expedition against Damascus, where a half-hearted siege was repulsed by a relief army under Nur-ed-Din. The Crusaders retreated with heavy losses and Conrad took his army back to Germany (23–28 July 1148).

Damascus ▮ 1401 ▮ Conquests of Tamerlane

The Turko-Mongol Tamerlane captured **Aleppo** (December 1400), then marched south towards Damascus. Mamluk Sultan Faraj gathered an Egyptian army to protect Syria's capital, but they fled when Tamerlane approached and the city surrendered. However, the citadel held out for a month against heavy assault. As punishment Damascus was sacked and stripped of its vast treasure (25 January 1401).

Damascus ▮ 1771 ▮ Mamluk-Ottoman Wars

With Cairo secured by victory at **Tanta**, the great Mamluk leader Ali Bey sent General Abu'l-Dhahab into Syria to support Shayk Zahir al-Umar against Uthman Pasha al-Sadiq, Ottoman Governor of Damascus. The combined Mamluk forces defeated the Ottoman army and captured Damascus. Abu'l-Dhahad then returned to Egypt to overthrow his master in **Cairo** (3 June 1771).

Damascus ▮ 1918 ▮ World War I (Middle East)

During his decisive broad offensive in Palestine through **Megiddo**, British General Sir Edmund Allenby sent his cavalry north in pursuit of the Turks, towards Damascus, while Arab forces further east advanced along the railway from **Dera**. After Australian troops entered Damascus, Prince Feisal secured the city. Beirut fell the same day and the fall of **Aleppo** ended the war (1 October 1918).

Damascus ▮ 1925 ▮ Druze Rebellion

Encouraged by Druze capture of **Suwayda** in southern Syria (24 September), rebellion broke out in Damascus, where looters destroyed the palace of French High Commissioner Maurice Sarrail. Withdrawing north, General Maurice Gamelin's artillery and aircraft bombarded the rebel quarter, with perhaps 1,000 killed and over 100 million francs of damage. Sarrail was recalled (18–20 October 1925).

Damascus I 1926 I Druze Rebellion

On the offensive against Druze rebels in Syria, French General Maurice Gamelin sent forces to retake **Suwayda**, then launched a fresh attack on rebel positions in the southern part of the capital, Damascus, where aerial bombardment with explosives and incendiaries caused massive damage and casualties. Druze Sultan al-Atrash soon fled to Jordan and the rebellion slowly ended (7 May 1926).

Damascus I 1941 I World War II (Middle East)

See **Syria**

Damdama I 1624 I Rebellion of Prince Shahjahan

During war against Persia in Afghanistan, Mughal Prince Shahjahan rebelled against his father, Emperor Jahangir and, despite defeat at **Balochpur** (March 1623), returned to advance up the Ganges and occupy Benares. At Damdama, near Allahabad, his General, Bhim Singh, was defeated and killed, crushing the rebellion. Shahjahan later made peace with his father and succeeded to the throne.

Damghan I 1528 I Persian-Uzbek Wars

A Persian force marching to relieve the Uzbek siege of **Herat** was beaten outside Damghan, in northeast Iran, by Uzbek commander Renish Behader Khan. The main Persian army of Shah Tahmasp then besieged Renish in Damghan, where he was defeated and killed along with most of the garrison. Ubaid Khan had to raise the siege of Herat and met the Persians in September at **Torbat-i-Jam**.

Damietta I 1169 I Crusader Invasion of Egypt

King Amalric of Jerusalem left a Crusader garrison in Cairo after his victory at **Alexandria** and two years later he and Turkish General Shirkuh returned to resume the struggle for the strategic Nile Delta. However, a combined Crusader-Latin army was badly repulsed besieging Damietta and Amalric withdrew. Shirkuh died and his nephew Saladin effectively secured Egypt and later Damascus.

Damietta I 1218–1219 I 5th Crusade

Crusaders from Palestine and Europe landed at the eastern mouth of the Nile, where they maintained a loose blockade of Damietta, later strengthened by fresh reinforcements and capture of the nearby fortress of **Adiliya**. Following a brutal siege with heavy losses on both sides, Damietta fell by storm. It was given up in 1221 after failure of the Crusade (May 1218–5 November 1219).

Damietta I 1249 I 7th Crusade

Louis IX of France assembled a massive Crusader army in Cyprus and sailed to Egypt. In a reprise of the Fifth Crusade, he landed near Damietta on the eastern Nile Delta, where the city was besieged and then captured when the garrison fled in panic. However, Damietta was surrendered by the French ten months later after disastrous Crusader defeats at **Mansura** and **Fariskur** (7 June 1249).

Damietta I 1250 I 7th Crusade

See **Fariskur**

Damme I 1213 I Anglo-French Wars

When Count Ferdinand of Flanders defected, Philip II of France diverted his fleet against Flanders before invading England. King John of England sent a large fleet under Count William of Holland and William Longsword Earl of Salisbury and, off Damme near Bruges, the French fleet was destroyed. Philip burned his remaining ships and abandoned his planned invasion (30 March 1213).

Dams Raid **|** 1943 **|** World War II (Western Europe)

One of the best-known British air exploits took place when Wing commander Guy Gibson led 17 bombers against five strategic dams in the Ruhr using the revolutionary "bouncing bombs." Eight aircraft and 53 aircrew were lost and only the Möhne and Eder dams were breached. While damage was soon repaired, the "Dam Busters" provided an important boost for Allied morale (16–17 May 1943).

Danang **|** 1847 **|** French Conquest of Indo-China

In a powerful demonstration against the anti-Christian Vietnamese Emperor Thieu Tri, Admiral Jean-Baptiste Cécille sent two warships against the key port of Danang, nominally to rescue a jailed missionary. While a massive French bombardment inflicted heavy damage and casualties, nothing substantial was achieved until a full-scale attack on the port 11 years later (15 April 1847).

Danang **|** 1858 **|** French Conquest of Indo-China

As supposed response to the execution of Spanish Bishop José María Díaz, 14 ships and 2,500 men under Admiral Charles Rigault de Genouilly bombarded and stormed Danang. Genouilly then sailed for **Saigon**. Meanwhile, Danang held out against Vietnamese Marshal Nguyen Tri Phuong despite terrible losses to disease, until it was abandoned in March 1860 (31 August–1 September 1858).

Danang **|** 1975 **|** Vietnam War

At the start of the offensive to conquer South Vietnam, up to 35,000 North Vietnamese with tanks and artillery converged on Danang, packed with civilian and military refugees fleeing the fall of **Hue**. As order in Danang broke down under heavy shelling, South Vietnamese officers fled, leaving a claimed 100,000 troops to surrender, effectively ending resistance in the north (28–29 March 1975).

Danbury Raid **|** 1777 **|** War of the American Revolution

Encouraged by the raid on **Peekskill** (23 March), British commander William Howe sent Colonel William Tryon against Danbury, Connecticut. Having burned buildings and stores, Tryon was blocked at nearby Ridgefield by Generals Benedict Arnold, David Wooster and Gold Silliman. Wooster was mortally wounded, yet the British eventually withdrew with heavy losses (25–27 April 1777).

Danchua **|** 1857 **|** Indian Mutiny

Amid sharp fighting west of Cawnpore, a local unit under Colonel Thomas Rattray—known as Rattray's Sikhs—repulsed a mutineer force at Akbarpur (7 October) and a month later finally met Tantia Topi's rebels at Danchua. The rebels suffered a decisive loss, though three weeks later they defeated General Charles Windham outside **Cawnpore** and seized the city (6 November 1857).

Dandanaqan **|** 1040 **|** Seljuk Wars of Expansion

The Seljuk brothers Toghril and Caghri Beg marched into Khorasan, in Turkish northeastern Iran and captured **Nishapur** (1037) before Ghaznavid Sultan Masud ibn Mahmud counter-attacked. Outside Dandanaqan, near Merv (modern Mary, Turkmenistan), Masud was routed and withdrew to India, leaving Caghri to rule Khorasan and Toghril to go on to capture **Isfahan** and **Baghdad** (23 May 1040).

Dandridge **|** 1864 **|** American Civil War (Western Theatre)

Campaigning east of Knoxville, Tennessee, Union General Samuel B. Sturgis advanced south from **Mossy Creek** towards Dandridge, where he was blocked by Confederate General James Longstreet. Sturgis was forced to withdraw west towards Strawberry Plains after sharp fighting and ten days later he had his revenge at **Fair Garden** (17 January 1864).

Danesmoor I 1469 I Wars of the Roses
See **Edgecote**

Danith I 1115 I Crusader-Muslim Wars
See **Tel-Danith**

Danj I 1447–1448 I Albanian-Venetian War
Venetian forces intervening to support the Zakarija Dynasty in northern Albania seized Danj fortress, where they were besieged by George Kastriote Skanderbeg. The Albanian commander defeated a relief force at the nearby Drin (July 1448), but with Turkey threatening after victory at **Svetigrad** he made peace with Venice and soon repulsed the Turks at **Dibra** (1447–4 October 1448).

Danli I 1844 I Central American National Wars
General Joaquín Rivera attempted an invasion of Honduras in the name of former President Francisco Morazán and raised insurrection in Texiguat. He suffered a heavy loss at **Nacaome** and, after gathering fresh forces in the east, he was decisively defeated at Danli by government troops under Colonel Julián Tercero. Rivera was later captured and executed in Comayagua (20 December 1844).

Dannevirke I 1848 I 1st Schleswig-Holstein War
Encouraged by Prussia, the Duchies of Schleswig and Holstein rose against Frederick VII of Denmark. Following their defeat at **Bov** (9 April), Prussia sent General Eduard von Bonin to occupy Holstein, while Count Friedrich Heinrich von Wrangel invaded Schleswig. As a result of hard fighting, Wrangel stormed the defensive line of the Dannevirke and Denmark withdrew (23 April 1848).

Dannoura I 1185 I Gempei War
Taira Tomomori was driven from his stronghold on the Inland Sea at **Yashima** (23 March) and withdrew to Dannoura, in far south Honshu, where he was attacked by Minamoto Yoshitsune. In a decisive and bloody sea battle, the boy-Emperor Antoku was drowned and the Taira nobility was virtually destroyed, establishing Minamoto as the greatest power in Japan (25 April 1185).

Danubyu I 1825 I 1st British-Burmese War
When Burma conquered Arakan and attacked British India, General Sir Archibald Campbell drove Burmese General Maha Bundoola away from **Rangoon**, then pursued him up the Irriwaddy to the stockade at Danubyu. British Colonel Willoughby Cotton was initially repulsed, but Campbell himself led a second attack and Bundoola was defeated and killed (7 March–1 April 1825).

Danubyu I 1853 I 2nd British-Burmese War
With Burma defeated at **Pegu** in late 1852, Britain faced continued resistance by Nya-Myat Toon in the jungle west of Danubyu. At the end of a hard-fought campaign, with costly losses from cholera, General Sir John Cheape finally took the Burmese Chieftain's stronghold at Kyoukazeen. Only scattered guerrilla opposition remained to British rule of Pegu Province (February–March 1853).

Danzig I 1308 I Wars of the Teutonic Knights
See **Gdansk**

Danzig I 1577 I Gdansk War
After Danzig declared for the Habsburg candidate for the throne of Poland (September 1576), King Stephen Bathory marched on the city with Jan Zborowski. While Bathory closed the siege after victory at **Lubieszow**, Danzig (modern Gdansk) held out with Danish support by sea. However, the city finally agreed to accept Bathory and pay him a substantial subsidy (11 June–12 December 1577).

Danzig I 1626–1630 I 2nd Polish-Swedish War
Gustavus Adolphus of Sweden intervened in Polish Prussia to blockade, then besiege, the

great Baltic port of Danzig (modern Gdansk), capturing the fortifications at Putzig and Danziger Haupt. Despite a naval loss off **Oliwa**, Sweden maintained the blockade. However, defeat at **Sztum** in June 1629 led Sweden to make separate peace with Poland and Danzig (3 July 1626–18 February 1630).

Danzig I 1733–1734 I War of the Polish Succession

Russian and Saxon troops under Count Burkhardt von Münnich invaded Poland in support of Augustus III of Saxony, claiming the throne and besieged the rival claimant and former King Stanislas Leszcynski in Danzig. Although Leszcynski's son-in-law, Louis XV of France, sent reinforcements by sea, Danzig fell and Leszcynski fled to Prussia (October 1733–30 June 1734).

Danzig I 1807 I Napoleonic Wars (4th Coalition)

Having bypassed Danzig (modern Gdansk) on his advance into eastern Prussia, Napoleon Bonaparte sent Marshal Francois Lefebvre against the port, held by Prussians under Count Friedrich von Kalckreuth. After a sustained Russian relief attempt by General Levin Bennigsen was eventually repulsed (15 May), Kalckreuth capitulated, marching out with all his arms (19 March–27 May 1807).

Danzig I 1813–1814 I Napoleonic Wars (War of Liberation)

As Napoleon Bonaparte's army withdrew west after the disastrous retreat from Moscow, General Jean Rapp took a large force to Danzig, where he was besieged by an Allied army under Prince Eugene of Württemberg. The prolonged siege denied Bonaparte experienced troops for his campaign in Germany and Rapp was eventually forced to surrender (21 January 1813–2 January 1814).

Danzig I 1945 I World War II (Eastern Front)

When the **Vistula-Oder** offensive had secured Poland, Soviet forces under Marshal Georgi Zhukov and General Konstantin Ro-

kossovksy drove north across East Pomerania to reach the Baltic, cutting off German-held Danzig. In heavy fighting they reduced nearby Gdynia and Danzig itself two days later. The Russian armies then joined the drive towards **Berlin** (13–30 March 1945).

Daosa I 1859 I Indian Mutiny
See **Dausa**

Dara I 530 I Byzantine-Persian Wars

Early in his career, the great Romano-Byzantine General Belisarius was posted as commander of the East to defend the border outpost at Dara, northwest of Nisibis (Nusaybin in modern Turkey). Outside the walls of the fortress, Belisarius secured a decisive victory against an attacking Sassanian Persian army. But, after defeat at **Callinicum** the next year, he was demoted and recalled (June 530).

Dara I 540 I Byzantine-Persian Wars

While returning from the sack of **Antioch**, Sassanian Shah Chosroes attacked the frontier fortress of Dara, where he burned gates in the outer wall but could not force an entry. He then attempted to tunnel under the walls, but the Romans discovered the strategy and built a counter-trench. Chosroes eventually agreed to withdraw in return for the payment of a reported 1,000 pounds of silver.

Dara I 573 I Byzantine-Persian Wars

When Justin II provoked a new war with Persia, Chosroes I routed the Romano-Byzantine army investing Nisibis, then besieged the key fortress at nearby Dara, held by General Marcian. After six months, the Sassanian Persians stormed the city, reputedly driving Justin insane. Dara remained Persian until Chosroes II returned it in 591 to secure Roman aid for his restoration at **Ganzak** (November 573).

Dara I 586 I Byzantine-Persian Wars
See **Solachon**

Daratoleh I 1903 I Wars of the Mad Mullah

A week after disaster at **Gumburu**, the third expedition against Muhammad Abdullah Hassan of Somaliland met Dervishes at Daratoleh, near Damot. Defending a square with Maxims, Major John Gough inflicted terrible losses for just 15 killed and 29 wounded. Three Victoria Crosses were won (including Gough) and the Mullah withdrew until his defeat in January 1904 at **Jidballi** (22 April 1903).

Darbytown Road (1st) I 1864 I American Civil War (Eastern Theatre)
  See **New Market Road**

Darbytown Road (2nd) I 1864 I American Civil War (Eastern Theatre)

Union forces under Generals Alfred H. Terry and Augustus V. Kautz successfully defended the **New Market Road**, southeast of Richmond, Virginia, then advanced on Confederate General Richard H. Anderson on the Darbytown Road. The Union troops were driven off after scattered action and another advance was checked two weeks later further north at **Fair Oaks** (13 October 1864).

Darda I 1687 I Later Turkish-Habsburg Wars
  See **Harkany**

Dardanelles I 1399 I Byzantine-Ottoman Wars

In a French effort to drive off another Ottoman advance against Constantinople, Jean le Maingre Marshal Boucicaut took six ships from Aigues-Mortes and sailed into the Dardanelles, supported by Venetian and Genoese galleys. During perhaps the first significant Ottoman naval battle, he defeated 17 Turkish galleys, then landed troops and archers at Constantinople to relieve the siege.

Dardanelles I 1654 I Venetian-Turkish Wars

On a fresh advance towards Constantinople, Venetian Captain-General Luigi Lionardo Mocenigo was confronted in the Dardanelles by a much larger Turkish fleet. Despite massive superiority in numbers and guns, the Turks suffered a bloody defeat, with a claimed 3,000 killed. The Ottoman fleet was defeated again in the Dardanelles two years later (16 March 1654).

Dardanelles I 1656 I Venetian-Turkish Wars

When Venetian Captain-General Lorenzo Marcello renewed the blockade of Constantinople, the Turks counter-attacked in the Dardanelles. While Marcello was killed, the Turks lost up to 10,000 dead and 400 prisoners. The Venetians freed 5,000 Christian galley slaves in captured ships, then seized Tenedos and Lemnos. It was the worst Ottoman naval defeat since 1571 at **Lepanto** (26 August 1656).

Dardanelles I 1657 I Venetian-Turkish Wars

After failed attempts to break the Venetian blockade of Constantinople, new Vizier Koprulu Mehmed Pasha rebuilt his fleet and attacked again in the Dardanelles. Venetian commander Lazzaro Mocenigo died when a lucky shot sank his flagship and Koprulu won a decisive victory. The Turks then recovered Tenedos (4 September) and Lemnos (15 November) after a 60-day siege (17–19 July 1657).

Dardanelles I 1912 I Italo-Turkish War

To support her war against Turkey in Libya, Italy sent a naval force against the Dardanelles. Although over 300 shells were fired from long range against the outer forts, little damage was caused and fear of Great Power intervention forced the Italians to withdraw. However, they then seized Rhodes and other islands in the Dodecanese and retained them at the end of the war (18 April 1912).

Dardanelles I 1915 I World War I (Gallipoli)

At the start of a misconceived naval plan to force the Dardanelles and attack Constantinople, 24 Anglo-French warships under Admirals Sackville Carden and Émile Guépratte bombarded the Turkish outer forts at the entrance to the Dardanelles. Two attacks caused considerable damage prior to an attempt to enter the straits and force the **Dardanelles Narrows** (19 & 25 February 1915).

Dardanelles Narrows ▮ 1915 ▮ World War I (Gallipoli)

After silencing the forts at the entrance to the **Dardanelles**, Anglo-French warships under Admirals John de Robeck and Émile Guépratte attempted to storm the Narrows. They bombarded Turkish coastal batteries, but withdrew with three battleships sunk and three badly damaged by mines and gunfire, leaving the army to later attack on land at **Helles** and **Anzac** (18 March 1915).

Dar es Salaam ▮ 1914 ▮ World War I (African Colonial Theatre)

The reputed first British action of the war saw the cruiser *Astraea* bombard Dar es Salaam in German East Africa to destroy the naval wireless. Governor Heinrich Schnee blew up the station and surrendered the city, which was later reoccupied by German forces. It was eventually recaptured by British General Jan Smuts (3 September 1916) during the **Morogoro** Offensive (8 August 1914).

Dargai ▮ 1897 ▮ Great Frontier Rising

Following capture of the Northwest Frontier Khyber Forts by Afridi tribesmen, General Sir William Lockhart was sent west from Kohat into the Tirah to subjugate the rebels. On the Dargai Heights, north of Thal, his Gordon Highlanders and Gurkhas inflicted a decisive defeat, after which he severely crushed the remaining rebellion and recaptured **Landi Kotal** (18–20 October 1897).

Darghiyya ▮ 1842 ▮ Russian Conquest of the Caucasus

On a determined expedition against the Muslims of Dagestan, Russian Baron Pavel Grabbe took 10,000 men south from Gurzul towards the rebel "capital" at Darghiyya. In the forest of Ichkeria, he was attacked and forced to retreat by Shu-ayb and Ulubey, lieutenants of the Imam

Shamil. Grabbe lost 1,800 men killed and wounded and was soon relieved of command (11–16 June 1842).

Darghiyya ▮ 1845 ▮ Russian Conquest of the Caucasus

Sent by the Tsar against Imam Shamil of Dagestan, Russian Count Mikhail Vorontsov led 20,000 men west from Gertme towards Darghiyya, which he captured, then abandoned and burned (18 July). Facing terrible losses, Vorontsov destroyed his supplies and withdrew north through the forest of Ichkeria, losing 4,000 men killed and wounded before reaching Gurzul (15 June–1 August 1845).

Dargo ▮ 1842 ▮ Russian Conquest of the Caucasus

See **Darghiyya**

Dark Water Creek ▮ 1875 ▮ Red River Indian War

See **Sappa Creek**

Daroca ▮ 1120 ▮ Early Christian Reconquest of Spain

See **Cutanda**

Dartanat ▮ 1488 ▮ Persian-Turkoman Wars

Sheikh Haidar of Ardabil in northern Iran led a campaign into Shirvan (modern Azerbaijan), where he besieged Shah Farrukh Yasar at Shemakha, 70 miles west of Baku. However, the Turkoman Sultan Yakub intervened and, near Dartanat, Sheikh Haidar suffered a devastating defeat and was killed. His son Ismail was avenged against Farrukh Yasar 12 years later at **Jabani** (9 July 1488).

Darwin, Australia ▮ 1942 ▮ World War II (Pacific)

As Japanese forces invaded **Papua**, Admiral Chuichi Nagumo sent over 200 land and carrier aircraft against Darwin Harbour in nearby northern Australia, sinking eight ships, including an American destroyer. This first and most serious attack on Australia killed about 250 and caused massive destruction in the town. Darwin was hit again 63 times in the next 12 months (19 February 1942).

Darwin, Falklands I 1982 I Falklands War
See **Goose Green**

Dashiqiao I 1904 I Russo-Japanese War
As they withdrew into Manchuria from defeat at **Delisi** (15 June), Russian Generals Nikolai Platonovich Zarubayev and Georg Karlovich Stackelberg tried to defend Dashiqiao (Ta-shih-ch'iao), 140 miles north of **Port Arthur**. Advancing from the south, General Yasukata Oku's Second Army smashed into the Russians and drove them back through Haicheng with about 3,000 casualties (24 July 1904).

Dasmariñas I 1897 I Philippines War of Independence
Recovering from a check at **Zapote Bridge**, Spanish General José Lachambre continued the offensive south of Manila, attacking Emilio Aguinaldo and 5,000 men at Dasmariñas. Following days of brutal fighting, and the heroic death of 23-year-old General Flaviano Yengco at nearby Pasang Santol, Aguinaldo evacuated the burning town and fell back on **Imus** (28 February–3 March 1897).

Dasymon I 838 I Byzantine-Muslim Wars
See **Dazimon**

Dathin I 634 I Muslim Conquest of Syria
See **Wadi al-Arabah**

Daulatabad I 1294 I Wars of the Delhi Sultanate
See **Deogiri**

Daulatabad I 1633 I Mughal-Ahmadnagar Wars
Mughal Governor Mahabat Khan of Punjab advanced into central India, where he besieged Daulatabad fortress, northwest of Aurangabad, defended by Fath Khan of Ahmadnagar. Mahabat Khan captured the outer defences and, four months later, Fath Khan and his son, the boy-King Husain Nizam Shah III, surrendered the citadel, ending the Sultanate of Ahmadnagar (28 June 1633).

Daulatabad I 1741 I Mughal Wars of Succession
Manipulated by scheming courtiers, the Mughal General Mir Ahmed Nasir Jang rose in rebellion against his father, Nizam-ul-Mulk of Hyderabad. When the contending armies eventually met at Daulatabad, near Aurangabad, the Nizam attempted reconciliation but failed. The ensuing battle saw Nasir Jang wounded and defeated, though he was later pardoned (23 July 1741).

Dausa I 1859 I Indian Mutiny
Rebel leader Firuz Shah lost at **Ranod** in December, then marched northwest to join Tantia Topi and Man Singh at Dausa, a fortified town east of Jaipur, where they were surprised by Brigadier St George Showers, sent in pursuit by General Sir Robert Napier. The rebels were beaten, losing about 300 casualties, but all three leaders escaped. Topi soon lost decisively at **Sikar** (14 January 1859).

Dau Tieng I 1966 I Vietnam War
Following action south of the DMZ at **Song Ngan**, American and South Vietnamese forces began an even larger offensive near the Cambodian border northwest of Saigon (Operation Attleboro). The heaviest fighting was at Ap Cha Do and against the huge supply base at Dau Tieng, where the Allies took heavy losses before the Communists withdrew (14 September–25 November 1966).

Davis' Cross Roads I 1863 I American Civil War (Western Theatre)
Soon after Union forces occupied **Chattanooga**, Tennessee, General James S. Negley marched south against Confederates concentrating near Lafayette. To the west at Davis' Cross Roads beyond Dug Gap, Negley checked Generals Thomas C. Hindman and John C. Breckinridge, then skillfully withdrew to establish a defensive line west of the **Chickamauga** (10–11 September 1863).

Dawson's Massacre I 1842 I Texan Wars of Independence

Texan Captain Nicholas Dawson marching to join battle at the **Salado**, northeast of **San Antonio**, was met two miles away by part of the Mexican army under Colonels Cayetano Montero and José María Carrasco. In a confused action, 36 out of 54 Texans were killed, apparently trying to surrender. Three escaped and the rest were taken as prisoners to Mexico (18 September 1842).

Dawston I 603 I Anglo-Saxon Territorial Wars

See **Daegsaston**

Dayr al-Jamajim I 701 I Muslim Civil Wars

In revolt against the Umayyad Caliphate, Ibn al-Ash'ath in the east raised an army of Arab Kufans and non-Arab Mawali and marched into Iraq to seize Kufa. He then took a claimed 200,000 men against Governor al-Hajjaj on the nearby plain at Dayr al-Jamajim. After lengthy negotiations, al-Hajjaj and his smaller Syrian-supported force defeated the rebel, who fled north to **Maskin** (September 701).

Day River I 1951 I French Indo-China War

Defeated in the **Red River Delta** at **Vinh Yen** and **Mao Khé**, Viet Minh commander Vo Nguyen Giap then attacked across the Day River, south of Hanoi. Crossing at Phu Ly, Ninh Binh and Phat Diem, the Communists advanced towards the Red River, but lacked resources across such a wide front. Facing his third defeat in five months, Giap disengaged and withdrew (29 May–18 June 1951).

Day's Gap I 1863 I American Civil War (Western Theatre)

On a raid into Confederate Alabama and Georgia, Union Colonel Abel D. Streight was attacked by General Nathan B. Forrest at Day's Gap on Sand Mountain, southwest of Chattanooga, Alabama. Streight fought a brilliant rearguard action, but he was pursued for days, and on 3 May his entire force of about 1,600 men surrendered west of Rome, Georgia (30 April 1863).

Dayuan I 102 BC I Wars of the Former Han

Han Emperor Wudi determined to expand his influence in Central Asia and sent General Li Guangli and a large force of conscripts against Dayuan (Ta-yüan) in the Ferghana Valley. After a failed expedition with very heavy losses (104–103 BC), Li Guangli returned the following year with a much larger force to besiege Dayuan. The city fell after 40 days and the King of Dayuan was executed.

Dazaifu I 1281 I Mongol Wars of Kubilai Khan

See **Hakata Bay**

Dazimon I 838 I Byzantine-Muslim Wars

When Emperor Theophilus raided into Syria, Caliph al-Mu'tasim led a counter-invasion into Anatolia and the Emperor advanced from the Halys to meet the Arabs on the Iris, east of Amasya. At Dazimon (modern Tokat), part of the Muslim army under Afshin Khaydar inflicted a disastrous defeat and Theophilus fled west to Constantinople, leaving the Caliph to seize Ancyra and besiege **Amorium**.

D-Day I 1944 I World War II (Western Europe)

See **Normandy**

Dead Buffalo Lake I 1863 I Sioux Indian Wars

General Henry Hastings Sibley advancing into central North Dakota in pursuit of Santee and Teton Sioux under Inkpaduta defeated the Indians at **Big Mound**. Two days later, he attacked again at **Dead Buffalo Lake**, northeast of Fort Rice in modern Kidder County. The Sioux were once more driven off and two days later Sibley had his third and largest victory at **Stony Lake** (26 July 1863).

Deal I 55 BC I Roman Invasion of Britain

Julius Caesar landed with just two Legions at Deal in Kent and there was sharp resistance before local British tribes began to surrender. However, when a storm damaged Caesar's ships and dispersed his reinforcements, he abandoned the campaign and sailed for Gaul. He returned with a larger force a year later and defeated Cassivellaunus at **Wheathampstead** (August–September 55 BC).

De'an I 1206–1207 I Jin-Song Wars

When Song forces tried to recover land in northern China, a massive Jin (Chin) army advanced to besiege **Xiangyang** and also De'an (Te-an) to the southeast, where Wang Yunchu led a courageous defence by a largely militia force. The Jin used incendiaries to burn the defences and undermined parts of the walls, but De'an held out. After 108 days, the enemy abandoned the siege and withdrew.

Dearborn I 1812 I War of 1812
See **Fort Dearborn**

Debar I 1448 I Albanian-Turkish Wars
See **Dibra**

Debra Sina I 1887 I Sudanese-Ethiopian War

With Abyssinia occupied by war with Italy, Mahdist Khalifa Abdullah sent 60,000 men into Abyssinia under General Hamdan Abu Anja. The army of King Yohannes IV, led by Ras Asdal, attempted to make a stand on the Plain of Debra Sina, northeast of Addis Ababba, but was crushed. The Dervishes entered Gondar, then returned to Omdurman with massive booty (July 1887).

Debra Tabor I 1941 I World War II (Northern Africa)

After Italian surrender at **Amba Alagi** in May, the Allied drive began against remnants in the Ethiopian mountains near Lake Tana. Advancing from **Dessie**, British-led Ethiopian forces attacked the fortified village of Debra Tabor, where Colonel Ignazio Angelini surrendered 3,000 Italians and 1,200 colonial troops. After the rains, the advance continued northwest to **Gondar** (3 July 1941).

Decatur I 1864 I American Civil War (Western Theatre)

Following the fall of **Atlanta**, Georgia, in July, Confederate General John B. Hood marched west from a repulse at **Allatoona** and tried to cross the Tennessee River at Decatur, Alabama, defended by General Robert S. Granger. Hood was driven off after some artillery fire and continued west to cross the river and occupy Florence before turning north towards **Columbia** (26–29 October 1864).

Decium I 533 I Vandal War in Africa
See **Ad Decimum**

Dee I 1308 I Rise of Robert the Bruce

While Robert the Bruce was campaigning in Argyle, his brother Edward marched into Galloway and, soon after victory at the **Cree**, attacked Sir Roland MacDougal of Galloway and Donald of the Isles on the banks of the Dee. The Lord of the Isles was routed and taken prisoner and Edward Bruce drove the native Irish Chiefs and their English allies out of Galloway (29 June 1308).

Dee I 1639 I 1st Bishops' War

Covenanters under James Graham Earl of Montrose opposed to Charles I's attempt to impose a new prayer book on Scotland advanced against Aberdeen and defeated James Gordon Viscount Aboyne at nearby **Megray Hill**. Days later, when Aboyne attempted to hold the Bridge on the Dee outside the city, he was driven off by heavy gunfire, although the war had already ended (18 June 1639).

Deeg I 1804 I 2nd British-Maratha War
See **Dieg**

Deep Bottom (1st) I 1864 I American Civil War (Eastern Theatre)

General Winfield Scott Hancock led a Union offensive to the southeast of Confederate Richmond, Virginia, crossing the James River to attack Confederate positions just north of Deep Bottom, defended by General Charles Field. Hancock secured initial success, but in the face of Confederate reinforcements he left a garrison at Deep Bottom and withdrew south (27–29 July 1864).

Deep Bottom (2nd) I 1864 I American Civil War (Eastern Theatre)

In a renewed Union offensive southeast of Confederate Richmond, Virginia, Generals Winfield S. Hancock and David B. Birney again crossed the James to support the Union garrison at Deep Bottom. After heavy fighting and almost 3,000 casualties, Hancock was once more driven off by Confederate General Charles Field and withdrew south, leaving his bridgehead (13–20 August 1864).

Deerfield I 1675 I King Philip's War

Amid a bitter war in colonial New England, Indians supporting Metacomet of the Wampanoag (King Philip) burned Deerfield, in western Massachusetts. Sent to recover the local harvest, Captain Thomas Lathrop was ambushed to the southwest and killed, along with almost all his 60 men (Bloody Brook Massacre) before Major Robert Treat arrived and drove the Indians off (18 September 1675).

Deerfield I 1704 I Queen Anne's War

In apparent retaliation for English attacks on Abnaki settlements, Major Jean-Baptiste Hertel de Rouville led 50 Canadians and 200 Indians in a night assault during a snowstorm on Deerfield in western Massachusetts. Of fewer than 300 residents, 54 were killed and 120 were captured, with 17 dying on the return to Canada. Hertel lost three killed and 20 wounded (28–29 February 1704).

Deganiya I 1948 I Israeli War of Independence

Syrian General Husni el Zaim advancing towards the Sea of Galilee seized the Israeli village of Zemach (18 May) then followed up a heavy artillery bombardment to attack the twin villages of Deganiya Alpha and Deganiya Beta. Facing a large Israeli counter-attack with artillery, the Syrians had to withdraw and never again attempted to attack south of the Sea of Galilee (20–23 May 1948).

Dego I 1796 I French Revolutionary Wars (1st Coalition)

Two days after defeat at **Montenotte**, west of Genoa, Austrian General Eugène von Argenteau withdrew to Dego, northwest of Savona, where he was defeated by part of the French army under General André Masséna. A hard-fought counter-attack by Baron Philip von Vukassovitch briefly regained the town until Napoleon Bonaparte arrived and Dego was recaptured (14–15 April 1796).

Deig I 1804 I 2nd British-Maratha War
See **Dieg**

Deining I 1796 I French Revolutionary Wars (1st Coalition)

While French General Jean-Baptise Jourdan advanced across the Rhine into Germany, Archduke Charles Louis of Austria counter-attacked from the Danube and fell with massively superior forces on General Jean Baptiste Bernadotte at Deining, southeast of Nuremburg. Bernadotte was heavily repulsed and was beaten again next day at **Neumarkt** (22 August 1796).

Deir Yassin I 1948 I Israeli War of Independence

Fighting was continuing for **Kastel**, just west of Jerusalem, when guerrillas of the Irgun and Stern Gang attacked the nearby Palestinian village of Deir Yassin, overlooking the strategic road to Tel Aviv. After crushing minimal resistance, the Jews killed a large but hotly disputed number of civilians, creating one of the most controversial incidents in all Arab-Israeli conflict (9 April 1948).

Dekemhare I 1990–1991 I Eritrean War of Independence

As rebel forces advanced on Asmara, there was heavy fighting on the Gura Plain to the south around Dekemhare, where the Ethiopian government had established powerful defences (August–September 1990). A second offensive by Eritrean liberation forces saw a massive artillery and tank battle to take Dekemhare. Asmara fell a few days later to virtually end the war (19–21 May 1991).

De Klipdrift I 1902 I 2nd Anglo-Boer War
See **Tweebosch**

Delaware Capes I 1781 I War of the American Revolution
See **Chesapeake Capes**

Delhi I 1398 I Conquests of Tamerlane
The Turko-Mongol Tamerlane marched into northern India, where he joined his troops who had captured **Multan** in October. He then advanced on the capital and, outside Delhi, he overwhelmed the army of Sultan Mahmud II Tugluk. After executing perhaps 50–80,000 prisoners, the Mongol conqueror sacked Delhi before turning north with his booty towards **Meerut** (17 December 1398).

Delhi I 1556 I Mughal Conquest of Northern India
The Hindu General Hemu and his Afghan allies took advantage of the death of Mughal Emperor Humayun (24 January 1556) to capture Agra, then marched on Delhi. Outside the walls of the city, Hemu defeated the Mughal Governor Tardi Beg Khan, who fled to the new Emperor Akbar and was assassinated. Late in the year, Akbar recovered Delhi with his decisive victory at **Panipat**.

Delhi I 1737 I Later Mughal-Maratha Wars
Expanding his power in northern India, Maratha Peshwa Baji Rao I attacked Delhi, where he defeated Imperial commander Amir Khan before being forced to withdraw to face the advancing forces of Wazir Qamar-ud-din Khan. While Baji Rao was driven off to the southeast at Badshahpur, Emperor Muhammad Shah eventually made peace and ceded Malwa to the Peshwar (28 March 1737).

Delhi I 1739 I Persian Invasion of India
See **Karnal**

Delhi I 1757 I Indian Campaigns of Ahmad Shah
On his fourth invasion of northern India, Afghan General Ahmad Shah Durrani—having gained the Punjab and Multan in 1752 at **Lahore**—marched east and captured Delhi. The Mughal capital was sacked and subjected to terrible massacre and pillage before Durrani returned home with a vast treasure. His next invasion brought decisive victory in 1761 at **Panipat** (January 1757).

Delhi I 1803 I 2nd British-Maratha War
General Sir Gerard Lake marched into Hindustan with British regulars and native troops to capture **Aligarh**, then pursued the defeated Maratha army under French General Louis Bourquien northwest to Delhi, where Lake soon defeated a much superior force. With Delhi secured and Bourquien a prisoner, Lake then marched south against the fortress city of **Agra** (11 September 1803).

Delhi I 1804 I 2nd British-Maratha War
Encouraged by destroying **Monson's Retreat** in August, Maratha leader Jaswant Rao Holkar of Indore took a large force to besiege Delhi, captured by the British just a year earlier. A brilliant defence saw Colonel David Ochterlony's vastly outnumbered garrison repulse the Marathas for nine days, until General Sir Gerard Lake approached and Holkar withdrew (7 October–2 November 1804).

Delhi I 1857 I Indian Mutiny
When rebels seized Delhi as the mutiny started, General Sir Henry Barnard and later General Archdale Wilson blockaded the city, held by King Bahadur Shah and his commander Bakht Khan. Reinforced by General John Nicholson, there was a bloody assault (September 14) with heavy losses on both sides including Nicholson killed. The city fell six days later (8 June–20 September 1857).

Delisi I 1904 I Russo-Japanese War
Russian General Georg Karlovich Stackelberg advancing from Manchuria was halted 80 miles north of **Port Arthur** (modern Lüshun) by General Yasukata Oku's Second Army at Delisi (Telissu) near Wafangdian. Oku counterattacked in force and, as a result of indecision,

the Russians withdrew to avoid encirclement. They fell back through **Dashiqiao** with over 3,000 casualties (14–15 June 1904).

Delium ∎ 424 BC ∎ Great Peloponnesian War

On a two-pronged Athenian offensive into Boeotia, in conjunction with Demosthenes' failed advance on **Megara**, the main Athenian army under Hippocrates captured Delium on the east coast of Boeotia. In a terrible rout nearby however, Hippocrates was defeated and killed by Theban General Pagondas. Delium fell after a 16-day siege and the survivors fled south to Athens (November 424 BC).

Delville Wood ∎ 1916 ∎ World War I (Western Front)

As part of the Battle of the **Somme**, South Africans under General Henry Lukin attacked east from Longueval against Germans at Delville Wood. South Africa's heaviest fighting on the Western Front cost both sides high losses, but reinforcements eventually helped the Allies capture the shattered remains of the Wood. They soon attacked again at nearby **Guillemont** (15 July–3 September 1916).

Dembeguina ∎ 1935 ∎ 2nd Italo-Ethiopian War

While Ethiopians tried to encircle Makale, Ras Imru attacked the pass at Dembeguina, west of Aksum, held by Major Luigi Criniti with an Italian-Askari force. Criniti was driven out and lost all his nine light tanks before Ras Imru was checked by the war's first use of mustard gas. The "Christmas Offensive" was finally halted and the Italians soon struck back in the **Tembien** (15–17 December 1935).

Demetritsa ∎ 1185 ∎ 2nd Byzantine-Sicilian War

Leading a fresh offensive against the Byzantine Empire, William II—the Good—of Sicily was defeated west of Constantinople at the **Strymon** (7 September) before his fleet was attacked off Greece near Demetritsa by Admiral-General Alexius Branas. The Normans were decisively defeated, checking their offensive. A few years later Norman Sicily was seized by Germans (7 November 1185).

Denain ∎ 1712 ∎ War of the Spanish Succession

When peace talks failed, Prince Eugène of Savoy led Austro-Dutch troops to the Netherlands, where part of his force under Arnold van Keppel Earl of Albermarle was attacked by Marshal Claude Villars at Denain, near Valenciennes. Before Eugène could intervene the Dutch were destroyed. It was the last major battle of the war and strengthened France in ensuing peace negotiations (24 July 1712).

Denia ∎ 1707 ∎ War of the Spanish Succession

Following French victory at **Almanza** in April, French forces under Irish General Daniel Mahony (later Claude-Francois Bidal Chevalier d'Asfeld) besieged Denia, held by Juan Bautista Basset y Ramos. After repeated assaults, Denia was reinforced by British naval Captain James Moodie and the French withdrew. The city eventually capitulated to d'Asfeld in November 1708 (June 1707).

Denmark Strait ∎ 1941 ∎ World War II (War at Sea)

See **Bismarck**

Dennewitz ∎ 1813 ∎ Napoleonic Wars (War of Liberation)

In the wake of defeat at **Dresden**, the Allies resumed their policy of attacking Napoleon Bonaparte's lieutenants. Marshal Michel Ney's attempt to march on Berlin was met southwest at Dennewitz by Swedes under former French Marshal Jean Baptiste Bernadotte and General Friedrich von Bulow's Prussians. Ney's Saxons fled and he lost heavily in men and guns (6 September 1813).

Denpasar ∎ 1906 ∎ Dutch Conquest of Bali

Dutch forces conquered northern Bali at **Jagaraga** (1849) and **Cakranegara** (1894), then used looting of a shipwreck in 1904 to justify attacking Badung in the south. They shelled Denpasar, where about 4,000 Balinese soldiers and civilians died in a ritual suicide battle (puputan). The kingdoms of Tabanan and Klungkung also fell and Balinese independence was finally crushed (20 September 1906).

Deogiri ∎ 1294 ∎ Wars of the Delhi Sultanate

Marking the first major Muslim offensive in the Deccan, Muslim Prince Ala-ud-din (nephew of Sultan Jalal-ud-din of Delhi) led 10,000 men through the Gavilgad Hills towards Deogiri (later Daulatabad) near Aurangabad. There he utterly routed the army of King Ramchandra (Ramdev) of the Hindu Yadav Dynasty and his son Prince Shankar. Ala-ud-din then returned with a massive treasure.

Deogiri ∎ 1307 ∎ Wars of the Delhi Sultanate

Despite defeat in 1294, King Ramchandra (Ramdev) of Deogiri eventually refused to pay tribute to Sultan Ala-ud-din, who sent an expedition under Malik Kafur. The army of Deogiri was defeated and Ramchandra was taken to Delhi to pay homage, as well as his arrears and a peace offer claimed to include 700 elephants. He was pardoned and returned as a vassal King (March 1307).

Deogiri ∎ 1318 ∎ Wars of the Delhi Sultanate

Taking advantage of a disputed succession in Delhi following the death of Ala-ud-din, Gujarat and Deogiri rose in revolt. New Sultan Mubarak Shah sent troops to restore order in Gujarat and personally led a force into Deogiri, where Harpal had usurped his father-in-law Ramchandra and proclaimed independence. The rebel was defeated and fled, but was later captured, flayed and beheaded.

Deols ∎ 469 ∎ Goth Invasion of the Roman Empire

After murdering his brother Theodoric II, the new Visigoth ruler Euric campaigned against King Riothamus of the Bretons, who attempted to defend Roman Aquitaine. At Deols, on the Indre, south of Orleans near Chateauroux, Riothamus was heavily defeated and fled to the Burgundians. Euric was checked by the Roman-Frank Paulus, though in 471 he defeated an Imperial army near **Arles**.

Deorai ∎ 1659 ∎ War of the Mughal Princes

In bitter war between the sons of ailing Mughal Emperor Shahjahan, Dara Shikoh the eldest, defeated at **Samugargh** (May 1658), raised a new army against Aurangzeb, who had seized the throne. Taking a powerful position in the pass at Deorai, south of Ajmer, Dara was defeated and fled after three days of fighting. He was later captured and executed by his brother Aurangzeb (12–14 April 1659).

Deorham ∎ 577 ∎ Anglo-Saxon Conquest of Britain

King Ceawlin of the West Saxons resumed the advance west into Gloucestershire after victory at **Wibbandun** in 568 and he defeated and killed three British Kings—Conmail, Condidan and Fairnmail—at Deorham (modern Dyrham), just north of Bath. Ceawlin's decisive victory led directly to the capture of Gloucester, Cirencester and Bath, and divided the British forces in Wales and Cornwall.

Deothal ∎ 1815 ∎ British-Gurkha War
See **Malaon**

Deptford Strand ∎ 1497 ∎ Flammock's Rebellion
See **Blackheath**

Dera ∎ 1918 ∎ World War I (Middle East)

Advancing north along the Jordan Valley, the Arab army of Prince Faisal attacked the key railway junction city of Dera (in modern Jordan), though was driven off by the Turkish garrison. Reinforced by British ground and air forces, the Arabs attacked again and eventually secured the town as the Turks evacuated north towards **Damascus** (18–28 September 1918).

Derby ∎ 917 ∎ Viking Wars in Britain

Following the death of Aethelred of Mercia in 911, his widow Aethelflaed—the Lady of Mercia—ruled in peace for many years, then turned against the Danish Confederacy of the Five Boroughs and laid siege to Derby. When Derby fell by storm, Leicester and York acknowledged her rule. Aethelflaed then joined with her brother, Edward of Wessex, against the Danes of East Anglia.

Dermbach ∎ 1866 ∎ Seven Weeks War

See **Wiesenthal**

Derna ∎ 1805 ∎ Tripolitan War

Six months after failing to destroy the pirate fleet at **Tripoli**, American forces turned against Derna, 500 miles to the west, attacked from the sea and by a land force from Alexandria under Captain William Eaton, Marine Lieutenant Preston O'Bannon and deposed Tripolitan ruler Hamet Karamanli. With Derna taken by storm, Peshwa Yusuf Karamanli sued for peace, ending the war (25 April 1805).

Derna ∎ 1912 ∎ Italo-Turkish War

In fighting around Derna, in eastern Libya, Italian General Tomasso Salsa drove off attacks by Turkish commander Enver Bey (10 February and 3 March), then received reinforcements and led a large-scale counter-offensive. Italian machine-guns and artillery inflicted terrible Turko-Arab losses and Enver Bey withdrew after three days. Peace was signed a month later (14–17 September 1912).

Derry ∎ 1600 ∎ Tyrone Rebellion

Sir Henry Docwra was sent from England to suppress Hugh O'Neill Earl of Tyrone and he held a strongly entrenched position at Derry (later Londonderry) against attacks by Gaill Narv (29 July) and O'Neill's cousin Hugh Roe O'Donnell (16 September). However, when Narv went over to the English, O'Donnell raised the siege and marched to aid the rebels at **Kinsale** (May–September 1600).

Dertosa ∎ 215 BC ∎ 2nd Punic War

See **Ibera**

Descarga ∎ 1835 ∎ 1st Carlist War

Soon after a Spanish Liberal government force marching to relieve the Carlist siege of **Villafranca de Oria** was repulsed at **Larrainzar**, a second much larger force under General Baldomero Espartero was attacked in camp at Descarga, just east of Vergara, by Carlist General Juan Benito Eraso. Espartero lost almost 2,000 men captured and Villafranca fell next day (2 June 1835).

Deschutes ∎ 1848 ∎ Cayuse Indian War

Colonel Cornelius Gilliam, marching east from Vancouver after Cayuse who had murdered Dr **Whitman** in November 1847, met an Indian force at the mouth of the Deschutes on the Washington-Oregon border. Major Henry Lee was repulsed in a skirmish, but next day, Gilliam's force pursued and beat the Indians, killing more than 20, then won again at the **Willow** (29–30 January 1848).

Desert Storm ∎ 1991 ∎ 1st Gulf War

Responding to Iraq's invasion of Kuwait, coalition General Norman Schwarzkopf determined not just to liberate Kuwait but to destroy the Iraqi army. Desert Storm saw a huge air campaign against **Baghdad**, victories at **Khafji** and **Bubiyan**, and a 100-hour ground offensive with victories such as **As-Salman, Wadi al-Batin** and **Kuwait** forced Iraq to make peace (17 January–28 February 1991).

Deskarti ∎ 1946 ∎ Greek Civil War

During a Communist offensive in Macedonia, one of the largest actions was at Deskarti, southeast of Grevena, where 1,500 well-armed insurgents attacked and seized the town. After five days of heavy fighting, government forces retook Deskarti. Martial law was then declared throughout northern Greece as the Communist offensive resumed at **Naoussa** (21–26 September 1946).

Despenaperros ∎ 1810 ∎ Napoleonic Wars (Peninsular Campaign)

See **La Carolina**

Dessau I 1626 I Thirty Years War (Saxon-Danish War)

When Christian IV of Denmark intervened in Germany, Protestant commander Count Ernst von Mansfeld attempted to cross the Elbe to join the Danes. Attacking the Catholic bridgehead north of Leipzig at Dessau, Mansfeld was utterly defeated by Imperial General Albrecht von Wallenstein, losing much of his army and withdrew into Silesia. Mansfeld died a few months later (25 April 1626).

Dessie I 1941 I World War II (Northern Africa)

With Ethiopia's capital **Addis Ababa** taken (6 April), South African Brigadier Dan Pienaar drove north against strong Italian defences at Combolchia Pass, outside Dessie. Very hard fighting saw Italy's accurate artillery eventually overcome and over 8,000 prisoners were captured, along with huge quantities of guns and vehicles. The survivors fled north towards **Amba Alagi** (17–22 April 1941).

Detmold I 783 I Wars of Charlemagne

Defeated by Pagan Saxons at **Suntel Hill** in 782, Charlemagne, King of the Franks, sent a large force to suppress the rebellion of Chief Widikund. The Saxons were beaten at Detmold in northern Germany and again a few days later, on the River Haase near Osnabruk. Intermittent fighting continued for several years before Widikund surrendered and accepted Christianity.

Detroit I 1763–1764 I Pontiac's War

The great Ottawa Chief Pontiac turned on his former British allies and led a surprise attack on Major Henry Gladwin at Fort Detroit. Despite initial failure, he established a siege and routed a British patrol at nearby **Bloody Run**. Though he eventually withdrew (28 November), the fort remained under loose blockade until finally relieved by Colonel John Bradstreet (7 May 1763–August 1764).

Detroit I 1812 I War of 1812

While withdrawing from a failed advance into Canada, American General William Hull was blockaded at Detroit by British regulars and militia under General Isaac Brock and Indians led by Tecumseh. After American defeats at **Brownstown** and **Magagua**, Hull disgracefully surrendered the fort. The British abandoned it in September 1813 following defeat on **Lake Erie** (16 August 1812).

Dettingen I 1743 I War of the Austrian Succession

George II of England and John Dalrymple Earl of Stair marching up the Rhine at the head of the Anglo-Hanoverian-Hessian "Pragmatic Army" were trapped on the Main at Dettingen by French Marshal Adrien de Noailles and his nephew Louis Comte de Gramont. A hard-fought action saw Gramont's line broken and the defeated French fell back behind the Rhine (27 June 1743).

Deutschbrod I 1422 I Hussite Wars

See **Nemecky Brod**

Devagiri I 1294 I Wars of the Delhi Sultanate

See **Deogiri**

Devernaki I 1822 I Greek War of Independence

Dramali (Mohamet Ali Pasha) advanced into eastern Peloponnesia and was repulsed at **Nauplia**. He then withdrew through the pass at Devernaki, where he was attacked by Nikitas Nikitaras and suffered terrible losses. The disastrous expedition cost 17,000 Turkish dead (including Dramali) out of 23,000, before the survivors were finally evacuated from Corinth (8 August 1822).

Devikota I 1749 I 2nd Carnatic War

Attempting to help deposed Raja Sauhojee of Tanjore against the French-appointed Raja Partab Singh, British forces failed to capture Devikota at the mouth of the Coleroon River in southeast India. Major Stringer Lawrence was then sent and, after a rash attack by Captain Robert Clive, Devikota was taken by assault.

Britain later abandoned Sauhojee in return for the fort (April 1749).

Devil's Backbone   I   1863   I   American Civil War (Trans-Mississippi)

After victory in July at **Honey Springs**, Oklahoma, Union General James G. Blunt entered western Arkansas, where he occupied Fort Smith, then sent Colonel William Cloud in pursuit of the retreating Confederates under General William L. Cabell. At nearby Devil's Backbone, close to Jenny Lind, Cabell ambushed Cloud, but was repulsed and had to continue withdrawing (1 September 1863).

Devil's Bridge   I   1799   I   French Revolutionary Wars (2nd Coalition)

As he crossed the Alps from Italy to aid General Alexander Korsakov in Switzerland, Russian General Alexander Suvorov repulsed General Claude Lecourbe at **Airolo**. Next day he met a desperate French defence of the Devil's Bridge over the Shöllenen Gorge on the Reuss. The French retreated after heavy losses on both sides and Suvorov advanced to the **Muottothal** (24 September 1799).

Devil's Hole   I   1763   I   Pontiac's War

During Ottawa Chief Pontiac's war against Britain, a supply train was ambushed near the Devil's Hole, at the foot of Niagara Falls, by Seneca Indians. Only a handful of the train and their escort escaped and, when two nearby companies of light infantry went to their aid, they too were ambushed. Most of the 60 men were killed, including all three subalterns (14 September 1763).

Devizes   I   1643   I   British Civil Wars
See **Roundway Down**

Dewangiri   I   1865   I   British-Bhutanese War

When Britain seized Assam, neighbouring Bhutan seized key mountain passes and refused to pay Britain tribute. A small British force was repulsed at Dewangiri, near Deothang, before Sir Henry Tombs led a second much larger force and recaptured Dewangiri after a brief campaign. Bhutan was forced to sue for peace and agreed to cede the passes in return for an annual subsidy from Britain.

Dhar   I   1857   I   Indian Mutiny

Mandasur rebels west of Indore occupied Dhar and Amjhera and, in response, Colonel Charles Stuart marched west from Mhow to Dhar, held mainly by Arab and Afghan mercenaries claiming allegiance to 13-year-old Rajah Anand Rao Puar of Dhar. Following a fierce action, Durand waited for siege guns. He then bombarded and stormed the fort but found it abandoned (22–31 October 1857).

Dharmat   I   1658   I   War of the Mughal Princes

Amid bitter war between the sons of the ailing Mughal Emperor Shahjahan, the younger brothers Aurangzeb and Murad Baksh united against an Imperial army led by Jaswant Singh, Rajput Raja of Marwar, in support of the eldest brother, Dara Shikoh. At Dharmat, near Ujjain, the Rajputs were heavily defeated and the rebels advanced for decisive battle in late May at **Samugargh** (15 April 1658).

Dharmkot   I   1846   I   1st British-Sikh War

When a large Sikh army crossed the Sutlej into British East Punjab to gather supplies, an Anglo-Indian force under Sir Harry Smith was sent against them at Dharmkot, between Ludhiana and Ferozepur. Smith captured the small fortress, with its massive supply of grain, though he was defeated a few days later at **Baddowal** as he marched east towards Ludhiana (18 January 1846).

Dhat al-Sawari   I   654   I   Early Byzantine-Muslim Wars
See **Mount Phoenix**

Dhodap   I   1768   I   Maratha Wars of Succession

Renewing war against Maratha Peshwa Madhav Rao after earlier victory at **Alegaon** (1762), his ambitious uncle Raghunath Rao challenged the Peshwa and found himself under attack at the hill fortress of Dhodap, northeast of Bombay near Nashik. Raghunath was defeated and imprisoned after a decisive action, but he later became Peshwa after murdering Madhav Rao's successor (10 June 1768).

Dhu al Quassa ■ 632 ■ Muslim Civil Wars

Immediately following the death of the Prophet Mohammed, the new Caliph Abu Bekr faced rebellion by Bedouin of the Abs and Dhobian tribes. The new Caliph dispersed the tribesmen in a surprise raid on the rebel camp at Dhu al Quassa, northeast of Medina. A second raid a month later a little further east utterly routed the dissidents and established the Caliph's authority (August 632).

Dhu-Kar ■ 610 ■ Persian-Arab Wars
See **Dhu-Qar**

Dhu-Qar ■ 610 ■ Persian-Arab Wars

Shah Chosroes II of Persia abolished the buffer Arab kingdom of Hira (between the lower Euphrates and northern Arabia) and executed its last king, provoking an incursion by the Bedouin of the Bakr ibn Wail. At Dhu-Qar the powerful sub-tribe of Bani Shaiban inflicted a heavy defeat on the Persian army, later greatly exaggerated as the first Arab victory over Persia.

Diamond Hill ■ 1900 ■ 2nd Anglo-Boer War

Shortly after capturing Pretoria (5 June), British commander Lord Frederick Roberts took 17,000 men and 70 guns against a strongly entrenched Boer position under General Louis Botha, ten miles to the east at Diamond Hill. After inflicting over 160 British casualties, Botha had to withdraw, although the action was seen by the Boers as showing that they could fight back (11–12 June 1900).

Diao Yu ■ 1258 ■ Mongol Conquest of China

In a large-scale assault on Song southern China, the Mongol Khan Mongke, a grandson of Genghis Khan, captured Chengdu, then besieged Song General Wang Jian at Diao Yu fortress, near modern Hechuan in central Sichuan. After

four months, Mongke's last assault was repulsed and he died soon afterwards. The war was then suspended until resumed by his brother Kubilai (May–August 1258).

Dibra ■ 1448 ■ Albanian-Turkish Wars

Ottoman Sultan Murad II invaded Albania to capture **Svetigrad**, then advanced against Dibra (modern Debar), northeast of Tirana. Albanian commander George Kastriote Skanderbeg broke off his siege of **Danj** and marched to meet the Turks, inflicting a very costly defeat. The Turks soon had to withdraw, lifting their siege of **Krujë**, to meet a Hungarian army at **Kossovo** (October 1448).

Didymoteichon ■ 1352 ■ Byzantine-Ottoman Wars

In the war between rival Byzantine Emperors, John V Palaeologus sought aid from Stephan Dushan of Serbia, while John VI Cantacuzenus was sent an Ottoman army under Suleyman Pasha, son of the Sultan Orchan. A decisive battle in Thrace at Didymoteichon, south of **Adrianople**, saw the Serbians under Borilovic routed. Cantacuzenus deposed Palaeologus and enthroned his son Mathew.

Diedenhofen ■ 1643 ■ Thirty Years War (Franco-Habsburg War)
See **Thionville**

Dieg (1st) ■ 1804 ■ 2nd British-Maratha War

Following the repulse of Maharaja Jaswant Rao Holkar at **Delhi**, British commander General Sir Gerard Lake sent General John Henry Fraser south against the mountain fortress of Dieg, where he soon met a massive Maratha army. When Fraser was fatally wounded, Colonel William Monson managed to scatter the Marathas. A month later Lake arrived with his siege train (14 November 1804).

Dieg (2nd) ■ 1804 ■ 2nd British-Maratha War

With Maharaja Jaswant Rao Holkar of Indore defeated at **Farrukhabab**, British commander

General Sir Gerard Lake took his siege train west against the fortress of Dieg, where a hard-fought battle had been won a month earlier. The garrison fled following a massive bombardment and Lake turned his attention to the remaining fortress at **Bharatpur** (1–13 December 1804).

Diégo Suarez ▮ 1942 ▮ World War II (Indian Ocean)

See **Madagascar**

Dien Bien Phu ▮ 1953–1954 ▮ French Indo-China War

To break Viet Minh control in northern Vietnam, French General Henri Navarre determined to hold the remote camp at Dien Bien Phu. Against all odds, General Vo Nguyen Giap moved heavy guns to the surrounding hills to lay siege. After massive bombardment and brutal hand-to-hand fighting 10,000 French surrendered, ending French rule in Indo-China (20 November 1953–7 May 1954).

Dieppe ▮ 1942 ▮ World War II (Western Europe)

Determined to demonstrate an Allied offensive in the west, over 6,000 Anglo-Canadian troops under Task Force commander General John Roberts attacked the well-defended French port of Dieppe. Over 3,500 were killed or captured, plus heavy losses in tanks, ships and aircraft. The disaster was later claimed to have provided valuable experience for subsequent landings in **Normandy** (19 August 1942).

Diersheim ▮ 1797 ▮ French Revolutionary Wars (1st Coalition)

After French victory on the lower Rhine at **Neuwied**, upstream beyond Strasbourg Generals Jean Moreau and Dominique Vandamme crossed the river before dawn and advanced under deadly Austrian fire towards Diersheim. A powerful counter-attack by Count Anton Sztaray that afternoon was repulsed with heavy losses on both sides, before an armistice halted further operations (21 April 1797).

Dig ▮ 1804 ▮ 2nd British-Maratha War

See **Dieg**

Dijon ▮ 500 ▮ Burgundian-Frankish War

Clovis, King of the Salian Franks, determined to launch a campaign against King Gundobad of Burgundy and enlisted the aid of Gundobad's brother, the Prince Godigisel. On the River Ouche at Dijon, Gundobad was heavily defeated by the Franks and his treacherous brother. Gundobad was then pursued down the Rhone to **Avignon** where he held out against a long siege.

Dijon (1st) ▮ 1870 ▮ Franco-Prussian War

With the French defeated near Besançon at **Chatillon-le-Duc**, German commander Karl August Werder marched west through **Gray** and sent General Gustav von Beyer probing towards the key city of Dijon. Following unexpectedly hard fighting at nearby St Apolinaire, Beyer bombarded Dijon into capitulation, though it was abandoned by the Germans after only a month (30 October 1870).

Dijon (2nd) ▮ 1870 ▮ Franco-Prussian War

Italian Liberator Giuseppe Garibaldi intervened to support France and followed a modest victory at **Chatillon-sur-Seine** with a rash attack on Dijon. After two days of fighting to the northwest near Pasques, Garibaldi's inadequate force was repulsed by General Karl August von Werder, who pursued Garibaldi back to Auton. The Germans later abandoned Dijon (26–27 November 1870).

Dijon ▮ 1871 ▮ Franco-Prussian War

After occupying Dijon following German withdrawal (28 December 1870), Italian Liberator Giuseppe Garibaldi, commanding the Army of the Vosges, was attacked by 4,000 men from General Edwin von Manteuffel's army under General Karl von Kettler. The Germans withdrew after three days of very heavy fighting and Garibaldi held the city until armistice a week later (21–23 January 1871).

Dilam ▮ 1902 ▮ Saudi-Rashidi Wars

Responding to the fall of **Riyadh** in January and the killing of its Rashidi Governor, Abd al-Aziz ibn Rashid marched south from Hail against the upstart Abd al-Aziz (Ibn Saud). Unwisely attacking Saudi and Kuwaiti forces in a strongly defended position at Dilam, 50 miles south of Riyadh, Ibn Rashid suffered heavy losses and withdrew. In June 1904 he advanced on **Unayzah** (November 1902).

Dimale ∎ **219** BC ∎ **2nd Illyrian War**
Demetrius of Pharos, the ruler of Illyria, began to threaten Roman territory and a massive land and naval force under Consuls Aemilius Paullus and Livius Salinator attacked his heavily fortified city of Dimale on the Illyrian mainland. The supposedly impregnable defences were breached after just seven days. The Romans then quickly stormed the island capital of Pharos (Lesina) and Demetrius fled.

Dinant ∎ **1466** ∎ **Franco-Burgundian Wars**
A year after crushing rebellion in Liège at **Montenaeken**, Philip Duke of Burgundy resolved to impose his will on rebellious Dinant, in the southeast of modern Belgium, and sent his son Charles the Bold. After besieging the city, Charles took it by storm, razed the walls and destroyed the citadel. A claimed 800 male prisoners were tied back to back and thrown into the Meuse (24–27 August 1466).

Dindori ∎ **1670** ∎ **Mughal-Maratha Wars**
When the great Maratha Shivaji sacked the Mughal city of **Surat**, General Daud Khan was sent to cut off his withdrawal to the southeast. Shivaji detached part of his force as a rearguard and Daud Khan was heavily defeated in the Chandvad range near Dindori, north of Deolali. Emperor Aurangzeb then sent a much larger army against the Maratha fortress of **Salher** (16–17 October 1670).

Dinghai ∎ **1840** ∎ **1st Opium War**
British Admiral Sir George Elliot arrived with a fresh fleet to reinforce the locals after victory at **Chuanbi** (November 1939) and sailed against Dinghai, on Zhoushan Island off the Yangzi, held by Zhang Chaofa. War junks were destroyed and Dinghai was bombarded and stormed by General George Burrell. A brief

truce followed and Britain withdrew but later had to retake the island (5 July 1840).

Dinghai ∎ **1841** ∎ **1st Opium War**
Leading a force northeast from Hong Kong, British Superintendent Sir Henry Pottinger, with General Sir Hugh Gough and Admiral Sir William Parker, captured **Xiamen**, then attacked Dinghai (Tinghai), on Zhoushan Island off the Yangzi. Chinese General Keo was defeated and killed after a courageous defence and the British attacked nearby **Zhenhai** (29 September–1 October 1841).

Dingjun ∎ **219** ∎ **Wars of the Three Kingdoms**
After defeating Cao Cao at **Red Cliffs** (208), the warlord Liu Bei consolidated power in southern China, then led a large army into disputed Hanzhou. In battle at Dingjun Mountain, Liu Bei's General, Huang Zhong, routed Cao Cao's vanguard and killed commander Xichou Yuan. Liu Bei secured Hanzhou and, a few months later, his ally Guan Yu attacked Cao Cao's forces at **Fancheng**.

Dinwiddie Court House ∎ **1865** ∎ **American Civil War (Eastern Theatre)**
With Union forces attacking his defences southwest of **Petersburg**, Virginia, Confederate commander Robert E. Lee sent Generals George Pickett and Fitzhugh Lee to block General Philip Sheridan at Dinwiddie Court House. Fighting in heavy mud, Pickett repulsed Sheridan's advance, but he was decisively beaten the following day to the northwest at **Five Forks** (31 March 1865).

Dipaea ∎ **471** BC ∎ **Arcadian War**
Following defeat at **Tegea**, the cities of Arcadia, in the mountainous central Peloponnese (except for Mantinea), joined forces against Sparta. With Argos apparently absent, Tegea and her allies were decisively beaten at Dipaea by disciplined Spartan Hoplites. The victory enabled Sparta to strengthen her grip on the Peloponnese and she soon turned west to secure Messenia (uncertain date c 471 BC).

Dire Dawa ▌ 1977–1978 ▌ Ogaden War

As the Somali army invaded Ethiopia's northern Ogaden in support of separatist rebels, an armoured force advanced on Dire Dawa, where repeated attacks were driven off with costly losses in men and tanks. The Somalis then turned their attention south to **Jijiga**, but Dire Dawa remained under virtual siege until relieved by a massive Soviet-led counter-offensive (August 1977–February 1978).

Dirnstein ▌ 1805 ▌ Napoleonic Wars (3rd Coalition)
See **Durrenstein**

Dirschau ▌ 1627 ▌ 2nd Polish-Swedish War
See **Tczew**

Distomo ▌ 1827 ▌ Greek War of Independence

To support Greek forces besieged at the **Acropolis**, Georgios Karaiskakis attacked Ottoman supply lines in the mountains west of Levadia. After victory at **Arachova** (December 1926) he attacked and defeated Omer Pasha of Negroponte to the southwest near Distomo and captured valuable baggage and artillery. Karaiskakis was killed in May near the Acropolis at **Analatos** (12 February 1827).

Ditmarschen ▌ 1500 ▌ Wars of the Kalmar Union
See **Hemmingstedt**

Diu ▌ 1509 ▌ Early Portuguese Colonial Wars in Asia

When Portugal seized **Cochin** in southern India, the deposed Raja sought aid from the Mamluk Sultan of Egypt, who sent a fleet advised by Venetians resentful of Portuguese interference. Off Diu, in the northwest, the allies were routed by Viceroy Francisco de Almeida, whose son had been killed at **Chaul**. Almeida then sacked Diu, which later became a Portuguese colony (3 February 1509).

Diu ▌ 1538–1539 ▌ Portuguese Colonial Wars in Asia

The Portuguese island colony of Diu, off northwest India, was attacked by a vastly superior force of Ottoman ships under Khedim Suleiman Pasha of Egypt and troops of Gujarati Sultan Bahadur Shah, led by Khadjar Safar. Defended by Sultan Muhammad Zaman Mirza and Antonio de Silveira, the three-month siege ended on reports of the Portuguese Viceroy approaching (25 February 1539).

Diu ▌ 1546 ▌ Portuguese Colonial Wars in Asia

Following a failed siege in 1538, the Portuguese island colony of Diu, off northwest India, was again besieged by Gujarati General Khadjar Safar. Defended by John de Mascarenhas, the fortress held out against seven months of starvation and assault and Safar was killed. A Portuguese fleet under Viceroy Juan de Castro eventually appeared and routed the Muslims (20 April–11 November 1546).

Djalula ▌ 637 ▌ Muslim Conquest of Iraq
See **Jalula**

Djerba ▌ 1560 ▌ Turkish-Habsburg Wars

Having lost **Tripoli** to Ottoman forces in 1551, Phillip II of Spain sent Juan Duke of Medinaceli, who captured the nearby island of Djerba (7 March 1560). The Christian fleet was soon destroyed at anchor by Admiral Pyale Pasha and the Corsair Turghud Re'is (11 May). The 5,000-strong garrison under Alvaro de Sande at Burdj al-Kabir was then besieged and captured (16 May–31 July 1560).

Djiddah ▌ 1916 ▌ World War I (Middle East)
See **Jeddah**

Djiddah ▌ 1925 ▌ Saudi-Hashemite Wars
See **Medina, Saudi Arabia**

Djidjelli I 1664 I North African War of Louis XIV
See **Jijelli**

Djorf I 1908 I French Colonial Wars in North Africa
After victory in May at **Bou Denib**, just inside Morocco's Algerian border, Major Jules Fesch's garrison came under attack by Moroccans until relieved by General César Alix and 4,000 men, who then assailed the siege force on the nearby Plain of Djorf. The Moroccans suffered severe losses to French artillery and machine-guns and the border area was largely secured (7 September 1908).

Djunis I 1876 I Serbo-Turkish War
Resuming war after a brief armistice, the Serb army under Colonel Djura Horvatovic and Russian General Mikhail Chernyayev attacked Turkish commander Abdul Kerim between Djunis and **Alexinatz**, southeast of Belgrade. The Turks took Alexinatz after very heavy fighting around Djunis and were threatening Belgrade when Russia intervened to enforce an armistice (29 October 1876).

Dnieper I 1788 I Catherine the Great's 2nd Turkish War
See **Liman**

Dnieper I 1943 I World War II (Eastern Front)
Having blunted the German offensive at **Kursk** and counter-attacked at **Orel** and **Kharkov**, Russian forces advanced on a broad front towards the German "eastern rampart" on the Dnieper. In the north the offensive secured **Smolensk**, in the centre it took **Kiev** and **Zhitomir** and in the south the Russians advanced through **Melitopol** to seal off the Crimea (7 August–31 December 1943).

Dniester I 1769 I Catherine the Great's 1st Turkish War
The invading Russian army under General Pyotr Rumyantsev secured victory at **Khotin**, then marched down the Dniester and set up camp, where they were subjected to a large-scale assault by Turkish Grand Vizier Moldovani Ali Pasha. The Turks were repulsed with heavy losses, after which Rumyantsev proceeded to capture Jassy and occupy Moldavia and Wallachia (9 September 1769).

Dobromierz I 1745 I War of the Austrian Succession
See **Hohenfriedberg**

Dobro Polje I 1918 I World War I (Balkan Front)
At the start of the Allies' Salonika offensive on the **Vardar**, Serbian Generals Petar Bojovic and Stepa Stepanovic smashed into the Bulgarians around Dobro Polje in mountains east of Bitola. Their brilliant victory secured a decisive breakthrough and Franco-Serb forces stormed into Bulgaria, which surrendered on 4 November after the fall of Nish and Belgrade (15 September 1918).

Dobrynitchi I 1605 I Russian Time of Troubles
A Polish-supported pretender claiming to be Dimitri—murdered son of former Tsar Ivan IV—invaded the Ukraine and, after victory at **Novgorod Seversk** (November 1604), attacked Tsarist leaders Fedor Mstislavski and Basil Shuiski at Dobrynitchi. The "First False Dimitri" was beaten, though with Cossack support eventually usurped the throne. He was later overthrown by Shuiski (21 January 1605).

Dodecanese Islands I 1943 I World War II (Southern Europe)
When Italy surrendered (8 September 1943), British forces seized several small islands of the Dodecanese, while the Germans held Rhodes. Churchill's doomed attempt to secure Aegean sea lanes ended in disaster when German airborne and amphibious attacks overwhelmed **Kos** (5–6 October) and a second larger assault took **Leros** after some very heavy fighting (12–16 November 1943).

Dodowa ▌ 1826 ▌ 1st British-Ashanti War

Reinforced by local auxiliaries, British troops in Gold Coast under Colonel Edward Purdon marched against the Ashanti, who had killed General Charles McCarthy two years earlier at **Bonsaso**, then threatened coastal tribes under British protection. On the Plain of Accra, just south of Dodowa, the Ashantene Obei Yaw was defeated and the hostile advance was repulsed (7 August 1826).

Doffingen ▌ 1388 ▌ German Towns War

Ten years after winning privileges at **Reutlingen**, the South German cities of the Swabian League renewed resistance against King Wenceslas. At Doffingen, near Stuttgart, their mercenary army was defeated by German Princes led by Eberhard of Württemberg. The Diet of Eger in 1389 dissolved the city leagues and princely privilege was gradually restored (28 August 1388).

Dogali ▌ 1887 ▌ 1st Italo-Ethiopian War

After Italian forces invaded Ethiopia's Eritrea Province against King Yohannes IV, Abyssinian commander Ras Alula besieged the Italian border post at Saati (24 January 1887). When a reinforcement of 500 troops was sent from Monkulla under Colonel Tommaso de Cristoforis, the Italians were ambushed and routed at Dogali, ten miles west of Massawa (26 January 1887).

Dogba ▌ 1892 ▌ 2nd Franco-Dahomean War

When King Behanzin of Dahomey (modern Benin) contested French occupation of **Cotonou**, war resumed and Colonel Alfred Dodds advanced inland with over 2,000 men towards Dogba, where the Dahomeans attacked. Dodds suffered heavy losses (including Colonel Marius-Paul Faurax killed) before his enemy were repulsed. He then continued on towards **Abomey** (19 September 1892).

Dogger Bank ▌ 1781 ▌ War of the American Revolution

British Admiral Hyde Parker was escorting a convoy from the Baltic when he met a Dutch convoy under Admiral Johann Zoutmann near the Dogger Bank in the North Sea. Both sides suffered heavy losses in a hard-fought but indecisive action before Parker drove the Dutch back to port. Parker blamed his incomplete victory on poorly equipped ships and resigned his commission (5 August 1781).

Dogger Bank ▌ 1904 ▌ Russo-Japanese War

As the Russian Baltic Fleet crossed the North Sea on its way to destiny off Japan at **Tsushima**, they mistakenly opened fire on the Hull fishing fleet on the Dogger Bank, sinking the trawler *Crane* and damaging several others. The incident threatened war with Britain and was settled only after the Tsar apologised and Russia paid 65,000 pounds compensation (21–22 October 1904).

Dogger Bank ▌ 1915 ▌ World War I (War at Sea)

Buoyed by success against **Scarborough**, German Admiral Fritz von Hipper led his battle fleet into the North Sea and was intercepted on Dogger Bank by Admiral Sir David Beatty, who sank one German battle-cruiser and severely damaged two others. However, after heavy damage to Beatty's own flagship, his deputy Admiral Archibald Moore allowed the Germans to escape (24 January 1915).

Dogoran ▌ 1097 ▌ 1st Crusade
See **Dorylaeum**

Dog's Field ▌ 1109 ▌ Polish-German Wars
See **Psie Pole**

Doiran ▌ 1917 ▌ World War I (Balkan Front)

While Franco-Serb forces attempted to advance into Macedonia around **Lake Prespa**, British General George Milne attacked north from Salonika towards Bulgarian positions near Doiran. The poorly co-ordinated attacks stalled and the front stabilised again until a fresh advance towards Doiran in 1918 as part of the successful offensive on the **Vardar** (24–25 April & 8–9 May 1917).

**Doiran I 1918 I World War I
(Balkan Front)**

As part of the great Allied offensive north from Salonika, British forces under General George Milne advanced against strong Bulgarian positions near Doiran. Milne was repulsed with almost 4,000 men lost in a frontal assault, though Franco-Serb victory further west on the **Vardar** forced the Bulgarians to withdraw and the British joined the pursuit (18–19 September 1918).

**Dol-de-Bretagne I 1793 I French
Revolutionary Wars (Vendée War)**

Royalist rebel Henri de la Rochejaquelein was marching south through Normandy soon after his repulse at **Granville**, when Republican Generals Jean Antoine Rossignol and Jean-Baptiste Kléber attempted to cut him off near the towns of Antrain and Dol. A premature attack cost the Republicans victory at Dol and they were driven out of Antrain with very heavy losses (22–23 November 1793).

Dole I 1668 I War of Devolution

After Philip IV of Spain died, his son-in-law Louis XIV of France claimed Spanish territory for his wife Maria Theresa. Having conquered Flanders, the King and Louis II de Bourbon Prince of Condé invaded Franche-Comte. Besançon capitulated and Dole, southeast of Dijon, surrendered after a costly siege. The ensuing peace saw Louis retain Flanders but lose Franche-Comte (14 February 1668).

Dollar I 875 I Viking Wars in Britain

Thorstein the Red, son of Olaf, continued the Viking War against Scotland by decisively defeating Constantine I on the border of Perthshire and Fife at Dollar, near the River Devon. Threatened by English Northumbria, Constantine gave up half his kingdom to Thorstein. However, within less than a year, the Viking leader was killed in battle by native Chiefs supporting their true King.

**Dolni-Dubnik I 1877 I Russo-Turkish
Wars**

See **Plevna**

Dolores, Chile I 1879 I War of the Pacific
See **San Francisco**

Dolores, Chile I 1891 I Chilean Civil War
See **San Francisco**

**Dolores, Mexico I 1810 I Mexican Wars of
Independence**

When the militant Mexican priest Miguel Hidalgo preached resistance to Spain, his followers seized the town and prison at Dolores (modern Dolores Hidalgo). Supported by his peasant army, Hidalgo then took San Miguel el Grande and Celaya without resistance before leading a bloody assault on **Guanajuato**, launching the first Mexican War of Independence (16 September 1810).

Domazlice I 1431 I Hussite Wars

In response to Hussite raids into eastern Germany, a huge new crusade invaded Bohemia under Frederick of Brandenburg. Southwest of Pilsen at Domazlice (German Taus) they were met by Prokob the Bald, supported by the Polish Hussite Sigismund Korybut. The Germans fled in disorder after only light fighting, reinforcing the need to negotiate with the heretics (14 August 1431).

**Dominica I 1761 I Seven Years War
(Caribbean)**

Following the conquest of French Canada, a British force of 26,000 men under Admiral Sir James Douglas and General Andrew Lord Rollo sailed against Dominica. After heavy naval gunfire destroyed the French positions, the island fell in just two days and Rollo went to support the attack on **Martinique**. At the war's end Britain retained possession of Dominica (7 June 1761).

**Dominica I 1778 I War of the
American Revolution**

Soon after France entered the war, French Admiral Francois-Claude de Bouillé at Martinique in the West Indies sailed with 2,000 men to nearby Dominica, where the 500-strong British garrison under Captain William Stewart was forced to surrender. Britain quickly responded by capturing **St Lucia**, south of Martinique, and regained the island at the war's end (8 September 1778).

Dominica I 1782 I War of the American Revolution

French Admiral Francois Comte de Grasse sailing from Martinique to join Spain against Jamaica was intercepted south of Dominica, where Rear Admiral Sir Samuel Hood (1724–1816) opened a long-range duel with Rear Admiral Louis Philippe Marquis de Vaudreuil. When Admiral George Rodney's main fleet came up, the French withdrew. Battle resumed three days later off the **Saints** (9 April 1782).

Dominica I 1805 I Napoleonic Wars (3rd Coalition)

The West Indian island of Dominica was awarded to Britain in 1763, though its possession remained disputed and, in 1805, five French warships under General Joseph Lagrange bombarded and took the capital, Roseau. However, Governor Sir George Prevost and his small garrison stubbornly fought on from a secondary position and the French eventually withdrew (22 February 1805).

Dominica I 1965 I Dominican Civil War
See **Santo Domingo**

Domitz I 1635 I Thirty Years War (Franco-Habsburg War)

John George of Saxony declared war on Sweden in Pomerania and advanced down the Elbe against Swedish General Johann Banér. In a mid-winter counter-offensive, Banér attacked across the Elbe at Domitz, northeast of Dannenberg, defeating a small Saxon force and opening way into Mecklenberg. The Saxons were beaten again in December at **Goldberg** and **Kyritz** (1 November 1635).

Domokos I 1897 I 1st Greco-Turkish War

Defeated in Thessaly at **Mati, Pharsalus** and **Velestino**, Crown Prince Constantine of Greece fell back on Domokos, north of Lamia, for a final stand against the victorious Ottoman army of Edhem Pasha. In a very large-scale action, the Turks were initially repulsed with heavy losses, but by nightfall, the defeated Greeks were forced to retreat and quickly ended their disastrous war (17 May 1897).

Domosdova I 1444 I Albanian-Turkish Wars

When an Ottoman army under Ali Pasha invaded Albania through Ohrid, they were met southeast of Elbasan on the plain of Tervol at Domosdova by an Albanian force under George Kastriote Skanderbeg. The Turks were heavily defeated in an unexpected reverse, encouraging King Ladislas of Poland to launch his fatal Crusade towards disaster at **Varna** (June 1444).

Domstadtl I 1758 I Seven Years War (Europe)

While Frederick II of Prussia besieged the Austrians at **Olmütz**, in eastern Bohemia, a Prussian supply convoy of 4,000 wagons tried to advance south from Niesse. After several attacks the convoy, claimed to be 40 miles long, was utterly destroyed at nearby Domstadtl by Austrian General Gideon von Loudon, aided by Croat auxiliaries. Frederick withdrew from Olmütz next day (30 June 1758).

Don I 1380 I Russian-Mongol Wars
See **Kulikovo**

Donabew I 1825 I 1st British-Burmese War
See **Danubyu**

Donaldsonville I 1862 I American Civil War (Lower Seaboard)

A few days after a failed Confederate advance on **Baton Rouge**, Louisiana, Union Admiral David G. Farragut attacked Donaldsonville, further down the Mississippi, which had fired on passing Union ships. After landing and exchanging fire with local Confederate patriots, Farragut persuaded the town leaders to halt attacks on Union shipping (9 August 1862).

Donaldsonville I 1863 I American Civil War (Lower Seaboard)

Confederate forces under General Thomas Green and Colonel James P. Major recovered from a repulse at **Lafourche Crossing**, in western Louisiana (21 June), then advanced on Donaldsonville, on the Mississippi, held by Major Joseph D. Bullen. Green retired after heavy fighting and over 300 Confederate casualties, but struck back two weeks later at nearby **Cox's Plantation** (28 June 1863).

Dona Maria I 1813 I Napoleonic Wars (Peninsular Campaign)

As the French army retreated during the week-long "Battles of the Pyrenees," General Sir Rowland Hill overtook Marshal Nicolas Soult's rearguard as it attempted to force the pass at Dona Maria. While the first British attack was repulsed, with General Sir William Stewart wounded, a second attack broke the French, though heavy fog hindered pursuit (31 July 1813).

Donauwörth I 1632 I Thirty Years War (Swedish War)

See **Rain**

Donauwörth I 1704 I War of the Spanish Succession

Advancing deep into Germany, Allied commander John Churchill Duke of Marlborough and Prince Louis of Baden attacked and defeated the army of Bavaria under Elector Maximilian Emanuel and Count Jean-Baptiste d'Arco on the Danube at the fortress of Schellenberg, outside Donauwörth. Marlborough then occupied Donauwörth and six weeks later won again at **Blenheim** (2 July 1704).

Don Basin I 1919 I Russian Civil War

Driven back from **Orel** (20 October), White commander Anton Denikin appointed Sergei Ulagai to defend the Don Basin (Donbas) against Generals Aleksandr Yegorov and Kliment Voroshilov. Ulagai's army lost 8,000 men in bloody fighting and retreated to **Rostov** and the Crimea as advancing Reds took key cities including Bakhmut, Popasnaya and Lugansk (25–31 December 1919).

Donegal Bay I 1798 I French Revolutionary Wars (Irish Rising)

In support of Irish Rebellion, Commodore Jean-Baptiste Bompart sailed for Lough Swilly with 3,000 troops in nine ships. However, in Donegal Bay, he was routed by British Admiral Sir John Borlase Warren. Only two French ships escaped and Irish rebel Wolfe Tone was captured in the flagship, *Hoche*. The French advance party had already surrendered at **Ballinamuck** (12 October 1798).

Donetz I 1943 I World War II (Eastern Front)

See **Kharkov (1st)**

Dong Ap Bia I 1969 I Vietnam War

Americans and South Vietnamese on a large-scale sweep into the A Shau Valley, southwest of Hue, attempted to capture the North Vietnamese fortified position on Mount Ap Bia. After repeated bloody assaults, the position was taken with terrible losses on both sides, raising intense American debate and virtually ending such costly search and destroy operations (10–20 May 1969).

Dong Bo Dau I 1258 I Mongol Wars of Kubilai Khan

See **Thang Long**

Dong-do I 1426–1427 I Sino-Vietnamese War

Ending his ten-year war against Chinese overlordship of Vietnam, Le Loi and General Nguyen Trai besieged Dong-do (later Thang Long and Hanoi), reinforced by Ming troops under Wang Tong. Defeated at nearby **Totdong**, and with reinforcements destroyed at **Chi Lang**, Wang Tong abandoned the city and China withdrew from Vietnam for the next 350 years (1426–December 1427).

Dong Ha I 1968 I Vietnam War

As the **Tet Offensive** wound down, up to 8,000 North Vietnamese regulars entered the A Shau Valley to attack the Dong Ha base and nearby Dai Do. Aided by air-strikes and artillery,

the outnumbered US Marines and South Vietnamese eventually repulsed the Communists
with over 1,000 killed, effectively ending the
threat of invasion across the DMZ until 1972 (29
April–15 May 1968).

Dong-Khé ▮ 1950 ▮ French Indo-China War

Encouraged by Communist victory in China,
Viet Minh under Vo Nguyen Giap attacked
French border fortresses in northern Vietnam,
where four battalions overwhelmed the 800-
strong garrison at Dong-Khé. The fortress was
retaken by French airborne troops at high cost
after two days, though was lost again four
months later in the Communist advance on **Cao-
Bang** (25–27 May 1950).

Dong Xoai ▮ 1965 ▮ Vietnam War

Following government failure at **Binh Gia**
and **Ba Gia**, about 1,500 Viet Cong attacked the
army base at Dong Xoai, 50 miles north of
Saigon. With heavy losses on both sides, the
Viet Cong were driven off by Allied air power
before government forces fled in the face of a
renewed attack, helping convince the US that
only major military intervention could save
South Vietnam (10–12 June 1965).

Donkerhoek ▮ 1900 ▮ 2nd Anglo-Boer War
See **Diamond Hill**

Doogaur ▮ 1780 ▮ 1st British-Maratha War

While British forces besieged **Bassein**, off
Bombay, Colonel James Hartley manoeuvred
against a Maratha relief army under Ramchandra
Ganesh. After a skirmish at Padaghe, Hartley
met a reported 20,000 Marathas northwest at
Doogaur, where Ganesh was fatally wounded.
Bassein fell following further fighting at Vaj-
reshwari and the Marathas withdrew (10–12
December 1780).

Doolittle Raid ▮ 1942 ▮ World War II (Pacific)

Determined to strike at the Japanese home-
land, 16 American B-25 bombers led by Colonel
James Doolittle took off from the carrier *Hornet*
and bombed Tokyo and other cities. With limited fuel, the crews bailed out or crash-landed in
China, with some captured and three executed.
The raid caused little material damage but
greatly affected both Japanese and American
morale (18 April 1942).

Doornkop ▮ 1896 ▮ Jameson's Raid
See **Krugersdorp**

Doornkop ▮ 1900 ▮ 2nd Anglo-Boer War

As General Lord Frederick Roberts advanced
on Johannesburg from the east through **Elandsfontein**, General Sir Ian Hamilton attacking from
the west was blocked at Doornkop by Jacobus de
la Rey and Ben Viljoen. Although Hamilton lost
300 men in a parade-ground frontal assault
against the ridge, the Boers withdrew and Johannesburg fell two days later (29 May 1900).

Doornkraal Farm ▮ 1900 ▮ 2nd Anglo-Boer War
See **Bothaville**

Dorchester Heights ▮ 1776 ▮ War of the American Revolution

During the siege of **Boston**, American General John Thomas attacked the Dorchester
Heights, on a peninsula, south of the harbour. In
a bold night assault with a large workparty and
wagon loads of materials, Thomas secured and
fortified the position. A snowstorm prevented a
British counter-attack and, within days, commander General William Howe decided to
evacuated Boston (4 March 1776).

Dormans ▮ 1575 ▮ 5th French War of Religion

Facing increasing Huguenot disorder, Henry
of Guise took a Catholic force against Henry of
Navarre and moderate French Catholics known
as Politiques. At Dormans, southwest of
Rheims, Guise intercepted and defeated German
Protestant reinforcements under John Casimir.
However, the newly crowned King Henry III
feared the Politiques and established a new
peace (10 October 1575).

Dornach I 1499 I Swabian War

In their final struggle for freedom, the Swiss cantons defeated the Habsburg Swabian League at **Frastenz** and **Calven** before Emperor Maximilian intervened a few months later and sent Count Henry of Furstenberg to besiege the castle of Dornach, south of Basel. Decisive defeat cost the Germans 3,000 killed, including Count Henry and war ended with virtual Swiss independence (22 July 1499).

Dorostalon I 971 I Byzantine-Russian Wars

Prince Sviatoslav of Kiev conquered Bulgaria, though he was repulsed by the Byzantine army at **Arcadiopolis** (970) and withdrew to the Danube, where he was beaten with terrible losses at Dorostalon by Emperor John Tzimisces. After a three-month siege, Sviatoslav was defeated again and sued for peace, but on the way home he was killed by Pecheneg Turks at the Dnieper (13 April–21 July 971).

Dorpat I 1603 I 1st Polish-Swedish War

After Swedish forces invaded and overran most of Livonia, they were defeated in March 1601 at **Kokenhausen** and new Polish commander Jan Karol Chodkiewicz gradually regained control. Attacking Dorpat (modern Tartu, Estonia)—which had been seized by the Swedes in December 1600—Chodkiewicz defeated General Arvid Stalarm and won again in 1609 at **Weissenstein** (13 April 1603).

Dorpat I 1625 I 2nd Polish-Swedish War

Gustavus Adolphus of Sweden resumed war against Poland in Livonia, where he captured Kokenhausen and Selburg, while further north in eastern Estonia, his forces under Gustavus Horn and Jakob de la Gardie besieged the key Catholic city of Dorpat (modern Tartu) on the Ema River. With the fall of Dorpat, Adolphus was able to turn south towards **Wallhof** (16 August 1625).

Dorpat I 1702 I 2nd "Great" Northern War

See **Erestfer**

Dorpat I 1704 I 2nd "Great" Northern War

On a fresh spring offensive through Ingria, Tsar Peter I sent Russian forces to besiege the powerful Swedish fortresses of **Narva** and Dorpat (modern Tartu) in eastern Estonia. Dorpat was invested by 23,000 men under Marshal Boris Sheremetev. When Peter personally arrived, a ruse encouraged a sortie, which was destroyed and the commander surrendered (June–24 July 1704).

Dorylaeum I 1097 I 1st Crusade

Crusaders under Bohemund of Taranto advancing into modern Turkey from the capture of **Nicaea** (19 June) were attacked by Sultan Kilij Arslan's Turkish cavalry near Dorylaeum (modern Eskisehir) and suffered severe casualties. Relieved by the arrival of Godfrey de Bouillon's heavy cavalry, the Crusaders beat the Turks before taking Dorylaeum and Arslan's rich treasure (1 July 1097).

Dorylaeum I 1147 I 2nd Crusade

Emperor Conrad III rejected advice to use the coastal route to Palestine and led his German Crusaders into central Turkey without waiting for Louis VII of France. While advancing past Nicaea to Dorylaeum, site of a great Crusader victory in 1097, Conrad's poorly provisioned force was destroyed by a massive Turkish army. The Emperor eventually reached Acre by ship (25 October 1147).

Dos Pilas I 679 I "Star" Wars

During war between Mayan cities (in modern Guatemala), with battles planned by the stars, rivals for Tikal fought for possession of Dos Pilas to the southeast. In 672 Nu Bak Chaak took the city from B'alaj Chan K'awiil then lost it again. In the decisive return battle, with aid from Calakmul, B'alaj Chan K'awiil defeated and killed Nu Bak Chaak, whose son was later avenged at **Calakmul**.

Dos Ríos I 1895 I 2nd Cuban War of Independence

Shortly after returning to Cuba to join renewed revolution, the Patriot leader and poet

José Martí was surprised in camp at Dos Ríos, ten miles east of Bayamo, by Spanish forces under Colonel Ximénez Sandoval. The Cubans suffered about 150 casualties, including Martí killed and Máximo Gómez wounded trying to recover his body. Cuban forces soon struck back at **Peralejo** (19 May 1895).

Douai ∎ 1710 ∎ War of the Spanish Succession

Imperial commander Prince Eugène of Savoy led a fresh offensive in the Netherlands to besiege Douai, south of Lille, held by French General Francois Albergotti. The town surrendered after a relief force was driven off, although Eugène had lost very heavy casualties in the siege. He then also took the Béthune, St Venant and Aire, though all were lost again in 1712 (25 April–26 June 1710).

Douala ∎ 1914 ∎ World War I (African Colonial Theatre)
See **Duala**

Douaumont (1st) ∎ 1916 ∎ World War I (Western Front)

At the start of the battle for **Verdun**, German forces under Crown Prince Wilhelm and General Konstantin Schmidt von Knobelsdorf attacked the key fortress of Douaumont, which fell after heavy fighting. French commander Philippe Petain himself tried to hold Douaumont village, but on 4 March it too fell to the German onslaught, which then turned against **Vaux** (21–25 February 1916).

Douaumont (2nd) ∎ 1916 ∎ World War I (Western Front)

While French forces defended desperately around **Vaux**, northeast of **Verdun**, General Charles Mangin attempted a counter-attack further north at Fort Douaumont. The French seized part of the fort before bloody fighting eventually drove them out with terrible losses. Mangin was relieved of command, but was soon recalled and secured success at **Fleury** and **Souville** (22–25 May 1916).

Douaumont (3rd) ∎ 1916 ∎ World War I (Western Front)

Following a lull in fighting around **Verdun**, after German failure at **Fleury** and **Souville**, new French commander Robert Nivelle determined to renew the offensive and ordered General Charles Mangin against the key fortress of Douaumont. The fort surrendered after massive bombardment and heavy fighting and the French turned south against **Vaux** (21–24 October 1916).

Dove Creek ∎ 1865 ∎ Kickapoo Indian Wars

A large party of Kickapoo under Papequah marching towards Mexico to escape Civil War in Kansas was attacked at Dove Creek, west of San Angelo, Texas, by Confederate Captain Henry Fossett. The badly outnumbered Americans lost 26 killed and 60 wounded for 15 Indian dead. This worst Texan defeat at Indian hands was avenged at **Nacimiento** in 1873 (8 January 1865).

Dover, England ∎ 1216–1217 ∎ 1st English Barons' War

Supported by English Barons rebelling against King John, Crown Prince Louis of France landed in England, where he captured **Rochester** and Winchester, then besieged Dover Castle, held by Hubert de Burgh. After the Royalist victory at **Lincoln**, and defeat of Louis' supply fleet off **South Foreland**, the Prince abandoned the siege and his claim to the throne (22 July 1216–August 1217).

Dover, England ∎ 1652 ∎ 1st Dutch War
See **Goodwin Sands**

Dover, Tennessee ∎ 1863 ∎ American Civil War (Western Theatre)
See **Fort Donelson**

Dover Straits ∎ 1666 ∎ 2nd Dutch War
See **Four Days Battle**

Dover Straits ∎ 1917 ∎ World War I (War at Sea)

Six German destroyers attacking the Dover barrage near the South Goodwins were met by the British destroyers *Broke* and *Swift*. A close-range night engagement saw *Swift* torpedo *G-85*, while *Broke* (Commander Edwards Evans) rammed *G-42*, which sank after hand-to-hand fighting to repel boarders. Both British ships were badly damaged but the other Germans withdrew (20–21 April 1917).

Downs ▌ 1639 ▌ Netherlands War of Independence

Spain determined to reinforce her army in the Netherlands and sent a fleet of over 70 ships and 24,000 men under the command of Admiral Antonio d'Oquendo, who anchored in the English Downs between Dover and Deal. In a brilliant attack with 30 ships, Dutch Admiral Maarten Tromp destroyed the Spanish fleet, killing over 7,000 and securing mastery of the sea (21 October 1639).

Drabescus ▌ 465–464 BC ▌ Wars of the Delian League

During the confrontation with Thasos over mineral-rich areas on the Thracian mainland, Athens sent 10,000 settlers to Ennea Hodoi at a crossing point on the lower River Strymon. After establishing a colony, settlers advanced into the interior, where they were annihilated by Thracian tribesmen at Drabescus. In 437 BC, the Athenians established a short-lived colony on the Strymon at Amphipolis.

Draco ▌ 553 ▌ Gothic War in Italy
See **Mount Lactarius**

Dragasani ▌ 1821 ▌ Greek War of Independence

In support of Greek Independence, Alexander Ipsilantis tried to raise rebellion in Romania, where he led over 5,000 men in a rash frontal assault on about 800 Turks on the Olte at Dragasani. Ipsilantis was driven off with terrible losses, including the "Sacred Band" of Greek youth annihilated, then fled to Austria, where he was imprisoned for seven years. His allies died at **Sekou** (19 June 1821).

Dranesville ▌ 1861 ▌ American Civil War (Eastern Theatre)

Union General Edward O. C. Ord recovered from the costly defeat in northern Virginia at **Ball's Bluff** (21 October) and met a large Confederate foraging expedition under General James "Jeb" Stuart northwest of Washington, D.C., near Dranesville, just south of the Potomac. Stuart lost almost 200 casualties before being forced to withdraw, though he managed to save his wagons (20 December 1861).

Drepanum ▌ 249 BC ▌ 1st Punic War

Supporting Rome's blockade of the Carthaginian fortress of **Lilybaeum** in western Sicily, Consul Publius Claudius Pulcher ill-advisedly took his fleet to attack Carthaginian ships at nearby Drepanum. Claudius was completely outmanoeuvred by Admiral Adherbal in a resounding defeat. Almost 100 Roman vessels were destroyed, while the Carthaginian fleet reputedly lost no ships.

Drepanum ▌ 1266 ▌ Venetian-Genoese War
See **Trapani**

Dresden ▌ 1760 ▌ Seven Years War (Europe)

Manoeuvring against the Austrians after a Prussian defeat in Silesia at **Landshut** (26 June), Frederick II of Prussia tried to divert his rivals by besieging and bombarding Dresden, held by General Johann Sigismund von Macquire. Austrian Marshal Leopold von Daun advanced to relieve the city and, with Silesia under threat, Frederick withdrew and marched to **Liegnitz** (12–29 July 1760).

Dresden ▌ 1813 ▌ Napoleonic Wars (War of Liberation)

Soon after French defeats at **Grossbeeren** and **Katzbach**, Austria joined the alliance and supported an attack on Napoleon Bonaparte at Dresden. Despite their superior numbers, the Russians of Prince Ludwig Wittgenstein, the Prussians of General Friedrich von Kleist, and

Prince Karl Philipp Schwarzenberg's Austrians suffered terrible losses and withdrew into Bohemia (26–27 August 1813).

Dreux ▌ 1562 ▌ 1st French War of Religion

Two months after Protestant defeat at **Rouen**, Huguenot leader Louis I de Bourbon Prince of Condé took German reinforcements to relieve Le Havre, but was defeated at Dreux, north of Chartres, by Anne Duke of Montmorency. However, the rival commanders were both captured and the later assassination of Catholic leader Francis of Guise brought temporary peace (19 December 1562).

Dreux ▌ 1870 ▌ Franco-Prussian War

When General Yves-Louis Fiereck directed a breakout west from besieged **Paris**, a mixed force of Gardes Mobiles and marines reached Dreux, where they were attacked by Germans under Grand Duke Friedrich Franz II of Mecklenburg. The French withdrew after a heavy defeat in fierce action south of Dreux, pursued next day through Chateauneuf (17 November 1870).

Drewry's Bluff ▌ 1862 ▌ American Civil War (Eastern Theatre)

As the Confederate army withdrew up the Virginia Peninsula from **Yorktown**, five Union gunboats under commander John Rodgers ascended the James River towards Richmond. Seven miles upriver the guns under General William Mahone at Fort Darling on Drewry's Bluff inflicted such heavy damage, especially on the iron-clad *Galena*, that Rodgers had to withdraw (15 May 1862).

Drewry's Bluff ▌ 1864 ▌ American Civil War (Eastern Theatre)

Union commander Benjamin F. Butler withdrawing from action at **Swift Creek**, north of Petersburg, Virginia, attempted a cautious advance against the Confederate line further north at Drewry's Bluff, on the James River. After initial Union success, Confederate General Pierre G. T. Beauregard led a bold counter-attack and repulsed the advance on Richmond (12–16 May 1864).

Driefontein ▌ 1900 ▌ 2nd Anglo-Boer War

As he advanced east from **Kimberley** through **Paardeberg** and **Poplar Grove**, General Lord Frederick Roberts was blocked by General Christiaan de Wet at Driefontein, defending Bloemfontein, capital of the Orange Free State. A sharp action cost 400 British and 100 Boer casualties before the Boers withdrew and Bloemfontein was abandoned three days later (10 March 1900).

Drin ▌ 1448 ▌ Albanian-Venetian War
See **Danj**

Drina ▌ 1914 ▌ World War I (Balkan Front)

Buoyed by success at **Cer** and **Sabac**, Serbian Marshal Radomir Putnik advanced into Syrmia, then had to withdraw in the face of a second Austrian invasion across the Drina by General Oskar Potiorek. Austrian General Artur Geisl secured Parasnica before a massive Serbian counter-offensive halted the invasion. Putnik later fell back to defend Belgrade at **Kolubara** (8–17 September 1914).

Driniumor ▌ 1944 ▌ World War II (Pacific)
See **Aitape**

Drogheda ▌ 1649 ▌ British Civil Wars

Oliver Cromwell led a campaign of destruction against Catholic-Royalist Ireland, where he attacked Drogheda on the Boyne, held by a 3,000-strong garrison under Sir Arthur Aston. The town was overwhelmed after a brief siege, followed by slaughter of the garrison and civilians, including Aston killed. Cromwell then advanced against **Wexford** (3–12 September 1649).

Droop Mountain ▌ 1863 ▌ American Civil War (Eastern Theatre)

Raiding against road and rail links in West Virginia near Lewisburg, Union Generals William W. Averell and French-born Alfred N. Duffié attacked Confederate General John Echols 20 miles to the north at Droop Mountain. The Confederate brigade was defeated and dispersed in a sharp action, though Averell soon withdrew and ended his raid (6 November 1863).

Drumclog ▪ 1679 ▪ Scottish Covenanter Rebellion

Despite defeat at **Rullion Green** (1666), non-conformist Covenanters renewed their rebellion against Episcopalianism and, on Drumclog Moor, southwest of Strathaven, met John Graham of Claverhouse. Led by John Balfour of Kinloch, the rebels repulsed the badly outnumbered government force, killing about 40, but they were destroyed three weeks later at **Bothwell Bridge** (1 June 1679).

Drummossie ▪ 1746 ▪ Jacobite Rebellion (The Forty-Five)
See **Culloden**

Dryfe Sands ▪ 1593 ▪ Later Scottish Clan Wars

In the so-called "last great Clan battle" on the border, John Lord Maxwell took 2,000 men against Sir James Johnston at Lockwood. But at Dryfe Sands, near Lockerbie, Maxwell was ambushed and killed along with many of his men. In 1608 Maxwell's son murdered Sir James in revenge but was subsequently hanged and James IV reconciled the Clans to end the feud (7 December 1593).

Dry Lake ▪ 1873 ▪ Modoc Indian War
See **Lava Beds (2nd)**

Dry Wood Creek ▪ 1861 ▪ American Civil War (Trans-Mississippi)

After victory in southwest Missouri at **Wilson's Creek**, 6,000 secessionist militia led by General Sterling Price marched to Dry Wood Creek, on the Kansas border, east of Fort Scott, where they were attacked by just 600 Kansas cavalry under Colonel James H. Lane (1814–1866). Despite the advantage of surprise, Lane was driven off and Price marched north to **Lexington, Missouri** (2 September 1861).

Duala ▪ 1914 ▪ World War I (African Colonial Theatre)

In the wake of a failed land assault in German Cameroon at **Garua**, Anglo-French forces under General Charles Dobell attacked by sea against

Duala. Naval bombardment forced the Germans to blow up the wireless station and surrender the port and its shipping, including nine liners. They then retreated inland to Yaunde and held out in the north at Garua and **Mora, Cameroon** (27 September 1914).

Dubba ▪ 1843 ▪ British Conquest of Sind
See **Hyderabad, Pakistan**

Dubienka ▪ 1792 ▪ Polish Rising

When Poland declared independence, Catherine the Great sent Marshal Alexander Suvorov to impose Russian authority. He fought the Poles at **Zielenice** before Tadeusz Kosciuszko brilliantly defended Dubienka, east of Chelm. However, Kosciuszko dispersed his outnumbered force when two Russian armies encircled and occupied Warsaw. The Second Polish partition followed (18 July 1792).

Dublin (1st) ▪ 1171 ▪ Anglo-Norman Conquest of Ireland

Following Norman capture of Dublin after victory at **Waterford**, Haskulf the Norse King of Dublin returned from overseas with fresh forces and attempted to retake the city. Outside Dublin, near the mouth of the Poddle, Haskulf was routed and captured by Normans under the brothers Miles and Richard de Cogan. He was later executed (May 1171).

Dublin (2nd) ▪ 1171 ▪ Anglo-Norman Conquest of Ireland

With the Norse King Haskulf captured attempting to retake Dublin from the Normans, Irish High King Rory O'Connor laid siege to the city, supported by leading Clan Chiefs. However, Norman leaders Raymond le Gros, Richard de Clare "Strongbow," Miles de Cogan and Maurice Fitzgerald led a powerful counterattack. The Irish King fled and his army was routed (September 1171).

Dublin ▪ 1803 ▪ Emmet's Insurrection

In the aftermath of the failed Irish rebellion of 1798, Nationalist leader Robert Emmet returned from France with pikes and muskets, hoping to trigger a fresh rising with French support. A premature march on Dublin Castle was bloodily dispersed after his rebels seized and killed the Lord Chief Justice. Emmet was soon captured and hanged for treason, as were many of his supporters (23 July 1803).

Dublin I 1916 I Easter Rising

In an insurrection against Britain, about 1,500 Irish Republicans under James Connolly and Patrick Pearse seized the General Post Office and other buildings in Dublin on Easter Monday. General Sir John Lowe's powerful response saw five days of street fighting and artillery fire force a surrender. Fifteen rebel leaders were executed and the rising was suppressed (24–29 April 1916).

Dublin I 1922 I Irish Civil War
See **Four Courts**

Dubrovnik I 1991–1992 I Croatian War

When Croatia broke away from Yugoslavia, the Adriatic port city of Dubrovnik came under siege as part of the Serb blockade of the Croatian coast. Heavy shelling by the Yugoslav army under General Pavle Strugar and navy under Admiral Miodrag Jokic caused civilian deaths and severe property damage, before a UN-mediated ceasefire finally ended the siege (October 1991–May 1992).

Duck Lake I 1885 I 2nd Riel Rebellion

Veteran Canadian rebel Louis Riel declared Saskatchewan independent and Méti led by Gabriel Dumont ambushed 56 Mounted Police and 43 Prince Albert settlers under Superintendent Leif Crozier near the Duck Lake Trading Post, on the South Saskatchewan, near **Batoche**. Crozier lost 12 killed and 11 wounded in sharp fighting and had to retreat. Dumont lost five killed (26 March 1885).

Dudley's Defeat I 1813 I War of 1812

During the British siege of **Fort Meigs**, a relief force arrived under General Green Clay of Kentucky, who sent 800 men under Colonel William Dudley to spike the British guns. With his mission accomplished, Dudley rashly pursued the British and their Indian allies. Lured into ambush, Dudley and about 200 men were killed and more than 400 were captured, but Fort Miegs was saved (5 May 1813).

Dug Gap I 1863 I American Civil War (Western Theatre)
See **Davis' Cross Roads**

Dujaila I 1916 I World War I (Mesopotamia)

Soon after failing at **Sheik Sa'ad, Wadi** and **Hanna**, General Sir Fenton Aylmer's Anglo-Indian force made a further attempt to break the Turkish siege of **Kut-al-Amara** near Es Sinn. But an attack on the powerful redoubt at Dujaila by General George Kemball was driven off with heavy losses. Aylmer was replaced by General George Gorringe, who in turn failed at **Sannaiyat** (8 March 1916).

Dul Madoba I 1913 I Wars of the Mad Mullah

When Muhammad Abdullah Hassan renewed war against friendly tribes in Somaliland, British Camel Constabulary under Richard Corfield attacked the Mullah's forces at Dul Madoba, near Idoweina. Corfield was killed and Captain Gerald Summers wounded before the Dervishes withdrew. The British lost 36 killed and 21 wounded out of 85 before returning to Burao (9 August 1913).

Dumanli Dag I 1916 I World War I (Caucasus Front)
See **Bayburt**

Dunaberg I 1915 I World War I (Eastern Front)
See **Dvinsk**

Dunajetz I 1915 I World War I (Eastern Front)
See **Gorlice-Tarnow**

Dunamunde I 1701 I 2nd "Great" Northern War

Charles XII of Sweden drove off a siege of the Baltic city of **Riga** by Russian, Polish and Saxon troops, then pursued his enemy to the nearby fortress port at Dunamunde (modern Daugavgriva, Latvia). Crossing the Dvina (Duna) in rafts and boats under heavy opposition fire, Charles won a great victory and went on to occupy Livonia and Courland (9 July 1701).

Dunanore I 1580 I Geraldine Rebellion
See **Fort del Or**

Dunbar I 1296 I English Invasion of Scotland

In reponse to Scotland's alliance with France and invasion of Cumberland, Edward I marched north to sack **Berwick**, then sent forces to Dunbar, east of Edinburgh, against the main Scottish army of King John Baliol, led by Thomas Durward Earl of Athol. English under John de Warenne Earl of Surrey overwhelmed the Scots and Edward declared himself King of Scotland (27 April 1296).

Dunbar I 1337–1338 I Anglo-Scottish War of Succession

Supporting his ally Edward Baliol against adherents of David II, Edward III of England sent William Montague Earl of Salisbury and Richard Fitzalan Earl of Arundel against Dunbar Castle, held by Countess Agnes of Dunbar for her absent husband. In a celebrated siege, "Black Agnes" resisted for six months before Sir Alexander Ramsay broke the blockade by sea and the English withdrew.

Dunbar I 1650 I British Civil Wars

The outnumbered Parliamentary army of Oliver Cromwell marched into Scotland against Royalists under General David Leslie and attacked the Scots outside Dunbar, on the Firth of Forth, east of Edinburgh. Leslie suffered an overwhelming defeat and withdrew north, leaving Cromwell and his commanders George Monck and John Lambert to seize Edinburgh (3 September 1650).

Dunblane I 1715 I Jacobite Rebellion (The Fifteen)
See **Sheriffmuir**

Duncrub I 965 I Scottish Dynastic Wars

Following the death of King Indulph of Scotland at **Invercullen** in 961, his throne passed to Duff (Dubh), son of Malcolm I, who found himself at war with Indulph's son Cullen. At Duncrub, in Perthshire, Cullen was heavily defeated, with his allies the Mormaor of Atholl and the Abbot of Dunkeld slain. Two years later Cullen killed Duff at Forres and seized the throne.

Dundalk I 1318 I Rise of Robert the Bruce

Edward Bruce, brother of Robert the Bruce, extending the Scottish War to Ireland, defeated local forces at **Ardscull** and was crowned at Dundalk, north of Dublin. Two years later, his small Scots force faced a much larger Anglo-Irish army loyal to Edward II, under Sir John de Bermingham, near Dundalk at Faughart. Bruce was killed and England re-established control of Ulster (14 October 1318).

Dundarg I 1334 I Anglo-Scottish War of Succession

In the war between adherents of young King David II and the English-backed Edward Baliol, Scottish Regent Sir Andrew Moray and Alexander de Mowbray marched into Buchan and besieged Henry de Beaumont in Dundarg Castle on Moray Firth. Beaumont was forced to surrender when his water supply was severed and was permitted to return to England (August–November 1334).

Dundee, Scotland I 1651 I British Civil Wars

Left to subjugate Scotland after victory at **Dunbar** (1650), Parliamentary General George Monck captured Stirling, then besieged Dundee, defended by Governor Robert Lumsden. The storming of Dundee was followed by heavy civilian deaths. With Royalist defeat at **Worcester** two days later, other Scottish towns quickly surrendered and the war came to an end (August–1 September 1651).

Dundee, South Africa ∎ 1899 ∎ 2nd Anglo-Boer War
See **Talana Hill**

Dundia Khera ∎ 1858 ∎ Indian Mutiny
Determined to pacify Oudh, General Sir Colin Campbell took Shankapur without a shot fired and drove Beni Madhav northwest towards Dundia Khera, on the Ganges, south of Cawnpore. The fleeing rebels were beaten nearby by Colonel Frederick Evelegh (10 November). Two weeks later, Campbell inflicted a decisive defeat with over 600 dead, and secured Oudh (24 November 1858).

Dunes ∎ 1600 ∎ Netherlands War of Independence
See **Nieuport**

Dunes ∎ 1658 ∎ Franco-Spanish War
French Marshal Henri de Turenne was besieging **Dunkirk**, aided by ships and troops from Cromwell's England, when a large Spanish relief force approached, led by Don John of Austria and Louis II de Bourbon Prince of Condé supported by English Royalists. On dunes between the beach and the port, the Spanish were routed and Dunkirk fell ten days later, ending the war (14 June 1658).

Dungan Hill ∎ 1647 ∎ British Civil Wars
On an offensive from Dublin, Parliamentary commander Colonel Michael Jones took a force northwest towards Trim and, at nearby Dungan (sometimes Dungan's) Hill, attacked a Catholic-Royalist force under Thomas Preston Viscount Tara. The Irish were virtually annihilated, losing over 3,000 killed and all their guns and baggage, and Tara retired to Kilkenny (8 August 1647).

Dungeness ∎ 1652 ∎ 1st Dutch War
After Admiral Witte Cornelius de With was repulsed at **Kentish Knock** (8 October), Maarten Tromp was recalled to lead the Dutch fleet and, off Dungeness headland in Kent, he engaged English Admiral Robert Blake, who had only half as many ships. With three vessels sunk and two captured, Blake withdrew defeated and

Tromp secured temporary command of the Channel (10 December 1652).

Dunkeld ∎ 1689 ∎ First Jacobite Rebellion
One month after victory at **Killiecrankie**, Scottish supporters of James II, led by Colonel Alexander Cannon, attacked Dunkeld, north of Perth, held for William III by the Cameronian Regiment under Colonel William Cleland. Although Cleland was killed, the Highlanders were heavily repulsed (despite a four to one advantage) and the Jacobite rising was virtually over (21 August 1689).

Dunkirk ∎ 1646 ∎ Thirty Years War (Franco-Habsburg War)
Gaston Duke d'Orleans (son of Henry IV of France), expanding French territory north into the Spanish Netherlands, captured **Gravelines** (1644) and later took Mardyk. He then left Louis II Duke d'Enghien to besiege the key Spanish port of Dunkirk. Supported at sea by a Dutch blockade under Admiral Martin Tromp, d'Enghien captured Dunkirk after a month (19 September–11 October 1646).

Dunkirk ∎ 1658 ∎ Franco-Spanish War
As France and Cromwell's England strengthened their alliance against Spain in northern France, French Marshal Henri de Turenne, aided by English troops under Sir William Lockhart, besieged Dunkirk, supported by the blockading English fleet. The port capitulated ten days after the nearby Battle of the **Dunes** and remained four years in English hands (24 June 1658).

Dunkirk ∎ 1793 ∎ French Revolutionary Wars (1st Coalition)
Attacking in northern France, Prince Frederick Augustus Duke of York and a strong British-Hanoverian force besieged Dunkirk by land and sea. French commander General Joseph Souham gallantly defended the port and, after the Allied covering force lost at nearby **Hondschoote**, the Duke lifted his siege and withdrew to Belgium (24 August–8 September 1793).

Dunkirk I 1940 I World War II (Western Europe)

With the Allies overwhelmed on all fronts by the German invasion of the Lowlands and the enemy race for the **Channel Ports**, French, British and Belgian troops withdrew to Dunkirk, which saw a bold defence and evacuation under General John Lord Gort (later General Harold Alexander). While almost 900 small ships and naval craft saved 338,000 men, France was doomed (28 May–4 June 1940).

Dunlawton I 1836 I 2nd Seminole Indian War

Marching south from St Augustine, Florida, 40 men of the independent St Augustine Guards under Major Benjamin Putnam went to Anderson's Plantation at Dunlawton on the Halifax, where Indians had fired on a boat the previous day. Attacked by 150 Seminoles under Coacoochee, Putnam was driven out with costly losses and fled to his boats (18 January 1836).

Dunnichen Moss I 685 I Anglo-Saxon Territorial Wars

King Ecgfrith of Northumbria had been defeated by the Kingdom of Mercia at **Trent** in 679 and unwisely turned north to invade Scotland, where he was overwhelmed and killed by Brude, King of the Picts. The battle at Dunnichen Moss (Nechtanesmere), east of modern Forfar, effectively signalled the end of Northumbrian power and secured Scotland against Anglo-Saxon England (20 May 685).

Dunnottar I 900 I Viking Wars in Britain

During a reign marked by increasing Viking attacks, Donald II of Scotland, son of Constantine I, had his capital at Forteviot burned by Norse raiders under Sitric, son of Imhair. Donald then marched to repulse a fresh Danish landing at the Tay, but at Dunnotar near Stonehaven in Kincardine, he was defeated and killed (some historians assert he died of old age, not in battle).

Dunsinane I 1054 I Scottish War of Succession

In support of his grandson Malcolm Canmore, Siward the Danish Earl of Northumberland invaded Scotland against the usurper King Macbeth (who had murdered Malcolm's father, Duncan I). At Dunsinane, near Perth, Macbeth was heavily defeated, reputedly losing 10,000 men. Malcolm took the throne three years later after Macbeth was killed at **Lumphanan** (27 July 1054).

Dunstable I 1461 I Wars of the Roses

The Lancastrian army of Henry Beaufort Duke of Somerset approaching the Yorkists at St Albans surprised an outpost 14 miles northwest at Dunstable, where every one of 200 men under Edward Poynings was killed or captured. Richard Neville Earl of Warwick apparently disbelieved reports of the loss and as a result he was surprised and defeated next day at **St Albans** (15 February 1461).

Duoro I 1809 I Napoleonic Wars (Peninsular Campaign)

See **Oporto**

Duppel I 1849 I 1st Schleswig-Holstein War

With the resumption of hostilities against Frederick VII of Denmark, the rebel Duchies of Schleswig and Holstein repulsed a Danish landing at **Eckenforde**, then joined German troops under General Eduard von Bonin and stormed the Danish entrenchments at Duppel, just west of Sonderborg. After further fighting the rebels advanced into Danish Jutland (13 April 1849).

Duppel I 1864 I 2nd Schleswig-Holstein War

Following the death of Frederick VII of Denmark, Prussian troops under Prince Friedrich Karl and General Leonhard von Blumenthal invaded Schleswig in support of the German claimant Prince Fredrick of Augustenburg and attacked the Danish lines at Duppel with heavy artillery fire. The Danes withdrew to **Alsen** after losing 5,000 casualties and prisoners (30 March–18 April 1864).

Dupplin I 1332 I Anglo-Scottish War of Succession

Edward Baliol, son of former King John Baliol, launched an attempt to seize the Scottish throne, invading with a mixed force of Scots and English adventurers against Donald Earl of Mar, Regent for the boy-King David II. On Dupplin Moor, west of Perth, Earl Donald was killed. Baliol had himself crowned, but he was defeated at **Annan** in December by the new Regent (12 August 1332).

Duquesne I 1758 I Seven Years War (North America)
See **Fort Duquesne**

Durango I 1808 I Napoleonic Wars (Peninsular Campaign)
Regrouping his forces after battle with Spanish General Joachim Blake southeast of Bilbao at **Zornoza**, French commander Eugène Villatte, supported by Generals Francois Sébastiani and Jean Francois Leval, launched a massive attack at Durango. In the face of heavy artillery fire the Spanish fell back to **Bilbao** and the next day they withdrew west towards **Valmaseda** (31 October 1808).

Durazzo I 1081 I 1st Byzantine-Norman War
See **Dyrrhachium**

Durbe I 1260 I Early Wars of the Teutonic Knights
After disaster at **Siauliai** (1236), the Livonian knights made peace with Duke Mindaugus of Lithuania, who adopted Christianity. But Pagan Samogitians advanced into Latvia and met the knights at Durbe. One of the worst German defeats in the east saw Master Burckhardt von Hornhausen among thousands killed. Mindaugus reverted to Paganism but was soon murdered in a coup (13 July 1260).

Durdah I 1781 I 1st British-Maratha War
With a British advance on Poona checked at **Bhorghat**, Major Jacob Camac crossed the Jumna into Malwar and, following repulse near Sironj, fell back on Mahadpur. Two weeks later, he surprised Mahadji Sindhia's camp at nearby Durdah and inflicted a severe defeat, capturing the Maratha horses and baggage. Mahadji sued

for peace and never again took arms against Britain (24 March 1781).

Durham I 1069 I Norman Conquest of Britain
Three years after his great victory at **Hastings** (October 1066), William I sent the Norman noble Robert de Comines north, where he seized the city of Durham. Northumbrian forces counter-attacked next day and Comines was killed in a disastrous defeat, along with most of his men, said to have numbered up to 500. Returning south from Hexham, William later retook the city by storm.

Durham I 1080 I Norman Conquest of Britain
Northumbrians in Durham renewed resistance against Norman rule, killing the tyrannical Earl-Bishop Walcher of Lorraine and about 100 of his supporters. King William's half-brother Odo (who was Bishop of Bayeaux and Earl of Kent) marched north and crushed the rebellion. However, Odo's corruption and cruelty shocked even William, and he was imprisoned throughout his brother's lifetime.

Durham I 1312 I Rise of Robert the Bruce
Robert the Bruce of Scotland led a powerful raid into England, crossing the border in force and sending his brother Edward and Sir James "Black" Douglas against Durham. The city was sacked amid widespread death and destruction. After Douglas also raided Hartlepool, the people of Durham agreed to pay a large tribute and the Scots withdrew (August 1312).

Durnkrut I 1278 I Bohemian Wars
See **Marchfeld**

Durrenstein I 1805 I Napoleonic Wars (3rd Coalition)
As Napoleon Bonaparte advanced towards Vienna after victory at **Ulm**, French General Honoré Gazan met a powerful Russian army under Prince Mikhail Kutuzov at Durrenstein (modern Durnstein), west of Vienna, near

Krems. The hard-fought delaying action is counted a Russian victory, yet Bonaparte continued on to the capture of Vienna and glory at **Austerlitz** (11 November 1805).

Dussindale I 1549 I Kett's Rebellion

Leading a rural insurrection from Norfolk, a landholder named Robert Kett took a reputed 20,000 against **Norwich**, where he defeated the incompetent William Parr Marquess of Northampton. John Dudley Earl of Warwick was then recalled from Scotland and routed the rebels at nearby Dussindale with more than 3,000 killed. Kett and several other leaders were hanged (27 August 1549).

Dvinsk I 1915 I World War I (Eastern Front)

On the northern flank of the **Triple Offensive**, General Otto von Below made a determined assault on the border city of Dvinsk (Daugavpils in modern Lithuania). The Germans were repulsed in heavy fighting and the offensive stalled. Despite further costly attacks in October 1915 and early 1916 the city remained in Russians hands until the general withdrawal in 1917 (24–25 September 1915).

Dwin I 624 I Byzantine-Persian Wars

On the second campaign of his counter-attack against the Persians after victory at **Ophlimos**, Emperor Heraclius advanced northeast from Ceasarea into the Araxes Valley to attack Dwin, capital of Persian Armenia. Sassanid King Chosroes II withdrew before the Emperor's continued advance towards Ganzak, where he seized massive booty. The following year Heraclius beat a Persian army at **Arcesh**.

Dybbol I 1864 I 2nd Schleswig-Holstein War

See **Duppel**

Dyle I 891 I Viking Raids on Germany

When Danish Vikings advancing up the Rhine heavily defeated a German force at **La Gueule** (26 June), German King Arnulf personally led an attack on the Norse camp on the Dyle, near Louvain. The invaders were routed in a violent repulse, with Danish King Godefrid and his brother Siegfried killed. The Vikings never again ventured so far inland and turned instead to Britain (September 891).

Dyle Line I 1940 I World War II (Western Europe)

Facing an overwhelming German invasion of **Belgium** and the fall of **Eben Emael**, the Belgian army fell back to the River Dyle, in central Belgium between Antwerp and Namur. Allied commander Maurice Gamelin ordered British and French forces to help hold the line, but the Germans broke through in force and the Allies soon fell back to the Escaut and then the Lys (15–17 May 1940).

Dylerschans I 1664 I 2nd Dutch War

Prince William Fredrick of Nassau led a counter-offensive in east Friesland, where he laid siege to Dylerschans, on the Ems near Papenburg, taken the previous year by Prince-Bishop Christof Bernhard van Galen of Munster. The small fortress was forced to surrender after six weeks. Its loss persuaded van Galen to support the English during the 2nd Dutch War (23 May–4 June 1664).

Dyme I 226 BC I Cleomenic War

See **Hecatombaeum**

Dyrham I 577 I Anglo-Saxon Conquest of Britain

See **Deorham**

Dyrrhachium I 49–48 BC I Wars of the First Triumvirate

Julius Caesar crossed the Adriatic and landed 25,000 men near Pompey's base at Dyrrhachium (modern Durres, Albania). Reinforced by Mark Antony, Caesar besieged Dyrrhachium, but Pompey's greatly superior force broke out and Caesar was heavily defeated on the nearby plains. He withdrew to Thessaly but had his revenge three months later at **Pharsalus** (December 49 BC–20 May 48 BC).

Dyrrhachium ▌ 1081 ▌ 1st
Byzantine-Norman War

Attacking the Byzantine Empire from Italy, the Norman Robert Guiscard besieged the Adriatic port of Dyrrhachium (modern Durres, Albania). While Venetian ships defeated Guiscard's son Bohemund at sea, a decisive battle on land saw Guiscard rout the relief army of Emperor Alexius I. The city fell by treachery a few months later and Alexius withdrew (18 October 1081).

Dyrrhachium ▌ 1083 ▌ 1st
Byzantine-Norman War

When the Norman Robert Guiscard seized the Byzantine Adriatic port of Dyrrhachium (modern Durres, Albania) in 1082, his son Bohemund was left in command and faced counter-attack by Emperor Alexius I. The Emperor was again heavily defeated in the field near Dyrrhachium, but the Normans withdrew from Byzantine territory two years later after losing to Alexius at **Larissa**.

Dyrrhachium ▌ 1107 ▌ 2nd
Byzantine-Norman War

The great Crusader Bohemund of Antioch was returning from Europe when he attacked Byzantium by besieging the fortress at Dyrrhachium (modern Durres, Albania). Cut off from Italy by Byzantine ships, Bohemund was forced to surrender and acknowledge Emperor Alexius I. He never returned to the Holy Land, leaving Antioch to his nephew Tancred (August–September 1107).

Dysert O'Dea ▌ 1318 ▌ English Invasion
of Ireland

Encouraged by Anglo-Norman defeat at **Ardscull** (1316), Murtough O'Brien attempted to recover Thomond (seized 150 years earlier by Richard de Clare "Strongbow" after victory at **Dublin**). Supported by Conor O'Dea at Dysert O'Dea near Ennis, King Murtough defeated and killed Strongbow's descendant Richard de Clare, driving the Normans out of County Clare (10 May 1318).

E

Eagle Creek ❚ 1877 ❚ Nez Percé Indian War
See **Bear Paw Mountains**

Eagle Hills ❚ 1885 ❚ 2nd Riel Rebellion
Days after defeating Colonel William Otter at **Cut Knife Creek**, in northwest Saskatchewan, Cree Indians under Poundmaker (Pitikwahana-piwiyin) marched east towards **Batoche** and, at Eagle Hills, met a wagon train carrying supplies to Otter. When the wagons were captured in a sharp action, Poundmaker intervened to prevent bloodshed and the 21 teamsters were taken prisoner (14 May 1885).

East China Sea ❚ 1945 ❚ World War II (Pacific)
Sent on a suicide mission to disrupt Allied landings on **Okinawa**, Japan's largest surviving battleship, *Yamato*, was met southwest of Kyushu in the East China Sea by American carrier-borne aircraft. With no air cover, *Yamato* was overwhelmed and sunk along with a cruiser and four out of eight destroyers. Admiral Sheiichi Ito and 3,500 men died for just ten US aircraft lost (7 April 1945).

Eastern Solomons ❚ 1942 ❚ World War II (Pacific)
Admiral Nobutake Kondo, advancing from Truk with a carrier force and transports to wrest the initiative at **Guadalcanal**, was met in the Eastern Solomons by American Admiral Frank Fletcher. A long-range duel between carrier-borne aircraft saw the US carrier *Enterprise* severely damaged, but Kondo lost a light carrier and 70 planes and had to withdraw (24–25 August 1942).

Eastertide Offensive ❚ 1972 ❚ Vietnam War
With America withdrawing from Vietnam, North Vietnamese General Vo Nguyen Giap launched a widespread offensive, taking cities including **Quang Tri**. The Eastertide Offensive was finally halted in the central highlands at **Kontum** and in the south at **An Loc** with 50,000 North Vietnamese and 40,000 South Vietnamese killed. Giap was dismissed (30 March–1 May 1972).

East Indies ❚ 1941–1942 ❚ World War II (Pacific)
While the Japanese advanced through the **Philippines** and **Malaya**, large forces under Admiral Ibo Takahashi converged on the Dutch East Indies and captured Borneo, Celebes and Timor. The Australian, British, Dutch and American Allies tried to halt the invasion at **Lombok Strait** and the **Java Sea**, but were badly beaten and the region was quickly occupied (16 December 1941–9 March 1942).

East Stoke ❚ 1487 ❚ Simnel's Rebellion
See **Stoke**

Ebelsberg ❚ 1809 ❚ Napoleonic Wars (5th Coalition)
After Austria's failed invasion of Bavaria, Baron Johann Hiller withdrew following defeat at **Landshut** and, after a tactical victory at **Neumarkt-St-Viet**, was attacked attempting to hold the bridge on the Danube at Ebelsberg, southeast of Linz. Despite inflicting heavy

French losses, the outnumbered Austrians were defeated by Marshal André Masséna and retired towards **Vienna** (3 May 1809).

Eben Emael ▮ 1940 ▮ World War II (Western Europe)

Airborne troops under Hauptmann Walter Koch opened Germany's lightning invasion of **Belgium**, landing at key bridges and on top of the vital fortress at Eben Emael commanding defences on the strategic Albert Canal. In little more than 24 hours, Major Jean Jottrand surrendered the supposedly impregnable fortress and the Belgian army fell back to defend the **Dyle Line** (10 May 1940).

Eben-ezer ▮ 1050 BC ▮ Philistine-Israel Wars

As Philistine invaders spread from Palestine into Israel, two decisive actions were fought at Eben-ezer, near Aphek (modern Ras el-Ain), east of Jaffa. Rashly accepting open battle, the tribes of Manasseh, Ephraim and Benjamin were routed. In a second action, the sacred Ark was brought as a rallying point, but the Israelites were defeated again, with the Ark captured and taken to Ashod.

Ebersberg ▮ 1809 ▮ Napoleonic Wars (5th Coalition)

See **Ebelsberg**

Ebro ▮ 217 BC ▮ 2nd Punic War

With Carthaginian General Hanno defeated by Roman invaders at **Tarraco** in northeast Spain, the great Carthaginian leader Hasdrubal took a large land and naval force north as far as the Ebro River. A small Roman fleet, aided by Massilia, attacked and destroyed Hasdrubal's ships in confined waters at the mouth of the river and the Carthaginians withdrew south to New Carthage (modern Cartagena).

Ebro ▮ 1084 ▮ Early Christian Reconquest of Spain

Following defeat at **Almenar** in 1082, al-Hayib, Taifa of Lérida, and King Sancho Ramirez of Aragon renewed their invasion of Muslim Saragossa. On the Ebro River, they were routed by Rodrigo Diaz de Bivar—El Cid—in service with al-Hayib's brother, al-Mutamin. El Cid's prisoners included the powerful Aragonese noble Count Sancho Sanchez of Pamplona (14 August 1084).

Ebro ▮ 1938 ▮ Spanish Civil War

With **Valencia** holding firm, Republican General Juan Modesto launched a final offensive across the Ebro to ease pressure on **Madrid**. Despite initial success, the Republicans were driven back by Nationalist General Juan Yagüe, suffering irreplaceable losses in men and equipment. The fate of the Republic was virtually sealed and the rebels marched on **Barcelona** (24 July–16 November 1938).

Ebsdorf ▮ 880 ▮ Viking Raids on Germany

Viking forces repulsed in England at **Edington** (878) turned against Europe and, at Ebsdorf, on Luneberg Heath, they attacked an army under Duke Bruno of Saxony. Caught in a snowstorm, the Germans were routed. Among the many dead, Bruno and the Bishops of Hildesheim and Ninden were canonised as martyrs. The Norsemen were checked a year later at **Saucourt** (2 February 880).

Ecbatana ▮ 129 BC ▮ Later Syrian-Parthian War

The Seleucid Antiochus VII campaigned from Syria into Mesopotamia, where he defeated Parthia at the **Zab** River (130 BC) and took Babylon and Ecbatana (modern Hamadan). After trying to impose a harsh peace, he faced a large Parthian army under Phraates II near Ecbatana. Antiochus died in a terrible rout, effectively ending Seleucid power east of the Euphrates (February 129 BC).

Echalar ▮ 1813 ▮ Napoleonic Wars (Peninsular Campaign)

During the week-long "Battles of the Pyrenees," Arthur Wellesley Lord Wellington was pursuing Marshal Nicolas Soult from defeat at **Sorauren**, when General Bertrand Clausel attempted to make a stand on the ridge at Ivantelly near Echalar. Wellington's outnumbered force won the ensuing struggle and Soult continued his retreat into France (2 August 1813).

Echmiadzin I 1804 I Russo-Persian Wars

When Russia annexed Georgia, local rebels sought Persian aid and Russian General Pavel Zitzianov besieged Erivan. In the ensuing battle 12 miles west at Echmiadzin, Russia secured a narrow victory over Persian Crown Prince Abbas Mirza. When Shah Fath Ali sent fresh forces, the Russian siege was lifted and war dragged on until the decisive battle at **Aslanduz** (20 June 1804).

Echmiadzin I 1827 I Russo-Persian Wars

After defeat in Azerbaijan near **Abbasabad**, Persian commander Abbas Mirza marched west into Armenia to threaten the rear of General Ivan Paskevich's Russian army. A small force under General Afanasi Ivanovich Krasovski near Echmiadzin was massively outnumbered, but after heavy losses on both sides, Abbas withdrew and Krasovski joined Paskevich at **Erivan** (August 1827).

Ecija I 711 I Muslim Conquest of Spain

Having beaten a Visigothic Spanish army near Cadiz in July 711 at Xeres (later known as **Guadalete**), invading Muslims under the brilliant General Tarik ibn Ziyad advanced into Spain and soon achieved another victory at Ecija, on the Genil River. The battle led directly to Muslim seizure of the Visigoth capital at Toledo.

Eckau I 1812 I Napoleonic Wars (Russian Campaign)

At the beginning of Napoleon Bonaparte's invasion of Russia, Prussians under General Friedrich von Kleist advanced in the north towards the Baltic port of Riga, defended by Russian and English forces. The Allies under General Feodor Lewis marched out to meet the invaders at Eckau, but after repeated assaults, they were driven back by Kleist, who then established a siege (18 July 1812).

Eckenforde I 1849 I 1st Schleswig-Holstein War

With the expiry of an armistice, Frederick VII of Denmark sent forces to recover Schleswig and Holstein, which had been seized by rebels with Prussian aid. The warships *Christian VIII* (84) and *Gefion* (46) escorted Danish troops to land at Eckenforde, northwest of Kiel. However, they were repulsed by small coastal batteries and were forced into a humiliating surrender (5 April 1849).

Eckmühl I 1809 I Napoleonic Wars (5th Coalition)

Archduke Charles of Austria invaded Bavaria, where he was defeated by Napoleon Bonaparte at **Abensberg** (20 April). While the Austrian left wing was then beaten to the southeast at **Landshut**, the right wing under Charles marched northeast towards Marshal Louis Davout at Eckmühl. Aided by Bonaparte himself, Davout crushed the Austrians, but they withdrew in good order (22 April 1809).

Ecnomus I 256 BC I 1st Punic War

When Roman Consuls Atilius Regulus and Lucius Vulso put into Phintias, near Mount Ecnomus in southern Sicily, to embark troops for Africa, their fleet was attacked by the Carthaginians Hamilcar and Hanno. In one of history's largest naval battles, with over 300 vessels on either side, both fleets suffered comparable losses, though more Carthaginian vessels were captured and Hamilcar fled.

Econochaca I 1813 I Creek Indian War
   See **Holy Ground**

Edessa I 260 I Roman-Persian Wars

Shapur I of Sassanid Persia seized Armenia and Mesopotamia and captured Antioch in Roman Syria, but he was driven out of Antioch by Emperor Valerian, who then unwisely advanced northeast to Edessa. With his incompetent commander Macrianus defeated, Valerian was surrounded and became the first Roman Emperor captured in battle. Ransom was refused and he died in Persian captivity.

Edessa I 503 I Byzantine-Persian Wars

Following success in Roman Mesopotamia at **Amida** and **Apadna**, Sassanid King Kawad was encouraged to attack Edessa by Arab leader Numan because of an Apocryphal letter from Christ guaranteeing King Abgar that the city would not be captured. After a short blockade and some skirmishing, the Persians withdrew following payment in gold and the war wound down (September 503).

Edessa | 544 | Byzantine-Persian Wars

Having earlier failed to capture **Dara**, Chosroes I of Persia invaded Roman Mesopotamia to attack Edessa, claimed to be protected by a legendary religious guarantee. Following a courageous defence—reputedly aided by divine intervention—Chosroes received payment in gold and withdrew. After a failed Roman incursion into Armenia, in 545 the two warring powers agreed to a truce.

Edessa | 1031 | Later Byzantine-Muslim Wars

Despite the terrible Christian defeat near Aleppo at **Azaz**, the great Byzantine commander George Maniaces led a force against Edessa (modern Urfa in southeastern Turkey), which was yielded to him by the Marwanid Emir of Mayyafariqin. When the Arab leader tried to retake the city, Maniaces defeated and repulsed him. Aleppo remained a Christian possession for the next 50 years.

Edessa | 1098 | 1st Crusade

Having detached himself from the main Crusader advance towards **Antioch, Syria** in order to capture **Tarsus**, Baldwin, brother of Godfrey of Bouillon, took his own expedition across the Euphrates, supposedly to assist the Christians of Edessa. He seized the city in a sharp campaign to establish the Latin Principality of Edessa and played no further part in the Crusade (February 1098).

Edessa | 1144 | Crusader-Muslim Wars

When the Turkish warrior Zengi and his son Nur-ed-Din attacked the northernmost Crusader city of Edessa, Count Joscelin of Edessa was away campaigning and his army was too small to relieve the garrison, under Archbishop Hugh. Edessa (modern Urfa, Turkey) fell on Christmas Eve, followed by a brutal massacre, leading to preaching of the 2nd Crusade (28 November–24 December 1144).

Edessa | 1146 | Crusader-Muslim Wars

When Zengi, the Turkish Governor of Mosul, was murdered, Count Joscelin of Edessa tried to recover Edessa, captured two years before. Aided by Lord Baldwin of Marash, he took the town, though the citadel held out and Zengi's son Nur-ed-Din counter-attacked a week later. With Baldwin killed and Joscelin wounded, Edessa was retaken by the Muslims and finally destroyed (3 November 1146).

Edgecote | 1469 | Wars of the Roses

Supporting George Duke of Clarence against his brother Edward IV, Yorkshire Lancastrians under Robin of Redesdale attacked a loyal force led by William Herbert Earl of Pembroke and Humphrey Stafford Earl of Devon. Northeast of Banbury on Danesmoor near Edgecote, the Welsh were routed with perhaps 4,000 killed. Pembroke, Devon and many others were later executed (26 July 1469).

Edgehill, England | 1642 | British Civil Wars

Parliamentary commander Robert Devereux Earl of Essex, attempting to intercept the Royalist march on London, met Charles I at Edgehill, near Kineton in Warwickshire. Despite the courage of Royalist cavalry under Prince Rupert, this first major action of the wars was confused and indecisive. Essex withdrew and the King advanced through **Brentford** (23 October 1642).

Edge Hill, Pennsylvania | 1763 | Pontiac's War

See **Bushy Run**

Edinburgh | 1314 | Rise of Robert the Bruce

As Scotland secured her border areas following victory at **Loudon Hill**, Thomas Randolph Earl of Moray (a nephew of Robert the Bruce) besieged Edinburgh Castle, lost to England in 1296. At the end of a futile six-week siege, Randolph and a handful of men scaled the walls in a brilliant night-assault to overpower the garrison, leading to surrender of the fortress (14 March 1314).

Edinburgh I 1335 I Anglo-Scottish War of Succession
See **Boroughmuir**

Edington I 878 I Viking Wars in Britain
With King Alfred of Wessex previously defeated at **Chippenham** in January, Danish King Guthrum faced the King of the West Saxons marching on Chippenham with a newly raised army. Alfred routed the Danes to the south near Westbury at Edington (Ethandun) and Guthrum sued for peace and withdrew. The action effectively settled the border between Saxon and Danish England (May 878).

Edo I 1868 I War of the Meiji Restoration
See **Ueno**

Eger I 1552 I Turkish-Habsburg Wars
Turkish forces under Kara Ahmed began a fresh offensive and captured **Temesvár**, then marched into eastern Hungary and joined the Pasha of Buda to take Szolnok and besiege Eger (Erlau), southwest of Miskolc, held by Stephan Dobo. After an heroic five-week defence, aided by the wives of the 2,500-strong Imperial garrison, the Ottomans were forced to withdraw (September–October 1552).

Egg Harbour I 1778 I War of the American Revolution
See **Little Egg Harbour**

Eggmühl I 1809 I Napoleonic Wars (5th Coalition)
See **Eckmühl**

Egmont-op-Zee I 1799 I French Revolutionary Wars (2nd Coalition)
See **Alkmaar**

Egorlyk I 1920 I Russian Civil War
See **Torgovaya**

Ekaterinburg I 1918 I Russian Civil War
Having seized **Chelyabinsk**, 40,000 Czech and Slovak former prisoners of war joined the anti-Bolshevik cause and secured much of the Trans-Siberian Railway. Colonel Sergei Voitsekhovsky then marched on nearby Ekaterinburg (modern Sverdlovsk), where the Imperial family had just been murdered. The city was taken and the Czechs continued west towards **Kazan** (25 July 1918).

Ekaterinburg I 1919 I Russian Civil War
As part of a massive counter-offensive in the Urals, Red commander Mikhail Tukhachevski sent General Vasilii Shorin to attack Ekaterinburg (modern Sverdlovsk), defended by 40,000 Whites under General Rudolf Gajda. The city was taken by storm with 3,500 Whites captured and, following further White defeat to the south at **Zlatoust**, the survivors withdrew east to the **Tobol** (15 July 1919).

Ekaterinodar (1st) I 1918 I Russian Civil War
At the start of a fresh offensive into the Kuban, White commander Lavr Kornilov led a strong force against Ekaterinodar (modern Krasnodar), supported by General Sergei Markov. A brutal action saw Kornilov killed by artillery fire on his headquarters and his Volunteer Army withdrew. However, the Whites soon secured success further north at **Novocherkassk** (10–13 April 1918).

Ekaterinodar (2nd) I 1918 I Russian Civil War
On the offensive in the Kuban, white commander Anton Denikin captured **Torgovaya** and **Belaya Glina**, then advanced on Red commander Ivan Sorokin at Ekaterinodar (modern Krasnodar). During a month-long campaign, Denikin captured nearby towns before Ekaterinodar fell by storm. Sorokin fell back on **Stavropol** and Whites reached the sea at Novorosissk (16 July–15 August 1918).

Ekeren I 1703 I War of the Spanish Succession
French Marshal Louis de Boufflers was sent against a Dutch army threatening Antwerp and led 40,000 men against a much smaller force

under Jacob van Wassanaer Heer van Opdam, south of Bergen-op-Zoom around Ekeren. Opdam withdrew prematurely in a confused and bloody action and left General Frederik Johan van Baer to save the defeated army. Opdam then resigned (30 June 1703).

El Agheila ▪ 1941 ▪ World War II (Northern Africa)

With an Italian army destroyed in Libya at **Bardia**, **Tobruk** and **Beda Fomm**, newly arrived German General Erwin Rommel launched an Axis offensive at El Agheila, where British General Richard O'Connor was thrown into headlong retreat. While **Tobruk** held out under siege, O'Connor was captured at the front and a British counter-attack failed at **Sollum-Halfaya** (24 March 1941).

El Agheila ▪ 1942 ▪ World War II (Northern Africa)

As they pursued Field Marshal Erwin Rommel across Libya after victory at **El Alamein**, British forces retook Tobruk (12 November) and Benghazi (19 November) before meeting sharp resistance at Agedabia, then a full-scale defence at El Agheila. Heavy fighting saw costly losses on both sides before Rommel withdrew through **Buerat** and entered **Tunisia** (23 November–15 December 1942).

El Alamein (1st) ▪ 1942 ▪ World War II (Northern Africa)

Falling back from defeat at **Gazala** and **Mersah Matruh**, new British commander Sir Claude Auchinleck committed his reserves to hold a defensive line west of Cairo at El Alamein. His great victory halted Field Marshal Erwin Rommel's advance into Egypt in arguably the most important strategic battle in the Desert war, followed by further Axis defeat at **Alam Halfa** (1–27 July 1942).

El Alamein (2nd) ▪ 1942 ▪ World War II (Northern Africa)

Having forced Field Marshal Erwin Rommel to withdraw at **Alam Halfa**, British General Bernard Montgomery built overwhelming su-

periority in men and armour, then attacked west of Cairo at El Alamein. Despite initial Allied failure and losses, Rommel was forced to disengage and begin retreating west across Libya through **El Agheila** and **Buerat** (23 October–4 November 1942).

Elandsfontein ▪ 1900 ▪ 2nd Anglo-Boer War

General Lord Frederick Roberts led the invasion of Transvaal by advancing on Elandsfontein, a vital railway junction just east of Johannesburg near Germiston, where he came under Boer fire and took some losses. However, the Boers withdrew and, after British victory the same day in the west at **Doornkop**, Roberts permitted the Boers to evacuate Johannesburg (29 May 1900).

Elandslaagte ▪ 1899 ▪ 2nd Anglo-Boer War

As Boers invaded Natal through **Talana Hill**, another column further west under General Johannes Kock was attacked on the railway at Elandslaagte by General John French. A British infantry assault and cavalry charge cost both sides heavy casualties, including Kock mortally wounded. His troops then surrendered, delaying the Boer advance on **Ladysmith** (21 October 1899).

Elands River Poort ▪ 1901 ▪ 2nd Anglo-Boer War

In command of a guerrilla raid into eastern Cape Colony, General Jan Smuts crossed the Orange and sent Deneys Reitz against 130 men of the 17th Lancers in camp at Elands River Poort, near Tarskastad. The British were routed, with 29 killed and 41 wounded including commander Captain Lord George Vivian. The Boers re-equipped themselves with captured supplies (17 September 1901).

Elands River Post ▪ 1900 ▪ 2nd Anglo-Boer War

Jacobus de la Rey captured **Zilikats Nek**, west of Pretoria, then besieged a garrison of 500 Australians and Rhodesians under Colonel Charles O. Hore further west at Elands River Post (modern Swartruggens). A relief attempt by General Sir Frederick Carrington was repulsed and the colonials lost 75 men before finally being relieved by General Robert Broadwood (4–15 August 1900).

El Arish **I** 1799 **I** French Revolutionary Wars (Middle East)

Opening Napoleon Bonaparte's invasion of Syria, advance units from Egypt under General Jean Reynier took El Arish town on the Palestine border, but could not dislodge the Mamluk and Albanian fortress garrison. When General Jean-Baptiste Kléber arrived with fresh troops, a relief force from **Jaffa** was heavily defeated (14–15 February) and the fort surrendered (8–20 February 1799).

El Arish **I** 1916 **I** World War I (Middle East)

See **Magdhaba**

El Arish **I** 1967 **I** Arab-Israeli Six Day War

See **Rafa**

Elasa **I** 161 BC **I** Maccabean War

When a Seleucid army was defeated at **Adasa** by Hebrew rebel Judas Maccabeus, a much larger force was sent later the same year under the powerful General Bacchides. He lured the outnumbered Jews from the hills onto a relatively open battlefield at Elasa, north of Jerusalem. Judas Maccabeus was defeated and killed, though his brothers Jonathon and Simon continued the rebellion.

El Ashmunien **I** 1167 **I** Crusader Invasion of Egypt

After marching into Fatimid Egypt and taking Cairo, Crusaders led by King Amalric of Jerusalem, aided by the deposed Egyptian Vizier Shawar, advanced up the Nile against Turkish General Shirkuh and his nephew Saladin. The Crusader-Egyptian army was badly defeated at El Ashmunien and withdrew to Cairo. But within weeks they besieged and later captured **Alexandria** (18 March 1167).

El Asnam **I** 740 **I** Berber Rebellion

Berbers in the Maghrib Province led by Maysara al-Matghari rebelled against the Arab rulers of North Africa and captured Tangier. After Maysara was deposed and killed by his followers, his successor, Khalid ibn Hamid al-Zanatai, defeated a large Arab army on the Wadi Chelif at El Asnam. Following the "Battle of the Noble Ones," the Arabs were defeated again the following year at **Bakdura**.

El Ayoun **I** 1958 **I** Western Sahara Wars

Soon after Morocco gained independence, Moroccan-backed guerrillas attacked in Spanish West Africa, with severe fighting at El Ayoun. A large-scale assault was repulsed, but next day a Spanish Legion patrol was ambushed and destroyed at nearby Edchera. Within weeks, a massive Spanish-French joint offensive (Ouragan) suppressed the Saharawi rebellion (12–13 January 1958).

Elba **I** 1652 **I** 1st Dutch War

Near the start of the war, Dutch Admiral Jan van Galen's Mediterranean squadron of ten warships attacked English Admiral Richard Badiley off Elba, with just four ships and four merchant vessels. After losing one warship captured, Badiley took refuge in Porto Longone, Elba. The captured ship was retaken in November and in March 1653, battle was resumed off **Leghorn** (28 August 1652).

Elba **I** 1801 **I** French Revolutionary Wars (2nd Coalition)

When the Italian island of Elba refused to surrender to France, the Tuscan garrison—supported by Lieutenant Colonel George Airey—was besieged at Porto Ferraio by French General Pierre Joseph Watrin. Admiral Sir John Warren drove off the French blockade and Watrin withdrew when a landing party under Captain John Chambers destroyed the French batteries (2 May–22 September 1801).

El Bodon **I** 1811 **I** Napoleonic Wars (Peninsular Campaign)

As French forces advanced to relieve the Anglo-Portuguese blockade of **Ciudad Rodrigo**, Marshal

Auguste Marmont crashed into British units under General Sir Thomas Picton eight miles southwest at El Bodon. The Allied army under Arthur Wellesley Lord Wellington withdrew after a courageous defensive victory and Ciudad Rodrigo was temporarily relieved (25 September 1811).

El Caney I 1898 I Spanish-American War

American commander William R. Shafter advanced through **Las Guásimas**, then despatched General Henry W. Lawton against El Caney, northeast of **Santiago de Cuba**. While the massively outnumbered Spanish force suffered heavy casualties, including General Joaquin Vara de Rey killed, the heroic action prevented Lawton joining the main assault that day at **San Juan Hill** (1 July 1898).

Elchingen I 1805 I Napoleonic Wars (3rd Coalition)

Advancing across the Rhine in force, Napoleon Bonaparte's Grand Army swung south to the Danube to cut off the Austrian invasion of Bavaria and trap General Karl Mack von Leiberich at **Ulm**. When Mack attempted to break out of encirclement seven miles east at Elchingen, he was heavily repulsed by General Michel Ney and the French swarmed across the Danube (14 October 1805).

El Ferrol I 1936 I Spanish Civil War

At the start of the war, heavy fighting took place for the key naval base and shipyard at El Ferrol in northwest Spain. The Nationalists eventually seized the port, capturing a battleship, four cruisers (two under construction almost complete) and a destroyer. These formed the backbone of their fleet and two cruisers secured the early strategic victory off **Cape Espartel** (20–21 July 1936).

Elgin I 1040 I Scottish War of Succession

Earl Macbeth of Moray rebelled against his cousin Duncan I of Scotland and allied himself with the Danish Earl Thorfinn to defeat and kill the King near Elgin on the River Lossie, traditionally at Pitgaveney. Macbeth seized the

Scottish throne, but he was eventually defeated by Duncan's son Malcolm at **Dunsinane** (1054) and was killed three years later at **Lumphanan** (14 August 1040).

El Guettar I 1943 I World War II (Northern Africa)

Recovering from disaster in southern Tunisia at **Kasserine**, new American commander George Patton attacked through Gafsa against Italians at El Guettar. After initial success, Patton met strong resistance from German tanks and artillery before breaking through. General Omar Bradley called it America's first "indisputable defeat" of German forces in the war (20 March–8 April 1943).

El Herri I 1914 I French Colonial Wars in North Africa

French forces determined to suppress the Zaia of central Morocco seized their capital at **Khenifra** (12 June) before Colonel René Laverdure marched south to attack the Zaian camp at nearby El Herri. A brutal counter-attack saw Laverdure and 600 of his men killed in the worst French defeat in Morocco, though some French prestige was restored a year later at **Sidi Sliman** (13 November 1914).

Elizabethville I 1961 I Congolese War

After Moise Tshombe proclaimed the secession of Katanga (11 July 1960), UN troops intervened to reintegrate the province. After two failed attempts (August and September 1961) to secure the Katangan capital Elizabethville (modern Lubumbashi), the UN attacked in force with artillery and jet bombers. After costly losses, Tshombe agreed to end the secession (5–18 December 1961).

Elizabethville I 1962–1963 I Congolese Civil War

Despite agreeing to end the secession of Katanga, Moise Tshombe failed to comply and, a year later, UN troops launched a fresh attack on Elizabethville (modern Lubumbashi). The secessionist capital fell after heavy fighting and Katanga was reunited with Congo. Tshombe went into exile but returned as leader to crush rebellion in the east at **Stanleyville** in late 1964 (29 December 1962–15 January 1963).

El Jícaro ▮ 1906 ▮ Guatemalan-Salvador War

When El Salvador supported efforts to overthrow President Manuel Estrada Cabrera of Guatemala, war was declared and Salvadoran General Tomás Regolado invaded eastern Guatemala. He was killed in the first major action at El Jícaro, just south of Tegucicalpa and, after further costly Salvadoran losses, US President Theodore Roosevelt intervened to restore peace (11 July 1906).

Elk Creek ▮ 1863 ▮ American Civil War (Trans-Mississippi)

See **Honey Springs**

Elkhorn Tavern ▮ 1862 ▮ American Civil War (Trans-Mississippi)

See **Pea Ridge**

Elkin's Ferry ▮ 1864 ▮ American Civil War (Trans-Mississippi)

At the start of an expedition southwest from Little Rock, Arkansas, towards **Camden**, Union General Frederick Steele was blocked near the Little Missouri by Confederates under General John S. Marmaduke. Repulsing a rearguard attack at Okolona, Steele fought his way across the river at nearby Elkin's Ferry, then continued south through **Prairie d'Ane** (3–4 April 1864).

El Ksiba ▮ 1913 ▮ French Colonial Wars in North Africa

Colonel Charles Mangin led an offensive against the Zaia of central Morocco and attacked Moussa ou Said's camp at El Ksiba, near Kasbah Tadla, southwest of the Zaian capital at Khenifra. While French cannon inflicted heavy loses, Mangin suffered badly with 63 killed and 153 wounded, many lost on the return march. **Khenifra** fell to a fresh offensive a year later (8–10 June 1913).

Ellandun ▮ 825 ▮ Later Wars of Wessex

Beornwulf of Mercia took advantage of the West Saxons being occupied against the Welsh at **Gafulford** and marched into Wessex to curtail the ambition of King Egbert. Supported by the East Angles, Egbert defeated Mercia in Wiltshire at Ellandun (possibly modern Wroughton near Swindon) and over-ran southeastern England. Beornwulf was killed later in the year during battle in East Anglia.

Elleporus ▮ 389 BC ▮ 2nd Dionysian War

When Dionysius of Syracuse invaded southern Italy he besieged Caulonia, near Locri, then turned against an Italiote League relief army advancing from Crotona under the Syracusan exile Heloris. Surprised at the Elleporus River, on the east coast of the "toe" of Italy, Heloris was defeated and killed. Rhegium itself accepted a truce but was captured two years later.

El Menabba ▮ 1908 ▮ French Colonial Wars in North Africa

Campaigning along Algeria's Moroccan border, Mulai Lahsin surprised a French supply column before dawn at El Menabba, north of Béchar. However, the Moroccans then stopped to loot and the Legionnaires recovered and drove them out. While the humiliating defeat cost 19 killed, 100 wounded and all their supplies, the French were avenged a month later at **Bou Denib** (17 April 1908).

Elmina ▮ 1782 ▮ Anglo-Dutch War

During a brief war against Holland, two British ships under Captain Thomas Shirley (*Leander*) and 500 men under Captain Alexander Mackenzie attacked Fort Conraadsburg at Elmina, on the Gold Coast (modern Ghana). The British were heavily repulsed, but later captured other Dutch forts at Mouree, Cormantine, Apam and Accra. All were returned by treaty in 1785 (16–21 February 1782).

El Moungar ▮ 1903 ▮ French Colonial Wars in North Africa

Driven off from **Taghit** near Algeria's western border, Dawi Mani and Oulad Djerir tribesmen attacked a French supply column and its 113-strong escort under Captain Marie Louis Vauchez further north at El Moungar. The Legion lost 38 killed (including Vauchez) and only 20 remained unwounded as the Moroccans made off with the convoy and its supplies (2 September 1903).

El Mughar I 1917 I World War I (Middle East)

With his cavalry advancing north along the Palestine coast from **Gaza**, British commander Sir Edmund Allenby struck the Turkish Eighth Army under Colonel Friedrich von Kressenstein trying to hold the railway west of Jerusalem near El Mughar. The Turks were driven back and the port city of Jaffa fell two days later as Allenby circled northeast to outflank **Jerusalem** (13–14 November 1917).

El Obeid I 1883 I British-Sudan Wars

Khedive Mohammad Ahmed of Egypt faced a rising in the Upper Sudan by the Mahdi and sent 10,000 Egyptians under General William Hicks, who reached Khartoum, then marched southwest towards the Dervish capital at El Obeid. In the desert nearby at Kashgil, Hicks was killed and his army was utterly destroyed, forcing an Anglo-Egyptian evacuation of the Sudan (4 November 1883).

El Potrero I 1840 I Central American National Wars

Defeated by Salvadoran invaders at **Soledad**, new Honduran President José Francisco Zelaya sought aid from Nicaragua, which sent a 500-strong force under General Manuel Quijano. Just south of Tegicucalpa at El Potrero, Salvadoran General José Trinidad Cabañas was defeated and driven out. Salvadoran forces then invaded Guatemala to take and then lose **Guatemala City** (31 January 1840).

El Ronquillo I 1810 I Napoleonic Wars (Peninsular Campaign)

Campaigning in southwestern Spain, General Francisco Ballesteros struck at the French forces of Honoré Théodore Gazan at El Ronquillo, 20 miles north of Seville, where he suffered an unexpected check and was driven off. Forces sent by Marshal Édouard Mortier then beat Ballesteros at Zalamea (15 April) and Aracena (26 May) before he withdrew to Gibraltar (25 March 1810).

El Sombrero I 1818 I Venezuelan War of Independence

See **Sombrero, Venezuela**

El Tambo I 1816 I Colombian War of Independence

Spanish commander Pablo Morillo recaptured **Cartagena** and Bogotá, then sent General Juan Samano to recover Popayán, lost following defeat at **Palo River**, and to reconquer the Cauca Valley. Marching west to meet the Royalists at El Tambo, 24-year-old Patriot Colonel Liborio Mejía suffered a terrible defeat and withdrew towards **La Plata** while Samano took Popayán (29 June 1816).

El Teb (1st) I 1884 I British-Sudan Wars

Advancing south from the Red Sea port of Trinkitat to relieve the Mahdist siege of **Tokar**, General Valentine Baker and more than 4,000 Turks, Sudanese and Egyptians were met at El Teb by a large Dervish army under Abdullah ibn Hamid. Baker lost two-thirds of his force to the Hadendowa warriors in a disastrous rout, but he was avenged three weeks later at the same site (4 February 1884).

El Teb (2nd) I 1884 I British-Sudan Wars

Determined to avenge British defeat at El Teb, Generals Sir Gerald Graham and Sir Redvers Buller left the Red Sea port of Trinkitat with 3,000 infantry and 900 cavalry to relieve the Mahdist siege of nearby **Tokar**. The Dervishes were defeated in hard fighting with 2,000 killed. Graham then relieved Tokar before returning to Trinkitat and in March he beat the Dervishes at **Tamai** (29 February 1884).

Eltekeh I 700 BC I Assyrian Wars

When Hezekiah of Judah refused tribute to Assyria, Senaccherib led a large force which routed the Judean King and his Egyptian allies at

Eltekeh, near Ekron, southeast of Joppa. Assyrian forces then besieged and captured Lachmish further south and Hezekiah paid a tribute to avoid the capture of Jerusalem. Senaccherib withdrew but assigned much of Judah to his allies in Palestine.

Eltham's Landing I 1862 I American Civil War (Eastern Theatre)
As the Confederate army withdrew up the Virginia Peninsula from **Yorktown**, a Union force under Brigadier General William B. Franklin attempted a flank attack, disembarking to the north on the York River at Eltham's Landing, near West Point. Marching towards Barhamsville, Franklin was intercepted by General Gustavus W. Smith and driven off with almost 200 casualties (7 May 1862).

El Uvero I 1957 I Cuban Revolution
Rebel leader Ernesto Che Guevara over-ran the garrison at **La Plata, Cuba** (16 January), then gathered a larger force and attacked the well-fortified Federal barracks further east at El Uvero. While both sides suffered unexpectedly high losses, the victorious rebels captured large quantities of arms. A year later, President Fulgencio Batista sent a major counter-offensive into the **Sierra Maestra** (27–28 May 1957).

Elvas I 1659 I Spanish-Portuguese Wars
When Portuguese forces under Joao Rodrigues de Vascondellos Conde de Castello-Melhor invaded Spain to besiege Badajoz, they were driven off by Luis Mendez de Haro, who unwisely pursued the Portuguese across the Guadiana into Portugal. At Elvas, 20 miles west of Badajoz, de Haro was routed by Castello-Melhor and Sancho de Villa Flor and fled in panic (14 January 1659).

Ely I 1071 I Norman Conquest of Britain
Supported by Danish King Sweyn Estridsen, the Saxon leader Hereward the Wake sacked Peterborough (1070). After King William I persuaded the Danes to withdraw, Hereward was left to

defend the fortified camp at Ely, Cambridgeshire. Hereward escaped when Normans stormed the stronghold, but over 1,000 Saxons were killed, crushing the final local resistance after **Hastings**.

Ely I 1267 I 2nd English Barons' War
With Baronial rebellion by Simon de Montfort Earl of Leicester routed at **Evesham** (August 1265), the remainder were defeated at **Axholme** and **Chesterfield** before Prince Edward moved against the last hold-outs under John d'Eyvill on the Isle of Ely in the Fens of Cambridgeshire. The disinherited rebels were crushed and forced to acknowledge Henry III as King, ending the war (11 July 1267).

Elz I 1796 I French Revolutionary Wars (1st Coalition)
See **Emmendingen**

Emaqongqo I 1840 I Zulu Wars of Succession
See **Maqonqo**

Embadeh I 1798 I French Revolutionary Wars (Middle East)
See **Pyramids**

Embata I 356 BC I 1st Greek Social War
A year after defeat off **Chios**, Athenian commander Chares was reinforced by Iphicrates and Timotheus and they met the combined forces of Chios, Rhodes, Cos and Byzantium in the Hellespont. Unwisely sailing out to battle while his colleagues were deterred by storms, Chares was badly defeated off Embata, near Chios. Athens soon made peace and recognised the independence of the allies.

Embudo Pass I 1847 I American-Mexican War
Facing a rising against the American annexation of New Mexico, Colonel Sterling Price dispersed a large insurgent force at **La Cañada**, near modern Santa Cruz, then advanced up the Rio Grande against a strong position at the Embudo Pass. The Mexicans were driven off with 20 killed and 60 wounded and Price con-

tinued northeast towards **Pueblo de Taos** (29 January 1847).

Emessa ∎ 272 ∎ Roman-Palmyrean War

When Emperor Aurelian invaded Syria against Queen Zenobia of Palmyra, he defeated her army at **Immae**, then pursued her south along the Orontes River. Palmyrean General Zabdas commanded a large army at Emessa (modern Homs in western Syria), but after the defeat of his cavalry, the Palmyreans fled. Zabdas withdrew into the desert to Zenobia's capital at **Palmyra**.

Emmaus ∎ 166 BC ∎ Maccabean War

Jewish rebel Judas Maccabeus defeated the Seleucids at **Beth Horon**, then later that year faced a large army sent under Seleucid Generals Nicanor and Gorgias. While Gorgias was unsuccessfully raiding the Jewish camp, Judas fought Nicanor at Emmaus (modern Imwas), west of Jerusalem. By the time Gorgias returned, the Seleucid camp at Emmaus had been destroyed and the government army put to flight.

Emmendingen ∎ 1796 ∎ French Revolutionary Wars (1st Coalition)

Driven back towards the Rhine by Archduke Charles Louis of Austria, despite a sharp victory at **Biberach**, French General Jean Victor Moreau suffered a costly defeat on the Elz at Emmendingen, just north of Freiburg. He then sent General Louis Desaix across the Rhine at Breisach and continued retreating south before crossing to the left bank after further defeat at **Schliengen** (19 October 1796).

Empadine ∎ 1893 ∎ Matabele War

Invading Matebeleland (in modern Zimbabwe) against King Lobengula, Colonel Goold Adams advanced north towards Empadine, where 600 Matabele under Gambo attacked a patrol led by Captain Thomas Tancred. They were then routed by the main British force, but the over-cautious Adams played no part in the capture of Bulawayo after the victory at **Imbembesi** (2 November 1893).

Empingham ∎ 1470 ∎ Wars of the Roses
See **Lose-Coat Field**

Empress Augusta Bay ∎ 1943 ∎ World War II (Pacific)

As American forces landed at Cape Torokina in Empress Augusta Bay on **Bougainville**, Japanese Admiral Sentaro Omori tried to disrupt the invasion and was attacked by the covering force under Admiral Stanton Merrill. With superior radar, Merrill sank a Japanese cruiser and a destroyer, forcing Omori to withdraw at the cost of just one American destroyer damaged (2 November 1943).

Emsdorf ∎ 1760 ∎ Seven Years War (Europe)

Despite defeat at **Korbach**, Duke Ferdinand of Brunswick sent Prince Karl Wilhelm Ferdinand south through Hesse against French communications. Northeast of Marburg, between Emsdorf and Erxdorf, the Hereditary Prince's German and English cavalry routed and captured French General Christian Glaubitz. The French were decisively defeated at **Warburg** two weeks later (16 July 1760).

Emuckfaw ∎ 1814 ∎ Creek Indian War

General Andrew Jackson led an inexperienced force against Creek Indians at **Horseshoe Bend**, on the Tallapoosa in Alabama, and came under severe attack at nearby Emuckfaw. With Major Alexander Donelson killed and lacking sufficient forces to take the Creek fortress, Jackson retreated towards Fort Strother, through another costly engagement at **Enotachopco** (22 January 1814).

Enderta ∎ 1936 ∎ 2nd Italo-Ethiopian War
See **Amba Aradam**

Engabeni ∎ 1837 ∎ Boer-Matabele War
See **Kapain**

Engen ∎ 1800 ∎ French Revolutionary Wars (2nd Coalition)

On a major French offensive across the Rhine, northwest of Lake Constance, General Jean

Victor Moreau was attacked by Austrian General Paul Kray in the Black Forest. During a prolonged and sprawling engagement, Moreau defeated Kray at Engen, taking a large number of prisoners, while General Claude-Jacques Lecourbe defeated the Austrian rearguard at nearby **Stockach** (3 May 1800).

Englefield ❚ 870 ❚ Viking Wars in Britain

With East Anglia secured following victory at **Hoxne**, Viking forces under Halfdan (son of Ragnar Lodbrok) and the warrior Bagsecq, invaded Wessex. West of Reading at Englefield, a Viking advance party was heavily repulsed by Aethelwulf, Ealdorman of Berkshire. However, an Anglo-Saxon attack on the invaders' camp at **Reading** a few days later was a costly failure (December 870).

English Channel ❚ 1588 ❚ Anglo-Spanish Wars
See **Spanish Armada**

Eniwetok ❚ 1944 ❚ World War II (Pacific)

Following capture of **Kwajalein**, in the central **Marshall Islands** (4 February), Americans under Admiral Harry Hill and General Thomas Watson moved 350 miles west against the well-fortified Eniwetok Atoll. A massive preliminary bombardment and very heavy fighting virtually annihilated the entire 4,000-man garrison, including commander General Yoshima Nishida (17–20 February 1944).

Enkhuizen ❚ 1573 ❚ Netherlands War of Independence
See **Zuyder Zee**

Enna ❚ 133 BC ❚ 1st Servile War

Veteran Roman General Publius Rupilius was sent to suppress a large-scale slave rebellion in Sicily, where he first captured the rebel city of **Tauromenium**. Later in the year, he stormed the mountain stronghold of Enna in central Sicily and the rebellion was brutally crushed. The insurgent leader Cleon of Cilicia was killed in the fighting and his ally Eunus the Syrian died in prison.

Enniscorthy ❚ 1798 ❚ Irish Rebellion

At the start of the rebellion in Ireland, a large rebel force under Father John Murphy attacked the town of Enniscorthy, 12 miles from Wexford on the River Slaney. North Cork militia and yeomanry infantry under Captain William Snowe held them off with heavy losses, then withdrew to Wexford. The rebels set up a major encampment on nearby **Vinegar Hill** (28 May 1798).

Enniskillen ❚ 1689 ❚ War of the Glorious Revolution
See **Newtown Butler**

Enogai Inlet ❚ 1943 ❚ World War II (Pacific)

During the assault on **New Georgia**, a Raider Battalion under Colonel Harry Liversidge landed behind enemy lines (5 July) and crossed the Dragons Peninsula for a rear attack on the Japanese coastal guns at Enogai Inlet, commanding the **Kula Gulf**. Heavy fighting cost the Americans 48 killed and 77 wounded, but the guns were silenced and the 350-man Japanese garrison was destroyed (10 July 1943).

Enotachopco ❚ 1814 ❚ Creek Indian War

After a failed advance against Creek Indians in Alabama, General Andrew Jackson withdrew from **Emuckfaw**, then came under attack at Enotachopco Creek, where his rearguard under Colonel William Carroll suffered heavy losses. Jackson rallied his inexperienced troops, but lost 20 dead and 75 wounded before extracting his force. He was soon avenged at **Horseshoe Bend** (24 January 1814).

Ensenada ❚ 1827 ❚ Argentine-Brazilian War
See **Monte Santiago**

Enslin ❚ 1899 ❚ 2nd Anglo-Boer War
See **Graspan**

Enterprise vs _Boxer_ ❚ 1813 ❚ War of 1812
See **Portland, Maine**

Entrammes I 1793 I French Revolutionary Wars (Vendée War)

Campaigning north of the Loire, Vendéean rebel Henri de la Rochejaquelein concentrated his force at Entrammes on the Mayenne to face the Republican army of General Jean Lechelle. Failing to wait for his full army to arrive, Lechelle attacked and was routed with the loss of 4,000 men and most of his guns and stores. He never again commanded in the field (26 October 1793).

Entshanana I 1884 I Zulu Civil War
See **Tshaneni**

Enugu I 1967 I Biafran War

Goaded by the abortive rebel invasion of Midwest State through **Benin**, the bulk of the Nigerian Federal army of General Yakubu Gowon advanced on the Biafran capital at Enugu. After heavy shelling, the coal and steel city fell to Colonel Theophilus Danjuma and rebel leader Colonel Chukwuemeka Ojukwu transferred his capital to **Umuahia** (26 September–4 October 1967).

Enzheim I 1674 I 3rd Dutch War

Marshal Henri de Turenne advanced along the Rhine after his victory at **Sinsheim** in June and captured Strasbourg for Louis XIV of France. He then marched southwest to nearby Enzheim against a superior Imperial force led by Prince Alexandre de Bournonville. While both sides withdrew after heavy casualties, Turenne is regarded as having won a narrow but costly victory (4 October 1674).

Épéhy I 1918 I World War I (Western Front)

Near the start of his assault on the **Hindenburg Line**, British commander Sir Douglas Haig launched a preliminary attack against outlying defences held by superior forces under General Max von Boehn. General Julian Byng took Havrincourt (18 September), then joined Sir Henry Rawlinson in the main attack around Épéhy, capturing 100 guns and over 11,000 prisoners (12–28 September 1918).

Ephesus I 498 BC I Greco-Persian Wars

When some Greek cities on Asia Minor's Ionian coast rebelled against Persia and secured aid from Athens, the Satrap Artaphernes (brother of King Darius) recovered Sardis, then attacked the Greeks near Ephesus. The Persians won a decisive victory though the Greek cities continued their revolt. Persia then turned to recover Cyprus with victory at **Salamis**, before resuming the war in Ionia at **Miletus**.

Ephesus I 406 BC I Great Peloponnesian War
See **Notium**

Epidaurus I 47 BC I Wars of the First Triumvirate
See **Tauris**

Epila I 1348 I Aragonese Civil War

When Pedro IV of Aragon named his daughter as heir, he faced open rebellion by Aragonese nobles exercising rights granted to them by previous Kings. After forcing the King to name a male heir, open war broke out and the nobles besieged Royalists under Lope de Luna at Epila, west of Zaragoza. Pedro arrived to secure a decisive victory and he severely curbed the power of the aristocracy (21 July 1348).

Epsom I 1944 I World War II (Western Europe)

As part of Montgomery's advance on **Caen**, General Miles Dempsey launched a large-scale offensive—Operation Epsom—along the Orne, southwest of the city. After very costly fighting, the British forced a salient into the German line before both sides fell back exhausted. Over 100 Panzers were lost and Marshal Gerd von Rundstedt was replaced. Caen fell a week later (26–29 June 1944).

Erbach I 1800 I French Revolutionary Wars (2nd Coalition)

With General Jean Victor Moreau invading southern Germany after victory at **Mosskirch**, Austrian commander Paul Kray counterattacked at **Biberach**, then in greater strength towards Erbach on the Danube, where Moreau was driven back. French reinforcements restored the line and Kray fell back through Delmensingen (20 May) and Kelmuntz (5 June) towards **Ulm** (16 May 1800).

Erdi ∎ 1986 ∎ Libyan-Chad War

As rival tribal leaders struggled for control of northern Chad, the mainly Arab forces of Libyan-backed Acheikh ibn Oumar seized Erdi, then faced a massive counter-attack by Toubou loyal to Goukouni Oueddei. Libyan tanks and aircraft intervened to rescue Acheikh and Erdi was saved but at very heavy cost. Full-scale war began when Libyan regulars advanced on **Zouar** (5 October 1986).

Erego ∎ 1902 ∎ Wars of the Mad Mullah

General Eric Swayne defeated Muhammad Abdullah Hassan of Somaliland at **Ferdiddin** (June 1901), then led a second expedition southeast from Bohotle towards Erego, near Mudug Oasis. Hard fighting saw almost 100 British killed and a Maxim lost before the Dervishes withdrew with 1,400 lost. Although Swayne was recalled, further action followed at **Gumburu** and **Daratoleh** (6 October 1902).

Eressos ∎ 1821 ∎ Greek War of Independence

In the first important naval action of the war, Greek Admiral Yakoumakis Tombazes met the Turkish fleet advancing from the Dardanelles and pursued a Turkish battleship to Eressos on southwestern Lesbos. After ineffective gunfire, the heroic Dimitris Papanikolis used a fireship to destroy the man-of-war, which was lost with about 400 lives. The Turkish fleet then withdrew (5–8 June 1821).

Erestfer ∎ 1702 ∎ 2nd "Great" Northern War

Despite his terrible defeat at **Narva** in 1700, Russian Tsar Peter I ordered General Boris Sheremetev into eastern Livonia, where he met Swedish General Anton von Schlippenbach at Erestfer, near Dorpat. Using infantry, dragoons and sledge-mounted cannon, Sheremetev won a decisive victory, with over 3,000 Swedes lost and 350 prisoners. He also gained his Marshal's baton (7 January 1702).

Eretria ∎ 411 BC ∎ Great Peloponnesian War

When Euboea threatened to revolt against Athens, a powerful fleet under Spartan Admiral Agesandridas was sent to aid the rebels. Forced to respond, Athenian Admiral Thymochares put to sea with an ill-trained squadron, which met the Spartans off the harbour of Eretria, south of modern Chalcis. The Athenians were crushed, with 22 ships and crews lost, and the Euboean rebellion spread.

Ergeme ∎ 1560 ∎ Livonian War
See **Oomuli**

Erie ∎ 1812 ∎ War of 1812
See **Fort Erie**

Erivan ∎ 1616–1618 ∎ Turko-Persian Wars

Advancing into Armenia to recover cities seized by Persia, Ottoman Grand Vizier Damad Mehmed Pasha was dismissed when he was repulsed assaulting Erivan and made peace. New Vizier Khalil Pasha and his Crimean Tatar allies renewed the siege, but after defeat by the Persians southeast near Arbadil (10 September 1618), Khalil was driven off and made peace (1616–September 1618).

Erivan ∎ 1635–1636 ∎ Turko-Persian Wars

Turkish Sultan Murad IV renewed his campaign against Persia, where he captured Tabriz in the northwest, then took Erivan in Armenia before returning to Constantinople. A hard-fought counter-offensive saw Persian Shah Safi march against Erivan, which fell after a long winter siege. While Erivan remained in Persian hands, Murad responded two years later by finally taking **Baghdad**.

Erivan ❙ 1724 ❙ Turko-Persian War

Launching a fresh invasion of Persian-held Armenia, Turkish forces besieged Erivan (modern Yerevan), said to be the most powerful fortress in the country. After a three-month siege and terrible Turkish losses in four failed assaults, the Persian garrison surrendered and was permitted to leave with the honours of war. The invaders then marched southeast against **Tabriz** (September 1724).

Erivan ❙ 1731 ❙ Turko-Persian War

Shah Tahmasp II defeated the Afghans in Persia, then marched into Turkish Armenia with 18,000 men against Hakimoglu Ali Pasha. Following defeat at Echmiadzin, the Turks fell back to Erivan (modern Yerevan), which Tahmasp besieged having failed to take it by assault. Faced by a separate Turkish threat to **Hamadan**, Tahmasp had to lift his siege and withdraw (March 1731).

Erivan ❙ 1804 ❙ Russo-Persian Wars
    See **Echmiadzin**

Erivan ❙ 1827 ❙ Russo-Persian Wars

On a new offensive against the Persian invasion of Armenia, Russian General Afanasi Ivanovich Krasovski blockaded Erivan, but had to withdraw when the Persians advanced towards **Echmiadzin**. Russian Commander Ivan Paskevich then resumed the siege (28 September) and took the city by storm, earning the title Count of Erivan. Persia soon sued for peace (July–1 October 1827).

Erlau ❙ 1552 ❙ Turkish-Habsburg Wars
    See **Eger**

Ermes ❙ 1560 ❙ Livonian War
    See **Oomuli**

Er Ridisiya ❙ 1799 ❙ French Revolutionary Wars (Middle East)

Having defeated Mamluk General Murad Bey on the left bank of the Nile at **Aswan**, French General Louis Desaix sent Louis-Nicolas Davout's cavalry across the river in pursuit of General Osman Bey. In some of the hardest fighting on the Upper Nile, Davout defeated the Mamluks during a sandstorm at Er Ridisiya Bihari, though at a heavy cost in French casualties (11 February 1799).

Erxdorf ❙ 1760 ❙ Seven Years War (Europe)
    See **Emsdorf**

Erzincan ❙ 1473 ❙ Ottoman-Turkoman War

When Uzun Hassan of the White Sheep Turkomans advanced from Azerbaijan into Anatolia and destroyed Tokat, Ottoman Sultan Mehmed II's army was checked at **Terjan**. However, the following year at Otluk Beli, northeast of Erzincan, the Turkoman army was destroyed by Mehmed and Vizier Ahmad Gedik Pasha, securing Turkish domination over Anatolia (11 August 1473).

Erzincan ❙ 1916 ❙ World War I (Caucasus Front)

Resuming his advance across the Caucasus from **Erzurum**, Russian commander Nikolai Yudenich split the Turkish defence at **Bayburt**, then advanced on General Abdul Kerim at Erzincan. The Turkish Third Army was utterly crushed, losing 17,000 casualties and another 17,000 captured. Yudenich then turned south against the Second Army around **Bitlis** (23–25 July 1916).

Erzurum ❙ 298 ❙ Roman-Persian Wars

The year after his disastrous defeat at **Callinicum**, Galerius Maximus secured reinforcements from the Danube and marched into Armenia against Narses of Persia. Near Erzurum, he inflicted a decisive defeat on the Persian army, capturing massive booty including the King's harem. He then raided towards Ctesiphon and Narses sued for peace, ceding Mesopotamia and other territory to Rome.

Erzurum ❙ 1821 ❙ Turko-Persian War in Azerbaijan

Facing an attack by the Turkish army of Dawud Pasha of Baghdad, Persian Prince Abbas Mirza marched west with 30,000 men in a counter-invasion and met the much larger force at Erzurum, north of Lake Van. The Turks were badly defeated in a decisive battle before Abbas was turned back by winter. He won again the next year at **Khoi** before both sides agreed to make peace.

Erzurum ∎ 1877–1878 ∎ Russo-Turkish Wars

As he advanced through the Caucasus from capturing **Kars**, Russian Grand Duke Michael pursued Turkish commander Ahmed Mukhtar Pasha, who had withdrawn following defeat at **Aladja Dagh** to the fortress of Erzurum. While investment of Erzurum was completed in December 1877, the Turks held out against a bitter winter siege until an armistice signed on 31 January 1878 ended the war.

Erzurum ∎ 1916 ∎ World War I (Caucasus Front)

Russian commander Nikolai Yudenich crushed the Turks at **Koprukoy** in January, then stormed west across the Caucasus in bitter winter conditions to attack Abdul Kerim at Erzurum. A three-day battle saw Yudenich break through the outer perimeter of fortresses and entrenchments, forcing the Turks to abandon the city and retreat towards **Bayburt** and **Erzincan** (11–16 February 1916).

Escobea ∎ 1873 ∎ 2nd British-Ashanti War

With Ashanti forces threatening the British at **Abakrampa**, north of Elmina in modern Ghana, further north at Dunquah Colonel (later Sir) Francis Festing led a force west against the nearby Ashanti camp at Escobea, held by the Chiefs Essaman Quantah and Quasi Doomfie. The Ashanti camp was destroyed and the survivors dispersed, withdrawing north through **Amoafo** (27 October 1873).

Eshowe ∎ 1879 ∎ Anglo-Zulu War

Soon after repulsing a Zulu force on the **Nyezane** in southern Zululand, Colonel Charles Pearson fortified the mission station at nearby Eshowe, which he held with about 1,400 troops and 460 native auxiliaries. After ten weeks' loose siege, Pearson was relieved following British victory to the southeast at **Gingindlovu** and the entire force returned south into Natal (23 January–3 April 1879).

Eski Hissarlik ∎ 1915 ∎ World War I (Gallipoli)

When Anglo-French forces landed on the Gallipoli Peninsula around **Helles**, the Turks repulsed an advance towards **Krithia**, then counter-attacked around Eski Hissarlik. The night action cost severe losses on both sides, especially among the French Senegalese. Following a second Allied offensive towards Krithia, the opposing forces dug in for virtual trench warfare (1–3 May 1915).

Eskisehir ∎ 1097 ∎ 1st Crusade
See **Dorylaeum**

Eskisehir ∎ 1147 ∎ 2nd Crusade
See **Dorylaeum**

Eskisehir ∎ 1921 ∎ 2nd Greco-Turkish War

With the Greek army checked in Anatolia at the **Inönü**, King Constantine took command and led his army against the Turks around nearby Eskisehir. Turkish General Ismet Pasha (later Inönü) fought a bloody defence before commander Mustafa Kemal had to order a withdrawal to prevent further losses. The Turks then fell back to a defensive position on the **Sakarya** (16–17 July 1921).

Eski Zagra ∎ 1122 ∎ Byzantine-Pecheneg Wars

Thirty years after the disastrous defeat at **Mount Leburnion**, a fresh horde of Pecheneg Turks invaded through Bulgaria and ravaged as far as Thrace and Macedonia before being met by Varangians and mercenary knights under John II Comnenus at Eski Zagra (modern Stara Zagora) in Bulgaria. The invaders were defeated with terrible slaughter and virtually disappeared from history.

Espinosa ▌ 1808 ▌ Napoleonic Wars (Peninsular Campaign)

Napoleon Bonaparte invaded Spain with a large army, sending Marshals Claude Victor and Francois Lefebvre through Old Castile, where they attacked General Joachim Blake in a strong position west of **Bilbao** at Espinosa de los Monteros. Despite an initial costly repulse, the French won a decisive victory next day and Blake's Galicians withdrew west to **Reynosa** (10–11 November 1808).

Espiritu Santo ▌ 1839 ▌ Central American National Wars

Facing an invasion of eastern El Salvador by Honduran-Nicaraguan troops under Francisco Ferrera, Liberal President Francisco Morazán of El Salvador lost at **Jicaral**. But at Espiritu Santo, northwest of San Miguel, Morazán and José Trinidad Cabanas routed the invaders. Morazán later beat Ferrera again at **San Pedro Perulapán** while Cabañas won in Honduras at **Tegucicalpa** (6 April 1839).

Esquiroz ▌ 1521 ▌ 1st Habsburg-Valois War

Francis I of France resolved to restore Henry d'Albert to the throne of Navarre and sent a large army under Andre de Foix de Lesparre to occupy Navarre and Castile, where they besieged Logrono. Two months later, a relief army under Antonio de Lara Duke of Najera routed the French at Esquiroz, northeast of Pamplona, capturing de Foix and repelling the invaders (May–30 June 1521).

Es Salt (1st) ▌ 1918 ▌ World War I (Middle East)

Having secured **Jerusalem** and **Jericho**, Sir Edmund Allenby sent General John Shea across the Jordan to support Arab forces around **Amman**. Costly fighting against Turks under Liman von Sanders won Es Salt, northwest of Amman, though heavy rain and bombing blocked further advance. Shea had to withdraw across the swollen Jordan with about 1,400 casualties (23–30 March 1918).

Es Salt (2nd) ▌ 1918 ▌ World War I (Middle East)

General Harry Chauvel led a second attempt to support Arab forces around Amman, crossing the Jordan with Australian, New Zealand and Imperial forces to take Es Salt, northwest of Amman, along with over 1,000 Turkish prisoners. However, he had to withdraw in the face of costly losses and Turkish reinforcements. **Amman** did not fall for another four months (30 April–4 May 1918).

Essaman ▌ 1873 ▌ 2nd British-Ashanti War

With Ashanti forces under Amonquatia threatening the coastal port at Elmina, in modern Ghana, General Sir Garnet Wolseley took an African auxiliary force sweeping north and west against the villages of Essaman and Amguana. Near Essaman, the Ashanti were defeated and driven away from the so-called Cape Coast. They were soon defeated again near **Abakrampa** (14 October 1873).

Essertenne ▌ 1870 ▌ Franco-Prussian War
See **Gray**

Essex vs *Phoebe* ▌ 1814 ▌ War of 1812
See **Valparaiso**

Essie ▌ 1058 ▌ Scottish War of Succession

When the usurper King Macbeth of Scotland was defeated at **Dunsinane** and killed at **Lumphanan**, his followers installed his stepson Lulach—the Simpleton—son of Queen Gruoch by her first husband. However, the victorious Malcolm Canmore soon defeated and killed Lulach at Essie in Strathbogie, Aberdeenshire, and was crowned as Malcolm III (17 March 1058).

Es Sinn ▌ 1916 ▌ World War I (Mesopotamia)
See **Dujaila**

Essling ▌ 1809 ▌ Napoleonic Wars (5th Coalition)
See **Aspern-Essling**

Estella I 1873 I 2nd Carlist War
See **Montejurra**

Estella I 1874 I 2nd Carlist War
Spanish Republican Marshal Francisco Serrano captured Carlist **Bilbao**, then sent General Manuel de la Concha against Estella, held by Carlist Generals Antonio Dorregaray and Torcuato Mendíri. Concha was killed in heavy fighting near Abárzuza and the Republicans were driven off with over 1,000 casualties. Estella was saved and Mendíri became Count of Abárzuza (25–28 June 1874).

Estella I 1876 I 2nd Carlist War
Near the end of the war in Spain, Republican General Fernando Primo de Rivera became commander in chief and advanced on the remaining Carlist stronghold at Estella. The city itself was taken by storm after bloody victory at nearby **Montejurra** and, a week later, Don Carlos VII fled Spain for good, ending the fighting. Primo de Rivera was created Marques de Estella (19 February 1876).

Estero Bellaco I 1866 I War of the Triple Alliance
A fresh Allied offensive into southwest Paraguay against President Francisco Solano López saw 45,000 Brazilians and Argentines led by General Venancio Flores surprised at Estero Bellaco, near the Upper Parana, by just 5,000 Paraguayans under General José Eduvigis Díaz. Fighting on marshy ground, Díaz had initial success before being forced to withdraw northeast to **Tuyutí** (2 May 1866).

Estero Rojas I 1867 I War of the Triple Alliance
A bold initiative from besieged **Humaitá** saw Paraguayan Colonel Valois Rivarola ambush a convoy led by Brigadier Alexandre Manuel Albino de Carvalho approaching the Allied base at **Tuyutí**. Attacking at nearby Estero Rojas, Rivarola inflicted about 300 casualties before the convoy was rescued by troops from Tuyutí under Brazilian General Manuel Marques de Sousa (24 September 1867).

Estill's Defeat I 1782 I War of the American Revolution
See **Little Mountain**

Esztergom I 1595 I Later Turkish-Habsburg Wars
Leading a fresh Imperial advance into Turkish Hungary, Prince Karl of Mansfeldt besieged the important fortress of Esztergom, north of Buda, held by the veteran warrior Kara Ali. A relief army led by the son of Grand Vizier Sinan Pasha was heavily defeated at the gates of the city and Kara Ali was killed as Esztergom fell by storm and was put to the sack (7 September 1595).

Esztergom I 1605 I Turkish-Habsburg Wars
Turkish Grand Vizier Lala Mehmed Pasha led a fresh offensive in Hungary to capture Pest, then marched north to besiege Esztergom, supported by Prince Stephan Bocskai of Transylvania, who was in revolt against the Emperor. The city fell by storm and the Habsburgs evacuated Transylvania, recognising Bocskai, who mediated peace between the Emperor and the Sultan (29 September 1604).

Esztergom I 1683 I Turkish-Habsburg Wars
Weeks after defeating the Turks at **Vienna** and **Parkany**, Charles V of Lorraine besieged the Danube fortress of Esztergom. When his artillery breached the walls, 4,000 Turks surrendered and were allowed to march out with their arms. Grand Vizier Kara Mustafa had three local commanders beheaded for cowardice, but he was himself later executed for failure (20–26 October 1683).

Etampes I 1652 I War of the 2nd Fronde
A month after defeating part of the army of Louis XIV and Cardinal Mazarin at **Blenau**, rebel French nobles under Louis II de Bourbon Prince of Condé and his Spanish allies were met south of Paris at Etampes by the main Royal army under Marshal Henri de Turenne. Condé was defeated and driven back to Paris, where he

was defeated again two months later at **St Antoine** (4 May 1652).

Etchoe | 1760 | Cherokee Indian Wars

With **Fort Prince George** and **Fort Loudoun** besieged by Cherokee Chief Oconostota, General Jeffrey Amherst in Charleston sent a large relief force of Scottish regulars under Colonel Archibald Montgomerie. Attacked on the Little Tennessee River near Etchoe (modern Franklin, North Carolina), Montgomerie withdrew with 20 killed and 76 wounded (27 June 1760).

Etchoe | 1761 | Cherokee Indian Wars

Following the **Fort Loudoun** massacre by Cherokee Chief Oconostota, General Jeffrey Amherst in Charleston eventually sent 2,600 regulars and local militia into North Carolina under Colonel James Grant. He won a hard-fought action on the Little Tennessee near Etchoe (modern Franklin), site of battle the previous year, and the Cherokee soon sued for peace (10 June 1761).

Ethaleni | 1838 | Boer-Zulu War

Boer leaders Piet Uys and Andries Potgieter led a counter-offensive against Zulu King Dingane after the massacre at **Bloukranz** (18 February), taking over 300 men across the Tugela. Ambushed by Chief Ndlela at Ethaleni, on the Mhlatuze, west of Gingindlovu, the Boers were routed and fled, with Uys and his son among the dead. The Zulus soon won again at the **Tugela** (11 April 1838).

Ethandun | 878 | Viking Wars in Britain

See **Edington**

Etival | 1870 | Franco-Prussian War

German commander Karl August von Werder campaigning west of **Strasbourg** sent General Alfred von Degenfeld towards Epinal. Between Etival and Nompatelize, south of Raon l'Etape, Degenfeld crashed into part of General Louis-Francois Dupré's Army of Lyons. The badly outnumbered French lost 2,000 casualties and prisoners and Dupré was severely wounded (6 October 1870).

Etshaneni | 1884 | Zulu Civil War

See **Tshaneni**

Ettlingen | 1796 | French Revolutionary Wars (1st Coalition)

See **Malsch**

Eupatoria | 1855 | Crimean War

Following failure at **Balaklava** and **Inkerman** to break the Allied siege of **Sevastopol**, Russian commander Prince Alexander Menshikov sent General Stepan Khrulev north against the Allied port of Eupatoria (Yevpatoriya). However, Khrulev was driven off with almost 800 killed by Turkish forces under Colonel Robert Cannon, who was in the Sultan's service as Bahram Pasha (17 February 1855).

Eureka Stockade | 1854 | Eureka Rebellion

Disenfranchised gold miners at Ballarat, Australia, rebelled in support of reformist grievances and about 250 "diggers" led by Peter Lalor manned a fortified stockade at Eureka. When police and soldiers under Captain John Thomas approached, fighting broke out with 22 miners and six soldiers killed. The failed resistance came to symbolise the cause of workers' freedom (3 December 1854).

Eurymedon | 466 BC | Greco-Persian Wars

Cimon of Athens commanding the Delian League fleet sailed along the south coast of Turkey to confront a massive Persian fleet assembled to avenge the humiliating defeats at **Plataea** and **Mycale** in 479 BC. At the mouth of the Eurymedon in Antalya Bay, Cimon won a decisive victory on land and sea and drove the Persians back from southeast Asia Minor, confirming Athenian mastery of the Aegean.

Eurymedon ▮ 190 BC ▮ Roman-Syrian War

War at sea between Rome and Antiochus III of Syria continued after the action at **Corycus** and Rome's Rhodian allies under Eudamas met the Seleucid fleet, now led by the exiled Hannibal, off the Eurymedon, in southern Turkey, near Side. Hannibal's larger fleet was badly handled and lost 20 ships disabled and one captured. The main decisive action came that September at **Myonnesus** (July 190 BC).

Eutaw Springs ▮ 1781 ▮ War of the American Revolution

Pursuing the British into South Carolina despite a check at **Fort Ninety-Six**, rebel General Nathanael Greene was met near the Santee River at Eutaw Springs by about 2,000 men under Colonel Alexander Stewart. Greene was eventually repulsed in a hard-fought action, although Stewart had also suffered very heavy losses and withdrew south to **Charleston** (8 September 1781).

Evesham ▮ 1265 ▮ 2nd English Barons' War

With King Henry III captured at **Lewes** by Simon de Montfort Earl of Leicester, his son Prince Edward gathered a powerful army. When de Montfort crossed the Severn and advanced towards Evesham, southeast of Worcester, he mistook Edward's force for his own son's army, defeated earlier at **Kenilworth**. The Earl was defeated and killed and King Henry was restored (4 August 1265).

Evora ▮ 1663 ▮ Spanish-Portuguese Wars
    See **Ameixial**

Evora ▮ 1808 ▮ Napoleonic Wars (Peninsular Campaign)

After marching into Portugal, French commander Androche Junot sent General Louis Loisson southeast to secure his communication with Spain. At the town of Evora, 70 miles southeast of Lisbon, Loisson routed an inexperienced Portuguese-Spanish force under General Francisco de Paula Leite. He then sacked Evora but withdrew when the British landed in Portugal (29 July 1808).

Exeter ▮ 1068 ▮ Norman Conquest of Britain

Renewing the war against William I after their father was killed at **Hastings**, the sons of former King Harold of England attacked Bristol with the Irish fleet, then joined Harold's mother Gytha at Exeter. Marching west against the rebels, William besieged Exeter and, after undermining its walls, took the town by storm. He then ravaged the countryside of Devon to impose Norman rule.

Exeter ▮ 1549 ▮ Western Rebellion

When Edward VI tried to enforce the new English prayer book, pro-Catholic forces in Cornwall and Devon rebelled under Sir Humphry Arundell and up to 10,000 besieged Exeter. Royal troops under Lord John Russell failed to raise the siege until reinforcements gave them victory at nearby **St Mary's Clyst**. The rebels withdrew and were routed at **Sampford Courtenay** (2 July–6 August 1549).

Exilles ▮ 1747 ▮ War of the Austrian Succession

Attempting to divert Austria's siege of **Genoa**, Louis-Charles Fouquet Comte de Belleisle (brother of Marshal Charles de Belleisle) invaded Piedmont. West of Turin near Exilles, Belleisle was killed in a rash frontal attack on Austrian General Rudolf Joseph Colloredo in entrenchments at the Col de l'Assiette. His routed army was then driven back to France (19 July 1747).

Eylau ▮ 1807 ▮ Napoleonic Wars (4th Coalition)

In their mid-winter offensive against the French invasion of eastern Prussia, Russians under General Levin Bennigsen met Napoleon Bonaparte's Grand Army in a snowstorm at Eylau (modern Bagrationovsk). Although General Anton Lestocq's Prussians arrived to assist, Bennigsen could not break through and withdrew to winter quarters, leaving Bonaparte to claim victory (8 February 1807).

Ezra Church I 1864 I American Civil War (Western Theatre)

While besieging the Confederate army at **Atlanta**, Georgia, Union commander William T. Sherman sent General Oliver O. Howard against the supply lines to the west, where he dug in at Ezra Church against Generals Stephen D. Lee and Aleander P. Stewart. The Confederates were repulsed with heavy losses and Sherman soon attacked again further west at **Utoy Creek** (28 July 1864).